Come Up to Stuart Island in Big ~~Bay, BC~~ & "Watch Us Grow!"

* General store with, 3,600 sq ft deck attached with outside covered seating.

* Profits from the Stuart Island Community Dock will go towards salmon enhancement and other community initiative programs.

* Fresh water to docks, showers, laundry, post office, ice, fresh crab and prawn sales, espresso bar and ice cream counter, fishing gear and licenses.

* Sport fishing guides for hire with 15 to 20 years experience, tidal and eagle eco-tours.

* Dock with 650 lineal feet and airplane float will be expanded to 1,050 lineal feet in 2006, accommodating boats over 100'.

* Walking trail to Eagle Lake.

* Future plans for 2007 – Liquor store if approved, expanded moorage, gift shop, bakery and pizzeria.

Reservations are suggested.

email: **stuartislandca@aol.com**

phone: **250 202-DOCK (3625)**

we monitor VHF channel 66A

2006 Northwest Boat Travel

Trusted Since 1978

General Information

Puget Sound

Gateway Area & San Juan Islands

Vancouver Island & Gulf Islands

City of Vancouver to Discovery Passage

North Vancouver Island & West Coast

Northern B.C. & Southeast Alaska

PUBLICATION   INFORMATION

ISBN: 0-945989-18-0
Founders: Phil & Gwen Cole
Publishers Emeritus: Hugo & Rachel Anderson
Customer Service Representative: Debbie Brickman
  (425) 488-3211 • Email: debbie@vernonpublications.com
Webmaster: Trisha Thomas • Email: trisha@nwboat.com
Editor: Kathy Newman
Editor Emeritus: Gwen Cole
Contributing Editors: See Page A-8
Circulation, Records: Janice Walters
Advertising & Marketing Manager: Michael Romoser
Canadian Sales: Dependable Ad Sales
U.S. Sales: Roger Hunsperger
Key Grip: Office Bob
Mailing Address: Post Office Box 970,
                Woodinville, WA 98072-0970
Business Office: Telephone: (425) 488-3211
                Fax: (425) 488-0946
                E-Mail: info@vernonpublications.com
Publishers: Robert Walters
            Trevor Vernon
Internet Home Page: www.boattravel.com

©2005 Vernon Publications, LLC All rights reserved.
Printed in U.S.A. Date of publication: November 2005
Cover: The sun sets over the Olympic Mountains and
    Shilshole Bay Marina in Seattle.

★ Keep this edition updated: See page A-10

©2005 Vernon Publications, LLC

2006 Northwest Boat Travel Featured Article

Northwest Boat Travel Welcomes Warren Miller

Warren Miller is......rather hard to describe! While most of us have one, possibly two, careers in our lifetimes, Warren Miller is an author, cartoonist, ski racer, newspaper columnist, photographer, cameraman, and director of movies and television productions, to name just a few. He is widely recognized and honored, not only for his professional achievements, but for his philanthropic endeavors as well. He is also an avid boater. We are honored to include this piece he wrote for *Northwest Boat Travel*. It epitomizes the way we feel about boating in the Pacific Northwest— life just doesn't get any better!

I WANT A BOAT WITH A HEAD AND A SHOWER

by Warren Miller

About twenty years ago I tied my boat trailer to the back of my van and drove north from Hermosa Beach, California to Anacortes, Washington. On the trailer was my 20 foot Pursuit that I had used as a camera boat for about six years. With me was my guide and future wife, Laurie and our destination was the San Juan Islands. I had never driven my boat anywhere except to Catalina Island, but it had been used in the production of about a dozen sailing films up and down the west coast.

As I was looking for a place to launch in Anacortes, I spotted the 110 foot Carideus which was a converted World War Two subchaser. It was identical to the one I had sunk out from under me in a South Pacific hurricane. Immediately we became friends with Pat and Maureen Dickson who owned the boat and ran the marina. Pat took good care of me before launch with a new battery, some charts to take the place of the road map I was going to use for navigation, a tank full of fuel, a Porta potty and Laurie and I were on our way.

That launch led to three summers of cruising as far north as Sullivan Bay. By the third summer we were using the same boat but had added a Gatorade jug for our water, a Porta potty, a Coleman stove to cook on and a Coleman lantern for heat.

Our inflatable was named Old Leaky because it did. We had a two horse power motor that had a three ounce gas tank. It was capable of getting you there, but not back. More than once I had to row us back from wherever we went. The inflatable would bend in the middle with each stroke of the oars.

When everyone else at Cape Mudge was catching salmon faster than they could haul them aboard, we caught our limit of Dog fish. Thirty seven I think it was in three hours.

We swam in warm water lakes, and the not so warm water of Princess Louisa. We sat and read in our canvas chairs when it was raining and some nights we lay on the foredeck and watched the satellites racing by in the black sky in front of twenty gazillion stars.

I didn't know the words difficult boating at the time because I was really enjoying every moment afloat. That first summer we had no radio, no radar, no spare motor, no depth sounder, just blind faith that everything would work and it did, but I certainly don't recommend such casual boating. I took pictures in the Octopus Islands when the water was so

Warren with the falls at Baranof Island, and Warm Springs in the background.

mirror like that I can turn the picture upside down and you can't tell the difference.

On the dock at April Point one Sunday morning Laurie, using our gasoline stove, cooked eggs Benedict with cracked crab on top, along with fresh squeezed orange juice and peanut butter on English muffins. A friend whose 87 foot boat was tied up down the dock stopped and had coffee with us. Sitting in our beach chairs on the dock, the other boaters had to carefully walk around us. When the "Whatcha been doing lately" conversation wound down he said, "You folks look like you're having a lot more fun than we are on our 87 footer." I can't respond to that statement, but I do know that our fun meter was way off of the scale for the six weeks we cruised that summer.

Is this kind of cruising expensive? The monthly payments for a 20 foot boat with a small cutty cabin to sleep in and a good outboard motor costs about the same as four one day ski lift tickets per month. A lot less if you buy a good used boat. Once your boat is in the water, the only expense is gasoline and the occasional ice cream cone at Lund or Friday Harbor or maybe even Sullivan Bay.

Many of the fuel docks you stop at will have showers for a buck or so, a grocery store and washing machines too. When Laurie occasionally did the laundry, I did some mainte-

nance on the boat or grabbed some sleep in the cutty cabin. The only risk in cruising north in British Columbia is a highly contagious disease called "Three foot fever."

The third season of what I considered real luxurious 20 foot cruising, we were caught in a pretty bad storm. When we finally made it to our destination, exhausted and sopping wet, Laurie announced, "I want a boat with a stand up shower and a sit down toilet." That was almost twenty years ago and this summer we completed our first trip to Glacier Bay, Alaska. About two thousand miles round trip, but we didn't do it in my old 20 foot camera boat. Instead last year we bought a seven year old 47 foot Bayliner with only 400 hours on the engines. The previous owner had used it as a Condo in Roche harbor for all of those years. His children were getting bigger and he needed a bigger boat and we were getting older and we needed a bigger boat. A used boat such as this can be bought for about one third of the price of a new one.

Would I go to Glacier Bay in my 20 foot Pursuit? At the drop of a hat, but I wouldn't want to go there without Laurie.

The freedom that the Northwest has to offer boaters is quite simply, some of the best cruising in the world. High snow capped mountains slope down to the stern of my boat where it is tied up. When the tide goes out, I can stand on the swim step and with a screw driver, pry off enough oysters and barbecue them for dinner. I have just spent a few hours this sunny afternoon writing about how this part of the world has changed my life.

Remember what I have been saying for years. "If you don't do it this year, you'll be one year older when you do."

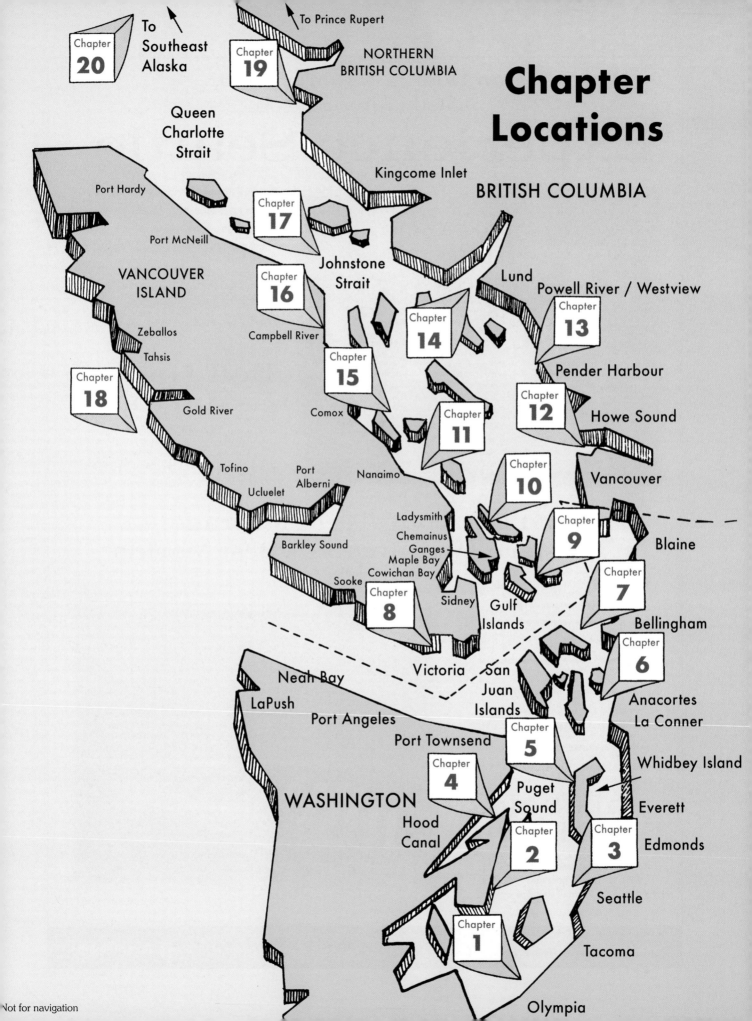

Chapter Locations

Chapter 20

To Southeast Alaska

To Prince Rupert

Chapter 19

NORTHERN BRITISH COLUMBIA

Queen Charlotte Strait

Kingcome Inlet

BRITISH COLUMBIA

Port Hardy

Chapter 17

Port McNeill

Johnstone Strait

Lund

Powell River / Westview

Chapter 13

VANCOUVER ISLAND

Chapter 16

Campbell River

Chapter 14

Pender Harbour

Zeballos

Chapter 15

Chapter 12

Howe Sound

Tahsis

Comox

Chapter 11

Chapter 18

Gold River

Chapter 10

Vancouver

Tofino

Port Alberni

Nanaimo

Chapter 9

Blaine

Ucluelet

Ladysmith

Chemainus

Barkley Sound

Ganges

Maple Bay

Chapter 7

Cowichan Bay

Bellingham

Sooke

Sidney

Chapter 8

Gulf Islands

Chapter 6

Victoria

San Juan Islands

Anacortes
La Conner

Neah Bay

Chapter 5

Whidbey Island

LaPush

Port Angeles

Port Townsend

Everett

Chapter 4

Puget Sound

Edmonds

WASHINGTON

Hood Canal

Chapter 2

Chapter 3

Seattle

Chapter 1

Tacoma

Olympia

WHAT IS NORTHWEST BOAT TRAVEL?

HOW TO USE THIS GUIDE

Now in its 28th year, *Northwest Boat Travel* is a unique cruising guide containing over 2,700 ports-of-call, anchorages, bays, inlets, waterways, marine parks, marina and resort facilities, fuel docks, services, and things to see and do along the coasts and islands of Washington, British Columbia, and Southeast Alaska.

Northwest Boat Travel is written by Northwest Boaters for Northwest Boaters. The original boater's guide to the Inside Passage waters, trusted since 1978. It is a compilation of information collected over years of boating experience, with thousands of additions and changes made yearly. Our own work is augmented by a growing list of contributing editors, most who are avid boates or boating support people. (See Page A-8).

Northwest Boat Travel Research Sources Since its inception, *Northwest Boat Travel* has striven to provide accurate, up-to-date information. Editing takes place year round. Many readers provide information and pictures for *CruiseGrams®*, on-line features, and the annual Guidebook. In addition, we receive updates from the *Recreational Boating Association of Washington, Women in Boating, British Columbia Shorelines,* the *Northwest and British Columbia Marine Trade Associations,* the *Department of Transportation,* the *U.S. Coast Guard Local Notice to Mariners,* the *Pacific Coast Congress of Harbormasters and Port Managers, Washington Water Trails Association* and others.

We contact Chambers of Commerce, Tourism Bureaus and VisitorInfo Centres who review our data for accuracy and provide additional up-dates. Over the years we have established dependable lines of communication with representatives of the Coast Guard, Customs Service, Immigration Department, Department of Natural Resources, Fisheries and Oceans, the Institute of Ocean Sciences, NOAA, the North Pacific Marine Radio Council, plus many city, state, and provincial departments. Additionally, representatives of yacht clubs, U.S. Power Squadrons, Coast Guard Auxiliaries, schools and colleges use *Northwest Boat Travel* as a teaching and information guide and reciprocate by providing additional or corrected information. All of this information is collected, sorted through, checked for accuracy, reported in four quarterly *CruiseGrams®* which are distributed to subscribing Members (See Page A-10), and posted in the member features on our website www.boattravel.com For Membership/Subscription ordering information, see the card at page 251.

To help our readers collect additional information on a variety of topics, *Northwest Boat Travel®* contains necessary contact information to obtain articles, documents, brochures, and information from tourism, government, and private agencies. Also, we provide a mail-in card offering free reader information, page A-17.

What is Northwest Boat Travel On-line?

Established in January, 1996, www.boattravel.com is "The northwest's most active Internet boating site." One popular feature is our Boater's Forum, with discussions of topics and issues such as *Breaking Boating News, Boating Events, for Sale or Wanted, Moorages Available or Wanted, Questions & Answers,* and more.

The site is constantly growing and contains a wide variety of information of interest to boaters. NBT Web Club Members enjoy their own password protected pages, including an on-line version of the printed guide and a growing list of continuously updated, essential boating information for viewing and printing.

See pages A-10 for more information about **www.boattravel.com.**

How To Use This Guide

How is the Information Presented?

The A-Pages: Located in the front of the book, these pages serve as the Table of Contents and introduce products, facilities, services, contacts for free Reader Service Information, and the Mariner's Library. Our featured article is also found here. Included in this section is a map (page A-6) which illustrates the chapter locations.

Chapter Organization and Content:
Twenty geographically arranged chapters, from south to north, present descriptions and useful information about the waterways, bays, anchorages, facilities, and services along the Inside Passage from Olympia, Washington to Skagway, Alaska.

Essential Supplies and Services:
At each chapter's end is a classified listing of contact information, including VHF Channels and phone numbers for commercial and government facilities and services including: Medical (Hospitals, Ambulances, Red-Tide and Poison Information Hot-Lines) and Boating (Repairs, Fuel, Towing) emergency facilities and services. Supplies (Groceries, Liquor, Propane, CNG). Plus Lodging, Marine Operator and Weather Channels, Moorages, Sportfishing, Tourist, and Transportation Information.

Important Notices: Located between Chapters 7 and 8 are pages containing information for U.S. and Canada regarding crossing the border, rules, regulations, contacts, procedures, and resources for a variety of subjects.

Tables, Indexes, and Articles: Included in the guide book are articles (*Crossing the Big Waters, Basic Anchoring*), Distance Tables, VHF Radio operation, Index of Sponsors, and and Index to places, facilities, and services.

Widely Diverse Area Of Coverage: The vast geographical area covered varies from cosmopolitan cities to out-of-the-way coves visited mostly by birds, deer, and bears. If, as you travel the Inside Passage with us, you can adapt your needs and desires to your surroundings, you will enjoy a variety of experiences, ranging from gourmet restaurants and posh hotels to remote anchorages and wilderness campsites. Please remember that buildings, floats, chefs, managers, and owners of facilities are subject to change. Therefore, it is impossible to guarantee the actual availability or nature of the services or facilities described. We can only describe our experiences and those our readers have shared with us. We can only invite you to explore these wonderful waters of adventure, as we have, and to partake of the good life along the way. We welcome your comments, information, and suggestions.

The ★ (Steering Star) symbol, used throughout this guide, was inspired by this John Masefield poem. The star guides readers to recommended destinations, facilities, and services.

*I must go down
to the sea again.
To the lonely sea
and sky,
And all that I ask
is a tall ship,
And a ★ to steer her by.*

—John Masefield

Meet Our On-The-Water Staff

Here is a list of some of the wonderful people who help us keep **Northwest Boat Travel**® Printed Guide and Website accurate and up-to-date. Together, they put in thousands of hours visiting sites, collecting information, taking pictures, and making suggestions. They include avid boaters, facility owners, government officials, Chambers of Commerce Directors, and representatives of private organizations. Our hats are off to each and everyone of our **Northwest Boat Travel**® Contributing Editors. Want to join our on-the-water staff? Email kathy@vernonpublications.com.

Al Francisco	Dennis LaPointe	Joanne McGovern	Peyton F Perry
Al & Mary Fox	Dependable Ad Sales	Jodye Erickson	Phil & Sandra Pidcock
Allistair Mclean	Don Wahlstrom	Joe Dusenbury	Phil & Shelagh Tucker
Andrew James	Doug & Diana Mitchell	Johan F Battie	Phil Richter
Andy Smith	Doug & Vicki Martin	John & Emilee Boyd	QMC Eileen Metzler
Anne Beach	Doug Bernard	John & Margaret Mills	R A Murray
April Curtis	Dr Bob Lordahl	John Groening	Ralph Linnmann
April Jones	Dr Ernest Plata	Jorge Rincon	Ralph Mackie
Art McGinnis	Dundee Woods	Judi Bowen	Randy Bauton
Barbara Hess	Dyan Freer	Karen Manhas	Ray Poorman
Barbara Williamson	Ed Barrett	Kathy Whitman	Regnor Reinholdtson
Becca Smucker	Elizabeth Harvey	Kaye Pennier	Remey Valenzuela
Ben Reams	Eric Elliott	Ken & Betty Moore	Rich & Stephanie Satter
Bernard Murray	Eugene Flath	Ken & Linda Rider	Rich Clement
Bernie & Mark Bouffiou	F P Fromhagen	Ken Radon	Richard A Satterberg
Betsy Crawford	Florence Lovric	Ken Stormans	Richard Field
Betsy Wareham	Fran Olsen	Ken Yick	Richard Heaton
Bill Diller	Fred & Marilyn Laba	Ken Zimmer	Richard Oliphant
Bill Golby	G.A. Buckingham	Kent Williams	Rob & Janice Metcalf
Bill Hawkins	Gail Quigg	Kori Ward	Robert C Miller
Bill Neapole	Gary Bradford	Larry Hemmerich	Robert F Annenberg
Bill Woolsey	Gary Titchkosky	Larry Rosencrantz	Robert G Patterson
Bob & Nancy Richter	Gary Utter	Lee & Kathy Downing	Roger L Johnson
Bob & Susie Valentine	Gene Fellerman	Lee Edmondson	Ron Williamson
Bob Cadieux	George Bayless	Leonard A Komor	Ron & Nancy Sefton
Bob Miller	George Hall	Lewis B. Harder	Ron Fraser
Bob Young	Gerald Mittet	Lieutenant Hunt	Ron Johnston
Brian Tetreault	Gerald Neault	Linda & John McKinnon	Ron McFarlane
Brian Watt	Gerri Dolman	Linda Barnes	Ron McLaren
Bruce & Kay Knierim	Glen & Verlie Carleton	Linda McKeag	Rondi Dyke
Bruce Jackman	Glen Hayes	Lisa Guzman	Ross King
Bruce Peterson	Gordon Fountain	Lisa Wells	Roy & Dawn Lambert
Bruce W Kilen	Graham Breeze	Lori Johnson	Sandie Floe
Bud Young	Greg Dickinson	Lori Zimmerman	Sandie Miller
Caleb Standafer	Greg Gillen	Lorna Hink	Sandy Bryant
Capt. Lawrence E Hirtzel	Hal & Drew Irwin	Lorraine Kopetzky	Sarah Fisken
Carin Perrins	Harold Manfred	Lynn Ove Mortensen	Scott & Kelly Foss
Carl Cederberg	Heather Pate	Margaret Wood	Scott Rowland
Carl & Gloria Tenning	Howard & Fairy Eskildsen	Marilyn Breeze	Spence & Linda Flegel
Carl R Bergman	I.V. Villani	Marilyn Bendotti	Steve Demopoulas
Cheryl & Iver Johnson	Iain Barr	Martin Mittet	Steve Hixson
Cheryl Nobel	Inspector Olsen	Martyn Daniel	Steve Laine
Chris Dysart	Ione and Richard Murray	Mary Allard	Steve Miller
Chris Keuss	J Boyer	Mary Fox	Steve Toms
Cindy Wagner	Jack & Helen Ross	Mary Lou Garrison	Susan Steele
Clive Cunningham	Jack Johnstone	Mel & Anita Berry	Terrance Berscheid
Colleen Kemp	Jack & Linda Schreiber	Michael Kampnich	Terry Dow
Connie Bennett	James E Joy	Mike Stokes	Terry McPhail
Connie Van Schenk	James MacDonell	Mr & Mrs Lintons	Terry O'Neill
Cynthia Koop	Jamie Mittet	Nadine Joientz	Theo Prystawik
Dale Fowler	Jamie Stephens	Nanci Cook	Tim Whelan
Dan Iverson	Jan Baunton	Nancy Chave	Todd Johnson
Dave Enabnit	Jan Searle	Nola & Robert Bachen	Todd Shannon
Dave Fisher	Jane Hannah	Norm Culver	Tom & Ann Taylor
Dave Walker	Jane Hemmerich	Norman R Nashem Jr	V C Bertelsen Jr
Dave Williams	Jay Randolph	Norman Watson	Vicky Lagos
David Hagiwara	Jeanne Moroney	P Maughan	Virginia Painter
David Kuntz	Jeff Waite	Pam Cunningham	Walter Jaster
David R & Irene Axup	Jim & Jeannie McFarland	Pam Taft	Will Carlson
Dawn and Roy Lambert	Jim Garrison	Patti Grant	William B A Botham
Dean Hofferth	Jim Chrysler	Paul A Croegaert	William R Sandifer II
Deborah Hopkins	Jim Cuthert	Peter Van Schenk	William Shang
Dennis Hazelton	Joan Sell	Peter Plath	Willis W Knight

Want to keep yourself & this book up-to-date? Here's how!

1. Subscribe to Northwest Boat Travel's® CruiseGrams® Inside Passage News & Information Newsletter... Supplement to this Guidebook

Available by mail, e-mail, or on our website. See top card at page 251

Or...

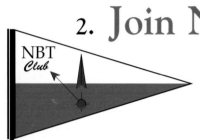

2. Join Northwest Boat Travel® Web Club®

See top card at page 251

★ *Receive CruiseGrams® via E-mail*

★ *Northwest Boat Travel e-Guide®*
NBT Guidebook to view, research, download, & print the pages you'd like.

★ Directories of Essential Supplies & Services For Each Chapter
To view, research, download, & print.

★ *Northwest Boat Travel On-line Magazine*
Articles, stories, logs, recipes, mini-cruises, Family Fun, personality portraits, & destinations.

★ Northwest Boating Forum
Breaking Northwest boating news; Boating Events; Boats For Sale, Rent, Wanted; Moorages Available, Wanted; General Boating Discussion.

★ Instantly Request Free Information From Facilities, Services, Suppliers
Your requests are automatically emailed to participating businesses you select.

★ Classified Directory Of CruiseLinks® To Boating Websites & Email Addresses
Thousands of links to marinas, resorts, government agencies, Chambers of Commerce, marine parks, restaurants, yacht clubs & organizations.

★ Boating Picture-of-the Day Members' Album
Over 1200 Inside Passage four color photos to view, download & print. Make your own album and screen savers.

★ *101 Places to Go, Things to See & Do®*
The name says it all for this popular feature.

★ Red Tide Warnings ★ Marine Weather & Tide Tables ★ Important Notices
All continuously updated, viewable, printable.

Much Much More... *Every Day is Boating Day With Us!*

To join, use top card at page 251 or order on-line at nwboat.com/shopping#membership

Cruise-In to Dine-Out...

From gourmet to take-out, these establishments are conveniently located for boaters.

FREE INFORMATION FOR OUR READERS

BOAT REPAIRS

Cove Yachts

Birds Eye Cove, Maple Bay: Complete yacht repair facilities, construction, all types of repairs. **Circle #61 on Reader Service Card.**

Lovric's Sea-Craft Inc.

Anacortes: Specializing in wooden boats, marine ways to 150-feet. Complete repair facility. **Circle #59 on Reader Service Card.**

West Sound Marina

Orcas Island. Complete repair facility. Permanent and guest moorage. Fuel. **Circle #40 on Reader Service Card.**

HOTELS, INNS, RESORTS, MARINAS

Beach Gardens Motel & Marina

Located just south of Grief Point near the gateway to Desolation sound. Gas, diesel, charters, lodging. **Circle #15 on Reader Service Card.**

Bell Harbor Marina

Prime Elliott Bay moorage location on the Seattle waterfront. Adjacent to Bell Street Pier development. **Circle #08 on Reader Service card.**

Bellingham Port of, Squalicum Harbor

Convenient location near San Juan Islands and Gateway to Canada. **Circle #25 on Reader Service Card.**

Blaine Harbor

Canadian/U.S. border: A customs port-of-entry with security protected transient and permanent moorage. **Circle #37 on Reader Service Card.**

Chinook Landing Marina

Tacoma: Modern, first-class guest and permanent moorage facility. **Circle #20 on Reader Service Card.**

Coast Victoria Harbourside Hotel & Marina

Located in Victoria's Inner Harbour. Modern marina with access to luxury hotel amenities and downtown Victoria. **Circle #16 on Reader Service card.**

Dawsons Landing General Store

Rivers Inlet, B C: Serving boaters and fishermen for the past 45 years. **Circle #50 on Reader Service Card.**

Deer Harbor Marina

Modern moorage floats accommodate boats to 150'. Located adjacent to Deer Harbor Resort and convenient to lodging and restaurants. **Circle #56 on Reader Service Card.**

Dent Island Lodge, The

Near Stuart Island, B C: A destination resort for boaters; a fishing lodge for the discriminating angler. **Circle #45 on Reader Service Card.**

Des Moines Marina, City of

18-miles south of Shilshole: Enjoy one of the finest views of the Olympic Mountains. Moorage, repairs. **Circle #26 on Reader Service Card.**

FREE INFORMATION FOR OUR READERS

Discovery Harbour Marina

Campbell River: Large, well-protected marina with 100 guest and 200 permanent berths. **Circle #06 on Reader Service Card.**

Echo Bay Resort

Noted marina and resort on Gilford Island in the center of good fishing grounds. Lodging, store. Owners retiring, facility listed for sale. **Circle #03 on Reader Service Card.**

Fairwinds Schooner Cove Resort

Hotel and Marina, Nanoose: 400 slip marina, 31 guest rooms, restaurant, pub, store, championship 18-hole golf course. **Circle #11 on Reader Service Card.**

Friday Harbor, Port Of

San Juan Island: Moorage at the heart of one of Washington's best tourist oriented communities in the beautiful San Juan Islands. **Circle #24 on Reader Service Card.**

Garden Bay Resort, Pub, & Marina

Pender Harbour: Great food, beverages, and live entertainment along with protected moorage. **Circle #41 on Reader Service Card.**

Heriot Bay Inn & Marina

Quadra Island: Over 100-years of old fashioned charm and hospitality are found at this lovely spot. **Circle #30 on Reader Service Card.**

Montague Harbour Marina

Galiano Island: Located in one of the Gulf Island's most beautiful harbors. Moorage (summer & winter), store, fuel, the Deck Restaurant, gift shop. **Circle #33 on Reader Service Card.**

Nanaimo, Port of Boat Basin

Northern Gulf Islands: A customs port-of-entry and popular
rendezvous for pleasure craft at hub of city. Request publication: Information on **Circle #80 on Reader Service Card.**

Point Baker, Alaska

The friendly folks at Point Baker Trading Post and Ruffie's Bed and Breakfast await you with homemade pies and the last floating saloon in Southeast Alaska. **Circle #54 on Reader Service Card.**

Point Hudson Marina & RV Park

Located in Port Townsend, convenient location for travels to Puget Sound, San Juan Islands, and points north. Open all year. For more information: **Circle #23 on Reader Service Card.**

Port Orchard Marina

Port Orchard: breakwater protected overnight and permanent moorage with state-of-the-art security, water, power. **Circle #22 on Reader Service Card.**

Port Townsend, Port of

Port Townsend: Permanent and transient moorage and repairs, behind a protective breakwater. **Circle #19 on Reader Service Card.**

Quamichan Inn

Memorable English Tudor country inn where boaters have returned year after year for the past 20-years to experience the gracious hospitality, enjoy a cool drink, dine on gourmet foods, and optionally stay in Ensuite Bed and Breakfast accommodations. **Circle #66 on Reader Service Card.**

Quarterdeck Marina, Inn, & I.V.'s Pub

Port Hardy, inner harbor of Hardy Bay: Permanent and transient moorage, floats, fuel, repairs, marine store, hotel, pub-restaurant. **Circle #55 on Reader Service Card.**

Sandspit Harbour

Moresby Island, Queen Charlotte Islands: Marina, power, water, showers, pumpout, launching in a picturesque island setting. **Circle #81 on Reader Service Card.**

Shelter Island Marina

Richmond, Fraser River: Relax in Tugboat Annie's, the marina pub, while mechanics and shipwrights repair your vessel. Convenient moorage available. **Circle #44 on Reader Service Card.**

Shilshole Bay Marina

Convenient Puget Sound location near the entrance to Seattle's Hiram M. Chittenden Locks, extensive permanent and guest moorage available for individuals and groups. **Circle #09 on Reader Service Card.**

Union Steamship Co. Marina

Bowen Island, adjacent to Snug Cove: Lots of transient space up to 200', parks, village, and boutiques. **Circle #12 on Reader Service Card.**

Mariner's Library
Recommended Publications

Editor's Note: The following books have been published or reprinted in recent years. They are recommended for your library. Because of rapid changes along the Inside Passage, not ALL necessarily recommended to be used as guides to current facilities, places, dangers, and conditions. Some are classics of primary value for their pictures, articles, and charts. Some are reprints from earlier editions while others, especially charts, are revised and reprinted annually or every few years. **The publications with a star (★) are updated and reprinted annually.**

Afoot & Afloat Series: By Ted & Marge Mueller. This series of books for land and sea travelers describes the terrain and covers activities for beachcombers, divers, walkers, and hikers from South Puget Sound through the San Juan Islands.

Alaska Harbors Directory: The Alaska Department of Transportation and Public Facilities offers this helpful guide that includes drawings and lists of available facilities. Download at www.dot.state.ak.us/stwddes/desports/resources.shtml

Alaska's Birds: (1998) By Robert Armstrong. Includes all 443 species with full color photos and detailed information on field marks, status, behavior, voice, and habitat.

Alaska's Southeast: (2004, 9th ed.) By Sarah Eppenbach. Information on history, geography, flora, fauna, and what to see while cruising.

Anchorages & Marine Parks: By Peter Vassilopoulos. A guide to sheltered anchorages and marine parks in the San Juan Islands, Gulf Islands, Desolation Sound, the West Coast of Vancouver Island, and the Inside Passage. Air photos. Includes recommended areas for kayaking and Scuba diving.

Birds of Coastal British Columbia: By Nancy Baron & John Acorn. Describes 435 birds and habitat. Organized by Diving Birds, Sea Birds, Gull-like Birds, Wading Birds. Coded by season.

British Columbia Tidal Water Sport Fishing Guide/Fresh Water Salmon Supplement: Fisheries and Oceans Canada, Communications Branch, Suite 200-401 Burrard Street, Vancouver, B.C. Canada V6C 3S4. Phone 604-666-0384.

Canadian Hydrographic Service, Official charts & publications for British Columbia waters: The free Pacific Coast Catalogue of Nautical Charts and Related Publications contains listings of chart dealers, numerical chart listings, photographs and descriptions of nautical publications, including electronic chart data on compact disc. Contact:

Canadian Hydrographic Chart Distribution Office, PO Box 6000, Sidney, British Columbia V8L 4B2. 250-363-6358. Fax: 250-363-6841. Email: chart-sales@pac.dfo-mpo.gc.ca Websites: www.charts.gc.ca.

★ Canadian Tide & Current Tables Volume 5: Covers Juan de Fuca Strait and the entire Strait of Georgia. Also includes tables for Seattle and Port Townsend and currents for Juan de Fuca Strait and Deception Pass. Daily tide and current tables. Available at marinas, chart dealers, or see Canadian Hydrographic contact numbers above.

★ Canadian Tide & Current Tables Volume 6: Covers West Coast of Vancouver Island and East Coast of Vancouver Island as far south as Campbell River. Daily tide and current tables. Full size, easy to read publication. See Canadian Hydrographic contact information above.

★ Canadian Tide & Current Tables Volume 7: Covers coast of Northern British Columbia, including the Queen Charlotte Islands to Dixon Entrance.. See Canadian Hydrographic contact information above.

Canadian Hydrographic Service, Official charts for British Columbia waters: Comprehensive chart collection. Recent release is Chart #3313, spiral bound, large size with comprehensive coverage Victoria to Nanaimo and Gulf Islands. See contact numbers above.

Challenge the Wilderness: By George D. Thomlinson. This is the true account of Robert and Alice Woods Thomlinson's life as missionaries along the Northern British Columbia coast. Contains historical facts about William Duncan's mission at Metlakatla. Describes Indian culture in the 1860's.

Cruising Guide to Puget Sound, A: (2nd ed., 2005) By Migael Scherer. Chart reproductions, harbor descriptions, historical information for coverage between Olympia to Blaine, Strait of Juan de Fuca, Lake Washington & Lake Union. Photographs. Contains a harbor rating system, aids to navigation.

Curve of Time: By M. Wylie Blanchett. Delightful accounts of a family's adventures when a widow and her five children cruise the British Columbia coast in the days when few pleasure craft plied these waters.

Day By Day To Alaska: By Dale R. Petersen. The author makes his 30-year dream cruise in the 21-ft Bayliner Trophy, Day by Day from his home in northern Puget Sound to Sitka, Alaska and return via the outside of Vancouver Island.

Continued on next page

Exploring Series: Vancouver Island's West Coast, Inside Passage to Alaska, South Coast of British Columbia, North Coast of British Columbia, San Juan Islands, Southeast Alaska: By Don Douglass & Reanne Hemingway-Douglass. Seven separate publications. Suggested itineraries, distance tables, background information, author's observations, detailed descriptions, diagrams and photos.

GPS Instant Navigation: By Kevin Monahan and Don Douglass. A great book for the GPS user to have on board.

GPS Waypoints: By Don Douglass. Three thousand waypoints for named positions, complete with chart number and horizontal datums. Companion book to GPS Instant Navigation. Includes all the great places for boaters on the British Columbia coast.

Guide to the Queen Charlotte Islands: By local residents. Resource guide, revised annually, contains maps and practical information. Includes camping locations, ferry schedules, drawings, and photographs. Order from 250-559-4680.

Gunkholing Series: *South Puget Sound, San Juan Islands, Gulf Islands, Desolation Sound and Princess Louisa Inlet:* By Jo Bailey, Al Cummings & Carl Nyberg. Four separate publications. By kayak and sailboats, these veteran writers explored the nooks and crannies of these areas. Interesting narratives, historical information and native lore.

Inside Passage To Alaska: A Short History by Hugo Anderson. Easy to read, interesting, narrative history of the fabled Inside Passage to Alaska in ten chapters, featuring Geological Formation, First Inhabitants, Wildlife, Climate, Plant Life, Explorers and Explorations, and the Industries such as Mining, Fishing, and Timber, which have helped shape the region into what it is today. Of interest to everyone boating, living, and/or visiting the Northwest. 6" X 9" size. Full color pictures. Plastic coated for durability. See order card at page A-17 or order at www.nwboat.com/shopping/#books

Marine Atlas, The Original: By George Bayless. Two volumes containing detailed cruise charts covering the waters of British Columbia, Puget Sound, and Alaska. Pre-plotted magnetic courses, aerial photos, and marine parks lists. Both volumes 14" x 11", plastic spiral (nonmagnetic) bound. Index and speed tables. Volume 1: Olympia to Malcolm Island, North end of Vancouver Island, B.C. 2005. Volume 2: Port Hardy to Skagway, Alaska. 2000. Bayless Enterprises, Inc. P O Box 4447, Sunriver, Oregon 97707. 541-593-6396. Fax: 541-593-1795.

Northwest Marine Weather: By Jeff Renner. Boater and Seattle TV meteorologist. An educational resource book about local northwest weather basics and forecasting tools from the Columbia River to Cape Scott.

Northwest Tugboat Captain: By Helen Leber. Narrative describes the life and times of Captain Martin Guchee, one of the northwest's legendary seaman. Encompasses both hair-raising and hilarious adventures. See order card at page A-17. Available at www.nwboat.com/shopping#books

Proven Cruising Routes, Seattle To Ketchikan, Vol. 1 : By Kevin Monahan and Don Douglass. Actual routes-waypoint to waypoint, with a diagram of each waypoint-from Seattle to Ketchikan.

Row To Alaska: By Wind & Oar: By Pete & Nancy Ashenfelter. This delightful book will keep you on the edge of your seat, and you will find yourself laughing out loud at the accounts of this retired couple's adventurous row from the San Juan Islands in Washington to Ketchikan, Alaska. For copy email author at nanmash@hotmail.com.

Sailing Directions, British Columbia Coast (South Portion), Vol. 1: Covers Vancouver Island and the coastal mainland to Cape Caution. Available at marinas, chart dealers, or from the Canadian Hydrographic Chart Distribution Office, Post Office Box 6000, Sidney British Columbia, V8L 4B2. Phone: 250-363-6368. Fax: 250-363-6841.

Sailing Directions, Inner Passage – Queen Charlotte Sound to Chatham Sound (PAC 205): Canadian Hydrographic Service. Covers the Inner Passage route from Cape Caution to Prince Rupert. Available at marinas, chart dealers, or from the Canadian Hydrographic Chart Distribution Office, Post Office Box 6000, Sidney British Columbia, V8L 4B2. Phone: 250-363-6368. Fax: 250-363-6841.

Sailing Directions, Hecate Strait, Dixon Entrance, Portland Inlet and Adjacent Waters and Queen Charlotte Islands (PAC 206): Covers Laredo Sound to Stewart, and the Queen Charlotte Islands. Available at marinas, chart dealers, or from the Canadian Hydrographic Chart Distribution Office, Post Office Box 6000, Sidney British Columbia, V8L 4B2. Phone: 250-363-6368. Fax: 250-363-6841.

Sailing Directions, General Information, Pacific Coast (PAC 200): Provides general navigational, geographic and emergency information, as well as information on the natural conditions for the coastal waters of British Columbia. Available at marinas, chart dealers, or from the Canadian Hydrographic Chart Distribution Office, Post Office Box 6000, Sidney British Columbia, V8L 4B2. Phone: 250-363-6368. Fax: 250-363-6841.

Secrets of Cruising #2... The New Frontier - B.C. Coast & Undiscovered Inlets: Author Hugo Anderson describes this frontier as "...the best cruising waters on this continent, if not the entire world." Discover pristine and memorable anchorages, fjords, sounds, bays, inlets, passages, villages, and communities not described in any other work. Includes firsthand, useful, knowledge of these inlets. See order card at page A-17. Available at www.nwboat.com/shopping#books

United States Coast Pilot: Published by the National Oceanographic Survey (NOAA). Depths, characteristics, hazards, anchorages, and navigational information for coastal waters. Volume 7 covers California, Oregon, Hawaii, and Washington. Volume 8, Dixon Entrance and Alaska to Cape Spencer. Volume 9, Cape Spencer, Alaska to the Bering Sea.

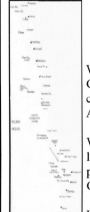

Boating Books From Northwest Boat Travel

These publications are not only entertaining and readable, they contain valuable, useful information. To quote the modern expression, *"They are great reads."*

The Inside Passage: A Short History

by Hugo Anderson.

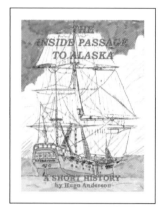

New release, August 1998. Full of fascinating adventures into the Inside Passage. A must for anyone who explores, or lives along, these waterways, islands, towns, villages, and cities. Ten chapters featuring Geological Formation, First Inhabitants, Wildlife, Climate, Plant Life, Explorers and Explorations, and the Industries such as Mining, Fishing, and Timber which have shaped the region. 128 pages. Prices include S&H. Mail Order Non-members: $15.95 U.S. **Members: $7.50** (Washington residents: add 8.8% sales tax).

Call: (425) 488-3211 or see below

Secrets of Cruising #2... The New Frontier: B.C. Coast & Undiscovered Inlets

by Hugo Anderson.

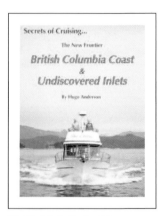

New release. Explore fjords, inlets, and bays yet undiscovered by most boaters. The Andersons are pioneers who have made writing the information about this territory the centerpiece of their boating years. Through their eyes you will be able to experience these inlets yourself, as you follow the vivid, meticulous, accurate, and informative detail. Useful listings of facilities and services. 240 pages, 4-color pictures. Prices include S&H. Mail Order Non-members: $19.50 U.S. **Members: $10.00** (Washington residents: add 8.8% sales tax.)

Call: (425) 488-3211 or see below

Northwest Tugboat Captain

by Helen Leber.

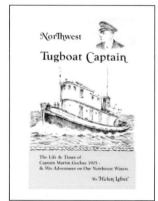

This narrative describes the life and times of Captain Martin Guchee, one of the northwest's legendary seamen. Encompasses both hair-raising and hilarious adventures, first as a deckhand and later as he commanded tugs along the north Pacific Coast, Aleutian Islands, and the Arctic Ocean.... both in times of peace and during World War II. Contains 160 pages. Prices include S&H. Mail Order Non-members: $12.95 U.S. **Members: $9.95** (Washington residents: add 8.8% sales tax.)

Call: (425) 488-3211 or see below

For fast service: Orders may be E-mailed to Janice@vernonpublications.com,, Faxed to (425) 488-0946, or Call Customer Service, (425) 488-3211. All prices are U.S. funds or Canadian equivalent . **To order by mail, send order to Vernon Publications, P.O. Box 970, Woodinville, WA 98072-0970.**

Chapter 1:

South Puget Sound

Vashon Island to Hammersley Inlet: Des Moines, Tacoma, Gig Harbor, Olympia, Shelton. Carr, Case, & Budd Inlets.

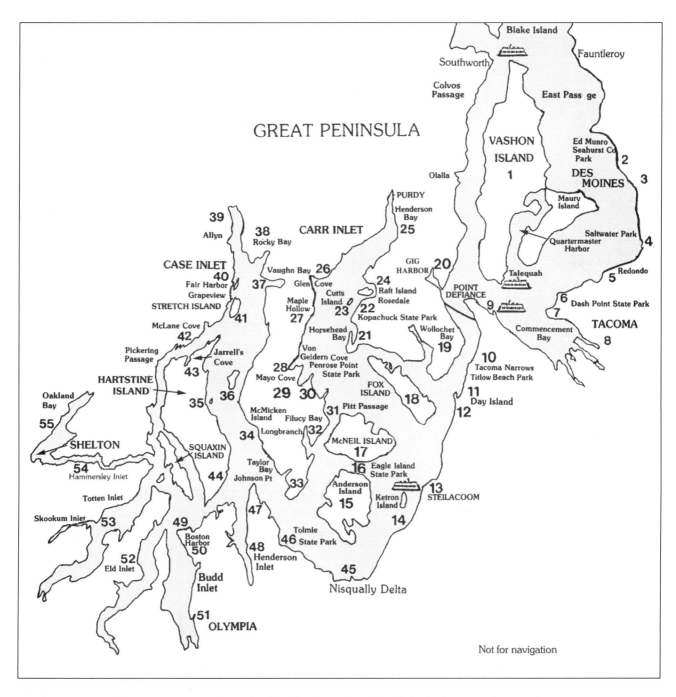

Not for navigation

Symbols

[ ]: Numbers between [ ] are chart numbers.

{ }: Numbers & letters between { } are waypoints.

⛰: Park, 🚤: Boat Launch, ▲: Campgrounds,
🥾: Hiking Trails, ⛱: Picnic Area, 🚲: Biking

Chart List

NOAA Charts:

18445, 18448, 18453, 18456, 18457, 18474

Marine Atlas (2005 ed.): Pages 2-3

★ **Important Notice:** See "Important Notices" between Chapters 7 and 8 in this guide for specific information on boating related topics such as: Canadian & U.S. Customs, boating safety and security, navigation, weather, U.S. & Canadian Coast Guard, U.S & Canadian marine radio use, Vessel Traffic Service and traffic separation plans, security zones, and internet access. Due to new Department of Homeland Security regulations, call ahead for latest customs information and/or see Northwest Boat Travel On-line, www.nwboat.com.

Puget Sound

[18445]

★ **Puget Sound:** When the glaciers dug deep troughs in the basin between the Cascade and Olympic Mountains, they left depths to 900 feet. Filled with the saltwater of the ocean, this sound extends nearly 90 miles from Olympia on the south to the Strait of Juan de Fuca on the north and affords over 2,000 miles of shoreline. In May of 1792, Captain George Vancouver named this extensive waterway "Puget Sound" in honor of Peter Puget, leader of the expedition to the southern portion of the sound.

Although much of Puget Sound is deep, the southernmost waters culminate in shoals and drying flats. Tidal differences vary greatly from north to south. At Port Townsend, on the north, the range is eight feet, while, on the south at Olympia, the change can be as much as 15 feet. Currents generally flow north or south with velocities of one-half knot to seven knots, depending on land constrictions. Current and tide tables are necessary publications to have on board. Storm winds usually blow from the south or southeast. In late spring and summer, the prevailing winds are from the west and northwest from Pacific highs. Except during storms, overnight winds are usually calm and there are rising afternoon breezes. In summer, a change to a southerly wind may indicate the approach of a storm front. Fog is common along the Puget Sound. April and May are the most fog-free months, while October, November, January and February tend to have the most fog. Weather conditions can be monitored on VHF Channel 1.

A variety of leisure, educational, and sports activities are available on and around Puget Sound. Each port-of-call is unique, with its own personality and attractions. Few cities can offer such an experience as locking your boat from saltwater through the locks to Lake Washington. Along with boating adventures from any size

craft, other activities include picnicking on a beach, hiking on the many trails, and camping at sites in state and county parks.

In addition to species of fish, the sound is home to several marine mammals. These include the harbor seal, harbor porpoise, Dall's porpoise, and Orca whale. Seasonal visitors include the Gray and Minke whales and California and Steller sea lions. Fish and shellfish harvesting is a big part of the state's economy. These include oysters, clams, scallops, crabs, geoducks, and shrimp. Several beaches offer shellfish harvesting to the public. Before digging, call the Shellfish Red-Tide Hot line, 1-800-562-5632, to check on beach closures. See www.doh.wa.gov/ehp/sf/biotoxin.htm.

Vashon & Maury Islands

[18445, 18448]

★ **Vashon Island & Vashon Center (1):** James Vashon, an officer with Peter Puget, was honored by Captain George Vancouver by giving his name to this large island. Steep cliffs and forested hillsides are prominent landmarks. Small coves, offering temporary anchorage, indent the shores. Quartermaster Harbor, a large natural anchorage, is located between Vashon and its neighbor, Maury Island. Agriculture, fruit and berry growing, and boat building have been traditional industries. Today, many residents commute to work in Seattle, while an equally large number are retired, having been attracted to the island because of its slow pace and its location only a few miles from a metropolitan city. Several artists reside on the island, many of whom display signs on their home studios welcoming visitors.

Washington State car/passenger ferries connect Vashon to the outside. The Washington State Ferry terminal is located at the wharf on the north shore between Dolphin Point and Point Vashon. Unless DOT budget cuts affect this route, a passenger-only ferry will continue to link downtown Seattle with the island. This ferry, designed for commuters, makes early morning and late afternoon runs on weekdays and a mid morning and five additional trips on Saturdays. Car/passenger ferries connect with Fauntleroy in West Seattle, and Southworth on the Kitsap Peninsula. Access to and from Tacoma is found at Tahlequah, on the extreme south end of the island, via a car/passenger ferry that makes regular crossings to, and from, Tacoma's Point Defiance.

The largest community, Vashon, sometimes called "The Center," is situated along the main north-south road near the center of the island. There are restaurants, a bakery, hardware, grocery, and liquor store, as well as specialty and antique shops, a gas station, theater, post office, and the noted Vashon Hardware and Tool Museum. Boaters and other tourists can travel to downtown Vashon by King County Metro bus from moorages at Burton and Dockton County Park. Route #119 makes weekday-only runs to Dockton County Park and Burton, a short walk from Quartermaster Marina. You can flag down the bus whether or not you are at a bus stop. Route #118 runs weekdays from the north end ferry terminal to the Tahlequah ferry. Each July, the community hosts the *Strawberry Festival*, a two day event filled with family fun.

In the days of the Mosquito Fleet, steamers plied the waters of Colvos, East, and Dalco Passages, which fringe the island, making regular stops at such ports of call as Olalla, Cove, and Lisabuela. Later, the Black Ball Line developed the ferry landing at the north end.

Colvos Passage: This mile-wide passage is free of obstructions and extends about 11 miles along the western shore of Vashon Island. The shoreline is indented with curving beaches, such as Fern Cove and Paradise Cove (site of the Campfire's Camp Sealth), and a few sharper niches such as Cove, and Lisabuela. Overnight anchorage is recommended only in settled weather. Ruins mark the wharf at Cove, where the Virginia V once made scheduled stops, and a scallop fisherman, with a distinctive one lunger boat engine, once sold gunny sacks full of scallops for 75 cents each.

Olalla: This small community is located on the opposite shore of the passage. There is a launch ramp, a picnic area, and waterfront grocery accessible by dinghy.

★⛰ **Lisabuela Park:** This Cascadia Marine Trail campsite is located on the west side of the island, 4.5 miles north of the south end of the island. There are three campsites and a launching ramp for hand carried craft. No open fires are permitted. Be aware of fast currents near shore. 206-463-9602. ▲

East Passage: [18474] See current tables for The Narrows, Washington. If currents are a consideration, most boaters heading south will go down East Passage and return north by Colvos Passage. This is because the current in Colvos nearly always flows north. Actually, currents in either passage are not strong. East Passage is a main shipping channel, with Vessel Traffic Separation lanes. Tugs and freighters are common sights.

★⛰ **Wingehaven Park:** This Cascadia Marine Trail site is in the first bay south of Dolphin Point. It has three campsites. No open fires permitted. The beach can be easily identified by the massive, sculptured bulkhead. It is accessible by beachable boat. Temporary anchorage is possible, with some protection from westerly winds. However, wakes from passing ships may be a nuisance. This park was once a large estate, and was named for the previous owners of the property. 360-902-8844. ▲

Tramp Harbor: Formed by the easternmost part of Vashon Island and the north end of Maury Island this curving beach has shoals along much of its length, extending about 0.2 mile from shore. Point Heyer is a sandspit to the north. Temporary anchorage is possible, but is open to north winds and wakes of passing ships. There is no moorage float. On shore, there is a fishing pier, with a picnic area at the head of it, and a good beach for beachcombing. Off shore, buoys mark the boundaries of an artificial reef that is popular with scuba divers.

Maury Island: [18474] This "island" is actually a five-mile long peninsula of Vashon Island, connected by a highway at a narrow neck of land. This is the site of the small community of Portage.

★⛰ **Point Robinson County Park:** Beachable boats can land here without difficulty. The park is situated on the hillside. Picnicking, beachcombing, fishing, and scuba diving are possible activities. A Cascadia Marine Trail campsite is also located here. In the summer, the Point Robinson Lighthouse, circa 1915, is open for public tours on Sundays from 12:30 pm to 4:00 pm. For information regarding private tours, call 206-463-9602. ⛱▲

★⛰ **Maury Island Marine Park:** One of King County's newest parks, it is located on the east side of Maury island on the site of an old gravel pit. This gravel operation may be the source of the high proportion of cobbles on the beach. The open location of the beach does not protect it from the surf. The wave action has created a beach steeper than most. The upper beach (above 0 feet) is composed mostly of loose gravel and cobbles while the lower beach (below 0 feet) is flatter and sandy in some areas. The adjoining upland was mined for gravel until a few years ago and the dock was used for loading barges.

★ **Quartermaster Harbor:** Vashon and Maury Islands come together to form this five-mile long harbor. When entering between Neill Point and Piner Point, be aware of a two fathom shoal off Neill Point, and a buoy-marked shoal off Manzanita, on Maury Island. Quartermaster Harbor is favored for its variety of anchoring sites and park lands. [North and south winds can enter, but one can usually select from the many available anchoring sites, one that is protected from a particular wind. Anchorage is on a mud bottom in depths of 20-50 feet.] The harbor shallows in the bay north of Burton Peninsula. Private homes, many with mooring buoys, a marina, and the nearby small community of Burton, with its stores, restaurant, post office and serveral B & B's are located in this area. Weekday bus service connects Burton with Dockton County Park and other sites on Vashon Island.

Several parks have waterfront access. A public tidelands beach, north of Neill Point and accessible only by small boat, has clams and geoducks. There is an undeveloped park at Lone Lake, north of the beach. Day use only, Burton Acre Park is on Burton Peninsula. There are restrooms, a swimming beach, hiking trails, picnic areas, and a launching ramp. Anchor some distance off shore to avoid shallow water at low tide. This is a popular site for dinghies, canoes, and inflatable craft. The largest park in the vicinity is

Maury Island's Dockton County Park.

Quartermaster Marina: Permanent moorage. 206-463-3624.

★⚓ **Dockton County Park:** This park, located on the east shore of the harbor, is protected from all but strong north winds. There are 58 moorage slips. Anchorage is also possible in 18-30 feet of water, on a mud bottom. Some boaters have reported problems with anchor dragging. Amenities include a paved launch ramp, parking, playground equipment, restrooms, showers, and a swimming beach. Because of this park's popularity, and its distance from the commercial center of Vashon, it is a scheduled stop for weekday bus service on the island. Picnic shelter reservations: 206-296-4287. In the 1890's schooners, and later steamboats, were constructed at a large shipyard in the area. ⚓

Tahlequah: This small community is the terminus of the ferry to Point Defiance. No marine facilities.

East Passage Mainland
[18445, 18448, 18474]

Fauntleroy: This is the site of the ferry terminal to Vashon Island and Southworth, on the Kitsap Peninsula. Lincoln Park is to the north, however Seattle City Park regulations prohibit the beaching of boats.

★⚓ **Ed Munro Seahurst County Beach Park (2):** This attractive acreage has no moorage, but small boats can be beached here. Offshore, buoys mark the site of a sunken barge. Skindiving is popular. Park facilities include picnic tables, barbecues, restrooms, and playground equipment. Tours of the Marine Technology Occupational Skills Center are available, with large viewing windows to see the sea life and a fish ladder. The park was named for a former King County Commissioner. ⚓

★ **Des Moines (3):** Des Moines, coined "The Waterland City," has an 840-slip marina and fishing pier. The area's gentle terrain, sloping westerly into Puget Sound, attracted early settlers and continues to attract residents today. Since its beginnings in 1889, the citizenry, now numbering nearly 30,000 have been occupied with activities along the waterfront. Des Moines Beach Park is to the north, Saltwater State Park to the south. In the middle of the shoreline sits the marina, restaurants, repair facilities, and marine store. The downtown shopping district is only a few blocks away and includes a variety of shops, services, lodging and dining establishments, as well as the Chamber of Commerce. Of special interest is the majestic Masonic Home of Washington that is open for tours. SeaTac International Airport is 15 minutes away by automobile, permitting possible flight access to this city, marina and shoreline. Annual festivals include the "Waterland Festival," a summer long event featuring special activities, contests, and other family fun.

★ **Des Moines Marina:** {47° 24.10' N, 122° 19.80' W} This well maintained, city-owned facility has moorage, 20, & 30 ampere power, gas, diesel, water, propane, repairs, haul-out, showers, waste pumpout, and restrooms. Enter south of the fishing pier, between the fishing pier and the north end of the rip rap breakwater. Convenient to restaurants, groceries, and downtown Des Moines. Reservations accepted for vessels 36' and greater in length and for groups of 5 or more boats. 24 hour notice for single boats and 2 weeks minimum notice for groups. See

---

★ **City of Des Moines Marina:** To enjoy one of the finest views of the Olympic Mountains, come to this marina facility located on the east side of Puget Sound, 18 miles south of Shilshole and 11 miles north of Point Defiance. (47-24' N lat. 22-20' long.) The marina entrance is between the fishing pier and the north end of the breakwater. At night, look for the three yellow navigation lights on the fishing pier and the single red marker light on the end of the breakwater. After clearing the breakwater, turn starboard and proceed to the fuel dock and guest moorage area. Approximately 1,500' of guest moorage is available on a first come, first served basis. Reservations accepted for vessels 36' and greater in length and for groups of 5 or more boats. 24 hour notice for single boats, two weeks minimum notice for groups. Vessels up to 60' can be accommodated. Water and 20, and 30 amp shore power are available. Check-in at the fuel facility. No time limit. There is a waiting list for permanent moorage. Since its opening in 1970, this well maintained facility has served the community of Des Moines and provided boaters access to the city's business district, located a few blocks east. Nearby are banks, shops, groceries, post office, restaurants, and lodging. Also at the marina are two restaurants, Milluzzo's, and Anthony's Home Port, Classic Yachts, a yacht brokerage, and CSR Marine South Boatyard. Repairs and a 37 ton Travel-lift with a beam capacity of 14' 6" are available. Boat launchers for small boats and a fuel dock with gas, diesel, propane, and lubricants are available. A pump-a-head and a "port-potty dump station are provided free of charge. Showers and restrooms. Families and large gatherings enjoy the picnic and meeting facilities at adjacent Des Moines Beach Park. Call the marina for information. Marina hours: Open all year. 6:00 a.m.-8:00 p.m. during the season and 8:00 a.m.-5:00 p.m. off season. **Circle #26 on Reader Service Card in A-Pages. Address: 22307 Dock Avenue, Des Moines, Washington 98198. Fax: 206-878-5940. Telephone: 206-824-5700. Internet: www.boattravel.com/desmoines & www.desmoineswa.gov.**

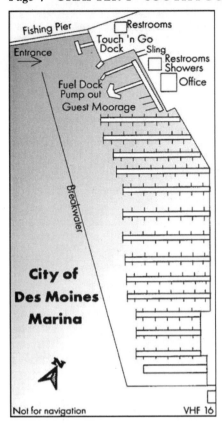

Fishing Pier
Restrooms
Touch 'n Go Dock
Entrance
Sling
Restrooms Showers
Office
Fuel Dock
Pump out
Guest Moorage

Breakwater

City of
Des Moines
Marina

Not for navigation   VHF 16

our Steering Star description in this chapter. Address: 22307 Dock Avenue South, Des Moines, Washington 98198. Fax: 206-878-5940. Telephone: 206-824-5700. VHF 16.

★⚓ **Saltwater Marine State Park (4):** Established in 1926, this 88 acre park is one of the state's oldest parks. It lies south of Des Moines in an attractive valley beside a salmon spawning creek called McSorely Creek. In the summer, the water that flows over the sandy flats is warm for wading. Facilities include tables, stoves, a kitchen shelter, food concession, pay phone, camping sites, showers, a swimming beach, mooring buoys, a scuba rinse station, underwater park with sunken barge and tire reef, and an RV dump station. The upper trails have beautiful views of Maury and Vashon Islands, the Olympic Mountains, and spectacular sunsets. This is a popular place for hiking and scuba diving. Fresh water is available. Summer hours are 8am - 9pm, winter hours are 8am - 5pm. Campground closed October - April. Call 206-592-0357 for general information. You will also find a year round educational facility with a "teach on the beach" progam for children which includes marine identification and beach walks. Summer camps also available.   206-824-0867, 360-902-8844, or 253-661-4956. ⚓🏕▲

★ **Redondo (5):** Anchoring is possible, or there is a seasonal mooring float and two concrete launching ramps, at this two-acre Redondo Beach Waterfront Park that is popular with scuba divers. There are shops, restaurants, a lighted T-shaped fishing pier, fish cleaning station, restrooms, boat parking, boat washing, and garbage containers. This site was originally named Poverty Bay by Captain Vancouver, because of a "poverty" of winds.

★⚓ **Dash Point State Park (6):** Near Dash Point, northeast of Tacoma, this park rims a warm, sandy beach. Fishing, scuba diving, swimming, and skim boarding are popular here. Because the water is shallow for some distance off

the beach, it is necessary to anchor quite a distance off the beach. The anchorage is open to winds and wakes. You will find 13 miles of hiking and mountain bike trails. There are picnic and campsites, hookups, fresh drinking water, and showers. Call for reservable shelter and group camp areas. Park is open year round but only available for reservations from May through September. The Trailer Dump Station will be closed for renovations through 2005. Call 253-661-4955 or 360-902-8844. ⚓🏕🚲

★⚓ **Dash Point Park & Pier:** A 200 foot fishing pier marks this site. Scuba diving is popular at a wreck off the park. No overnight camping is allowed on shore. There are picnic sites, a sandy beach for portable boats, a playground, and protected waters for swimming. Shallow water extends some distance offshore.

★⚓ **Browns Point Lighthouse Park (7):** This park has 1,500 feet of waterfront and offshore buoys for day use. Anchorage, open to the north, is possible in the deeper water offshore. This historic beacon, marking the entrance to Commencement Bay, was first constructed in 1903 and replaced in 1933 with today's concrete tower. Besides the beacon, this attractive three-acre park is home to the Points Northeast Historical Society Interpretive Center, open Sunday afternoons. The former lighthouse keeper's cabin is now available for weekly rental. Call 253-927-2536. A small shopping center is nearby.

Tacoma & Commencement Bay
[18445, 18448, 18453, 18474]

★ **Tacoma (8):** [18453] Although Tacoma's renaissance is the talk of the town, this city has been on the cutting edge for years. It is the first city in Washington to offer light rail service, is home to the nations's sixth largest port, and boasts the largest municipally owned telecommunications system in the U.S. By boat, entry is from Puget Sound, via Commencement Bay to Hylebos and Thea Foss Waterways. A five knot speed limit is enforced. Tacoma is a U.S. Customs & Border Protection designated Port of Entry. To report in-person to a CBP officer call 253-593-6338. At the head of Commencement Bay there are several small marinas along Hylebos and Thea Foss Waterways. Marinas along the Thea Foss Waterway offer access to repair facilities, chandleries, museums, shops, art galleries, specialty boutiques, restaurants, and waterfront parks. A new public dock in front of the Museum of Glass now lets boaters arrive in Tacoma's Museum District by water. From there, they can easily walk across the Chihuly Bridge of Glass to the Washington State History Museum, historic Union Station (filled with Chihuly glass art) and the Tacoma Art Museum. There are no longer any moorages in the Blair Waterway. The Blair Bridge was taken out to accommodate large freighters. The trip in, and out, of Blair Waterway permits seeing the rails at the mouth where the Todd Shipyards built the "Baby Flattops" during World War II. Metropolitan Park District mooring buoys are located along the south shore of Commencement Bay between Point Defiance Park and Old Town Dock. With its location on Commencement Bay, one of the largest natural deep-water ports in the world, much of the commercial development by the Port of Tacoma is on the flatlands at the mouth of the Puyallup River.

Each April, Commencement Bay is the site of the *Daffodil Festival Marine Parade.* Another event centered around Commencement Bay and Ruston Way parks is an annual *Fourth of July Extravaganza.* This features an air show, arts and crafts booths, and fireworks. The last weekend of June, The *Taste of Tacoma,* featuring food booths, live entertainment, Art a la Carte, and the Kids Art Festival, is held at Point Defiance Park.

The *Maritime Fest* is held in late September, with event headquarters at Thea's Park and Commencement Bay Maritime Center. An art show, tug boat race, free tours of the Port of Tacoma facilities, historical information, Wooden Boat Fair, salmon bake, food vendors, and a parade of vintage craft and fishing boats are planned attractions. Usually, a concert is the main event on Friday evening. Most of the other activities take place on the weekend, with the tug boat race on Sunday, followed by the Wooden Boat Parade. Many sailing races and regattas are held on Commencement Bay throughout the year. To highlight the holiday season, there is a marine Christmas parade along the Ruston Way shore and into Thea Foss Waterway. By car, Tacoma is approached from the north or south via Interstate 5, from the west via State Highway 16, or from the east via State Highway 410.

The Port of Tacoma: A major gateway to Asia and Alaska, the Port of Tacoma is a leading seaport in the Pacific Northwest and the fifth-largest container port in North America, handling more than $29 billion in annual trade and an estimated 2.3 million TEUs (Twenty-foot Equivalent container Units) in 2005. In addition to containers, the Port is a center for bulk, break-bulk and project/heavy-lift cargoes, as well as automobiles. The Port's Observation Tower, located next to the Port Administration Building (just off East 11th Street), gives visitors an up-close view of cargo handling activity. The Tower also features videos and displays show the history, development, and future plans for the Port.

Puyallup River: The Puyallup River system is one of Puget Sound's largest. It supports a large fish run, and much of the river basin has historical and archaeological significance.

Marine View Drive & Hylebos Waterway

[18445, 18448]

★ **Marine View Drive, Hylebos Waterway:** [18453] Marinas along Hylebos Waterway offer moorage, launching, provisions, and repairs, along with views of downtown Tacoma, the Port of Tacoma, and Mount Rainier. Indians once called the area, Tahoma, meaning Mother of Waters. Marine View Drive, along the northeast shore of Commencement Bay, is an aptly named street which ascends the edge of a bluff.

★ **J & G Marine Supply (8):** Your one stop shop for marine accessories and marine electronics. Authorized sales, service and installation of Big Bay Technologies, Inc., KVH, Nobeltec, Shakespeare, ComNav, Icom, Northstar, Simrad, Furuno, Lowrance, Nauticomp, JRC, Raymarine, Si-Tex, Garmin, Navman, Standard Horizon. We are located on Tacoma's Marine View Drive near the Hylebos Waterway. See our advertisement in this chapter. Email: jgmarinesupply.com. Address: 1690 Marine View Dr. Tacoma, WA 98422. Fax: 253-627-1344. Telephone: 253-572-4217, Toll Free: 1-800-381-4217.

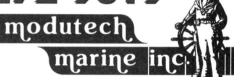

★ **Modutech Marine Inc.:** Family owned since 1970, Modutech is Tacoma's only full service boat yard. Dedicated to providing the highest quality repair and custom build services to fit any request, quotes are gladly given for any size project. We feature a 100 ton railway, insurance repair, custom fiberglass, aluminum, steel and custom woodwork. New construction from 26' to 70', offloads and commissioning. Covered moorage, 3 marine lifts, and heated painting booths. See our advertisement in this chapter. Address 2218 Marine View Dr., Tacoma, WA 98422. Website: www.modutech.marine.com. Telephone: 253-272-9319. Fax: 253-272-9337.

★ **Tyee Marina:** Located near Brown's Point, this moorage facility has covered and uncovered permanent moorage floats for boats 20'-50' in length. Storage units are available. Twenty-four hour security gate with card access to parking and floats. Boating services close by. Address: 5618 Marine View Drive, Tacoma, Washington, 98422. Fax: 253-838-2280. Telephone: 253-383-5321.

★ **Chinook Landing Marina:** {47° 16.90' N, 122° 24.20' W} Permanent and transient moorage is available at this modern marina. 125 volt, 30 & 50 ampere power, water, restrooms, store, laundry, showers, cable, pump out, convenience store, and phone service available. Twenty-four hour security. Open all year. Enter at the north-west side. See our Steering Star description and advertisement in this chapter. Website: www.boattravel.com/chinook/. Email: clm@puyallupinternational.com. Address: 3702 Marine View Drive, Tacoma, Washington 98422. Fax: 253-779-0576. Telephone: 253-627-7676. VHF 79.

Crow's Nest Marina: Limited moorage for overnight stays. Pump-out, dump, water, showers, laundry, restrooms. Friendly atmosphere with secured parking. 253-272-2827.

Hylebos Marina: Permanent moorage, haul-outs, repairs, parts. 253-272-6623.

Ole & Charlie's Marinas: Permanent & limited guest moorage only. 253-272-1173. VHF 16.

Thea Foss Waterway
[18453]

★ **Thea Foss Waterway:** [18453] No anchoring is permitted along the waterway. In 1900, when the Puyallup River was channeled into a straight course, two large waterways were formed. One of these, called City Waterway, was home to the Tacoma Municipal Dock. In 1989, City Waterway was renamed, "Thea Foss Waterway", in honor of the pioneer tug boating family headed by Thea Foss. The movie character, Tugboat Annie, is based on the life of Thea Foss. There is an attractive walkway along the shore.

Thea's Park is at the north end of the Thea Foss Waterway. At the head of Thea Foss Waterway is the Tacoma Dome. Freighthouse Square, near the dome, is an indoor mall with international food booths and shops. Also within

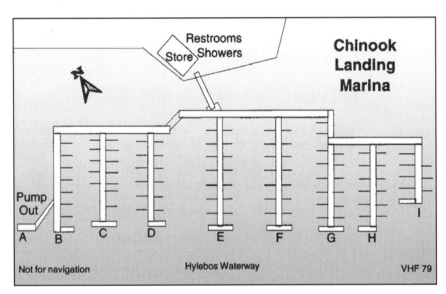

Chinook Landing Marina

Restrooms
Store Showers

Pump Out

A B C D E F G H I

Not for navigation   Hylebos Waterway   VHF 79

★ **Chinook Landing Marina:** At this modern marina in the Tacoma area, the management, security, and maintenance personnel take pride in operating a first class moorage facility where customer service is very important to the staff. The 213 slip, $3.6 million dollar marina has both permanent and transient moorage on a state-of-the-art concrete float system. Twenty-four hour security is provided. The marina, located near the Port of Tacoma, is found just as you enter Hylebos Waterway, off the starboard side. When approaching by auto, you will see a sand-blasted sign done in Native American Coastal Design-Chinook. There is extensive guest moorage with 430' available and no limitation regarding the length of stay. Tie to "A"-Dock and check in at the marina office, located in the longhouse-style building. Water, 125 volt, 30 and 50 ampere power, restrooms, showers, laundry, and waste pump-out are on the premises. A small retail store, which stocks some marine parts and provisions most commonly requested by boaters, also sells books, clothing, gifts, souvenirs, and charts. The staff will be happy to assist with land transportation needs so that it is possible to visit nearby restaurants, tourist attractions, golf courses, shops, museums, and theatrical events in downtown Tacoma. When arriving by car, follow Hwy 509 north until you come to Marine View Drive. Turn left and travel just past Old 11th Street Bridge to the marina. **Circle #20 on Reader Service Card in A-Pages. Website: www.boattravel.com/chinook/ Email: clm@puyallupinternational.com Address: 3702 Marine View Drive, Tacoma, Washington 98422. FAX: 253-779-0576. Telephone: 253-627-7676.**

walking distance of the downtown shoreline are hotels, Antique Row, and the Tacoma Farmer's Market, June to mid-September. Within walking distance of moorage on Thea Foss Waterway are the Tacoma Art Museum, the Broadway Center for the Performing Arts, Broadway Plaza, Commencement Bay Maritime Center, and Fireman's Park with its 105-foot high totem pole and a photography exhibit depicting the history of Tacoma.

Many changes, including additional moorage, are in store. On site is the Tacoma Maritime Center with its classrooms and boat building space. A pedestrian Bridge of Glass runs across

the I-705 freeway from the History Museum's Plaza to an International Glass Museum.

Foss Waterway Development Corp. manages several floats. Information: 253-597-8122 9-5 daily.

★ **Dock Street Marina:** Tacoma's preeminent "Destination Marina". Host to Tall Ships 2005, mooring 22 of the 30 visiting ships. Located closer than ANY marina to Tacoma's world-class museums, terrific restaurants, Theatre District and Antique Row. Walk two blocks to the free LightRail system to effortlessly extend your reach. Spacious and ample guest moorage - book

your cruisng clubs now. Gated access to state-of-the-art concrete docks, with extensive ADA features. 36' to 60' slips, with pier ends to 127'. 30 amp, 50 amp and 100 amp power. Cable TV and wireless internet connectivity. Slip-side pumpouts by marina staff - you don't even have to be there. Clean laundry facilities and restrooms, with free showers. Pet friendly and environmentally sensitive staff - an EnviroStars marina! See our Steering Star description in this chapter. Address: 1817 Dock Street, Tacoma WA 98402. Office 253-272-4352. Fax 253-272-4784. Dockmaster 253-250-1906.

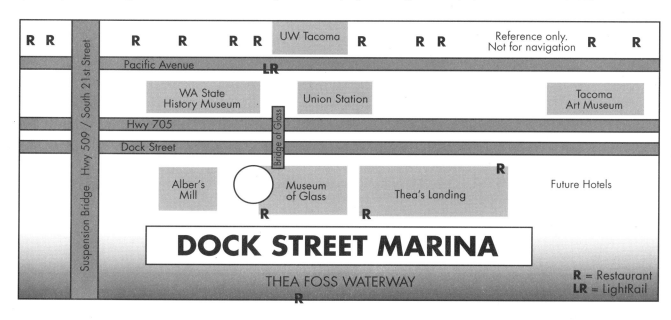

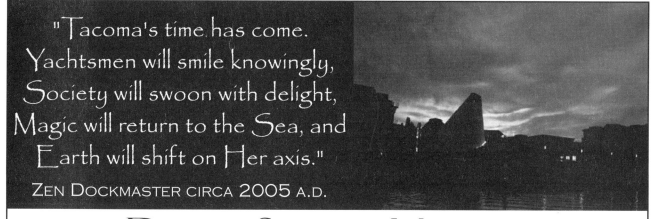

Tacoma's Museum of Glass   *Roger Hunsperger Photo*

★ **Foss Landing Marina:** Conveniently located just north of the Tacoma Dome on the east side of the Thea Foss Waterway, you will find the perfect combination of quality facilities, outstanding service, and reasonable rates. We offer an impressive array of boating services and amenities to make your boating experience as pleasurable as possible. See our advertisement in this chapter, or visit www.fosslanding.com for a complete list of the ways our friendly and knowledgeable staff can assist you. Address: 1940 E "D" St., Tacoma, WA 98421. Phone: 253-627-4343. fax: 253-627-4878. Email: info@fosslanding.com.

Johnny's Dock Marina: Temporary moorage while dining and 60 permanent, month to month, moorage slips. 253-627-3186.

Totem Fuel Dock : Gas, diesel, oil, snacks, ice, frozen herring. 253-383-0851.

★ **Foss Waterway Marina:** Best access to Downtown Tacoma's shops & restaurants. Fuel dock, showers, restrooms, full service marina with 480 slips, pump out & security. See our advertisement in this chapter. Address: 821 Dock St. Tacoma, WA 98402. Telephone: 253-272-4404. Fax: 253-272-0367. www.fosswaterwaymarina.com.

★ **15th Street Public Dock:** Open all year. No power or water. 240' of visitor's moorage, is located at 15th Street on the west side of Thea Foss Waterway, within easy walking distance of many points of interest in downtown Tacoma. There is a 24 hour moorage limit.

★ **Walk-around:** Bayside Trail system is located on the banks of the steep slopes between downtown Tacoma and the Old Town Historic District and runs for two and one-half miles, ending at Garfield Gulch. There are good views of Port of Tacoma, Commencement Bay, the Cascades and Mount Rainier along this trail. A large variety of plant and animal life exists in this 20 acre greenbelt.

Old Town & Ruston Way

[18445, 18448]

★ **Ruston Way [18453]:** Mooring buoys are offshore of this two mile stretch of beach, which has sandy and rocky stretches for beach walking or combing. This shoreline is part of scenic Kla How Ya Drive and offers panoramic views of Commencement Bay, Vashon Island, Port of Tacoma, Olympic and Cascade mountain ranges, including Mount Rainier, and the city skyline. There are parks, picnic tables, restaurants, a jogging and bicycle trail, a fishing pier, and public parking.

★⚓ **Commencement Park:** Mooring buoys are offshore along Commencement Bay, at the south end of Ruston Way. A large sundial is a landmark. Picnic area available. ⛩🚶

★ **Old Town Historic District:** The shopping district, one block from the Ruston Way waterfront and the Old Town Dock visitor moorage float, offer specialty foods, gifts, and artists' wares. In 1864, when Job Carr established claim to the land now known as Old Town, it was the beginning of Tacoma. The first house, church, post office, school, hospital, and lumber mill were built here. Many old homes and buildings, dating to this first port in Tacoma, remain, including St. Peter's Church. At the turn of the century, Slavonian immigrants settled in the Old Town, near Ruston Way. They introduced purse seining, a new and better method of fishing. This sparked a boom in commercial fishing, boat building and shipping along the shoreline.

★ **Old Town Dock:** Wharf and float are open. There is a sandy beach with picnic tables and restrooms nearby. An underwater artificial reef makes an excellent habitat and feeding ground for fish and other sea life. The original dock was built in 1873. By 1880, it was possible to rent a boat, board a steamer for Puget Sound cruising to other ports, or purchase wood, grains and farm produce from the many stores and businesses operating on the dock.

★⚓ **Hamilton Park:** This is a small park with promenades, benches, gardens and a fitness station.

★⚓ **Puget Gardens:** This nine-acre park is located on Alder Street, just 600-feet across Ruston Way. The three acres of beautiful gardens are bisected by a small stream. The gardens are espe-

cially lovely in the spring when the rhododendron and azalea shrubs are in bloom. Miles of trails wind through Puget Gulch to Puget Park. ⚓

Fire Station No. 5: Once an active fireboat station, Fire Station #5 now serves as administrative offices for the fire department. The high-speed fireboat/harbor service craft that was moored here from 1982 through 1999 has been relocated to the Thea Foss Waterway. Although Fire Station No. 5 is no longer open to the public, visitors can still enjoy the small park with unique walk-through seashell sculptures. The Tacoma Firefighters' Memorial nearby features a bronze sculpture of three firefighters advancing a hose line. Across the parking lot, retired Tacoma Fireboat #1 rests in permanent dry dock. Built in 1929, this familiar red and white vessel is designated as a National Historical landmark. The 96-foot Tacoma Fireboat #1 served the City of Tacoma for 54 years.

★⚓ **Marine Park, Tacoma:** As part of the city's dream to revitalize the Ruston Way shoreline, this 2,000 foot park has benches, lawn areas, restrooms, and access to the Les Davis Fishing Pier. It is a popular embarkation point for scuba divers. Tacoma's original fireboat has been permanently berthed at the east end of Marine Park. A memorial sculpture recognizes the sister city relationship between Tacoma and Kunsan City, Korea. There is also a memorial sculpture for the sister port of Kitakyushu, Japan. Several restaurants are nearby.

★ **Les Davis Fishing Pier:** This public fishing pier is a major attraction in the area. It is open 24 hours, with shelters, rod holders, and night lights. Restrooms are available. An underwater artificial reef provides an excellent habitat and feeding ground for fish and other sea life. During summer months concessions and skate rentals are offered nearby.

★⚓ **Knox Park:** Located on Ruston Way, this park has picnic sites, a sandy beach, and a mooring buoy. ⚓

★⚓ **Point Defiance Park (9):** Transient moorage is available adjacent to the launch ramp next to the Point Defiance-Vashon Island Ferry Terminal. Moorage is limited to 72 consecutive hours. A public launch ramp can be used for a nominal fee. Point Defiance Park is accessible by land and sea, and offers seasonal activities and special events for visitors of every age. This is the site of the Tacoma Yacht Club and two marinas, a restaurant, and Point Defiance Park. The 702-acre park has panoramic vistas of the water, Vashon Island, and the mountains. The formal rose, rhododendron, azalea, native herb iris, and Japanese gardens, and 20 miles of trails through old growth forest and a shoreline promenade offer peaceful moments in the park. Nearby are sandy

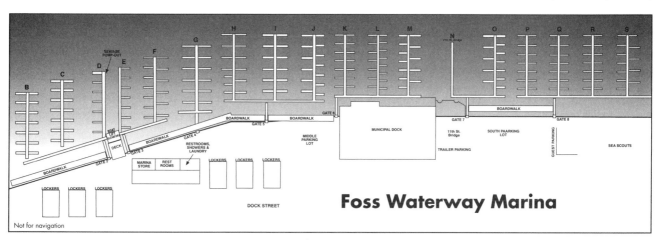

Foss Waterway Marina

Not for navigation

beaches, tennis courts, playgrounds, and picnic facilities. Extensive hiking running, walking and bicycling routes are accessible. Pont Defiance Park, with its Zoo and Aquarium, and historic Fort Nisqually, is rated as one of the best parks in the country. Activities include Taste of Tacoma and Art a la Carte the Friday, Saturday, and Sunday before the Fourth of July, Candlelight Tours held in October at Fort Nisqually, and Zoolights at Point Defiance Zoo during the month of December. Parks & Rec.: 253-305-1000. Zoo: 253-591-5337. www.metroparkstacoma.org

Point Defiance Boathouse Marina: Guest moorage, gas, water, pump-out, 4-lane launch ramp, provisions and bait. Located in Point Definance Park and close to Anthony's Restaurant. 253-591-5325.

Breakwater Marina: Limited guest moorage. Reservations requested. Gas, diesel, propane, limited power, grid, repairs, restrooms, showers, laundry, pump-out, ice, snacks. 253-752-6663.

Salmon Beach: When rounding Point Defiance and heading south toward the Narrows, one passes the unique, turn of the century Salmon Beach residential community. This small community of over-water cabins is in the State and National Register of Historic Places.

Tacoma Narrows (10): [18445, 18448] See The Narrows, Washington current tables. Because the water from the up-to-12 foot tidal changes in the South Sound area flows through this passage, currents run more than five knots. Currents generally flow northerly along the east side of the passage and southerly on the west side. Maximum flood and ebb currents occur about four hours after low and high tides in Seattle. These waters lead to the

South Sound, Longbranch Peninsula, Olympia, Horsehead Bay, Wollochet Bay, and more. By highway, the Narrows Bridge is the gateway to the Kitsap Peninsula and on to the Olympic Peninsula.

The bridge that spans nearly 6,000 feet across the Narrows is the fifth longest suspension bridge in the world. First built in 1940, it quickly became known as Galloping Gertie because of its tendency to sway and buckle. It collapsed within three months after its completion. Ten years later, a new steel span reconnected the peninsula to Tacoma. Today, the Narrows Bridge has a new nickname, Sturdy Gertie. A second bridge is currently under construction. All mariners must maintain a 500' distance within the right of way where boats and equipment are stored during construction. War Memorial Park is at the Tacoma end of the bridge. Visitors enjoy the flower beds and picnic sites.

★ Titlow Park (11): Pilings of the former Olympic Peninsula Ferry Landing mark the location of this 58-acre park. There are mooring buoys, an outdoor swimming pool, athletic field, fitness trail, volleyball and tennis courts, picnic, and scuba diving areas. Cousteau used the Titlow Beach area to study the native octopus. Since this area is a marine preserve, marine animals and plants may be studied but not removed, harvested, or harmed. Restaurants and a small grocery store are nearby.

Days Island (12): A 5-knot speed limit is enforced in the area. A dredged waterway, spanned by a bridge, separates this island (actually a peninsula) from the mainland. There are several permanent moorage facilities. Some local residents anchor shallow draft boats in Days Island Lagoon. The best course favors the Days Island side. There is a minimum low tide depth of one

foot. It is also possible to anchor east of the north tip of Days Island.

★ Day Island Boatworks, Narrows Marina and Narrows Bait & Tackle Store: Provide various amenities to boaters cruising south of the Tacoma Narrows Bridge. The offerings include moorage, winter storage, fuel, bait, tackle, beverages, restrooms, food, boats, service and parts. No transient moorage is available, but boaters are encouraged to tie-up at the Bait & Tackle Store to explore the facilities. Please call ahead for hours. Telephone: 253-564-1468. Website: www.dayislandboatworks.com. Address: 9004 19th W, Tacoma, WA 98466

Day Island Yacht Harbor: Permanent moorage. 253-565-4814.

Narrows Marina: Permanent moorage, gas, diesel, water, restrooms, launch ramp, full service with boat sales. 253-564-3032.

★ Steilacoom (13): This is the terminus for the ferry plying between Anderson, Ketron, and McNeil Islands. There is anchorage off Sunnyside Beach Park. There is a small pebble beach with picnic facilities, float, launching ramp, and fishing pier. A marina is located south of the ferry landing. There is short-term visitor moorage, for small and medium-sized boats, at a small float tucked in near the ferry landing. Founded by Lafayette Balch, a sea captain, Steilacoom began as a bustling frontier seaport. It was the first incorporated town (1854) in Washington Territory. Several homes have been restored, and 32 buildings are on the National Registry of Historic Places. A self-guided walking or driving tour is possible. The Historical Museum (Open 1-4:00 p.m. Wednesday-Sunday), and the Steilacoom Tribal Cultural Center are on site. The Cultural Center features a changing gallery, exhibits, gift shop and Fry Bread Café. Open Thursday-Saturday from 10am-4pm, phone: 253-584-6308. An ice cream stop is in the Blair Drug and Hardware Store. Built in 1895, it includes an early day post office, hardware, patent medicines, and 1906 soda fountain. A Salmon Bake is held the last Sunday in July and, for a fall visit, have fresh cider at the *Apple Squeeze* held the first Sunday in October.

Steilacoom Marina: Limited moorage, 20 ampere power, water, provisions. 253-582-2600.

Ketron Island (14): This is a private island with no public facilities.

★ Anderson Island, Oro Bay, & Amsterdam Bay (15): Anderson Island is the southernmost island in Puget Sound. It is a small, densely wooded island, encircled by 14 miles of beachfront property. Known for its serene pastureland and casual lifestyle, it is popular with bicyclists and boaters, though its shoreline is mostly private. A ferry connects Anderson Island to Steilacoom. A 5-knot speed limit is enforced in the area. There is anchorage in Oro and Amsterdam Bays. Thomson Bay has underwater cables. Oro Bay, on the southeast side is shallow. Amsterdam Bay, to port, in the inner harbor, has a shallow entrance. Favored anchorage is near the center of the bay. This bay is shallow at low tides. Good fishing is found year-round in the vicinity.

★ Eagle Island Marine State Park (16): This ten acre island in Balch Passage, between Anderson and McNeil Islands, is accessible only by boat. A buoy marks a reef nearby. Mooring buoys are provided. There are some sandy beaches. No drinking water or restrooms available. Currents may be strong in Balch Passage between

Anderson Island and McNeil Island. Currents have been known to shift the location of the buoys into areas with shallow water at low tides. The island may have been named by the Wilkes Expedition for a member in their party, Harry Eagle. 360-426-9226, 360-902-8844.

McNeil Island (17): This former Territorial Jail (1867) and Federal Penitentiary (1879-1980) is now a State Penitentiary. Maintain a distance of at least 100 yards off the island. Nearby Pitt and Gertrude Islands are undeveloped. McNeil Island is also home to many bald eagles and blue herons.

★ **Fox Island & Tanglewood Island (18):** If the red light is on, passage is prohibited in the Naval Testing Area on the southwest side of Fox Island. Fox Island is a peaceful residential island and was once home to Governor Dixie Lee Ray. It is connected to the mainland by a bridge. (See Hale Passage below.) Strong currents in this vicinity can affect launching from the ramp on the Fox Island shore. There are no public floats on the Island. Echo Bay, behind Tanglewood Island, is good anchorage. It is possible to land a dingy of in the southeast corner of this bay where there are no homes. One block up from the shore, on 6th Avenue, is a deli/grocery store that also sells gas and propane. Because of aquaculture operations, anchor on the west side of Tanglewood Island, and also farther in, behind the island. All shorelines and floats are private. Caution advised because several private buoys are in the bay. Nearns Point has a curving sandspit which cradles an anchorage basin.

Hale Passage: Separating Fox Island from the mainland, this four mile passage has maximum currents in excess of three knots. The ebb flows east and is stronger than the westerly flood current. Near the west end of the passage, a fixed highway bridge has a clearance of 31' at mean high water. A drying shoal, marked on its northeast side by a green buoy, is 350 yards southeast of the bridge and near the middle of the channel. Pass north of the buoy.

★ **Wollochet Bay (19):** [18445] This two-mile-long inlet, located off Hale Passage, is the site of many private homes and private mooring buoys. Anchorage is possible near the center farther into the bay, where the bay narrows abruptly. Private buoys and a yacht club outstation occupy most of the shallow basin at the head. There are launching ramps to starboard at the mouth of the bay and on the west shore in the inner harbor.

Gig Harbor
[18445, 18448, 18474]

★ **Gig Harbor (20):** A 5-knot speed limit is enforced including an area extending 200-feet outside the entrance. When traversing the narrow, 100-yard-wide channel that rims the spit at the entrance, keep to mid-channel if possible. Tidal currents can affect maneuvering near the spit. Within the harbor, shallow areas extend from shore and a drying flat is at the extreme head. Good anchorage, on a mud bottom, is found in the center, however, be aware that a thick layer of weeds on the bottom can foul some patent anchors. Anchorage is permitted on the north side and center of the harbor, not on the south side. Visitor moorage is relatively scarce because much of the dock space is reserved for permanent moorage and fishing boats. Marinas have transient moorage when permanent tenants are away from port. Jerisich Park, on the southern shore has guest moorage, and some restaurants have moorage floats for customers. A launch ramp is located on the northeast shore at the end of Randall Road. No fuel available in Gig Harbor.

Located at the southern end of the Kitsap Peninsula, Gig Harbor is home to spectacular views of Mount Rainier, the Olympics and the Cascades. Coined "The Maritime City," the harbor was so sheltered that in 1851, Captain Wilkes refused to enter until his gig was dispatched to explore the entry channel. The picturesque and photogenic waterfront, complete with fishing fleet, is often featured in magazines. Croatian and Yugoslavian descendants have given this community a European heritage, with fishing and tourism as major industries. A variety of seafood is available in the restaurants. Shopping includes wearable art, quilts, antiques, photographs, original paintings, pottery, concrete sculptures and books. An excellent brochure, published by the Gig Harbor Peninsula Historical Society and Museum, details a walking tour. The museum (253-858-6722) also features exhibits of the early settlement.

From May through October, a Farmer's Market operates each Saturday from 8:30am - 2:00pm, near Hwy 16 West, off Hunt Street. Annual events feature a parade in June, Art Festival in mid July, and a lighted boat parade at Christmas. By car, Gig Harbor is reached by State Highway 16 west from Interstate 5 in Tacoma. Gig Harbor, 30 minutes from Bremerton, is accessible via the Seattle-Bremerton ferry.

★⚓ **Jerisich Park:** Look for the large American flag and long moorage float extending from the southern shore. The pier has been widened and lengthened to more than double moorage space. Guest moorage permitted south side only. Check depth and low tide prediction. Rafting is permitted. Restrooms, picnic areas. Pump-out, (closed December 1 - April 1.) Dump open all year, 48 hour short stay. 253-851-8136. ⚓

★ **Arabella's Landing:** This new marina has security protected permanent and transient moorage (1,500 feet), 125 and 250 volt, 20, 30, and 50 ampere power, fresh water, showers, laundry, and waste pump-out. Reservations accepted. Relax on the waterfront deck for parties or your morning coffee. Downtown Gig Harbor is just a few steps away. See our advertisement in this chapter. Address: 3323 Harborview Drive, Gig Harbor, Washington 98335. Fax and telephone: 253-851-1793.

Lighthouse Marine Inc: Gig Harbor's marine hardware place to shop. Specializing in outboards and stern drives. 253-858-7280.

★ **Mostly Books:** Browse this very complete general interest book store, with its emphasis on northwest titles, travel, and marine books. New books for all ages. Mail orders welcome. See our advertisement in the A pages at the front of this book. Located near marina and public dock. Internet sites: www.mostlybooks.com & www.boattravel.com/mostlybooks. Address: 3126 Harborview Drive, Gig Harbor, Washington 98335. Fax: 206-851-7323. Telephone: 253-851-3219.

★ **Ship To Shore Marine Supply:** "The Biggest Little Marine Store On The Peninsula." Bait, fishing tackle, charts & maps, hardware, supplies and accessories. Located in downtown Gig Harbor. See our advertisement in this chapter. Address: 4021 Harborview Drive, Gig Harbor WA 98332. Telephone: 253-858-6090. Fax: 253-858-7104.

Gig Harbor Marina: Permanent moorage, haul-out, repairs, boat yard. 253-851-7157.

Murphy's Landing: Permanent moorage. 253-851-3093.

Peninsula Yacht Basin: Guest moorage, 30 ampere power, restrooms, showers, water. 253-858-2250.

Pleasurecraft Marina: Permanent moorage. 253-858-2350.

West Shore Marina: Permanent moorage. 253-858-3953.

Carr Inlet

[18445, 18448, 18474]

★ **Horsehead Bay (21):** Good, but limited, anchorage is found on a sandy mud bottom in 15-25 feet of water. A sandspit, in the shape of a horse head restricts the entrance and cuts off westerly seas. Private homes are located around the bay. A launching ramp is to port upon entry.

★⚓ **Kopachuck Marine State Park (22):** Located .7 miles north of Horsehead Bay, there are views of beautiful sunsets from the camping and picnicking sites among this park's 109 acres. Mooring buoys are available. Anchorage is possible on a good mud bottom. No protection from winds. Shore facilities include overnight campsites, RV facilities, showers, pay phone, picnic areas, forest trails, and water. About one mile from the park, groceries are available at a small store. A Cascadia Marine Trail campsite at the south end of the park has one group camp area and four tent sites. There is a sunken artificial reef offshore. Avoid the area near the white buoy. Scuba diving is popular in the Kopachuck-Cutts Island vicinity. 253-265-3606, 360-902-8844. ⚓▲🏕

★⚓ **Cutts Island (Deadman Island) Marine State Park (23):** Located in Carr Inlet, this park offers mooring buoys and a beach for picnicking. A drying spit connects Raft Island with Cutts Island. The six acre island is undeveloped except for pit toilets. No drinking water. 360-902-8844, 206-265-3606. 🏕

★ **Rosedale (24):** Good anchorage is possible in the lee of Raft Island. A bridge, with vertical clearance of 17 feet, connects the south shore of Raft Island to the mainland. Shoal areas dry in this channel and passage cannot be made at low water. Recommended entry is around the north side of Raft Island.

★ **Henderson Bay (25):** Leading to the community of Purdy, this bay stretches to Burley Lagoon at the extreme head. The lagoon dries and is private oyster lease land. Purdy has no marine facilities, however anchorage is good. Open to the south. A boat launching ramp is located at Wauna, near the highway bridge. Caution advised regarding low hanging electrical wires near the bridge. Department of Natural Resources beaches, found along the north shore of Henderson Bay, are posted with white posts.

Glen Cove (26): A spit protects the entrance to this very shallow bay. Do not attempt entry on a minus tide. A launching ramp is located to port near the entrance. There is limited, if any, anchorage.

★ **Maple Hollow (27):** Anchorage in the bay is possible. Avoid the Naval Acoustic Range marked by a red triangle with a flashing red light. Located on a steep, thickly forested hillside. As of March 1, 1999, this Department of Natural Resources acreage has been closed indefinitely.

★ **Von Geldern Cove (28):** Limited anchorage

space lies near the entrance to this shallow cove. A shoal extends from the north shore and the area is also exposed to north winds. A launching ramp is located on the west shore. In 1897, a commune settled here, but today, this is a quiet residential community with a store and service station located at the site of Home.

★ **Mayo Cove (29):** Shoals off Penrose Point restrict the port side when entering this shallow cove. Stay in center channel. The channel makes a bend to starboard. A marina and private homes lie to starboard near the head. Penrose Point State Park is located on the east shore.

Lakebay Marina: Gas, moorage, restrooms, provisions. Ramp. 253-884-3350.

★⚓ **Penrose Point Marine State Park (30):** Caution advised when approaching this area. To avoid unmarked shoals, the safest passage dictates keeping Penrose Point well off to port. There is over 10,000 feet of shoreline with extensive beaches at this lovely state park. There are mooring floats in Mayo Cove. The floats dry on extreme low tides. The tidal range is 12 feet. Mooring buoys are in outer Mayo Cove and along the east shore toward Delano Bay. Anchorage is possible in Mayo Cove, but be aware of pilings and an unmarked rock off Delano Beach. A park ranger is on duty. Showers, restrooms, RV facilities, hiking trails, pump-out, dump, and over 83 campsites with no hookups. Fresh water. Open seven days a week April-September. 253-884-2514, 360-902-8844. ⚓

Walk-around: Meander through attractive hillside trails and second generation stands of Douglas Fir, Western Red Cedar, Red Alders, Madronas, Rhododendrons, ferns, and Maples.

Pitt Passage (31): [18445] See current table for The Narrows, Washington. This narrow, two-mile-long channel is on the west side of McNeil Island. The ebb current flows north through Pitt Passage at the maximum rate of two and one-half knots. When traversing the passage, avoid the buoy-marked Pitt Passage Rocks, located off the McNeil Island shore, south of Pitt Island. At Pitt Island itself, pass in the channel on the east side of the island. Least depth within the passage at zero tide is 11 feet. Another buoy-marked shoal is a hazard north of Pitt Island. White posts on the beach along the west side of the Pitt Passage mark a public beach.

Many groundings occur at Wyckoff Shoal, a drying shoal located farther north of Pitt Island. Watch the depths and use chart. Pass west of green buoy #3 and north of green buoy #1. Wyckoff Shoal is a public beach, managed by the Department of Natural Resources. It is marked by white and red buoys. Clams, crabs, and sea cucumbers are plentiful.

★ **Filucy Bay & Longbranch (32):** Filucy Bay is a lovely, sheltered bay with good anchorage in 25-35 feet of water on a mud bottom. Anchorage, with protection from southeast winds, may be found in fairly shallow water inside the spit at McDermott Point and in the inlet that extends to the north. A launching ramp is south of McDermott Point.

Longbranch Marina: Moorage, 30 ampere power, covered pavilion. 253-884-5137.

Case Inlet

[18445, 18448]

Taylor Bay (33): There is limited anchorage

near the entrance. Some Department of Natural Resources public beaches are in the vicinity. Much of the shoreline is private.

★⚓ **Joemma Beach State Park (34):** Located in Whitman Cove (named for a local family), this Cascadia Marine Trail Campsite has a large camp, 2 primitive sites & 2 water trail sites. A pier, floats, restrooms, and picnic sites are available. Fees charged. Open year round. Floats removed in winter. 253-884-1944, 360-902-8844. 🏕

★⚓ **McMicken Island Marine State Park (35):** Mooring buoys are north and south of the island. There is good anchorage on a mud bottom. This 11 acre park is located off the east shore of Hartstine Island. It is accessible only by boat. There is a drying shoal and an uncharted rock between Hartstine and McMicken Islands. An artificial reef, constructed of old tires, lies north of the island. On Hartstine Island, behind the reef, is a public beach marked by white posts. There are clams, oysters, rock crab, and mussels here. Divers are likely to be in the vicinity. Pit toilets, and hiking trails are on park land. No fresh water. The extreme south tip of the island is privately owned. Originally, a Swedish sailor named Lundquist jumped ship, settled on the island, and gave it his name. However, when Mr. Lundquist contacted the government to get legal claim of the island, they said they had no record of its existence. A surveyor was dispatched to record the island on U.S. maps, and, in the process, he named the island, McMicken, after himself. 360-426-9226, 360-902-8844. ⚓

★⚓ **Hartstine Island State Park:** (Sometimes referred to as "Hartstene.") Located near the center of the east side of the island, this park has 1,600 feet of saltwater shoreline on Case Inlet. It is accessible by land and sea. Approaching by land, a parking lot is at trail head and a one half mile trail leads down to the beach. Hiking, beachcombing, clamming, and fishing are popular. The Department of Natural Resources manages the tidelands. 360-426-9226, 360-902-8844. ⚓

Herron Island (36): A ferry connects this private island with the mainland.

★ **Vaughn Bay (37):** Only shallow draft boats should explore this good, protected anchorage. The entrance is shallow, except above half tide. Enter mid-channel off the spit and follow the north shore for 200 yards. Then turn south, cross the bay staying parallel to the spit. When near the south shore, turn to port and follow the shore to the deeper water at the head of the bay. A concrete launching ramp and the small community of Vaughn are located on the north shore. A public beach is located on the outside of Vaughn Spit. There are littleneck and butter clams, and red rock crabs here.

Rocky Bay (38): Rocky Point provides some protection in north and west winds, however it is exposed to southerlies. A very shallow channel leads into the lagoon back of the sandspit. Watch for rocks. Travel around the small sandy island before turning to go behind the sandspit.

★ **Allyn (39):** A long dock with mooring float extends from shore. Some transient moorage is available. Caution advised because the bay is shallow. Deeper draft boats should not attempt it. Approach along the east side of the bay until opposite the pier, then turn in toward the pier. Drying flats extend from the head of Case Inlet. This public port on North Bay is the site of a new boat launch and float, as well as a city park.

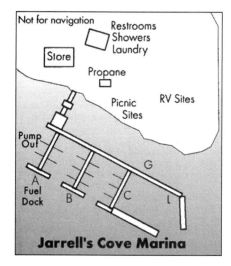

Jarrell's Cove Marina

Restrooms and fresh water are available, but no fuel. Restaurants and stores are within walking distance. Visitors will enjoy the fresh local oysters. The popular *Allyn Day Salmon Bake & Brew Festival* celebrated on Saturday, the third weekend in July, is held at the waterfront park and features food, vendors, and entertainment.

Port of Allyn: Limited moorage, ramps, water, restrooms, pump-out. Five feet of water at dock at low tide. 360-275-2430.

★ **Fair Harbor & Grapeview (40):** Enter from the south, in the channel between Stretch Island and Reach Island (also known as Treasure Island). The waterway under the bridge to Reach Island is dry on a minus tide. Deeper water is found near the marina. This harbor offers limited anchorage. Additional anchorage is found between the north tip of Reach Island and the mainland. Approach from the north. Reach Island is the name that commonly appears on marine charts, but the island is known locally as "Treasure Island", the name chosen by a development group that purchased the island in 1952. Across from the Island, farming once fueled the economy of the now residential community of Grapeview. The name reflects the grapes that became the number one crop. Today, local grape farms supply Hoodsport Winery and others. Many new, expensive waterfront homes are lining the shores as people discover the beauty and serenity of the area.

Fair Harbor Marina: Permanent and guest moorage, gas, power, water, showers, restrooms, launch ramp, minor repairs, provisions. 360-426-4028.

★ **Stretch Island (41):** Stretch Island is connected to the mainland by a bridge. There is no clear channel on the west side of the island and the area dries on any low tide. This is the site of the Museum of Puget Sound and Stretch Island State Park. The famous "Island Belle" grape used for winemaking is grown here.

★⚓ **Stretch Point Marine State Park:** Mooring buoys are at the site. This four acre park is accessible only by boat. It lies near Stretch Point on the northeast corner of Stretch Island. There is no fresh water, but mussels, swimming beaches, and scuba diving spots are plentiful. The island was named by Captain John Wilkes during an exploratory journey in 1841 for a gunner's mate, Samuel Stretch. 360-426-9226, 360-902-8844.

★ **McLane Cove (42):** This small indent off Pickering Passage has adequate depths for anchorage. A shoal is on the east side.

Pickering Passage: [18448] This nine-mile-long passage connects Case Inlet with Peale Passage and Totten Inlet (See current table for The Narrows, Washington). Pass mid channel. The flood current sets to the south toward Hammersley Inlet. Velocities in the area of Hammersley Inlet can reach 2.5 knots. A fixed bridge at Graham Point, clearance 31' at mean high water, connects Hartstine Island with the mainland. At Latimer's Landing Public Launch, near Graham Point, the concrete launching ramp can handle somewhat larger boats. About one mile west of Dougall Point on the north shore of Hartstine, is a private marina with moorage open only to property owners.

★⚓ **Jarrell's Cove Marine State Park (43):** This park is in the lovely inlet on the northern side of Hartstine Island. Beware of the shallow waters at minus tides and near the head of the cove. There are moorage floats. The first float is to port near the entrance. Fresh water is available. Another larger moorage float lies to port farther into the bay and there are numerous mooring buoys located in deeper water. The 43-acre park is accessible to visitors by land or by boat. Stoves, shelters, restrooms, showers, 20 campsites, waste pump, and dump. Anglers of all ages fish for perch and other marine creatures. Activities include canoeing, fishing, scuba diving, and hiking. User fees are charged year around. The Cascadia Marine Trail is north of the state park dock. The park was named after pioneer, Philora Jarrell. 360-426-9226, 360-902-8844. ⚓⛺▲⚓

★ **Jarrell's Cove Marina:** {47° 17.00' N, 122° 53.40' W} Located on Hartstine Island, opposite Jarrell's Cove State Park, this very clean marina has permanent and guest moorage, 30 ampere power, fresh water, diesel, gas, propane, ice, bait, fishing tackle and licenses, laundry, showers, waste pump-out and dump, picnic sites, and a nice beach. Three RV sites are equipped with electricity, water, and a dump station. The well stocked store has groceries, beer, wine, pop, and gifts. Moorage is available on a first come-first serve basis. Open every day in the summer and by appointment in the winter. Address: 220 E. Wilson Road, Shelton, Washington 98584. Fax: 360-432-8494. Telephone: 360-426-8823. 1-800-362-8823.

★ **Squaxin Island (44):** Squaxin Island is no longer a state park.

★⚓ **Hope Island Marine State Park:** Peace and serenity can be found at this lovely 106 acre state park. A resident caretaker is on the premises. No facilities. Hiking trails. No pets allowed, even on leash. No fires. Mooring buoys are available. Anchorage is possible off the eastern shore. Watch depths. 360-426-9226, 360-902-8844. ⚓

Nisqually Delta, Budd Inlet, & Olympia
[18445, 18448, 18456]

Nisqually Delta (45): This is a wildlife refuge with an outstanding accumulation of shore birds. A launching ramp at Luhr Beach, on Nisqually Head, provides access at high water. At the refuge, Nisqually Interpretive Center has guided tours which may be arranged by calling in advance. 360-753-9467. See current tables for The Narrows, Washington.

★⚓ **Tolmie Marine State Park (46):** Mooring buoys lie well out from shore, because the beach extends some distance. Anchorage is possible.

Named after a Hudson's Bay Company officer, this park has a picturesque saltwater lagoon and one of the finest sandy beaches in South Sound. It is located on the mainland about half way between Johnson Point and the Nisqually River delta. The beach is accessible by land and sea. Hiking is possible on over three miles of trails. A man-made reef provides scuba diving territory. A small footbridge leads to picnic facilities. There are tables, stoves, kitchens, restrooms, and outdoor showers, available for day use only. 360-456-6464, 360-902-8844. ⚓⚓⚓

Johnson Point (47): Site of two ramps.

Zittel's Marina: Permanent and guest moorage, 20 & 30 ampere power, gas, diesel, lift, provisions, ramp, pump-out, restrooms. 360-459-1950.

★ **Henderson Inlet (48):** Locally known as South Bay, Henderson Inlet extends over four miles to extensive drying flats. Keep to the center, avoiding private buoys and submerged pilings on the west. There is good anchorage inside the entrance in 35 feet of water on a mud bottom. Open to north winds. This is a wildlife conservation area. It is possible to explore Woodard Bay by dinghy.

★ **Boston Harbor (49):** The entrance to this attractive half-moon shaped harbor is identified by a lighthouse on Dofflemyer Point, at the mouth of Budd Inlet. There is a county launch ramp and marina for access to Nisqually Reach and other nearby attractions. Around the turn of the century this site was frequented by smugglers.

Boston Harbor Marina: Moorage, gas, diesel, 20 ampere power, water, provisions, service deli, kayak rentals, restrooms, CNG, launch. 360-357-5670. VHF 16.

★ **Budd Inlet [18448, 18456]:** The entrance to Budd Inlet is a mile wide between Dofflemyer and Cooper Points and is deep enough for all recreational vessels. To reach downtown Olympia from the north, round Dofflemyer Point and head toward Olympia by continuing past Olympia Shoal, marked by lighted beacons on the shoal's east and west sides. From Olympia Shoal, pick up the 28' dredged and buoyed channel that leads into the harbor. A spoils bank from channel dredging, lies east of the channel. This bank is quite shoal, with parts of it drying, so stay in the channel. The channel branches at a piling intersection market. Follow the eastern leg to Swantown Marina and Boatworks.

★⚓ **Burfoot County Park (50):** This is a 50-acre day-use park in a small niche south of Boston Harbor. There are trails, picnic areas, volleyball courts, and horseshoes. It can be accessed by land or water. An artificial reef is marked by buoys. ⚓⚓

Walk-around: Several trails in and around Burfoot County Park offer views.

★⚓ **Priest Point Park:** This 250 acre park on East Bay Drive is supplied with picnic tables, shelters, playgrounds, water, restrooms, and Ellis Cove Trail. A good beach and extensive tide flats are within this park acreage. ⚓

Walk-around: The Ellis Cove Trail is a three mile, loop design trail which takes approximately one hour to walk. There are Interpretive Stations describing different aspects of the ecology, forest, birds, plant life, wildlife, and history of the area. Beach access is possible in several places. All boardwalks, bridges, railings, and structures were designed to compliment the landscape. For a brochure about the City of Olympia

Boatswap & Chowder Challenge. *Lakefair* is held in July, and *Harbor Days*, with the Vintage Tugboat Race on Labor Day weekend. Contact the Olympia Thurston County Visitor & Convention Bureau for information regarding area events, attractions, and transportation. 360-704-7544, www.visitolympia.com.

Bayview Thriftway: Located at the end of Percival Landing. Beef, seafood, produce. 1-800-385-9875.

★ **Pettit Marine, LLC: (51)** This full service Marine Center specializes in Electric, Mechanical, Installation & Repair. They feature years of experience in custom wood replacement and repair. Upholstery cushions & covers, glass repair and hull bottom painting. Located in Olympia's Swantown Boatworks. There is access to a 77-ton travelift and 24 hour emergency haul out response. See our advertisement in this chapter. Website: www.pettitmarine.com. Address: 710 Marine Dr NE, Olympia, WA 98501, Telephone: 360-561-5780.

★ **Port Plaza (Port of Olympia):** Located north of Percival Landing. Water, no power. Free four-hour moorage, then guest rate for over four hours. This multi-use, natural park-like space serves as a concert and event site for outdoor events. Bronze artwork reflects maritime and natural history. The colored and textured concrete and paved surfaces, unique planting areas and raised lawn invite visitors to enjoy a relaxing respite onshore. For more information, call Swantown Marina 360-528-8049.

★ **Swantown Marina and Boatworks:** {47° 03.50' N, 122° 36.65' W} Owned and operated by Port of Olympia. Recent expansions provide over 700 slips for permanent and guest moorage. Amenities include security, 30 & 50 ampere shore power, concrete two-lane launch ramp, Porta-Potty and waste pump out station, restrooms, showers, laundry facilities, parking areas, pedestrian walkways, recycle services, complete repairs, 24-hour emergency haul-out. Open all year. See our Steering Star description in this chapter. Websites: http://www.portolympia.com/swantown/swantown.htm & www.boattravel.com/swantown/. Email: marina@portolympia.com. Marina address: 1022 Marine Drive N.E., Olympia, Washington 98501. Marina Telephone: 360-528-8049. Fax: 360-528-8094. Boatworks address: 650 Marine Drive NE, Olympia, Washington 98501. Boatworks Telephone: 360-528-8059. Fax: 360-528-8095. VHF 16 & 65A.

Martin Marina: Permanent moorage. 360-357-5433.

Percival Landing Marine Park: This city owned recreation area offers both electrical and non-electrical moorage. Free daytime guest moorage on non-electrical floats. Fees collected for floats equipped with 30-ampere power, regardless of length of stay. Maximum stay is seven days within any 30-day period. Showers, restrooms (open dawn to dusk), waste pump-out, and dump. Check in and make payment at the Olympia Center Pay Station on Columbia Street and Olympia Avenue. When the Olympia Center is closed, place moorage payments in provided dock boxes. Code locks on the showers open with access codes that are provided at registration or by staff that make daily rounds on the dock. Between the months of October and March the City of Olympia Parks & Rec accepts moorage reservations for Percival Landing. They can be made up to one year in advance for groups of more than five boats. Call 360-753-8380. Playfields, an observation tower, the Olympia

Regional Trail Guide call 360-753-8380.

★ **Olympia (51)** (See Budd Inlett chart numbers and navigation information above): There is overnight moorage at Swantown Marina, Port Plaza, and Percival Landing Park. Swantown, operated by the Port of Olympia, is located on the east side of the peninsula that juts out from the head of Budd Inlet. The other Port of Olympia facility, Port Plaza, with moorage and viewing tower, is on the main channel, past the marine shipping terminal. At the head of the inlet, next to the boat houses, is City of Olympia's Percival Landing Park.

The downtown heart of Olympia has many restored buildings which house gift shops, grocery stores, a Farmers Market, book shops, marine businesses, art galleries, antique shops, clothing and specialty shops, and a variety of popular restaurants and bars featuring live entertainment. Rimming the waterfront is a landscaped, mile-long, wooden promenade with benches and tables built over pilings along shore. The main promenade heads north, past a carved Orca Whale and a tangle of docks, to a tower that offers gulls-eye, 360 degree view of the Olympics and the port. At the corner of Fourth and Water Streets, a life-sized sculptured couple leans against the boardwalk rail, locked in an endless kiss while the boats come and go. This historically significant site, was named in 1853 after Captain Samuel Percival.

Parks, within easy walking distance, include Capitol Lake, Sylvester, and Port Plaza. At the former, sunbathers enjoy the beach, the boating and sailing activities, picnic areas, and trails where they can watch the reflections of the Capitol Buildings sparkling in the waters of the lake. The lake was created in 1951 by damming the mouth of the Deschutes River. Music-In-The-Park concerts entertain visitors every

Wednesday evening at 7pm during July and August at Sylvester Park. Nearby is the Old Capitol, all stone arches and gargoyles. Built in 1892 as the Thurston County Courthouse, this served as capitol from 1905 to 1928. Self-guided tours are possible. The Washington Center For The Performing Arts feature live stage productions with local and regional actors. The Hands On Children Museum is a special attraction, designed to entertain and educate children of all ages.

The Capitol Campus has lovely trees and gardens. Built in 1928, the Legislative Building, with a design reminiscent of the U.S. Capitol in Washington DC, is the last great domed capitol built in America. Louis Comfort Tiffany designed the building's floor lamps, sconces, and chandeliers. Tours offered daily on the hour from 10 am to 3 pm. Next to the capitol stands the red brick, Georgian Style home of the governor. Tours of the Executive Mansion are conducted each Wednesday, by reservation only. Call 360-902-8880 for information on capitol campus tours. The Capitol Conservatory, constructed in 1939, is a greenhouse containing tropical plants and bedding plants for the Capitol grounds. It is usually open Monday through Friday 8:00 a.m.-3:15 p.m. and weekends from Memorial Day through Labor Day. The Temple of Justice, completed in 1920, houses the Washington State Supreme Court and the State Law Library. Finally, the State Capitol Museum, south of the Capitol Campus on 21st Avenue, is open from 10:00 a.m. to 4:00 p.m. Tuesday through Friday and 12:00 to 4:00 p.m. Saturday. Closed Sun/Mon. 360-753-2580. For more information about Capitol facilities or events contact the State Capitol Visitor Center at 360-586-3460.

Special events featured during the month of May include the *Wooden Boat Fair, Capital City Marathon* (3rd weekend), and *Swantown*

Farmers Market, restaurants, and grocery store are in and around the park.

Westbay Marina: Permanent moorage and pump-out. 360-943-2080. 1-800-884-2080.

★ **Eld Inlet (52):** This inlet extends five miles. Limited anchorage is possible, however caution advised because of shallow depths and a lack of protection from winds. A spit extends some distance off Cooper Point. Favor mid channel when entering and enter on an incoming tide. Homes are along the shore. The east shore is undeveloped and offers niches for anchoring. Frye Cove County Park, a 90 acre undeveloped park, is north of Flapjack Point. Anchorage is possible. There is an artificial reef for swimming and scuba diving. A pay launching ramp is on the north shore of Young Bay, south of Flapjack Point. It is best to enter this cove on an incoming tide. Limited anchorage is possible. The campus of Evergreen Community College is on the south shore. See Current Table for The Narrows, Washington.

Totten Inlet (53): [18448] The warm waters of Totten and Skookum Inlets have been oyster producing grounds since the mid-1800's. Rock walls and poles used to mark the beds can be hazards for boats. There are no public beaches in the inlet. Anchorage is possible away from obstructions. A launching ramp is located at Arcadia Point on the eastern entrance to Totten Inlet. The word, Skookum, means strong water. Depths in Skookum Inlet allow for dinghy exploration only. Tidal range is 12 feet. See Current Table for The Narrows, Washington.

★ **Hammersley Inlet (54):** [18445, 18448, 18457] See Current Table for The Narrows, Washington. This six mile, narrow, fish-hook shaped passage leads to Oakland Bay and the City of Shelton. Controlling depth in the inlet is eight feet. Flood tides flow toward the head at a maximum rate of two and one half knots and are strongest near Cape Horn. The shallowest portion of the inlet is near the entrance, where there are drying flats. When entering, stay close to the north shore. Silting makes it important to make a wide turn and stay close to the Hungerford Side. At present, no navigation buoys are in the inlet. Some aids are marked on shore. After Church Point, passage is easier. Vessels with tows have the right of way. Traverse near the end of the flood tide when the tide is high and currents are weakest.

★ **Shelton & Oakland Bay (55):** Moorage is very limited, but anchorage is possible on a mud bottom. The marina is approximately one half mile from town. A launching ramp, inactive at low tides, picnic sites, and playground are at Jacoby Shore Crest County Park, across the bay from Shelton. There is a Visitor Center in an historic Peninsula Railway Caboose #700. Take a self guided walking tour and take time to discover the hidden creeks, inquire about the timber industry, and browse the quaint shops along the main street. Car rentals are available for sightseeing. Much of Oakland Bay is devoted to log storage and oyster cultivation. Shelton, coined the Christmas Tree Capital of the World, celebrates a *Forest Festival* in June and *OysterFest* the first weekend in October. Walker Park, Cascadia Marine Trail, is east of Shelton. Reservations: 360-427-9670 Ext. 535.

Port of Shelton Marina: Operated by the Shelton Yacht Club. Limited guest moorage, 30 ampere power, water, pump-out. No fuel. The visitor's dock is open at all times. 360-426-6435 after 5 p.m.

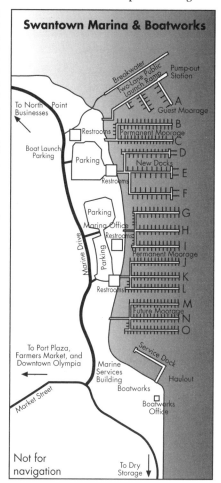

Swantown Marina & Boatworks

Not for navigation

★ **Swantown Marina and Boatworks:** Whether it's a visit, permanent moorage or vessel haulout, Swantown offers full-service boating convenience in a park-like setting. This modern Port of Olympia facility includes both permanent and guest moorage. A breakwater shelters security protected, concrete docks. Permanent moorage capacity is 645 slips for boats up to 80 feet. The guest dock offers slips for boats to 100 feet in length. Water and 30 or 50 ampere shore power are available. Other facilities include public telephones, restrooms, showers, laundry, garbage, recycle services, used oil recycle, a pump-out station, and Port-a-Potty. A

double-lane concrete launch ramp and parking area are available. Additional day-use moorage is available at the Port Plaza, located on the west side of the Port Peninsula.

Swantown Boatworks features a 77-ton Travelift and washdown with 24-hour emergency haul-out services. The 2.9-acre boatyard is fenced and lighted with capacity for 45 vessels. Other boatyard amenities include electricity, water and compressed air at all work areas. Repair vendors are available on-site and by referral.

Located on the East Bay of Budd Inlet, Swantown is picturesque and within easy walking distance to downtown, the Olympia Farmers Market (open April through December), and several restaurants. Olympia is a great year-round destination. Festivals during the year include the *Olympia Wooden Boat Fair* in May, the annual *Swantown BoatSwap & Chowder Challenge* in May, *Capital Lakefair* in July, and *Harbor Days* during Labor Day weekend. For information, go to www.visitolympia.com. **Websites: www.portolympia.com/swantown/swantown.htm & www.boattravel.com/swantown/ MARINA: Address: 1022 Marine Drive NE, Olympia, Washington 98501. Telephone: 360-528-8049. Marina Fax: 360-528-8094. Email: marina@portolympia.com BOATWORKS: Address: 650 Marine Drive NE, Olympia, Washington 98501. Telephone: 360-528-8059. Fax: 360-528-8095. Email: boatworks@portolympia.com VHF 16 and 65A.**

Essential Supplies & Services

AIR TRANSPORTATION
Seattle Seaplanes **1-800-637-5553**
AMBULANCES. . . . . **Call 911**
BOOKS / BOOK STORES
The Marine Atlas. **541-593-6396**
Mostly Books **253-851-3219**
BUS TRANSPORTATION
Greyhound 1-800-231-2222
Mason County Transit 1-800-374-3747
Olympia Intercity Transit 360-786-1881
Pierce Co. Transit 253-581-8000
Vashon Metro Rider. 206-553-3000
COAST GUARD
VHF 16 Seattle. 206-217-6000
Customer Information 1-800-368-5647
Vessel Traffic. 206-217-6151
CUSTOMS/BORDER PROTECTION
Tacoma 253-593-6338
FERRY TRANSPORTATION
Washington State 1-800-843-3779
FUELS
Boathouse Marina, Point Defiance: Gas . 253-591-5325
Boston Harbor Marina, Olympia: Gas. Diesel. 360-357-5670
Breakwater Marina, Point Defiance: Gas, Diesel
. . . . 253-752-6663
Des Moines: Gas, Diesel . . . 206-824-5700 VHF 16
Fair Harbor Marina, Grapeview: Gas 360-426-4028
Jarrell's Cove Marina: Hartstine Island. Gas,
Diesel 360-426-8823
Lakebay Marina, Mayo Cove: Gas 253-884-3350
Narrows Marina, Tacoma: Gas, Diesel. 253-564-3032
Totem Fuel Dock, Tacoma: Gas, diesel, oils. 253-383-0851
Zittel's Marina, Olympia: Gas, Diesel 360-459-1950
GOLF COURSES
Capitol City: from Olympia. 360-491-5111
Lakeland Village: from Allyn or Fair Harbor. 360-275-6100
North Shore: from Tacoma Marine Drive Moorages
. . . . 253-927-1375
Shelton Bayshore: from Shelton Yacht Club 360-426-1271
Tumwater Valley: from Olympia. 360-943-9500
HOSPITALS
Capitol Medical Center. 360-754-5858
Providence St Peters Olympia 360-491-9480
Mason General Hospital Shelton 360-426-1611
Tacoma General Hospital 253-403-1000
INSURANCE
Boat Insurance Agency 206-285-1350
Or Call 1-800-828-2446
MARINAS / MOORAGE FLOATS
Arabella's Landing Marina, Gig Harbor. 253-851-1793
Boathouse Marina, Point Defiance. 253-591-5325
Boston Harbor Marina, Olympia . 360-357-5670 VHF 16
Breakwater Marina, Point Defiance 253-752-6663
Chinook Landing, Tacoma . . 253-627-7676 VHF 79
Des Moines Marina . . . . . . 206-824-5700 VHF 16
Dock Street Marina 253-250-1906
Dockton County Park, Maury Island
Fair Harbor Marina, Grapeview 360-426-4028
Foss Developement Corporation 253-597-8122
Foss Landing Marina 253-627-4344
Foss Waterway Marina. 253-272-4404
Jarrell's Cove, Hartstine Is. 360-426-8823
Jerisich Park, Gig Harbor 253-851-8136
Lakebay Marina, Mayo Cove 253-884-3350
Longbranch Marina. . . . . 253-884-5137 VHF 16
Ole & Charlies, Tacoma 253-272-1173
Peninsula Yacht Basin, Gig Harbor 253-858-2250
Penrose Point Park
Percival Landing, Olympia 360-753-8380

Shelton: 360-426-9476(Port of Shelton: 360-426-1151)
Steilacoom Marina. 253-582-2600
Swantown Marina, Olympia 360-528-8049
. . . . **VHF 16 & 65A**
Thea Foss Development Corp: Tacoma . . 253-597-8122
(Water Development Authority)
Tyee Marina, Tacoma. 253-383-5321
Zittel's Marina, Olympia 360-459-1950
MARINE SUPPLIES
J & G Marine Supply 253-572-4217
Or Toll Free: 1-800-381-4217
Ship to Shore Marine Supply, Gig Harbor 253-858-6090
PARKS
Camping Reservations 1-888-226-7688
Department of Natural Resources 1-800-527-3305
Tacoma Metropolitan. 253-305-1000
Washington State 360-902-8844
POISON INFO: 1-800-222-1222
PROPANE
Breakwater Marina, Pt. Defiance 253-752-6663
Des Moines Marina. . . . . . 206-824-5700 VHF 16
Jarrell's Cove, Hartstine Island. . . . 360-426-8823
RAMPS/HAUL-OUTS
Allyn
Boathouse Marina, Point Defiance. 253-591-5325
Boatyard, The, Tacoma 253-565-6333
Boston Harbor Marina, Olympia 360-357-5670
Burton County Park
Des Moines Marina. . . . . . 206-824-5700 VHF 16
Dockton County Park
Eld Inlet
Fair Harbor Marina, Grapeview 360-426-4028
Foss Waterway Marina. 253-272-4404
Fox Island
Gig Harbor VHF 68
Glen Cove
Graham Point, Pickering Passage
Henderson Bay
Horsehead Bay
Hylebos Marina, Tacoma 253-272-6623
Johnson Point
Lakebay
Longbranch VHF 16
Luhr Beach, Nisqually Delta
Modutech Marine Inc. 253-272-9319
Narrows Marina, Tacoma 253-564-3032
Olalla
Ole & Charlies Marina 253-272-1173
Point Defiance
Redondo Beach
Shelton
Steilacoom
Sunnfjord, Tacoma 253-627-1742
Swantown Boatworks, Olympia
. . . . **360-528-8059 VHF 16 & 65 A**
Totten Inlet, Arcadia Point
Vaughn Bay
Von Geldern Cove
Wauna
Westbay Marina, Olympia 360-943-2080
Wollochet Bay
Young Point, Eld Inlet
Zittel's, Olympia 360-459-1950
RED TIDE HOTLINE 1-800-562-5632
REPAIRS & SERVICES
Breakwater Marina, Point Defiance 253-752-6663
Boatyard, The, Tacoma 253-565-6333
Day Island Boatworks 253-564-1468
Des Moines Marina. . . . . . 206-824-5700 VHF 16
Fair Harbor Marina, Grapeview 360-426-4028
Gig Harbor Marine 253-851-7157

Hylebos Marina, Tacoma 253-272-6623
J & G Marine Supply 253-572-4217
Or Toll Free: 1-800-381-4217
Modutech Marine Inc. 253-272-9319
Pettit Marine LLC 360-561-5780
Sunnfjord, Tacoma 253-627-1742
Swantown Boatworks: Olympia . . . 360-528-8059
Tyee Marina, Tacoma. 253-383-5321
Westbay Marina, Olympia 360-943-2080
Zittel's Marina, Olympia. 360-459-1950
RV FACILITIES
Dash Point Park
Jarrell's Cove, Hartstine Island 360-426-8823
Kopachuck State Park
Penrose Point State Park
SCUBA SITES
Dash Point State Park   Saltwater State Park
Eld Inlet   Stretch Island State Park
Jarrell's Cove State Park   Titlow Beach
Kopachuck State Park   Tolmie State Park
Point Robinson County Park   Tramp Harbor, Vashon
Ruston Way, Tacoma   Island
SEWAGE DISPOSAL SITES
Allyn: Pump. 360-275-2430
Arabella's Landing, Gig Harbor: Pump . . 253-851-1793
Boathouse Marina, Point Defiance: Pump . 253-591-5325
Breakwater Marina, Point Defiance: Pump. 253-752-6663
Chinook Landing, Tacoma: Pump. . . 253-627-7676
Des Moines Marina: Pump, Dump. . . 206-824-5700
Crow's Nest, Tacoma: Pump, Dump. 253-272-2827
Dock Street Marina 253-250-1906
Dockton County Park, Maury Island: Pump.
Foss Landing Marina 253-627-4344
Foss Waterway Marina, Tacoma: Pump. 253-272-4404
Jarrell's Cove Marina: Pump, Dump. 360-426-8823
Jarrell's Cove State Park: Pump, Dump. . 360-426-9226
Jeresich Park, Gig Harbor: Pump, Dump. 253-851-8136
Penrose Point Mayo Cove: Pump, Dump. 253-884-2514
Percival Landing, Olympia: Pump, Dump.. 253-753-8380
Shelton Marina: Pump.
Swantown Marina, Olympia: Pump. 360-528-8049
Westbay Marina, Olympia: Pump 360-943-2080
Zittel's Marina, Olympia, Pump 360-459-1950
SHELLFISH HOTLINE 360-796-3215
24-hour Red Tide Information Line 800-562-5232
For local area closures/information, call County Health Depts.:
King County Health Dept 206-296-4632
Mason County Health Dept 360-427-9670
Pierce County Health Dept. 253-591-6470
Thurston County Health Dept 360-754-4111
TAXI
Olympia 360-786-5226
Tacoma 253-472-3303
TOWING
C-TOW. 1-888-354-5554
VESSEL ASSIST . . . . Tacoma 253-312-2927
VHF MARINE OPERATOR
Whidbey Island: 87
Note: MariTel has shut down all other Washington State
     VHF Marine Operator channels.
VISITOR INFORMATION
Gig Harbor. 253-851-6865, 1-888-553-5438
Metropolitan Park District, Tacoma 253-305-1000
Olympia / Thurston County. 360-704-7544,
. . . . 1-877-704-7500
Shelton C of C 360-426-2021, 1-800-576-2021
Shelton Tourist Info. 360-427-8168
Tacoma C of C 253-627-2175
Tacoma/Pierce County 1-800-272-2662
WEATHER . . . . VHF WX-1, WX-3

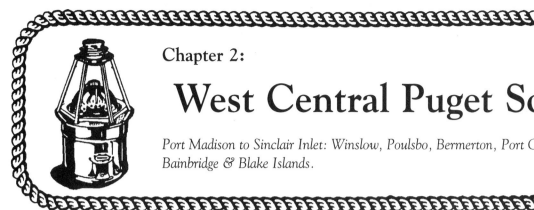

Chapter 2:

West Central Puget Sound

Port Madison to Sinclair Inlet: Winslow, Poulsbo, Bermerton, Port Orchard.
Bainbridge & Blake Islands.

Symbols

[   ]: Numbers between [   ] are chart numbers.

{   }: Numbers & letters between {   } are waypoints.

⚓: Park, ⛵: Boat Launch, ▲: Campgrounds,
𝕏: Hiking Trails, ⚏: Picnic Area, ☙: Biking

★ **Important Notice:** See "Important Notices" between Chapters 7 and 8 in this guide for specific information on boating related topics such as: Canadian & U.S. Customs, boating safety and security, navigation, weather, U.S. & Canadian Coast Guard, U.S & Canadian marine radio use, Vessel Traffic Service and traffic separation plans, security zones, and internet access. Due to new Department of Homeland Security regulations, call ahead for latest customs information and/or see Northwest Boat Travel On-line, www.nwboat.com.

Bainbridge Island

[18441, 18445, 18448]

★ **Bainbridge Island:** Circumnavigating Bainbridge Island is a boater's delight. One can anchor in a bay where the atmosphere seems to hang heavy with memories of the past and, at the same time, one can view the setting sun on today's Seattle skyscrapers and enjoy the twinkling night lights of the metropolis, just across Puget Sound. One could easily spend several days just exploring the many bays, parks, and the community of Winslow. For a shore excursion from moorage at Winslow, it is possible to rent a car or bicycle and ride along the relatively flat road which heads north toward Murden Cove. On the water, places of interest include Eagle Harbor, Fay Bainbridge State Park, Point Monroe, Port Madison, Agate Passage, Manzanita Bay, Fort Ward State Park, and Blakely Harbor.

Chart List

NOAA Charts:

18441, 18445-46, 18448-49, 18452, 18474

Marine Atlas (2005 ed.):

Page 4

Bainbridge Islanders are extremely proud of their home and its colorful history of Native settlements, shipyards, sawmills, and agriculture. Traces of its heritage are found among the 48 square miles of gently rolling hills, farms, vineyards, pristine seashore, and abundant streams to which salmon return during the spawning season.

History records that over 130 years ago, timber and ship building industries thrived. Although one will not see the square riggers and down-easters that once loaded lumber at the Port Madison mill and plied the waters of Puget Sound en route to far corners of the world, it is easy to imagine them sailing by. The Blakely Harbor docks, which provided moorage for ships, are also gone as is Hall Brother's Shipyard, once an Eagle Harbor landmark. Port Blakely, once a thriving and wide-open town, has only a few crumbling pilings as souvenirs of those days.

★ **Blakely Harbor (1):** This one mile indentation has a wide entrance that narrows to a lagoon at the head. Good anchorage may be found well into the harbor. Favor the center of the bay and southern shore. There are shoals and submerged pilings near shore. Private homes edge the low bank shore line. The sawmill located here in the 1800's was one of the world's largest. The mill buildings and employee houses once fronted along a boardwalk that rimmed the town and har-

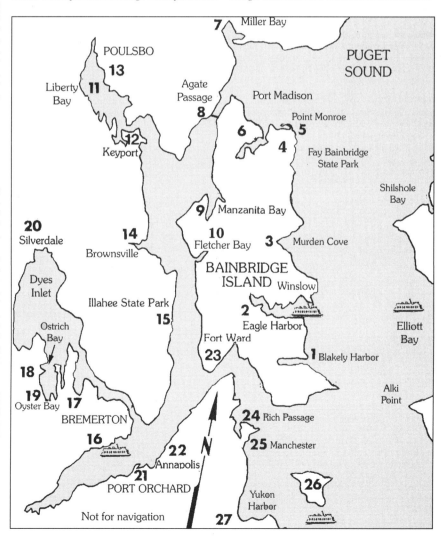

Not for navigation

bor. Paintings of the harbor show it filled to capacity with windjammers, flying the flags of many nations.

★ **Eagle Harbor (2):** [18449] Terminus for the Winslow-Seattle ferry, Eagle Harbor has a great deal of vessel traffic. The harbor is located on the eastern shore opposite Seattle's Elliott Bay. When approaching, note the obstructions on the northern side of the entrance at Wing Point. This tree-lined point is about 30 feet in height. There are about 500 yards of rocks and foul ground extending in a southerly direction from this point. The number '2' buoy marks the end of the foul area. Round this buoy, keeping it to starboard. Turn west in the channel, keeping markers '3' and '5' to port. The harbor speed limit of 5 knots begins at the U.S. Coast Guard Buoy #5. Ferries traversing this narrow corridor have the right-of-way. The two-mile-long harbor narrows, curves, and ends in a drying flat. No fuel facilities. There is good anchorage well into the bay, in 30-45 feet of water, avoiding the private buoys. Public Mooring is available at the 100' City Dock and Offshore 200' linear moorage system for 48 hours at $0.25/foot/day.

The Harbour Public House: Waterfront dining located on the north side of Eagle Harbor. 60' of designated dock space at Harbour Marina. 206-842-0969.

Harbour Marina: Located on the north shore of Eagle Harbor. Permanent and limited guest moorage, 30 ampere power, water, showers, restrooms, laundry, new holding tank and pump-out. Open all year. 206-842-6502. Dock Master: 206-842-5340.

Eagle Harbor Marina: Located on the south shore of Eagle Harbor. Limited guest moorage, 20, 30, & 50 ampere power, showers, restrooms, laundry, pump-out. Open all year. 206-842-4003.

Winslow Wharf Marina: Located on the north shore of Eagle Harbor. Limited guest moorage, 20 & 30 ampere power, water, showers, restrooms, laundry, pump-out & dump, provisions. Open all year. 206-842-4202. VHF 09.

★ **Winslow:** Winslow is the terminal city for the Bainbridge Island-Seattle ferry and the gateway to the Olympic Peninsula via Bainbridge Island and the Hood Canal Bridge. Explore specialty shops, retail stores, restaurants, art galleries and museums along the main street within walking distance of moorage. A walking tour brochure is available in most stores and at the Chamber of Commerce. 206-842-2982.

Walk-Around: A mile-long footpath, called the Walkabout, rims the waterfront, passes the site of historic Hall Brothers Shipyard, and leads to Eagle Harbor Waterfront Park.

★ **Eagle Harbor Waterfront Park Float:** Madronas overhanging the water and a long float mark the site of Eagle Harbor Waterfront Park. A moorage system with 200' of lines and buoys lies southwest of the park. A concrete launch ramp is near the moorage. Currently there is no under cover area during remodel. Port-a-potties available. The lighted dock has moorage, 48 hour limit. No power or water. Dump, pump-out. Watch the depths and the tide chart. A dinghy dock is provided. Playground equipment, picnic sites, tennis courts. On Wednesday evenings in July and August a Summer Concert Series is performed here. Shops and restaurants are within walking distance from the park. Parks: 206-842-1212, Harbor Master: 206-780-3733. Small boat rentals are available. ⛵🎣

Murden Cove (3): This bowl-shaped bay can be used to drop a lunch hook, but it is not a good overnight moorage. Much of the inner bay dries at low tide. Skiff Point, farther north, has a shoal area that is constantly shifting. Clearance of at least 250 yards is advisable. There is good crabbing in this area.

★🎣 **Fay Bainbridge State Park (4):** Mooring buoys are provided, however they are open to winds and wakes. As part of the Cascadia Marine Trail, one group camp and one tent site at the southern end of the day-use area, are provided. A steep hillside is the backdrop for this 17 acre park. The driftwood and sand beach is good for clamming. Overnight spaces for campers, trailers, and tents are available. Park facilities include stoves, picnic tables, fire pits and hot showers. 206-842-3931, 360-902-8844. 🎣▲

Point Monroe (5): This low, narrow, curving sand spit curves like a hooked finger. The entrance dries at low spring tides. It is possible to anchor in the bay. Enter at high water and check the expected low tide with present depth readings. The bay is exposed to winds from the north. Private floats extend from shore into the bay. Tightly clustered homes rim the spit and shore. A lagoon-like bay is between the spit and shore. There is fishing off Point Monroe. Bottom fish such as perch and ling cod are prevalent nearby.

★ **Port Madison (6):** [18446, 18478] Port Madison is actually the body of water that separates Bainbridge Island from the mainland shore to the north. For many, many years, local fishermen have relied on a secret fishing hole in this vicinity.

★ **Inner Port Madison & Hidden Cove:** To the south, the mile long indentation into Bainbridge Island is known as either Port Madison or Inner Port Madison, depending upon the source of information. This lovely inlet is very popular, and is the site of summer homes, yacht club facilities, and the residential community of Port Madison. The entrance is fairly narrow with shallow water to starboard near Treasure Island and a cluster of rocks 100 yards off the entrance. A marked rock, covered six feet, is south-southwest of Treasure Island. Caution is advised regarding other sunken debris, created because ballast was dumped from early-day ships. A bight on the port side just inside the entrance has adequate depths, but limited room for anchorage. Because of boat traffic, the more popular anchorages are farther in, closer to the head of the bay, especially in an area known as Hidden Cove. The historical plaque tells that, in 1841, Wilkes named the site after the fourth president, James Madison. A sawmill was in operation from 1853-1892, the first brass and iron foundry in the territory opened in 1859, and shipyards were on both sides of the harbor. Later, it became home to the first fish oil refinery north of San Francisco, and, for 36 years it was the Kitsap County seat. Today it is a peaceful, relatively serene place to visit.

Indianola: [18473, 18446] This rural community is situated within the borders of the Port Madison Reservation. Located on the north shore of Port Madison, a long pier serves as a fishing pier and viewing site. This area landmark, now rebuilt, marks the spot where the Mosquito Fleet and later a ferry to and from Seattle use to stop. A small float gives short-term shore access during summer months. Check depths when approaching. No overnight moorage and the beach is private. Anchorage is possible outside of the pier, however it is exposed. The dock, a country store, and post office are found nearby.

Miller Bay (7): Much of this bay, including the entrance, is shallow and some of it dries on low tides. It is advisable to enter only near high tide. Shallow anchorage is possible.

Bay Marine: Permanent moorage, repairs, ramp to 34'. 360-598-4900.

Agate Passage (8): See current table for Admiralty Inlet. Agate Passage connects Port Orchard and Port Madison. It is a straight channel about one mile in length. Depths average 20 feet. Currents run to six knots at springs, ebbing northeast and flooding southwest. The Agate Pass Bridge, with a 75 foot clearance at mean high water, connects Bainbridge to the peninsula. Shoal areas fringe both shores. Buoys mark some of the shoals. Scuba divers spear fish here for cod, sole, and flounder. In 1841, Wilkes named Agate Pass, not for the rocks, but for Alfred Agate, an itinerant artist along on the expedition.

Suquamish: Suquamish is the site of a wharf and launch ramp. No moorage float. Chief Sealth's (Chief Seattle) grave is located at Suquamish, on the Port Madison Indian Reservation. Temporary anchorage only, paying attention to the status of currents in Agate Passage. Annual community events include *"A Northwest Indian Festival"* held in August to honor Chief Seattle. Traditional food, dances, art, canoe races and more mark this special celebration.

★🎣 **Old Man House Park & Chief Seattle Park:** Owned and operated by the Suquamish Tribe, this park is approximately one half mile south of Suquamish, on the west shore of Agate Passage. Temporary anchorage may be possible, depending on currents. Dinghy to the sandy beach where water, a fire ring, toilet, and picnic facilities are available. A cable sign marks the northern boundary of the park. Do not anchor in this vicinity. 🎣

Suquamish Tribal Headquarters: Located just above and behind the beach farther south on Agate Passage's west shore, this building is the site of the Suquamish Museum. This museum is well known for its extensive collection of artifacts. It is accessible by Highway 305, turn off on Sandy Hook Road, or by beachable boat. Watch depths as shallows extend some distance. It is open daily, 10am to 5pm, from May to September. From October to April the hours are 11am to 4pm on Fridays, Saturdays, and Sundays. 360-598-3311 ext. 422.

★ **Manzanita Bay (9):** [18446] This bay is next to Arrow Point. There is good anchorage in 25-30 feet on a mud bottom at the center of the bay. Once a stop on the Mosquito Fleet, submerged pilings are near the shore.

Walk-around: It is possible to row to a public access area in the northeast corner of the bay. Look for the road end where concrete formations with steps are set between rock walls.

Fletcher Bay (10): This shallow bay is used extensively by local residents. Property is private, with no public access. It is limited both in shelter and in swinging room. The entrance dries at half tide.

Liberty Bay
[18441, 18445]

★ **Liberty Bay (11):** Once known as Dog Fish Bay, this four mile indentation is the water access to the City of Poulsbo. History tells that the rendered oil from dog fish caught in the bay was sold to logging camps. The Keyport Naval Facility lies in the entrance channel. When Navy torpedo practice is in progress, there is a flashing red light on the ATF (Acoustic Test Facility) barge. To avoid the area, stay to the east of the channel. The head of the bay is a drying flat. Anchorage is good near the head in the shelter of Port of Poulsbo yacht basin. The bay is open to southeast winds. The bay is closed to shellfish harvesting.

★ **Keyport Naval Facility:** Slow to three knots in this vicinity. Moor at the Keyport Marina, located east of the Naval Facility, on Grandview Blvd. Exhibits include the nation's best collection of historic torpedoes as well as displays about submarine history, the Ocean Environment, diving and salvage, and a reproduction of the control room from the submarine Greenling. Outdoor exhibits include the deep submergence vehicles Trieste II and Deep Quest. Admission is free. Open year round. Hours: June – September, 10 am to 4 pm daily. October – May, 10 am to 4 pm, every day but Tuesday. Closed Easter, Thanksgiving, Christmas, and New Year's Day. For information call 360-396-4148. http://naval.undersea.museum.

★ Keyport (12): This community is next to the navy base. Restaurants, church, parks, auto repair shop, Post Office. Permanently moored boats fill most of the moorage slips, however there is a 40 foot guest dock and some slips may be open for transient moorage. A fishing pier marks the spot. Provisions are found within walking distance.

Port of Keyport: Limited 40' guest moorage, launch ramp, 30 ampere power, water. 360-779-4259.

Keyport Marine: Permanent and limited moorage, haul-out, repairs (call ahead). 360-779-4360, 360-779-6206.

★ **Poulsbo (13):** This delightful community, located on the Kitsap Peninsula, is accessible by both land and sea. Boaters proceed through four-mile-long Liberty Bay when approaching this picturesque town. Marinas are adjacent to downtown. Coined *Little Norway On The Fjord*, Poulsbo is reminiscent of fishing villages in Norway. The town was founded in the 1880's by Norwegian cod fishermen and today a large Norwegian population still exists. Many of the buildings are painted with rosemaling, Nordic peasant designs. During the Christmas season, shop windows are painted with Norwegian Christmas scenes. *Norway's Independence Day, Sytennde Mai* (Seventeenth of May) is the reason for *Viking Fest*, held each year the weekend closest to May 17. Other annual events include *Skandia Midsommarfest* (June), *Fireworks on the Fjord* (July 3), *Arts by the Bay* (July and August), *Poulsbo Boat Rendezvous* (July), *Annual Lutefisk Dinner* (October), *Christmas Bazaars* (November and December), and *Yule Fest* (December).

There is an array of picturesque and inviting shops featuring antiques, arts, crafts, and fine gifts and collectibles. Home style delis, a tearoom, and restaurants will appeal to any palate. Six parks within the town blend with the green of surrounding hillsides and encourage visitors to picnic. An 800-foot-long pedestrian boardwalk connects waterfront parks. Liberty Bay Park, adjacent to downtown, has picnic facilities, Kvelstad Pavilion for entertainment, folk dancing, weddings, and camp fire pits. By car, three ferry routes bring visitors to the Kitsap Peninsula from the Greater Seattle area: the Edmonds-Kingston ferry, the Seattle-Winslow ferry, and the Seattle-Bremerton ferry. Bus travelers are served by Kitsap Transit with connections to Winslow, Kingston, Bremerton, and Silverdale.

Liberty Bay Marina: Permanent moorage. 360-779-7762.

★ **Port of Poulsbo** has 130 guest moorage slips (11 foot depths at low tide) and is open 7 days a week, all year. Call ahead to be sure the marina isn't completely taken by a rendezvous. 30 amp power is available on all docks. The fuel dock has gasoline and diesel. Register by 2000 hours to get the combination for the showers and restroom locks. On location are good restrooms and showers, laundry, pump out, portpotty dump, launch ramp and picnic area. Takes reservations for groups of 15 or more and limited single reservations for 30 foot slips. See our Steering Star description this chapter. Addres: 18809 Front St., Poulsbo, WA 98370; 360-779-3505 M-Sun 0800-2000; E-mail: port@poulsbo.net.

Bremerton Area
[18441, 18445]

★ **Brownsville (14):** Although Burke Bay is shallow with drying areas, it is the site of a large marina and launching ramps. A deli with sandwiches and beverages is near the docks. A Cascadia Marine Trail System campsite is located in Brownsville.

Port of Brownsville: [18446, 18449] Guest and permanent moorage, 120 volt and 30 ampere power, water, gas, diesel, oils, propane, launching, pump-out, dump site, showers, laundry. Wheelchair accessible. Open all year. 360-692-5498. VHF 16, 66.

Illahee: Illahee is an Indian word meaning

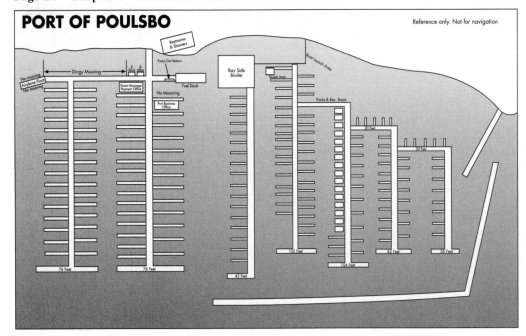

PORT OF POULSBO

Reference only. Not for navigation

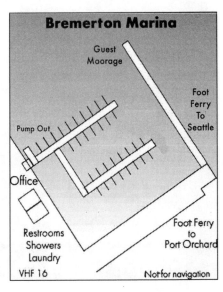

Bremerton Marina

Guest Moorage

Foot Ferry To Seattle

Pump Out

Office

Restrooms Showers Laundry

VHF 16

Foot Ferry to Port Orchard

Not for navigation

to attractions described above. Good cell phone coverage. Website: www.portofbremerton.org & www.boattravel.com/bremerton. Mailing address: 8850 SW State Highway 3, Port Orchard, Washington 98367. Street Address: Washington Beach, Bremerton. Telephone: 360-373-1035. Fax: 360-479-2928. VHF - Currently monitors channel 16, 68. Effective June 1, 2006 channel 66A.

Stephanie Satter Photography: A boater, free-lance travel and scenic photographer. Collection includes an extensive selection of beautiful marine views of Washington and British Columbia. Address: 8996 Utah Street NE, Bremerton, Washington 98311. E-mail: shutterbugtaffy@comcast.net. Telephone: 360-692-5893.

Port Washington Narrows: [#18449, #18452] See current table for Admiralty Inlet. This waterway, approximately three miles long, leads to Dyes Inlet. Currents, which run to approximately four knots, occasional rips, shallow areas, an unmarked, drying shoal on the north shore, and a large amount of boat traffic make caution necessary when navigating this channel. Because of these conditions, and the numerous piers and moorage floats, wakes must be minimized. The Manette and Warren Bridges traverse the channel; clearance is not a concern. A partially submerged footing for Pier 6 at the east end of the Manette Bridge is a hazard at mid-to-low-tide. The footing extends outward about ten feet in all directions. A warning sign is lighted, but the footing is unmarked.

★⚓ **Evergreen City Park:** The launching ramp is popular at this city park, located on the west side, between the two bridges. Picnic tables, 4 B-B-Q's, group shelter, sand volleyball and half-court basketball.

Port Washington Marina: Permanent moorage, pump-out. 360-479-3037.

★⚓ **Lions Park:** This 15-acre park includes nearly 2,000 feet of shoreline on the north side of Port

"earth" or "country." A fishing pier with floats and a buoy-marked artificial reef are located at this community. Watch depths when approaching the floats. Shoals are south of the pier. No overnight moorage. Provisions and gas, in portable cans, can be obtained nearby.

★⚓ **Illahee Marine State Park (15):** This 75-acre park contains a boat launch ramp, five mooring buoys, a 360' pier with 120' of floats, restrooms, campsites, covered kitchen shelters, horseshoe pits, and athletic fields. Overnight moorage fees. A rock has been reported to be about 50 yards southeast of the pier. A floating breakwater gives some protection, however vessel wakes enter this bay. The park has a memorial honoring members of the armed services from Bremerton who gave their lives in World War I. It is also home to one of the nation's largest Yew trees and Kitsap County's last stand of old growth timber. Water activities include fishing, water-skiing, swimming and diving, clamming and crabbing. Horseshoe pits, volleyball and softball fields, geocaching, and beachcombing are popular onshore pastimes. Call 360-478-6460 for kitchen shelter reservations, 360-902-8844 for moorage information.

★ **Bremerton & Bremerton Waterfront Park (16):** When cruising along the north shore of Sinclair Inlet, maintain a 1,500 foot distance from the shore, especially near the Puget Sound Naval Shipyard and its ships. This yard includes several miles of waterfront, 688 acres of land, 268 buildings, six dry docks and seven piers. The mothball fleet is located at the west end of the shipyard.

Although the shipyard is not open to the public, visitors can tour the USS *Turner Joy* (DD-951), a destroyer moored northeast of the ferry terminal on the Bremerton waterfront. Built in Seattle and commissioned in 1959, the *Turner Joy* saw combat in the Gulf of Tonkin at the onset of the Vietnam War. The ship and its crew earned nine battle stars in that conflict. Most spaces on the ship are accessible on the self-guided tour, including the engine room, bridge, and berths. The ship also features a Vietnam POW memorial. 360-792-2457.

A few blocks above the waterfront, at 402 Pacific Avenue, the Bremerton Naval Museum displays naval artifacts and memorabilia, including models of aircraft carriers. Open 10 am to 4 pm daily, except on Sunday 1 pm to 4 pm. 360-479-7447. The four-block Bremerton Waterfront Park offers spectacular views of Puget Sound as well as picnic sites, statues, and an observation platform. Look for the enormous propeller. The Bremerton Harborside, with conference center, hotel, restaurant, shops and musical fountains is located here. Beyond the Bremerton Marina at the south terminus of the waterfront, the Bremerton Transportation Center is the connection point for ferry travelers going to and from Seattle, and also for Kitsap Transit bus passengers.

Downtown Bremerton, a few blocks up from the waterfront, offers good browsing with art galleries featuring Northwest artists, restaurants, a used-book store, a coin shop and other specialty stores as well as the Kitsap County Museum. The museum displays vignettes of the early days of the county along with rotating exhibits. 360-479-6226. A showcase of the downtown area is the renovated Admiral Theatre, now a handsome art-deco performing arts venue. A block up from the Admiral, at 5th and Pacific, look for the plaque commemorating the speech given by Harry S. Truman when a spectator shouted "Give 'em hell, Harry!"

Come to Bremerton the third weekend in May for the *Armed Forces Festival and Parade*, one of the country's largest Armed Forces celebrations with more than 100 parade units. The day begins with a pancake breakfast and continues with the parade, displays of military equipment, a vintage car show, ship open houses, food cook-offs, and concerts. The *Blackberry Festival* on Labor Day weekends is a popular end-of-summer event with food and craft booths, kid's activities, live entertainment, and outdoor movies. During the summer, Bremerton offers free outdoor concerts at Evergreen Park on Tuesday evenings and on the waterfront on Friday evenings. Bremerton got its start in 1891 when founder, William Bremer, sold a 190 acre parcel to the US Navy for a shipyard.

★ **Bremerton Marina:** Located next to the ferry dock on the Bremerton waterfront. Secured guest moorage with 30 ampere power, water, restrooms, showers, laundry, pump-out, and Port a Potti dump. Fuel is available across Sinclair Inlet at Port Orchard Marina. Kitsap Transit buses service the marina and all of Kitsap County. Hours vary, call for seasonal hours of operation. Convenient

Washington Narrows. Fishing pier, float, launch ramp, picnic tables, restrooms, walking trail, ballfield.

★ **Phinney Bay (17):** [18449] This is the site of a private yacht club and sheltered anchorage found beyond the club, toward the head of the bay. Anchor in about 30 feet of water. An uncharted wreck is in the southern area of the bay. Shoals extend from shore. It has adequate water above it, even at a minus tide, however it can catch ground tackle. Mud Bay, back-to-back with Phinney Bay, dries on a low tide, however it can be explored by dinghy or shallow draft boats on higher tides.

★ **Ostrich Bay (18):** This long indentation near Madrona Point, has anchorage at the head of the bay. Caution advised of shoals off the point. An undeveloped park, with public tidelands, is on the west shore. A narrow passage, with a minimum depth of ten feet, leads farther inland to Oyster Bay.

★ **Oyster Bay (19):** High hills surround this beautiful, sheltered anchorage. Depths are 25-35 feet.

★ **Dyes Inlet (20):** The inlet is a wide, shallow bay that is exposed to most winds. Because of contamination, shellfish harvesting is prohibited. Caution advised regarding a drying shoal, known as Clam Island, in the east half of the inlet.

Chico: There is a launching ramp on Chico Bay.

Tracyton: Located on the east side of Dyes Inlet, a launching ramp gives trailerable boats access to the many bays on the opposite shore, and also provides shore access for those who may want to drop a lunch hook and walk onshore.

★⚓ **Anna Smith County Park:** Located near Barker Creek on the northeast side of Dyes Inlet, this interesting county park has 600' of public beach. Adjacent beach is private and no trespassing is allowed. Look for the old concrete wall south of Barker Creek. Temporary anchorage is possible, however avoid the drying shoal. The park is known for its gardens, flowers, and herbs. Picnic tables and restrooms are provided.

★ **Silverdale:** [18449] This community lies at the head of Dyes Inlet. Look for the gazebo that marks the location of the Port of Silverdale Waterfront Park. Adjacent to the park, Old Towne features historic murals and unique shops. Diehard shoppers can also visit the extensive Kitsap Shopping Mall. In the mid-1800's logging was the area's major industry. Later agriculture flourished. With the advent of the Naval Submarine Base at Bangor, the military became one of the area's largest employers. This unincorporated town of nearly 16,000 residents offers many of the conveniences of the "big city" yet retains hometown appeal. The *Whaling Days Community Festival* is held the last weekend in July and includes street fair, entertainment, parade and fireworks. The popular *quicksilver hydro-races & Watersports Festival* occurs in August.

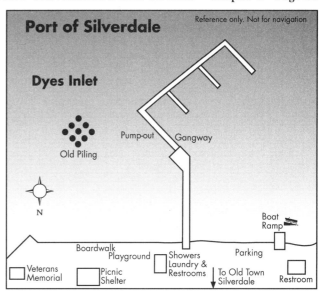

★⚓ **Silverdale Waterfront Park:** The park has good moorage floats, picnic area with a shelter, restrooms, fresh water, a playground, beach access and fishing pier. Close to shopping.

★ **Port of Silverdale:** 1,300 feet of lineal moorage, transient moorage for up to three consecutive nights, $5.00 per night for boats under 28 feet in length and $10.00 per night for those 28 feet and over. Port amenities include 30 amp power, fresh water, pump-out facility, new restroom/shower/laundry facilities, security cameras, security guards who make random nightly foot patrols, parking for vehicles with boat trailers. A two-lane boat launch is accessible during low tides and has a

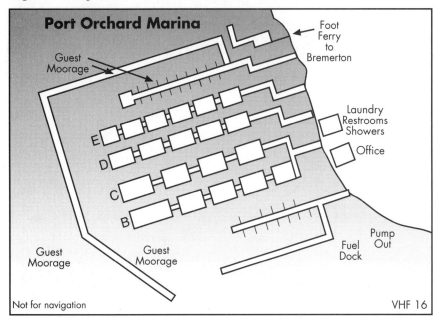

Port Orchard Marina

Guest Moorage

Foot Ferry to Bremerton

E
D
C
B

Laundry Restrooms Showers

Office

Guest Moorage

Guest Moorage

Pump Out

Fuel Dock

Not for navigation

VHF 16

convenient handling pier available from April through October. Enjoy nearby beach, playground, picnic area, veteran's memorial and various eateries and shops (books, flowers, gifts, food, hair, clothing, wine, legal, dental, and more). See our Steering Star description this chapter. Phone: 360-698-4918. Fax: 360-698-2402.   PO Box 310, Silverdale WA 98383. www.portofsilverdale.com. Email: portsilv@tscnet.com

Sinclair Inlet & Port Orchard

[18441, 18445]

★ **Port Orchard:** This waterway extends along the coast of Kitsap Peninsula, separating the mainland from Bainbridge Island. It turns toward the southwest, extending a branch into Port Washington Narrows to the northwest, passing the City of Bremerton to starboard, the City of Port Orchard to port, and ending in Sinclair

Inlet. Along the southern shore, fishing piers with floats are located at Annapolis, close to the launch ramp site at nearby Port Orchard Marina. While the float that was at the fishing pier at Waterman is gone, the pier is still available for fishing. Be aware of the shoal between Annapolis and the marina. The Gorst Aquatic Preserve, a fish and wildlife refuge, is at the head. It is accessible by car or beachable boat. Views of migratory waterfowl are possible. Near the Gorst Aquatic Preserve is Elandan Gardens with unique Bonsai Garden, Sculptures Garden, and specialty plantings, some of which can be seen from the water. 360-373-8260. Because of exposure to winds and highway noise, anchorage in this area is not recommended.

★ **City of Port Orchard:** Directly west of Seattle across Puget Sound on the shores of Sinclair Inlet lies Port Orchard, a city that boasts "19th century charm in a 21st century world." Residents here enjoy the relaxed rural pace and varied recreational opportunities of the beautiful Kitsap and Olympic Peninsulas.

The City of Port Orchard has long been a

popular boating destination. The Water Street launching ramp hooks into the marina and is equipped with a 1.5 acre parking lot, bathrooms with wheelchair access, park benches, picnic tables, and a trail. Anchorage can be found at the head of Sinclair Inlet.

Nearly all of the attractions in Port Orchard are within easy distance of the marina. Bay Street, with its historic buildings, is a photographer's delight. Browse through more than 50 shops and restaurants; there's something for everyone. If visiting during April-October, take in the Port Orchard Farmer's Market each Saturday from 9:00 a.m.- 3:00 p.m. Parks and playgrounds offer swimming, picnic sites, and tennis courts. Take a picnic lunch and enjoy the view at the Port Orchard Pedestrian Pier.

This is the Port of Arts and Antiques. Special city events include the *Seagull Calling Festival* on the first Saturday in May. *Concerts by the Bay* are free and are held downtown on Thursdays from mid-July through August. Summer festival *Fathoms O' Fun*, with parades, fireworks, and carnivals is the last weekend in June through July 4th. The second Sunday in August brings *The Cruz* hot rod and custom car show and *The Great Ball Race*. Five thousand brightly colored balls roll downhill. You've got to be there to believe it! During the summer, scheduled harbor tours leave from the Port Orchard waterfront. Port Orchard, the first city incorporated in Kitsap County, was originally named Sidney. Port Orchard became the Kitsap County Seat in 1893 and, with its beautiful Sidney Hotel, was the scene of fashion and entertainment for naval officers and their families. Port Orchard was a stop in the string of other Puget Sound ports served by passenger-carrying steamers of the *Mosquito Fleet*. The *Carlisle II* spearheads the last of Washington's original operating *Mosquito Fleet* that moved people and goods by water, long before roads were built. The Sidney Hotel is gone, but the past is immortalized in the restored buildings and in the popular craft and antique shops with their unique wares.

Port Orchard is connected to Bremerton by highway and also by a passenger-only ferry which departs for the 12 minute ride on the hour and half hour from near the Port Orchard Marina. 360-373-2877. The city can also be reached by air at the Bremerton airport, and by car via the Fauntleroy-Southworth ferry from Seattle, the Seattle-Bremerton ferry, and from Tacoma via Highway 16. Transit buses stop near the floats with service in the Port Orchard/South Kitsap area. For more information visit www.cityofportorchard.us.

★ **Port Orchard Marina:** This modern marina has extensive guest moorage. Thirty and 50 amp power, water, restrooms, free showers, laundry, fuel, waste pump-out and dump. Open all year. Summer hours 8:00 a.m. – 7:00 p.m. Winter hours: 8:00 a.m.—6:00 p.m. Good cell phone coverage. Conveniently located to all Port Orchard attractions. Kitsap Transit buses service the Marina and all of Kitsap County. Farmers Market open April 30 through October. Free summer concerts at Marina Park.   Website: www.portofbremerton.org   & www.boattravel.com/portorchard.   Mailing Address: 8850 SW State Highway 3, Port Orchard WA 98367. Street address: 707 Sidney Pkwy, Port Orchard. Telephone: 360-876-5535. Fax: 360-895-0291. VHF - Currently monitors channel 16, 68. Effective June 1, 2006 channel 66A.

Port Orchard Railway Marina: GPS N-47° 32.452 W-122° 38.637. 30 and 50 ampere power, water, restrooms, showers, laundry, waste pump-out. Conveniently located to all Port Orchard attrac-

quicksilver hydroplane races   Courtesy Gary Bowlby--Sure Shots Fine Photography tions. Moorage up to 150 feet, open and covered. 360-876-2522. VHF 16, 66A.

Dockside Marina: Permanent moorage, haul-out, repairs. 360-876-9016.

Sinclair Inlet Marina: Permanent moorage. 360-895-5167.

Annapolis (22): A public float and launching ramp are east of the old ferry pier at the site of Retsil. The float grounds at low water, and is open to northerly winds. Kitsap Transit Buses leave from the Park & Ride lot at the Annapolis Ferry in Retsil. 1-800-501-RIDE.

Waterman: Once a steamer stop, the 200-foot-long pier now serves as a public recreational and fishing pier. Limited beach area.

Rich Passage: See current table for Admiralty Inlet. This passage separates Kitsap Peninsula from Bainbridge Island. Frequent ferry traffic can be a hazard.

★⚓Fort Ward State Marine Park (23): Located on Bainbridge Island, this day use park has boat launching, vault toilets, walking trails, picnic tables, and water on site. Mooring buoys fringe the shoreline. Because of traffic in Rich Passage, and strong currents, anchoring and/or overnight stays are not advised. As part of the Cascadia Marine Trail, the park has one group camp area. Two gun batteries in the park recall the establishment of Fort Ward in 1903 to protect the Bremerton Naval Shipyard. During World War II, the site housed a Naval radio station and communications training center. After decommissioning, the Fort became a state park in 1960. A walk along the beach reveals unusual sandstone formations carved by wind and water erosion. Scuba diving is popular off Orchard Rocks. Fishing, crabbing, and sailboarding are also enjoyed in the area. 360-902-8844. ⚓⛱

Walk-around: Begin at the boat launch site. Walk up the hill to the left and go around the road barrier to the first gun bunker. A marker explains the history of the fort, and shows a map for the rest of the tour.

★⚓ Manchester State Park (24): Extensive eddies and strong currents often make this bight between Middle Point and Point Glover inhospitable, but temporary anchorage is possible. The park, on Middle Point, six miles northeast of Port Orchard, is part of the Cascadia Marine Trail. There are over 100 acres, with hiking trails and small beaches. Manchester has campsites, including a group camping site, plus restrooms. There is an unguarded swimming beach and bathhouse with showers, picnic sites, a volleyball field, horseshoe pits, and two small picnic shelters for daytime use. Displays tell the history of the brick torpedo warehouse, which now serves as a large, reservable picnic shelter. 360-871-4065, 360-902-8844. ⚓⛱▲

★ Manchester (25): In the late 1800's the residents of this small town chose the name of "Manchester," reflecting their vision of creating a busy seaport equal to the namesake port of Manchester, England. Today, the community of Manchester is largely residential, but does offer retail services. Annual community events include a *Salmon Bake* in June and the *Manchester Festival* in August. On the waterfront there is a pier, children's fishing pier, and a 200-foot day use moorage float. No fresh water or overnight parking. The float is in shallow water and is not usable at low tide. A launching ramp and park are adjacent. Restrooms, deli,

Big Dyes Inlet with Mount Rainier in the background   Photo Courtesy Ted Moore

restaurant, library, grocery nearby.   Port of Manchester: 360-871-2510. 🚢

★⚓ Blake Island Marine State Park (26): This popular park hosts over 13,000 visiting vessels a year. It is located two miles south of Bainbridge Island and five miles west of Seattle. There are no natural harbors, but 20 moorage buoys are scattered off shore and there are beaches for landing dinghies. A breakwater, on the northeast side of the island, protects the moorage floats, but not in all winds. The floats are approached through a shallow, dredged channel. Overnight moorage fees are collected year around. A moorage system that provides a 200 foot complex of lines and buoys, instead of traditional mooring buoys, is off the northwest shore. The Linear Mooring System provides 400 linear feet of actual tie-up space and serves up to a dozen 30 foot boats. An artificial reef, for scuba divers, lies on the south side of the island. Strong currents in the area can be hazardous.

Camping sites, picnic areas, shelters, waste pump out, porta potti dump, volleyball courts, hiking trails, restrooms, fresh water, and hot showers are provided. For reservations, call 888-226-7688. Swimming and clamming are possible on some of the beaches. This site was the ancestral camping ground of the Suquamish tribe, and it is believed that Chief Seattle was born here. Tillacum Village with its Indian Longhouse offers traditional native dance performances and salmon bake. 206-933-8600 or 800-426-1205. As part of the Cascadia Marine Trail, there is a group camp and a tent site at the northwest corner of the island.

First named by Captain Wilkes after George Blake, who was in charge of a survey from 1837-1848, it was purchased at the turn of the century by William Trimble. It was renamed Trimble Island and became one of the most beautiful private estates in the country, housing a magnificent

library collection. After Mrs. Trimble drowned in a freak accident, when the family car plunged off an Elliott Bay pier in 1929, Mr. Trimble never returned to the island. Some remains of the Trimble home and garden are still visable not far from the floats. The island served as the meeting site for a conference of world leaders in 1994. This 476 acre island has been a state park since 1959. Blake Island State Park Info: 360-731-8330. For general Information regarding Washington State Parks: 360-902-8844. ⚓⛱▲

Southworth: This is the terminus for the Kitsap Peninsula-Vashon Island-Fauntleroy (West Seattle) ferry. Small downtown area includes a grocery store and post office.

Harper: The tiny town of Harper is located on the south shore of Yukon Harbor. The abandoned ferry landing at Harper, with a fishing pier and nearby launch ramp is for day use only. Pier has very limited parking. The gravel launching ramp is accessible at higher tides. No moorage float. Small boats can be beached. Scuba divers often use the waters surrounding the pier.

★ Yukon Harbor (27): Anchorage is possible in this wide bight with protection from southwest winds. Tide flats extend from the head.

Cruising by Manette in Bremerton   Photo Courtesy City of Bremerton

Essential Supplies & Services

AIR TRANSPORTATION
Seattle Seaplanes **1-800-637-5553**

AMBULANCES . . . . All 911

BOOKS / BOOK STORES
The Marine Atlas. **541-593-6396**

BUS TRANSPORTATION
Kitsap Transit 1-800-501-7433
Poulsbo 360-697-2877, 1-800-501-7433
Southworth/Winslow 1-800-501-7433

COAST GUARD
VHF 16, Seattle 206-217-6000
Customer Information 1-800-368-5647
Seattle Station 206-217-6754
Vessel Traffic 206-217-6050

FERRY TRANSPORTATION
Bremerton-Port Orchard, Passenger only
. . . . 1-800-501-7433
Washington State 1-800-843-3779

FUELS
Brownsville Marina: Gas, Diesel 360-692-5498
Port Orchard Marina: Gas, Diesel . . 360-876-5535
Port of Poulsbo Marina: Poulsbo. Gas, Diesel.
. 360-779-3505

GOLF COURSES
(These courses are accessible from moorage and have
   rental clubs)
Gold Mountain: Port Orchard/Bremerton
. . . . 360-415-5432
Horseshoe Lake: Gig Harbor/Port Orchard
. . . . 253-857-3326
McCormick Woods: Port Orchard moorage
. . . . 800-323-0130
Meadowmeer: Winslow/Poulsbo 206-842-2218
Rolling Hills: Silverdale/Bremerton 360-479-1212
Village Greens: Port Orchard. 360-871-1222

HOSPITALS:
Bremerton 360-377-3911
Port Orchard (clinic) 360-895-6250
Silverdale. 360-377-8800

INSURANCE
Boat Insurance Agency 206-285-1350
   Or Call 1-800-828-2446

MARINAS / MOORAGE FLOATS
Blake Island State Park
Bremerton Marina. . . . . 360-373-1035 VHF 16, 68
Brownsville Marina: Brownsville
. . . . 360-692-5498 VHF 16, 66
Eagle Harbor Marina 206-842-4003
Eagle Harbor Waterfront Park: Winslow . 206-842-1212
Harbour Marina: Eagle Harbor. 206-842-6502
Illahee State Park
Keyport Marine 360-779-4360, 360-779-6206
Keyport, Port of: Keyport. 360-394-2474
Port Orchard Marina . . . 360-876-5535 VHF 16, 68
Port Orchard Railway Marina. 360-876-2522
Port of Poulsbo Marina 360-779-3505
Silverdale, Port of 360-698-4918
Winslow Wharf Marina: Winslow...206-842-4202 VHF 9

PARKS
Department of Natural Resources 360-825-1631
. . . . 1-800-527-3305
Washington State 360-902-8844

Camping Reservations 888--226-7688

PHOTOGRAPHERS
Stephanie Satter: Bremerton 360-692-5893

PROPANE:
Brownsville Marina 360-692-5498

POISON INFORMATION:
. . . . 800-222-1222

RAMPS / HAUL-OUTS
Annapolis
Bay Marina 360-598-4900
Brownsville Marina. . . . . 360-692-5498 VHF 16, 66
Chico
Eagle Harbor Waterfront Park
Evergreen City Park: Bremerton
Fay Bainbridge State Park
Fort Ward State Park
Harper Park, Southworth
Illahee State Park
Keyport Marine 360-779-4360, 360-779-6206
Lebo Street, Washington Narrows
Manchester
Miller Bay
Port Orchard
Poulsbo Marina. 360-779-9905
Retsil: Sinclair Inlet
Silverdale, Port of 360-698-4918
Suquamish
Tracyton

RECOMPRESSION CHAMBER
Keyport 360-396-2522
Virginia Mason . . . . Seattle. 206-583-6433

RED TIDE HOT LINE: 800-562-5632

REPAIRS / SERVICE
Bay Marine: Miller Bay. 360-598-4900
Dockside: Port Orchard 360-876-9016
Keyport Marine 360-779-4360, 360-779-6206

RESTAURANT / PUB
Harbour Public House, Eagle Harbor
. . . . 206-842-0969

SEWAGE DISPOSALS
Bainbridge Island City Dock: Pump, Dump.
. . . . 206-842-1212
Blake Island State Park: Pump, Dump. . 360-731-8330
Brownsville Marina: Pump, Dump . . 360-692-5498
Eagle Harbor Marina: Pump 206-842-4003
Eagle Harbor Waterfront Park: Winslow. Pump, Dump.
. . . . 206-842-1212
Harbour Marina: Eagle Harbor. Pump. . . 206-842-6502
Port Orchard Marina: Pump, Dump . 360-876-5535
Port Washington Marina: Pump 360-479-3037
Poulsbo Marina: Poulsbo. Pump . . . 360-779-3505
Silverdale, Port of: Pump, Dump . . . 360-698-4918
Winslow Wharf Marina: Pump, Dump. . . 206-842-4202

SHELLFISH HOTLINE: . . . 360-796-3215
24-hr Red Tide Hotline. 800-562-5232
For local area closures/information, call County Health Depts.:
Kitsap County Health Dept. 360-692-3611

SPORTFISHING: 360-902-2500

TAXI
Bainbridge Island. 206-842-1021
Port Orchard 360-876-4949
Poulsbo 360-698-7660

TOWING
C-TOW. 1-888-354-5554
VESSEL ASSIST . . . Lake Washington 206-793-7372
   Seattle (Puget Sound Area) 206-300-0486

VHF OPERATOR:
Whidbey Island: 87
Note: MariTel has shut down all other Washington State
   VHF Marine Operator channels until further notice.

VISITOR INFORMATION
Bainbridge Island. 206-842-3700
Bremerton 360-479-3579
Kitsap Peninsula 1-800-416-5615, 360-297-8200
Port Orchard 1-800-982-8139, 360-876-3505
Poulsbo 360-779-4848
Silverdale. 360-692-6800

WEATHER:
VHF WX-1

Bremerton Conference Center & Boardwalk   *City of Bremerton Photo*

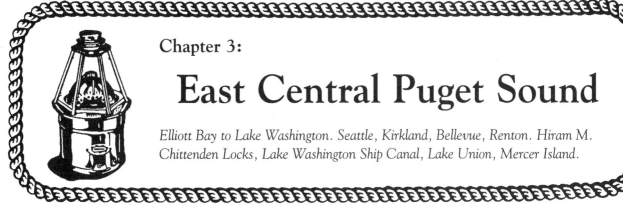

Chapter 3:
East Central Puget Sound

Elliott Bay to Lake Washington. Seattle, Kirkland, Bellevue, Renton. Hiram M. Chittenden Locks, Lake Washington Ship Canal, Lake Union, Mercer Island.

Symbols

[   ]: Numbers between [ ] are chart numbers.

{   }: Numbers & letters between { } are waypoints.

⚑: Park, ⛴: Boat Launch, ▲: Campgrounds, ⚲: Hiking Trails, ⚘: Picnic Area, ⚙: Biking

★ **Important Notice:** See "Important Notices" between Chapters 7 and 8 in this guide for specific information on boating related topics such as: Canadian & U.S. Customs, boating safety and security, navigation, weather, U.S. & Canadian Coast Guard, U.S & Canadian marine radio use, Vessel Traffic Service and traffic separation plans, security zones, and internet access. Due to new Department of Homeland Security regulations, call ahead for latest customs information and/or see Northwest Boat Travel On-line, www.nwboat.com.

★ **The Lakes to Locks Water Trail:** This regional freshwater trail stretches from the Eastside's Lake Sammamish, north along the Sammamish River around Lake Washington, through the Montlake Cut to Lake Union, then west to the Hiram M. Chittenden Locks to make a saltwater connection with Puget Sound and the Cascadia Marine Trail. The water trail is designed for small, non-motorized boats, canoes, kayaks, rowboats, and sailboats. Section maps have detailed information about campsites, rest stops, launch and landing sites, parks, etc. Contact Washington Water Trails Association 206-545-9161, www.wwta.org, E-mail: wwta@wwta.org.

Seattle
[18441, 18445, 18450, 18474]

★ **Seattle:** When you sail into Seattle, you are reaching a destination city that is one of the most beautiful in the world. Resembling an hourglass

Chart List

NOAA Charts:

18441, 18445-450, 18474

Marine Atlas (2005 ed.):

Pages 1, 4

fitted between Puget Sound and Lake Washington, it is the air and sea gateway to Alaska and Asia. Seattle is a cosmopolitan center, with great natural beauty, intriguing points-of-interest, and many attractions. Because of its location, there are hundreds of marine related businesses, industries, and services. The Port of Seattle alone operates 19 major terminals, including Bell Harbor Marina for pleasure boats, located on Elliott Bay; Shilshole Bay Marina, for pleasure boats; and Fishermen's Terminal, for commercial fishing vessels and pleasure boats. The shorelines of Portage Bay, Salmon Bay, and Lake Union are lined with marine supply stores, moorage facilities, and boat yards. Several tours are available through arrangements with the Seattle Convention and Visitor's Bureau.

Traversing the locks, from the salt water of Puget Sound to the lake waters inland, is a unique experience possible in only a few places in the world. Restaurants, stores, theaters, major hotels, night life, tours, 2 state of the art sports facilities, and beautiful parks, all await exploration. Each May, the *Opening Day Parade* ushers in the yachting season. Since the 1950's, *Seafair*, with its parades, crew races, unlimited Hydroplane races, and community celebrations is a major attraction each August.

Coined *The Emerald City*, Seattle, named after Indian Chief Sealth, has what many people consider to be an unusually romantic history. In 1851, Seattle's first white settlers arrived at Alki Point on the schooner *Exact*. Their primary source of revenue was the selling of logs for pilings for the San Francisco docks. They cleared land for homesteads and businesses along what is now Elliott Bay and a sawmill operated in the location of Pioneer Square. By 1889, the settlement, population 20,000, was a regular stop on shipping routes. In June 1889, however, fire destroyed 50 downtown blocks. Undaunted, the re-building began immediately. On July 17, 1897, the steamship *Portland*, arrived with $1 million in gold from the Yukon. The subsequent Alaska Gold Rush boosted the area's economy and focused attention on Seattle's strategic location. Many men, whose destination had been the gold fields in Alaska, changed their minds and stayed to help build the town. Immigrants came from around the world, especially from Scandinavian countries because the climate and surroundings were similar to their homelands. Other large migrations have come from Asia, as exemplified in the International District of today. Another feather in Seattle's cap came with winning the right to host the Alaska Yukon Exhibition in 1909. The site is now the University of Washington campus. By 1910, the population had grown to 235,000. Then, in 1962, came Century 21, *Seattle's World's Fair*, another event designed to attract international attention. The Space Needle and Pacific Science Center stand as a trib-

Brian Huntoon Photo

ute to this event. This international flavor is exemplified by the fact that Seattle has 21 sister cities around the world.

During World War II, Seattle, with its deep water port, became a center for naval operations and ship building. Without a doubt, the Boeing Airplane Company has played a major role in Seattle's growth.

Today, Seattle is a leader in a number of industries including aerospace, software, and biotechnology. It is also considered to be a leading center for the arts, with hundreds of galleries and museums. In professional sports, it has Mariners baseball, Sonics and Storm basketball, and Seahawks football, Sounders soccer and Thunderbirds hockey.

Seattle is a designated port of entry for Customs and Border Protection. Call 206-553-4406.

Alki Point: In 1851, white settlers landed on the sandy beach of this point. The name came from the Chinook word meaning "by and by." Today, it is the site of a park and a lighthouse. No floats or mooring buoys. Power boats may not come ashore at the public beach area. Only hand carried, non-motorized small boats can be beached in a designated area northeast of the open sandy public beach. City of Seattle policy designates that no anchoring is permitted off Seattle's shorelines. The lighthouse is open for tours each weekend from June through August, 12-3:30pm. 206-217-6124. Extending around Duwamish Head, the park's designated beach reaches Don Armeni Park and Seacrest Park.

Elliott Bay

[18441, 18445, 18450]

★ **Elliott Bay (1):** Speed limit is seven knots within 200 yards of shore. More and more pleasure craft are cruising into this, Seattle's major harbor, and the center of maritime commerce. Moorage is available at several sites. Anchoring by pleasure craft is not permitted. Notable are the large freighters, frequently at anchor, and large cranes, which may faintly resemble huge insect-like creatures, as they manipulate containers into the cargo ships. Cruise Ship piers await passenger arrivals, fireboats practice streaming water out over the harbor, kayaks and canoes maneuver in and out among the piers and, amidst it all, a steady parade of Washington State ferries arrive and depart to and from Puget Sound destinations. The following description of Elliott Bay attractions begins on the West Seattle shore and circles around through the downtown core to the north-ern shore and Magnolia Bluff. See current tide table for Admiralty Inlet.

★⚓ **Don Armeni Park:** On the west shore of Elliott Bay, Don Armeni Park is located just inside Duwamish Head. Named for a Deputy Sheriff, the park has a four lane launch ramp with side floats, view points, picnic tables, and restrooms. Daily or annual launch fees. There are spectacular views of the Seattle shoreline, especially at sunset when the setting sun reflects off the skyscrapers. ⚓🌲

★⚓ **Seacrest Park:** Located immediately south of Don Armeni Park, this park has a boathouse with concessions, boat rentals, restrooms, fishing pier, bait, restaurant, and picnic facilities. Call 206-938-0975 for boat rentals or information. 🌲

★ **Harbor Island & Duwamish Waterway:** Watch the commercial operations of this port facility and enjoy a change of scenery by explor-ing the Duwamish River vicinity. A marina, with floating breakwater, is located at the southern tip of Harbor Island where the Duwamish River separates into the East and West Waterways before flowing around Harbor Island and meeting the salt water of Elliott Bay. Port of Seattle operated parks are found along the Duwamish River. Mainly accessible by car, in the vicinity of East Marginal Way and West Marginal Way SW, these parks include a variety of amenities such as picnic areas, waterfront shoreline, benches, fishing piers, look-outs, and some launch ramps for hand carried craft. For information call 206-728-3654. Because of wildlife habitats, some areas restrict motor vehicle traffic. Port parks and Shoreline Paths are found at Terminals 115, 108, 107, 105, 102, and 30. From these vantages visitors enjoy up-close views of shipping operations, harbor tour boats, and an occasional canoe or kayak wending its way among the piers.

Harbor Island Marina: Permanent moorage, pump-out, restrooms, no fuel. 206-728-3006. VHF 17

Downtown Seattle Waterfront

★ **Downtown Seattle Waterfront:** Downtown is the epicenter of Seattle's culture and commerce. Its vibrant urban lifestyle continues to grow in popularity. Visitors enjoy the area's 500 restaurants, 15 theatres, 7 museums, 77 art galleries and 1800 plus shops and retail stores–all mostly found within walking distance.

The piers along the waterfront are numbered progressively from south to north. A great way to get a general lay-of-the land is to take a bus tour or a harbor cruise on a sight-seeing boat.

Beginning at Pier 36, is the Vessel Traffic Center (206-217-6050) and the Coast Guard Museum. The museum is open Monday, Wednesday, and Friday from 9:00 a.m. to 3:00 p.m. and Saturday and Sunday from 1:00-5:00 p.m. 206-217-6993. Proceeding north, and curving with the shoreline to the northwest, are the main working piers of the Port of Seattle. Upon reaching Pier 48, the industry begins to change to tourism. Walk to the head of this pier and use a 25-35 foot periscope for a closer look at trade activities. An interpretive exhibit explains terminal operations and Seattle's history as a port city. Alaska Square Park at Pier 49 is open 6:00 a.m.-11:00 p.m. with pedestrian access only. Benches are provided. Native American art is displayed along with a totem. From this location, it is possible to walk to Pioneer Square. Pioneer Square is considered by many to be the heart of Seattle. When visiting, pick up a copy of the informative map and guide publication entitled *Discovering Pioneer Square*. Visit restored buildings housing pubs, restaurants, antique stores, and other area shops. Parks provide benches and statues. The Pioneer Building, on the east border of Pioneer Square, is one of the oldest and most ornate.

The International District, or Chinatown, is a vibrant inner-city neighborhood. It is a jumble of Korean, Vietnamese, Chinese and Japanese restaurants, unique specialty shops and grocery stores. The Wing Luke Asian Museum and the Nippon Kan Theatre are located in this neighborhood. This is the cultural hub for Asian Americans in the area. The Lunar New Year Celebration and Annual Summer Festival are popular community events.

The Waterfront Trolley, with its Vintage 1920's cars, operates on a route that begins near Pier 70, parallels the waterfront, passes through Pioneer Square to 5th Avenue, and ends at Jackson Street in the International District. Streetcars come along every 20 minutes or so and

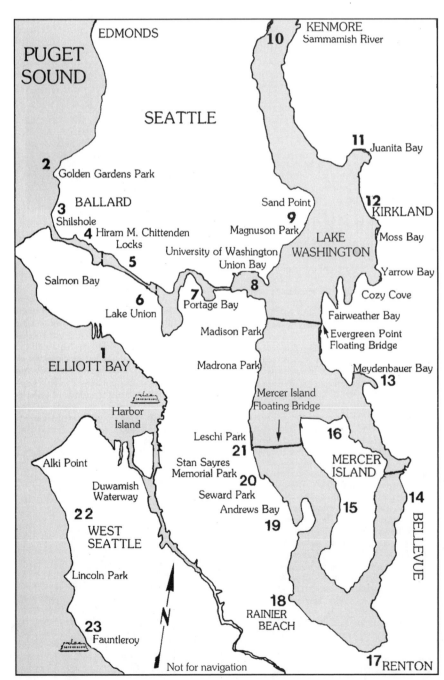

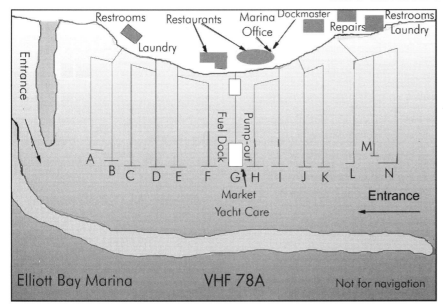

Restrooms Restaurants Marina Office Dockmaster Repairs Restrooms Laundry

Laundry

Entrance

Fuel Dock Pump-out

A B C D E F G H I J K L M N

Market Yacht Care

Entrance

Elliott Bay Marina   VHF 78A   Not for navigation

the architecturally acclaimed Central Library, Safeco and Qwest Fields, Benaroya Hall, medical facilities, churches, and historic residential neighborhoods, or to the 74 acre Seattle Center with its 605 foot high Space Needle. Its observation platform and revolving restaurant at the top provide panoramic views of the city, Puget Sound, and the Cascade and Olympic Mountain ranges. Also at Seattle Center is a children's museum and theater, the Seattle Opera House, Experience Music Project, the Key Arena, and the Pacific Science Center. Center information: 206-684-7200. The Monorail, a legacy from the 1962 World's Fair, runs from Seattle Center into downtown Seattle where it is possible to take the bus, or even walk back down to the waterfront. Monorail information: 206-905-2620.

Continuing north along the waterfront, other retail outlets and cruise lines occupy space to Pier 70. As the beach curves northwest, it becomes a 1.25 mile stretch of waterfront known as Myrtle Edwards Park featuring picnic tables and benches, biking lanes, and walkways. New in the summer of 2006, the unique Olympic Sculpture Park will open adjacent to Myrtle Edwards Park. From here, the shoreline winds around, past the grain elevators and Elliott Bay Park. A 400-foot fishing pier, tackle shop, restrooms, rose garden, exercise station, and trails are accessible at this Pier 86 location. Hours are 6am to 11pm. An underwater reef on the north end is marked by orange buoys. This park-like waterfront ends at massive Piers 90 and 91. Smith Cove Park, a small park with big views and shore access, is tucked between Pier 91 and the Elliott Bay Marina complex. www.portseattle.org/community/resources/. A 4,000 foot paved pathway connects with Elliott Bay and Myrtle Edwards Parks, Interbay and Fishermen's Terminal, and a bike route to Hiram Chittenden Locks.

★ **Bell Harbor Marina:** {47° 36.6' N, 122° 20.9' W NAD 83} This Port of Seattle marina offers moorage, power, water, showers, restrooms, garbage deposit and waste pump-out. Reservations advised. Individuals and groups are welcome. Marina open year round. Now reserve your slip on-line at www.portseattle.org or by calling Marina at 206-615-3952. Moorage is equipped with 30/110, 50/220 ampere/voltage power, drinking and hose down water. The wide, concrete docks are wheelchair accessible. Locked gates, security cameras, and 24 hour staffing provide security protection. Boaters advised to radio ahead on VHF Channel 66A for guidance into the marina and then check in with the Harbor Master. Dockside service. Check-out time at noon, check-in time 1:00 pm. Anthony's Pier 66 offers 3 dining options adjacent to Marina. Walking distance to the Seattle Aquarium, Pike Place Market, up scale dining. Taxis and Waterfront Trolleys are accessible. See our advertisement in the A pages at the front of this book. Circle #08 on Reader Service Card. Websites:

stop several times along the waterfront. For information call 206-553-3000. One stop is near the Pike Street Hillclimb, where you can walk to Pike Place Market. World famous, Pike Place Market is still going strong as one of the greatest Farmer's Markets. Much of the vehicular traffic along the waterfront will turn into the large Washington State Ferry Terminal on Coleman Dock, located at Piers 50 and 52. Ferries depart for Winslow, Bremerton, and (passenger only) to Vashon Island.

Continuing northwest, a fun stop is Pier 53 to see the fireboats. Then, for the next few blocks, there are restaurants and sightseeing tour opportunities to fill every wish. The chance to relax and watch the water comes between Piers 57-59 where a waterfront park provides picnic sites, a statue of Christopher Columbus, and a public fishing pier. Piers 59 and 60 house the highly respected Seattle Aquarium and Omnidome Theatre. The Aquarium features award-winning exhibits of marine life, including an Underwater

Glassed-in Dome. 206-386-4320. Nearby, a waterfront park is located at Piers 62/63, close to the Port of Seattle's short-stay moorage at Bell Harbor Marina at Pier 66. The Bell Street Pier development includes restaurants, a gourmet grocery/deli, ATM machine, cruise ship terminal, the Bell Harbor International Conference Center, and the Odyssey Maritime Discovery Center. In Odyssey, 33,000 square feet are filled with hands-on activities, sights, and sounds about the importance of the sea and maritime industry. Panoramic views, telescopes, historical information, and outdoor seating are found at the Public Plaza, located on the roof of the center. The main plaza on the pier level features an interactive children's fountain. Pedestrian bridges at the site and at Lenora Street, a few blocks to the south, allow convenient access. Moorage is within walking distance to the Pike Place Market, grocery store, hotels, restaurants, jogging paths, parks, and the Seattle Aquarium. If you are moored at Bell Harbor, a short bus or taxi ride could take you to

Bell Harbor & Seattle Waterfront   Photo © Brian Huntoon

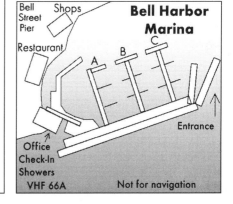

Bell Street Pier Shops **Bell Harbor Marina**

Restaurant

A B C

Entrance

Office Check-In Showers VHF 66A   Not for navigation

www.portseattle.org/seaport/marinas, www.nwboattravel.com/bellharbor. Email: bhm@portseattle.org. Address: Pier 66, 2003 Alaksan Way, Seattle, Washington 98121. Telephone: 206-615-3952 or 1-800-426-7817 Ext. 3952. VHF 66A.

★ **Elliott Bay Fuel Dock & YachtCare:** Located on "G" dock, right in the middle of Elliott Bay Marina. Gas, diesel, soy diesel, oil, sewage pumpout, confections, beer & wine, ice, and food area available. Friendly service and quantity discounts. The Elliott Bay Fuel Dock is also home to YachtCare, a full service mechanical and yacht repair facility. The dock opens at 8:00 a.m. seven days a week. Closing hours vary with sunset. Year around. Address: 2601 West Marina Place, Suite K, Seattle, Washington 98199. Fax: 206-285-2610. Email: eric@yachtcare.com Telephone: 206-282-8424. VHF 78A.

★ **Elliott Bay Marina:** Permanent and guest moorage. 30 amp, 125 volt or 50 amp 125/250 volt power. Gas, diesel, bio-diesel, propane (nearby), water. Pumpout, showers, laundry, provisions, repairs, restaurants. See our Steering Star description in this chapter. 206-285-4817. VHF 78A.

Shilshole Bay

[18441, 18446, 18447]

★⚓ **Golden Gardens Park (2):** This 87.8-acre park, known for swimming, sunbathing, sandy beaches, and sweeping views, stretches from Shilshole Bay to Meadow Point. There is a multi-lane launch ramp, picnic shelters, tables, concessions, fishing pier, off-leash dog area and play equipment. Meadow Point has been noted for good fishing. As one of Seattle City Parks' Marine Reserves, any harvesting other than hook

and line fin fishing is prohibited. Hours: 6am - 11:30pm. Parking lot is locked when closed. ⚓⛴

★ **Shilshole Bay (3):** Located near the entrance to the locks, this curving shoreline is home to the large Port of Seattle marina. Speed limit within 200 yards of shore is seven knots. Stay in the marked channel because of shallow water and a drying flat off the bluff that is directly across from the marina breakwater. In addition to the marina, a condominium development, an assortment of restaurants, and marine-related businesses are located here. A statue of Leif Ericson overlooks the moorage basin. Buses run along the waterfront into Ballard where riders can easily transfer to other city locales. See current table for Admiralty Inlet.

★ **Shilshole Bay Marina:** {47° 41' N, 122° 24.50' W} This Port of Seattle facility, with its convenient location on Central Puget Sound, has been called the *Gateway to Puget Sound Recreational Cruising.* Floating concrete piers are fully equipped with all the conveniences boaters require. Power and water equipped guest moorage is found at several locations. Shilshole Bay Marina is being rebuilt between June 2005 and July 2008. During construction displaced permanent boats will be relocated to visitor moorage, seriously limiting space available for guest boats. Individual and groups should call ahead for availability. Please contact the guest moorage attendant at 206-728-3006 or VHF 17. On-site laundry, showers, restrooms, recycling, and trash receptacles. Gas diesel, oils, small grocery, beer, wine, ice, and pump-outs for sewage and bilge are available at the fuel facility. Sewage pump at Central Pier. Launch ramps and a 25 ton marine crane accommodate haul outs. Marina open year-round. Walking distance to Anthony's Restaurant Shilshole, Ray's Boathouse and Little Coney.

Regular bus service to Ballard and Seattle. See our full page advertisement in the A pages at the front of this book. Circle #09 on Reader Service Card. Website: www.boattravel.com/shilshole & www.portseattle.org/seaport. E-mail: sbm@portseattle.org. Mailing address: 7001 Seaview Avenue Northwest, Seattle, Washington 98117. Fax: 206-728-3391. Telephone: 206-728-3006 or 1-800-426-7817 ext. 3006. Staff on duty 24 hours a day, 7-days a week. VHF 17.

Shilshole Bay Fuel Dock: Gas, bio-diesel, diesel #1, #2, bilge and sewage pump-outs, Porta Potti dump, confections. 206-783-7555

Hiram M. Chittenden Locks

[18441, 18447]

★ **Hiram M. Chittenden Locks (4):** [18447] Built in 1916, these locks are also known as the "Government" or "Ballard Locks." More than a million visitors a year watch the boats being raised or lowered to the levels of either Lake Washington or Puget Sound. By allowing gravity to move water into and out of lock chambers, the two locks lift and lower vessels navigating between the sea level of Puget Sound and the higher elevation of the ship canal and Lakes Union and Washington, a difference of as much as 26 feet, depending on tide and lake level fluctuations. The locks are in operation 24 hours a day, unless closed for maintenance. Locking time is about 25 minutes for the large lock and ten minutes for the small lock.

The locks handle a large volume of traffic and it may be necessary to wait for a turn, so it is wise to be flexible and plan to take more time.

Being prepared with the proper equipment is also important. Boaters need two 50-foot lines with 12-inch eye splices for locking. Lines, one in the bow and one in the stern, should be arranged neatly in preparation. Because your final placement in the locks is unknown, fenders are vital equipment and should be placed on both sides of the boat prior to entry. The lock authority also recommends that the captain check the reverse gear at this time. Crewmembers should be stationed at both the bow and the stern of the boat, and children should be inside the cabin. Be careful to keep hands away from cleats and do not hang arms or legs over the sides of the boat.

Do not use sound signals to signal a lock tender. Gather at the waiting piers and wait for the green lights. Directions given over a public address system tell boaters to proceed at 2½ knots into the appropriate lock. If your boat is larger than 85' in length, wait for the entrance to the big lock. If your boat's draft is over 14', you will need to request that the salt water barrier be lowered.

Small lock: Most pleasure boat traffic is accommodated in the small lock which has usable space of 123 feet in length, 28 feet in width. Boaters are directed to the moss covered sides, the boater wraps his line around one of the mushroom-shaped buttons attached to the movable inner walls. These tie-up posts will raise or lower along with the water. This eliminates the work and danger of a fixed tie-up, like the ones used in the big lock. The attendant will instruct boats about rafting to other boats. During the locking process boaters should keep an eye on the lines just in case the floating wall hang-ups. In that case, slacken the lines as needed and notify a lock attendant. When the water levels are equal, boaters will be asked to tie-down their lines while awaiting their turn to leave the chamber. When the locks are opened, strong currents occur due to the flow of a large volume of water.

Large lock: Commercial traffic, large ships, and sometimes, pleasure boats are directed to use the large lock. It has usable space of 760 feet in length and 80 feet in width, and can accommodate up to 100 boats. The procedures differ in the large lock because there is no movable inner wall with tie-up posts on it. When entering from Puget Sound, the lock attendant will throw a line down to the boat. The boater uses a slip knot to tie the eye of his line to the lock attendant's line. The attendant then hauls up the line to his level and secures it to his cleat. On the boat, the crewman will wrap his end around the deck cleat and tend the line, bringing it in as the water rises in the lock. Keep the line taut around the cleat at all

Elliott Bay   Photo courtesy of the Elliott Bay Marina

times, but do not tie down. When at lake level, the attendant will release the line from his cleat and hand it to you.

When heading out from the lake, you are at the higher water level, you will hand the line to the lock attendant when requested to do so. The attendant will wrap his end around his cleat, while you wrap your end around the deck cleat. Do not tie. The line must be tended and paid-out as the water level falls. Keep the line taut around the cleat at all times. Serious damage or injury can result from a line that snags on a cleat or other object, or a person during the descent.

When the water levels are equal, boaters will be asked to tie off their lines or the lines of another vessel rafting alongside while awaiting their turns to exit the lock chamber. To inquire about the free *Locking Through* program or to order *Guidelines for Boaters*, call the Lockmaster 206-783-7000. Classes are conducted January-September. For more information, visit www.nws.usace.army.mil/opdiv/lwsc.

Walk around: Tourists visiting the locks park in a lot located at 3015 NW 54th in Ballard. A walkway leads to the locks and Visitors Center wtih exhibits and gift shop. Commodore Park and the

Carl S. English Jr. Gardens are adjacent. The fish ladder with underwater viewing rooms is a favorite with visitors. For information or tours: 206-783-7059.

★ **Lake Washington Ship Canal:** [18447] Construction of this eight mile long canal was completed on July 4, 1917. Minimum width is 100 feet, with depths dredged to 30 feet. The waterway extends from Puget Sound through Shilshole Bay, Salmon Bay, Lake Union, Portage Bay, Union Bay to Lake Washington. A speed limit of seven knots is enforced in the canal and on the lakes within 100 yards of any shoreline, pier, or shore installation. No anchoring is permitted along the canal or off the Seattle shoreline. However, an exception to this policy is Andrews Bay at Seward Park. See #19.

Several bridges affect passage of tall masted vessels. Minimum clearances are: Burlington Northern Bridge (west of the locks) 42 feet (check the Clearance Gauge since clearance may vary as much as two feet), Ballard Bridge 44 feet, Fremont Bridge 30 feet, University Bridge 42 feet 6 inches; and Montlake Bridge 46 feet. On weekdays, except national holidays, the Ballard, Fremont, and University Bridges remain closed

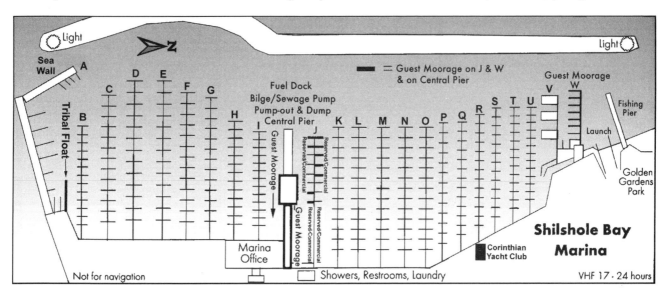

during peak rush hours (7 a.m. – 9 a.m. and 4 p.m. – 6 p.m.). Otherwise, from 7 a.m. to 11 p.m. boaters should signal the bridge operator by horn, using one long blast (four to six seconds) followed by one short blast (one second) when the vessel is at least 100 yards from the bridge. The bridge operator will acknowledge the signal and open the bridge as soon as possible. If the bridge cannot be opened immediately, the bridge operator will respond with five or more shore blasts (danger signal). If you hear the danger signal, stand off. The bridge operator will signal with one prolonged and one short blast once the bridge can be opened. From ll p.m. – 7 a.m., bridge openings are made by appointment. Call one hour ahead of time by phone (206-386-4251), or by radio (Marine Channel 13) to the "Bridge Shop." For more information or to request a copy of Seattle's Moveable Bridges Guide For Vessels call 206-386-4251.

The Montlake Bridge is state operated and has a seasonal schedule. Weekdays from May through August the bridge is open by request, except during the following hours: 7 a.m. – 9 a.m. bridge is closed; 12:30 p.m. – 3:30 p.m. bridge opens on the hour and half hour; 3:30 p.m. – 6:30 p.m. bridge is closed. There are no closures on weekends or national holidays. From September through April, weekday rush hour closures are extended from 7 a.m. – 10 a.m. and 3:30 p.m. – 7 p.m. To contact the Montlake Bridge to request an opening, signal by horn, call by phone (425-739-3700), or radio (Marine Channel 13).

★ **Ballard (5):** Ballard was settled by Scandinavians, many of whom became loggers and fishermen. By the 1890's, logging and Stimson's Mill supported nearly 2,500 residents. The Ballard vicinity includes the downtown center along Market Street, the marine-oriented companies along the Salmon Bay waterfront, and the residential area on the hills above the shoreline that curves south and then westward to Shilshole Bay on Puget Sound. Shops, restaurants, and parks in the downtown core retain much of their Scandinavian heritage, including Scandinavian products, foods, and decorations.

Ride-around: It is possible to walk from the Ballard Pier-24th Avenue Landing to Market Street and take the #17 Sunset Hill bus north to the renowned Nordic Heritage Museum at 3014 NW 67th. 206-789-5707.

★ **Ballard Pier - 24th Avenue Landing:** Community volunteers spear-headed the renovation of the old Ballard Pier, located at the foot of 24th Avenue. From the water, it is identified by the 300-foot-long dock wedged between a repair facility and a large restaurant. Side and end ties available for boats less than 40 feet in length with adequate depths. No power or water. Day use only. Two hour free moorage for patrons of the shops and restaurants of downtown Ballard. Donations are taken at the site.

★ **Salmon Bay (5):** This bay extends from the east end of the locks to the Ballard Bridge. Before the locks and the Lake Washington Ship Canal were built, this was a shallow, unnavigable harbor. Today, it is an active marine supply and industrial center. There are fuel docks, and permanent moorage facilities for pleasure and commercial boats along the shore. Fishermen's Terminal is on the southern shore.

★ **Fishermen's Terminal Moorage:** Located just inside the Ballard Locks next to the Ballard Bridge, this Port of Seattle Marina welcomes pleasure craft for both transient and permanent freshwater moorage. Note that the slips are sawtooth style (not finger piers) with easy tie up and

Lake Union with Elliott Bay in the foreground   *Staff Photo*

access off either the stern or bow. Dock power is 20, 30, and 50 ampere, water, showers, laundry, three day parking, 24 hour security, bilge and sewage pump out, Travel Lift rental, marine repairs, groceries, and delightful dining at Chinooks, with side-tie moorage in front of the restaurant. This site was dedicated in 1913 and is now home to the world's largest salmon and halibut fishing fleets, groundfish longliners, and factory trawlers. Staff on duty 24 hours/seven days a week. Open year around. E-mail: ft@portseattle.org. Address: 3919 18th Avenue West, Seattle, Washington 98119. Telephone: 206-728-3395, 1-800-426-7817 Ext. 3395. Fax: 206-728-3393. Website: www.portseattle.org/seaport. VHF 17.

Ballard Mill Marina: Very limited guest moorage, 20 & 30 ampere power, water, restrooms, laundry, showers, pump-out. 206-789-4777.

Ballard Oil: Diesel. 206-783-0241.

Covich-Williams Chevron (Ballard): Gas, diesel, oils, filters, water. Open weekdays, Saturday a.m. 206-784-0171, 1-800-833-3132.

14th Avenue Boat Ramp: This renovated Seattle Parks Department launch site is located at the foot of 14th Avenue in Ballard.

Ewing Street Moorings: Very limited guest moorage, 20 & 30 ampere power, restrooms, water. 206-283-1075.

Morrison's North Star Marine: Gas, diesel, oils, oil changes, pump-out, provisions, water. Open seven days all year. 206-284-6600.

Lake Union

[18441, 18447]

★ **Lake Union (6):** In 1854, Thomas Mercer a prominent Seattleite, named this lake in anticipation of the day when a canal would create a "union" between the lakes and the Puget Sound. Years later his vision would be realized and since that day Lake Union's waterfront has been continuously changing. Moorages, condos, floathouses, restaurants, marine supply stores, boat brokerages, charter agencies, boatyards, and marine repair

businesses thrive. Transient moorage may be arranged at some marinas when slips of permanent tenants are vacant. Temporary moorage can be found at several waterfront restaurants. Speed limit is seven knots and no anchoring is permitted.

The Seattle Police Harbor Patrol Office, Gas Works Park, and a Seattle Parks and Recreation boat launch off Northlake Way, at the foot of Sunnyside Street, are on the north shore. Gas Works Park is easy to locate by the large remnants of machinery from the days when the plant manufactured gas from coal. The park features a Play Barn for children, picnic sites, trails and restrooms, and one of the cities best kite flying hills. Off shore, four yellow buoys mark an area for boat testing on this north side of the lake. Caution advised.

On the east shore, a fleet of ships marks the site of the National Oceanic and Atmospheric Association (NOAA). Restaurants, boatyards, a seaplane base, and a U.S. Navy Reserve Center are also found along this shoreline. A buoy-marked shoal is near the southwest shore. A waterfront park and the Center for Wooden Boats are located on the southern shore.

The Center for Wooden Boats is a maze of docks loaded with classic wooden craft of all kinds. The Victorian-style buildings house the boat shop, the library, the general offices, and the boat house. In the boat shop, on any given day, you can see a class of students building a boat from the keel up, or volunteers restoring one of the Center's many boats. The library contains hard-to-find resources and has a lovely view of Lake Union. The boat house is home to a wonderful collection of old photographs from the Oregon Historical Society, and hanging from the ceiling, are old rowing shells, a Greenland kayak, and the driftwood skeleton of an old Eskimo kayak. This is a museum where you can play with the exhibits. There are over a hundred boats of historic significance which you can row or sail. Choose from a classic steamer or a sailboat and go for a ride. 206-382-BOAT.

Nearby, the Puget Sound Maritime Historical Society Museum, which houses ship models, paintings, photographs, and artifacts, is open Mon-Sun noon-5pm. 206-624-3028.

★ **Armchair Sailor, Inc.:** Located along the West Side of Lake Union, just north of downtown Seattle, our shop has been serving the boating community in the Pacific Northwest since 1987. We are a friendly, independently-owned store spe-

Husky Stadium from Union Bay   *Don Newman Photo*

cializing in nautical books, charts, videos, weather & nautical instruments, clocks, clock repair, gifts, and much more. We have the greatest customers that any business could have. They love boating and love feeding their boating habit in our shop! So selling nautical books, charts, and other related stuff is more fun than work! We're open seven days a week to best serve you. (9:30 am to 6:00 pm, Monday through Friday, 9:30 am to 5:00 pm on Saturday and Noon to 5:00 pm on Sunday.) See our advertisement in the A Pages at the front of this book. Website: www.armchairsailorseatttle.com. Address: 2110 Westlake Ave N., Seattle, WA 98109. Telephone: 206-283-0858 or 1-800-875-0852. Fax: 206-285-1935.

★ **Boat Insurance Agency** is an independent agency representing several quality marine insurance companies. We carefully compare a number of policies to find the lowest premiums, thereby providing you with proper marine coverages at the very best price. After placing your insurance with us, you can count on superior service from our helpful and knowledgeable staff. Whether you have a claim, a billing question or a coverage question, we are there to help. Owned and operated by Northwest boaters, we possess the local knowledge necessary to understand the special nature of boating in the West. Let our knowledge and expertise go to work for you! See our advertisement in the A Pages at the front of this book. 1500 Westlake Avenue N. #102, Seattle WA 98109. Phone: 800-828-2446, 206-285-1350. www.boatinsurance.net. email: info@boatinsurance.net.

★ **Seattle Seaplanes:** Located on Lake Union, this company's motto is "We Fly Everywhere!" Scheduled and charter flights in Washington, to and from British Columbia, and Alaska. Fly-in passenger, parts, and supply service direct to your boat. See our advertisement in this chapter. Website: www.seattleseaplanes.com Address: 1325 Fairview Avenue East, Seattle, Washington 98102. Fax: 206-329-9617. Telephones: 206-329-9638, 1-800-637-5553.

Chandler's Cove: Permanent. No overnight guest moorage, 30 & 50 ampere power, water. 206-262-8800.

Marina Mart: Permanent moorage, pump-out.

Marine Servicenter: Sales (new, used, power, sail). 206-323-2405.

Nautical Landing: Guest moorage for boats over 100' in length only. Secured gates. 50-200 ampere power. Call ahead. 206-284-2308.

Portage Bay (7): This bay is almost entirely filled with yacht club facilities and houseboats. Montlake Cut, a concrete-sided man-made canal, connects Portage Bay with Union Bay. See directions for bridge openings included in this chapter in the entry for Lake Washington Ship Canal.

Union Bay (8): This shallow bay, next to the University of Washington, has mooring buoys and a dock that is not attached to shore. This is a popular destination whenever the University of Washington has a sporting event at the stadium. Anchoring is permitted only during Husky football games. According to the Seattle Police Department, boats visiting Husky Stadium must be kept out of the area north and west of the green buoy. Anchorage is possible in other areas. Use a heavy anchor and adequate chain because the bottom is poor holding. Flag down a U of W shuttle boat to make the trip ashore. The price is $5 for a round trip. Only boats with permits are allowed to land on the Husky docks. For permit information call: 206-543-2234. Restrooms and a telephone are on shore.

The Washington Park Arboretum, a botanical research center, is located on the southern shore. Rent a canoe at the University Waterfront Activities Center 206-543-9433 and paddle across the ship canal to explore the Arboretum's secluded waterways. The Graham Visitor Center 206-543-8800 is open 10am - 4pm daily and has interpretive displays as well as a free guided tour at 1:00 p.m. on the first and third Sunday of each month.

Lake Washington
[18441, 18447, 18448]

★ **Lake Washington:** Nearly 17 miles in length, Lake Washington stretches from the communities of Kenmore on the north to Renton on the south. Seattle borders the lake on the west, while Kirkland and Bellevue rim the eastern shore. Mercer Island, located in the southern portion of the lake, is connected by bridges to the mainland. City of Seattle policy does not allow anchoring along its shores, whether in Lake Washington or on Puget Sound. Andrews Bay is an exception, and a specific code of conduct is in force. See entry for Seward Park in this chapter. On the eastern shore, opposite Seattle, Meydenbauer Bay, Fairweather Bay, Cozy Cove, Yarrow Bay, and Juanita Bay are the main anchorages. When anchoring along this eastern side, stay at least 100 yards off shore. Many parks with swimming beaches and fishing piers line the lake shore. Private docks, often extending out from beautifully landscaped properties, jut into the lake. Swimming, sailing, cruising, water-skiing, and fishing are popular activities. Launching ramp sites include the Sammamish River, Magnuson Park at Sand Point, Moss Bay, Stan Sayres Park, Newport Shores, Atlantic City Park, Ferdinand Street at Seward Park (hand launch only), and east of the Boeing plant at Renton. Small boats out on the lake also use these ramp sites for access to shore. Fishing piers are located at North Leschi Moorage, Madison Park, Mount Baker Park, Madrona Park, and Seward Park on Bailey Peninsula.

Swimming beaches, some on park land and some owned by private concessions, dot the shore between houses. These are usually marked by buoys, anchored rafts, or floats. Seattle Park and

Portage Bay, Lake Washington
Jason Paur Photo

Recreation Beaches operate from the end of June through Labor Day, 11:00 a.m.-8:00 p.m. daily, weather permitting. Beaches are located at Matthews Beach, Magnuson Park, Madison Park, Madrona Park, Mount Baker Park, Seward Park, and Pritchard Beach. Hydroplane activity reaches a peak in August during the *Seafair* celebration. The headquarters for the Hydroplane installation is in the Stan Sayres Memorial Park on the west shore, south of the Mercer Island Floating Bridge. The University of Washington crew team races on the lake.

The southernmost bridge is the Mercer Island Floating Bridge (Interstate 90) connecting Seattle with Mercer Island. Vertical clearance at either end is 29 feet. Keep clear of anchor cables which are within 1250 feet of both sides of the bridge. Underwater remains of piers of a former fixed bridge are southeast of the I-90 bridge. Stay in the main navigation channel. The Evergreen Point Bridge (State Route 520) is the northernmost bridge. It extends from Foster Island to Fairweather Point on the east. Vertical clearance is 44 feet on the west end and 57 feet on the east. Marked nautical mile check courses are on both bridges. A third bridge, the East Channel Bridge, with a vertical clearance of 65 feet, extends from Barnabie Point on Mercer Island to the mainland at Bellevue. Enforced seven knot speed restrictions exist within 100 yards of shore and under the bridges. The Seattle Police Harbor Patrol, a branch of the Seattle Police Department, supervises traffic and handles requests for aid. 206-684-4071. VHF 16.

★⚓ **Sand Point & Magnuson Park (9):** Sand Point, site of a former Naval Air Station, is now NW District Headquarters for NOAA, the National Oceanic and Atmospheric Administration. Many of the buildings were constructed by the Navy in 1930's and 40's. A small marina belongs to the Navy. Also located at Sand Point is Seattle's second largest park, Magnuson Park. Within the boundaries of its 350 acres there is something for everyone--sports courts and fields, sailing center, swimming beach, biking and walking trails, off-leash dog area, picnic sites, playground and wading pools. There are three long piers and four boat launch lanes near the NE 65th Street entrance. Hand-Carried, non-motorized vessels can be launched in two areas, one just south of the public piers and one south of the swimming beach. Hours: Gates are locked between 11pm - 4am. ⛴⚓🚲

Kenmore (10): Located at the extreme north end of the lake, Kenmore is the gateway to the Sammamish River. Observe a five mile speed limit in the area and be on the alert for floatplanes landing and taking off. Lighted markers outline the channel, however, there is shoaling and grounding has occurred.

★⚓ **Tracy Owen Station:** Formerly known as Log Boom Park. Day moorage is available. No power. Picnic tables, outdoor cooking facilities, restrooms, trails, fishing, and childrens' play equipment are available at this Kenmore City park. This is the start of the northern end of the 12 mile Burke Gilman Trail to Gas Works Park in Seattle. Anchorage is possible south of the park. ⚓🚶

★ **Cap Sante Marine - Seattle/Lake Washington:** Located at the north end of Lake Washington, adjacent to Kenmore Air. Fuel dock with supreme and unleaded gas, permanent moorage marina, dry storage racks (maximum boat length 23'), and indoor dry storage. Evinrude/Johnson (Bombardier), Volvo, Cummins, Mercruiser, Mercury outboards, Honda, Boss Boats, Duroboat Marine, Onan, Kohler Generators dealer. Factory trained technicians. Engine surveys, warranty repairs, engine, outboard, and generator repowers. Trailer, fiberglass, prop repairs. Haul-outs to 30,000 lbs, 12'8" beam. Painting, pressure washing, mast stepping and unstepping, detailing. Fully stocked parts store and chandlery. Open all year. See our Steering Star description in Chapter 6. Email: info@capsante.com. Websites: www.capsante.com and www.nwboattravel.com/capsante. Address: 6201 NE 175th Street, Kenmore, Washington 98028. Telephone: 425-482-9465. VHF 16.

Harbour Village Marina: Permanent moorage, pump-out. 425-485-7557.

★⚓ **Saint Edwards Park:** This day-use park contains 316 acres and is primarily accessed by car. Site of a former seminary, there are trails to the beach where good fishing is found. Equestrian and hiking trails, picnic sites, playground, sports fields, horseshoe pits. When arriving by water, look for the park sign. Because of shoaling and uneven depths, anchoring may be difficult. Anchor out in deeper water. ⚓🚶

★ **Sammamish River (10):** It is possible for flat bottom, shallow draft boats to navigate the dredged and cleared waterway all the way to Redmond. Bothell's first settler, Columbus Greenleaf, arrived in 1870 and built a cabin on the river. The river played an important role in commerce and, for awhile, was navigable by large barges up to Bothell Landing. This made Bothell an important steamboat landing. Farther up the river is Redmond.

★⚓ **Bothell Landing:** Located about two miles up the Sammamish River, this city park has a float, playground, restrooms, trails, picnic tables and BBQ. It also has an historical museum that is open on Sundays from 1-4pm from May 2 - Sept. 26. Admission is free. 425-486-1889. The amphitheater at the park is the site of a number of popular community events including the Summer Music In The Park Series. Canoes and small boats tie to the public pier, and visitors can wander into town or bike ride near the landing or on trails along the river. 🚶⚓🚲

★⚓ **Marymoor Park:** Located at the north end of Sammamish Lake, Marymoor Park is King County's largest park. Portable boats can be launched here and floated down the eight-mile stretch, past Bothell and Woodinville, to Lake Washington. The park features a climbing rock, exercise circuit, sports fields, picnic areas, off-

leash dog area, and trails. It is also the site of the state's only Velodrome that hosts competitve racing as well as public drop-in use. 206-975-4555. During summer months the popular Picnic In The Park Concert Series features internationally known acts. www.concertsatmarymoor.com.

★ **Juanita Beach (11):** Anchorage is possible in Juanita Bay. Shallow areas are near Nelson Point. Small boats can be beached at Juanita Beach Park. In the early 1900's this beach was a private resort. Today, after extensive renovation by the City of Kirkland, the beach is as popular as ever and features a pier, swimming beach, picnic shelters, tennis courts, ball fields, salmon stream, and the historic Forbes House. Anchorage is possible in the shallow area near the beach. There is another park with good swimming north of Champaign Point. Anchor at least 100 yards off shore. ⚓

★ **Kirkland (12):** Kirkland has over four miles of waterfront on Lake Washington. Moss Bay has marina facilities and Kirkland's Marina Park with moorage, a launching facility, sandy beach, waterfowl, and parks. Parks include Marina Park, Park Place, and Carillon Point, where the Summer Arts In The Park and other programs are held. Several waterfront restaurants maintain private floats for guest moorage while dining.

In the late 1880's, Peter Kirk, the city's namesake and industrialist, envisioned the area as the "Pittsburgh of the West" after veins of iron ore were discovered in the nearby Cascade mountains. Kirk had been the owner of Moss Bay Hermatite Iron and Steel Ltd. in Workington, England, and had invented steel sleeper cars and steel rails to be used in countries where wooden ties were not practical. He came to America to try to expand world trade, and eventually did open a steel mill here. Kirkland's population rose quickly to 5,000, however, because of the economic depression in 1893, the mill failed without ever producing an ounce of steel. Later, a woolen mill was established. The town began to prosper as a ship building center, attracting real estate sales and land development interests, and serving as the gateway for ferry traffic across the lake. When the first floating bridge opened in 1940, ferry service terminated. Today, Kirkland is primarily a residential area with an extensive variety of stores, restaurants, and services. Over 25% of the waterfront has been preserved by the city.

Carillon Point: Moorage by reservation only, showers, restrooms, 30 & 50 ampere power, pump-out. 425-822-1110.

Marina Park: Guest moorage, 77 slips. 72 hour maximum stay in any seven day period. Nominal fee. Water during most months, no power, restrooms. Launch ramp for boats under 24'. (Key card required for access April 1-October 31. Cards must be purchased at the Kirkland Parks Office. Bring registration or certificate of title. Sold to registered owner only. Resident, non-resident fees applied.) 425-587-3347. www.ci.kirkland.wa.us

Villagio on Yarrow Bay: Private moorage, water, electricity.

Wilcox's Yarrow Bay Marina: Permanent moorage, gas, diesel, boat rentals, repairs, pump-out. 425-822-6066.

★ **Cozy Cove:** There is anchorage here, as well as in adjacent Yarrow and Fairweather Bays. Cozy Cove is preferred because it is more protected and the bottom slopes gradually. Caution advised to allow adequate distance from private mooring buoys and docks.

★ **Fairweather Bay:** Give a wide berth to Hunts Point when crossing between Cozy Cove to Fairweather Bay. This bay, open to westerly winds, has anchorage on the west side.

★ **Meydenbauer Bay (13):** Limited anchorage is possible. Meydenbauer Bay Marina and the smaller Bellevue Marina are now owned by the City of Bellevue and future plans are being made for the facilities. A private yacht club is also located in the area, as is Meydenbauer Beach Park, the site of a swimming beach, picnic area and playground. William Meydenbauer established a claim in 1869, marking the beginning of Bellevue. Meydenbauer Bay was the site of a whaling ship station as recently as the 1930's. The American-Pacific Whaling Company operated a fleet of six steamers that whaled in the North Pacific and the Bering Sea. Beaux Arts Village, south of Meydenbauer Bay, is the site of a private marina.

Meydenbauer Bay Marina: Permanent moorage. 425-452-4883.

Bellevue (14): Bellevue, incorporated in 1953, is now the fifth largest city in the state. Enetai Beach, a park south of the East Channel Bridge has a dock, swimming beaches, picnic area, restrooms, and seasonal canoe and kayak rentals. Newcastle Beach is the largest city park on Lake Washington. Beautiful lake views, a swimming beach, picnic and playground areas, and nature trail are popular features. A 300-foot fishing dock and two floats offer boat access. The SE 40th Boat Launch, located at 118th and SE 40th St. also provides access to Lake Washington. Parking is available, fee charged. 425 452-6117.

Mercer Marine: Located at Newport Yacht Basin. Gas, diesel (call ahead), repairs, haul-out. No guest moorage. 425-641-2090.

Newport Yacht Basin: Permanent moorage. 425-746-7225.

★ **Mercer Island (15):** This beautiful island was named after Judge Thomas Mercer, who captained a wagon train to Seattle in 1853. Luxurious homes front the shoreline, many with private docks extending into the lake. Luther Burbank Park, on the north shore, has facilities for boaters. A launch ramp is found at Barnabie Point where the East Channel Bridge (vertical clearance 65') crosses East Channel.

★⚓ **Luther Burbank Park (16):** The City of Mercer Island manages this park and is currently reviewing plans for a grand new redesign. This extensive waterfront park, situated north of Barnabie Point, stretches all the way to Calkins Point. Docks with finger floats can accommodate 30 boats. Day moorage only. Grasslands near Calkins Point and trails encourage hiking and jogging. Attractions include tennis courts, fishing pier, off-leash dog area, picnic sites, restrooms, a bathhouse at the swimming beach, an amphitheater with covered walkway. 206-236-3545. ⚞🧍

Renton (17): A surfaced ramp on the east side of the Boeing facility is next to a parking lot and park with views of aircraft take-offs and landings.

★⚓ **Gene Coulon Memorial Park:** The Renton Parks Department has developed a mile and a half of waterfront property into a beautiful park with a fishing pier, floating boardwalk, and some moorage slips. No power. An eight lane boat launch ramp is open 24 hours a day, fee charged. Call 425-430-6700. On shore are swimming beaches, paths, tennis courts, horseshoe pits, sand volleyball courts, a playground, a viewing tower, restaurant, picnic sites, a bathhouse with hot showers

and restrooms. Of special interest are the bronze statues and the unusual floating patio-decks, connected by ramps with the main walkway. A number of community events are hosted here, including a summer concert series and the *Limited Hydroplane Races.* ⛴🧍

Rainier Beach (18): Speed limit three knots within 100 yards of shore. The only public facility located here is the Atlantic City launching ramp found in the cove south of Beer Sheva Park. This facility is maintained by the City of Seattle and has ramp and dock space accommodating up to six launches/retrievals at a time. Fee applies. Other facilities are private yacht clubs and marinas.

Parkshore Marina: Permanent moorage, pump-out. 206-725-3330.

★⚓ **Seward Park & Andrews Bay (19):** A three knot speed limit is enforced in this area. This park encompasses Andrews Bay and Bailey Peninsula. A Code of Conduct is enforced regarding noise, speed, pollution, and environmental damage. The anchorage area can accommodate approximately 80 vessels. It extends from the Seward Park shoreline, out to buoys that are placed 150 yards off the western shore. There is a 300 yard buffer zone off the extreme head of the bay. The approved area is defined by two buoys marked with an "A" (indicating the northwest and southwest corners) and two shore markers (indicating northeast and southeast corners). Place the hook where you are assured of not swinging out of the designated area or against your neighbor. Anchoring is limited to 72 hours within any 7 day period. There is a launching ramp for hand carried boats. The only access to land is at the site of the launch ramp on the western shore, however there is no float for dinghy-ties. In the park are picnic spots, tennis courts, swimming beach, an art studio, and environmental learning center. A nature trail skirts the peninsula. Bird watchers will enjoy this park since over 100 species of birds live in the area. 🧍⚞⛴

Lakewood Moorage: Permanent and limited guest moorage, 20, 30 ampere power, water, provisions. No fuel. 206-722-3887.

★⚓ **Stan Sayres Memorial Park (20):** This park is located a mile south of the I-90 bridge on a

north facing point. The peninsula upon which this park sits was created when water levels in Lake Washington lowered with the building of the Ship Canal in 1917. Named for hydroplane racer, Stan Sayres, this park has a launching ramp, walking trails, restrooms, and day moorage facilities for small boats. It is also the site of the Mount Baker Rowing and Sailing Center. 206-386-1913. ⛴🧍

★ **Leschi (21):** Leschi is located between the Mount Baker and Madrona neighborhoods along the shores of Lake Washington. In the late 1800's an amusement park, serviced by a cable-car system running between Leschi and Pioneer Square, was located here. The park is long gone, but people still enjoy the tranquility and beauty of this neighborhood. This is the site of a marina, gas dock, a fishing pier, and Seattle Park Department moorage.

Leschi Yacht Basin: Call 206-328-6777 ext.102 for information.

West Seattle
[18445, 18448]

West Seattle's Western Shore (22): See current table for Admiralty Inlet. This is the site of several saltwater parks. Alki Point, where, in 1851, white settlers landed, is the site of Alki Beach Park and lighthouse. No mooring facilities. Only hand carried, non-motorized small boats may be beached in a designated area northeast of the open public sandy beach. Me-Kwa-Mooks Natural Area is to the south, as are Lowman Beach Park and Lincoln Park.

★⚓ **Lincoln Park:** This lovely 135-acre park, accessible by car, borders Puget Sound north of the Fauntleroy-Vashon Island ferry landing. Per City of Seattle policy, anchoring, or the beaching of power craft is not permitted. In the park are landscaped grounds, trails, athletic fields, horseshoe pits, tennis courts, picnic sites, a seasonal heated saltwater pool, and locales for scuba diving, beachcombing, and fishing. ⚞🧍

Fauntleroy (23): Site of the Fauntleroy Vashon-Southworth ferry. No marine facilities.

Meydenbauer Bay   *Don Newman Photo*

Essential Supplies & Services

AIR TRANSPORTATION
Kenmore Air: 1-800-543-9595
Seattle Seaplanes . 206-329-9638, 1-800-637-5553

AMBULANCES: Medic 1   911

BUS TRANSPORTATION
Gray Line of Seattle 1-800-426-7532
Metro. 206-553-3000
Monorail information. 206-905-2620

BOOKS / BOOK STORES
Armchair Sailor: 206-283-0858, 800-875-0852
Evergreen Pacific Publications 206-368-8157
The Marine Atlas. 541-593-6396

CNG CYLINDERS
Shilshole Bay Fuel Dock 206-783-7555

COAST GUARD
Cell phones: #24, #CG
Emergencies: VHF 16 Seattle. 206-217-6000
Customer Information 1-800-368-5647
District Office. 206-220-7000
Vessel Traffic 206-217-6050

CUSTOMS
US Customs / Border Protection
   7277 Perimeter Road, Rm. 116 Seattle, WA 98108
   (To procure I-68 Forms Hours 8:00 a.m.-2:30 p.m.)
   206-553-0667
In-person report to CBP officer 206-553-4406

FERRY TRANSPORTATION
Victoria Clipper (passenger only) 206-448-5000
. . . . 800-888-2535
Washington State 206-464-6400; 1-800-843-3779

FISHING INFO . 360-902-2700. 360-902-2500

FUELS
Ballard Oil: Ballard. Diesel 206-783-0241
Cap Sante-Kenmore: Gas 425-482-9465
Covich-Williams: Ballard. Gas, Diesel . . . 206-784-0171
Elliott Bay Marina: Gas, Diesel 206-285-4817
Elliott Bay Yacht Care: Gas, Diesel . 206-285-8424
. . . . VHF 78A
Mercer Marine: Bellevue. Gas 425-641-2090
Morrison's North Star: Lake Union. Gas, Diesel.
. . . . 206-284-6600
Shilshole Bay Fuel Dock: Ballard. Gas, Diesel
. . . . **206-783-7555**
Yarrow Bay Marina: Kirkland. Gas, Diesel . 425-822-6066

INSURANCE
Boat Insurance Agency 206-285-1350
   Or Call 1-800-828-2446

HOSPITALS
Swedish Ballard. 206-782-2700
Bellevue. 425-688-5000
Swedish. 206-386-6000
Virginia Mason 206-624-1144

LIQUOR STORE
Elliott Bay Marina 206-285-4817

MARINAS / MOORAGE FLOATS
Ballard Mill Marina 206-789-4777
Bell Harbor: Pier 66 . . . . 206-615-3952 VHF 66A
Carillon Point Marina: Kirkland 425-822-1110
Chandler's Cove. 206-262-8800
Elliott Bay Marina. . . . . . . 206-285-4817 VHF 78A

Ewing Street Moorings: Seattle 206-283-1075
Fisherman's Terminal: Seattle. 206-728-3395
. . . . **VHF 17**
Gene Coulon Memorial Park: Renton
Marina Park: Kirkland 425-587-3300
Lakewood Moorage: Andrews Bay 206-722-3887
Luther Burbank Park: Mercer Island. (day only)
Nautical Landing (over 100' only): 206-284-2308
Shilshole Bay Marina: Ballard
. . . . **206-728-3006 VHF 17**

PARKS
Department of Natural Resources 1-800-527-3305
King County Parks. 206-296-4232
Washington Camping Reservations . . . 1-888-226-7688
Washington State Parks 360-902-8844

POISON CONTROL 1-800-222-1222

POLICE:
Seattle Harbor: . . . . 206-684-4071 VHF 16

RAMPS / HAUL-OUTS
Atlantic City Park: Southwest shore Lake Washington
Barnabie Point: Mercer Island
Don Armeni Park: Duwamish Head, Elliott Bay
14th Avenue Ramp: Ballard
Gene Coulon Park, Renton
Golden Gardens Park: Eddie Vine Ramp, Ballard
Kirkland Marina Park: Moss Bay
Lake Union: North shore at Sunnyside Street
Magnuson Park: Sand Point
Marymoor Park: Sammamish River
Newport Yacht Basin: Bellevue
Rainier Beach
Renton
Seattle Parks Ramps: 206-684-7249
Seward Park: Andrews Bay
Shilshole Bay Marina: Ballard 206-728-3006
Sixty Acres: Sammamish River
Stan Sayres Park: West shore Lake Washington

RECOMPRESSION CHAMBER
Virginia Mason, Seattle 206-583-6433

RED TIDE HOTLINE: 800-562-5632

REPAIRS / SERVICE
Cap Sante Marine: Kenmore 425-482-9465
Elliott Bay Yacht Care: . . . 206-285-2600 VHF 78A
Gallery Marine: Lake Union. 206-547-2477
Shilshole Bay Marina: Ballard. 206-728-3006

SEWAGE DISPOSALS
Ballard Mill Marina: Ballard. Pump 206-789-4777
Bell Harbor: Pier 66, Pump 206-615-3952
Carillon Point: Kirkland. Pump 425-822-1110
Elliott Bay Yacht Care: Pump 206-285-2600
Harbor Island Marina: Pump 206-728-3387
Harbor Village Marina: Kenmore. Pump . 425-485-7557
Morrison's North Star: Pump 206-284-6600
Parkshore: Rainier Beach. Pump 206-725-3330
Shilshole Bay Fuel Dock: Pump, Dump 206-783-7555
Yarrow Bay Marine: Pump. 425-822-6066

SHELLFISH HOTLINE: . . . 360-796-3215
For local area closures/information, call County Health Depts.:
King County Dept. of Health 206-296-4632

TAXI
Seattle. 206-622-6500; 206-622-1717

TOWING
C-TOW. 1-888-354-5554
VESSEL ASSIST . . Lake Washington 206-793-7375
Seattle (Puget Sound Area). 206-300-0486

VHF MARINE OPERATOR
Whidbey Island: 87
Note: MariTel has shut down all other Washington State
   VHF Marine Operator channels until further notice.

VISITOR INFORMATION
Ballard 206-784-9705
Kirkland 425-822-7066
Seattle 206-461-5840

WEATHER
VHF: WX1

Duck Dodge Sailboat Races on Lake Union   *Photo © Brian Huntooon*

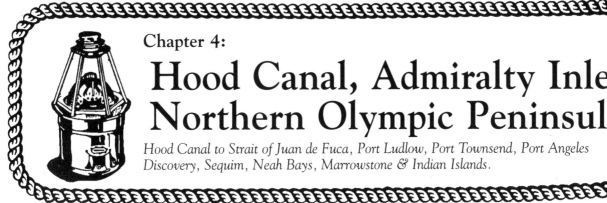

Chapter 4:

Hood Canal, Admiralty Inlet Northern Olympic Peninsula

Hood Canal to Strait of Juan de Fuca, Port Ludlow, Port Townsend, Port Angeles Discovery, Sequim, Neah Bays, Marrowstone & Indian Islands.

★ **Important Notice:** See "Important Notices" between Chapters 7 and 8 in this guide for specific information on boating related topics such as: Canadian & U.S. Customs, boating safety and security, navigation, weather, U.S. & Canadian Coast Guard, U.S & Canadian marine radio use, Vessel Traffic Service and traffic separation plans, security zones, and internet access. Due to new Department of Homeland Security regulations, call ahead for latest customs information and/or see Northwest Boat Travel On-line, www..nwboat.com.

Symbols

[   ]: Numbers between [ ] are chart numbers.

{   }: Numbers & letters between { } are waypoints.

⚓: Park, ⛵: Boat Launch, ▲: Campgrounds, 𝑥: Hiking Trails, 𝔸: Picnic Area, 🚲: Biking

Makah Whale Hunt Regulations: The Makah Tribe of Washington State is currently seeking a waiver from the National Marine Fisheries Service in order to resume whaling activities. A review process that includes public hearings and the preparation of an environmental impact statement will have to be completed before a final ruling is made. This process is expected to be complete by October 2006.

Hood Canal

[18441, 18445, 18448, 18458, 18476, 18477]

★ **Hood Canal:** Discovered in 1792, this picturesque fjord indents into the mainland 44 miles, curving at the Great Bend and extending another 11 miles. It ends in tide flats at Lynch Cove. Interestingly, only a few land miles separate Lynch Cove from the head of Case Inlet in South Sound, making one ponder what it would have been like had the waterways met and made the Kitsap Peninsula into a huge island. Hood Canal could be the destination for either an extended vacation or a short get-away cruise.

The shores are high and wooded and, except for the heads of bays and river mouths, the water is deep. U.S. Highway 101 rims much of the west shore. For many years Hood Canal has been a prime vacation area with summer cabins and permanent residences lining the shores. Tidal currents seldom can exceed more than two knots. There can be heavy, dangerous rips north of and around Foulweather Bluff when the ebb current of Puget Sound meets the ebb from Hood Canal. Winds in various parts of the canal affect water conditions greatly.   In the case of Foulweather Bluff, the rips become even more dangerous during an opposing strong north or northwesterly wind. Further into the canal, in Dabob Bay, rips can occur if a wind blowing from the north meets an opposing southwest wind within the canal.

HOOD CANAL

OLYMPIC PENINSULA

Foulweather Bluff

Bywater Bay

Salsbury Point

Twin Spits

Dabob Bay   **9**

Quilcene Bay   **10**

PORT GAMBLE

Floating Bridge

Kitsap Memorial State Park

BANGOR

Point Whitney   **11**

Fisherman Harbor
Dosewallips State Park   **12**

8

7

Pleasant Harbor   **13**

SEABECK

14

15
Scenic Beach

KITSAP PENINSULA

Lilliwaup

Belfair State Park   **20**

16   HOODSPORT

Tahuya   **19**
Twanoh State Park

Potlatch Park
17   **18** UNION   Alderbrook

Not for navigation

Chart List

NOAA Charts:

18423, 18441, 18445, 18448, 18458, 18460, 18464, 18465, 18468, 18471, 18476-77, 18484-85

Marine Atlas (2005 ed.):

Pages 13-19

Marina on the Peninsula   Photo © Carmen Scott

The Great Bend vicinity is also open to conflicting wind patterns. In these cases, smoother waters are found closer to shore.

The Hood Canal Bridge, a fixed pontoon bridge, crosses the canal between Termination and Salsbury Points. Clearance at the western end is 35 feet and, at the eastern end, is 55 feet. Construction currently underway to retrofit or replace parts of the bridge is not expected to be completed until 2009. Highlighted by a stop at the marine resort facility in Pleasant Harbor, there are also several marine state parks, Department of Natural Resources shellfish harvesting beaches, and beautiful bays to visit. To add history and variety to the cruise, visit the communities of Port Gamble, Quilcene, Seabeck, Hoodsport, and Union. Finally, Bangor is home port to naval nuclear submarines, and it is possible to see a submarine underway in the canal. Be aware of the designated restricted areas shown on NOAA chart 18476. During shrimp harvesting season (Wednesdays and Saturdays during three weeks in May), be watchful of shrimp pot markers, which can foul your propeller. Before harvesting shellfish, procure the Washington State Department of Fish & Wildlife brochure, "Fishing In Washington," available in marine supply stores and fuel outlets. Special regulations are enforced in this area. Before considering harvesting of shellfish, call the Red Tide Hot Line at 800-562-5632.

Over the years, photographers have often captured the canal's rich views of the Kitsap Peninsula to the east and the foothills of the Olympic Mountains to the west. This lush, relatively undeveloped playground is close to the metropolitan cities of Puget Sound. Hood Canal attractions include fishing, camping, beachcombing, clam digging, swimming, shrimping, mussel and oyster harvesting, dining, wildlife viewing, and just lazy gunkholing.

Foulweather Bluff (1): See current tables for Admiralty Inlet. Like so many other places where large amounts of water move rapidly, this vicinity can be either glassy smooth or rough and very uncomfortable, depending upon wind and tide. Off the point, the ebb current from Puget Sound meets the up to two-and-one-half knot current from Hood Canal. When a north or northwest wind blows during these ebb flows, the rips may be uncomfortable or even dangerous to small vessels. Then it is indeed Foulweather Bluff. During these wind conditions , travel during flood tide or close to slack water if possible.

Twin Spits (2): Temporary anchorage in 40 to 50-foot depths, is found south of the spits. This is often a good spot to wait for a tide change or the wind to lay down outside.

★⚓ Shine Tidelands State Park and Wolfe Property (3): Bywater Bay lies behind Hood Head, about three miles south of the entrance to Hood Canal. Very shallow, the bay nearly dries at lowest tides, making it suitable only for beachable boats. There are miles of sandy beaches, a lagoon, and nature trails in the 130-acres of undeveloped state park property known as Wolfe Property Park. Day use only, no camping, no fresh water. Crabbing, clamming and fishing are popular. Shine Tidelands State Park, developed from a portion of Wolfe Property, sits between the spit and the bridge and features 5,000 feet of tideland, picnic tables, and crude personal watercraft launch. There are 20 primitive campsites on the western shore of the canal. RV's are limited to 25 feet in length. Vault toilets provided. Fires are not permitted. A launch ramp, usable at all tides, is farther south, near the bridge site. Tidelands from Bywater Bay to this launch site are managed by the state and are open for shellfish harvesting. ⚓⚑⚓

Squamish Harbor: When heading south into the canal, this harbor is to starboard. Limited, exposed anchorage is possible on a mud bottom off the north shore and near the head of the harbor. Case Shoal is an extensive, marked, shoal on the southeast side that fills a great part of the bay and dries at a minus tide. Deeper water is along the north shore, and a launch ramp is found at the site of a park. Department of Natural Resources beaches offer shellfish harvesting, including crab and oysters. 360-825-1631.

★⚓ Salsbury Point County Park (4): This day use park lies outside of Port Gamble, at the western end of Teekalet Bluff. There is a good beach, restrooms, launch ramps, picnic and playground areas, fishing pier. No pets. ⚓⚑

★ Port Gamble (5): This is a favored anchorage. Strong currents occur in the entry channel and shoals extend off both sides. The lights on the east side are on shoal. and do not mark the exact boundary of the channel. Line up to the range markers for guidance through mid-channel.

Beware of the covered shoal about 500 yards northeast from the north end of the lumber mill wharf. There is good anchorage inside the entrance, on the port side opposite the mill and in the southern portion. Anchor in 25 to 40 foot depths, mud bottom. Do not tie to the floating bridge pontoon.

Nearby, historic Port Gamble is a restored 1850's company mill town founded by the owners of the Pope and Talbot Lumber Company. The mill closed in 1995, after 142 years of operation. A walking tour through town features many interesting structures including St. Paul's Episcopal Church and the Walker-Ames Home. The elm trees along Main Street came from Maine by way of Cape Horn in 1872.

The historic museum chronicles Port Gamble's development through exhibits of memorabilia owned by generations of mill families. A second museum, located in the general store, features shells and marine life specimens. There is a post office, lodging, day spa and shops selling antiques, art, books, chocolates, and coffee.

Hood Canal Floating Bridge: [18476] Constructed from over 20 concrete floating pontoons that are linked together, this one and one quarter mile bridge connects Kitsap and Olympic Peninsulas. Boats pass under the raised portions at either end of the bridge. Vertical clearance is 35' at the west end and 55' at the east end. Shoals are hazards and strong currents are often present. Because of the shoals, the eastern high span is the recommended passage. The vicinity of Sisters Rocks, south of the bridge and off the west shore, is extremely hazardous. Shown on the chart, these two rocks dry at half tide. A large lighted beacon is on the southernmost rock, however its neighbor is unmarked. If traveling south along the west side of the canal, turn east immediately after passing under the bridge and hug the bridge until midspan before turning south again. If traveling north, aim for mid-span until very close to the bridge, turn east and hug the bridge until turning north to go under the span. If it is imperative that the bridge be opened for your vessel, call on VHF 13. If not answered, call the Tacoma office of the State Department of Transportation, 1-800-419-9085. Allow about an hour for the bridge crew to arrive. On shore, on the east side, it is possible to stroll on the walkway. A concrete launch ramp, usable at all tides, lies north of the western end of the bridge. Because of anchor cables, do not anchor in the vicinity.

★⚓ Kitsap Memorial Marine State Park (6): This 58 acre park, three miles south of the bridge on the eastern shore of the canal, contains campsites, a mile of hiking trails, picnic facilities, swimming beach, showers, and mooring buoys. 360-779-3205, 360-902-8844. ⚓⚑⚑⚑

Thorndike Bay: This bay is too open and shallow for anchorage.

Bangor (7): [18476] Site of the Naval Nuclear Submarine Station. A new outer security area with 17 buoys has been established. A restricted naval operating area extends nearly four miles, north and south of the pier. Avoid this patrolled stretch by staying on the western shore of the canal. If a submarine is in the area, boaters must give it a berth of more than 1,000 yards.

★ Fisherman Harbor (8): [18476] When approaching Fisherman Harbor, aim north, traveling opposite the spit. The immediate vicinity is shallow, especially directly opposite the entry. Passage into the harbor must be made near high tide, because the entrance dries. There is a natural entry channel. After entering, turn hard to port and follow the spit, then turn to starboard. Depths

Port Townsend Wooden Boat Festival   Photo © Carmen Scott

range from four to 17 feet. The oyster beds are private. Toandos State Park Recreational Tidelands are outside the harbor, west of the harbor entrance and extending around Tskutsko Point at the west side of Oak Head. Adjacent tidelands are private. Ask prior to taking any shellfish in the vicinity. If permission is granted cover all holes.

★ **Dabob Bay (9):** In season, commercial shrimp pots, with floating buoys attached, are hazards in the bay. Broad Spit, on the western shore, provides some shelter from winds. Naval operations use much of the bay. There are warning lights on Whitney Point, Sylopash Point, and Zelatched Point. The lights flash green when caution is required and red if the area is definitely closed to navigation.

A Department of Natural Resources beach at the end of Bolton Peninsula is open to shellfish harvesting, as is another state managed beach on the east shore of Jackson Cove, below Pulali Point. These are marked by white and black posts. Anchorage can be found in Jackson Cove. 360-374-6131. See Red Tide Hotline on last page of this chapter.

★ **Quilcene Bay (10):** Quilcene Bay is open to southerly winds, dries at the head, and is often used for log storage. It does contain a breakwater-surrounded boat basin, and an adjacent park with picnic facilities.

Quilcene Boat Haven: Limited transient moorage, 20 & 30 ampere power, water, ice, launching, gas, diesel, showers, campground, limited RV spaces (reservations required), pump-out, repairs, emergency service, towing, boat transport. 360-765-3131.

Walk-around: Quilcene, a pleasant mile and a quarter walk from moorage, is known for its restaurants and markets which feature oysters and other sea foods. Take a little extra time to linger on Linger Longer Road.

★ **Whitney Point (11):** The State Shellfish Laboratory offers educational displays, restrooms, and a launch ramp. Take the self-guided tour. A sand spit encloses a lagoon, used for research. Swimming, beachcombing, and shellfish harvesting are possible on the Dabob Bay side of the spit. A restricted area for Naval operations is off the point.

Pulali Point: A Department of Fisheries beach is on the western side of Pulali Point in Jackson Cove. Shellfish harvesting is accessible only by boat. Scuba divers often explore the rocks and steep cliffs off the point for spear fishing and shellfish gathering. The area from Point Whitney south to Dosewallips Flats is noted for above average salmon fishing. The Olympic National Forest Service Campground is a good place for clam digging and oyster harvesting. 360-374-6131.

★⚓ **Dosewallips State Park (12):** Located one mile south of the town of Brinnon, this 425 acre park is accessible mostly by car. There are 5,500 feet of shoreline on Hood Canal and 5,400 feet of freshwater frontage on both sides of the Dosewallips River. Tables, stoves, restrooms, showers, drinking water, and campsites, 40 hookups are available. Both fresh and salt water fishing are popular. The part of the beach open for shellfish harvest is marked with orange posts. Hard shell clams, geoducks, and oysters are found. Anyone harvesting shellfish is reminded that the Washington Department of Fish and Wildlife requires a shellfish license before digging or taking shellfish. 360-902-8844, 360-796-4415. ▲⚓

★ **Pleasant Harbor (13):** [18476] This is an attractive and protected harbor on the west side of Hood Canal, 18 miles south of the bridge. When entering the harbor, stay in mid-channel. The entrance is narrow at low tide, but there is a minimum depth of seven feet. Anchorage is good in depths of 20 to 40 feet on a mud bottom.

Pleasant Harbor Marina: {47° 39.17' N, 122° 55.05' W} Resort marina with guest and permanent moorage, power, water, deli, store, bait and tackle, showers, laundry, gas, diesel, pump-out. Open all year. 360-796-4611. VHF 16, 09.

Homeport Marina: Permanent moorage only. 360-796-4040.

★⚓ **Pleasant Harbor Marine State Park:** Tucked in behind the sand and gravel spit to the right of the harbor entrance is a small dock. No power. Nightly moorage fees May-September. There is a pit toilet. Pump-out and dump site provided. No camping permitted. 360-902-8844.

★ **Seabeck Bay (14):** As early as 1853, Seabeck was an active timber town and busy seaport. Today it is a residential community with a marina, general store, restaurant, gallery, post office, and excellent fishing grounds. Anchorage, with protection from west and south winds, is possible inside Misery Point. It is open to the north.

Shoals extend from the head of the bay. An artificial reef is located off Misery Point, and an excellent launch site is located south of the Point.

Seabeck Marina: Gas, moorage, lift to 18', provisions, restrooms. CB 13, VHF 16, 68.

★⚓ **Scenic Beach State Park (15):** This park lies one mile southwest of the town of Seabeck. Originally a homestead and later a resort, the 88-acre park has tables and stoves, a kitchen shelter, children's playground, volley ball, horseshoe pit, campsites, and hot showers. Activities include swimming, fishing, hiking, and scuba diving. A surfaced boat ramp is 1 mile east of park. Campground closed in winter. This beach is excellent for oyster harvesting in season. Check the Red Tide Hot Line 1-800-562-5632. There is also above average salmon fishing off Misery Point, Scenic Beach, and in Stavis Bay to the south. 360-830-5079, 888-226-7688, 360-902-8844. ⚓▲⚓

Hood Canal from Scenic Beach south to Hoodsport: There are several small resort facilities along the western shore of the canal. Most of the harbors are actually estuaries where the rivers empty into the canal.

★⚓ **Triton Cove State Park:** There is anchorage with some protection from south winds. Five miles north of Eldon, a 29 acre site has been designated as Triton Cove State Park. It was once the site of a school, a motel, and a post office, and later a trailer park. The property includes a parking lot, launch ramp, picnic area, campsites, and restroom. Day use only. ⚓⚓▲

Eagle Creek: About 2 miles from Lilliwaup, there are tidelands for shellfish harvesting located on the south side of Eagle Creek. The north side of the creek is private.

Lilliwaup: This is a small town at the mouth of Lilliwaup Creek. The bay is very shallow. There is a launching ramp. Scuba diving and swimming are popular in this area. No drinking water is available. On the eastern shore, between Tekiu Point and Anderson Cove, and opposite Ayock Point, there are good clam and oyster harvesting spots. At least six beaches have tidelands managed by the Department of Natural Resources. They are bordered by black and white marker posts. Caution advised regarding trespassing on adjacent private property. Directly opposite Lilliwaup is Dewatto Bay. Good clam and oyster beaches are on the north and south shores of this bay. 360-825-1631.

Rest-A-While Resort: Day use dock, sling haul-out, showers, restrooms, RV park, provisions. 360-877-9474.

★ **Hoodsport (16):** Originally named Slalatlat-ltulhu, this is an interesting little town with friendly people. A State Fish Hatchery is nearby, and tours can be arranged. The beach in front of the hatchery is open to the public. No overnight moorage is permitted on the city dock. A liquor store, hardware, grocery, and launch ramp are available.

Hoodsport City Dock: Day moorage.

Sunrise Motel & Resort: Moorage (24' maximum), scuba air. 360-877-5301.

★⚓ **Potlatch Marine State Park (17):** Located 3 miles south of Hoodsport, at a site where local tribes once held their potlatch ceremony, this 57 acre park has many facilities. Mooring buoys, well offshore in Annas Bay, mark the site. There are tables, stoves, restrooms, hot showers, and campsites, some with hookups. Activities include swimming, fishing, Scuba diving, and hiking. Canoes or kayaks can be used to explore the estuary of the Skokomish River. Wildlife is plentiful in the vicinity. 360-877-5361, 360-902-8844. 🛶▲🏊

★ **Union (18):** See current tables for Admiralty Inlet. This tiny town, circa 1890 Union Pacific Railway days, is located at the Great Bend of the canal.

★ **Alderbrook Resort & Spa:** A Luxury Hotel Resort on beautiful Hood Canal, overlooking the spectacular Olympic Mountains and the glistening waters of the canal. Located just 90 miles west of Seattle, Alderbrook offers a full service spa, 1,500' linear dock, waterfront restaurant, boating facilities, golf course and many other recreational amenities. Recreated in 4 star luxury, the "new" Alderbrook Resort & Spa is the Northwest's premier destination of choice for both leisure travelers and boaters alike. See our advertisement in this chapter. Address: 10 E Alderbrook Dr, Union, WA 98592. Website: www.alderbrookresort.com. Telephone: 360-898-2200. For Reservations: 1-800-622-9370.

Hood Canal Marina: Permanent moorage, repairs, RV parking, ramp, water, and electricity. 360-898-2252.

Tahuya: This small settlement on the north shore has a pier and a launching ramp.

Summertide Resort and Marina: Moorage to 26-feet, lodging, provisions, RV park, launching, showers, propane, laundry. 360-275-9313.

★⚓ **Twanoh Marine State Park (19):** Over 182 acres in size, this well established park property has campsites, RV sites, hot showers, two excellent launch ramps, a dock with float, mooring buoys, kitchens, shelters, tables, and stoves. Look for the rustic stone and rock restrooms that were constructed in 1936 by the Civilian Conservation Corps. A display area describes CCC activities. Families enjoy tennis, horseshoes, the swimming beach and wading pool. Hiking, fishing, swimming, and crabbing are possible. Sewage pump and dump. Campground closed from October to mid-April. 360-275-2222, 360-902-8844. ▲⚓🏊

Walk-around: Walk Twanoh Park's trails upland along Twanoh Creek and the rain forest-like growth of moss, thick trees, and sprawling ferns. Observe second-growth cedar, fir, and hemlock.

★ **Port of Allyn Moorage Near Belfair:** North Shore Dock: Ten slips with power. Call ahead to arrange power. No water. Launch ramp and pump-out. Located five miles from Belfair on North Shore Road, about one mile past the state park. Moor here to visit Belfair State Park. 360-275-2430.

★⚓ **Belfair State Park (20):** This park lies on the north shore, near the extreme end of Hood Canal. It has campsites, RV sites, some hookups, stoves, tables, and restrooms. Lynch Cove, which borders the park, is a drying mud flat. Anchorage must be well off shore. No shellfish harvesting permitted. An unusual, man-made beach and gravel lined pool has been created to make swimming possible. Campsite reservations necessary Memorial Day through Labor Day. Campground open all year. 360-275-0668, 360-902-8844. Reservations: 1-888-226-7688. ▲🏊

Northern Puget Sound

★ **Kingston:** See Chapter 5

Admiralty Inlet
[18441, 18464, 18473, 18477]

★ **Port Ludlow (1):** Port Ludlow, a two-mile indention, is the site of a marina, resort, and anchorage. Shoals extend to the north. When entering or leaving, give at least a 200-yard clearance of Ala Point. Speed restrictions of five miles per hour are in force south of a line extending east of the marina to the east shore of Ludlow Bay. Anchorage in 4 to 8 fathoms is possible in several locations in the outer harbor. The most popular anchorage, however, is a beautiful, usually serene spot in the extreme southwest sector behind the Twin Islands. Enter between the Twin Islands and watch for the rock that is just south of the smaller island. Anchorage is excellent in 4 to 16 feet on a mud bottom. Port Ludlow, bearing the name of a naval officer who died in the War of 1812, is rich in historical significance. Boat building was among its earliest industries. A sawmill, operated by Pope and Talbot helped to make it one of the first logging communities on Puget Sound. While these industries declined a number of years ago, Port Ludlow emerged with a new focus—as a master planned community. To explore the area from Poulsbo to Port Townsend, take one of the transit buses that run on Oak Bay Road near the marina. Call 800-371-0497 or visit www.jeffersontransit.com for schedules.

Port Ludlow Marina: {47° 55.5' N, 122° 40.8' W} Permanent and transient moorage, power, water, showers, laundry, restrooms, store, gas, diesel, pump-out, porta potty dump, restaurants, lodging, golf, picnic areas.   360-437-0513, 1-800-308-7991. VHF 16, 68.

★ **Mats Mats (2):** [18441, 18473] Beware of Snake Rock, Colvos Rocks, and Klas Rock when traveling the 2.5 miles north from Port Ludlow to Mats Mats. When entering, pass east of the buoy marking Klas Rock. The two buoys marking Klas Rock have been removed and replaced with a single buoy east and south of Klas Rock. Mats Mats is a very tiny bay entered through a tricky 100-yard-wide, well marked, dredged channel from Admiralty Inlet. A day and night range marks center channel. Minimum depths are five feet in the channel. A red nun Coast Guard buoy "8" marks the sandbar on the western shore at the northern entrance to the bay. Depths in the bay range from three to 13 feet with the best anchorage in the center. A launch ramp is best used at higher tides.

★⚓ **Oak Bay County Park (3):** Anchorage is possible in Oak Bay or smaller boats can be beached on the good sand and gravel beach. Site of a rock jetty. Campsites, picnic tables, swimming, crabbing, clamming, launch ramp. No fresh water. 🛥🏕⚓

★ **Port Townsend Canal (4):** [18441, 18473] This canal connects Port Townsend with Oak Bay to the south. Separating Quimper Peninsula on the mainland from Indian and Marrowstone Islands, it is a short-cut for boaters and is particularly helpful when seas in Admiralty Inlet are rough and uninviting. The dredged canal is marked by a light at the north entrance, and a light and a day beacon at the south entrance. The passage is about 75 feet wide with a controlling depth of 13 feet. Currents run to three knots, and are strongest on the south end at ebb tide. A fixed bridge with a vertical clearance of about 58 feet crosses the canal. The shoreline surrounding both north and south entrances to the canal offers excellent clam and crab harvesting. Much of this land is county park and open to the public.

★⚓ **South Indian Island County Park (5):** Small boats can be beached at this park located across Oak Bay from Oak Bay County Park. Good clamming, crabbing, scuba diving, picnic tables. 🏕

★ **Hadlock (6):** There are floats during summer months, giving access to this small community. Beware of submerged pilings in the area. There is a sandy beach, launch ramp, and marina. Businesses in town include a coffee shop, post office, lodging, and dry cleaner.

Port Hadlock Inn & Marina (at the site of the old Alcohol Plant): Private moorage only. Power, restrooms, showers, water, pump-out, lodging, restaurant, lounge. 360-385-6368. VHF 16.

★ **Irondale (7):** There is an underwater recreation area at a wreck off Irondale. Bottle collecting, spear fishing, and shellfish gathering are popular. At the turn-of-the-century, Homer H. Swaney came from Pennsylvania to create a rail and steel manufacturing center. Swaney founded the Pacific Steel Company, believing the venture would be the largest in the west. By 1900, Irondale was a thriving community. Today only a small dock marks the spot where large sailing vessels once moored.

★⚓ **Old Fort Townsend State Park (8):** Park land between Glen Cove and Kala Point is a recreational area. Mooring buoys are available. Old pilings, once the fort's wharf, extend into the bay and mark the spot. Old Fort Townsend is located south of Port Townsend with access to Highway 20. The 377 acre park includes tent campsites and picnic sites. View campsites are on top of a bluff. Activities include swimming, fishing, hiking on over six miles of trails, meandering along a nature trail on self-guided walking tour, and scuba diving. There are showers, restrooms, and playgrounds. Fort Townsend was built in 1856 when, after the Battle of Seattle, Port Townsend residents became alarmed and demanded protection from the Indians. 360-344-4400, 360-902-8844. ⚓🏕🧗

Indian & Marrowstone Islands

[18441, 18464]

Indian Island: Because of naval installations, give Indian Island a wide berth. The only part of this island open to the public is South Indian Island County Park. A man-made causeway connects Indian and Marrowstone Islands and forms the head of Kilisut Harbor. The U.S. Navy has an ordnance handling and storage mission at Naval Magazine Indian Island. No private vessel of any size is allowed within 1,000 yards of the ammunition pier, 100 yards of the island's shore (except when transiting Portage Canal), or 100 yards from any naval vessel in Port Townsend Bay.

★⚓ **Fort Flagler Marine State Park (9):** Enter Kilisut Harbor in the S-curved channel that is protected by Scow Bay Spit. Boaters will find a boat launch, mooring buoys, fish cleaning station, and fishing pier at the park site. Nightly moorage fees May-September. Floats may be removed in winter. There are groceries, food concessions, fishing supplies, and overnight lodging available in season. Hot showers, over 100 campsites, restrooms, tables, stoves, cooking shelters, interpretive displays, and U.S. Fish and Wildlife Service marine lab. Campsites can be reserved. The Cascadia Marine Trail has one campsite northeast of the campground. Fishing, hiking, swimming, and scuba diving are popular. An old pier extends into Admiralty Inlet and is the location of an underwater park for divers. Together with the heavy batteries of Fort Worden and Fort Casey, this turn-of-the-century Army post guarded the entrance to Puget Sound. Construction began in 1897. It was named for Brigadier General Daniel Webster Flagler. The facility was finally closed in 1953 and, in 1955, became a 783-acre state park. 360-902-8844. 🛥⚓🏕🧗

★ **Kilisut Harbor (10):** [18423, 18464] This long, narrow bay indents four miles between Indian Island and Marrowstone Island. Depths in the entry channel average 11 feet. When following the S-curved entrance between the buoys and markers, refer to charts. Scow Bay Spit is approximately three quarters of a mile in length and is partially submerged at high water. Fort Flagler State Park is to port when entering. There is a mud bottom for anchorage.

★ **Mystery Bay (11):** Mystery Bay is on the east side of Kilisut Harbor, about two miles from the entrance. It is protected in most winds and has anchorage in depths of five to 25 feet. Shellfish harvesting may be possible. Check the Red Tide Hot Line 1-800-562-5632.

★⚓ **Mystery Bay Marine State Park:** Located on the northeastern portion of the bay. A dock, that also serves as a fishing pier, has a long moor-age float parallel to shore. Nightly moorage fees charged year around. Mooring buoys are provided. There are vault toilets, a pump-out, and dump site. This day-use park has no campsites. Activities include clamming, swimming, scuba diving, and picnicking. Launching is possible. The area once belonged to the U.S. Navy. It housed repair shops and service floats to take care of the Mothball Fleet anchored in Kilisut Harbor. It received its name during Prohibition days when smugglers of alcohol used Kilisut Harbor to hide from the U.S. Coast Guard. Overhanging trees at the north end provided perfect shelter for shallow draft boats. Concluding that the disappearance of the smugglers was indeed mysterious, the bay was referred to as Mystery Bay. 360-902-8844. 🏕

Nordland General Store: Mooring float, tie up dock, provisions. 360-385-0777.

Walk-around: Walk on the road two miles to the gate of Fort Flagler. Continue until a Y is reached. The right fork will go to the lighthouse. Go straight ahead to the park's main office and to several trails. The left fork ends at the beach.

Port Townsend

[18441, 18464]

★ **Port Townsend (12):** Port Townsend Bay is a large body of water that separates the Quimper Peninsula from Indian and Marrowstone Islands. See current tables for Admiralty Inlet.

★ **City of Port Townsend:** This city rims the waterfront on the northwest shore of the large harbor. Pleasure craft moorage is available at the Port of Port Townsend Boat Haven and at Point Hudson Resort and Marina. Enter the Port of Port Townsend Basin on the northeast side of the breakwater. In summer months, anchorage is possible in the bay, with protection from the prevailing west to southwest winds.

Victorian-era buildings dot the hillside above this inviting National Historic Landmark City and Gateway to the Olympic Peninsula. Many of these homes are open for viewing during the *Parade of Homes* held each May and September. In the historic district along Water Street, merchants have paid particular attention to detail and historical accuracy in restoring the old buildings. Union Wharf, located at Water and Taylor Streets, originally constructed in 1867, and then rebuilt in 1932 is seeing new life again. In addition to the wharf and moorage float, there are a variety of restaurants, shops, art galleries, antiques, clothing, and gift shops along the colorful waterfront. At the north end of Water Street, next to Point Hudson Marina, a 290' dock is being constructed. It will be included in the two acre site designated as the future home of the Northwest Maritime Center. The Center is scheduled to open in 2005, 360-379-2629, www.nwmaritime.org. Overnight accommodations are available, many in bed and breakfast inns. Points-of-interest include the Victorian houses in Uptown, Rothschild House and Rose Garden, Haller Fountain, Courthouse, Bell Tower, and the Jefferson County Historical Museum which displays many nautical, Native American, Pioneer, and Victorian artifacts. Popular events include the *Victorian Festival,* the *Rhododendron Parade, Chamber Music Festivals, Old Fashioned Fourth of July Celebration, Fiddler's Tunes Fest, Writers Conference, Mariner's Regatta, Jazz Festival, Air Fair, Theater Festival, County Fair, Salmon Derby, Bike Tour, Folk Dance and Music Festival, Wooden Boat Festival, Homes Tour, Kinetic Sculpture Race,* and *Cabin Fever Quilt Show.* Chetzemoka Park and John Pope Marine

Park, both located on the waterfront, have playgrounds, picnic, and barbecue facilities. State parks nearby include Fort Worden and Old Fort Townsend. The Coast Guard Cutter Point Bennett is berthed at this town.

First sighted by explorer Captain Vancouver in 1792, Port Townsend was named for the Marquis de Townsend. The city was founded in 1851, six months before Seattle. During the next several decades it developed into one of the leading northwestern seaports of that time. With the discovery of copper and iron nearby and the development of lumbering and trade, the harbor of Port Townsend became host to many foreign

ships. By the 1880's this city was larger than Seattle. Life amid the wealthy merchants and seamen fashioned a style of architecture still present in the city today. With a current population of over 8,700, the city's economy is centered around paper making, tourism, seafood packing, lumbering, fishing, and marine-oriented businesses such as boat repair and boat building.

Jefferson Transit offers excellent bus service within the city itself and through connecting routes to other communities. By bus it is possible to explore Fort Worden, Old Fort Townsend, Hadlock, Port Ludlow, Sequim, and Port Angeles. Port Townsend also has an airport.

Walk-around: The charm of Port Townsend intrigues visitors and lures them into sightseeing and touring. Be sure to visit Rothschild House, a half acre state park at the corner of Franklin and Taylor Streets. It is a good example of the decor and architecture of the period, and includes original furnishings, carpets, and wallpaper. Built in 1868, this residence and its ghosts are on the National Register of Historic Places.

★ **Port of Port Townsend:** {48° 07'N, 122° 54' W} Permanent and guest moorage, water, showers, laundry, gas, diesel, 20 & 30 ampere power, hoist, 70 and 300 ton lift capacity, repairs, launch, pump-out. See our Steering Star description in this chapter. Mailing address: Post Office Box 1180, Port Townsend, Washington 98368. E-mail: into@portofpt.com. Web Sites: www.portofpt.com & www.boattravel.com/port-townsend. Circle #19 on Reader Service Card on page 251. Fax: 360-379-8205. Telephone: 360-385-2355. VHF 9, 16, 66A.

★ **Fleet Marine Inc.:** Established in 1975, this full service boat yard and repair facility includes a chandlery, brokerage, CNG, propane, bait, ice, haul-outs, dry storage, indoor paint shop, fiberglass and wood repairs, and mast painting. Simrad, Walken Bay Dinghy, MMC and Webasto sales and service. Fleet Marine is located at Point Hudson, one block northeast from the Downtown Historical District. Prompt professional service at a fair price. Lift capacity 30 tons. Open six days a week. Web site: www.fleetmarine.com. Address: 419 Jackson Street, Port Townsend Washington 98368. Email: fleetmarine@waypt.com. Fax: 360-385-2178. Telephones: 360-385-4000 1-800-952-6962.

Fishin' Hole Fuel Dock: Gas, diesel, pump-out. Open all year. 360-385-7031. VHF 09.

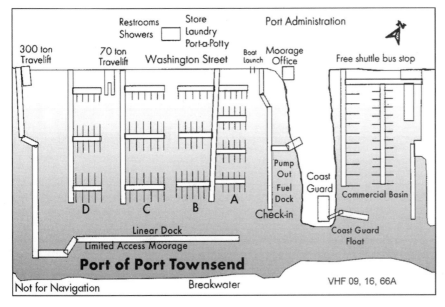

★ **Port of Port Townsend:** Located in historic Port Townsend on a main route to and from the San Juan Islands, this customs port-of-entry has both permanent and transient moorage available. The rock breakwater, which protects Port Townsend Boathaven, is located 1.1 miles southwest of Point Hudson. Entrance is at the south east end of the marina. Pass the Coast Guard station and tie up at the west end of the fuel/registration dock. For slip assignment, check in at the Moorage Office immediately upon arrival. The office is in the white, one story building at the head of the ramp. Twenty, 30, and 50 ampere power and abundant water are supplied to the floats. The fuel dock has gas, diesel, stove oil, propane, and waste pump-out. Other facilities include a launch ramp and dump station. One of the largest upland storage facilities on the west coast, serviced by 100 marine trade service providers for vessels weighing up to 330 tons. All types of marine repairs can be accommodated on site, and do-it-yourself space is available. Marine

parts, charts, and supplies, showers, and laundry are available, and towing and water taxi services can be arranged. Within easy walking distance are lodging facilities, groceries, and restaurants serving breakfast, lunch, and dinner. Port Townsend is a favorite destination for those who enjoy touring the picturesque buildings and learning about the city's prominence in the 19th century as one of the leading seaports in the northwest. Marina hours are 8:00 a.m.- 4:30 p.m. seven days a week in summer, Monday through Friday in winter. Open all year. **Circle #19 on Reader Service Card. Web Sites: www.portofpt.com & www.boattravel.com/porttownsend   E-mail: info@portofpt.com Mailing address: Post Office Box 1180, Port Townsend, Washington 98368. FAX: 360-379-8205. Telephone: 360-385-2355. VHF 9, 16, 66A.** Soundview Aerial Photo

★ **Union Wharf:** Located at the foot of Taylor, the main cross street in Port Townsend, this restored wharf is the pride of downtown. Its 7,000 square feet extend 200 feet into the bay. Temporary moorage (110 feet) is found on floats adjacent to the wharf. Floats removed in winter. Built in 1867 and once the home for steamships and cargo laden vessels, the decrepit wharf sat in disrepair for many years. It closed in 1981, after a semi truck loaded with dogfish fell through the decayed planking. Today, visitors stroll the pier and gather at the end in the covered, open-sided pavilion to view the city and Port Townsend Bay.

★ **Point Hudson (13):** This dredged boat harbor is protected by a rock breakwater and has good moorage floats. This is a public port and customs port-of-entry. The Harbor Master's office is on the fixed wharf, just off the starboard shore to the head of the harbor. Repair facilities are convenient. No fuel is available. Customs 360-385-3777. See current tables for Admiralty Inlet. Due to new Department of Homeland Security regulations, call ahead for latest customs information and/or see Northwest Boat Travel On-Line www.nwboat.com

★ **Point Hudson Marina & RV Park:** This marina, RV Park, and event facility is located at Point Hudson Harbor, at the east end of Water Street. Open all year, slip reservations accepted. 45 slips for boats to 40'LOA, plus 800' for larger vessels. Free launch ramp. Power and potable water, showers, heated restrooms accessible 24 hours with security code. Laundromat. Three restaurants on site. Propane, marine services, chandlery, travel-lift adjacent to resort. Short walk to shops, galleries, theaters, clubs. Circle #23 on Reader Service card on page 251. See our advertisement in this chapter. Websites: www.boattravel. pointhudson and www.portofpt.com Email: info@portofpt.com Address: 103 Hudson Street, Port Townsend, Washington 98368. For marina and RV Park reservations call 1-800-228-2803.

Walk-arounds: Point Hudson Marina is at the end of Water Street in downtown Port Townsend, one of only three nationally designated Victorian Seaports in the United States, featuring scores of Victorian buildings. Easy walks north, along the beach to Fort Warden and Point Wilson, or south along the city's waterfront, commercial district to Union Wharf Lookout. Parks and historical markers dot this pedestrian-sized little city.

★⚓ **Chetzemoka City Park (14):** Picnic tables, restrooms, fresh water, a playground, rose garden, and bandstand. The park was named for a Klallum Indian chief who befriended early white settlers. ⚓

★⚓ **Fort Worden Marine State Park (15):** A 400-foot long, L-shaped pier extends from shore and offers some protection. Mooring buoys, floats, and a ramp are available. Nightly moorage fees. Floats may be removed in winter. Two launching ramps are nearby. Fee charged. Temporary anchorage is possible in the buoy area, however winds can pick up and the bottom does not hold well. This 433 acre park is the gem of the park system. Over a million visitors visit Fort Worden each year. There are overnight accommodations, tables and stoves, kitchens, restrooms, tennis courts, athletic fields, 80 RV sites, hot showers, laundromat, snack bar/grocery, heritage sites, Coast Artillery Museum, marine interpretive displays, and learning center. Swimming, fishing, and scuba diving at the underwater park are popular activities. Fort Worden has landscaped grounds, old barracks, and renovated officer's quarters available for vacation housing. This site

is headquarters for the Centrum Foundation. Each summer there is a series of workshops and symposiums featuring famous musicians, dancers, and writers. The Marine Science Center is located on the Fort Worden Pier. Besides viewing, visitors can touch marine life specimens.

Fort Worden was one of the three primary forts built in the early 1900's to guard against enemy infiltration into Puget Sound. The armaments are a study in naval strategy of the time. During World War I, many anti-aircraft guns were sent to Europe. They were then mounted on railroad cars as mobile heavy artillery. During World War II the fort was the headquarters of the Harbor Defense of Puget Sound. Underwater sonar, sensing devices, and radar were used at the site.

Fort Worden has a reservation system for campsites, recreation housing, and conference facilities 1-888-226-7688, or write Fort Worden State Park, 200 Battery Way, Port Townsend, Washington 98368. Washington State Parks: 360-902-8844, 360-344-4400. ⚓🪝🧍🚲🅿️▲

Point Wilson (16): See current tables for Admiralty Inlet. A wind-swept lighthouse is a landmark to boaters traversing the Strait of Juan de Fuca and Admiralty Inlet. It is at this point that the Strait turns and aims southeasterly to become Admiralty Inlet, leading into Puget Sound. There are strong tide rips off the point. When ocean swells and adverse wind conditions exist, seas are uncomfortable and can be hazardous. When the wind is coming from the west and there is an ebb current, tide rips are especially heavy north of the shoals marked by the buoy northwest of Point Wilson light. This rip can be avoided by planning to cross the area near slack

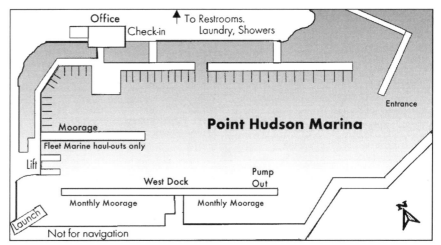

Point Hudson Marina

Office
Check-in
↑ To Restrooms. Laundry, Showers
Entrance
Moorage
Fleet Marine haul-outs only
Lift
West Dock
Pump Out
Launch
Monthly Moorage
Monthly Moorage
Not for navigation

water, or by staying close to Whidbey Island until the Point is passed. Some captains suggest passing close to Point Wilson itself, with careful attention to the depth sounder and to charted rocks off the Point. The Point Wilson Lighthouse, commissioned in 1879, has an intriguing history of sightings of a woman's ghost walking the grounds and entering the lighthouse to search for her daughter who was lost when a steamship sank in Puget Sound. Since the 1970's, the lighthouse has been automated and closed to the public.

Northern Olympic Peninsula

[18460, 18465, 18468, 18471, 18484, 18485]

★ **Discovery Bay (17):** Captain Vancouver found this anchorage when re-fitting his ships during his 1792 expedition. Today it remains relatively undiscovered. This inlet, with steep, tree-covered hillsides, is reminiscent of inlets much farther north. Unlike its neighbor Sequim Bay which hosts a large marina, many private waterfront homes, and a state park, Discovery Bay has only a few homes and a timeshare development with a private dock. Protection Island, near the entrance of the bay cuts off the prevailing west wind and can offer calm waters when winds in the Strait of Juan De Fuca kick up. This island is a National Wildlife Refuge. Anchorage can be found in several places in Discovery Bay, but avoid shoaling areas and the extreme head where remnants of a sawmill are found. Launching takes place at Gardiner, on the west shore. Within walking distance, on Old Gardiner Road, is Trollhaven, a creation of buildings and trolls created by a local resident.

★ **Sequim Bay (18):** The narrow entry passage is between the buoy off Gibson Spit to starboard and Travis Spit to port. The well-marked channel curves around Kiapot Point. Depths average nine feet, but shoals extend from both shores. Keep the "N" buoys to starboard and the "C" buoys to port. Once inside, good anchorage on a mud bottom can be found in about 35-50 feet of water. An 1800-foot breakwater along the access channel protects the boat moorage at John Wayne Marina. The marina is three miles from the community of Sequim. Formed in the shape of a vial, the bay is four miles in length. Sequim is an Indian word meaning "Quiet Water." With its overlapping spits, which leave only a zig-zag entrance into the bay from the Strait of Juan de Fuca, this refuge is quiet indeed.

Ride-around: Visit Sequim. Transportation from John Wayne Marina or Sequim Bay State Park is available by taxi or bus. (No bus on Sundays.) Rental cars are also accessible.

★ **Sequim:** Located approximately three miles from Sequim Bay, this is an interesting town with restaurants, groceries, shops, and tourist attractions. Impressive, huge murals depict historical scenes. There are two award winning wineries, an Aquatic Recreation Center, and a salmon hatchery. For those who like to study prehistoric creatures, the Museum and Arts Center on West Cedar Street has specimens, found locally, that prove man hunted the mastodon in North America 12,000-14,000 years ago. Land surrounding Sequim has so many irrigation ditches and lines (more than 300 miles) to water the valley's farmlands, that an *Irrigation Festival* is held in May. It is the oldest continuous festival in the state and includes the biggest parade on the

Olympic Peninsula. Just west of Sequim, visit the Dungeness River's Railroad Bridge Park with its restored railroad bridge, hiking trails, and picnic areas. Go bike or horseback riding and even drop a hook in the river to try your luck. Also the Olympic Game Farm with a three mile drive through, is nearby.

★ **John Wayne Marina:** {48° 03.95' N, 123° 02.31' W} This modern marina has both permanent and guest moorage with power and water. Gas, diesel, oils, restrooms, pump-out, waste dump, showers, laundry, and a restaurant are at the site. See our Steering Star description in this chapter. Internet Sites: www.portofpa.com/ & www.boattravel.com/johnwayne/. Email: info@portofpa.com. Address: 2577 West Sequim Bay Road, Sequim, Washington 98382. Fax: 360-417-3442. Telephone: 360-417-3440.

★⚓ **Sequim Bay Marine State Park:** [18471] Encompassing 92 acres, this park is located north of Schoolhouse Point. Tables, stoves, reservable kitchens (888-226-7688), restrooms, showers, campsites, RV sites, some with hookups, sewage dump, a 1 lane launching ramp with side float, and mooring buoys (in deeper water) are available. Moorage is available at floats, however depths are shallow at low tide. Floats removed in winter. Nightly fees May-September. Fishing from the pier, tennis, swimming, hiking, ball games, and scuba diving are possible. An interpretive kiosk details information about shellfish harvesting. 360-683-4235, 360-902-8844. ⚓▲⛟⚓

★ **Dungeness Bay (19):** [18465] Boaters must have a reservation to land on the spit. Call 360-457-8451. The designated landing spot is a 100 yard area near the lighthouse, on the bay side of

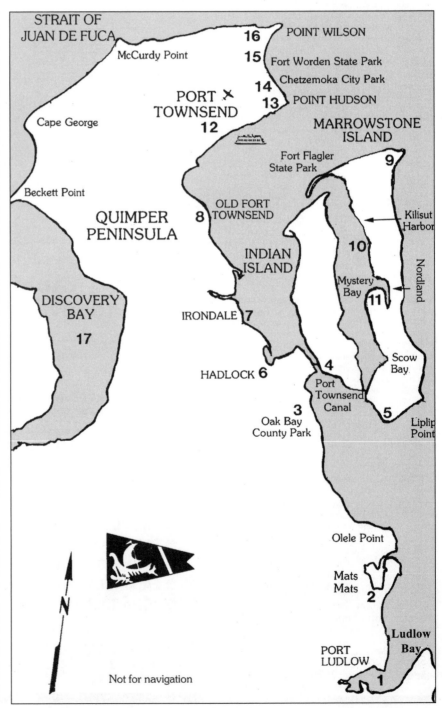

Not for navigation

the spit. The picturesque, automated lighthouse is at the tip of the spit. A shoal, marked by a buoy, extends northeast from the spit. The twisted spit forms a bay and an inner lagoon suitable for shallow draft anchorage. The best anchorage is in five to nine fathoms about one mile southwest of the tip. Avoid the marked cable area. The bay is sheltered from west winds, but east and north winds invade the area. The shallow lagoon at the head may be entered by very small boats. Public boat launches are found at Cline Spit County Park, Dungeness Boat Ramp at Oyster House Road, and Port Williams County Park. Dungeness Spit, six miles in length, is the longest natural spit in the world. Dungeness means Sandy Cape.

Walk-around: It is possible to walk to the New Dungeness Lighthouse at the tip. A fee is charged to hike the six miles to the Dungeness Lighthouse where a volunteer from the Lighthouse Society will show the visitor the secrets of the oldest (1857) light north of the Columbia River.

⚓ **Dungeness County Park Recreation Area:** This park is on a bluff. Although there is no direct access to the water, the spit and adjacent tidelands may be explored. There are views of the spit, picnic facilities, RV pump-out, playground, modern restrooms, and fresh water. ⚓

Port Angeles
[18465, 18468]

★ **Port Angeles (20):** A customs port-of-entry, Port Angeles is the last major fueling and supply station for those heading for the coast, across the ocean, or around Vancouver Island. It is also the site of the ferry to Victoria, Canada. The harbor is protected by Ediz Hook, a narrow, over three-

mile-long natural sand spit that nearly encircles it. There is protection in all but east winds. Much of the harbor is used for log booming operations. Moorage is available at the Port of Port Angeles Boat Haven, located in the southwest portion of the harbor, behind the breakwater, and at the municipal pier, west of the ferry landing. Anchorage is prohibited in the eastern end and off the north side. This city is the commercial center for the Olympic Peninsula and headquarters for the Olympic National Park. There are restaurants and stores. There is a currency exchange at the Landing Mall. Hours 7:00 a.m. to 5:00 p.m. During the summer, tour vans and Clallam Transit buses provide access to the entire peninsula from the ferries and moorage. For information regarding live theater productions at the

Union Warf   *Gwen Cole Photo*

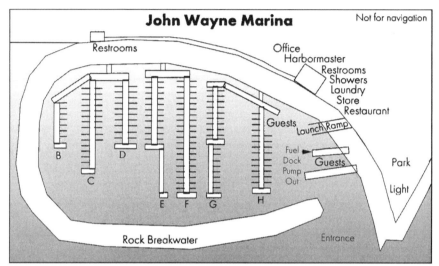

★ **John Wayne Marina:** *The Duke* was right. Sequim Bay is a special place. It is a beautiful, peaceful bay, almost equally accessible to Seattle, the San Juan Islands, and the wide Pacific. While anchored aboard his Wild Goose in Sequim Bay, the movie great envisioned a marina in the scenic, protected waters. The family donated 22

acres of land, and, under the ownership and auspices of the Port of Port Angeles, this facility is indeed, a special place to visit. Permanent and transient moorage is available. Moorage slips are assigned on a first-come-first-serve basis. Power and water are easily accessible. The fuel dock dispenses gas, diesel, and oils. Restrooms, showers, laundry facilities, dump station, and waste pump-out are on-site. Towing can be arranged. Other amenities include a restaurant and grocery. Provisions, charts, gifts, souvenirs, ice, and charters are accessible. Nearby attractions include golf courses, lodging, a casino, airport,

state park, and marine repairs. Attractively landscaped picnic areas are provided, and shellfish harvesting is possible along the beach. For those who would like to know the history of the area, an information kiosk is featured. A bronze statue of *The Duke*, from a favorite role in *She Wore a Yellow Ribbon*, is on display. The main building has a social center with banquet rooms and a dance floor for public use. This is becoming popular with yacht clubs for rendezvous parties and cruise destinations. If arriving by car with a trailerable boat, there is paved parking for cars and trailers, and an excellent launch ramp. The marina is only three miles from the community of Sequim. **Internet Sites: www.portofpa.com/ & www.boattravel.com/johnwayne/ Email: info@portofpa.com Address: 2577 West Sequim Bay Road, Sequim, Washington 98382. Telephone: 360-417-3440. Fax: 360-417-3442.**

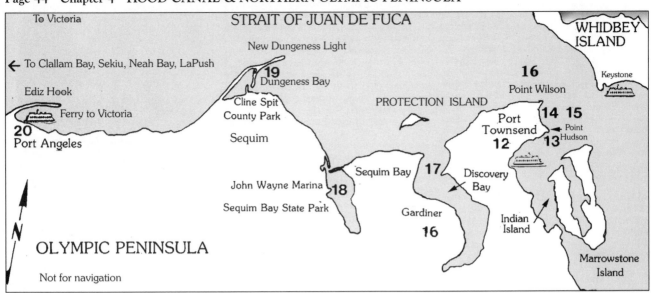

Port Angeles Community Playhouse call 360-452-6651. An Estuary Project on Port of Port Angeles property west of the center is an attractive commercial/industrial buffer, including an environmental showcase and interpretive center.

U.S. Customs & Border Protection Designated Port-of-Entry: For in-person inspection by CBP officer call 360-457-4311. Due to new Department of Homeland Security regulations, call ahead for latest customs information.

★ Port Angeles Boat Haven: {48° 07.7' N, 123° 27' W} Transient moorage, gas, diesel and mix, power, ice, fresh water, boat hoist, launching ramp, restrooms, showers, and waste pump-out, bait, and tackle are available. Adjacent to the Boat Haven, the Port operates a public boat yard for maintenance and repairs. The Boat Yard provides both covered and open work areas. There is a 133 ton marine railway and a 70 ton mobile straddle hoist, as well as hydro-blasting equipment. All maintenance work is performed by boat owners or independent contractors. Nearby businesses include a marine supply, charter service and restaurants. Operated by the Port of Port Angeles, this marina is located on 16 acres on the south shore of Port Angeles Harbor. See our advertisement in this chapter. Websites: www.portofpa.com & www.boattravel.com/portangeles/. Email: info@portofpa.com. Address: 832 Boathaven Drive, Port Angeles, Washington 98362. Telephone: 360-457-4505. Fax: 360-457-4921.

★⚓ Port Angeles Municipal Park and City Pier: Moorage is seasonal from April to October. Floats are removed in the winter. Pleasure boats up to 40 feet in length can find moorage on the concrete floats which lie parallel to the pier. No power. 24 hour limit for moorage. A 50 foot-tall observation tower marks this two acre waterfront park which has a maritime museum, sandy beach, landscaped grounds, fire pits, sheltered picnic area, and wood-decked pier. Elegant bronze statues of cormorants decorate the grounds. Fishing is permitted off the pier. The Arthur D. Feiro Marine Laboratory, a highlight of the pier, is a working lab, open to the public all year. The Visitor Center is within walking distance where you can pick up maps, brochures, and information about a walking tour. ⛺🚶

Ediz Hook (21): This three and one half-mile-long spit has a lumber mill at the shore end with adjacent log storage. Currents can be strong in this area. A large, four lane launch ramp, a small summer-only marina, restrooms, and the Coast Guard Air Rescue Station are located on the spit. The 110' ship, Cutty Hunk is stationed here. The original lighthouse was authorized in 1862, when President Lincoln declared the hook a military preserve. Lighthouses were built in 1865 and 1908. In 1945 the lighthouse was razed. Its beacon is now at the tower of the Coast Guard Air Station. A signal beacon is now located at the spot of the lighthouse.

Thunderbird Boathouse: Located on Ediz Hook. Summers only. Dump, launch, gas, moorage to 30'.

Freshwater Bay: Located about four miles east of Crescent Bay, this is a broad open bight, affording anchorage in six to ten fathoms.

Crescent Bay: This is a small semi-circular bight approximately one mile in diameter. The east part is shoal. Remains of a wharf on the west shore are to be avoided. This bay only provides shelter in southerly winds.

★⚓ Salt Creek County Park: Located in Crescent Bay, this park is accessible by beachable boat and has limited anchorage. There are hazards at the entrance to the bay. There are campsites, picnic shelters, playgrounds, an RV pump-

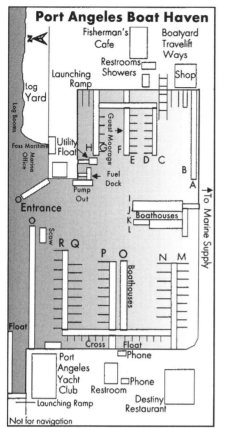

Port Angeles Boat Haven

Fisherman's Cafe

Boatyard Travelift Ways

Restrooms Showers

Shop

Launching Ramp

Log Yard

Log Booms

Foss Maritime

Marina Office

Utility Float

Guest Moorage

H G F E D C B A

Fuel Dock

Pump Out

Entrance

Scow

R Q P O N M

Boathouses

I J K L Boathouses

Float

Cross Float

Phone

Port Angeles Yacht Club

Restroom

Phone

Destiny Restaurant

Launching Ramp

Not for navigation

To Marine Supply

Port Angeles   *Northwest Air Photo*

out, and hiking trails. Tongue Point is the site of a marine life sanctuary with tidepool life. ▲🎣🥾

Pillar Point: Good anchorage can be found with shelter from westerlies. However, it is open to east and northeast winds.

★ **Clallam Bay:** [18460] Clallam Bay is located about 15 miles southeast of Neah Bay. Clallam Bay is a broad bay about two miles long and one mile wide. A signal beacon and fog horn are located in a square, white tower on Slip Point. Give Slip Point a wide berth of at least one quarter mile to avoid the reef west of it. The reef is marked by a bell buoy. The small towns of Clallam Bay and Sekiu are on the shore of Clallam Bay. There is often good fishing for salmon and halibut in this area. There is anchorage east of Van Riper's Rocks and off the rocky point, near the middle of the semi-circular beach on the southern shore of the bay. Anchorage is in 20-40 feet of water over a sand bottom and is protected from all but east winds.

★ **Sekiu:** This interesting town wakes up early during the fishing season. Restaurants, hardware, groceries, and lodging can be found. The waterfront resorts cater to boats less than 22 feet, whose owners have fishing in mind. Moorage may be available for larger craft. Most facilities operate April-October on a first-come-first-serve basis.

Cains Marine Service: Repairs. 360-963-2894.

Coho Resort: Moorage to 25', RV park, gas, launch, showers, laundry. 360-963-2333.

Curley's: Resort & Dive Center: Moorage, lodging. 800-542-9680, 360-963-2281. VHF 16.

Olson's Resort: Gas, diesel, water, launch, moorage to 40', provisions, lodging, showers, RV, laundry. 360-963-2311.

Straitside Resort: Limited moorage, lodging. 360-963-2100.

Van Riper's: Moorage, ramp, provisions, lodging, RV park, dump. 1-888-462-0803, 360-963-2334.

★⚓ **Hoko River State Park:** This park, located two miles west of Sekiu, contains 1,500 feet of shoreline on the Strait of Juan de Fuca and over 18,000 feet of freshwater shoreline along the Hoko and Little Hoko Rivers. An archeological site, at the mouth of the Hoko River, has remains of a 2500 year old Makah Indian village.

Snow Creek Resort: Located three miles east of Neah Bay. Moorage for boats to 25', water, showers, rail and strap to 30' launch, diver's air, RV park. 360-645-2284, 1-800-883-1464. VHF 16.

★ **Neah Bay:** [18484, 18485] {48° 23' N, 124° 36' W} Located about five miles east of Cape Flattery, this is a customs port-of-entry. Neah Bay has good but limited anchorage and a moorage facility. Enter between Waadah Island and Baadah Point. Favor the south side. There is a resort, sportfishing, shopping center, and provision stores. Many resorts in this area operate April to October. This is Makah Indian Reserve land. The tribe once used sea-going canoes for whale hunting. At the museum, there are preserved fish hooks, seal clubs, harpoons, nets, paddles, boxes, and baskets that were unearthed at the Ozette Archaeological site, where they had been covered by a mud slide, perhaps 500 years ago. Replicas depict whaling canoes and, in the longhouse, salmon drying on overhead racks. A typical Makah conversation is replicated. The museum is open daily from 10:00 a.m.-5:00 p.m. 5/31 -9/16, Closed Mon/Tues in winter. 360-645-2711. Due to new Department of Homeland Security regulations, call ahead for latest customs information and/or see Important Notice Section.

Makah Marina: Moorage, diesel, oils, power, water, pump-out, restrooms, showers, ramp. 360-645-3015. Fuel: 360-645-2749. VHF 16, 66.

Big Salmon Resort: Gas, diesel, ramp, moorage, water, power. 1-866-787-1900. VHF 68.

★ **LaPush:** [18480] LaPush is located on the Washington Coast about 30 miles south of Cape Flattery. It is an important sportfishing center and the site of a marina at the Quileute village on the Quileute River's east bank, about 0.4 of a mile above the entrance to the river. Nearby facilities include the Lonesome Creek Grocery and RV Park and motel accommodations. If trailering your boat to LaPush and launching at the marina, take Highway 101 from Port Angeles and, just north of Forks, take Highway 110 (the LaPush turnoff) and proceed 16 miles on this good road to LaPush.

Arriving by sea, locate the river channel near the southeast shore of James Island. At low tide, James Island is joined to the beach. The river channel is protected on the southeast side by a jetty. Note that at high water, about 250 feet of the outer end of the jetty is awash. The jetty is gradually settling, causing shoaling and breakers in the area that should be avoided. A rock dike protects the northwest side of the river channel. Give it wide berth due to river currents that can easily sweep vessels onto the rocks. There is a directional light in the channel. Inside the entrance, stay on the jetty side of mid-channel. A light and seasonal buoys are also in the channel that leads to the small craft basin. In season, floodlights also illuminate the entrance channel between James Island and the jetty. When winds and waves are from the south, entry into the channel can be dangerous. If there are breakers of any size across the entrance, entry should not be attempted except at better than half tide and with a well powered boat. If in question, contact the Quileute River Coast Guard Station by VHF 16 or 22. Look for the prominent tank that marks the location of the Coast Guard Station.

The Coast Guard has established a rough bar advisory sign to aid boaters when exiting the river. It is located about 34 feet above the water on the side of the old Coast Guard boathouse. It is visible from the channel when looking out to sea. The diamond shaped, white with International Yellow bordered sign, has *Rough Bar* in black letters. If two alternating flashing

Downtown Historic Port Townsend   Gwen Cole Photo

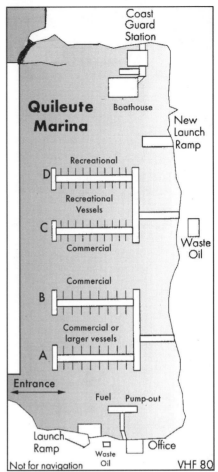

lights are on, the seas are more than four feet in height and should be considered dangerous for small craft. Even with the sign, caution is advised in the area because the lighting may not be all that dependable. Caution also advised in late summer and fall, when fish nets may be in the area.

The Quileute Tribe participates in Native American gatherings promoting traditions of Pacific Northwest canoe voyaging. In recent years, handmade cedar canoes from LaPush have been paddled to Seattle in 1989, to Bella Bella, British Columbia in 1993, and to the Commonwealth Games in Victoria in 1994 and 1997. *Quileute Days* are held in mid-July with fireworks, field sports, music entertainment, slow pitch and horseshoe tournaments, Indian dancing, arts and crafts, and the *World Famous Fish Bake* made the Quileute way. For more informa-

tion about the community and events, call the Quileute Tribal Office: 360-374-6163.

★ **Quileute Marina:** [18480] Located on the Quileute River about 0.4 mile above the entrance to the river. Ninety-six slips with modern concrete floats offer moorage, 30 ampere power, and fresh water. Chevron 87 octane gas, red diesel, hydraulic oil, two cycle oil available. Restrooms, laundromat, large launch ramp, sewage pump-out, and waste oil tank on site. Propane accessible. River's Edge Restaurant features fresh seafood, burgers, and views of the river. 360-374-5777. Store, campground, cabins, and motel located one-half mile from the marina. Access to LaPush by car with trailerable boat is by Highway 101, across northern Olympic Peninsula to just north of Forks and then west on Highway 110. Excellent fishing, inquire about

fishing derbies. Post Office Box 279, LaPush, Washington 98350. Fax: 360-374-4153. Telephone: Marina 360-374-5392, Ocean Park Resort: 1-800-487-1267. VHF 80.

★ For coverage of the Vancouver Island side of the Strait of Juan de Fuca, see Chapters 8 and 18. Individual sites are listed in the Index.

Essential Supplies & Services

AIR TRANSPORTATION
Seattle Seaplanes 1-800-637-5553

AMBULANCES . . . . All 911

BOOKS / BOOK STORES
The Marine Atlas. 541-593-6396

BUS TRANSPORTATION
Clallam Transit: Port Angeles 1-800-858-3747
Jefferson Transit: Port Townsend 360-385-4777

CNG CYLINDERS
Fleet Marine: Point Hudson **360-385-4000**
Port Ludlow Marina . . . . 360-437-0513 VHF 16, 68

COAST GUARD
VHF 16
Neah Bay 360-645-2236
Port Angeles 360-417-5840
Port Townsend 360-385-3070
Quileute 360-374-6469
Seattle 206-217-6000

CUSTOMS / BORDER PROTECTION
Due to new Department of Homeland Security regulations, call ahead for latest customs information and/or see Northwest Boat Travel On-Line www.nwboat.com
Port Angeles 360-457-4311
Port Townsend 360-385-3777
24 hours 800-562-5943
I-68 form: Call ahead 8:30 a.m.-5:00 p.m.
Box 1402J (Fairchild International Airport)
Port Angeles, Washington 98362 360-457-7414

FERRY TRANSPORTATION
Pt. Angeles-Victoria 360-457-4491
Pt. Townsend-Keystone 800-843-3779
Victoria Express (passenger only) 1-800-633-1589

FISHING INFO . 360-902-2700, 360-902-2500

FUELS
Big Salmon: Makah Marina, Neah Bay. Gas, Diesel.
. . . . 1-866-787-1900 VHF 68
Coho Resort: Sekiu: Gas 360-963-2333

John Wayne: Sequim Bay. Gas, Diesel.
. . . . **360-417-3440**
Olson's Resort: Sekiu. Gas, Diesel. 360-963-2311
Pleasant Harbor: Gas, Diesel. . 360-796-4611 VHF 16,9
Port Angeles Boat Haven: Gas, Diesel.
. . . . **360-457-4505**
Port Ludlow Marina . . . . 360-437-0513 VHF 16, 68
Port of Port Townsend: Gas, Diesel.
. . . . **360-385-7031 VHF 68**
Quilcene Boat Haven: Hood Canal. Gas, Diesel.
. . . . 360-765-3131
Quileute Marina: Gas, Diesel 360-374-5392 VHF 80
Thunderbird: Ediz Hook. Summers. Port Angeles. Gas.

GOLF COURSES
(These courses are accessible from moorage and have rental clubs)
Alderbrook: Hood Canal. 360-898-2560
Chevy Chase: Port Townsend 360-385-0704
Dungeness: Sequim. 800-447-6826
Port Ludlow Resort 360-437-0272
Port Townsend 360-385-4547

HOSPITALS

Hoodsport (Mason General) 360-426-1611
Port Angeles 360-457-8513
Port Townsend (Jefferson Health) 360-385-2200

IMMIGRATION SERVICE OFFICE

I-68 form: Call ahead 8:30 a.m.-5:00 p.m.
Box 1402J (Fairchild International Airport)
Port Angeles, Washington 98362 360-457-7414

INSURANCE

Boat Insurance Agency 206-285-1350
Or Call 1-800-828-2446

LODGING

Alderbrook Resort & Spa 360-898-2200
Curley's: Sekiu. 360-963-2281

MARINAS / MOORAGE FLOATS

Big Salmon: Neah Bay. . . . . . . 1-866-787-1900 VHF 68
Fort Flagler State Park: Marrowstone Island
Fort Worden State Park: Point Wilson
Hansville
Hood Canal Marina: Union. 360-898-2252
Hoodsport: Day only
John Wayne Marina: Sequim Bay . . . 360-417-3440
Makah Marina: Neah Bay1-866-787-1900 VHF 68, CB16
Mystery Bay State Park: Marrowstone Island
Olson's Resort: Sekiu 360-963-2311
Pleasant Harbor Marina . . . . . 360-796-4611 VHF 16, 9
Pleasant Harbor State Park: Hood Canal
Point Hudson Marina: Port Townsend
. . . . **1-800-228-2803**
Port Angeles Boat Haven 360-457-4505
Port Hadlock Marina 360-385-6368 VHF16
Port Ludlow Marina . . . . 360-437-0513 VHF 16, 68
Port of Port Townsend. . . 360-385-2355 VHF 16, 9
Quilcene Boat Haven: Hood Canal 360-765-3131
Quileute Marina: La Push . . 360-374-5392 VHF 80
Rest-a-While: Lilliwaup 360-877-9474
Sequim Bay State Park
Snow Creek Resort: Neah Bay . . 360-645-2284 VHF 16
Summertide Resort: Tahuya 360-275-9313
Thunderbird Boat House: Ediz Hook.
Van Riper's: Sekiu. Small boats. 360-963-2334

PARKS

Department of Natural Resources 360-374-6131
. . . . 360-825-1631, 1-800-527-3305.
Washington State 360-902-8844
Washington Camping Reservations . . . 1-888-226-7688

POISON INFO 1-800-222-1222

PROPANE

Fleet Marine: Point Hudson 360-385-4000
Point Hudson Marina (nearby). 800-228-2803
Port Ludlow Marina . . . . 360-437-0513 VHF 16, 68
Port of Port Townsend. . . 360-385-2355 VHF 16, 9
Quileute Marina: La Push . . 360-374-5392 VHF 80
Summertide Resort: Tahuya 360-275-9313

RV FACILITIES

Belfair State Park: Hood Canal
Dosewallips State Park: Hood Canal
Dungeness County Park: Dungeness Bay
Fort Worden State Park: Point Wilson
Hansville
Hood Canal Marina, Union. 360-898-2252
Olson's: Sekiu 360-963-2311
Point Hudson Marina & RV Park . . . 800-228-2803
Potlatch State Park: Hood Canal
Rest-a-While: Lilliwaup 360-877-9474
Salt Creek County Park: Crescent Bay
Sequim Bay State Park

Shine Tidelands: Hood Canal
Twanoh State Park: Hood Canal
Van Rippers, Sekiu 888-462-0803

RAMPS / HAUL-OUTS

Belfair State Park
Big Salmon: Neah Bay . . . . 360-645-2374 VHF 68
Bywater Bay: Hood Canal
Cline Spit County Park: Dungeness Bay
Coho Resort: Sekiu 360-963-2333
Dungeness Boat Ramp: Dungeness Bay
Ediz Hook: Port Angeles
Fleet Marine: Point Hudson 360-385-4000
Fort Flagler State Park: Marrowstone Island
Fort Worden State Park: Point Wilson
Gardiner: Discovery Bay
Hadlock Hood Canal Bridge, West End
Hansville
Hood Canal Marina: Union. 360-898-2252
Hoodsport: Hood Canal
Lilliwaup: Hood Canal
John Wayne Marina: Sequim Bay . . . 360-417-3440
Makah Marina: Neah Bay . . . 360-645-3015 VHF 16, 66
Mats Mats
Mystery Bay State Park: Marrowstone Island
Oak Bay County Park
Olson's Resort: Sekiu 360-963-2311
Point Hudson Marina & RV Park . . 1-800-228-2803
Point Whitney: Hood Canal
Port Angeles Boat Haven 360-457-4505
Port of Allyn Moorage: Hood Canal
Port of Port Townsend. . . 360-385-2355 VHF 16, 9
Quilcene Boat Haven: Hood Canal 360-765-3131
Quilcene Marina . . . . 360-374-5392 VHF 80
Rest-A-While: Lilliwaup 360-877-9474
Salsbury Point County Park: Hood Canal
Scenic Beach State Park: Hood Canal . . . 360-830-5079
Sequim Bay State Park 360-683-4235
Snow Creek Resort: near Neah Bay. 360-645-2284 VHF 16
Squamish Harbor: Hood Canal
Summertide Resort: Tahuya 360-275-9313
Tahuya: Hood Canal
Triton Cove: Hood Canal
Twanoh State Park: Hood Canal
Van Riper's: Sekiu 360-963-2334

RED TIDE HOT-LINE 800-562-5632

REPAIRS

Fleet Marine: Point Hudson 360-385-4000
Hood Canal Marina: Union. 360-898-2252
Port Angeles Boat Haven 360-457-4505
Port of Port Townsend. . . 360-385-2355 VHF 16, 9
Quilcene Boat Haven 360-765-3131

SCUBA AIR

Curley's: Sekiu. 360-963-2281
Snow Creek Resort: Neah Bay . . 360-645-2284 VHF 16
Sunrise Resort: Hood Canal 360-877-5301

SCUBA / DIVING SITES

Fort Flagler State Park: Marrowstone Island
Fort Worden State Park: Point Wilson
Lilliwaup: Hood Canal
Mystery Bay State Park: Marrowstone Island
Old Fort Townsend State Park: Irondale
Potlatch State Park: Hood Canal
Pulali Point: Hood Canal
Scenic Beach State Park: Hood Canal
Sequim Bay State Park
South Indian Island County Park

SEWAGE DISPOSALS

Fort Flagler: Marrowstone Island. Dump
John Wayne Marina: Pump, Dump . . 360-417-3440

Makah Marina: Pump, Dump. 360-645-3015
Mystery Bay State Park: Marrowstone Island. Pump. Dump
Pleasant Harbor Marina: Hood Canal. Pump, Dump. . . .
  360-796-4611
Pleasant Harbor State Park: Pump, Dump
Point Hudson Marina: Pump, Dump
. . . . **1-800-228-2803**
Port of Allyn Near Belfair: Pump
Port Angeles Boat Haven: Pump . . . 360-457-4505
Port Hadlock Marina: Pump. 360-385-6368
Port Ludlow Marina . . . . 360-437-0513 VHF 16, 68
Port of Port Townsend: Pump 360-385-2355
Quilcene Boat Haven: Pump. 360-765-3131
Quileute Marina: La Push. Pump.
. . . . **360-374-5392 VHF 80**
Sequim Bay State Park: Dump 360-683-4235
Thunderbird Boat House: Ediz Hook. Dump.
Twanoh State Park: Hood Canal. Pump, Dump

SHELLFISH HOTLINE 360-796-3215

For local area closures/information, call County Health Depts.:
Clallam County Health Dept. 360-417-2258
Mason County Health Dept. 360-427-9670

TAXI

Port Angeles 360-452-2223
Port Townsend 360-385-1872
Sequim 360-683-1872

TOWING

C-TOW. 1-888-354-5554
VESSEL ASSIST . . . Port Townsend, Port Hadlock,
** North Puget Sound 360-301-9764**
Quilcene Boat Haven 360-785-3131

VHF MARINE OPERATOR

Whidbey Island: 87
Note: MariTel has shut down all other Washington State
  VHF Marine Operator channels until further notice.

VISITOR INFORMATION

Clallam Bay / Sekiu 360-963-2339
La Push 360-374-4260
Port Angeles 360-452-2363
Port Townsend 360-385-2722, 1-888-365-6978
Victoria Tourist Bureau 1-866-457-5432
Sequim Chamber of Commerce. 360-683-6197
. . . . 1-800-737-8462
Sequim Visitors Bureau. 360-683-6690

WEATHER

VHF WX-1, WX-4

Dungeness Spit   Lynn Mortensen Photo

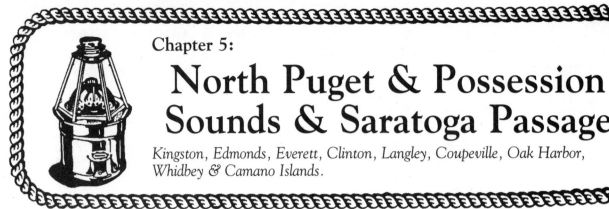

Chapter 5:
North Puget & Possession Sounds & Saratoga Passage

Kingston, Edmonds, Everett, Clinton, Langley, Coupeville, Oak Harbor, Whidbey & Camano Islands.

Symbols

[   ]: Numbers between [ ] are chart numbers.

{   }: Numbers & letters between { } are waypoints.

⚓: Park, ⛵: Boat Launch, ▲: Campgrounds, 🥾: Hiking Trails, ⛱: Picnic Area, 🚲: Biking

★ **Important Notice:** See "Important Notices" between Chapters 7 and 8 in this guide for specific information on boating related topics such as: Canadian & U.S. Customs, boating safety and security, navigation, weather, U.S. & Canadian Coast Guard, U.S & Canadian marine radio use, Vessel Traffic Service and traffic separation plans, security zones, and internet access. Due to new Department of Homeland Security regulations, call ahead for latest customs information and/or see Northwest Boat Travel On-line, www.nwboat.com.

Northern Puget Sound & Admiralty Inlet
[18441, 18445, 18446, 18473]

★ **Port Ludlow:** See Chapter 4

★ **Kingston & Appletree Cove (1):** [18446] Kingston is a North Kitsap town situated on the hillside surrounding the shores of Appletree Cove. The Mosquito Fleet provided early freight and passenger services here until the ferries began running in 1923. Today Kingston is the western terminus of the Edmonds-Kingston ferry, making it the gateway for visitors to the Olympic Peninsula.

Next to the ferry terminal is a port-operated, breakwater-protected marina. The visitor's float is parallel to the breakwater. Limited anchorage has protection from prevailing winds, however it is exposed to the southeast. Repair facilities and marine supplies are available. Mike Wallace

Chart List

NOAA Charts:

18423, 18428, 18441, 18443, 18444, 18445, 18556, 18473, 18477

Marine Atlas (2005 ed.):

Pages 5-6

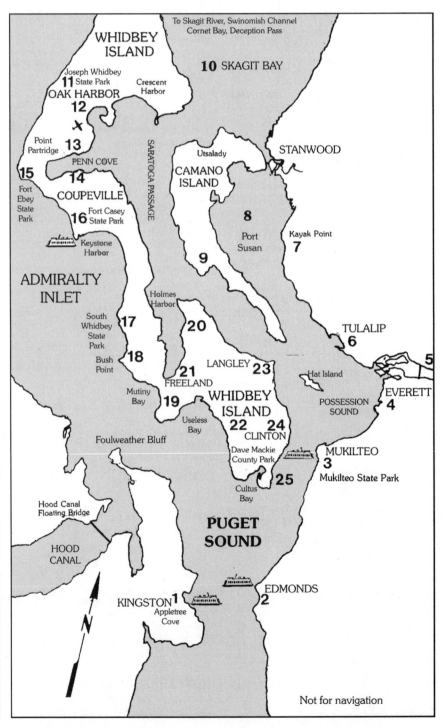

WHIDBEY ISLAND

To Skagit River, Swinomish Channel
Cornet Bay, Deception Pass

10 SKAGIT BAY

Joseph Whidbey
11 State Park

Crescent Harbor

OAK HARBOR

12

Point Partridge

13

PENN COVE

14

15

Fort Ebey State Park

COUPEVILLE

Fort Casey State Park

16

Keystone Harbor

ADMIRALTY INLET

SARATOGA PASSAGE

Utsalady

CAMANO ISLAND

STANWOOD

Port Susan

8

9

Kayak Point

7

Holmes Harbor

South Whidbey State Park

17

20

TULALIP

6

Bush Point

18

LANGLEY

23

Hat Island

21   FREELAND

Mutiny Bay

19

WHIDBEY ISLAND

POSSESSION SOUND

EVERETT

4

5

Useless Bay

22   CLINTON   **24**

Dave Mackie County Park

MUKILTEO

3

Mukilteo State Park

Foulweather Bluff

25

Cultus Bay

Hood Canal Floating Bridge

PUGET SOUND

HOOD CANAL

EDMONDS

2

KINGSTON **1**
Appletree Cove

N

Not for navigation

Memorial Park, located at the head of the visitor's dock, offers picnic and restroom facilities. From April through October the Kingston Farmers Market operates at the park on Saturdays from 9:00 a.m. to 2:30 p.m. 360-297-7683. The park also hosts the "Kingston Tunes on Tuesday," with performances from 6:30 p.m. to 8:00 p.m. each Tuesday in August. 360-337-5350. Restaurants, a coffee shop and gift shop are located nearby. Adjacent to the ferry dock is a community-fishing pier. A bank and post office, as well as stores (hardware, liquor, and grocery) are within a half a mile.

★⚓ **Arness County Park:** Wetlands containing significant wildlife are at the back of the bay, near Arness County Park. Picnic areas and fireplaces

are available. It is also possible to take a motor powered dinghy through a culvert under the road to explore a drying lagoon, which is a popular swimming hole when the tide is right. If exploring, go on a rising tide that is close to at least a 10-foot high tide. Currents can be strong through the culvert. 🌲

Port of Kingston: Permanent & guest moorage, 75-ft linear float for larger boats, gas, diesel, 30 ampere power, water, showers, laundry, waste pump-out, dumpsters, launch ramp, propane available. 360-297-3545

Walk-around: There is a pleasant beach walk north of Kingston.

Edmonds
[18441, 18445, 18446, 18473]

★ **Edmonds (2):** Site of a large, port operated marina. There are many attractions in this city. Restaurants, shopping, lodging, repairs, and dry boat storage are all near the marina. Edmonds is celebrated for its public art. European-style streets, spoke out from a central fountain. Old-time streetlights draped with hanging baskets accent these streets. The *Edmonds in Bloom* competition gardens have been featured in Sunset Magazine. Four parks lie along the waterfront, and an underwater park with an artificial reef, to

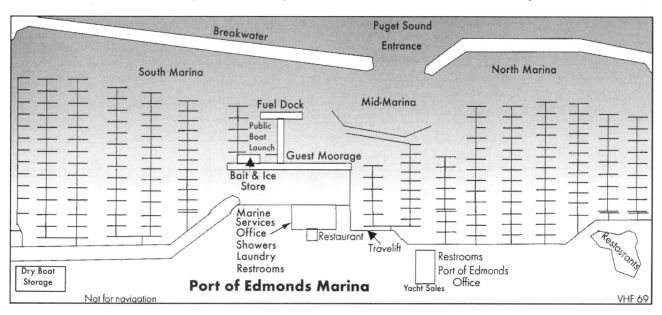

Port of Edmonds Marina
Not for navigation
VHF 69

attract salmon and bottom fish, is strategically placed near the 950 foot public fishing pier. To discover the marine life at low tide, wander along the beach with the *Edmonds Beach Rangers*, as they give guided walks and informative tours. The Ranger Visitor Station at Olympic Beach is open summer weekends, 425-771-0227. A swimming pool, 13 parks, and tennis courts are within the city limits. Edmonds is well known for its art galleries and artworks which adorn the downtown streets. Activities include the *Waterfront Festival* in late May, *Edmonds Arts Festival* in mid-June, *Taste of Edmonds* in August, and the *Fourth of July Celebration*. For live theater productions, call the Driftwood Players, 425-774-9600, or the Edge of the World Theater, 206-542-7529. The eastern terminus for the Edmonds-Kingston ferry route, by highway this picturesque community is 15 miles north of Seattle, west of Interstate 5.

Edmonds has many historic sites. Visitors may enjoy leisurely walks, lovely sunsets over the distant Olympic Mountain range, and wandering where turn-of-the-century ship building wharves and shingle mills once flourished. In the foreground are the ferries, making their two dozen daily trips to the Kitsap Peninsula, *The Gateway to the Olympic Peninsula*. If you begin your walk from Brackett's Landing and walk Main Street, pretend you are back in time when the gas lamps were lit and the town crier announced the news of the day. Near the center of town, visit the museum with a room dedicated to marine artifacts.

★ **Port of Edmonds:** {47° 48.5' N, 122° 23.4' W} This facility offers permanent and guest moorage, water, power, showers, restrooms, laundry, travelift, workyard, dry storage, launch, gas, diesel, and pump-out. Restaurants and shops are within walking distance of the marina. Courtesy van available. See our Steering Star description in this chapter. Website: www.portofedmonds.org & www.boattravel.com/edmonds/ 336 Admiral Way, Edmonds, Washington 98020. Fax: 425-670-0583. Telephone: Marina Operations: 425-775-4588. VHF 69

★⚓ **Richmond Beach County Park:** Located somewhat over a mile south of Edmond's Pt. Wells, this King County Park is used for scuba diving and swimming, has hiking trails, restrooms, picnic sites, and fireplaces. There is a concrete path on the bank. Practical anchorage is limited to a lunch hook. ⛫🧍

Possession Sound Vicinity

[18423, 18441, 18443, 18445]

★ **Possession Sound:** See current tables for Admiralty Inlet. Possession Sound joins Puget Sound at the southern point of Whidbey Island and extends in a general northerly direction for ten miles to its junction with Saratoga Passage and Port Susan.

Elliott Point (3): Elliott Point is a low spit projecting approximately 200 yards from the high land. Mukilteo Light, 33 feet above the water, is shown from a white octagonal tower on the point. A fog signal is at the station.

★⚓ **Lighthouse Park:** This day-use park land is near the lighthouse. In season, the lighthouse, built in 1905, is open for tours on Saturdays, Sundays, and holidays. 425-513-9602. Fourteen acres have launching ramps with side floats (seasonal floats), tables, fireplaces, stoves, and restrooms. If winds are strong, go to Everett to launch. No campsites. Mooring buoys may be

Edmonds Ferry Dock

available, however this area is open to winds and wakes. Scuba diving and fishing are popular. 425-355-4141. ⛴🏕

★ **Mukilteo (3):** [18443] Located at Elliott Point, this residential community is the terminus for the Mukilteo-Columbia Beach (Whidbey Island) ferry. An L-shaped fishing pier is near the landing. Port owned mooring floats are tucked in on the north side of the ferry landing. These seasonal floats are open to visiting boats for short stays. Overnight moorage may be available. Restaurants are within walking distance.

Walk-around: It is a three-mile walk north from Mukilteo State Park to Howarth City Park. The route is north on the road around the oil terminal and along the beach and the railroad tracks.

Everett & Vicinity

[18423, 18443, 18444]

★ **Everett (4):** [18444] Everett is the county seat of Snohomish county, one of the fastest-growing counties in the nation. Located 25 miles north of Seattle, Everett is home to Naval Station Everett, the world's most-modern Navy base, as well as the world's largest aircraft manufacturer, the Boeing Company. The Port of Everett links the community to international shipping from around the world. The city's transportation center and higher education facility, Everett Station, is a model of ingenuity and design. It was named one of the 10 All-America Cities in the nation in 2002.

Extensive permanent and guest moorage is available at the Port of Everett, located on the east shore of Port Gardner, about one half mile into the mouth of the Snohomish River. If on an ebb tide, currents can be strong. When landing, dock into the current. On approach, you will pass the U.S. Navy Homeport facility. Do not pass within 300-yards of the piers, when approaching the river entrance. Because of the channel buoys, which may be confusing, reflections of lights on the water, and debris from up-river, plan to arrive during daylight hours. When entering the channel, keep buoy #5 to port.

The list of things-to-do and places-to-see in and around Everett is extensive. Beginning with the attractions just at the port facility itself, one can enjoy hours of entertainment. The 10th Street Marine Park has picnic and BarBQ facilities. A free ferry to Jetty Island departs from the park's boat ramp. A Farmers Market at the marina is open each Sunday from Memorial Day through Labor Day. During *Salty Sea Days* in June, activities including the fireworks and the *"On The Waterfront Festival"* are held here. On Thursday nights in July and August there are waterfront concerts at Port Gardner Landing. The annual *Fresh Paint Arts Festival* occurs each August. Up from the waterfront, a visit to the newly revitalized downtown area will reveal a variety of stores and restaurants amid the historic buildings and viewpoints. The Everett Public Market on Grand Avenue houses antique shops, a restaurant, deli, and an organic food store. The Everett Events Center (425-322-2600) on Hewitt Avenue hosts concerts, rodeos, circuses, and other exciting events. Taxi, limousine, and bus transportation are available to and from the waterfront. Call 425-257-8803. The *Music in the Parks* concert series is held at Forest Park each Sunday in July and August. The park is also home to the Animal Farm, open June, July and August. This free petting zoo features farm animals and pony rides. Call 425-257-8300. Other local attractions include Boeing Plant Tours (800-464-1476) and Everett Aquasox baseball games (800-463-7647). Visit www.ci.everett.wa.us/visitor/ for additional information.

Captain Vancouver landed at the site of Everett in 1792. A hundred years later, visionaries dreamed of Everett as the western destination of the Great Northern Railroad's transcontinental route. Eastern investors, including John D. Rockefeller, were influential in Everett's early history. More recently, Everett was known as the home of the late U.S. Senator Henry M. Jackson. A trident submarine is named after him, the only person to have been bestowed this honor.

Everett is strategically located just off the I-5 corridor, approximately a 30 minute drive north of Seattle. By car, the port is reached from Interstate 5 southbound, via exit 194 to Everett

Avenue and driving west toward the waterfront to West Marine View Drive. Northbound, take exit 193 to Pacific Avenue and drive west toward the waterfront to West Marine View Drive.

U.S. Customs & Border Protection Designated Port-of-Entry: For in-person report to a CBP officer call 425-259-0246. Due to new Homeland Security regulations, call ahead.

★ **Port of Everett:** {47° 59' N, 122° 14.1' W} Everett Marina is the largest marina on the Pacific Coast. Two lighted markers show the marina entrance. The extensive Marina Village and the Landing at Port Gardner with hotel, shops, chandlery, and restaurants are a strollers and shoppers paradise. The port has permanent and guest moorage, power, gas, diesel, laundry, restrooms, showers, haul-out, repairs, waste pump-out. A guest float, also designed for wheel chair access, is near the head of the basin, providing access to the Landing at Port Gardner. See our full page advertisement on Page A-2. Address: 1720 West Marine View Drive (Post Office Box 538), Everett, Washington 98201. E-mail to: marina@ portofeverett.com Websites: www.portofeverett.com & www.boattravel.com/everett/ Fax: 425-259-0860. Telephones: 1-800-729-7678, 425-259-6001. VHF 16, 68, 69.

Walk-around: Several points of interest are within walking distance of moorage. These include Marina Village, the Landing at Port Gardner. Marine-oriented businesses wrap around the port basin. Many shops and services are located on 14th Street. A visit to the Firefighter's Museum on 13th Street is another possibility.

Naval Base Everett: Restricted area withn 300-yards of piers. 425-304-3000 (general information).

Naval Station Everett Marina: The marina is accessible to DoD civilian, reservists, active duty, and retired military only. Any vessel, prior to transmitting to or from the marina, must contact Everett Control on VHF 74. This Navy installation contains 90 slips. Permanent moorage, water, power, pump-out. 425-304-3909.

★ **Jetty Island:** When the Port of Everett basin was created, two-mile-long Jetty Island also came into being. It shelters the port facility from a short distance offshore, and is only a five minute boat ride away. Small boats can be beached easily and some moorage may be available. Caution advised regarding strong currents in the area and, from February through June, you might encounter the California Sea Lions who feed near the island. The picnic areas and sandy beaches of Jetty Island attract thousands of visitors each year. From July to September, Wednesdays-Sundays, *Jetty Island Days* feature treasure hunts, sandcastle building contests, and concerts. There is hourly transportation to Jetty Island from The 10th Street Boat Launch. For schedule and programs available after July 4, call 425-257-8304.

★⚓ **Everett Marine Parks & Everett Boat Launch:** Three parks are north of the moorage basin. The first park is the port-operated boat launch, rated one of the best in the northwest. There are 13 ramps with side floats, and guest moorage floats. Restrooms and picnic sites are available. April-October hours are 4:00 a.m.-11:00 p.m. A metal sculpture is an attraction. North and South Marine Parks are farther north. They are primarily designed for strolling and sight-seeing along the 1,200 feet of waterfront. ⚓☂

★ **Snohomish River (5):** The Snohomish is navigable for some distance by canoe, kayak, and

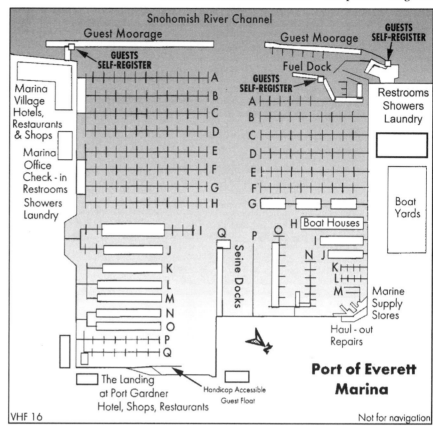

Snohomish River Channel
Guest Moorage
Guest Moorage
GUESTS SELF-REGISTER
GUESTS SELF-REGISTER
Fuel Dock
GUESTS SELF-REGISTER
Marina Village Hotels, Restaurants & Shops
Marina Office Check - in Restrooms Showers Laundry
Restrooms Showers Laundry
Boat Yards
Seine Docks
Boat Houses
Marine Supply Stores
Haul - out Repairs
The Landing at Port Gardner Hotel, Shops, Restaurants
Handicap Accessible Guest Float
Port of Everett Marina
VHF 16
Not for navigation

shallow draft power boats. Explore the main channel for approximately three quarters of a mile past the I-5 overpass. The first bridge to be encountered is a railroad swing bridge with a least clearance of nine feet. It is located a little over one half mile east of Preston Point. Next, just past the railroad bridge, is the U.S. Highway 529 bridge with a least clearance of 38 feet. The next bridge, the I-5 overpass with a clearance of 66 feet, is inland about a mile and one half. On Smith Island, the Smith Island Boat Launch Park and Langus Waterfront Park offer picnic sites and launch ramps.

Dagmar's Marina: Located on Smith Island. Permanent boat storage, haul-outs, launching, repairs. 425-259-6124. VHF 77.

Ebey's Slough: Caution advised crossing the shallow flats leading to Steamboat and Ebey Sloughs. The bar must be crossed at high tide. It is possible to navigate Ebey Slough to the city of Marysville. Two fixed bridges, with clearance of 41 feet, and two swing bridges cross the slough. Moorage and repairs can be obtained in Marysville.

Geddes Marina: Haul-outs, prop, outboard, trailer repairs, moorage. 360-659-2575.

Gedney Island (Hat Island): This high, wooded island is residential property, and the marina on it is privately owned. Foul ground extends from the south side of the eastern half of the island. Caution advised. An artificial reef for Scuba diving is 3,000 feet south of the island.

★ **Tulalip (6):** Caution advised because of rocks and extensive shoals. Limited anchorage in the shallow bay, located about four miles northwest of Everett. Minimum depths are three feet in most of the bay, however floats near shore may dry. A marina, with limited guest moorage, is on the eastern shore. Moorage chances are better from spring to August, because fishing boats may have

vacated their slips. A concrete launch ramp, with boarding float, is south of the marina. On the hillside, there is an historic Catholic Mission. The surrounding land is Indian reservation. The word Tulalip means "almost landlocked bay."

Tulalip Marina: Limited moorage for small boats may be possible. Launch ramp, restrooms. Call ahead. 360-651-4047.

★⚓ **Kayak Point County Park (7):** Tall trees line the extensive gravel beach at Kayak Point. Anchorage is close to shore at the park, or in the bays north and south of the point. There is a launching ramp and fishing pier. The float is for loading and unloading only. There are cooking facilities, restrooms, picnic shelters, and fresh water. Kayak Point, a golf course, is nearby. ⚓☂

★ **Port Susan (8):** [18423, 18441] Port Susan is a 12-mile long, 1-mile wide body of water between Camano Island and the mainland. Boaters traveling north from Everett occasionally enter Port Susan by mistake, missing Saratoga Passage. If exploring Port Susan, temporary anchorage is found in the bay on the mainland shore, south of Kayak Point. There is little protection here from southeast winds. A better anchoring spot is off Camano Island, across from and south of Kayak Point. This is Gerde Cove. Although unmarked on charts, it was named in honor of the Gerde family, a seafaring people with many generations fishing the west coast and finally settling on Camano Island. Water depths are 15 to 20 feet with anchorage on a mud bottom. A launching ramp is located at Cavelero Beach County Park on the west shore of Port Susan, south of Triangle Cove. Anchorage is possible. Picnic facilities. Because of the sun-heated tide flats that warm the shallow water in much of the bay, swimming is good.

Everett's Inland Waterway   *Roger Hunsperger Photo*

Saratoga Passage & Camano Island

[18423, 18441]

★ **Saratoga Passage:** See current table for Admiralty Inlet. Rimming the west side of Camano Island, Saratoga Passage extends approximately 18 miles in a northwesterly direction from its entrance between Sandy Point and Camano Head. At its north end, this deep waterway connects with Penn Cove and Oak and Crescent Harbors, and leads into Skagit Bay. Winds can funnel through this waterway, and rough water can be encountered when winds meet an opposing tide.

★ **Camano Island:** This appendage is an island only because the channels at the mouth of the Stillaguamish River separate it from the mainland shore near the town of Stanwood. These river sloughs are navigable only at the highest tides and in shallow draft boats. The beach below 340 foot high Camano Head, at the southern tip of the island, is a geoduck and butter clam digging spot. Camano Island was named after a Spanish explorer by the name of Caamano. Indians used to dive into the water off this Head and hold their breaths while trying to touch the bottom. Accomplishing this task was believed to give them supernatural power.

Elger Bay: This bay lies on the Saratoga Passage side of the island. There is temporary anchorage with protection from northwesterly winds. The northern extent of the bay is shallow. Favor the Lowell Point side, avoiding some foul ground off the point.

★⚓ **Camano Island State Park (9):** This Cascadia Marine Trail park is north of Lowell Point on Saratoga Passage. The trail sites include one group camp area and seven tent sites at the far south end of the day-use area at Point Lowell beach, along the cliff. The 134 acre park has a beach, 87 campsites, water, 2 kitchens with shelters, restrooms, a boat launching ramp, 5 kayak sites, and showers. Hiking and Scuba diving are popular in the area. 360-387-3031, 360-902-8844 ▲⛺🛥🚶

Onamac Point: This point is the site of an artificial reef. There are a variety of bottom fish nearby.

★ **Utsalady:** Primarily a summer home settlement, there is a launch ramp at the small county park on the west side of the bay. Another ramp is farther west, around Utsalady Point. Utsalady Bay is formed between Utsalady Point and Brown Point with depths of 10 to 20 feet. Anchorage is on a mud bottom. The bay is exposed to north and northwest winds and seas from shallow Skagit Bay. Adjoining land is private. A century ago, the area was a center for lumber milling and ship building. In 1857, the enterprising mill owner, Lawrence Gremman, envisioned a canal dug through the middle of Whidbey Island to make a direct shipping lane to the Strait of Juan de Fuca. Select timbers, as much as 125 feet in length and 50 inches in diameter, were shipped as spars to the British and American Navies. One flag staff, made at Utsalady, appeared at the Paris Exposition. The mill closed in 1896. Utsalady means land of the berries.

Skagit Bay & Skagit River

[18423, 18427]

★ **Skagit Bay (10):** See current tables for Deception Pass. This bay extends north from Saratoga Passage about 12 miles in a west-north-west direction. The bottom of much of the bay is mud flats that are bare at low water. The mud is intersected by numerous channels caused by the Skagit River outflow. Shoals also extend into the bay from Whidbey Island. A natural channel, marked by buoys and lights, follows the eastern shore of Whidbey Island to the northern point where the channel turns west through Deception Pass. Stay in the marked channel. Approaching from the south, the red nun buoys are to starboard and green cans to port. Velocity and direction of the currents vary throughout the channel. The flood enters through Deception Pass and sets in a generally southern direction. The ebb flows north. This can be important to know if west winds are blowing in Juan de Fuca Strait and will clash with an ebb current in the vicinity of Deception Pass.

★ **Skagit River:** The South Fork and North Fork of the Skagit River empty into Skagit Bay, leaving the rich farmlands of Fir Island as a triangle-shaped island between them. The North and South Forks meet about a mile and one half south of Mount Vernon. The South Fork empties through the flats north of Camano Island. Navigation of the South Fork is not recommended, except for occasional use by canoeists and kayakers. Launch ramps are at Utsalady.

The North Fork, however, offers an opportunity for owners of small, hand-carried or small-medium sized boats to explore the Skagit River. It is possible to enter the river at most times of the year on a high tide of eight feet or better. The problem spot is the approach channel in Skagit Bay. Entrance to the North Fork is in the channel along the south side of the man-made jetty. Go slow and stay fairly close to the jetty. Once in the river itself, depths are adequate, and unless it is a time of extremely low river height, it is even possible to navigate inland by small craft past the city of Mount Vernon. In Skagit Bay, however, the river shallows to wadeable depths at low tide. According to Mary Blake, whose family has owned a resort and marina on the North Fork for many years, it is possible to launch a boat (to 30 feet) at the ramp at their facility and to exit on an 11 or 12 foot tide, go to La Conner to explore, and return at a regular tide with no problem. She also recommends fishing for Humpies in August and September because they are easy to catch, and it is possible to anchor and let the current do all of the work.

The remainder of Skagit Bay, including Swinomish Channel and Similk Bay, are farther north and are described at the beginning of Chapter 6.

Blake's RV Fishing Resort: Full RV hookups, limited moorage, launch ramp, snack shop, showers, laundry, camping, propane. 360-445-6533.

Whidbey Island

[18423, 18441]

★ **Whidbey Island:** Whidbey Island is described in two chapters in this book. The area along the northern shore, Cornet Bay, and Deception Pass, is outlined in Chapter 6. The area south from Joseph Whidbey State Park and Oak Harbor is described here

Approximately 55 miles in length, this is the largest salt water island in the contiguous United States. In February, 1985 the Supreme Court, in a 9-0 decision, ruled that Long Island, New York is a peninsula rather than an island, leaving the largest island honors to Whidbey. It was named for Joseph Whidbey, a sailing master with Captain George Vancouver in the 1790's. It was Whidbey who discovered Deception Pass between Whidbey and Fidalgo Islands. On the north, Whidbey Island is connected to Fidalgo Island by the Deception Pass Bridge. On the west and south, ferry service connects the island with Port Townsend and the Olympic Peninsula mainland from Keystone Harbor, and with the mainland at Mukilteo from the town of Clinton.

In climate and economy, the northern half of Whidbey Island is quite different from the southern half. North Whidbey falls within the lee of the Olympic Rain Shadow. This results in arid grazing land with an average rainfall of only 17 inches. Even some forms of cacti flourish here.

On the southern half of the island, the annual rainfall is 35 inches, contributing to the agricultural economic base of this part of the island. Real Estate development, logging, and ship building are other south-island industries. The largest employer and economic factor on the island is the Naval Air Station, north of Oak Harbor.

★⚓ **Joseph Whidbey State Park (11):** Located on the Strait of Juan de Fuca, on the west shore of the island, this park is primarily accessible by car. There is a beach for small, beachable boats. Picnic sites and restrooms are available. As part of the Cascadia Marine Trail, one group camp area is provided. 360-902-8844 ⛺🏕

Oak Harbor & Vicinity

[18423, 18428, 18441]

Crescent Harbor (12): [18428] Oak and Crescent Harbors are adjacent to each other. Crescent Harbor, a semicircular bight two miles in diameter, is immediately east of Oak Harbor. Shoal areas are identified on the chart. The pier and hangars at the Sea Plane Base are navy property. No marine facilities for pleasure craft. A proposed restricted area would be from a line drawn from the Polnell Point Light (48 degrees 16' 22"N, 122 degrees 33' 32" W) west-southwest to a point in central Crescent Harbor (48 degrees 16' 00" N, 122 degrees 36' 00" W) and then due north to a point along Crescent Harbor's shoreline on Whidbey Island (48 degrees 17' 55" N, 122 degrees 36' 00" W). Prior to the area being restricted, the navy would search the vicinity to assure that the area is clear. Any nearby vessels would be contacted by a Navy patrol boat and be advised to steer clear. If exercises were in progress, a solid red Bravo flag would be flown

from a patrol boat and/or a buoy would be placed at the southwest corner of the restricted area (48 degrees 16' 00" N, 122 degrees 36' 00" W).

★ **Oak Harbor (12):** [18428] Enter Oak Harbor in the marked channel between Blower's Bluff and Forbe's Point. Check depths and stay in the dredged channel between the red and green markers. Do not go between buoy #2 and Maylor Point. Shoaling and rocks make passage near high tide advisable. Once clear of the last starboard marker, turn sharply to starboard. The city will be on the port side and the marina, with abundant visitor moorage, is at the head of the bay. This marina is about ¹/₄ mile from downtown shops and restaurants. Taxi and Bus service are available. The bus is free and runs Tuesday through Saturday with stops at the marina every two hours at 20 minutes to the hour. Destinations of interest include Deception Pass, Ft. Casey and Coupeville. There is a float for small dinghies at the downtown waterfront. Depths are shallow and the float dries at a minus tide.

★ **City of Oak Harbor:** The city of Oak Harbor was once called "Paradise of Puget Sound." It has many amenities, including restaurants, motels, liquor store, gift shops, theaters, and grocery stores. City Beach Park, with its landmark windmill, has pads for RV's, bathhouses, a swimming pool, kitchens, fire pits, tennis courts, and ball fields. The grounds are open year around while the buildings and facilities are open from May-October. A pier, with a float for fishing and landing dinghies, lies along this shore at Flintstone Park. Depths are shallow and the float dries at a minus tide. Annual Oak Harbor Events include *Holland Happening* during the last week of April, an *Old-Fashioned Fourth of July Parade and Celebration*, the *Whidbey Island Race Week* and

the Naval Air Station's *Sea and Sky Festival* all in July, the *Lion's Club Car Show* in August, and the *Artichokes and Arts Festival* in September. Island Transit buses provide free transportation throughout Whidbey Island.

The town site, first settled by a Swiss Army officer, a New England gentleman and a shoemaker from Norway, was named for the preponderance of Garry Oaks in the mid-1800's. The Dutch arrived in 1894 from Michigan and the Dakotas. They were searching for land where they would be free from the age-old fear of floods. The Dutch have continued to be a very important influence in the community, as evidenced by the farms, architecture, and gardens. By 1891, the downtown waterfront of Oak Harbor was booming when steamers made regular freight and passenger runs between here and Bellingham, Everett, Seattle, and Olympia.

★ **Oak Harbor Marina:** {48° 17.12' N, 122° 38.03' W} This recently expanded facility has permanent and guest moorage with 20 and 30 ampere power, showers, laundry, gas, diesel, LP refills, haul-outs, launch ramp, waste pump-out and dump. Use the south entrance for guest moorage slips F-18 through F-52, and the north entrance for slips F-1 through F-13 and for side ties along the north side of the main walkway. See map and Steering Star description in this chapter for entry directions. Pay stations are on the breakwater dock adjacent to F-27 and F-52 or at the marina office. Relax at the spacious picnic sites located on the floats. This is a popular center for July sailing races and other activities. Closed Sundays November through February. Internet: www.whidbey.com/ohmarina E-mail: ohmarina@whidbey.net Address: 865 SE Barrington Drive, Oak Harbor, Washington 98277. Fax: 360-240-0603. Telephone: 360-679-2628. VHF 16, working 68.

★ **Oak Harbor Marina:** The award-winning city marina has been the pride of Oak Harbor residents for many years. First completed in 1974, expansion and modernization have developed it into a 434 boat facility with moorage

for boats up to 50' in length. The breakwater dock, (F-Dock), runs north to south. It is 900' in length and offers 52 open slips for guest moorage. The main entrance is from the south. To avoid running aground, if using the north entrance, approach from the south end of breakwater dock, turning parallel to the outside (west side) of this dock. Head north, keeping the piling to port. Enter the marked and dredged channel around the north end. Departure is the reverse of this procedure. Additional side ties are found along walkways. Moorage pay stations are located on the breakwater dock at F-27 and F-52, or check-in at the Harbor Master's Office in the two-story gray building adjacent to the flagstaff. Twenty and 30 ampere power, drinking water, hose-down water, gas, diesel, propane, lubricants, a dump station, and waste pump-out available. Showers and laundromat available. For trailer boats, the large launch ramp is well known as one of the finest in the northwest. Adjacent to the marina is a marine chandlery, engine repair

facility, and a privately owned and operated boat storage yard which also offers trailer haul-outs for boat to approx. 40'. An overhead crane provide haul-outs for boats to 6,500 pounds. Having become the center for popular community events, the marina sponsors the Old-fashioned Fourth of July extravaganza and the Race Week in mid-July. Taxi and bus service connects with the downtown core, approximately 1-mile away. Restaurants, banks, groceries, liquor store, and all city amenities are found downtown. Rental cars are available, or take Island Transit, which offers complimentary bus service to parks and communities all around Whidbey Island. Bus schedules are available at the Harbor Master's Office. This facility, designed to please the vacationing family, has picnic tables, barbecues, horseshoes, volley ball, playground equipment, and even a fishing pier. Open all year. Hours: 8:00 a.m.-6:00 p.m. Memorial Day-Labor Day, 8:00 a.m.-5:00 p.m. the remainder of the year. Closed Sundays November-February. **E-mail: ohmarina@whidbey.net   Internet: www.whidbey.com/ohmarina & www.boattravel.com/oakharbor/ Address: 865 S E Barrington Drive, Oak Harbor, Washington 98277. FAX: 360-240-0603. Telephone: 360-679-2628. VHF 16 (switch to 68).**

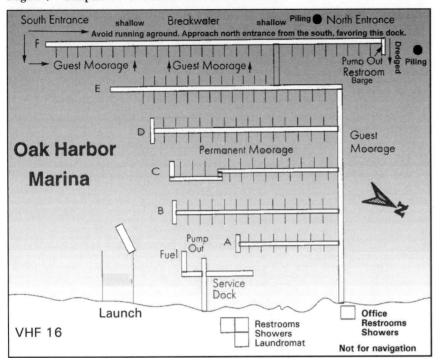

Oak Harbor
Marina

South Entrance   shallow   Breakwater   shallow Piling North Entrance
Avoid running aground. Approach north entrance from the south, favoring this dock.

F

← Guest Moorage →   ← Guest Moorage →   Pump Out   Piling
Restroom   Dredged
Barge

E

D

Permanent Moorage   Guest
Moorage

C

B

A

Pump
Out

Fuel

Service
Dock

Launch

VHF 16

Restrooms
Showers
Laundromat

Office
Restrooms
Showers

Not for navigation

Penn Cove & Coupeville

[18423, 18441]

★ **Penn Cove (13):** Penn Cove indents three and a half miles, nearly cutting Whidbey Island in two. It is about one mile wide. Anchorage is possible in several locations in 30-45 feet of water. Most of the bottom is good holding mud. Snatelum Point, at the southern entrance to Penn Cove, is a narrow spit that extends north for over a half mile. The spit is marked by a buoy. Beware of a wreck in the vicinity. Private homes line this spit. On the north shore, Monroe Landing is home to a launch ramp and picnic area. Also on the northern shore are old wharfs and pilings, reminders of the 1890's when the community of San de Fuca was established on this hillside. The boom came when a survey proposed a railway could travel north on Whidbey Island and link the island to the mainland. At one time San de Fuca had the first schoolhouse on the island, a general store, furniture, and jewelry shops, a tavern, and a fine hotel. However, the railroad plan died within a year. Through the years, several promoters have expounded ideas such as digging a canal at the island's narrowest part to link Saratoga Passage with the Strait of Juan de Fuca, thus enabling direct shipping lanes from Everett. A Wyoming millionaire was one who was willing to fund the project, however he died suddenly. The San de Fuca Fire Department building marks the spot today, and the landmark Armstrong House on the hill, has been restored as a residence. On the opposite shore is the historic town of Coupeville.

Farther into Penn Cove, private buoys and aquaculture operations are at the southwest corner. Madrona trees decorate the surrounding hillside approaching Kennedy's Lagoon, at the head of the cove. At the turn-of-the-century, a Seattle company offered $100 in prize money for the best essay describing the beauty of these trees, the surrounding waterfront, and lagoon. Postcards with the winning essay were sent to prospective buyers of the development. An inn was built and is still in operation. It is interesting to note that Madronas, the deciduous evergreens which peel red bark and leaves year around, also produce

white blossoms in the spring and poisonous red berries in autumn.

★ **Coupeville (14):** Overnight moorage is available first come-first served at the Port of Coupeville floats, adjacent to the historic city wharf. Water depths are minimal at very low tides. Be sure to read the sign at the head of the floats for information regarding depths. 400 feet of moorage is available and four mooring buoys are just northwest of the wharf. Adequate depths for anchoring.

Coupeville's attractions include information kiosks at the shore-end of the wharf, Front Street with its picturesque shops and restaurants, art galleries, a museum, historic exhibits, and Victorian era homes. Many of the buildings have been restored and are bed and breakfast inns. A liquor store, grocery, post office, and bank are accessible. The town celebrates an *Arts and Crafts Festival* in August with a tour of homes, exhibits, and a salmon bake. *Art Walks* are held quarterly. *Dance Bonanza* is a 4-day, 20-event dance festival held the first Thursday-Sunday in November (360-678-5434). Coupeville is the county seat for Island County. The town was founded by Captain Thomas Coupe. He sailed through Deception Pass in his vessel Success and then, in 1852, swallowed the anchor, bought a homestead, and became one of the town's earliest settlers. At that time about 300 Skagit Indians lived on the lands surrounding Penn Cove.

Walk-around: A walking tour takes about an hour and includes many of the restored Victorian homes of the community. Plaques on these buildings give historical information. The Island County Museum exhibits illustrate the era when Coupeville was a leading shipping port in the days of the tall ships. Indian dugout canoes and the Alexander Blockhouse are interesting to study. Another walk is to a large grocery up the hill. If too far, they will pick-up and deliver. 360-678-5611.

Port of Coupeville: Transient moorage only, no power or water, gas, diesel, store, showers, restaurant, ice, marine supplies. 360-678-5020. Store: 360-678-3625.

★⚓ **Captain Coupe Park:** A launch ramp is on the eastern side of town at Captain Coupe Park. A ramp with side float marks this site. Parking is provided for cars and boat trailers. The pump-out is for RV's only, not accessible from the water. A dump site is available, restrooms. Anchorage in the immediate area is limited because of shallow water. 360-678-4461. ⚓

★⚓ **Point Partridge Park (15):** Located close to Fort Ebey on the west side of the island, this park has primitive campsites. Picnic tables, beach trails, and pit toilets are available. No fresh water. Primary access is by car.⊞▲

Ebey's Landing (15): A parking lot, vault toilet, interpretive display, and one and one half miles of hiking trail are provided. Hiking, surf fishing, and beachcombing are popular. There are no mooring buoys, however small boats can be beached. A memorial set above the beach depicts the life of Colonel Ebey, pioneer commander of an 1855 Militia station who was slain by Haida Indians from the north, when they raided and sought revenge for the death of their chief.

★⚓ **Fort Ebey State Park:** Eagles, bluffs, army bunkers, wild rhododendrons, and sandy beaches can all be found at this 226 acre park on the west side of Whidbey Island. There are over 50 campsites with restrooms and showers, fresh water, and 10 hookups. As part of the Cascadia Marine Trail, four sites are provided on a steep bluff that affords beautiful views. Fort Ebey, built in 1942, joined Fort Casey, Fort Worden and Fort Flagler as the four corners in the defense system of Puget Sound. Gun batteries and bunkers still remain. It became a park in 1981 and was named for Colonel Ebey. 360-678-4636, 360-902-8844. ▲⊞⚓

Keystone Harbor (16): Fairly protected by Admiralty Head, Keystone has a small spot for temporary anchorage. The controlling depth at the entrance is 18 feet, with 15 to 18 foot depths in the harbor. Use caution when the tide rips are frothing at the entrance. This small harbor is the Whidbey Island terminus for the Port Townsend-Keystone ferry. Allow sufficient maneuvering room for the ferry to land. There is a paved launch ramp with a boarding dock and trailer parking space.

★⚓ **Fort Casey State Park:** There are 60 picnic sites, 35 campsites, restrooms, showers, and water. Activities include hiking on the trails, Scuba diving at the underwater marine park, visiting the interpretive center in the Admiralty Head Lighthouse, and exploring in the underground rooms. The park's 137 acres include the concrete bunkers and gun stations from the days of the 1890's when the fort was used in the defense system protecting the entrance to Puget Sound. Because of the crowded bay, access to the park is primarily by car. 360-678-4519, 360-902-8844.⊞⚓

Walk-around: A four-mile walk north along the beach leads to Ebey's Landing. The walk farther north leads to Perrigo's Lagoon and on to Point Partridge.

Walk-around: Crockett Lake, and the stretch of saltwater beach on Keystone Spit, are park land within walking distance of Fort Casey. In the 1850's, a community named New Chicago was located on the spit. Lots were platted and brought high prices. A wharf and hotel were built, however, a windstorm leveled the hotel, and a proposed railway system never materialized. Crockett Lake is a popular site for birdwatchers.

★⚓ **South Whidbey State Park (17):** This 347 acre park is near Bush Point. Facilities include campsites, tables, shelters, showers, and restrooms. All campsites are available for individual and family reservations between May 1 and September 15. One group camp, accommodating up to 100 persons, can also be reserved, and a reserve picnic shelter is available for groups to 30. Artificial reef for divers. No mooring buoys, however small boats can be beached. A public beach, accessible only by boat, is one mile south of the point. Diggers will find several varieties of clams. 360-331-4559, 360-902-8844. ▲🏕

Bush Point (18): This picturesque point is identified by homes rimming the beach and a larger building, the site of a restaurant during summer season. During summer months, launching has been possible by sling for boats up to 22 feet, or 4,000 pounds. The Bush Point Lighthouse, built in 1933, marks the spot where residents once hung a kerosene lantern on a long pole during dark nights. Watch for rocks offshore.

Mutiny Bay (19): It is possible to anchor in this indentation between Bush Point and Double Bluff. A launching ramp is available. Watch for tide rips off Double Bluff. Shoals extend 600' off the bluff.

Mutiny Bay Resort: Limited guest moorage, (no overnight, nothing over 20'), showers, lodging. Buoys for resort guests only. 360-331-4500.

Greenbank: Located north of Holmes Harbor on the island's east shore, this farming settlement, well known for the cultivation of loganberries and for loganberry liqueur, does not have facilities for boaters. In the early days of the century, a wharf and a store were established, and the site was a regular steamer stop. By 1908 several Finnish

families had settled, and a hotel and school stood near the beach. Today, Greenbank Beach County Park has swimming and picnic sites. Fairly deep water anchorage on a mud bottom, offering some protection in west winds. No marine facilites.

★ **Holmes Harbor (20):** This six mile long inlet was named by Wilkes in 1841. Private homes and floats dot the shore. Anchorage is in Honeymoon Bay and off the head, opposite Freeland Park. Open to winds from the north.

★ **Honeymoon Bay:** Anchorage is in a bight on the west shore, south of Dines Point. No floats or docks are available.

★ **Freeland (21):** The town of Freeland is located at the head of Holmes Harbor. Anchorage can be found at the head, opposite the park. It is possible to dinghy ashore and walk to the town center where one will find restaurants, marine supplies, banks, and grocery stores. Freeland was settled in 1900 when large tracts of land were sold to disenchanted Socialists from the Equality colony. Each family grew crops and contributed both money and man power to be used for machinery and construction. A community sawmill was utilized for many years. Today, Freeland is a commercial center and residential community, and is home to the nationally recognized Nichols Brothers Shipyard. No marine facilities.

★⚓ **Freeland Park:** Located at the head of Holmes Harbor, facilities include a launching ramp, picnic sites, playground, and restrooms. The ramp has been extended over 100 feet to permit access at all tides, and floats have been added. ⚓🏕

Useless Bay (22): Shallow flats extend from shore and then drop-off abruptly to depths of

more than 12 fathoms. This vicinity has been a private summer home haven for many years.

★⚓ **Dave Mackie County Park:** A launching ramp is on the east shore at Dave Mackie County Park near Maxwelton. It is possible to launch smaller trailer boats above half tide, but silting makes the depth and condition of the bottom difficult to predict. The park has picnic tables, restrooms, fresh water, and a playground. ⚓🏕

Langley
[18423, 18441]

★ **Langley (23):** A breakwater protects the City of Langley moorage basin, where both permanent and guest moorage can be found. Anchorage is possible in the bay, but it is open to winds. No fuel.

This town site lies on a hillside overlooking Saratoga Passage, with the Cascade Mountains in the distance. In May and June, watch for whales. Popular attractions are the bronze statues of a boy and his dog looking at the marvelous view. There are gift, antique, clothing, jewelry, book, and pharmacy shops, as well as a general store and several good restaurants. Along the seawall, Phil Simon Waterfront Park has picnic and barbecue sites. Special annual events include *Mystery Weekend* in February, an art festival held around the Fourth of July, and an old-fashioned County Fair, where neighbors gather to celebrate summer in country tradition, during the third weekend of August. Langley has had wharves in the bay since the 1880's when it became a cord wood supply center for the steamer traffic plying Puget Sound.

★ **Langley Boat Harbor:** {48° 02' N, 122° 24' W} A 100-foot float provides 200 lineal feet of addi-

★ **Langley Boat Harbor:** Great little getaway whether close to home or as a stopping place on a longer journey. This breakwater-protected facility offers transient moorage May to September and permanent moorage from October through April. Large float provides 200' of visitor moorage uninterrupted by pilings. No reservations taken, although limited rafting possibilities assure that most, if not all, can find moorage. Twenty and 30 amp power available, as well as water, waste pump-out barge, showers, and a launch ramp. No fuel. Located on the southeast shore of Whidbey Island, this is a perfect stopover. The charming town of Langley overlooks Saratoga Passage and is a short walk from the waterfront. Restaurant offerings range from gourmet pizza to seafood, Mediterranean to pub food, and several options in between. Excellent wine selection, fresh produce, and gourmet goodies available at the general store. Several coffee shops and a bakery offering delectable pastries. Shops include bookstore, grocery, and pharmacy, as well as several galleries, clothing shops, and antique stores. Library provides internet access

and US Post Office is across the street from City Hall. Special times of the year include: last weekend in February (Mystery Weekend); March-May when gray whales visit the shallow Langley shoreline to feed on sand shrimp; second weekend in July for the annual Choochokam arts and music festival; and third weekend in August for the Island County Fair. At all times of the year, visitors will enjoy beautiful vistas of the Cascade Mountains, eagles in flight, herons along the shoreline, and both sunsets and sunrises over Saratoga Passage. Walking tour map is available at the Chamber of Commerce (near corner of Second and Anthes), and their number is 360-221-5676. **City's mailing address: P.O. Box 366, Langley WA 98260. Harbor phone: 360-221-2611. Also see City website: www.langleywa.org.**

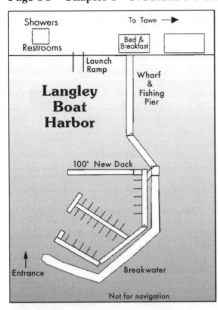

Langley Boat Harbor

Showers
Restrooms
To Town →
Bed & Breakfast
Launch Ramp
Wharf & Fishing Pier
100' New Dock
Entrance
Breakwater
Not for navigation

tional visitor moorage, uninterrupted by pilings. Slips are labeled according to the size of boats that can be accommodated. No reservations can be made. Twenty and 30 ampere power, launch ramp, and waste pump-out barge. Permanent moorage is also available. The boat basin is sheltered by a pile and plank breakwater. No fuel. See our Steering Star description in this chapter. Mailing address: Box 366, Langley, WA 98260. Fax: 360-221-4265. Telephones: 360-221-2611.

★♨ Seawall Park: This park rims the waterfront below the town of Langley. A wooden staircase descends the bank. There is a northwest Indian-motif seawall, large fire pit, and boat ramp. ⬗

Clinton (24): A summer only, 30-minute-stay float for loading is located adjacent to the north side of the ferry wharf. Recreational Pier. This is the western terminus for the Clinton-Mukilteo ferry route. The town lies along Highway 525 on the hillside above the ferry terminal. Grocery stores, banks, retail shops, restaurants, and Dan Porter Memorial Park, the pride of local residents, are accessible.

★♨ Possession Point Waterfront Park: Located south of Clinton, this park has picnic tables, a concrete launch ramp, recreational pier. Two Department of Natural Resources beaches are also on this shore and marked by white posts. Red rock and Dungeness crabs are found, along with abundant horse clams. 🜨⬗

Possession Point & Cultus Bay (25): [18441, 18445] Prominent white bluffs provide the backdrop for the popular fishing grounds off this point. A shoal extends one-half mile from shore, west of Scatchet Head. There is a bell buoy. Another shoal juts 2¼-mile offshore from Possession Point. Another lighted bell buoy marks the end of this foul ground. An artificial reef with a 240-foot sunken ship is 600 feet west of the buoy. Water depths here are 55 to 100 feet. Anchorage in settled weather can be found fairly close to shore, off the southeast tip of Whidbey, north of Possession Point. Beach homes on shore mark this location. Cultus Bay contains shoals and dries on low tides. A dredged channel on the east side of the bay leads to a private development.

Essential Supplies & Services

AIR TRANSPORTATION
Seattle Seaplanes **1-800-637-5553**

AMBULANCES . . . . All 911

BOOKS / BOOK STORES
The Marine Atlas **541-593-6396**

BUS TRANSPORTATION
Everett 425-257-8803
Greyhound 425-252-2143
Snohomish County 425-353-7433
Whidbey Island 1-800-240-8747

COAST GUARD
VHF 16 or 21
Bellingham 360-734-1692
Seattle 206-217-6000

CUSTOMS/BORDER PROTECTION
Everett 425-259-0246

FERRY INFORMATION . 1-800-843-3779

FISHING INFO 360-902-2500

FUELS
Coupeville, Port of: Gas, Diesel 360-678-3625
Edmonds, Port of: Gas, Diesel.
. . . . **425-775-4588 VHF 69**
Everett, Port of: Gas, Diesel. 425-259-6001 VHF 16
Kingston, Port of: Gas, Diesel. 360-297-3545
Oak Harbor: Gas, Diesel . . . 360-679-2628 VHF 16

HOSPITALS
Edmonds 425-640-4000
Everett 425-261-2000
Coupeville 360-321-5151, 360-678-5151
N Whidbey Community Clinic 360-679-5590

INSURANCE
Boat Insurance Agency **206-285-1350**
   Or Call **1-800-828-2446**

MARINAS / MOORAGE FLOATS
Coupeville, Port of 360-678-5020
Edmonds, Port of . . . . **425-775-4588 VHF 69**

Everett, Port of . . . . **425-259-6001 VHF 16**
Geddes Marina: Marysville 360-659-2575
Kingston, Port of 360-297-3545
Langley Boat Harbor **360-221-2611**
Oak Harbor Marina . . . . **360-679-2628 VHF 16**
Tulalip Marina 360-651-4047

PARKS
Department of Natural Resources:
. . . . 360-856-3500, 1-800-527-3305
Washington State 360-902-8844
Washington Camping Reservations . . . 1-888-226-7688

POISON INFO 1-800-222-1222

RAMPS / HAUL-OUTS
Bush Point: Whidbey Island
Camano Island State Park
Cavelero Beach: Port Susan
Captain Coupe Park: Coupeville
Dagmar's Landing: Smith Island. 425-259-6124 VHF 77
Dave Mackie Park: Maxwelton
Edmonds, Port of . . . . **425-775-4588 VHF 69**
Everett Bayside Marine 425-252-3088
Everett, Port of . . . . **425-259-6001 VHF 16**
Fort Casey State Park: Keystone
Freeland Park: Whidbey Island
Geddes Marina: Marysville 360-659-2575
Kayak Point: Port Susan
Kingston, Port of 360-297-3545
Langley Boat Harbor **360-221-2611**
Langus Waterfront Park: Snohomish River
Lighthouse Park, Mukilteo
Mariner's Haven 360-675-2659
Mutiny Bay: Whidbey Island
Oak Harbor Marina . . . . **360-679-2628 VHF 16**
Possesson Point Waterfront Park
Smith Island Boat Launch
Tulalip Marina
Utsalady: Camano Island

RV PARKS
Fort Ebey State Park
Oak Harbor City Beach Park

RECOMPRESSION CHAMBER
Virginia Mason: Seattle 206-583-6433

RED TIDE HOT-LINE 1-800-562-5632

REPAIRS / SERVICE
Dagmar's Landing: Smith Island. 425-259-6124 VHF 77
Edmonds, Port of . . . . **425-775-4588 VHF 69**
Everett Bayside Marine 425-252-3088
Everett, Port of . . . . **425-259-6001 VHF 16**
Mariners Haven 360-675-2659

SCUBA / DIVING SITES
Camano Island State Park
Edmonds Underwater Park
Fort Casey State Park
Hat Island
Mukilteo State Park

SEWAGE DISPOSALS
Captain Coupe Park: Dump 360-678-4461
Oak Harbor Marina: Pump, Dump . . . 360-679-2628
Edmonds, Port of: Pump 425-775-4588
Everett, Port of: Pump, Dump 425-259-6001
Kingston, Port of: Pump, Dump 360-297-3545
Langley Boat Harbor: Pump 360-221-2611

SHELLFISH HOTLINE 360-796-3215
For local area closures/information, call County Health Depts.:
Island County Health Dept 360-679-7350
Snohomish County Health Dept 425-339-5250

TOWING
C-TOW **1-888-354-5554**
CATeam Marine Assistance 360-378-9636
VESSEL ASSIST Everett **425-344-3056**
Whidbey Island **360-675-7900**

VHF MARINE OPERATOR
Whidbey Island: 87
Note: MariTel has shut down all other Washington State VHF Marine Operator channels.

VISITOR INFORMATION
Central Whidbey 360-678-5434
Edmonds, Port of . . . . **425-775-4588 VHF 69**
Edmonds 425-776-6711

WEATHER . . . . VHF W-1

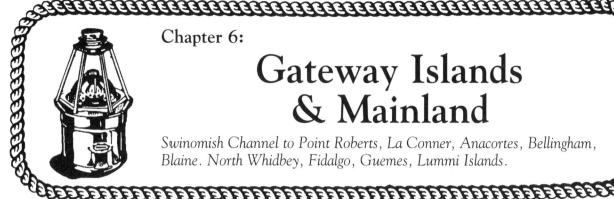

Chapter 6:

Gateway Islands & Mainland

Swinomish Channel to Point Roberts, La Conner, Anacortes, Bellingham, Blaine. North Whidbey, Fidalgo, Guemes, Lummi Islands.

Symbols

[   ]: Numbers between [ ] are chart numbers.

{   }: Numbers & letters between { } are waypoints.

⚓: Park, ⛴: Boat Launch, ▲: Campgrounds, ⚡: Hiking Trails, ⟊: Picnic Area, ⬭: Biking

★ **Important Notice:** See "Important Notices" between Chapters 7 and 8 in this guide for specific information on boating related topics such as: Canadian & U.S. Customs, boating safety and security, navigation, weather, U.S. & Canadian Coast Guard, U.S & Canadian marine radio use, Vessel Traffic Service and traffic separation plans, security zones, and internet access. Due to new Department of Homeland Security regulations, call ahead for latest customs information and/or see Northwest Boat Travel On-line, www.nwboat.com.

Skagit Valley
[18400]

★ **Skagit Valley:** The Skagit River descends from the mountains and passes several communities as it meanders through this fertile valley to its mouth at Skagit Bay. See Chapter 5. Dairy, bulb, seed, and vegetable farms predominate the landscape. *The Daffodils In Bloom Festival* is held in March and *The Tulip Festival* in April. The Skagit County Bus System, SKAT, offers transportation from moorages in La Conner and Anacortes to nearly all corners of Skagit County. This enables visitors to connect with Mount Vernon, the Bayview Airport, and outlet and shopping malls.

Chart List

NOAA Charts:

  18400, 18421-23, 18424, 18427, 18429-32

Marine Atlas (2005 ed.):

  Pages 6-7, 12

★ **Mount Vernon (1):** See Skagit River information in Chapter 5. Mount Vernon is the county's largest city and the mainland hub for the Skagit Valley. Much of the downtown core lies along the east bank of the Skagit River, and a promenade provides views of the river. Travel on the Skagit River by small boat is possible in the vicinity and also along the North Fork and for some distance

La Conner's Rainbow Bridge   Debbie Brickman Photo

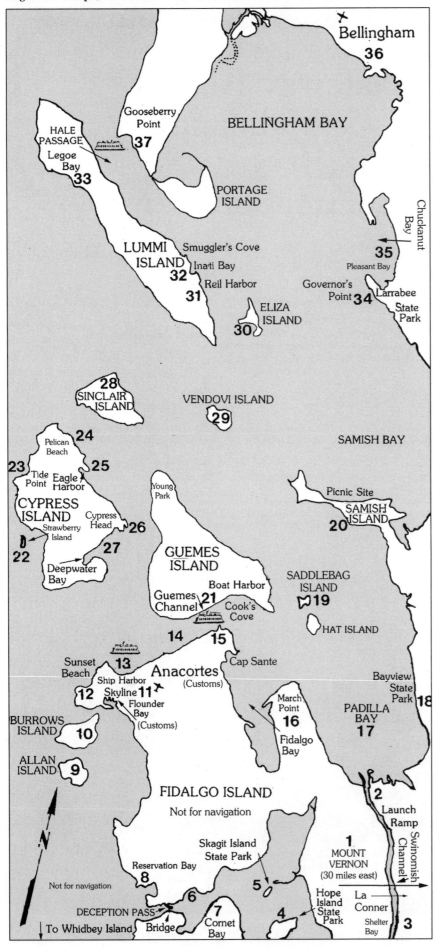

into the South Fork to Conway. Some moorage floats for small boats are located along the river bank. Edgewater Park, in West Mount Vernon, south of the bridge, has a launching ramp into the river. Fishermen catch several types of salmon, steelhead, and sometimes sturgeon in the Skagit. For information regarding licenses and seasons, contact the Washington Department of Fish and Wildlife in Olympia, or a sporting goods store.

Swinomish Channel

[18421, 18423, 18427]

★ **Swinomish Channel (2):** Previously named Swinomish Slough, this natural channel has been dredged for many years. Recently the controlling depth of the entire channel has been changed from 8 feet to 7.3 feet. It connects Skagit Bay on the south with Padilla Bay, near Anacortes, on the north. At the northern end, currents flood south and ebb north. The opposite is true at the southern end, resulting in the currents meeting at about the halfway point in the channel. Marked courses for both north and south approaches help boaters avoid the drying tidal flats and rocks that surround the entrances. See entry descriptions below. Minimum depth in the canal course is about eight feet. Because of extensive boat traffic, keep the boat's wake as low as possible. If docking at the town of La Conner, located along the channel, it is advisable to head into the current when approaching the dock.

Entry from the south: Yachtsmen should not turn into the marked channel until the range markers in Dugualla Bay on Whidbey Island are lined up. Before turning east, the boat must be north of the red buoy that marks the southern side of the channel. Next, proceed eastward in the channel, passing to the north of Goat Island. The channel turns to port at Hole In The Wall. A small fork of the Skagit River empties into the channel at this point, however this is not the North Fork and entry is not recommended. Steep banks are on both sides after the channel curves to port. A small Indian settlement is on the port side, behind a breakwater. The passage then turns to starboard and leads past Shelter Bay, also to port. Shelter Bay is a well established residential community located on Swinomish Indian lease land. It is home to a yacht club and many moorage floats. Favor the east side of the channel when passing Shelter Bay. The town of La Conner lies to starboard, beyond the Rainbow Bridge. There is a launching ramp and a storage and repair facility on the waterfront at the base of the Rainbow Bridge. Moorage is available at La Conner Marina and city-owned private floats along the channel.

Entry from the north: From Padilla Bay, keep the red buoys, which line the channel, to starboard, and the cans to port. Do not attempt to cut inside the first (northernmost) red buoy. Keep a watch for commercial crab pot markers. The first bridge is a seldom used railroad bridge. A large concrete obstruction, which bares at low tide, lies on the east shore of the channel between the highway bridges and the railroad swing bridge. The Swinomish Channel Boat Launch is at the east approach to the bridge over the channel. Navigational range markers for the channel lead to a turn to starboard at the northerly entrance to the town of La Conner. The two Port of Skagit County's La Conner Marinas are to port after this turn as is the town of La Conner. An Indian community is on the west shore.

Twin Bridges Marina: North Swinomish Channel. Full service, indoor dry stacked storage. 360-466-1443.

La Conner
[18427]

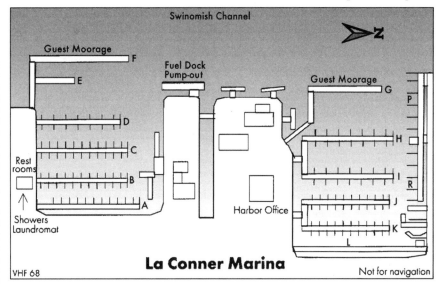

★ **La Conner (3):** The Rainbow Bridge, built in 1958 and named for its graceful shape, is a distinctive landmark for this friendly town and historic village on the Swinomish Channel. Boat moorage is available at both basins in the Port of Skagit County's La Conner Marina, at city owned floats along the Swinomish Channel, and at restaurant facilities. Specialty shops are open year around, seven days-a-week, along the waterfront and side streets. Quality goods, art galleries, and a variety of restaurants attract thousands of visitors from distant places. The town has provided off-street and on-street parking.

La Conner is the oldest town in Skagit County, with a heritage dating to the first white settlers in 1864. Thomas Hayes opened a trading post on the site that is now Totem Pole Park. Shortly after, John S. Conner and his wife, Louisa, purchased the post and established a post office. The town's original name of Swinomish was changed to La Conner. From its heritage as a trading post and port-of-call for steamships, the town has retained and restored much of its picturesque New England waterfront flavor. The surrounding farmlands were reclaimed from the river and the sea by diking and draining the land. In spring, extensive bulb fields bloom into a maze of yellow, red, and lavender.

Points of interest include the Skagit County Historical Museum and the 1891 Gaches Mansion. The county museum offers a large selection of memorabilia from pioneer days, and affords beautiful views of farmlands, looking east to the Skagit Valley. Museum hours are Tuesday-Sunday 10:00 a.m. to 5:00 p.m. The Gaches Mansion, built in 1891, is home to the La Conner Quilt Museum, showing quilts from around the world.

The Museum of Northwest Art features noted artists from the Pacific Northwest. On First Street, the Fireman's Museum houses a fire engine built in New York in 1848. Before coming to La Conner, the engine was shipped around the horn and was used during the San Francisco earthquake fires of 1906.

Activities include the *Smelt Derby* in February, *Grapes and Plates* in March, *Tulip Festival* in April, *Elements* - La Conner's Art Festival in June, *Fireworks at Dark* on July 4th, the *La Conner Classic Yacht and Car Show* in September, *Art's Alive* - an art festival and invitational art show in November, and the *Christmas Lighted Boat Parade*

with Santa coming to town in December.

Enjoy a half-hour ride on the authentic steamboat, Liberty Bell, or a relaxing lunch cruise on the Viking Cruise boat while learning about wildlife and the history of the area.

Walk-around: La Conner is easy to walk around. Take a picnic lunch and walk to Sylvan Pioneer Park, located at the eastern entrance to the Rainbow Bridge. There are kitchen facilities, picnic tables, fireplaces, restrooms, and an amphitheater.

★ **Boater's Discount Center:** Complete marine supply and chandlery located between the two boat basins at La Conner Marina. A large moor-

★ **Boater's Discount Center and Yacht Sales:** Let us sell your yacht for less. Located in La Conner, between the two marinas on Swinomish Channel, is a very unique marine store. It is easy to tie up to their dock to go shopping. The store is well-stocked with hardware, marine parts and supplies, propane and CNG tanks, galley equipment, kitchen utensils, clocks, barometers, fishing licenses, fishing and crabbing gear and bait, NOAA and Canadian charts, books, and nautical gifts. Dealer for Achilles and Flexboat Inflatable dinghies and Nissan outboards. Dealer and Installer for Seawise & Pacific Fabrication low profile davits and Sealand Vac-U-Flush systems. An unusual sideline is the manufacture of their own fiberglass adjustable radar arches, dock boxes, storage boxes, and piling caps. They have an expanded line and custom-made ordering of hardtop extensions for Bayliners, and can now accommodate 28', 32', 33', 37', 38' and 39' models. Boater's Discount Center is becoming known as the place to go to find an ever-changing inventory of supplies. Crushed and block ice, pop, juice, and a variety of snacks and chips are available. You can explore the shops and restaurants in downtown La Conner. If arriving by car, as you are coming into town on Morris Street, turn right on Third Street, and then left on Dunlap. Open all year, seven days a week. Summer hours 8:00 a.m.-6:00 p.m. Winter hours 9:00 a.m.-4:30 p.m. Sundays 9:00 a.m.-3:00 p.m. **E-Mail: boatersd@cnw.com Website: www.boathardtop.com Mailing address: Post Office Box 1590. Address: 601 Dunlap Street, La Conner, Washington 98257. Fax: 360-466-5350. Telephones: 360-466-3540, 1-800-488-0245.**

age float provides direct access. See our Steering Star description in this chapter. Email: boatersd@cnw.com Website: www.boathardtop.com Address: 601 Dunlap Street, La Conner, Washington 98257. Fax: 360-466-5350. Telephone: 360-466-3540, 1-800-488-0245.

★ **L & T Canvas & Upholstery:** {48° 24' N, 122° 30' W} Located on the channel at La Conner Marina, this facility offers a convenient private dock for one-stop custom marine canvas, interior and exterior upholstery work. See our advertisement in this chapter. Address: La Conner Marina, 601-C Dunlap, La Conner, Washington 98257. Telephone: 360-466-3295.

La Conner Maritime Service: Complete boatyard service & repair. Found on Swinomish Channel in La Conner, adjacent to La Conner Marina. 360-466-3629

La Conner Landing: Gas, diesel, convenience store. 360-466-4478.

Port of Skagit County, La Conner Marina: Two large boat basins offer permanent and transient moorage. Gas, diesel, waste pump-out, repairs, haul-outs to 100 tons, restrooms, showers, laundry, power, fresh water. 360-466-3118. VHF 66A.

⚓ Swinomish Indian Tribal Park Floats: Moorage on west shore of channel for tribal members only.

★⚓ **Hope Island Marine State Park (4):** Located in Skagit Bay, this island park has mooring buoys on the north side in Lang Bay. Anchoring is also possible. There are campsites, picnic sites, and a sandy beach, but no fresh water is available. 360-902-8844. ▲⚲

★⚓ **Skagit Island Marine State Park (5):** Mooring buoys are located on the northwest side

of this state park island. Campsites are primitive, with no fresh water. A trail encircles the island. Depths between Skagit and Kiket Islands do not permit passage. Skagit Island was the hideout for turn of the century burglar/smuggler, Henry The Flying Dutchman Ferguson, a member of Butch Cassidy's Hole In The Wall Gang. 360-902-8844. ▲⚲

★ **Similk Bay (5):** This wide, shallow bay has calm weather anchorage in the outer portion. Often used for log storage, it is open to south winds.

Dewey Beach: Once a mill townsite, today this is residential area. Shoals extend some distance off the beach and drop off suddenly. Anchorage is possible outside these shoals, but the area is open to strong currents and winds.

Deception Pass Vicinity

[18421, 18423, 18427]

Deception Pass & Canoe Pass (6): The pass narrows to 200 yards at Pass Island. Passage at or near slack water is recommended. Currents run to eight knots and eddies form near the shores. Passage need not be difficult if wind and tide are considered. Do not traverse the pass during strong westerlies because dangerous swells, tide rips, and overfalls may be encountered. Canoe Pass, the narrowest portion, is located on the north side of the main pass. Some boaters prefer it, believing that currents are milder. It has a submerged rock lying on its north side, at the bend. West of the bridge, Lottie Bay, an indentation on Fidalgo Island, offers shelter in an emergency, but nearly dries on a minus tide. If traversing the pass after dark, be aware that lights from the bridge and the head-

lights of passing cars do not help, but instead create an eerie picture when looking up from the water.

The passage, first charted by a Spanish exploration in 1791, was named Boca de Flon. In 1792, Captain George Vancouver sighted the indentation, however, he did not recognize it as a passage separating two land masses. Master Joseph Whidbey discovered its true significance and Vancouver then named it Deception Pass. He also named the large island to the south in honor of Whidbey. Before the turn-of-the-century, Whidbey pioneers envisioned a bridge to link Whidbey and Fidalgo Islands. Captain George Morse, credited as the original promoter of the project, cruised through many times and told his children that Pass Island was placed there to be a pier for the bridge. A miniature model of the proposed bridge was exhibited at the Alaskan-Yukon Exposition in 1909. However, it was 1934 before the federal, state, and county governments funded the project. A Public Works Project, the bridge was built with young workers from the Civilian Conservation Corp and from a penal colony located at a quarry near the site. When completed in 1935, 700 cars passed over the span during the first hour. Today, over 5.7 million vehicles use the bridge annually. The bridge was declared a National Monument in 1982, and was the scene of a 50th birthday party celebration on July 31, 1984.

★⚓ **Deception Pass Marine State Park (Cornet Bay):** Several large concrete launch ramps are equipped with side floats. Improved park floats, floating islands, dinghy float and mooring buoys, restrooms, and waste pump and dump are provided. Moorage fees collected year around. Other state park acreage with saltwater access is on Fidalgo Island. See Bowman's Bay description below. 360-675-2417, 360-902-8844. ⚲⛵

★⚓ **Deception Pass State Park:** This thickly forested 4,300 acre park covers much of northern Whidbey Island and some land on Fidalgo Island. It has 246 campsites, kitchens with shelters, restrooms, hot showers, a group camp, and a learning center. Facilities for boaters are found in Cornet Bay and in Bowman's Bay (Sharpe Cove) on Fidalgo Island. ▲⛺

★ **Cornet Bay (7):** Located at the head of the bay are a marina and repair services. Because of shallow water and shoaling, proceed in the channel between the markers. Deception Pass State Park land rims the bay. When entering or exiting Cornet Bay, shoals make the west side of Ben Ure Island unnavigable.

★ **Deception Pass Marina:** Located in Cornet Bay. Permanent and transient moorage, 30 ampere power, water, gas, diesel, propane, kerosene, and repairs. Vessel Assist, rescue and towing are available. This is a pleasant stop, and is within walking distance of park amenities. The general store has gear, groceries, beer, ice, a wine cellar, fishing tackle, and a friendly staff. Call for any questions or reservations. Address: 200 West Cornet Bay Road, Oak Harbor, Washington 98277. Telephone: 360-675-5411. VHF 16 CB 10.

Walk-around: It is a pleasant stroll along the road to Hoypus Point. Here one will find a road-end turn around. Until the completion of the Deception Pass Bridge in 1935, a ferry connected Whidbey Island with Blaine Point on Fidalgo Island from this site. Ferry fares were 50 cents per vehicle and 10 cents per passenger. When the bridge opened, the ferry owners received $375 compensation from each county government for lost business. A small gravel beach has views of Mount Baker, Fidalgo, Skagit, and Hope Islands.

Fidalgo Island

[18421, 18423, 18427]

★ **Fidalgo Island:** This island, which some say resembles the shape of a dog's head, is separated from the mainland on the east by the Swinomish Channel. Bridges cross the channel. To the south, the Deception Pass Bridge connects Fidalgo with Whidbey Island. Fidalgo received its name from Lieutenant Salvador Fidalgo of the Spanish ship San Carlos. It is known as The Heart of the Island Empire.

★ **Bowman Bay (Reservation Bay) (8):** Check your charts and beware of Coffin and Gull Rocks in the entrance. Some of the entrance rocks are covered at higher tides and, near high tide, it is easy to mistake Gull Rocks for Coffin Rocks. It is possible to anchor in the bay, but it is exposed to swells from the strait. Once inside, favor the southeast area of the bay in depths of 12-18 feet. There are mooring buoys, campsites, launch ramp, and restrooms. The bay is on the Cascadia Marine Trail. There are six tent sites at the far east end of grass. There is also a group camp. Sharpe Cove Marine State Park is located behind some rock out-croppings, in a niche on the northwest side of the bay. 360-902-8844.

★⚓ **Sharpe Cove Marine State Park (8):** A wharf with floats and mooring buoys are found in this protected cove. Floats removed in winter. Anchorage is not recommended in this area of Bowman Bay. Moorage fees are charged May through September. On shore are cookout shelters, tables, showers, restrooms, and a waste dump. 360-902-8844. ⚞

Walk-around: A short walk away is Pass Lake, a serene, pastoral lake where fishing is limited to non-powered boats and the use of artificial flies. Another walk is to Rosario Bay to view the statue of The Maiden of Deception Pass.

Rosario Bay: Anchorage is not recommended. There are picnic sites, a kitchen, and mooring buoys that are seasonally available. This area is popular for scuba diving. An underwater park is located south of Rosario Head. Private homes, state park lands, and a college marine facility occupy the shore. There is also a red cedar, carved statue of The Maiden of Deception Pass. It symbolizes the Samish Tribe's legend that a mythical, self-sacrificing Indian gave herself to the gods of the sea, and that Ko-kwal-alwoot safely guides travelers through the passage. Scenes for the movie, The Postman, were filmed here.

★ **Burrows Bay:** This long, steep-sided bay on the west shore of Fidalgo Island, stretches from Langley Bay, on the south, to Flounder Bay on the north. Avoid Williamson Rocks, a National Wildlife Refuge. Biz Point shelters a community-owned wharf with private mooring float and several private buoys. Beware of reefs in this vicinity. Much of Burrows Bay is open to the southwest and is seldom used as an anchorage. A portion, Alexander Beach, has homes fronting a lovely sandy beach. Temporary anchorage, perhaps as a dinner stop in settled weather to enjoy the sunset, is possible.

Allan Island (9): A small bay on the northeast side of Allan Island has private floats that block the anchorage area.

★⚓ **Burrows Island Marine State Park (10):** Anchorage is found fairly close to shore in Alice Bight, a niche on the northeast side of the island.

Deception Pass   U.S. Navy Photo

Tidelands are private. The park land around Burrows Island Lighthouse is nearly inaccessible, except for beachable craft landing in tiny Short Bay. Overnight camping, but no fresh water. Halibut fishing is good off Burrows Point and fishing for Chinook is often good off Fidalgo Head. ▲

Anacortes

[18423, 18421]

★ **Anacortes:** This friendly city is a center for tourist facilities, restaurants, retail stores, and anything boating. Thousands of boats are moored on a permanent basis and hundreds more arrive to visit this "boater's paradise." Four full-service marinas, three public boat launches, boat storage, boat building and repair, diving and salvage, marine lumber, marine surveyors, and the list goes on. Because of its strategic location on the northern and western shores of Fidalgo Island, Anacortes is also frequented by larger vessels like the State Ferries. The city is the terminus for ferries to the San Juan Islands and Sidney, British Columbia. See the Important Notices between Chapters 7 and 8 for the latest information regarding the ferry service to Sidney.

★ **Flounder Bay & Skyline (11) [18421]:** This well sheltered basin is accessed from an entrance on the northern shore of Burrows Bay. There are port and starboard lights at the entrance. Reduce speed before entry to avoid making a wake that will disturb or damage boats moored just inside. The channel has not been dredged in recent years so boats with drafts of five feet or more should use depth soundings and avoid the east side of the channel. At low tide, deep draft boats should favor the west side of the channel. Skyline is a large residential development. Many residents are retirees who have been drawn to the area and its beautiful views. Skyline is augmented by marine businesses, including a large marina, stores, and yacht club facilities. The marina fuel float is visible once making the turn into the inner bay from the entry channel.

Customs inspection and clearance: Daytime hours 8am-5pm. Telephone: 360-293-2331. If no answer, call 1-800-562-5943. Summer Hours 7am-8pm. If after hours, stay on your boat.

Penmar Marine Co. at Skyline Marina: Permanent & guest moorage, 120 volt, 20/30/50 ampere power, gas, diesel, CNG, propane, waste pump-out, showers, laundry, repairs, haul-outs. Customs clearance. 360-293-5134. VHF 16. Summer hours 8 a.m.-5 p.m. If after hours, stay on your boat.

Walk-around: Walk north on Skyline Way to Sunset Avenue. Turn left and walk down the hill to Washington Park and Sunset Beach. See description below.

★⚓ **Washington Park & Sunset Beach (12):** This 220-acre park, owned by the City of Anacortes, sits on the western shores of Fidalgo Island. It offers trailer hookups, campsites, boat launching ramp with side boarding floats, sheltered stoves, tables, playground areas, showers, restrooms, and laundry facilities. A 2.3-mile loop road, ideal for hiking or biking, encircles the park. Beaches of small gravel make landing small boats feasible. Campground and boat lot information 360-293-1927; Other information 360-293-1918. ▲⚓⚞⚘

Ship Harbor (13): This is the eastern terminus of the ferries to the San Juan Islands and Sidney, British Columbia. Once named Squaw Harbor, whalers beached their boats here to scrape bottoms and make repairs. Later, fish canneries stood on pilings in the harbor. A passenger only ferry, Chinook, has joined the Anacortes to San Juan Islands fleet.

Guemes Channel (14): Stretching from Shannon Point on the west to Cap Sante on the east, this channel separates Fidalgo and Guemes Islands. Currents exceed five knots at times, flooding east, ebbing west. If winds are strong from the west and you are heading west on a flood tide, heavy rips can be expected where Bellingham Channel (See current tables for Rosario Strait) meets Rosario Strait and Guemes Channel.

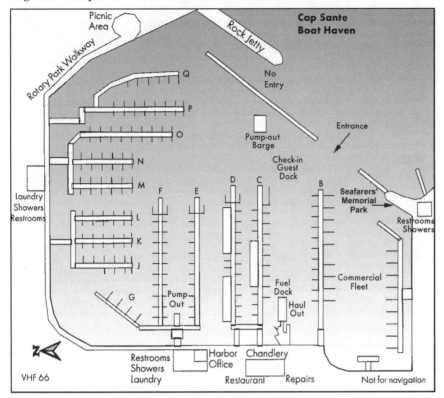

and stretches southward to the residential hillside.

Anacortes is sometimes known as *The City Within A Park*, because it is surrounded by natural beauty. Lakes, salt-water shore, forest and parklands that encompass the area are filled with recreational opportunities including boating, fishing, scuba diving, whale and wildlife watching, camping, hiking, and biking. Within the city itself, there are twenty parks.

Seafarer's Memorial Park, occupying three acres of waterfront south of Cap Sante Boat Haven, has a 200' dock to accommodate rowing and sailing dinghies, canoes, and kayaks. Showers, restrooms, and meeting rooms are included in the park property. The sculpture *The Lady of the Sea*, dedicated to those who wait for those who make their living off the sea, and the *Seafarer's Memorial*, dedicated to those who, while engaged in marine oriented occupations have lost their lives, are park landmarks.

Nearby, at 7th and R Avenue, take a self-guided tour of the W.T. Preston, a historic steam paddlewheeler that plied the waters of the Skagit River for many years, serving to clear debris that threatened safe navigation. The new W.T. Preston Snagboat Heritage Center features artifacts and displays illustrating the historical significance of the snagboat. Adjacent, the restored Railway Depot now houses an art gallery, and a Saturday Farmer's Market during summer months. The Jim Rice Park provides benches and view sites. Other parks include Lower Cap Sante Bluff (Rotary) Park and Causland Park, on 8th Street. Causland Park, designed by a French architect who chose to use native stone mosaics to depict the walls of a park in an old Austrian city, has long been a tourist attraction. The Anacortes Museum, located in a landmark Carnegie Library, is across the street. 360-293-1915.

★ **Downtown Anacortes (15):** Transient moorage is found at the Port of Anacortes Cap Sante Boat Haven, tucked in west of the bluff of Cap Sante. Adjacent to downtown Anacortes, this moorage is within easy walking distance of grocery stores, barber and beauty shops, library with internet, hardware stores, marine chandleries, restaurants, pharmacies, post office, liquor store, banks, furniture and antique dealers, real estate offices, and specialty shops. Many are located on Commercial Avenue, the 40-block-long street which begins at Guemes Channel on the north

★ **Cap Sante Boat Haven:** This Port of Anacortes marina is a customs port-of-entry located in the heart of downtown Anacortes. Permanent and transient moorage is available, with 150-200 berths used for guest moorage. Floats, with 20, 30, and 50 ampere power and water accommodate vessels to 110'. Visitors' Check-In Float is "C" dock. For slip assignment, call on VHF 66 US, or call 360-293-0694, or

walk to the shore end of "C" dock, turn right, and proceed to the Harbor Master's Office. Clean restrooms, showers and laundry facilities are located in the west and north basin. Portable pump-outs are located at the head of docks E–Q. A floating pumpout barge is located just inside the breakwater. There is no charge. A marine supply company, repair yard, prop repair, yacht brokerages, restaurant, fuel dock, propane, haul-outs to 35 ton are on the premises. All supplies and repairs are accessible. The marina is within easy walking distance of parks, museums, restaurants, grocery, drug, hardware, liquor store, post office, and the downtown shopping center. Open seven days a week from 7:00 a.m.-5:00 p.m. **E-mail: marina@portofanacortes.com Internet: portofanacortes.com & www.boattravel.com/anacortes/ Address: 1019 "Q" Avenue Suite C, Post Office Box 297, Anacortes, Washington 98221. Fax: 360-299-0998. Harbor Office Telephone: 360-293-0694. VHF 66 US.**

Popular events include an in-water boat show in March, the *Skagit Valley Tulip Festival* and *Anacortes Quilt Show and Walk in* April, the *Waterfront Festival* in May, the *4th of July Celebration*, *Shipwreck Days* in mid-July, the *Pull and Be Damned Rowboat Race* in late July, and the Anacortes *Arts Festival* the first weekend in August. A *Lighted Christmas Ship Parade* is held in mid-December. In addition, Anacortes Community Theatre presents outstanding plays during the year, capped by a musical during the summer. 360-293-6829.

There are over 90 murals on downtown buildings portraying Anacortes pioneers and historical scenes reproduced from actual photographs. Settled in 1860, this town was first known as Ship Harbor. The townsite was platted in 1876, when Amos Bowman, here on a Canadian Government geological survey, envisioned Anacortes as the terminus for the transcontinental railroad. He established a post office, wharf, and store at what is now the site of the Guemes Island Ferry landing. He dedicated the post office the "Anna Curtis Post Office." The name was later modified and contracted into "Anacortes." It is possible that the name was given the Spanish ending in order to make it blend with Fidalgo, which had been named in 1792 by Spanish Explorers after Captain Salvador Fidalgo.

The city grew by leaps and bounds and by 1890 Anacortes was a bustling, thriving community. Fortunes changed with an unsuccessful attempt to move the county seat to Anacortes, and the knowledge that Anacortes was not to be the Trans-Pacific port for the northwest. The economy deflated, many people left, and the city was a near ghost town. True to its pioneering spirit residents turned to fishing, fish processing, building cold storage facilities, lumbering, millworking, manufacturing boxes, and eventually, to ship building. By 1912, the prosperous communi-

ty had water and electric plants, and streets paved with asphalt. World War I added to the economy when ships were built in Anacortes shipyards and on marine ways on Guemes Island. The next boom came during the 1950's when Texaco and Shell established refineries. Today, the refineries and related businesses are still prominent in the economy, as is tourism, fishing, ship building, repair, and other marine-oriented businesses. Anacortes is also building a reputation as a haven for artists, many who display their works at local shops and at the popular *Anacortes Arts Festival*.

Customs inspection and clearance: Boaters entering from Canada (see Important Notices pages between Chapter 7 and 8) may clear customs at Cap Sante Boat Haven or Skyline Marina. Daytime hours 8am-5pm, Summer 7am-8pm. Telephone: 360-293-2331. If no answer, call 1-800-562- 5943. If after hours, stay on your boat.

★ **Cap Sante Boat Haven:** {48° 30.70' N, 122° 36.18' W} Enter between the pile and plank breakwaters. There is extensive transient and permanent moorage with power, water, laundry, showers, pump-out. If in need of 220 volt power, request at time of reservation. See our Steering Star description in this chapter. This Port of Anacortes marina has received the nationally acclaimed Clean Marina Award. Websites: www.portofanacortes.com & www.boattravel.com/anacortes/ Email: marina@portofanacortes.com Address: 1019 "Q" Avenue, Post Office Box 297, Anacortes, Washington 98221. Fax: 360-299-0998. Harbormaster's Office Telephone: 360-293-0694. VHF 66 U.S.

★ **Cap Sante Marine Ltd:** Three separate locations. Anacortes-Cap Sante Boat Haven 360-293-3145, Anacortes-South Yard 360-293-3732,

Lovric's Sea Craft Marina   Roger Hunsperger Photo

and Seattle/Lake Washington-Kenmore 425-482-9465. Cap Sante Boat Haven location has gas, diesel, propane, launch, marine supply, repairs. Email: info@capsante.com Websites: www.cap-sante.com & www.nwboattravel.com/capsante. See our Steering Star description in this chapter. 1-800-422-5794. 360-293-3145. VHF 16.

★ **Cap Sante Marine-South Yard:** Haul-out, launch, repairs. 360-293-3732. VHF 16.

★ **Cap Sante Marine Ltd.:** This company's reputation, built over the last 25 years, has made them an excellent choice among Northwest boaters for refits, rebuilds, and all manner of custom projects. The company has over 70 employees based in 3 separate locations. Anacortes-Cap Sante Boat Haven (360-293-3145), Anacortes-South Yard (360-293-3732), and Seattle/Lake Washington-Kenmore (425-482-9465). All

locations feature fully stocked parts departments with knowledgeable "solution oriented" staff. Mechanics are factory trained and certified technicians for: Volvo, Mercruiser, Mercury Marine, Honda, Bombadier/OMC, Cummins, Onan, Vacuflush and Raytheon. Cap Sante is the west coast's leading installer of bow thrusters and the nation's only installer of shallow draft stern thrusters. Cap Sante's capabilities also include fiberglass, electronics, shaft, rudder, propeller repairs, and sanitation system repairs and installation. Painting, bottom cleaning, woodworking, canvas work, power washing, waxing, and boat detailing are all available. All work is 100% guaranteed. Registered dealer for Boss Boats and Duroboat Marine. Launching facilities accommodate boats up to 50-tons. Multiple storage facilities also available. Chandlery with charts, marine parts and supplies. Gas, diesel, and oils are conveniently located. Open all year. **Telephones: 1-800-422-5794, 360-293-3145. Fax: 360-293-2804. Websites: www.capsante.com & www.nwboattravel.com/capsante/ E-mail: info@capsante.com Address: Cap Sante Waterway, Post Office Box 607, Anacortes, Washington 98221. VHF 16.**

Seafarer's Memorial   Howard Eskilsen Photo

★ **Lovric's Sea Craft Inc.:** Located on the Anacortes waterfront on Guemes Channel, this family owned and operated yard has experienced, complete marine repair and maintenance for wood, fiberglass, aluminum, and steel vessels. Marine Railways up to 150' vessels. Small, floating dry-dock up to 45'. See our advertisement in this chapter. Circle #59 on Reader Service Card on page 251. Address: Located on Guemes Channel. 3022 Oakes Avenue, Anacortes, Washington 98221. Telephone: 360-293-2042.

★ **Marine Supply and Hardware Co.:** Few marine stores anywhere can offer the vast collection of items that have made this store famous. Family owned since 1913, the oldest marine supplier operating on the West Coast. Enjoy the flavor of times gone by, the oiled wood floors, and the thousands of bins stocked with items too numerous to count. Rope, blocks (of every size), hardware, fasteners, chain, crab pots, brass, decor accessories, galley ware, lamps, rain gear, charts, marine paint. You name it and, chances are, they'll have it. Internet: www.marinesupplyand-hardware.com Email: info@marinesupplyand-hardware.com Mailing address: Post Office Box 350. Address: 202 Commercial Avenue, Anacortes, Washington 98221. Fax: 360-293-4014. Telephone: 360-293-3014.

Anacortes Marina: Permanent moorage. 360-293-4543.

Fidalgo Marina: Permanent moorage. 360-299-0873.

Marine Servicenter, Anacortes Marina: Full service boatyard, 55 ton TravelLift, dry storage, indoor paint shop, custom installs, welding, s/s fabrication. Located next to Anacortes Marina. 360-293-8200.

March Point (16): Two oil refineries, a waterfront beach area with parking, launching ramp, and RV parking are found on this peninsula.

Padilla Bay To Boundary Bay
[18421, 18423, 18427, 18429, 18430]

Padilla Bay (17): [18427] The entrance to Swinomish Channel is in the southwest part of this shallow bay. The Brezeale Interpretive Center and Bayview State Park are on the eastern shore. This park is accessible by road or by sea via flat bottom boats at high water only. This is one of 17 Natural Estuarine Preserves in the United States.

★⚓**Bayview State Park (18):** Located on Padilla Bay, west of the city of Burlington, this park is often isolated from navigable water by extensive drying flats and at high water is only accessed by shallow draft boats. There are several furnished cabins with heat and electricity, 90 tent sites, nine hook-up sites, picnic sites with kitchens, and restrooms with hot showers. Activities include fishing, swimming, hiking, and scuba diving. A high-tide only use boat launch, operated by the Department of Ecology, is located one block south of the park. 360-902-8844.▲⚓⚓

Hat Island: Drying flats of Padilla Bay rim the eastern shore of this island. Crabbing is popular. The lack of beaches or coves, and direct exposure to Guemes Channel winds and currents makes this spot unattractive for anchorage.

★⚓ **Saddlebag Island Marine State Park (19):** This 23 acre Cascadia Marine Trail park is east of Guemes Island and north of Anacortes. There is a bay on the north side and another on the south. Anchor in either one, depending on wind direction. On shore are picnic tables, a vault toilet, and campsites, but no fresh water. Marine trail sites include one group camp area and two tent sites on the south side of the island. Surrounding waters are good crab fishing grounds. The Padilla Bay tide flats make the eastern side of the islands unnavigable.▲🏕🏃

★⚓**Huckleberry Island State Park:** A day-use park, the island's ten acres are undeveloped. Limited anchoring restricts usage, however there is a small beach for beachable boats. No camping or fires.

Samish Island (20): Drying flats prevent anchorage along much of the shore, except at high-tide. On the north, toward shore, there is a Department of Natural Resources picnic spot on a wooded cliff with steps leading down to the beach. The island's name means hunter. 360-856-3500.

Guemes Island (21): Family farms and homesteads predominate and there are few tourist attractions. No facilities for boats, except for a small resort with launching ramp that is located near the north shore. In Young Park, at North Beach, there are picnic sites, pit toilets, and a swimming beach. On the east side, temporary anchorage can be found at Boat Harbor. Often called Square Harbor, this bay is about 400 yards deep and 400 yards wide with six foot depths at a minus tide. Farther south, Long Bay and Cook's Cove provide temporary anchorage on either side of Southeast Point. Open to southeast winds. Currents can be strong in Guemes Channel, thus affecting anchorage. The island was named for Spanish explorer, Don Juan Vincente de Guemes Pachec y Orcas y Aguayo. Fortunately, the name was shortened. Car ferry service connects the south shore of the island with Anacortes.

★⚓ **Cone Islands State Park:** Three lovely islets in Bellingham Channel off the east side of Cypress Island are used by owners of small, beachable boats. Good fishing is often found in the vicinity.

★ **Cypress Island:** This 6,000 acre island is located between Rosario Strait and Bellingham Channel, about six nautical miles northwest of Anacortes. It is a Natural Resources Conservation Area. The thick forested hills rise to heights of over 1,500 feet. Local residents refer to the waters at the southern end of Cypress at Reef Point as the Devil's Hell Hole. The devil appears in the form of waves when strong winds meet opposing tide rips in this vicinity. It is claimed that Cypress has unusual geological characteristics which affect the varieties and growth rates of the plants and trees. There are more than 100 different species of birds living here. Salmon fishing is excellent in season along the west side from Tide Point to Towhead Island. Bottom fishing is popular in several areas around the island. There are anchorage or moorage facilities at Pelican Beach State Park, Eagle Harbor, Cypress Head, and Deepwater Bay, Secret Harbor.

★⚓**Strawberry Island Park (22):** Included as a Natural Resources Conservation Area, Strawberry (Loon Island) is a Department of Natural Resources recreation area and is on the Cascadia Marine Trail. It has three campsites and a vault toilet. There is a beach on the southeast side for beaching small boats and dinghies. No fresh water. Anchorage is possible off the Cypress shore, but it is open to south winds. There are strong currents and submerged rocks near shore. In the 1920's there was a health resort on the west side of Cypress. Fishing and scuba diving are popular. 360-856-3500. ▲

Tide Point (23): North of this legendary fishing ground is a curving indentation which provides temporary anchorage. Try fishing along the shore from Tide Point to Eagle Cliff and the north tip of Cypress. An indentation near Eagle Cliff can be used for temporary anchorage.

★ **Pelican Beach Recreation Area (24):** This Department of Natural Resources land was named for a Pelican sail boating group which has made this a traditional camping site. Anchorage and mooring buoys (if available) are open to north winds. Gravel beach. Check swinging room to make sure there is adequate clearance from the beach. Small boats can be beached. There are campsites, picnic sites, fire pits, tables, and vault toilets. As part of the Cascadia Marine Trail, five tent sites are provided. No fresh water. 360-856-3500.

Walk-around: A 1 mile trail leads to Eagle Cliff. Closed February 1 to July 15.

★ **Eagle Harbor (25):** A favorite anchorage for local boaters, this tiny spot has limited room. It is protected from all but southeast winds. Parts of the harbor are shallow at low tide. The surrounding land is a Natural Resources Conservation Area. No camping or fires on shore.

★ **Cypress Head (26):** Cypress Head is a tombolo, a land mass separated from land by a sandspit. It is the site of a Department of Natural Resources park and is a site on the Cascadia Marine Trail. Mooring buoys are in the northern bay. Anchorage is best in the northern bight also. The southern bay shallows and has stronger currents. Currents affect anchorage and the swing of the buoys. On low tides, check depths and the swing of the buoys that are near shore. There are trails, campsites, fire pits, a vault toilet, and 16 acres of park lands. No fresh water. 360-856-3500.

★ **Deepwater Bay, Secret Harbor (27):** This bay on the eastern side of Cypress provides good, but limited anchorage for small craft. Fish pens are located here and the inner bay is shallow at low tide. This is the site of a private school. No trespassing.

Sinclair Island (28): Caution advised because of extensive shoals off the west and north shores. A small dock, located at Urban, is for loading and day-use only. Limited anchorage can be found off the float. The sandy spit on the southwest tip provides some protection from northwesterly winds. At the turn of the century, Smuggler Kelly's farm was located here.

Vendovi Island (29): Private island. A caretaker is on the premises.

Eliza Island (30): This is a private island with a resident caretaker. There is a private dock with moorage floats on the west side of the island. Temporary anchorage is good both north and south of the peninsula that extends to the west and near Eliza Rocks. The eastern shoreline is lined with shoals and rocks, however, good crabbing can be found. The island's interesting history includes a time when fish traps were used and Eliza was home to the Pacific American Fish Company. Ironically, cats were also raised here and sold for their pelts. Presumably the cats and the fish company flourished together.

★ **Lummi Island:** This long, mountainous island is easy to identify. Anchorages are found in Legoe Bay on the west side, in small niches along the east shore, and on Hale Passage in a spot north of Lummi Point. Lummi Island is connected by car ferry to the mainland at Gooseberry Point. For fares and schedules, call 360-676-6759. The small, very rural community of Lummi includes a general store, post office, library, two restaurants and several B & B's. Local artists host three "Art Tours" annually over Memorial and Labor Day weekends and the first weekend in December. The Lummi Indian Reservation is also located on the island.

★ **Lummi Recreation Site (31):** This Department of Natural Resources recreation area is located in a small inlet on the southeast shore, not quite two miles from the southern tip of the island. Anchorage is fair on a rock bottom. It is one mile south of Reil Harbor. There are campsites, vault toilets, and trails. As part of the Cascadia Marine Trail, five tent sites are provided. No drinking water. 360-856-3500.

Reil Harbor: Fair weather anchorage.

★ **Inati Bay (32):** This bay is located about a third of the way up the island from Carter Point on the Hale Passage side. A rock in the entrance is barely covered at high-tide. Enter south of the white buoy. The bay is sheltered from all but northeast winds and offers good anchorage in 30-40 feet of water. There are pit toilets, trails, and a beach. No garbage facilities. An old story tells of a bootlegger who, while being chased by the Coast Guard, went over the entrance rock in his small, flat-bottomed boat, while the Coast Guard boat, in hot pursuit, was not as lucky.

Smuggler's Cove: Limited anchorage.

Legoe Bay (33): There is anchorage inside Village Point, but it is open to west winds.

★⚓ **Larrabee State Park (34):** Dedicated in 1923, Larrabee was the first state park in Washington. Having recently undergone extensive restoration, the 2,500 acre camper and small boat facility, is accessible primarily by land access from Chuckanut Drive. It is located seven miles south of Bellingham. There are shelters, tables, stoves, hot showers, campsites, several with hookups, restrooms, and a launching ramp into Wildcat Cove south of Governor's Point. Swimming, scuba diving, and hiking are popular activities. 360-902-8844. 🏕▲⛴🏃

★ **Chuckanut Bay & Pleasant Bay (35):** While open to the west, this long indentation in the eastern shore of Bellingham Bay, offers shelter on both the north and south ends. Houses fronting along Chuckanut Drive on the hillside behind the bay, look down the steep sided walls to the waters below. The northern portion has anchorage behind the peninsula, offering protection from northwest winds. Anchorage is good, mud bottom. It is possible to dinghy to public tidelands north of the trestle. Because it dries, enter this lagoon on an incoming tide. A second, tiny anchorage with some protection from the north, is found at the tip of the peninsula, north of Chuckanut Rocks. Chuckanut Rocks, which rim the outer edge of the bay, are hazards as are rocks in the vicinity of Chuckanut Island, farther south. Caution advised. The third anchorage is in Pleasant Bay, inside Governor's Point. It offers good anchorage with protection from south winds. Salmon fishing is often good in the immediate area.

Bellingham

[18421, 18423, 18424]

★ **City of Bellingham (36):** Moorage is available at Port of Bellingham's Squalicum Harbor and Fairhaven moorage. Bellingham is the southern terminus for the Alaskan Marine Highway ferry system and the last major United States city before the Washington coastline meets the Canadian Border. It is also the site of companies operating small cruiseships which cruise through the San Juan Islands and link with Victoria, British Columbia. Located on Bellingham Bay, this city is in a strategic location for visiting the San Juan Islands, the Canadian Gulf Islands, and the mainland coast northward to the City of Vancouver and Desolation Sound. There is moorage at Squalicum Harbor and at Boulevard Park in south Bellingham. The city contains a lively mix of excellent restaurants, art galleries, specialty shops, department stores, motels, hotels, bed and breakfast inns, schools, and colleges. Taxi and bus service connect the harbor with downtown Bellingham. In addition to shopping and educational tours, other activities include whale watching tours, tennis, swimming, golfing, fishing, waterskiing, sailing races, beachcombing, picnicking, kite flying, sail boarding, rowing, hiking, camping at state parks in the vicinity, and playing on playground equipment in the many parks within the city. There are waterfront activities during the Maritime Month of May. This event packed month focuses the region's attention on Bellingham's historic and present connection to Puget Sound. Activities include classic sailing vessel races, a salmon bake and art exhibit. An annual boat show and other water activities take place in Squalicum Harbor. A 2 mile promenade rims Squalicum Harbor, providing opportunities for exercise, shopping, and dining.

Points of interest include the National Historical Registered and elaborate Mount Baker Theater. Music from a Wurlitzer Pipe Organ is played before the evening shows. A second point of interest is Western Washington University with the Western Outdoor Museum and its collection of art works and sculptures. There is also Summer Stock Theatre at the University. The Whatcom Maritime Historical Society Museum, on the corner of Central and Roeder Streets, has a collection of steam and outboard engines, and nautical artifacts. The Whatcom County Museum of History and Art is housed in the former Bellingham City Hall. In this old, red brick landmark, there are exhibits featuring northwest artists and regional history. Of special interest is the H.C. Hanson Naval Architecture Collection. During his career, Hanson produced from 2,500-3,000 designs for wooden watercraft. Closer to downtown, on "C" Street, The Maritime Heritage Center is a park and hatchery where visitors can fish for steelhead and trout and watch salmon spawn. Other interesting sites include the Roeder Home on Sunset Drive, the Eldridge Avenue National Historic District, and the historic landmark Fairhaven District in South Bellingham. On his 1792 voyage,

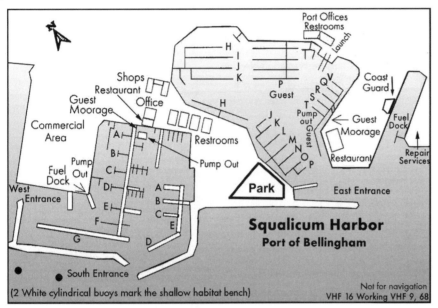

Squalicum Harbor
Port of Bellingham

(2 White cylindrical buoys mark the shallow habitat bench)

Not for navigation
VHF 16 Working VHF 9, 68

Sunset over Squalicum Harbor   Carl & Gloria Tenning Photo

Captain George Vancouver named Bellingham Bay in honor of Sir William Bellingham. Settlement at Bellingham began in 1852 when a lumber mill was established at the site. Bellingham is adjacent to Highway I-5, 54 miles from Vancouver, British Columbia, to the north, and 86 miles from Seattle, Washington, to the south.

★ **Squalicum Harbor, Port of Bellingham:** {48° 45' N, 122° 30.5' W} Permanent & guest moorage, 110/120 volt, 20/30/50 ampere power, water, gas, diesel, propane, repairs, showers, laundry, provisions. Visitor floats at Gates 3, 9, 10 and 12. Pump-outs at Gates 1, 3, 5, 6, 19 and 12. Seasonal complimentary shuttle. Community meeting facility on the waterfront. Hotel and restaurants nearby. Additional moorage is found on buoys at the Port's Fairhaven moorage in South Bellingham Bay. See our Steering Star description in this chapter. Websites: www.portofbellingham.com and www.boattravel.com/squalicum. E-mail: squalicum@portofbellingham.com. Address: 722 Coho Way, Bellingham, Washington 98225. Fax: 360-671-6149. Telephone: 360-676-2542. VHF Channels 16.

Harbor Marine Fuel: Gas, diesel #2, restrooms, oils, water. 360-734-1710.

Hilton Harbor: Gas, haulouts, dry storage, repairs. 360-733-1110.

★ **Fairhaven:** Fairhaven is an historic district in South Bellingham which has become the center for cruise-ferry traffic north to the Alaska Marine Highway, and passenger ferry service west through the San Juan Islands to Victoria. A covered walkway, from the ferry terminal, connects Fairhaven Station and the Amtrak and bus terminal. Fairhaven's rather wild history is vividly described in the Walking Tour Brochure, sponsored by the Old Fairhaven Association. Read the brass plaques on many of the buildings to learn more about life in the late 1890's, when over 35 hotels and boardinghouses were built to handle the influx of new settlers. The community grew ninefold in less than a year. Today, Fairhaven is known for its preservation of historic buildings, the likes of which once accommodated such notables as Jim Hill and Mark Twain. Numerous restaurants, specialty shops and theaters are attractions.

★ **Fairhaven Moorage:** Located opposite the community of Fairhaven on South Bellingham Bay. 600 feet of side-tie linear moorage and 10 moorage buoys. Water, garbage drop on shore. Open May through October. Port of Bellingham: Phone: 360-319-9081.

Walk-around: Nearby is the Interurban Trail, off Old Fairhaven Parkway and 24th Street. It is ideal for hiking and jogging.

Bellingham Cruise Ship Terminal: Terminus for the Alaska Marine Highway Ferry. 1-800-642-0066. Website: www. alaska.gov/ferry

★⚓ **Boulevard Park:** This park in South Bellingham is a beautiful two level park with a lookout and gazebo. The lower section has a pier with floats for day moorage. There is a red buoy off the park. Open to winds.

Gooseberry Point (37): Ferry terminus of mainland-Lummi Island ferry. 360-676-6759.

Fisherman's Cove Marina: Gas, launching, repairs, propane. 360-758-2450.

Sandy Point: This private residential development is located along the beach and along an inland waterway. Considerable shoaling occurs at the entrance. No marine facilities. If hoped to be used in an emergency, discern the depth of the tide. Do not enter unless it is a high tide.

Birch Bay (38): Birch Bay is very shallow. Summer cabins, sandy beaches, and swimming are popular here. Birch Bay State Park has extensive shore side development, however, it does not have marine facilities. Campsites, kitchens, hook-ups and hot showers are available in the 179 acre park. Campsite reservations: 1-888-226-7688.

Birch Bay Village Marina: Private facility, but is a harbor of refuge in an emergency.

Boundary Bay & Drayton Harbor

[18421, 18423, Canadian Chart: 3463]

★ **Blaine (39):** Blaine, "The Peace Arch City," is a major customs port-of-entry for those crossing the border by boat or by car. For land travelers, the Interstate 5 crossing is at International Peace Arch Park. For boaters, Blaine is a stop for those heading north or south along the mainland coast to and from Bellingham, the San Juan Islands, Point Roberts, and Vancouver, British Columbia. Boaters approach Blaine by entering Semiahmoo Bay, passing Semiahmoo Spit and then proceeding in the channel to moorage at Drayton Harbor. Semiahmoo, a resort and marina development is to starboard. To port is Blaine Harbor with its large moorage basin for small craft. Customs clearance can be arranged. A two lane public boat launch ramp is located at the end of Milhollin Drive and a Seafarer's Memorial is an attraction near the port facility. During the summer, a bicycle and foot passenger ferry service links Semiahmoo Spit with Blaine Harbor, allowing

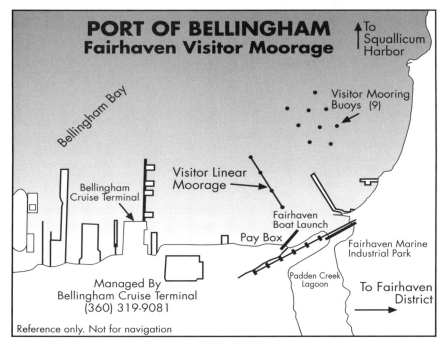

PORT OF BELLINGHAM
Fairhaven Visitor Moorage

↑ To Squallicum Harbor

Bellingham Bay

Visitor Mooring Buoys (9)

Visitor Linear Moorage

Bellingham Cruise Terminal

Fairhaven Boat Launch

Pay Box

Fairhaven Marine Industrial Park

Padden Creek Lagoon

To Fairhaven District →

Managed By Bellingham Cruise Terminal (360) 319-9081

Reference only. Not for navigation

boaters to explore the resort, park, and beaches on the west side of Drayton Harbor, and the town of Blaine on the east. The *Plover Beach Gang*, an energetic group of volunteers under the sponsorship of the Whatcom County Historical Museum, restored the historic boat Plover. Built during World War II, this classic, cedar-planked boat is 30 feet in length. Blaine's festivals include the *Peace Arch Celebration* and *Skywater Festival* in June, a *Salmon Bake* and *War Canoe Races* in July, and a *Kite Fly-In* in August.

★ **Blaine Harbor:** {48° 59.30' N, 122° 46' W} Operated by the Port of Bellingham, this facility has moorage, gas, diesel, lubricants, laundry, showers, repairs, waste pump-out and dump. During summer, a passenger ferry connects with Semiahmoo. See our Steering Star description in this chapter. Internet site: www.portofbellingham.com & www.boattravel.com/blaineharbor E-

mail: blaineharbor@portofbellingham.com Mailing address: P O Box 1245, Blaine, Washington 98231. Fax: 360-332-1043. Telephone: 360-647-6176. VHF 16.

★ **Blaine Marina Fuel:** Gas, diesel, oils, water. 360-332-8425.

Semiahmoo Marina: {48° 59.30' N, 122° 46'W} Moorage, gas, diesel, propane, showers, laundry, power, water, provisions, boat yard with 35 ton haul-out. 360-371-0440. VHF 68.

★⚓ **Semiahmoo Park:** Identified by its totem pole, this park is found at the base of Semiahmoo Spit. There is an interpretive center, picnic sites, and a good beach at this site of a 19th century Indian trading post. ▲

Clearing United States Customs: 360-332-6318.

If no answer, call 1-800-562-5943. Summer Hours 7am-8pm. If after hours, stay on your boat.

★ **White Rock, British Columbia (40):** [18421, Canadian 3463] The International Boundary, separating the United States from Canada, passes through Semiahmoo and Boundary Bays. The community of White Rock is located in Semiahmoo Bay, just north of the border. A long T-shaped wharf, over 1,500 feet in length, has floats that are managed by the White Rock Sailing Club. The eastern floats are for two-hour visitor moorage and the western floats are for permanent moorage.

A promenade encourages strolling along the waterfront and among the numerous waterfront shops and restaurants. The White Rock Museum, located near the foot of the pier, features displays and photos of southwestern British Columbia. Another attraction is the Station Art Centre, housed in a restored 1913 BNR Station. There are many year-round activities including the annual *Polar Bear Swim, Mayfair Trade Show* and *Family Fair,* and the *Sea Festival* held during the long weekend in August. White Rock is named for the very large white boulder on the beach, just east of the pier. Visitors disagree about whether the community has a New England or a European atmosphere, but it's true in either case, that it has had great appeal to vacationers as a resort community since the early 1900's.

★ **Clearing Canadian Customs:** When calling customs, two public phones are located on shore, just across the railroad tracks. See Customs information in Important Notices at the beginning of Chapter 8. Telephone: 1-888-226-7277.

★ **Boundary Bay and Crescent Beach (41):** [Canadian 3463] Boundary Bay lies between the white cliffs at the eastern extremity of Point

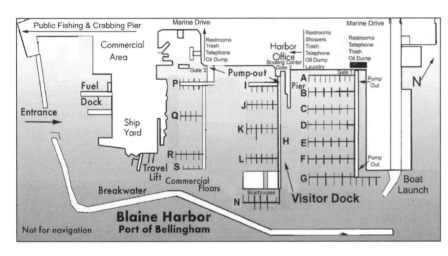

Blaine Harbor
Port of Bellingham
Not for navigation

★ **Blaine Harbor:** Moorage Available: Call 360-647-6176 for more information. Boaters approaching Blaine pass Semiahmoo Spit and then enter Drayton Harbor. The entrance to the harbor is marked by a red triangle to port. Blaine Harbor, a port-operated facility, is at the northeast end of the harbor, past numerous marine repair facilities and floats for commercial craft. The sign also points the way to the transient moorage float. 860-feet of guest moorage is found on the long float directly in front of the office. All moorage is security protected. This is a U.S. Customs port-of-entry. Blaine Harbor is a year-round full service marina. There is a sewage pump-out, sanitary dump, fuel, gas, diesel, 30/50 ampere, 110 volt power, fresh drinking water, showers, and a laundry facility. Vessel repair facilities. Families enjoy visiting this friendly marina. It offers plenty of space to get off the boat and explore neighboring attractions in the town of Blaine. Restaurants, lodging, grocery, chandlery and liquor store are within walking distance. For those who wish to try their luck at the fishing pier, tackle is in stock. In summer, a bicycle and foot passenger ferry connects Blaine Harbor with the Inn at Semiahmoo and other recreational activities. Office hours are Monday through Sunday 8:00 a.m.-5:00 p.m. See map for new harbor layout. **Internet: www.portofbellingham.com & www.portofbellingham.com/blaine.html & www.nwboattravel.com/blaineharbor/ E-mail: blaineharbor@portofbellingham.com Circle #37 on Reader Service Card. Address: 235 Marine Drive, Blaine, Washington 98230. Mailing Address: P O Box 1245 98231. Telephone: 360-647-6176. Fax: 360-332-1043. Monitor VHF 16.**

Roberts and Kwomais Point, 6.6 miles east-northeast. Much of the bay is filled with mud and sand flats. Boundary Bay Regional Park is on the western side of the bay. This region is rich in wildlife and has good fishing grounds. Marsh lands are home to herons, ducks, eagles, and geese. Salmon, steelhead and cutthroat trout are abundant in the rivers which empty into Boundary Bay. Commercial crabbing may be present. Caution advised regarding traps and floats.

The Nicomekl and Serpentine River channels flow through Mud Bay, the northeast part of Boundary Bay. A marked channel leads to Crescent Beach, Blackie's Spit, and Crescent Beach Marina. Navigation is not difficult. Crescent Beach light, a flashing red light in the outer approach to Mud Bay, is shown from a dolphin with a starboard hand daymark. The channel is marked by port and starboard hand daymarks on piles or dolphins. Keep the red triangles to starboard when entering, and the green squares to port. (Red right returning.) Favor the port side because some of the red markers are now on drying sand/mud. If possible, traverse the channel at half tide or better and on an incoming tide. A swimming and sailing area is in the channel. No wakes. A long government wharf, with a 40' side float, extends from shore at the site of Crescent Beach. This residential and resort area has stores and restaurants near the wharf. Day anchorage can be found on the east side of the wharf. Depths are approximately nine feet. The beach is good for swimming and a large municipal park is on shore. Crescent Channel light, 0.4 mile southwest of Blackie's Spit is shown from a dolphin with a starboard hand daymark. Blackie's Spit is a nature park and bird sanctuary with walking trails. After rounding Blackie's Spit and entering the Nicomekl River, a Burlington Northern Railroad Bridge comes into view. Crescent Beach Marina is on the south shore, just past the bridge. This is a swing bridge and when closed, the swing span has a clearance of nine feet at high water. The trestle has a vertical clearance of 12 feet at high water. A height clearance gauge is located on the northwest end of the bridge. The swing span shows a red light when closed, and a green light when open. To have the swing span opened, signal three long blasts on the horn or call Crescent Beach Marina 604-538-9666 at least one hour before arrival time and before 1530 hours. The bridge is manned seven days-a-week from 6:30 a.m. to 10:30 p.m. Pass on the east side of the bridge both coming and going. A speed limit of four knots is posted in the Nicomekl River.

★ **Crescent Beach Marina:** Located in historic Crescent Beach, marina is the Customs port-of-entry. Moorage from 20' - 50' (year round), transient moorage, 15 & 30 amp power, water, fuel-diesel, regular & premium, full chandlery store, washrooms, laundromat, showers, repairs, parts, haul-outs, dry storage compound, launch ramp. Close to shopping, fine dining, golfing. Thirty minutes to Vancouver. Please see Steering Star and Marina Map in Chapter 12. Address: 12555 Crescent Rd, Surrey, B.C. V4A 2V4. Website: www.crescentbeachmarina.com. Telephone: 604-538-9666. Fax: 604-538-7724. VHF 66A.

★ **Point Roberts (42):** [18421] Point Roberts is a peninsula and is an unconnected portion of United States territory, located on the western shore of Boundary Bay. This "dissection" came about because the 49th parallel was used as the boundary between Canada and the United States. Access to this 4.9 square mile peninsula is possible by a 23 mile highway trip from Blaine, or by air to the private airstrip, or by boat to the large marina facility. To get there by land it is necessary to cross the U.S.-Canada border at Blaine, go

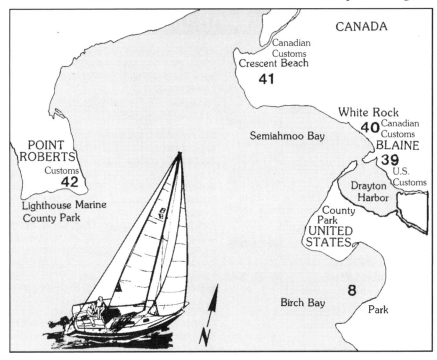

west to Tsawwassen, British Columbia, and then cross the border again. Point Roberts is a United States port-of-entry. A large marina and a repair facility are located here. Lighthouse Marine Park is a stretch of beach that is ideal for beachcombing. A launch ramp is located at the park. For those who enjoy nature walks, the area is rich in wildlife including deer, eagles, herons, raccoons, and other wild animals. The tide at Boundary Bay comes in over a square mile of firm sandbars, making it an ideal walking beach. Panoramic views are of Mount Baker, the Cascades Mountains, San Juan Islands, and Vancouver Island. Restaurants, grocery and liquor store, mobile home and RV parks, a campground, and a post office are also within walking distance of moorage.

★ **Westwind Marine:** {48° 58.3' N, 123° 03.6' W} Located at the Point Roberts Marina. The convenient, well stocked marine store features a large inventory and friendly, knowledgeable staff. The service division, a dealership for Volvo, Mercury/MerCruiser, OMC, Johnson/Evinrude and more, is staffed by factory certified mechanics and uses genuine parts. Full service and do-it-yourself haul-out packages are available with 35 ton Travelift, power washing, and mast tower. Yacht Brokerage on-site. Address: 721 Simundson Drive, Point Roberts, Washington 98281. Telephone: 360-945-5523. Fax: 360-945-5525. E-mail: westwindmarine@dccnet.com

Point Roberts Marina Resort: Permanent and guest moorage, power, gas, diesel, pump-out, propane, repairs, laundry, restaurant, showers, provisions. 35-ton lift, haul-out sling. 360-945-2255. VHF 68.

★⚓ **Lighthouse Marine County Park:** Lighthouse Park lies at the southwest tip of Point Roberts. There are launch ramps with floats, parking for trailers, stoves, picnic shelters, fire pits, gravel beach, and view tower. Look for unusual black rocks that are found here and the exhibit featuring whales. 360-733-2900, 360-945-4911. ⚓⛱

Mount Baker viewed from James Island   *Carl & Gloria Tenning Photo*

Essential Supplies & Services

AIR TRANSPORTATION
Seattle Seaplanes 1-800-637-5553

AMBULANCES 911

BOOKS / BOOK STORES
The Marine Atlas. 541-593-6396

BUS TRANSPORTATION
Bellingham. 360-733-5251
Greyline 1-800-426-7532
Mount Vernon 360-336-5111
Skagit Transit 360-757-4433, 360-299-2424
Whatcom County. 360-676-RIDE

CANVAS/UPHOLSTERY
L & T Canvas . . . . La Conner. 360-466-3295

CNG CYLINDERS
Boaters Discount: LaConner 360-466-3540
Penmar Marine at Skyline. . . . . . 360-293-5134 VHF 16

COAST GUARD
VHF 16, 21, 22, CB 09
Bellingham. 360-734-1692

CUSTOMS/BORDER PROTECTION
Due to new Department of Homeland Security regula-
tions, call ahead for latest customs information.
. . . . 1-800-562-5943 8:00 a.m.-10:00 p.m.
Anacortes 360-293-2331
Bellingham. 360-734-5463
Peace Arch 360-332-7650
Crescent Beach, B.C. 1-888-226-7277
Point Roberts 360-945-2314

FERRY INFORMATION
Guemes Island. 360-293-6356
Lummi Island 360-676-6759
Washington State. 1-800-843-3779

FUELS
Bellingham Harbor Marine: Gas, Diesel. . 360-734-1710
Blaine: Gas, Diesel. 360-332-8425
CATeam Marine Assistance (Fuel Delivery) . 360-378-9636
Cap Sante Marine: Anacortes. Gas, Diesel.
. . . . 360-293-3145
Crescent Beach Marina . . . 604-538-9666 VHF 66A
Deception Pass: Gas, Diesel 360-675-5411 VHF 16
Fisherman's Cove: Gooseberry Pt. Gas . . 360-758-2450
Hilton Harbor: Bellingham. Gas. 360-733-1110
La Conner Landing: Gas, Diesel 360-466-4478
La Conner Marina: Gas, Diesel . 360-466-3118 VHF 66A
Marine Service Center - Anacortes: Gas, Diesel.
. . . . 360-293-8200
Penmar Marine at Skyline. . . . . . 360-293-5134 VHF 16
Point Roberts Marina: Gas, Diesel. 360-945-2255
Semiahmoo Marina: Gas, Diesel. 360-371-0440 VHF 68
Westwind Marine: Point Roberts . . . 360-945-5523

HOSPITALS
Anacortes 360-299-1300
Bellingham. 360-734-5400
Mount Vernon 360-424-4111

INSURANCE
Boat Insurance Agency 206-285-1350
Or Call 1-800-828-2446

BORDER PROTECTION IMMI-GRATION OFFICES (I-68 form)
Bellingham: 104 West Magnolia, Room 201 (Post Office
Box 2055), Bellingham, WA 98227 . . . 360-676-8411

Blaine: U.S. Immigration Service, Peace Arch, 100
Peace Portal Drive, Blaine, WA 98230 . 360-332-8511
Blaine: Pacific Highway Station, 9950 Pacific Highway,
Blaine, WA 98230. 360-332-6091
Point Roberts: U.S. Immigration Service, 50 Tyee Drive,
Point Roberts, WA 98281 360-945-5211

MARINAS / MOORAGE FLOATS
Blaine Harbor. . . . . 360-647-6176 VHF 16
Cap Sante Boat Haven: Anacortes.
. . . . 360-293-0694 VHF 66
Crescent Beach Marina . . . 604-538-9666 VHF 66A
Deception Pass Marina . . . . 360-675-5411 VHF 16
Deception Pass State Park: Sharp Cove
Fairhaven Visitor Moorage . 360-676-2542 VHF 16
La Conner Marina. . . . . 360-466-3118 VHF 66A
Penmar Marine at Skyline. . . . . 360-293-5134 VHF 16
Point Roberts Marina 360-945-2255
Semiahmoo Marina. . . . . 360-371-0440 VHF 68
Squalicum Harbor . . . . 360-676-2542 VHF 16

MARINE SUPPLY STORES
Boater's Discount: La Conner 800-488-0245
Cap Sante Marine: Anacortes 360-293-3145
Marine Supply & Hardware: Anacortes
. . . . 360-293-3014
Penmar Marine at Skyline. . . . . 360-293-5134 VHF 16
West Marine: Anacortes 360-293-4262
Westwind Marine: Point Roberts . . . 360-945-5523

PARKS
Department of Natural Resources 360-856-3500
. . . . 1-800-527-3305
Washington State 360-902-8444
Washington Camping Reservations . . . 1-888-226-7688

POISON INFO 1-800-222-1222

PROPANE
Boater's Discount: La Conner 800-488-0245
Cap Sante Marine: Anacortes . 360-293-3145 VHF 16
Deception Pass Marina . . . . 360-675-5411 VHF 16
La Conner Marina. . . . . 360-466-3118 VHF 66
Marine Service Center: Anacortes 360-293-8200
Penmar Marine Co. at Skyline. . . 360-293-5134 VHF 16
Point Roberts Marina 360-945-2255
Semiahmoo Marina. . . . . 360-371-0440 VHF 68
Squalicum Harbor . . . . 360-676-2542 VHF 16

RAMPS / HAUL-OUTS
Anacortes Marina 360-293-4543
Bayview State Park: Padilla Bay
Berentsen Bridge: Swinomish Channel
Blaine Harbor. . . . . 360-647-6176 VHF 16
Blaine: Milhollin Road
Cap Sante Marine: Anacortes 360-293-3145
Cap Sante Marine-South Yard 360-293-3732
Crescent Beach: Boundary Bay . . . 604-538-9666
Deception Pass Marina . . . . 360-675-5411 VHF 16
Deception Pass State Park: Bowman Bay, Cornet Bay
Fisherman's Cove: Gooseberry Pt 360-758-2450
La Conner Marina. . . . . 360-466-3118 VHF 66A
Larrabee State Park: Bellingham
Lighthouse Marine Park: Point Roberts
Lovric's Sea Craft 360-293-2042
Penmar Marine at Skyline. . . . . 360-293-5134 VHF 16
Pioneer Point, San Juan Marine: LaConner . . . .
. . . . 360-466-1314 VHF 68
Point Roberts Marina 360-945-2255
Rainbow Bridge: Swinomish Channel
Semiahmoo Marina: Blaine. . . . . 360-371-0440 VHF 68
Squalicum Harbor . . . . 360-676-2542 VHF 16

Twin Bridges Marina: Swinomish Channel . 360-466-1443
Washington Park: Anacortes
Westwind Marine: Point Roberts . . . 360-945-5523

RECOMPRESSION CHAMBER
Virginia Mason 206-583-6433

RED TIDE HOT-LINE 1-800-562-5632

REPAIRS & SERVICE
Blaine Harbor. . . . . 360-647-6176 VHF 16
Blaine Marine Services 360-332-3324
Cap Sante Marine: Anacortes 360-293-3145
Cap Sante Marine South Yard 360-293-3732
CATeam Marine Assistance 360-378-9636
Crescent Beach Marina . . . . 604-538-9666 VHF 66
Deception Pass Marina . . . . 360-675-5411 VHF 16
L & T Canvas: La Conner 360-466-3295
La Conner Marina . . . . 360-466-3118 VHF 66
La Conner Maritime Services 360-466-3629
Lovric's Sea Craft: Anacortes 360-293-2042
Marine ServiCenter, Anacortes 360-293-8200
North Harbor Diesel: Anacortes. 360-293-5551
Penmar Marine at Skyline. . . . . 360-293-5134 VHF 16
Semiahmoo Marina . . . . 360-371-0440 VHF 68A
Squalicum Harbor . . . . 360-676-2542 VHF 16
Westwind Marine: Point Roberts . . . 360-945-5523

SEWAGE DISPOSALS
Blaine Harbor: Pump, Dump 360-647-6176
Cap Sante Boat Haven: Pump, Dump 360-293-0694
Deception Pass State Park: Cornet Bay. . . Pump, Dump
Deception Pass State Park: Sharpe Cove. Dump
La Conner Marina: Pump. 360-466-3118
La Conner Public Guest Dock
Marine Service Center: Pump 360-293-8200
Penmar Marine/Skyline: Pump 360-293-5134
Point Roberts Marina: Pump, Dump 360-945-2255
Semiahmoo Marina: Pump, Dump 360-371-0440
Squalicum Harbor: Pump, Dump . . . 360-676-2542

SHELLFISH HOTLINE 360-796-3215
For local area closures/information, call County Health Depts.:
Skagit County Health Dept. 360-336-9380
Whatcom County Health Dept 360-676-6724

SPORTFISHING 360-902-2500

TAXIS & RENTAL CARS
Anacortes 360-293-3979
Bellingham. 360-734-8294, 1-800-281-5430

TOWING
C-TOW. 1-888-354-5554
CATeam Marine Assistance 360-378-9636
VESSEL ASSIST   Anacortes. 360-675-7900
Friday Harbor 360-378-4588

VHF MARINE OPERATOR
Whidbey Island: 87
Note: MariTel has shut down all other Washington State
VHF Marine Operator channels until further notice.

VISITOR INFORMATION
Anacortes 360-293-3832, 360-293-7911
Bellingham C of C 360-734-1330
Bellingham-Whatcom 360-671-3990
Blaine Visitors Bureau 1-800-624-3555
La Conner 360-466-4778, 1-888-642-9284
Mount Vernon 360-428-8547

WEATHER VHF
Seattle: WX-1
Victoria: WX-3

Chapter 7:

San Juan Islands

Blakeley, Decatur, Lopez, Shaw, Orcas, San Juan, Stuart, Waldron, Patos, Sucia, Matia, Barnes, & Clark Islands.

Symbols

[   ]: Numbers between [ ] are chart numbers.

{   }: Numbers & letters between { } are waypoints.

⚓: Park, 🚤: Boat Launch, ▲: Campgrounds, 🥾: Hiking Trails, 🌲: Picnic Area, 🚲: Biking

---

★ **Important Notice:** See "Important Notices" between Chapters 7 and 8 in this guide for specific information on boating related topics such as: Canadian & U.S. Customs, boating safety and security, navigation, weather, U.S. & Canadian Coast Guard, U.S & Canadian marine radio use, Vessel Traffic Service and traffic separation plans, security zones, and internet access. Due to new Department of Homeland Security regulations, call ahead for latest customs information and/or see Northwest Boat Travel On-line, www.nwboat.com.

National Wildlife Refuges: Areas designated on charts by the initials NWR are National Wildlife Refuge lands. These are closed to the public to protect breeding colonies of seabirds, endangered and threatened species, and marine mammals. Boaters are requested to stay at least 200 yards away from these rocks and islands.

Unnamed Rocks State Parks: Several rocks and islets in the San Juan archipelago are designated as state park properties, open for visitors. These are often unnamed and are known by a specific number. Such areas are undeveloped and are for day use only. No fires or overnight camping. Boaters are asked to take any garbage with them, and to leave them in a pristine condition.

Chart List

NOAA Charts:

18400, 18421, 18423, 18429-34

Canadian Hydrographic Charts:

3462

Marine Atlas (2005 ed.):

Pages 7-9, 12

San Juan Islands

[18421, 18423, 18429, 18430, 18431, 18432, 18433, 18434, Canadian 3462]

★ **The San Juan Islands:** First surveyed into townships in 1874, as many as 750 reefs, islets, and rocks can be seen at a minus tide, giving ample reason for more than a casual look at the charts. The commonly accepted number of islands is 457, with approximately 175 being of sufficient size to have been named. The San Juan Archipelago is a prized destination, not only for the residents, but also for boaters and other visitors. Sometimes called the *Magic Islands*, the San Juan Islands do seem to have mystical powers, luring thousands of visitors each year from all over the world. This is a vacationer's paradise and boater's dream come true. In truth, these islands have everything a water lover could want. There are quiet bays with splendid and dependable anchorages, marine parks with docks and facilities, picturesque towns with friendly people and shops, almost inexhaustible beds of shellfish, favored salmon fishing holes, a number of resorts, and an abundance of restaurants and inns. Major communities are found at Eastsound on Orcas Island, and on San Juan Island at Friday Harbor,

the county seat of San Juan County. There is ferry service to the four major islands.

The waters of the San Juan Islands embrace the passages and bays north of the east end of the Strait of Juan de Fuca, and are bounded on the west by Haro Strait and on the north by Boundary Pass. This area is sometimes referred to as *Washington Sound*. The International Boundary line, which separates Canada from the United States, runs through Boundary Pass and Haro Strait. Tidal currents set north in Haro Strait and Boundary Pass, and ebb to the south with a velocity of one to two knots.

These waterways are used extensively by pleasure craft, ferries, fishing boats, as well as commercial ocean going vessels. Recreational boats abound in June, July, August, and September, but are not totally missing in any month of the year. Ferries run regular trips from Anacortes through Thatcher Pass, Harney Channel, Wasp Passage, San Juan Channel, Spieden Channel, and across Haro Strait to Sidney, British Columbia. Ferry landings are at Upright Head on Lopez Island, at the east entrance to Shaw Island's Blind Bay, at Orcas, on the southern shore of Orcas Island, and at Friday Harbor on San Juan Island.

Oceangoing vessels normally use Haro and Rosario Straits and do not traverse the channels

San Juan Islands   *Northwest Air Photo*

Fisherman Bay Entrance Channel *(For orientation only, not for navigation)*   Northwest Air Photo

and passes through the islands. Sailing craft, without motors, should not attempt the passages against the current, unless the wind is fresh. A reliable auxiliary engine for sailboats is a necessity in this area. During fishing season, purse seiners and gill netters may be found, especially in the vicinity of the Salmon Banks, south of San Juan Island. There are several marina facilities and hundreds of anchorages. When anchoring, boaters are cautioned to watch for signs posted on shore, and notations on charts, indicating the placement of underwater cables.

For bird-watchers, more than 80 of the islands, rocks, reefs, and islets have been removed from private ownership to form the San Juan Islands National Wildlife Refuge. Those wishing to identify or count the tufted puffins, cormorants, glaucous winged gulls, and eagles can do so to their heart's content. Except for Alaska, the San Juan Islands have the largest concentration of nesting bald eagles in the nation. In the summer, golden eagles join the bald eagles. There are also harbor seals, porpoises, and whales. For information, map, and regulations write Wildlife Refuge, c/o Washington Maritime NWR Complex, 33 S. Barr Road, Port Angeles, WA 98362. 360-457-8451.

★⚓ **James Island Marine State Park (1):** This 113 acre hourglass-shaped island has back-to-back bays on the southwest and northeast sides. The western bay faces Decatur Head and is the most popular. There is a dock large enough for four medium-sized boats. The floats are in place year around. Moorage fees are charged all year. The bottom is rock and gravel making anchoring difficult. At times a few state park mooring buoys may be present. Strong currents often swirl through the narrow passage between the island and Decatur. There are campsites with tables and cooking facilities. Designated as a site on the Cascadia Marine Trail, a group camp area and tent sites are at the south end of the southwestern bay. No fresh water is available in this tent camping area. On the opposite side of the island, the bay on the northeast side has as many as five mooring buoys. Open to the north and northeast, it gets wave action from the wakes of passing boats, and less shelter from winds. Gravel beaches on both sides of the island make it possible to

beach small boats. If the dock and buoys are full, overnight anchorage is possible opposite James Island, along the Decatur Island shore, along the curving beach adjacent to Decatur Head. Good fishing can be found along the Decatur Island shore in Thatcher Pass and near James Island. ⚓🍴🧍

Walk-around: Several trails offer good hiking and views from the 200-foot-high hills. Vine maples regally arch the trail.

Decatur Island

[18421, 18423, 18429, Canadian 3462]

★ **Sylvan Cove (2):** When heading west in Thatcher Pass and approaching this bay, caution advised regarding a reef known as Lawson Rock. Marked by a day beacon, this reef is off the Decatur Island shore and is longer than might be obvious. Sylvan Cove was known as San Elmo for many years. Boaters visited in the 40's-50's to enjoy chicken dinners at the farmhouse at the head. Today it is the site of a private development. The dock is private. The view from this bay is a changing scene of passing vessels and a background of radiant sunsets. Open to the northwest, but good protection from southeasterly winds. Depths in most of the bay are about 20 feet. Limited anchorage is possible.

★ **Brigantine Bay (3):** There is good anchorage with protection from northern winds. Anchor close to the beach in about 15 feet of water. This is an attractive half-moon shaped indentation with a private, gravel beach on the southwest shore of Decatur, opposite Trump Island. Shrimping is possible southwest of Trump Island near the Lopez shore in 20 fathoms.

★ **Center Island & Reads Bay (4):** Anchorage, offshore from this private island, is possible in the northern part of Reads Bay, south of Center Island and north of Ram Island, in the passage between Decatur and Center Islands. Note charted hazards.

Blakely Island

[18421, 18430, Canadian 3462]

★ **Behind Armitage Island (5):** Off Thatcher Pass, the waters between Armitage Island and the southeastern tip of Blakely offer shelter. Limited anchorage is possible. Cruise around the bay while checking the depth sounder for suitable depths. There are several private buoys and shallow areas. Both Armitage and Blakely Islands are private. No shore access.

★ **Thatcher Bay (6):** In the spring, a visible waterfall from Spencer Lake marks this wide bay on the west side of Blakely Island. Temporary anchorage is recommended because it is exposed to boat wakes and both southwest and westerly winds. The 12-15 foot depths are fairly consistent. Watch for submerged pilings along the north shore.

★ **Blakely Harbor (7):** This harbor is located off the west end of Peavine Pass. The entrance channel is narrow and sometimes busy with local traffic. Tidal currents can affect maneuvering.

Blakely Island Marina: Guest moorage, gas, diesel, 30 ampere power, water, showers, laundry, provisions, picnic shelter. Call ahead as may be closing in 2006. 360-375-6121. VHF 66A.

Lopez Island

[18421, 18423, 18429, Canadian 3462]

★ **Hunter Bay (8):** Fairly even depths, a mud bottom, protection from all but north winds, and plenty of room to swing, make this an excellent anchorage. The beach is posted and there is no shore access. A day-use county dock and launching ramp are near the tip of the peninsula that separates Hunter Bay from Mud Bay.

★ **Mud Bay (8):** Mud Bay has drying flats, however anchorage is possible in the northern portion. Open to winds. Note a rock off the eastern shore, well into the bay. Mud Bay Park, with state owned beach and tidelands, is on the southeastern shore. Uplands are private. A launching ramp is on the northeast shore. In 1893, there was a store and post office at Mud Bay.

Lopez Pass (9): See tables for Rosario Strait. This pass connects Lopez Sound with Rosario Strait. A flashing light is on Decatur at the Rosario Strait side of the pass. Lopez Pass is deep with no charted hazards. A tombolo of land extending from Decatur and three islets border the pass opposite Lopez Island. The three islets are Ram, Cayou, and Rim. Passage is between Decatur and Rim or between Lopez and Ram. When rounding Ram, give plenty of berth to the charted, kelp-marked rock.

★ **Watmough Bay (10):** A steep-sided bay, this is protected on the south by Watmough Head and gives good shelter in westerly winds. The bottom shoals quickly before the gravel beach at the head. Tricky, overnight anchorage is possible on a rock bottom in about 15 feet of water. The beach is a good spot for an afternoon picnic. A few walking trails allow for exploration.

★ **Southern Lopez Island:** Rainfall is less on this wind-swept shore, because it is in the lee of the Olympic Rain Shadow. Cactus grow in profusion. Protected anchorage (exposed to southerlies) is possible in several bays. These include McArdle Bay, Hughes Bay, Aleck Bay, and MacKaye Harbor.

★ **McArdle Bay (11):** When approaching from Point Colville, a picturesque, cliff-lined passage between Castle Island and Lopez Island leads to this bay. Private homes look down from the hills to the basin. Open to the Strait of Juan de Fuca and to southwest winds. There is a charted rock and marsh areas are at both ends of the bay. The bottom is good holding mud. Anchoring depths are 25-35 feet.

Hughes Bay (12): Open to southerly winds, an islet to port upon entry has some protection. Anchor far into the bay.

★ **Aleck Bay (13):** The hills which separate Aleck Bay and Barlow Bay are low and do not

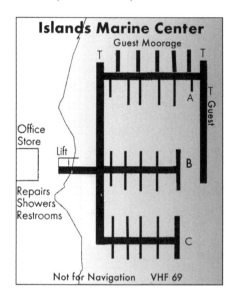

Islands Marine Center
Guest Moorage
A
Guest
Office
Store
Lift
B
Repairs
Showers
Restrooms
C
Not for Navigation   VHF 69

offer much protection from west winds. The bay is completely open to the east. The bottom is good holding mud. Favored anchorage is off the southern shore.

Outer Bay: Outer Bay lies between Iceberg Point and Johns Point. Look for the large rock that is directly opposite Agate Beach Park. This small county park is for day-use only. It provides a beautiful beach, pit toilets, picnic facilities, and sensational views of the cormorants and puffins which nest offshore on nearby rocks. There are rocks, but, in season, kelp marks many of them. Temporary anchoring on a rock bottom is possible only in settled weather. Private property borders the park.

★⚓ **Iceberg Island State Park:** Located in Outer Bay, this undeveloped island is open for day use only. Anchorage possible. No fires or overnight camping.

Davis Bay: This wide bay offers temporary anchorage only, with protection from north winds. Open to Cattle Pass currents and conditions on the Strait of Juan de Fuca. Avoid the rocky areas north of Buck Island and off the western shore. The indentations on the eastern shore are drying flats. Stay in the center in approximately 25' of water. Hard bottom, make sure anchor is hooked.

★ **MacKaye Harbor (14):** [18429] For years, Richardson, located near Charles Island at the western entrance to the harbor, was the site of an old-fashioned general store which was destroyed by fire. There is a commercial fuel facility. This spot, named for the island's first settler, was a major port for steamship travel in the early 1900's. Good anchorage is found in the bays next to the old store site. Avoid rocks near the entrance to

Jones Bay. The harbor is large with good anchorage in several spots, especially at the eastern end. Barlow Bay, the southern portion, is shallow and has private docks.

Richardson Fuel Dock: Gas, diesel. 360-468-2275.

Walk-around: Anchor at the eastern end and row ashore. Walk up to MacKaye Harbor Road and walk south toward Outer Bay and Agate Beach Park.

★ **Fisherman Bay (15):** [18434] Visitors will find moorage, anchorage, repairs, and restaurants in this long indentation into the western shore of Lopez Island. If approaching from the north, along the Lopez Island shore, give the shore a wide berth to avoid rocks. Most hazardous is a drying rock about three quarters of a mile north of the entrance to the bay. If approaching from the west, give the sand spit a wide berth. Entry into the bay is not difficult. Stay in the narrow, marked channel. If there is any question about adequate depths due to an extreme low tide, enter on an incoming tide. Entry is on a line which divides the approach bay about in half and heads toward the channel and past the end of the spit guarding the entrance. Entry channel markers are on concrete pillars and continue after passing the spit. Sandbars and shallows lie outside these markers. The first marker to starboard is red and white checkerboard. Stay close to all markers and keep in a straight line between them down the center of the channel (red right returning). Keep green (1,5,7) to port. Currents may be strong in this corridor. While transiting this channel, look to port to see the village of Lopez. Winds from the southwest can enter. If anchored, allow adequate room to swing. A low wake maximum speed of six knots is enforced in Fisherman Bay.

★ **Islands Marine Center:** Islands Marine Center is the first marina on the left once you have entered Fisherman Bay. It is recommended that you reference a chart before entering the bay, and be aware that, at times, strong currents and winds may affect docking. This marina and repair facility is regarded as one of the finest in

the San Juan Islands. Permanent, daily, and temporary moorage is available on modern floats. Water, 30 amp power, and a pump-out are accessible. Yacht club rendezvous can be accommodated on the front lawn with barbecue pit and tents upon request. Two rental apartments, with kitchens, bath, and beautiful views are available at modest rates. The marine store and service shop are across the street from moorage. Bathrooms with coin-operated showers, limited garbage deposit, and recycling available. A fuel dock is located next door. The fully-stocked marine chandlery contains hardware, paint and supplies, fishing tackle, bait, ice, clothing, charts, gifts, electronics, and a complete NAPA auto parts store. Authorized boat dealers for Ocean Sport Boats, Pursuit, Avon, Duroboat, and authorized sales and service for Yamaha, OMC, Volvo Penta, and MerCruiser. Factory-trained technicians handle major to minor repairs, rigging, electronic installations, bottom painting and detailing. Haul-outs to 15 tons and a 13' beam, may depend on tides. Dry storage available for short or long term. Lopez Village is a short walk and offers many shops, grocery store, and liquor store. The village hosts a Farmer's Market on Saturdays. Other restaurants, bike, and kayak rentals nearby. The Washington State ferry dock is 4.5 miles from the marina. Kenmore Air float planes stop next door. **Websites: www.islandsmarinecenter.com and www.boattravel.com/islandsmarine Email: imc@rockisland.com and imcservice@rockisland.com Address: 2793 Fisherman Bay Road, Post Office Box 88, Lopez, Washington 98261. Fax: 360-468-2283. Telephone: 360-468-3377. VHF 69.**

Several points of interest are accessible from moorage. First is the town of Lopez, within walking distance (see Walk-Around below). Taxi service is also available on the island. Several bed and breakfast inns and a golf course are nearby. Only four and one/half miles from Fisherman Bay is the Washington State ferry landing at Upright Head. Daily floatplane flights connect with other islands and major cities. An airport is also located on the island.

★ **Galley Restaurant & Lounge:** Located on Fisherman Bay, the Galley Restaurant has been a northwest destination since 1971. The beautiful, newly rebuilt dock has 14 boat slips, combining long term, short term, and guest moorage. There are also two mooring buoys and a dinghy dock available to Galley guests. Call ahead for availability. Ownership of the Galley changed in 2001, and is now operated by Jeff and Kim Nichols, who operated the beloved New Bay Cafe in Lopez Village from 1977 to 1989. With a fabulous view of sunsets over Fisherman Bay, Galley's dining room is totally non-smoking. Breakfast, lunch, dinner, and a great kid's menu are available year round, with an emphasis on fresh and local. Fresh seafood and natural beef are menu features, (you've probably heard of our grilled halibut tacos with mango salsa...) and we have a great selection of fine beers, wines, and cocktails. The main dining room can accommodate groups of eighty. Contact us with your group's needs. Cocktail Lounge with pool, games, six beers on tap, great company, and occasional live entertainment. Visa and Mastercard.   See our advertisement in this chapter. Email: galley@rockisland.com. Internet: www.rockisland.com/~galley. Mailing Address: 3365 Fisherman Bay Road, Lopez Island, Washington 98261. Fax: 360-468-2221. Telephone: 360-468-2713.

Cruising the San Juans   *VPLLC Staff*

★ **Islands Marine Center:** {48° 31.5' N, 122° 55.2' W} Founded in 1972 by Ron and Jennifer Meng. Complete repair facility with permanent, daily, and temporary moorage. Water, showers, ice, pump-out. Marine parts store, chandlery, and NAPA auto parts store. Haul-outs, dry storage. Authorized boat dealer for Ocean Sport Boats, Pursuit, Avon, Duroboat, and authorized sales and service for Yamaha, OMC, VolvoPenta, and MerCruiser. See our Steering Star description in this chapter. Websites: www.islandsmarinecenter.com and www.boat-travel.com/islandsmarine Email: imc@rock-island.com and imcservice@rockisland.com. Address: 2793 Fisherman Bay Road, Post Office Box 88, Lopez, Washington 98261. Fax: 360-468-2283. Telephone: 360-468-3377. VHF 69.

★ **Lopez Islander Bay Resort & Marina:** {48° 31.5' N, 122° 55.2'W} The Islander espresso bar offers fresh baked cinnamon rolls each morning. Guest moorage at floats, 30 and 50 ampere power, water, restrooms, showers, laundry and a dock store with provisions. Gas and diesel are available at the fuel float located at the north end of the 60 berth marina. Propane is accessible on the island. The Islander Waterfront Restaurant with deck for outdoor seasonal dining and Bay Cocktail Lounge with live music on summer weekends is located at the head of the pier.   The extensive menu features seafood, steaks, gourmet burgers, and signature clam chowder. Banquet facilities for group functions. Amenities for resort guests include barbeque and picnic area, a jacuzzi hot tub, seasonally heated swimming pool, and scenic bay view accommodations.   RV and camping sites are available onsite. Bicycle and kayak rentals, tennis courts and Lopez Golf Course add to the fun. Arrive by Washington State Ferry from Anacortes to Lopez Island or by Kenmore Air Services connecting the resort with Seattle via float plane. Complimentary guest shuttle service from the ferry landing or Lopez airport provided. Yacht clubs and rendezvous welcome. Marina, restaurant, bar and hotel open all year. See our Steering Star description in this chapter. Internet: www.lopezislander.com & www.boat-

travel.com/lopezislander. Email: desk@lopezislander.com Address: Fisherman Bay Road, P.O. Box 459, Lopez, WA 98261. Telephone: 360-468-2233. VHF 78.

Walk-around: Walks are possible along the main road which skirts the bay. One walk leads south to a restaurant and lounge, the other north, to the Village of Lopez, with shops and restaurants. The road meanders through pasture land, passing the library and a picturesque church.

★ **Lopez Village:** No floats give direct access to town. It is, however, an interesting and easy walk from moorages at Islands Marine Center or Lopez Islander Resort in Fisherman Bay. The townsite was chosen by early settler and Indian fighter, H.E. Hutchenson. There are several specialty shops, restaurants, bakery, galleries, hardware, pharmacy, liquor store, and grocery.

★ **Upright Channel Recreation Area:** This Department of Natural Resources recreation area is located on the north side of Flat Point. It has a day-use picnic area and mooring buoys. The 20 acre site allows access to about three miles of public beach. Surrounding land is private. The uplands site is open May-September only. 360-856-3500.

★▲ **Odlin Park (16):** This popular 82 acre park is located on the west side of Lopez, between Flat Point and Upright Head. There is a small float for shore access and a launching ramp. Anchorage off the park is possible. A sand and mud beach extends into tide flats off shore. Campsites, picnic tables, plentiful fresh water, and toilets. Children often enjoy playing on unusual playground structures which include a cannon and an old beached boat.⊓▲

★ **Shoal Bay (17):** Located between Upright Head and Humphrey Head, shoals extend off the shore. Anchorage is possible in depths of 10-25 feet. Open to north winds. A small private marina and aquaculture operations are located near the low-land which adjoins Humphrey Head. Tidelands are private. No facilities for transient boaters.

★ **Swift's Bay (18):** Although wide and open to ferry wakes and north winds, this bay does offer anchorage. Enter at a lower tide to identify rocks. Leo Reef and Flower Island are opposite the head. Rocky patches, barely covered at high tide, are off Flower Island on a line to the reef. Anchorage is possible in 12-20 foot depths. The shore shoals for some distance. Private homes overlook the bay. A lagoon at Swift's Bay was once the site of Port Stanley, a thriving town until the depression of 1893.

★▲ **Spencer Spit Marine State Park (19):** Encompassing a large sand and gravel spit and a lagoon on the eastern side of Lopez Island, this park contains 130 acres. Sufficient depths permit passage between Frost Island and the spit at any tide. Stay close to Frost Island. Mooring buoys border both sides of the spit. Because of the park's popularity, it is best to arrive earlier in the day in order to find an empty buoy. Park buoys are often empty between 10:30 a.m. and noon, after the previous night's boats have departed and before new occupants arrive for the next night. Anchorage is excellent on both sides of the spit. Often, wind direction is the deciding factor. No dock. Campgrounds are accessible for car and bike travelers. Spencer Spit is also a member of the Cascadia Marine Trail and, as such, has one group camp area and tent sites on the south side of the hill directly west of the spit. Closed for winter. There are trails, shelters, and fire rings. Water is available, however it is scarce. Swimming in the shallow, sun-warmed waters along the spit is a popular activity. A log cabin, vintage 1913, serves as a picnic shelter. Migratory waterfowl inhabit this lagoon refuge in season. Great blue herons, Canada geese and kingfishers are familiar sights. Rabbits, deer, and raccoons frequent the area. The area was homesteaded in 1860 by the Troxell family and, in 1869, was sold to the Spencer family. It became a park in 1967. 360-468-2251, 360-902-8844. ▲⊓

Walk-around: Hiking trails climb the banks and edge the lagoon.

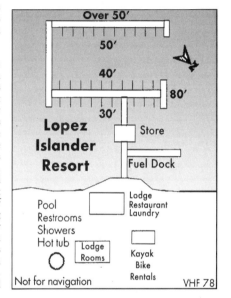

★ **Lopez Islander Bay Resort and Marina:** Family owned and operated for eight years. Boating visitors moor at modern concrete floats equipped with 30 and 50 ampere power and water. Gas and diesel are available at the fuel float located at the north end of the 60 berth marina. Propane is accessible on the island. Facilities include restrooms, showers, laundry and a dock store with provisions and condiments. The lodge building, at the head of the pier, includes the resort lobby, restaurant, and Bay Lounge, with live music on summer weekends. Enjoy seafood, steaks, gourmet burgers, and the world famous fish and chips. A large deck provides summertime waterfront dining with views of sunsets reflecting in the waters of Fisherman Bay. Banquet facilities are available as are meeting rooms to accommodate large groups and rendezvous. A barbecue and picnic area is provided for resort guests. The waterview lodging units have been upgraded. In the center of the complex, the pool pavilion contains a Jacuzzi hot tub and a seasonally heated swimming pool. Known as the bicycle island of the San Juans, bicycle rentals are available as are Kayak rentals for those who want to enjoy the serenity of a quiet time exploring the bay. Other attractions include RV and camping sites, and a nearby golf course. A large grocery store, bakery, pharmacy, galleries, and liquor store are located in the nearby village of Lopez. The resort's 15 acres of pastoral grounds are perfect for evening walks in search of the resident deer.  By land, easy access is by Washington State ferry from Anacortes. Kenmore Air Services connects the resort with Seattle via float plane. Yacht Clubs and rendezvous accommodated. Call ahead for reservations. Marina, restaurant and motel open all year. **Internet: http:// lopezislander.com & www.boattravel.com/lopezislander/ Email: bill@lopezislander.com Address: Fisherman Bay Road, Post Office Box 459, Lopez, Washington 98261. Fax: 360-468-3382. Telephone: 360-468-2233. VHF 78.**

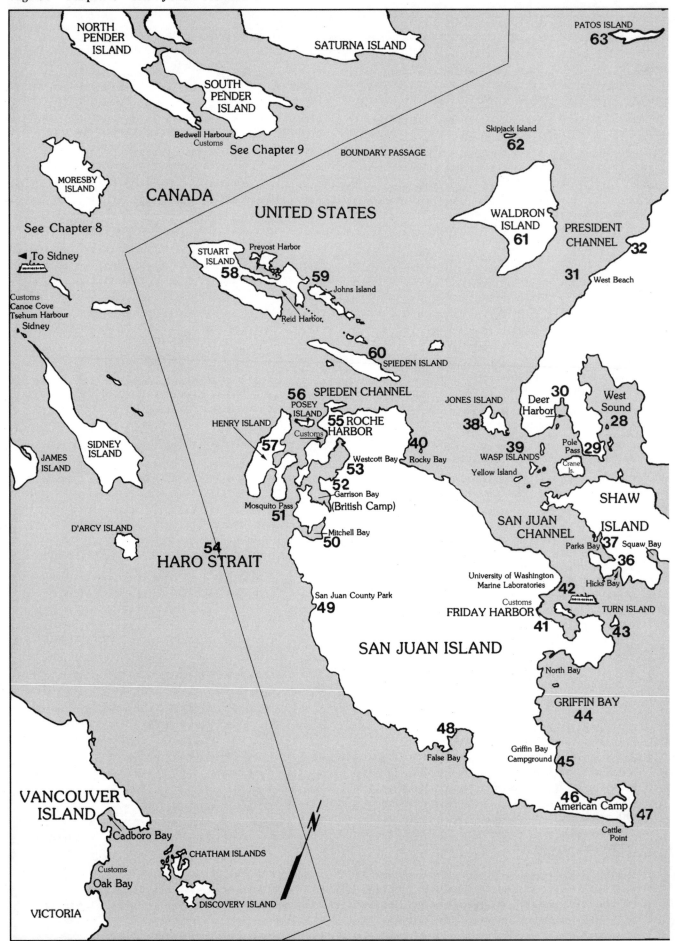

NORTH
PENDER
ISLAND

SOUTH
PENDER
ISLAND

SATURNA ISLAND

PATOS ISLAND
63

Bedwell Harbour
Customs   See Chapter 9

Skipjack Island
62

BOUNDARY PASSAGE

MORESBY
ISLAND

CANADA

UNITED STATES

WALDRON
ISLAND
61

PRESIDENT
CHANNEL

See Chapter 8

To Sidney

STUART
ISLAND   Prevost Harbor
58   59

Johns Island

31   32

West Beach

Customs
Canoe Cove
Tsehum Harbour
Sidney

Reid Harbor

Deer
Harbor   30

West
Sound
28

SPIEDEN ISLAND
60

JONES ISLAND

56   SPIEDEN CHANNEL
POSEY
ISLAND
55 ROCHE
HARBOR
Customs
38

39
WASP ISLANDS
Yellow Island

Pole
Pass
29

Crane
Is.

HENRY ISLAND
57

Westcott Bay   40
53   Rocky Bay

JAMES
ISLAND

SIDNEY
ISLAND

52
Garrison Bay
(British Camp)

SHAW
ISLAND
37   Squaw Bay
36

SAN JUAN
CHANNEL

D'ARCY ISLAND

Mosquito Pass
51

Mitchell Bay
50

Parks Bay
Hicks Bay

54
HARO STRAIT

University of Washington
Marine Laboratories

42

TURN ISLAND

Customs
FRIDAY HARBOR
41   43

San Juan County Park
49

SAN JUAN ISLAND

North Bay

GRIFFIN BAY
44

48
False Bay

Griffin Bay
Campground   45

VANCOUVER
ISLAND

Cadboro Bay

N

46
American Camp   47

Cattle
Point

Customs
Oak Bay

CHATHAM ISLANDS

VICTORIA

DISCOVERY ISLAND

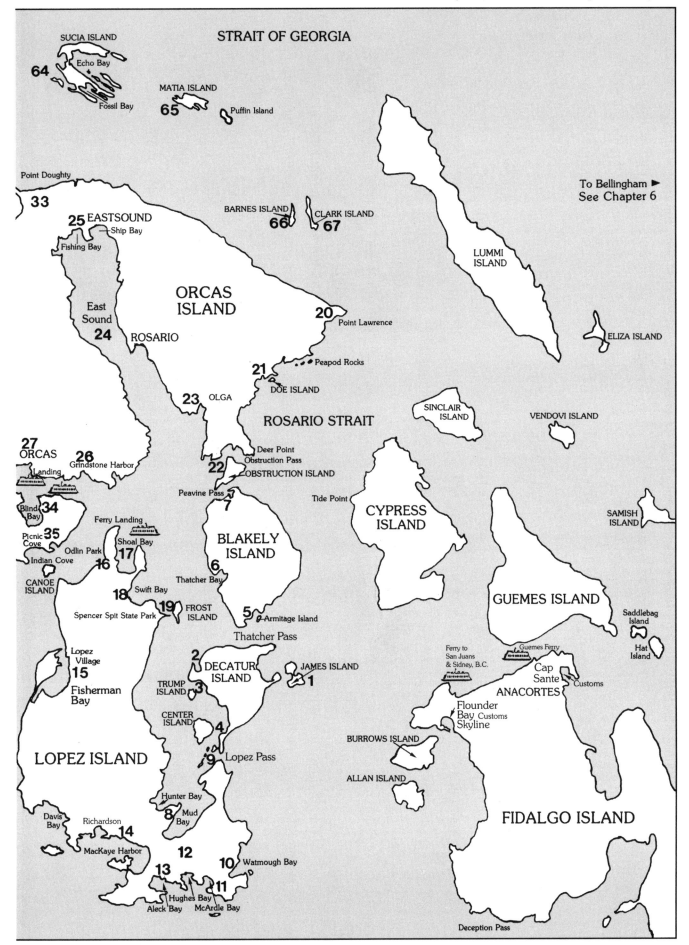

STRAIT OF GEORGIA

SUCIA ISLAND
Echo Bay
64
Fossil Bay

MATIA ISLAND
65
Puffin Island

Point Doughty
33

25 EASTSOUND
Ship Bay
Fishing Bay

BARNES ISLAND
66
CLARK ISLAND
67

To Bellingham ►
See Chapter 6

LUMMI ISLAND

ORCAS ISLAND

East Sound
24
ROSARIO

20
Point Lawrence

Peapod Rocks

21
DOE ISLAND

ELIZA ISLAND

23 OLGA

ROSARIO STRAIT

SINCLAIR ISLAND

VENDOVI ISLAND

27 ORCAS
Landing

26
Grindstone Harbor

Deer Point
Obstruction Pass
22 OBSTRUCTION ISLAND

Blind Bay **34**

Peavine Pass
7

Tide Point

CYPRESS ISLAND

SAMISH ISLAND

Picnic Cove **35**
Ferry Landing
Shoal Bay
17

BLAKELY ISLAND

Odlin Park
16
Indian Cove

18 Swift Bay

6
Thatcher Bay

CANOE ISLAND

19 FROST ISLAND

Spencer Spit State Park

5
Armitage Island

Thatcher Pass

GUEMES ISLAND

Saddlebag Island

Lopez Village
15

Fisherman Bay

2 DECATUR ISLAND

JAMES ISLAND
1

Ferry to San Juans & Sidney, B.C.

Guemes Ferry

Cap Sante

Hat Island

TRUMP ISLAND **3**

CENTER ISLAND

4

Customs

ANACORTES

LOPEZ ISLAND

Lopez Pass
9

Flounder Bay Customs
Skyline

BURROWS ISLAND

Davis Bay
Richardson **14**

Hunter Bay
8 Mud Bay

ALLAN ISLAND

MacKaye Harbor

12

10 Watmough Bay

FIDALGO ISLAND

13
Hughes Bay
Aleck Bay   **11**
McArdle Bay

Deception Pass

Orcas Island

[18421, 18423, 18430, 18434, Canadian 3462]

★ Orcas Island: This 59 square mile, saddlebag-shaped island is the largest in the San Juan Archipelago. It is one square mile larger than San Juan Island. Four main communities are spread out over this island. These are Deer Harbor, Orcas, Eastsound, and Olga. For the boater, there are many inviting bays which indent into the island, and several notable facilities. The name, Orcas, means large marine animals. The island was named for a Spanish explorer whose nine-name surname included Orcas, Guemes, and Padilla.

Point Lawrence (20): This point was named for James Lawrence, whose dying words were "Don't Give Up The Ship." The rugged, steep hillside is a landmark for fishermen who frequent this area.

Peapod Rocks: This is an Underwater Recreation Park. Shore access prohibited. Diving is popular here and in Doe Bay.

★ Doe Bay: Doe Bay, although exposed to the east and Rosario Strait, provides anchorage.

★⚓ Doe Island Marine State Park (21): Six-acre Doe Island is a relatively secluded park offering a pier and mooring float on the southeast side of Orcas Island. Approach the dock from the northeast to avoid shallows off the Orcas shore, west of Doe Island. Floats removed in winter. Private homes line the shore. There are many private mooring buoys. Campsites, each with table, a vault toilet, and picnic areas are available. No fresh water. Scuba diving is popular. 360-902-8844. ▲⚓

Walk-around: A trail circles Doe Island with access to several small beaches.

★ Obstruction Pass & Peavine Pass (22): See current tables for Rosario Strait. These two passes separate Obstruction Island from Orcas and Blakely Islands. When approaching from the west, the view over Obstruction Island toward distant Mount Baker is a photographer's delight. Of the two waterways, Peavine Pass, while narrower, is the easiest to navigate. It is shorter and free of hazards. Rocks south of the eastern entrance are marked. Currents run to four knots at springs. Obstruction Pass, to the north of Obstruction Island, curves and has rocks off the Orcas shore. A launching ramp is on the Orcas shore near the Volunteer Fire Department building. Fishing is popular in and near both passes.

★⚓ Obstruction Pass State Park: Now under state parks management. Containing 80 acres, this park is in a tiny nook on Orcas Island, at the northwest end of Obstruction Pass. The park sign is on a bluff. Anchor as close to the shore as depths will permit. Mooring buoys are available. This park has campsites, fireplaces, tables, and vault toilets. No fresh water. As part of the Cascadia Marine Trail, campsites are provided. 360-755-9231, 360-376-2326, 360-902-8844. ▲⚓

Lieber Haven Resort: Moorage, power, provisions, lodging, boat & kayak rentals. 360-376-2472.

★ Olga (23): The pastoral charm of another era is still found at Olga. Named after the mother of the village's first postmaster, the community has a dock with about 90 feet of moorage. Fresh water may be available at the head of the dock.

Peavine and Obstruction Passes, East Sound in the distance.   *Northwest Air Photo*

Anchorage is possible along the shore south of the dock area. Buck Bay, is a drying lagoon.

★ East Sound (24): [18430] East Sound is a steep sided, forested indentation extending over six miles into the island. Excellent for sailing, the topography of East Sound is such that winds are often present even though surrounding waters are calm. The town of Eastsound (one word) lies at the head.

★ Cascade Bay: Cascade Bay, formed by Rosario Point, extends from the eastern shore of East Sound. Anchorage and Rosario Resort buoys are found in the bay.

Rosario Resort: Moorage, mooring buoys, gas, diesel, provisions, laundry, showers, power, water, restaurant, lodging. 360-376-2222. VHF 78A.

★⚓ Moran State Park: Two mountains and five lakes are included in this park. It contains campsites, trout- stocked lakes and the famous lookout tower at Mount Constitution. A trail, covered and planked much of the way, leads up the hill to the dam and the tennis courts near Rosario Lagoon. The trail continues around the north end of Cascade Lake to a swimming beach. At the Y one may veer to the right, cross the Cascade Lake Bridge, and hike around Rosario Lagoon to the main path. ▲⚓

★ Eastsound (25): A day-use float on the eastern shore gives boaters access to this intriguing community. Small boats can be beached. Ship Bay has anchorage off Madrona Point in 20-35 feet of water. Fishing Bay has anchorage near Indian Island. Another niche, Judd Bay, may have anchorage for a few boats. Boating families will find all services, a great variety of stores, restaurants, the Orcas Historical Museum and Community Theater in Eastsound.

Walk-around: Dinghy to the public float from Ship Bay Anchorage. It is about a 5-minute walk to downtown Eastsound's shops, large grocery store, and liquor store. Walk up North Beach Road to see Victorian homes and the historical museum and its six log cabins with themes depict-

ing the history of Orcas.

Guthrie Bay: There is some anchorage in the area marked four fathoms on the chart. This spot is open to the southeast and to wakes from passing boats. There are rocks on the port side and shallows at the head of the bay.

★ Twin Rocks: Located opposite Olga, off the west shore of East Sound, this is the site of a day-use park with 800 feet of shoreline. Anchorage is possible, with caution advised regarding shoals off the islands. No fires or camping.

★ Grindstone Harbor (26): [18434, 18430] Two reefs, covered at high tide, appear to block the entrance to this bay, but safe passage is possible on either side of the entry by staying close to the Orcas shore. A drying flat extends from the northeastern side of the bay. The bay is open to winds from the southeast. Grindstone was named because a gentleman named Paul Hubbs operated a trading post with a much valued grindstone at the site in the 1860's. The harbor received prominence again when a wayward Washington State Ferry tried, but failed, to pass safely between the reefs at the entrance.

★ Orcas Landing (27): Site of the Orcas Ferry Landing, a fuel dock, grocery, and liquor store. Located west of the Washington State Ferry Landing are limited stay mooring floats which are open to the wakes of passing boats and ferries. On the hillside above the moorage are specialty shops, a hotel, and food concessions.

Island Petroleum: Gas, diesel, oils, deliveries. 360-376-3883.

★ West Sound (28): Framed by an irregular, winding coastline, this three mile indentation into Orcas Island is especially appealing to those who enjoy exploring nooks and crannies without going ashore. Prevailing north and south winds funnel into the sound, creating ideal sailing conditions. This is the site of a cafe, yacht club, and marina. There is a dock with moorage float for shore access. The marina is on the east shore, behind Picnic Island.

Orcas Island   Michael Romoser Photo

mouth of West Sound, there is good anchorage in about 40 feet of water in a small bay on the northwest side. Anchorage is also possible along the Orcas shore, opposite the north tip of Double Island and south of the dock with boathouses. Passage between Orcas and Double Island, even at high tide, is not recommended. Double Island, and Alegria Island to the south, are privately owned.

★ Victim Island State Park: Located off the western shore of West Sound, this undeveloped park offers day use. No fires or overnight camping. Good anchorage and beach for landing small boats.

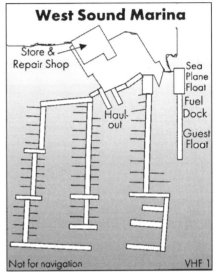

Place names such as Massacre Bay and Skull and Victim Islands, tell of the bloody battles here between the Lummi and Haida tribes. Skull and Victim Islands are undeveloped park lands. There is anchorage in the vicinity of Skull Island in Massacre Bay. Give a wide berth to the rock at the entrance to Massacre Bay. The west shore of West Sound has several small bights for anchorage. Explore the intended anchorage carefully to avoid charted rocks and shoals. Victim Island is an underwater state park. No facilities, and open for day-use only. Skull Island is another day-use park. No camping or fires. Anchorage is possible.

★ West Sound Marina: {48° 37' N, 122° 57' W} Located in the lee of Picnic Island. Stay wide, and to the west of Picnic. Approach close to the south float for guest moorage. Family owned and operated full service marina with moorage, gas, diesel, ice, chandlery, haul-outs, pump-out, and complete repair service. Open all year. See our Steering Star description in this chapter. Website: www.boattravel.com/westsound/ Mailing Address: Post Office Box 119, Orcas, Washington 98280. Telephone: 360-376-2314. Fax: 360-376-4634.

★ Double Island: Located near the western

★ **West Sound Marina:** Located on the northeast side of West Sound, in the lee of Picnic Island. Enter from the west. Look for the high bay building, gray with green trim, and the landmark weather vane and windsock. Guest moorage is found at a 250' float on the south side of the marina, closest to Picnic Island. You may tie on both sides of the float. Thirty amp power, drinking water, and showers are available to moorage patrons. Call on VHF 16. Check in at the marina office on arrival. The fuel dock is adjacent to the guest moorage and dispenses gas and diesel. Waste pump-out is also available at the fuel dock. Expanded in 1999, West Sound Marina is the largest moorage facility on Orcas Island with 180 permanent moorage slips. Some summer sublets are available. West Sound Marina is also the largest repair facility in the San Juans. In addition to the 30 ton hoist, which can handle boats to 18' beam, the yard is an authorized repair facility for MerCruiser, Volvo, Yanmar, Ford, Force, and Johnson/Evinrude engines and products. Boats to 60' in length can be repaired under cover in the high bay building on the wharf. The marina store has an extensive inven-

tory as well as a complete stock of engine parts. Ice, propane, charts, and snacks are sold. The Orcas Island Yacht Club and West Sound Cafe are only a short walk. Kenmore Air provides scheduled service. Open all year. Hours: Monday-Friday 8:00 a.m.- 4:45 p.m. Saturday 10:00 a.m.- 3:00 p.m. Sunday (July and August) 10:00 a.m.-3:00 p.m. Closed Sunday in off season. Emergency services can be provided. **Circle #40 on Reader Service Card.   Website: www.boattravel.com/westsound/ Mailing address: Post Office Box 119, Orcas, Washington 98280. FAX: 360-376-4634, Telephone: 360-376-2314.**

★⚓ **Skull Island State Park:** Located in Massacre Bay near the head of West Sound, anchorage is easily found at this undeveloped park. No fires or overnight camping.

★ **Pole Pass (29):** A county ordinance specifies a low-wake and maximum speed of six knots in Pole Pass. This passage separates Crane Island from Orcas Island. The Sheriff patrols this area. Few dangers are found on the eastern approach, however rocks are off the Orcas shore at the western entrance and a shoal extends north off Crane Island just west of the indentation that houses a private float. When heading west into Deer Harbor, avoid this shoal and the kelp beds off Orcas Island by maintaining a course about half-way between Crane Island and Orcas Island until clear of the passage about 75 yards before aiming to port toward Reef Island or into Deer Harbor. Strong currents occur on spring tides, however they are navigable at the reduced speed of six knots. Pole Pass was named because Indians tied nets between a pole and a tree across the passage to catch sea birds flying through.

★ **Deer Harbor (30):** {48° 37' N, 123° 00 W} Deer Harbor indents into the western side of Orcas Island. The harbor is entered from Pole Pass to the southeast or from North Pass to the west. There are marina, resort, and repair facilities. Watch for crab and shrimp pots off the eastern shore. While anchoring is possible, the bay is open to winds from the south. Cormorant Bay, a scenic shallow area near the head of the harbor, may be explored by canoe or dinghy. In 1853 four men came to Orcas Island to hunt deer for the Hudson's Bay Company. They found a beautiful, protected harbor which provided easy access to the plentiful deer on the island. Anchorage is good off Fawn Island.

★ **Deer Harbor Marina:** (48° 37'N, 123° 00W) Open year round, the marina has permanent & guest moorage available, with power, water, gas & diesel, pump-out, restrooms, showers, laundry, groceries & deli store. The marina is adjacent to the Resort at Deer Harbor. See our Steering Star description in this chapter. Internet: www.deerharbormarina.com, www.bellportgroup.com. Email: info@bellportgroup.com. Mailing address: P.O. Box 344, Deer Harbor, WA 98243 Telephone: 360-376-3037. Fax: 360-376-6091. VHF 78A.

★ **President Channel (31):** [18432] This five-mile-long waterway separates Orcas and Waldron Islands. Currents run two to five knots. In the early 1900's, this coast was mined for limestone, and ruins of the quarries are visible.

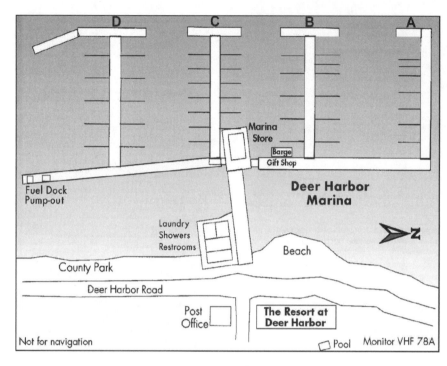

Deer Harbor Marina

West Beach Resort: Moorage, gas, limited provisions, showers, laundry. 360-376-2240.

Freeman Island (32): It is possible to anchor and explore this federally owned park land. Anchor between the island and the Orcas shore. No fires or overnight camping.

★⚓ **Point Doughty State Park (33):** Located on the northwestern tip of Orcas Island, Washington State Parks now manages this small, four-acre recreation site. Because of very rocky approaches, the site is primarily used by small boats and kayaks. It is part of the Cascadia Marine Trail and, as such, has campsites, picnic area, and fire rings. Anchorage is difficult because of strong currents and hard bottom. Recreation includes beachcombing, scuba diving, and fishing. There is above average salmon fishing off the point. Super-sized ling cod often bite the hook here. No fresh drinking water. A state Natural Area Preserve is south of the recreation site and is open only by permission for educational and research activities. These restrictions protect wildlife nesting areas and sensitive resources on the preserve. Preserve boundaries are posted. 360-376-2073, 360-902-8844. ⚓▲

Bartwood Lodge: Temporary moorage, buoys, launch, open during restoration. 360-376-2242.

Shaw Island

[18421, 18423, 18434, Canadian 3462]

★ **Shaw Island:** Known as "The Hub", this island is the smallest of the four islands served by Washington State Ferries. This is a residential island with no community center except for the area at the ferry landing. There is a county park at Indian Cove.

Shaw General Store: Limited moorage (call ahead). Power, water, fuel or launch ramp. Provisions, hardware items, post office. Hours: 9am-7pm, Sundays 9am-5pm. 360-468-2288.

★ **Blind Bay (34):** Blind Bay, adjacent to the Shaw Island ferry landing, has good anchorage. The bay is about one half mile in width. Depths in the anchoring basin are approximately 12 to 18 feet, except for a deeper spot south of Blind Island. Being mindful of overnight depths, and the charted rock and shoal area, anchor about 150-200 feet off shore. Be aware of another charted drying rock located south of Blind Island, not far from the state park buoys. Along the south shore is a very small, state-owned, island. It is an Oyster Catcher rookery and is marked "No Trespassing."

There are hazards to consider before entering the bay. Drying rocks nearly fill the entry to the west between Blind Island and Shaw Island, and passage is not recommended. The safest entry is east of Blind Island, however there is a drying rock (marked by a pole with white day beacon and the words "Danger Rock") located approximately mid-channel. Pass to the west of this rock (between the rock and Blind Island).

★⚓ **Blind Island Marine State Park:** Blind Island is designated a Cascadia Marine Trail site. All campsites are reserved for use by boaters whose primary mode of transportation is human powered watercraft. No fresh water. There is a group camp, in addition to tent sites. Mooring buoys are tucked in south of Blind Island - fees are charged. These offer some protection from north winds and some views of passing traffic in Harney Channel. In the early part of the century, a squatter settled on the two acre island building a small

The San Juan Islands as they appear from Anacortes   Roger Hunsperger Photo

house and storage sheds and set up housekeeping. His hermit lifestyle was supported by fishing and tilling a small garden spot, evidence of which still remains today. He dug several holes into the rock, evidently to be used as cisterns. Around a small spring he built a concrete retainer that is still visible. Because of their poor condition, all buildings were removed in 1972. Water from the spring is not safe for human use. 360-902-8844. ▲

★ **Picnic Cove:** Picnic Cove, north of Indian Cove, has depths of six to ten feet at most low tides. There are shoals, especially near the entrance. Anchorage is possible.

★ **Indian Cove (35):** This cove, known locally as South Beach, lies on the southeast side of Shaw Island. This is the site of Shaw Island County Park. When entering from the north, favor the Canoe Island side of the channel to avoid a shallow spot in mid-channel. When entering from the south, note the shoal that extends southeast for some distance off Canoe Island and also a rock marked by kelp south of Canoe Island. The cove has a lovely white-sand swimming beach perfect for swimming. The cove waters are warmed by the effect of the sun on the water in the shallow shoal areas. Reasonably good anchorage may be obtained, but it is open to south winds. Canoe Island is private.

★⚓ **Shaw Island County Park:** This county park has a picnic area, boat launching ramp, eight campsites, and fresh water. Squaw Bay is not a good anchorage. ⚓🛶▲

Hicks Bay (36): Frequently used as a haven by fishermen, this small bay has temporary anchorage with protection from westerlies. It is open to southeasterlies. Rocks to starboard near the entrance are covered at high tide. Tide rips form in the area.

★ **Parks Bay (37):** This is an excellent overnight anchorage. It is sheltered on the southwest by Point George. The bottom is good holding mud. The bay is spacious with anchorage for many boats. Check the chart for the location of old pilings. The western exposure often results in spellbinding sunsets. Deer, eagles, and wild mink inhabit the area. There are no facilities and the

land surrounding the bay and the island near the entrance, is a "no trespassing" biological reserve.

★⚓ **Jones Island Marine State Park (38):** Located outside North Pass at the southwestern end of Orcas Island, moorage is possible in bays on the south and north sides. A valley between the two hills connects North and South Coves, and walking trails crisscross the area. Mooring buoys are in the southern bay, and anchorage is good on a sand and mud bottom. Picnic sites on the grassy meadow above the bay have good views of the Wasp Islands. The anchorage is open to southerly winds and to the wakes of boats. In the northern bay are several mooring buoys and a dock with 275 feet of moorage. Fees are charged all year. Floats are removed in winter. When entering, avoid the marked drying rock about 150 yards off the island's northeast point. The bottom of this northern bay is rock, making anchoring difficult. The favored procedure is to try to secure the hook behind a rock on the bottom and complete a tie to shore to keep the boat from swinging. There is tidal action in the bay, adding to the problems of anchoring. Campsites, fresh water, pit toilets, and fire rings are available. Designated as a site on the Cascadia Marine Trail, one group camp area and two tent sites are at the west side of the southern bay. Scuba diving is popular. Because this is a wildlife refuge (deer are especially plentiful) pets must be on a leash on shore. The island is named for Jacob Jones, captain of the 1812 warship Wasp. Ruins of a homestead and a few fruit trees on the south side are evidence that a hearty soul settled on this isolated island many years ago. ⚓▲🎣

Wasp Islands (39): [18434] Also called, *The Rock Pile*, this vicinity has been more profanely named by those who have hit upon one of the many rocks in the area. Even some Washington State Ferries have not escaped the area uninjured. There are many covered and some uncharted rocks and shoals. For example, at or near high tide, rocks lie just under the surface of the water and extend for some distance to the northeast of Bird Rock. Reduced speed, careful attention to chart and sounder, and a visual watch are the only prudent procedures for venturing into this rock pile. Crane Island is the largest and most developed of the Wasps. McConnell, Cliff, Yellow,

Reef, Coon, and Bell are the others. There are isolated, one-boat anchorages in the bights around these islands. All, except Yellow Island, are privately owned. There is some unidentified, day use, state parks land on islands northwest and east of McConnell Island.

McConnell Island: Good anchorage is found in the wide bay on the northeast side of McConnell. The shore is private property.

Yellow Island: Yellow Buttercups that grow profusely each spring inspired the name "Yellow Island." Purchased in 1980 by the Nature Conservancy, the Island is now a nature preserve with beautiful meadows of wildflowers and birds. It is open to limited public exploration keeping strictly on the trails. A caretaker is on the premises and should be contacted when you come ashore. There are no campsites or picnic facilities, and no pets are allowed. Anchor in the southern bay and row ashore.

San Juan Island

[18421, 18423, 18434, Canadian 3462]

★ **San Juan Island:** Second largest in the San Juan group, this island boasts an average of 55 more sunny days per year than Seattle to the south. Most of the population lives around Friday Harbor, the county seat, only incorporated city, and center of commerce for the San Juan Islands.

Friday Harbor is reached by boat, ferry, and airplane. Agriculture, real estate, and tourism are the major industries.

About seven miles wide and 15 miles in length, the island has 70 miles of waterfront. The topography varies, with heavily forested hills and shoreline in the northern area, rolling, rich farmlands along the San Juan Valley in the center of the island, and barren wind-swept bluffs and treeless pastures along the southernmost shoreline.

Rocky Bay (40): O'Neal Island lies in the middle of this large indentation into the north shore of San Juan Island. Although there are rocks near shore, anchorage is possible in small coves. Reuben Tarte Memorial Park is on shore.

★ **Friday Harbor (41):** [18434] This harbor is sheltered on the east by Brown Island, sometimes known as "Friday Island". The passage on the northwest side of Brown Island into Friday Harbor is also used for ferry traffic. The University of Washington Oceanographic Laboratories and Cantilever Pier are to starboard. On the southeast side of Brown Island, the passage into the harbor is narrow and restricted by shoals off the Brown Island side. Shallow ground and rocks are marked. Favor the San Juan Island side when traversing this waterway. The southeastern portion of Friday Harbor, known as Shipyard Cove, houses shipyards and repair facilities.

Anchorage is possible in several locations, however space is limited. Avoid anchoring near the breakwater cables at the port facility, and in the traffic lanes of the ferry. Caution is advised because the ferry often backs out toward the south to turn around. Favored anchorage is in the southernmost portion of the harbor, or in the niche between the Marine Laboratories and the port marina. A cable which supplies power (7,200 volts), telephone, and water to Brown Island, from Friday Harbor is shown on recent charts. It is also marked with lighted signs on shore. The Brown Island Owner's Association has installed four small marker buoys, with the warning "Do not anchor-cable area," to help boaters avoid the hazard.

Theories abound about the naming of this area. One is that it received the name from Joe Friday, a Kanaka, who was one of many brought to the island from Hawaii by the Hudson's Bay Company. Joe's real last name was unpronounceable so, having just read Robinson Crusoe, the paymaster at Hudson's Bay called him "Joe Friday". The Kanakas were sheepherders and their main settlement was near Kanaka Bay, near False Bay, at the southern shore of the island. Another theory is that someone called ashore, "What bay is this?", and after hearing the question incorrectly and replying "Friday," the sailor recorded that answer on the chart.

★ **City of Friday Harbor:** This is one of the most popular tourist destinations in the northwest. Shopping and dining top the list of reasons given for visiting this port. Other activities include bowling at the new alley, window shopping, exploring the Whale Museum, touring the San Juan Island Historical Society Museum, playing tennis, watching ferry and small cruise ship vessels arrive and depart, visiting the National Park Service Interpretive Center, looking for souvenirs and items in the attractive shops on and near Spring Street, watching a movie in the vintage theatre, playing golf at the course south of town, having a stylish hairset, and enjoying the leisurely pace of the town. The community theater offers excellent live theater and other performances. Annual events include the *San Juan County Fair.*

An increasing number of small cruise ships are including this port-of-call on their itineraries, linking Seattle, Victoria, and Bellingham. The island is also served by Washington State Ferries from Anacortes, on the east, and from Sidney, British Columbia, on the west. An inter-island ferry connects Friday Harbor with Orcas, Shaw and Lopez Islands. Floatplanes are active in the vicinity of the harbor. An airport, located fairly close to town, has scheduled and charter services to other islands and metropolitan cities in the northwest.

Customs check-in: See information in the Important Notices section between Chapter 7 and Chapter 8 in this book. Report to the station on Breakwater B, near the seaplane float. The customs office is open 8:00 a.m.- 5:00 p.m., seven days a week. Telephone: 360-378-2080. If no answer call: 1-800-562-5943. May not be operational if Homeland Security requires all boats to be inspected.

CATeam (Tim's Marine): Towing, light salvage, and general assistance. Dispatch: 360-378-9636. VHF 16.

★ **Friday Harbor, Port of:** {48° 32.12' N, 123° 01' W} This marina is convenient to attractions in the town of Friday Harbor. Customs port-of-entry. Permanent and overnight moorage is available with water and power. Gas, diesel, showers, laundry, waterfront park are at the site. When departing, notify attendant on VHF 66. See our Steering Star description in this chapter. Websites: www.portfridayharbor.org & www.boat-travel.com/fridayharbor.   Address: 204 Front

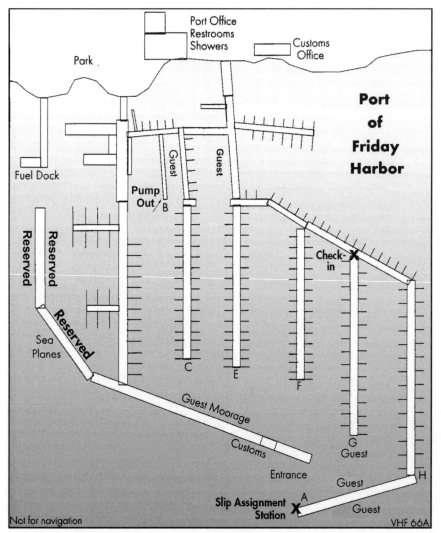

Not for navigation

Street, Post Office Box 889, Friday Harbor, Washington 98250. Fax: 360-378-6114. Telephone: 360-378-2688. VHF 66

Port of Friday Harbor Fuel Dock: Gas, diesel, lubricants, propane, water. 360-378-3114.

Walk-around: Beginning at the Port of Friday Harbor moorage, walk through the park at the head of the ramp, and look along the shore to see the piers and developments for small cruiseships and visiting vessels. Stroll along Front Street to Spring Street. The latter was named because a large spring was located at what is now Spring and Second Streets. While in Turn-around Park, at the foot of Spring Street, look up the hill to get an overall picture of the buildings along the main street. Go to the south side of Spring Street and continue up the hill. At First Street, a turn to the left will take you to Sunken Park and the restored home of the Churchill family. This is known as Churchill Square. Walking back to the corner of Spring and First, you will be standing in front of the historic San Juan County Bank building. Cross the street and proceed up the North First Street hillside to the Whale Museum. The noteworthy museum features carvings, lithographs, scale models, and video displays of both Orca and Humpback whales. Nearby are the vintage San Juan County Courthouse and the Community Theater. Returning down the hill to Spring Street, a right turn will take you past a variety of shops and provisioning stores. The liquor store is found farther up Spring Street and other shops are near the area of the "Y".

★ **University of Washington Oceanographic Laboratory (42):** Established in 1902, this renowned marine laboratory is about 1-mile from town.

★⚓ **Turn Island Marine Park (43):** Located to the east of Friday Harbor, at Turn Point, this popular park has campsites, pit toilets, and picnic facilities. No fresh water. Mooring buoys on the west side are somewhat protected, however tidal currents sweep through this area. There is anchorage in the bay south of Turn Island where several private buoys are located. Watch for shallow spots, especially off the southern point. Beaches in the north and west bays are fine gravel and good for beaching small boats. A tide flat on the southwest side of the island has clams. Turn Island is a wildlife refuge. In 1841, it was originally mapped by the Wilkes Expedition as a point of land on San Juan Island and named Point Salsbury. When it was found to be an island, it was named Turn because it was at the turn in the channel, and was so noted on British charts of 1858. ▲☂

Walk-around: Trails encircle the 35 acre island.

★ **Griffin Bay (44):** [18434] Anchorage is possible in several niches, such as the bight inside Pear Point, the indentation near the quarry on the north shore, Merrifield Cove along the western shore, and along the Fish Creek shoreline near Cattle Point. North Bay has some protection in westerlies. Little Island, connected by a spit of land to the mainland, has long been the site of cannery operations. The spit near this cannery is the location of Jackson Beach Park. Directly behind the spit is a drying lagoon which is also a biological preserve. While in this vicinity, caution is advised near Dinner Island, a pretty islet to see, but keep your eyes focused on the water for hazardous rocks. An unnamed island, south of Dinner, is a day use park.

Land surrounding Griffin Bay has historical significance. The bay was named after Charles Griffin, an influential sheep herder and farmer

sent to the island by the Hudson's Bay Company prior to the Pig War. The British fleet trained here with its guns aimed at American Camp. San Juan Town, which burned in 1890, and the settlement of Argyle, were once established communities along the shoreline.

★⚓ **Jackson Beach Park:** A log-strewn beach, launch ramp, and picnic tables are found. ⚓☂

★⚓ **Griffin Bay State Park (45):** This site is located on the western shore. The park is available only by boat and may be difficult to spot. It is about 1/2 mile north of American Camp, in from Halftide Rocks. There are submerged hazards and a charted foul area with pilings. The 19 acre park is part of the Cascadia Marine Trail and has one trail campsite, picnic areas, fire rings, fresh water, and other campsites. Mooring buoys may be available. Anchorage is possible. Surrounding lands and the Fish Creek property nearby, are private. 360-755-9231, 360-376-2073, 360-902-8844. ▲☂

★⚓ **San Juan Island National Historical Park:** Designated as park lands in 1966, two historical parks are found on San Juan Island, British Camp at Garrison Bay (52) and American Camp (46) along the southern shore of Griffin Bay to Cattle Point. These camps were part of the Pig War of 1860, the border-setting confrontation between the United States and Canada. This dispute began when an American settler shot a British neighbor's pig. Except for the ill-fated pig, no other shots were fired and there were no human casualties in this 12-year war. Facilities were constructed to house the troops at both island locations and from time to time, warships stood-at-the ready. Kaiser Wilhelm I of Germany was finally accepted by both sides as the arbitrator. In 1872, he ruled in favor of the United States, set-

★ **Port of Friday Harbor:** Located on the northwest shore of Friday Harbor, this port-operated marina facility has permanent, overnight, and temporary moorage available. Reservations can be obtained by telephone up to 24 hours ahead of arrival. As you enter the harbor, call port staffers for slip assignment on VHF Channel 66 U.S. The slip assignment station is located on Breakwater A in the north end of the facility, right across from "G" and "H" docks. Enter at the northern entrance by the slip assignment station for "H", "G", "F", "M", "E" or "C" docks, or at the southern end by the fuel dock for "J" or "K" docks. Transient moorage is on both sides of "G" dock (40' slips) or the inside of "H" dock (30' slips). At the direction of the Harbor Master, short term moorage (four hours or less) and transients may also tie to the inside of the floating breakwaters. The outside of the floating breakwaters is designed for seaplanes, larger ships, excursion vessels and assigned large vessels seeking overnight moorage.

The southern breakwaters are reserved for large vessels. The port is a U.S. Customs Port-of-Entry with a check-in station on Breakwater B near the front of the facility. 110 volt, 30 ampere and limited 240, 50ampere Power, water, pump out, gas, diesel, and propane. The marina has a two ton jib crane on the main pier for loading and repairs. **Circle #24 on Reader Service Card. Websites: www.portfridayharbor.org & www.boattravel.com/fridayharbor/ Address: 204 Front Street, Post Office Box 889, Friday Harbor, Washington 98250. Fax: 360-378-6114. Telephone: 360-378-2688. VHF 66.**

ting the boundary in Haro Strait. This put the San Juan Islands in the United States. Literature about the Pig War is available at the park.

★⚓ American Camp (46): This part of the park is primarily accessed by land. There are picnic facilities and beaches. No buildings remain. Fresh water is available except during the mid-winter months. No camping is permitted. The park is open daily. Anchorage is possible along the park's shoreline on Griffin Bay. There are no dock facilities. A staffed Interpretive Center is open seasonally. ⚓

Walk-around: There is a historical trail at American Camp with 22 marked points of interest, including photographs, descriptions, and exhibits.

Cattle Point Picnic Area (47): Situated atop a large sand dune, picturesque Cattle Point Light House marks the entrance to Cattle Pass. Cattle Pass is said to have received its name when a boat load of cattle was wrecked and the cattle had to swim ashore. It is possible to picnic on the Cattle Pass shore, about 1/4 mile north of the light. A wooden stairway down the bank marks the spot. This Department of Natural Resources Recreation Area has a group shelter, picnic tables, and vault toilets. Fresh water is available. Small boats may be beached. Currents are often strong in the pass. Anchoring is not recommended. 360-856-3500.

False Bay (48): This curving bay well deserves its name. Boaters who enter the shallows often find themselves high-and-dry. Nearly all of the bay dries. The land is owned by the University of Washington and is used for marine biological study.

Kanaka Bay: On the chart Kanaka Bay shows as the third indentation north of False Bay. Temporary anchorage only, with some protection from northwest winds. Use Charts 18433 and 18434.

Deadman Bay: Temporary anchorage is possible, settled weather only. Avoid shoal areas along north shore.

★⚓ Lime Kiln Point State Park: Accessed by land, this whale-watching park is the first of its kind in the United States. Thirty-nine acres of land with 2,500 feet of waterfront are devoted to this sport. Displays illustrate kinds of whales which frequent the area. There are picnic sites, restrooms, and trails. A lighthouse, built around 1880, is on the point. No marine facilities are provided. 360-378-2044. ⚓🏃

★⚓ San Juan County Park & Small Pox Bay (49): [18433] This park has a launching ramp, campsites, fireplaces, park office, picnic facilities, and restrooms. Temporary anchorage in the bay is possible close to shore, however it is open to winds and wakes from Haro Strait. Scuba diving and snorkeling are popular. There are panoramic views of Saanich Peninsula and the lights of Victoria. The bay was named when an epidemic swept through the Indian tribe which inhabited the area. Story tells that in a fever-fighting attempt, the Indians sought relief by diving into the bay, only to contact pneumonia as a result. ⛵ ▲⚓

Smuggler's Cove: This tiny niche has limited usage for the boater, however it has been witness to the smuggling in of Chinese laborers, opium and diamonds, and during the Prohibition years, liquor from Puerto Rico, Scotland, and Canada.

★ Mitchell Bay (50): Located on the west side of San Juan Island, this bay is near the southern entrance to Mosquito Pass. A channel leads through rocky patches to the inner bay. Although the entry may appear tricky, there is no problem if the boater stays in the channel. As the sign on the largest rocky patch states, the 200 foot-wide entrance channel is north of the sign. The center of the bay has a minimum depth of six feet at an extreme low tide.

Snug Harbor Marina Resort: Gas, boat launch, power, water, provisions, lodging, gas docks. No showers. 360-378-4762. VHF 16.

★ Mosquito Pass (51): [18433] This narrow, shallow waterway stretches over a mile from Hanbury Point on the south to Bazalgette Point on the north. There are both charted and

uncharted rocks in the pass. Although hazards are marked, caution is advised. In summer, kelp marks most rocky patches. At times of maximum tidal flow, strong currents are present. Flood tide sets north, ebb south. A county ordinance specifies a low-wake and maximum speed of six knots in Mosquito Pass. The Sheriff patrols this area.

★ Garrison Bay (52): [18433] Garrison Bay and Westcott Bay indent into the San Juan Island shore about midway through Mosquito Pass. Garrison Bay is shallow, however anchorage is good if attention is paid to overnight depths. Check the chart for submerged rocks on the starboard side of the bay. Anchorage is possible in the center near the entrance or to port in the vicinity of Guss Island.

★ British Camp: This historic site, also known as English Camp, housed British troops during the Pig War. The British Royal Marines landed here March 21, 1860. Several of the original buildings have been restored. These include a barracks, blockhouse, and commissary. A display is housed in one of the buildings. Programs with historical themes are presented every Saturday night during the summer. The first gardens were established here in the 1860's. Each autumn the leaves on the 100-foot tall maple tree display a blaze of colors. There are many deer and small animals in the area. No hunting permitted. A dinghy dock gives access. No fresh water or overnight camping. 360-378-2902

Walk-around: One walk begins at the British Camp parking lot, crosses Beaverton Valley Road, and continues on the trail to the cemetery. The old cemetery lies in a clearing, near the base of Young Hill. It is maintained for seven Royal Marines and a civilian who died while at the camp. For spectacular views of the islands, continue hiking to the summit of 680' Young Hill.

★ Westcott Bay (53): This bay is larger than Garrison and somewhat deeper in the center. Grass marks shallow spots. A depth sounder or lead line can be used to check the depth within the scope of the overnight anchor rode. Much of the shoreline is private. There is public access and good clamming on the south shore near Bell Point.

Walk-around: A trail connects Bell Point with British Camp.

Haro Strait (54): When traversing Haro Strait, note that the ebb sets south and the flood to the north. Currents at springs reach five knots. The deepest water in Haro Strait is off Stuart Island where depths reach 1,356 feet.

★ Roche Harbor (55): [18433] The harbor is protected by Pearl Island on the north and Henry Island on the west. Entry from the north is made by passing either side of Pearl Island. On low and minus tides, the western passage is preferred because depths in the eastern pass are shallow to four feet of water. Steer mid-channel in either pass. Entry from the south is made from Mosquito Pass. There is anchorage in the bay in depths of 15-50 feet on a good bottom. Give a wide berth to private docks which extend from shore and from the resort floats.

Customs: Status uncertain due to new Deptarment of Homeland Security changes. Has generally been open June to Mid-September from 8:30 a.m. to 4:30 p.m. but call 360-378-2080 to verify hours of operation during those months. This office and Friday Harbor office have customs and immigration officers on duty. See Important Notices in the section between Chapter 7 and

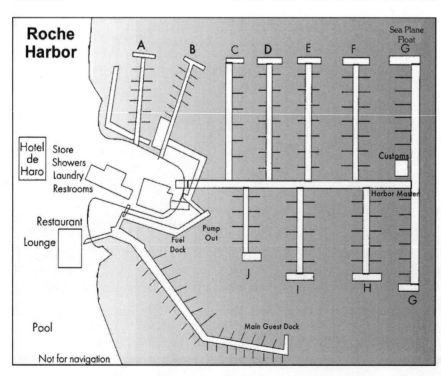

Roche Harbor

Hotel de Haro

Store
Showers
Laundry
Restrooms

Restaurant

Lounge

Pool

Fuel Dock

Pump Out

Sea Plane Float

Customs

Harbor Master

Main Guest Dock

Not for navigation

Chapter 8 in this book, 8:00 a.m.-5:00 p.m. seven days a week. 360-378-2080. After hours and holidays call 1-800-562-5943 except may not be operational due to new Department of Homeland Security regulations requiring that all boats be inspected.

★ **Roche Harbor:** {48° 36.45' N, 123° 09.30' W} Customs-port-of-entry. This large marina resort accommodates an extensive number of vessels for permanent and guest moorage. Check in with the Harbormaster at the end of the center float. Power, water, gas, diesel, propane, launch, showers, laundry, pool, restaurants, lounge, lodging in the historic Hotel de Haro, cottages, condominiums, and McMillin Suites. A paved, lighted airstrip services the resort. See our Steering Star description in this chapter. Websites: www.boattravel.com/rocheharbor/ andwww.rocheharbor.com. Email: roche@rocheharbor.com. Mailing address: Post Office Box 4001, Roche Harbor, Washington 98250. Fax: 360-378-9800. Telephone: 360-378-2155 Ext. 450, 1-800-451-8910. VHF 78A.

Walk-around: Near the entry arches to Roche Harbor is Westcott Bay Reserve Art and Nature Sculpture Park, a 19 acre reserve operated by the Westcott Bay Institute. Stroll through the reserve and view the northwest artists' sculptures on display.

★⚓ **Posey Island Marine State Park (56):** Named because the locals went to this spot to pick wildflowers, this one-acre state park is part of the Cascadia Marine Trail. A group campsite and four tent sites are provided, as well as pit toilets and picnic facilities. A wooden structure, historically used as a tidally-flushed outhouse, is now being evaluated for addition to the historic register. Because the passage between Posey and Pearl Islands is shallow and strewn with rocks, this park

Orcas Breach Near Blakeley Island   *Jason Paur Photo*

is used primarily by canoe and kayak recreationists. 360-902-8844. ⚓▲

★ **Henry Island (57):** It is possible to imagine that this island is in the form of the letter H. Open Bay and Nelson Bay indent the shores of this island. Open Bay is popular for fishing. Beware of the rocks off the southeast tip of the island. They extend some distance from shore, are covered at high tide, and are not well marked. Anchorage with protection from northerly winds is possible near the head of the bay. Nelson Bay has anchorage near its entrance. The inner bay is shallow. A more preferred anchorage in this bay is farther north, past the site of the Seattle Yacht Club out-station.

★ **Roche Harbor:** This premier *Village* has a state-of-the-art marina. While still maintaining the charm and traditions of the historic site established in 1886, new moorage facilities offer both permanent and guest moorage, restroom and shower facilities, power, water, and offices for the Harbormaster and U.S. Customs. Dinner is served in the first-class *McMillins Dining Room and Madrona Grill*, featuring live entertainment on weekends during summer. Traditional entrees include roast prime rib of beef, salmon, sizzling steaks, plus a variety of Northwest specialties. Spectacular sunsets, the lingering afterglow, and the nightly flag lowering ceremony add to the experiences that make a visit so memorable. Also on shore is a well stocked grocery store, a swimming pool, tennis courts, gift and specialty shops, showers, laundry, and lodging in cottages, the *Hotel de Haro*, modern condominiums, and new McMillin Suites. Breakfast, lunch, dinner are served in the *Lime Kiln Cafe*. Guided kayak and whale watching tours are available in summer. The fuel dock dispenses gas, diesel, oils, and propane, and has fixed and floating waste pump-out facilities. Adjacent to the resort is a 4,500' airstrip, and regularly scheduled float plane flights offer service right to the harbor. Moorage reservations are advised and can be arranged now. **Websites: www.rocheharbor.com and www.boattravel.com/ rocheharbor/ Mailing address: Post Office Box 4001, Roche Harbor, Washington 98250. Fax: 360-378-9800. Telephone: 1-800-451-8910 or 360-378-2155 Ext. 450. E-Mail: marina@rocheharbor.com VHF 78A**

Reid and Prevost Harbors, Stuart Island   ABC Charters Photo

Stuart Island

[18421, 18423, 18432, Canadian 3462]

★ **Stuart Island (58):** [18423] Home to several families who reside on private land, it is also the site of Stuart Island Marine Park with facilities in Prevost Harbor and Reid Harbor. See descriptions below. This beautiful island is composed of sedimentary rocks that were deposited about 70 million years ago. These softer rocks eroded, leaving a very irregular and picturesque shoreline. Douglas fir, madrona, red cedar, juniper, and oak provide a lush forest. Wildflowers are common in spring, and several varieties of mushroom grow in spring and fall. Shellfish and sports fishing regulations are posted within the park. Deer and raccoon, as well as eagles, ravens, and a variety of gulls are commonly seen. Disturbing wildlife and vegetation is prohibited. There is debate whether the island was named for Captain Charles Edward Stuart of the Hudson's Bay Company in Victoria or for Frederick D. Stuart who, in 1841, was captain's clerk on the Wilkes Expedition. Early settlers on Stuart Island were fishermen and ranchers, as are many of the current residents. An interesting pioneer cemetery includes plots over 100 years old. Other points of interest include a school that serves the local population and Turn Point Lighthouse overlooking Haro Straight. Currents in this vicinity can run to six knots and dangerous rips form. By water, it is a short three to four miles from Turn Point to the southern Gulf Islands in Canada. Turn Point, a blind point is a Special Operating Area so monitor VHF 11 when in this vicinity to be aware of approaching vessel traffic.

★ **Prevost Harbor Marine State Park:** This 40 acre marine park, located on the north side of Stuart Island, is protected by Satellite Island. Enter between Charles Point on Stuart and the northwest end of Satellite. Do not use the rock strewn pass southeast of Satellite Island. There are several mooring buoys, a dock with moorage floats, and a linear mooring system. Moorage fees are charged all year. There is anchorage in several places. The grassy bottom may foul your patent anchor. Many prefer to anchor in the bight near Satellite's west end. There is a drying rock in the entrance to this bight. In the summer, this rock is marked by kelp in season. A pier, used by the Coast Guard and San Juan Country, is on the west shore. 360-902-8844.

Walk-around: Take the trail inside Charles Point that leads to the lighthouse. The correct road is the one straight ahead, not the one to the left past the cemetery.

★⚓ **Reid Harbor Marine State Park:** Over 1 mile long, Reid Harbor indents like a crooked finger into Stuart Island. Cemetery and Gossip Islands, near the entrance, are undeveloped marine parks. The bay lies in a northwest to southeast direction. Private homes and Reid Harbor State Park are on shore. On the north side at the head of the bay, a dock with a mooring float extends from shore. Moorage fees are charged all year. Anchorage is possible in four to five fathoms, mud bottom. There is a linear mooring system, as well as several mooring buoys that are spaced strategically throughout the harbor. Facilities ashore include campsites, firerings, shelters, picnic tables, pit toilets, and fresh water. A waste pump and dump are available. Blacktail deer and raccoon are often seen in the park, as are bald eagles, ravens, and seagulls of many varieties. A colony of prickly pear cactus, not a native species, are of special note. Divers enjoy the surrounding Underwater Marine Recreation Area. 360-378-2044, 360-902-8844. ⚓▲

Walk-around: A trail at the head diverts foot traffic away from private land between the park and the school house. It winds through woods and marsh and crosses a low, gracefully curved bridge. At the intersection with the public road, hand painted signs, made by the school children,

point the way to Turn Point Lighthouse where visitors are treated to views stretching into British Columbia.

★ **Johns Pass (59):** This pass separates Stuart Island from Johns Island. Depths are 4 to 11 fathoms. Stay in mid-channel to avoid kelp-marked rocky patches. Currents run to five knots on spring tides, ebbing north, flooding south. An extensive reef stretches southeast for over one-half mile from the Stuart Island shore. Foul ground is marked by kelp, but extends farther out than one might expect. When heading southeast from the pass, aim toward Gull Reef, which has a drying islet. Stay on this heading until well clear of the kelp patches.

★ **Spieden Channel & Spieden Island (60):** The flood current flows east from Haro Strait and west from San Juan Channel often causing heavy rips in Spieden Channel and off Green Point. There are several homes on this 2 mile long island. Green Point on the east tip shelters a small harbor. Spieden is dry and barren on the south side, green and thickly forested on the north. There is no good anchorage. In the early 1970's, the island was stocked with exotic wildlife and birds. Hunting excursions were promoted on the then renamed, Safari Island. The venture was short lived, but the Island still remains private. Sixteen acre Sentinel Island has been purchased by the Nature Conservancy.

Northern Islands

[18421, 18423, 18431, 18432,

Canadian 3462]

★ **Waldron Island (61):** North Bay and Cowlitz Bay offer some anchorage in settled weather. Mail Bay, a tiny niche in the east shore, is rock strewn and has only limited anchorage in the northern section. Minimum depth is six feet. This bay was named because mail was delivered here from Orcas. Sandstone bricks were exported from Waldron near the turn of the century.

Skipjack Island (62): Named in the 1850's for the skipjack fish caught in the area, this, and neighboring Bare Island, are now wildlife preserves. Boat landing is prohibited. Underwater reefs located here are favorites of divers.

★⚓ **Patos Island Marine State Park & Active Cove (63):** This park lies a few miles northwest of Sucia Island. Facilities include four campsites with cooking facilities, pit toilets, no fresh water. Beachcombing, above average cod and salmon fishing, and collecting marine life specimens found in the tide pools among the rocks are popular activities. Rock walls line the cove. Entry into Active Cove should only be made off the west end of Little Patos Island at the foot of the wooded hill that bends to the beach. Mooring buoys are the best choice for overnight stays since the currents can run fairly strong in the cove. Rocks and ruins of a dock restrict the anchoring area. A sandy beach is at the head of the bay. The word "Patos" means ducks in Spanish. This island is a breeding ground for birds, especially seagulls which enjoy flying bombing missions over peaceful boaters anchored nearby. The automated light at Alden Point is a Lighthouse Reserve. ▲⚓

★⚓ **Sucia Island Marine State Park (64):** [18431, 18421] Sucia Island Marine State Park includes several islands: Sucia, Little Sucia, Ewing, and the Clusters. North and South Finger Islands and Harnden are private and are not open to the public. The island group is located 2¹/₂ miles north from Orcas Island. Several bays have anchorage, park buoys, and shore facilities. These include Echo Bay, Snoring Bay, Fossil Bay, Fox Cove, and Shallow Bay. In many places, small boats can be beached easily. Sucia has an extensive number of campsites with tables and stoves. Fees are charged. Fresh water is available during summer. Primitive roads and hiking trails wind around most of the islands, and fine beaches provide sunbathing and picnic sites.

The park was acquired from 1952 to 1974, for a total cost of $6,818.67. At one time Lummi Indians used Sucia for summer hunting and foraging. Erosion, caused by water, has created hundreds of tide pools in the sandstone. Here, limpets, starfish, snails, sea urchins, sea anemone, and crabs delight old and young marine biologists. Fishing is often good for cod, rockfish, and salmon. Irregular coastlines with spectacular rock formations and picturesque bays are a photographer's paradise. An underwater park, in Ewing Cove, is a favorite for divers. It is marked with a locator buoy. Scuba diving and swimming are popular activities. In the early 1900's sandstone bricks from Sucia were used to pave the streets in many Puget Sound towns. Earlier, smugglers used the sandstone crevices as hiding places for their hoards of silk, opium, and whiskey. The island's name originated with the Spanish Captain Eliza who labeled it *Isla Sucia* on his map of 1790. In the nautical sense, Sucia means *foul*. The name was probably chosen because the shore was reef strewn. 360-376-2073, 360-902-8844. ⊀

★ **Echo Bay:** [18431] Largest in size, this is a favorite destination for many, although swells often enter from Rosario Strait. Good holding bottom. If anchoring, favor the area behind the Finger Islands. Several buoys stretch along the west shore and a linear mooring system expands moorage possibilities. North and South Finger Islands are privately owned. Justice Island, the small island off the tip of South Finger is owned by the state, however, because of the protected wildlife on the island, this site is closed to the public.

Walk-around: There are over six miles of hiking trails and logging roads. An enjoyable walk is from Echo Bay to Fossil Bay.

★ **Ewing Cove:** This hideaway cove is found in the north portion of Echo Bay. Caution advised regarding a rock in the entrance from Echo Bay, near the area marked "Fish Haven" on the chart. It is just underwater at low tide. The few buoys here have more protection than those in the wide bay to the south. There are primitive campsites and a nice beach. This is an underwater park, with three sunken vessels on the bottom for divers.

★ **Snoring Bay:** Nearly parallel to Fossil Bay, narrow Snoring Bay is home to buoys and campsites. It is steep-sided and open to east and southeast winds. Anchoring space is limited, but there is protection during summer months from the prevailing northwest winds.

★ **Fossil Bay:** Perhaps the busiest area is Fossil Bay with its docks, floats, and large number of mooring buoys. The anchorage basin is a wide area with good bottom. Anchoring depths are adequate, but because this is a relatively shallow bay and winds can enter, especially from the south and southeast, anchorage can be uncomfortable in unsettled conditions. The float behind Harnden Island remains in place all year. Moorage fees are charged all year. Many campsites and picnic areas are on shore and fresh water is available all year. As in most parks, fresh water

Sucia Island Marine State Park   *Northwest Air Photo*

is turned off during winter months. Mud Bay, next to Fossil Bay, is a favorite for those who enjoy exploring by dinghy. It is too shallow for anchorage and dries on low tides.

★ **Fox Cove:** Back-to-back with Fossil Bay, anchorage and buoys are found in this picturesque cove. Little Sucia Island offers some protection. Pay close attention to the chart to avoid extensive reefs off the island.

★ **Shallow Bay:** As its name implies, this popular destination offers anchorage and buoys in its one to two fathom depths. The southern portion and much of the bay close to shore is too shallow for overnight anchorage. Located on Sucia Island's west coast, it has the best protection in south and southeast winds. Watch out for strong northwesterlies. Enter between the green and red markers, keeping the green to port. The markers indicate reefs which extend from shore. Campsites are available. Hiking the trails and swimming in the warm water are favorite pastimes. A scenic marshland at the southern end is popular with photographers, as are China Rock and sunsets framed through the bay's entrance.

★⬥ **Matia Island Marine State Park (65):** This sandstone island is two and one half miles north of Orcas Island and one and one half miles east of Sucia Island. Two bights indent the shore near Eagle Point on the island's west side. One is quite small. The other, Rolfe Cove, is a deeper indentation that houses a dock and floats. Floats removed in winter. Buoys snuggle near the wharf. Moorage fees are charged all year. Anchorage is difficult because the bottom is rock. Because this is a bird sanctuary, only the five acres surrounding Rolfe Cove are open for camping. A Porta Potti dump is available. No fresh water. Both of these bays are open to winds from the west and northwest.

A small bight on the south side is a beautiful anchorage for a small boat. This bay is sheltered from west and northwest winds. Anchorage for larger boats is in the deeper indentation at the southeast tip of the island. This secluded harbor is unnamed and appears on the chart with a 2.3 fathom mark, and 0 at the head. With the exception of extremely low summer tides, depths are adequate, except at the head of the bay. Check sounder and expected overnight tide depths.

The area between Puffin and Matia is foul with many reefs and kelp beds to mark underwater dangers. If approaching from the direction of Puffin Island, there is a reef with a light on it. There is a passage through the floating kelp between Puffin and a curving bay on Matia's eastern shore. Temporary anchorage is possible in this bight, also marked two fathoms on the chart.

Captain Eliza of the Spanish Expedition of 1792 named the island *Isle de Matia*. The name, pronounced Mah-tee-ah, has many meanings in Spanish, most having to do with lush plant growth. Interestingly, the island was once a fox farm. Puffin Island is a bird sanctuary. Cormorants, puffins and playful seals abound in the area. ▲

Barnes Island (66): This privately-owned island lies parallel to Clark Island. Water depth is more than adequate for passage in the channel between the two islands. Reefs lie along the Barnes shore.

★⬥ **Clark Island Marine State Park (67):** This is one of the lesser known havens for boaters. It stretches lengthwise in a northwest to southsoutheast direction. The island resembles the shape of a slender rocket with its exhaust sprinkled out like the cluster of rocks known as The Sisters. When encircling the island, avoid the long reef which extends from the northwestern tip of the island. While there are no well protected bays on Clark's shoreline, there are indentations which offer some shelter. State park mooring buoys are placed in the passage close to Clark's western shore. A gravel and sand beach is excellent for beaching small boats. Another set of buoys is on the eastern side of the island. They sit temptingly in the wide curving bay that is formed by the sweep of beach that extends out from the southeast tip of the island. This mooring is exposed to winds from several directions and to wakes from passing freighters. Sandy beaches on the south have good clamming. Campsites and pit toilets are provided.▲

Essential Supplies & Services

AIR TRANSPORTATION
Seattle Seaplanes 1-800-637-5553

AMBULANCES 911

BOOKS / BOOK STORES
The Marine Atlas 541-593-6396

COAST GUARD
VHF 16 or 22
Bellingham: 360-734-1692

CUSTOMS / BORDER PROTECTION
Due to new Department of Homeland Security regulations, call ahead for latest customs information.
. . . . 1-800-562-5943 8:00 a.m.-10:00 p.m.
After hours, stay on your boat.
Anacortes 360-293-2331
Friday Harbor 360-378-2080
Roche Harbor 360-378-2080

FERRY INFORMATION
Friday Harbor 360-378-8665
Lopez Island 360-468-4095
Orcas Island 360-376-6253, 360-376-4389
Shaw Island 360-468-2288
Washington State 1-800-843-3779

FUELS
Blakely Island General Store: Gas, Diesel. 360-375-6121 VHF 66A
Deer Harbor Marina: Gas, Diesel.
. . . . 360-376-3037 VHF 78A
Friday Harbor: Gas, Diesel . . 360-378-3114 VHF 66
Lopez Islander Bay: Gas, Diesel . . . .
. . . . 360-468-2233 VHF 78
Island Petroleum: Orcas Landing. Gas, Diesel.
. . . . 360-376-3883
Richardson's Fuel Dock: Lopez. Gas, Diesel.
. . . . 360-468-2275
Roche Harbor: Gas, Diesel . 360-378-2155 VHF 78A
Rosario Resort: Gas, Diesel . . . 360-376-2222 VHF 78A
Snug Harbor Resort: Gas . . . . . 360-378-4762 VHF 16
West Beach Resort: Orcas Island. Gas . . 360-376-2240
West Sound Marina: Gas, Diesel.
. . . . 360-376-2314 VHF 16, 9

GOLF COURSES
(These courses are accessible from moorage and have rental clubs available)
Lopez Island 360-468-2679
Orcas Island 360-376-4400
San Juan Island 360-378-2254

HOSPITALS/CLINICS
Anacortes 360-299-1300
Bellingham 360-734-5400
Friday Harbor 360-378-2141
Lopez Island 360-468-2245
Orcas Island 360-376-2561

INSURANCE
Boat Insurance Agency 206-285-1350
Or Call 1-800-828-2446

LIQUOR STORES
Eastsound
Friday Harbor
Lopez Village
Orcas Landing

LODGING/INNS
Islands Marine Center 360-468-3377
Lopez Islander Bay . . . . 360-468-2233 VHF 78
Roche Harbor . . . . 360-378-2155 VHF 78A

MARINAS / MOORAGE FLOATS
Blakely General Store & Marina . 360-375-6121 VHF 66A
Deer Harbor Marina . . . . . 360-376-3037 VHF 78A
Friday Harbor, Port of . . . . 360-378-2688 VHF 66
Islands Marine Center . . 360-468-3377 VHF 69, 16
James Island State Park
Jones Island State Park
Little Portion Store: Shaw Landing 360-468-2288
Lopez Islander Bay . . . . 360-468-2233 VHF 78
Matia Island State Park
Olga Community Float
Orcas Landing
Prevost Harbor State Park: Stuart Island
Reid Harbor State Park: Stuart Island
Roche Harbor . . . . 360-378-2155 VHF 78A
Rosario Resort . . . . 360-376-2222 VHF 78A
Snug Harbor Resort: San Juan Island . . . 360-378-4762
Sucia Island State Park
West Beach Resort: Orcas Island 360-376-2240
West Sound Marina . . . . . 360-376-2314 VHF 16, 9

MARINE SUPPLY STORES
Islands Marine Center . . 360-468-3377 VHF 16, 69
West Sound Marina . . . . . 360-376-2314 VHF 16, 9

PARKS
Department of Natural Resources 360-856-3500
Washington State 360-902-8844
Washington Camping Reservations . . . 1-888-226-7688

POISON INFO 1-800-222-1222

PROPANE
Friday Harbor, Port of 360-378-3114
Lopez Islander Bay . . . . 360-468-2233 VHF 78
Roche Harbor . . . . 360-378-2155 VHF 78A
West Beach Resort: Orcas Island 360-376-2240
West Sound Marina . . . . . 360-376-2314 VHF 16, 9

PROVISIONS
Deer Harbor Marina: . . . . . 360-376-3037 VHF 78A
Lopez Islander Bay . . . . 360-468-2233 VHF 78
Roche Harbor . . . . 360-378-2155 VHF 78A

RAMPS / HAUL-OUTS
Bartwood Lodge: Orcas Island 360-376-2242
Indian Cove: Shaw Island
Islands Marine Center . . 360-468-3377 VHF 69, 16
Jackson Beach: Griffin Bay
MacKaye Harbor: Lopez Island
Mud Bay: Lopez Island
Obstruction Pass: Orcas Island
Odlin Park: Lopez Island
Roche Harbor . . . . 360-378-2155 VHF 78A
Rosario Resort: Orcas Island . . . 360-376-2222 VHF 78
San Juan County Park
Shipyard Cove: Friday Harbor 360-378-5101
Snug Harbor Resort: San Juan Island.
. . . . 360-378-4762 VHF 16
West Beach Resort: Orcas 360-376-2240
West Sound Marina . . . . . 360-376-2314 VHF 16, 9

RECOMPRESSION CHAMBER
Virginia Mason: Seattle 206-583-6433

RED TIDE HOT-LINE 1-800-562-5632

REPAIRS/SERVICE
Islands Marine Center . . 360-468-3377 VHF 69, 16
West Sound Marina . . . . . 360-376-2314 VHF 16, 9

RESTAURANTS
Galley Restaurant & Lounge 360-468-2713
Lopez Islander Bay . . . . . . 360-468-2233 VHF 78A
Roche Harbor . . . . 360-378-2155 VHF 78A

SCUBA SITES
Doe Island
Jones Island
Point Doughty: Orcas Island
San Juan County Park
Sucia Island

SEWAGE DISPOSAL
Deer Harbor Marina: Pump 360-376-3037
Friday Harbor, Port of: Pump, Dump. 360-378-2688
Islands Marine: Lopez Island. Pump. 360-468-3377
Matia Island State Park: Dump.
Reid Harbor State Park: Stuart Island. Pump, Dump
Roche Harbor: Pump, Dump 360-378-2155
West Sound Marina: Pump 360-376-2314

SHELLFISH HOTLINE 360-796-3215
For local area closures/information, call County Health Depts.:
San Juan Island County Health Dept 360-378-4474

SPORTFISHING 360-902-2500

TAXI
Lopez Island 360-468-2227
Orcas Island 360-376-8294
San Juan Island 360-378-3550, 360-378-8887

TOWING
C-TOW 1-888-354-5554
CATeam Marine Assistance 360-378-9636
VESSEL ASSIST . . . . . Friday Harbor 360-378-4588
Anacortes 360-675-7900

VHF MARINE OPERATOR
Whidbey Island: 87
Note: MariTel has shut down all other Washington State VHF Marine Operator channels until further notice.

VISITOR INFORMATION
All Islands 360-378-9551, 1-888-468-3701
Lopez 360-468-4664
Orcas 360-376-2273
San Juan 360-378-5240
Washington State 1-800-544-1800

WEATHER:
Port Angeles: WX-4
Seattle: WX-1
Victoria: WX-3

Important Notices

CROSSING THE BORDER

Canada Customs

All vessels must report to a designated Customs Port-of-Entry. Only the captain, or his designate, may leave the vessel. No baggage or merchandise may be unloaded.

If landing at an unmanned station: Call: 1-888-226-7277. Officers may visit any of these sites if the occasion warrants. Be prepared with the following information: Vessel name and length, vessel registration number, estimated number of days to be spent in Canada, and the names, addresses, birthdates, and citizenship of all aboard.

The following ports-of-entry are arranged by Chapters in *Northwest Boat Travel Guide.*

Unless otherwise specified, customs hours are 8:00 a.m. to midnight, seven days a week. The Telephone Reporting Centre is open 24 hours. 1-888-226-7277.

Chapter 8:
Victoria Inner Harbour
Sidney
Canoe Cove Marina
Oak Bay Marina
Port Sidney Marina
Royal Victoria YC Cadboro Bay (CANPASS only)
Royal Victoria YC Tsehum Harbour (CANPASS only)
Van Isle Marina

Chapter 9:
Bedwell Harbour (May 1-September 30) 8:00 a.m.- 10:00 p.m. daily, 8:00 a.m.- 5:00 p.m. after Labor Day. Closure September 30.
Cabbage Island (CANPASS only)
Horton Bay (CANPASS only)
Miner's Bay (CANPASS only)

Port Browning (CANPASS only)
Chapter 10:
Ganges- Breakwater Float (CANPASS only)
Montague Harbour Marina (CANPASS only)

Chapter 11:
Nanaimo, Port of Harbour Basin
Nanaimo, Assembly Wharves
Nanaimo-Brechin Pt. Marina
Nanaimo, Townsite (CANPASS only)

Chapter 12:
Canada Parks Welcome Dock   (Coal Harbour, foot of Bute Street)
Crescent Beach Marina
Delta River Marina, Fraser River, Richmond
Steveston Government Dock
White Rock Government Dock

Chapter 16:
Campbell River Coast Marina
Discovery Harbour Marina

Internet Access While Cruising

There are numerous wired and wireless options becoming available to boaters. See nwboat.com/#forum for a continuously updated list.

Alpha List of Internet Connection Locations:

Alert Bay
Anacortes
Bainbridge Island
Bedwell Harbour
Bellingham
Blaine
Blind Channel
Bowen Island
Bremerton
Campbell River
Chemainus
Coal Harbour
Comox
Craig
Deer Harbor
Echo Bay
Edmonds
Egmont
Elliott Bay
Fisherman Bay
Friday Harbor
Ganges
Ketchikan
Lund
Maple Bay
Minstrel Island
Nanaimo
Oak Harbor
Olympia
Oyster River
Pelican

Pender Harbour
Petersburg
Point Roberts
Port Hardy
Port McNeill
Port Orchard
Port Townsend
Poulsbo
Prince Rupert
Quadra Island
Richmond
Roche Harbor
Rosario
San Juan Island
Sandspit
Schooner Cove
Scott Cove
Seattle
Shawl Bay
Shearwater
Sidney
Sitka
Tahsis
Telegraph Cove
Tsehum Harbour
Ucluelet
West Thurlow Island
Westview
Vancouver
Victoria

Generally speaking, libraries and museums in most cities have Internet access. Also check with Visitor Bureaus and Chambers of Commerce. (See numbers in the End of Chapter Listings in this book.) There are also Internet Cafes in many locations. For more information, go to http://www.bbxpress.net/

Washington:
Anacortes Marina
Blaine Harbor
Bremerton Marina
Cap Sante Boat Haven (Anacortes)
Deer Harbor Marina (Orcas Island)
Edmonds, Port of
Elliott Bay Marina (Seattle)
Everett, Port of
Friday Harbor, Port of (San Juan Island)
Liberty Bay Marina (Poulsbo)
Lopez Islander Resort & Marina
Oak Harbor Y.C.
Port Townsend, Port of
Poulsbo, Port of
Poulsbo Y.C.
Roche Harbor Village (San Juan Island)
Rosario Resort (Orcas Island)
Semiahmoo Marina (Blaine)
Shilshole Bay Marina (Seattle)
Skyline Marina (Anacortes)
Squalicum Harbor, Port of Bellingham
Swantown Marina (Olympia)

British Columbia
Alert Bay Boat Harbour
April Point Lodge & Marina (Quadra Island)
Bathgate General Store & Marina (Egmont)
Bayshore West (Vancouver)
Beach Gardens Motel & Marina (Westview)
Bear Cove Petro (Port Hardy)
Blind Channel Resort (West Thurlow Island)
Campbell River Harbour Authority
Captains Cove Marina (Richmond)
Coal Harbour Marina (Vancouver
Comox: Library
Discovery Harbour Marina (Campbell River)
Duncan Cove Marina (Pender Harbour)
Echo Bay Resort (Gilford Island)
Fairwinds Schooner Cove (Schooner Cove)
Fisherman's Cove Marina (Pender Harbour)
Ganges Marina

Garden Bay Marina (Pender Harbour)
Glen Lyon Inn (Port Hardy)
Great Canadian Marina (Richmond)
Heriot Bay Store
John Henry's Marina (Pender Harbour)
Lund
Maple Bay Marina
Minstrel Island
Nanaimo, Port of
Painter's Lodge (Campbell River)
Pierre's Bay Lodge
Poet's Cove Resort & Spa (Bedwell Harbour)
Port McNeill Boat Harbour
Port Sidney Marina
Prince Rupert Yacht Club
Ridor Fuels (Port Hardy)
Sandspit Marina (Queen Charlotte Islands)
Scott Cove
Shawl Bay Marina
Shearwater Resort
Silva Bay Resort (Gabriola Island)
Stone's Marina (Nanaimo)
Sundowner Inn, Pender Harbour
Quarterdeck Inn & Marina (Port Hardy)
Telegraph Cove Resort
Union Steamship Marina (Bowen Island)
Van Isle Marina (Sidney, Tsehum Harbour)
Vancouver Y.C. (Coal Harbour)
West Bay Marine (Village Victoria)
Westin Bayshore (Vancouver)

Alaska:
Auke Bay Harbor
Craig
Gustavus
Hyder
Juneau: Copy Express, Soapy's Station
Ketchikan: Thomas Basin, Bar Harbor
Pelican
Petersburg
Sitka
Skagway

Chapter 18:
Ucluelet RCMP Otter Street Dock

Chapter 19:
Prince Rupert: Fairview Government Dock
Prince Rupert Yacht Club
Rushbrooke Government Dock

Customs requirements: The following information covers a few of the issues you might encounter at the Canadian Border. For more detailed information visit www.ccra.gc.ca.

Proper Identification: Everyone entering Canada must satisfy Immigration or Customs of their citizenship. Identification in the form of photo ID and birth certificate, passport, or visa, is required and may be requested. When bringing children, including your own, into Canada, you must carry ID for each minor. If the children are not your own or you are not the custodial parent, you must carry a notarized statement from the custodial parent authorizing you to take the child into Canada. Proof, such as a copy of a divorce decree granting custody, is recommended to verify that the person signing the authorization is the custodial parent. Lack of the proper papers may result in unnecessary delays or denied entrance into Canada.

Duty Free Entitlements: Fuel that is in the vessel's tanks, clothing, camping and sporting equipment, and a supply of food appropriate to the nature, purpose, and length of stay in Canada may enter duty free. Pitted fruits, apples, pears, onions, and potatoes may not be imported. The legal age to purchase alcohol or tobacco in Canada is 19. Each adult is permitted 40 fluid ounces of liquor, 1.5 litres of wine, or 24 – 12 ounce bottles of beer or ale. Adults may bring tobacco products for their own use into Canada, but are limited to 50 cigars, 200 cigarettes, 7 ounces of manufactured tobacco, and 200 tobacco sticks (the stick goes into a tube to make a cigarette).

Pets: Dogs and cats, aged three months and older, must be current (within the last three years) on their rabies vaccinations. Carry a signed and dated certificate from a veterinarian verifying this fact and clearly identifying the animal. For all other animals, contact www.inspection.gc.ca or 1-888-732-6222 for information.

Firearms: Handguns and automatic firearms are not permitted. If you carry a firearm aboard your vessel, you must go to a manned station and fill out Non-resident Declaration Form and pay the $25 Cdn. fee. The permit is good for one year; renewable every 60 days at no additional cost. To comply with safety storage and transportation laws, the gun must be unloaded and unable to fire (bolt removed, or trigger or cable lock) and unless in wilderness areas, stored in a locked unit. Mace and pepper spray are also prohibited, but bear sprays are allowed. Call 1-800-731-4000, www.cfc.gca.ca.

Prescription Drugs: All prescription drugs should be clearly labeled in the original packaging. If possible, carry copies of the prescription or a letter from your doctor.

After clearing Customs: Follow directions given at Customs in regards to posting the clearance number on your boat. Note the time and date you cleared, and the clearance number in your logbook.

U.S. boats may be left in Canada temporarily: If a U.S. visitor plans to leave his boat unattended in Canada, advise Canada Customs of this fact upon arrival into Canada. Advise Customs as to the location of moorage and who will be responsible for looking after the boat. Display the Canada Customs clearance number prominently on the boat and also leave it with the marina. Customs: 1-888-226-7277.

Customs booklet-USA Bound: This informative booklet is written for Canadians traveling to the United States. To request a copy call 1-800-267-8376; write to Enquires Service, Foreign Affairs Canada, 125 Sussex Dr., Ottawa ON Canada, K1A   0G2;   or   visit www.voyage.gc.ca/main/pubs/usa_bound-en.asp.

CANPASS: This program offered jointly by the Canadian Border Services Agency and Citizenship and Immigration Canada is designed specifically for frequent travelers to Canada. The CANPASS "prescreens" low risk travelers in an effort to expedite the clearance process at Customs. Citizens and/or permanent residents of the U.S. and Canada who have no record of criminal activities, or illegal customs or immigration activities are eligible to apply for the program.

Applying For A CANPASS: Apply as early as possible to allow for verification of information and processing of paperwork. Forms are available online at www.cbsa-asfc.gc.ca/formspubs/request-e.html, or by telephone at 1-800-959-2221. Mail completed form, photocopies of requested documents, and non-refundable fee of $40 Cdn ($50 Cnd. for Air CANPASS) to Customs Processing Centre, 28 176th St., Surrey BC Canada V3S 9R9.

CANPASS Private Boats: Participants in this program enjoy simplified clearance procedures when entering Canada, as well as access to three Ports-of-Entry dedicated solely to processing CANPASS holders. CANPASS holders save time by calling ahead (from one to four hours prior to arriving in Canada) to the Telephone Reporting Centre at 1-888-226-7277 to request clearance before leaving the United States. After reporting by telephone, the vessel may proceed to a designated Customs Port-of-Entry.

Only the captain, or his designate, may leave the vessel. No baggage or merchandise may be unloaded. Be prepared to provide the following: ETA; vessel registration number; proposed initial Canadian docking site; final destination in Canada; the names, dates of birth, and citizenship of everyone aboard, purpose and length of stay in Canada. Once cleared, the customs official will give the captain a report number as proof of presentation. Note: This procedure applies only when everyone aboard is a CANPASS holder. If cruising in Canada longer than six months, you must apply for a Visitor's Permit. Within Canada call 1-888-242-2100. For questions regarding CANPASS Private Boats call 1-800-461-9999 from inside Canada. From outside of Canada call (204) 983-3500 or (506) 636-5064. Also visit www.cbsaasfc.gc.ca/travel/canpass/canpassprivateboat-e.html. Another helpful resource, The CANPASS-Private Boats brochure is available at customs offices or online.

United States Customs & Border Protection

Customs & Border Protection and Immigration are now Bureaus within the U.S. Department of Homeland Security. To report suspicious activity, call 1-800-BE-ALERT (after hours, 1-800-562-5943).

Customs Information: Clearing customs is fairly straight forward if you are prepared, so become knowledgeable about requirements before you travel. Contact U.S. Customs & Border Protection at www.cbp.gov/ (go to the travel tab) for helpful information and brochures such as "Know Before You Go" and "Pleasure Boats." For questions regarding reporting requirements for private boat operators, contact a Customs & Border Protection Office near you.

Reporting to Customs is the Law: As a general rule of law, it is incumbent upon the master of every vessel arriving in the U.S. from a foreign place or port to report to U.S. Customs at a designated port-of-entry. Everyone, even I-68 and NEXUS holders must report their arrival to Customs. I-68 and NEXUS holders may do so by telephone, all others must report in person. The master must keep all persons and articles onboard the vessel until released by U.S. Customs. Proof of citizenship (passport and/or birth certificates) along with photo ID may be required. A driver's license alone may not suffice. Penalties for failing to report properly or not following procedures may result in $5,000 fine, seizure, or criminal penalties.

It will significantly speed your clearance entering the U.S. from Canada if you have a Private Vessel Decal (see below) and if you know what items are allowed to cross the border. Some specific items to be aware of include: Fuel that is in the vessel's tanks, apparel, sporting equipment, and a two days supply of food can enter duty free. Live plants potted in soil require a phyto-sanitary certificate. Many Canadian grown fruit and vegetables are allowed. Beef, lamb, fish, and pork, including bacon and ham, for personal consumption (50 lbs or less) may be imported. No fresh chicken. Merchandise made in North Korea, Vietnam, Cambodia, or Cuba may not enter the U.S. Each adult is entitled to one liter of alcoholic beverages, including beer or wine, as well as 100 non-Cuban cigars, 200 cigarettes, or 2 lbs of tobacco. The dollar amount of duty free imported merchandise, including gifts, onboard cannot exceed $200 per person, if out of the country less than 48 hours. If out of the country for more than 48 hours the amount is $800, but this exemption may only be used once every 30 days.

U.S. Customs Decals: All pleasure boats, 30 feet or longer, crossing the U.S. border must display a Private Vessel Decal. This annual $25 decal may be purchased from U.S. Customs offices, or online a   t www.cbp.gov/xp/cgov/travel/pleasure_boats/user_fee_decal.xml. For other options or question regarding decals, call 317-298-1245 or email decals@dhs.gov. Purchasing the decal prior to the cruise is recommended. It is possible to apply and pay for decals upon re-entry to the U.S., but most ports don't issue the actual decal. Once cleared for re-entry, the decal will be mailed to your address.

PIN System: PINs (Personal Identification Numbers) used in prior years as part of the Small Boat Reporting System by U.S. Customs are no longer valid. Other "trusted travel programs" such as I-68 or NEXUS/SENTRI represent the current options for boaters interested in expediting customs clearance with a call-in procedure.

U.S. Immigration Form I-68: I-68 is designed to provide recreational boaters with pre-clearance when reporting back into the U.S. Under this program, I-68 permit holders (like all recreational boaters) are still required to report to U.S. Customs, but they may do so by telephone instead of in-person.

The information provided has been verified with appropriate agencies and is believed to be correct as of October 2005

Eligibility: The I-68 program is open to U.S. and Canadian citizens and lawful residents.

How To Get an I-68: To obtain an I-68 form, call ahead to a U.S. Customs and Border Protection office and make an appointment for a personal interview. Bring proof of citizenship such as birth certificate or passport, photo ID, and vessel registration number to the interview. To view an online version of the I-68 form for informational purposes only, visit http://uscis.gov/graphics/formsfee/forms/i-68.htm. The CBP Office at King County International Airport (206-553-0667; address: 7277 Perimeter Rd., Room 112, Seattle WA 98108) is able to process I-68 requests digitally. This eliminates the usual requirement for applicants to provide three passport style photos. Look for other CBP offices to up-grade in the future.

Cost of I-68: The cost for this one-year permit is $16 per individual or $32 per family (includes all children under 21 years of age). Children under 14 years can be listed on their parents' I-68 form; children 14 and older require their own form.

How to Report With I-68: In order to utilize the phone-in arrival advantage offered by I-68, everyone onboard the vessel must be an I-68 permit holder. You may call the Small Boat Reporting System at 1-800-562-5943 to notify Customs of your arrival (see below) or you may call a designated port of entry (see below). Most port offices are open from 8am – 8pm, so after hours reporting requires use of the 1-800 number. If an in-person report is requested, I-68 permit holders must comply. Only the captain or designated permit holder may go ashore to report. No passengers, luggage or merchandise may be unloaded until vessel is released by Customs.

NEXUS: NEXUS, a bi-national program, is another "trusted traveler" option aimed at lessening delays at the U.S./ Canadian border. On land, special lanes are dedicated at border crossings for the use of NEXUS holders. On the water, boaters with NEXUS card may report arrival by telephone. To obtain a NEXUS card, visithttp://www.cbsa-asfc.gc.ca/travel/nexus/menu-e.html to download an application, or call 1-800-959-2221 and request the RC 4209 NEXUS. Mail completed form and $50 U.S. fee to the Canadian Border Services Agency listed. Next, the U.S. Customs & Border Protection contacts applicants to schedule an interview. Interviews are in-person and conducted at the NEXUS Processing Center in Blaine, Washington. Once issued, NEXUS cards are good for 5 years. For more information call 1-800-639-8726 or visit http://www.cbp.gov/xp/cgov/travel/frequent_traveler/nexus.xml.

U.S. Customs & Border Protection Designated Port-of-Entry: These sites are arranged by chapter locations in this edition of Northwest Boat Travel. If planning to report in person to a CBP officer, local numbers are included for reference. Some are small, one-man offices and are not always on a fixed schedule, but in general, hours are from 8am – 8 pm. To be on the safe side, call ahead for hours at smaller stations. Customs recommends that boaters check-in with the first site upon crossing the border. For after hours reporting or further questions, call 1-800-562-5943.

Chapter 1: Tacoma 253-593-6338
Chapter 3: Seattle 206-553-4406
Chapter 4: Neah Bay 360-457-4311
   Port Angeles Marina 360-457-4311
   Port Townsend Boat Haven 360-385-3777
Chapter 5: Everett 425-259-0246
Chapter 6: Anacortes 360-293-2331

Bellingham 360-734-5463
Blaine 360-332-6318
Point Roberts 360-945-2314
Chapter 7: Friday Harbor 360-378-2080
Roche Harbor (Call before expecting to clear at Roche Harbor mid-June to mid-September) 360-378-2080
Chapter 20 (Alaska): Ketchikan 907-225-2254
Juneau 907-586 7211

Vessels in Washington State: Most vessels in Washington must be titled and registered. Vessel 10 horsepower or less and under 16 feet long are generally exempt. Contact the Department of Licensing at www.boatwashington.org/tax_title__registration_of_boats.htm or 360-902-3770 for specifics.

Non-resident vessels in Washington: If a vessel is legally registered in the state of principal use, it may be operated in Washington waters for a maximum of six months in any 12 month period. An Identification Document can be purchased for $30, on or prior to the 61st day, that extends the use by another two months. There is a limit of two Identification Documents per 12-month period. Visit http://www.dol.wa.gov/vs/tr-ves.htm.

Purchasing or Repairing a non-resident vessel in Washington: Non-residents purchasing a boat in Washington are exempt from retail sales tax when the boat is US Coast Guard documented or pre-registered by the state or country in which the boat will be principally used subsequent to sale and the boat will be removed from Washington within 45 days of delivery. This exemption is available for sale of vessels to non-residents even when delivery is made in Washington. To learn whether you qualify, call the Washington Department of Revenue at 1-800-647-7706. Also contact The Department of Revenue if you plan to bring a vessel into Washington for repairs. For non-resident registration requirements, obtain a copy of the publication Tax, License, and Registration of Boats at http://dor.wa.gov/docs/pubs/excisetax/retailsales_usetax/boatbroc.pdf.

U.S. & Washington Notices, Regulations, Resource Materials

Boating Safety

Boating Safety Program: "Adventures in Boating" is a terrific resource for the Washington boater. It contains rules, regulations, safely tips, a pump-out locations map and more. Download a copy at http://boat-ed.com/wa/handbook/ or call 360-586-6592. This brochure contains the course material necessary to receive a Washington Boater Education Certificate. This certificate may reduce boat insurance rates and fulfills requirements for a Boater Education Card. http://boat-ed.com/wa/.

United States Power Squadrons: USPS offers public boating classes on a variety of subjects. 1-888-367-8777, www.usps.org.

United States Coast Guard Auxiliary and Power Squadron Courses: Call 1-800-336-2628. Website: www.boatus.com/courseline/

Life Jacket Requirement: The law requires every vessel to carry a U.S. Coast Guard approved (Types I, II, or III) life jacket for every person onboard. On vessels under 19 feet in length, all children aged 12 and younger must wear life jackets whenever the vessel is underway unless they are in a fully enclosed area.

Mandatory Boater Safety Education Law: Beginning in 2008, Washington State will start phasing in a new law requiring boaters to pass an approved boater safety education course to obtain a Boater Education Card. Each phase applies to a different age group and by 2016 every boater over age 12 will be required to acquire this card. For more information visit http://www.parks.wa.gov/boatsafefaq.asp. Boater Education Cards cost $10 and are good for life. Boaters born before January 1, 1955 are exempt, as are operators of boats with less than 15 horsepower. Washington boaters who have already received a certificate of completion from a Coast Guard Auxiliary or U.S. Power Squadron boating safety class need only to provide a copy of it along with an application form and $10 to receive a Boater Education Card from the Washington State Parks and Recreation. Cards from other states and Canada are recognized as well. Boater Education Cards will be available starting January 1, 2006. For information and application forms contact 360-586-592, www.parks.wa.gov/boating.asp.

Charts & Weather

NOAA National Oceanic & Atmospheric Administration. Website www.noaa.gov.

NOAA's National Weather Service. Website www. nws.noaa.gov.

Charts: NOAA Raster Nautical Charts: In the past, charts have only been available as a printed-paper product. Over time, NOAA developed a prototype digital version of its nautical charts in a raster format. A raster chart is an electronic picture of the chart and is suitable for uses in computer-based navigation systems and geographic information systems. Today, raster charts being manufactured and distributed by MapTech are full color images at a resolution of 254 pixels per inch. They are available on CD/ROM (50 charts per CD average). The target price is less than or equal to the paper chart. For information visit http://nauticalcharts.noaa.gov/ocs/rnc/raster1.htm or contact David Enabnit, NOAA 1313 East-West Highway, Silver Spring MD 20910. Phone: 301-713-2770. Fax: 301-713-4019.

Electronic Charts: Where Raster charts are basically pictures of charts, the electronic charts contain more information, such as being able to click on a buoy and get the information about that buoy. Proper hardware is necessary to use electronic navigational charts. To download these charts at no cost, visit http://chartmaker.ncd.noaa.gov/MCD/enc/index.htm.

Print on Demand (POD) Charts: POD charts are paper charts that are updated with all the LNM and NM corrections by NOAA every week, thus they are fully corrected when purchased. The prudent mariner only has to maintain, not "catch up" the chart. This is especially useful when many changes take place, such as the implementation of the security zones and Vessel Traffic Scheme changes. Contact NOAA for more information at 301-713-2770 or visit http://nauticalcharts.noaa.gov/pod/currency.htm

Reporting Chart Discrepancies: Boaters who find discrepancies on charts can help by reporting to NOAA, http://ocsdata.ncd.noaa.gov/dr/ or 301-713-2724 x123.

NOAA Publications: A variety of informational publications of interest to Pacific Northwest boaters are available at www.nws.noaa.gov/om/marine/pub.htm, Marine Weather Service Charts MSC-10 (Point St. George, CA to the Canadian border) and MSC-15 (Alaskan waters) cover the geographical areas included in Northwest Boat Travel. Download or order by phone 1-800-638-8972 or 301-436-8301. The cost is $1.25 per chart. "A Mariners Guide to Marine Weather Services – Coastal, Offshore, and High Seas" (NOAAPA 98054) is free and available online or from the National Weather Service, 7600 Sand Point Way NE, Seattle WA 98115-6349, 206-526-6087. "Safe Boating Weather Tips" is found at www.weather.gov/os/brochures/safeboat.htm.

NOAA Weather Channel-Continuous Reporting WWG-24, 161.425 Mhz: Located on Miller Peak, on the northeast slopes of the Olympic Mountains, offers 24 hour, continuous broadcasts to mariners. The listening area includes as far south as Olympia and north into Southern British Columbia. Content includes regional and Western Washington's 3-5 day and extended forecasts, marine weather synopsis, warnings, watches, and advisories for conditions, such as severe thunderstorms, high winds, and flooding. www.nws.noaa.gov/nwr.

Distances Between United States Ports, 2002 (9th Edition): This NOAA publication is available on the Internet at http://chartmaker.ncd.noaa.gov/NSD/welcome.htm. Click on "index" and choose the entry for "port distance table."

Live Sea/Weather Conditions by Phone or Internet: Live information, such as wind direction and speed, air temperature and pressure, visibility and more is relayed from specific buoys and Coastal-Marine Automated Network Stations (C-MAN) to the National Data Buoy Center. Mariners can access this helpful information online at www.ndbc.noaa.gov/index.shtml or by cell or touch tone phone. The phone procedure is as follows:

1. Dial 228-688-1948. Enter the number 1 if you know the station ID Number (See Below). Enter the number 2 if you prefer to use latitude and longitude.

2. Enter the station ID number, followed by the # sign. (See below) For the letter Q press the number 7, for Z press 9.

3. Some stations also offer marine forecasts. If so, you will be prompted to press #.

4. Press 6 to hear reports from another station or hang up.

WA Buoy/Station Locations and Identification Numbers:
1. Smith Island (Strait of Juan de Fuca, west of Whidbey Island): enter 74791# (SISW1)
2. West Point (West of Discovery Park): enter 97691# (WPOW1)
3. New Dungeness, WA (Hein Bank): enter 46088#
4. Neah Bay, WA: enter 46087#
5. Tatoosh Island: (mouth of Strait of Juan de Fuca) enter 88491# (TTIW1)
6. Destruction Island (La Push): enter 33791# (DESW1)
7. Cape Elizabeth (45NM northwest of Aberdeen, WA): enter 46041#

8. Columbia Bar (mouth of the Columbia River): enter 46029#

Coast Guard

U.S. Coast Guard Info Hotline: Call from a touch tone phone to request information about boating safety classes, marine radio licensing, rules of navigation, and scheduling a courtesy examination. 1-800-368-5647. Lines open 8:00 a.m.- 5:00 p.m. EST. No weekends or holidays. Web site: www.uscgboating.org

U.S. Coast Guard Auxiliary: The Auxiliary consists of volunteers who aid the Coast Guard in a non-law enforcement capacity. Their efforts ease the burden on the Coast Guard by assisting in areas such as Homeland Security activities, patrols, boaters' safety education, emergency rescues and more. The opportunities for involvement, both on and off the water, are endless. Groups of volunteer form "Flotillas" in local areas. Full time Washington State Flotillas include Anacortes, Bellingham, Blaine, Edmonds, Everett, and Port Ludlow, and the lists continues to grow. For questions, contact USCG Customer Information at 1-877-875-6296 or visit www.cgaux.org/.

U.S. Coast Guard Navigation Information Service: 24-hour navigation information service. 703-313-5900. Fax: 703-313-5920. www.navcen.uscg.gov.

U.S. Coast Guard Notice to Mariners: Also known as LNMs, these weekly notices can be downloaded www.navcen.uscg.gov/lnm/d13/default.htm. There are specific LNMs for each USCG District. The LNM for District 13 covers the waters of Oregon, Washington, Idaho, and Montana, while the LNM for District 17 covers Alaskan waters. GPS, DGPS, and Loran-C information is also available.

U.S. Coast Guard Towing Policy: Unless in grave or imminent danger, the Coast Guard and Coast Guard Auxiliary are no longer authorized to tow disabled vessels. See End of Chapter listings under "Towing" and "Repairs".

Ferries-Washington State

Contact Information: For schedules, fares, route maps and other information visit www.wsdot.wa.gov/ferries or call the following numbers: In Seattle call 206-464-6400, in WA State call 1-888-808-7977 or 1-800-843-3779 (automated). Outside WA State call 206-464-6400.

For automated travel information (including ferries) from the Dept. of Transportation, dial 5-1-1. Local telephone numbers for the terminals at Friday Harbor, Lopez, Shaw and Orcas Islands are found on the Essential Services & Supplies page at the end of Chapter 7, but general questions should be directed to the main ferry system numbers above.

Fish and Wildlife, Washington State

Vehicle Use Permit: A Vehicle Use Permit is required at all sites, including nearly 625 boat launches and access sites, owned by WDFW. The cost for the permit is $10.95 (free with the purchase of a hunting or fishing license) and two vehicles may be designated on a single permit.

Additional permits cost $5.48. Parking in a signed WDFW access site without a permit could result in a $66 fine. Permits can be obtained online at www.fishhunt.dfw.wa.gov, by telephone at 1-866-246-9453, or where hunting and fishing licenses are sold.

Puget Sound Recreational Salmon Marine Fish Enhancement Program: For a brochure explaining the program, rules, and regulations, write: Washington Department of Fish and Wildlife, Program Coordinator, 600 Capitol Way North, Olympia, WA 98501-1091.

Sportfishing / Shellfish Information: WDFW Fish Program: 360-902-2700 or www.wdfw.wa.gov/fishcorn.htm. WDFW Fishing Hotline (request regulation pamphlet, receive regulation updates, ask fishing/shellfishing regulation questions): 360-902-2500. Shellfish Rule Change Hotline: 1-866-880-5431. Shellfish Hotline (Dept. of Health Marine Toxins/PSP alerts): 1-800-562-5632.

Sports Fishing Regulations: For a copy of the current State Fishing Regulations pamphlet, "Fishing In Washington," call 360-902-2700, download at www.wdfw.wa.gov/fishcorn.htm, or request a copy by mail from WDFW Fish Program, 600 Capitol Way N, Olympia WA 98501-1091. They are also available at tackle shops and other places where fishing licenses are sold. Regulation pamphlets are generally valid from and including May 1 through and including April 30.

Sport Fishing Licenses: Angler Sports Fishers, 15 years or older, must have a fishing license and carry it on their person when fishing. In the case of shellfish/seaweed, licenses must be displayed on the outside of clothing while harvesting or transporting catch. Licenses are valid from April 1 – March 31. A sampling of some of the current prices for fishing licenses for Resident Adults include:

Annual Freshwater	$21.90
Annual Saltwater	$19.71
Annual Shellfish/Seaweed	$10.95
Annual Combination	$41.61
1 day combination	$ 7.00
5 day combination	$17.00

For more information on license types, prices, regulations and more refer to the State Fishing Regulations Pamphlet. To purchase a license: online visit http://fishhunt.dfw.wa.gov; telephone sales 866-246-9453; 500 statewide vendors (for locations call 360-902-2464 or check WDFW website).

Along with a license, when fishing for salmon, sturgeon, steelhead, Dungeness crab, or halibut (areas 5-13), everyone must carry a Catch Record Card. A Catch Record Card is available for free with the purchase of a license, $10.95 for each additional card.

Fuel Tax

Fuel tax refund: Fuels purchased in Washington are taxed by the state, a large portion of which is a road tax aimed at drivers using roads and highways. Since boats do not use these facilities, boaters who have paid these taxes may apply for a refund. As a general rule of thumb, fuel tax is always charged for gas and, depending on the vendor, is sometimes charged for diesel. If the boat is registered and a minimum of 64 gallons of fuel have been purchased, owners may call the Fuel Tax Refunds Section of the Washington Department of Licensing at 360-664-1838 or visit ww.dol.wa.gov/forms/forms.htm#Prorate to obtain an "Application for Fuel Tax Refund Permit Account." Once the DOL receives the completed application, they will mail out a refund claim form. Fill it out and return with the requested copies of receipts showing the name and address of the seller, date of sale, type of fuel, total number of gallons purchased, price per gallon, and total amount of sale. Receipts can be dated up to 13 months prior to the date the application is mailed. Refunds do not reflect the total amount taxed. State sales or excise tax is deducted from a 31-cent tax rate for a refunded amount of about 14 - 16 cents per gallon. Mail: Department of Licensing Fuel Tax Section, Refund Unit, P.O. Box 9228, Olympia WA 98507-9228.

Health Department- Washington State

Shellfish Harvesting: The Washington Department of Health's website, www.doh.wa.gov/ehp/sf/default.htm, is a great resource for information, including a helpful "Harvest Checklist." For the latest biotoxin closure information call the 24 hour "Red Tide" Hotline, 800-562-5632. For up-to-date shellfish rule changes call 866-880-5431. The WDFW Shellfish Regulation Hotline at 360-796-3215 provides information on seasons and limits. The WDFW Fishing Hotline at 360-902-2500 provides recreational fishing/shellfishing rules and regulations. Shellfish Beach Maps and Rules are included in the current WDFW fishing regulations pamphlet, "Fishing In Washington" (to obtain a copy see previous entry, "sports fishing regulations").

Paralytic Poisoning (PSP): This hazard has been reported in many Pacific Northwest coastal areas. Before harvesting any shellfish call the local health department (many are listed on the Essential Supplies & Services page at the end of each chapter in this guide). In Washington, call the Shellfish "Red Tide" Hotline at 800-562-5632. Visit www.doh.wa.gov/ehp/sf/recshell.htm to download a copy of the latest Biotoxin Bulletin or to check on the health status of beaches in Washington counties.

Homeland Security The Boater's Role

All boaters are reminded to: 1) keep your distance from all military, cruise line, ferries, or commercial shipping (see Security Zones below), 2) avoid commercial port operations, 3) not stop or anchor beneath bridges or in the channel, 4) stay vigilant, keeping a sharp eye-out for anything unusual, and finally, 5) keep an eye on your boat and/or boat and trailer. Make sure it is not an easy target for thieves. When storing your boat, make sure it is secure and its engine disabled. Always take the keys with you.

Boats larger than 65 feet: In Puget Sound and the Strait of Juan de Fuca, during times of high security levels, captains of boats larger than 65 feet in length are to make contact with Seattle Traffic (VHF 14 south of Possession Point and VHF 05 north of Bush Point) or call 206-217-6050 (using a cell phone or Whidbey Island's Marine Operator on VHF 87). Check the latest Local Notice to Mariners or listen for the Broadcast Notice to Mariners for the current status of this requirement.

How Boaters Can Help: We can help the Coast Guard by distributing educational materials, especially in the form of posters or decals. View them at www.safeboatingcouncil.org/brochures.htm They can be downloaded individually or ordered for a large group.

Coast Guard Auxiliary: Consider becoming a volunteer and join an area Flotilla. (See previous entry for U.S. Coast Guard Auxiliary).

Security Zones in Washington State: Security Zones affecting both commercial and pleasure craft have been designated in Puget Sound and the Strait of Juan de Fuca. These zones, intended to help reduce dangers to people, property, and natural resources include the implementation of 500-yard security zones affecting three primary types of vessels: military vessels, tank ships (either loaded or empty), and passenger vessels (ferries, passenger boats more than 100' in length, cruise ships, excursion vessels). These permanent exclusionary zones apply whether the ship is underway, anchored, or moored.

Do not approach within 100 yards: If you have no choice but to pass within 500 yards of a naval vessel or within 100 yards of a designated passenger vessel, contact the vessel or the Coast Guard escort vessel in advance on VHF 13 or 16. Always operate at minimum speed within 500 yards of any affected vessel and proceed as directed by the Commanding Officer or official patrol. The official will consist of a Coast Guard patrol, General or Limited Authority Washington Peace Officer, or a specially commissioned Washington Peace Officer. Violators may be charged with criminal penalties of up to six years in prison and $250,000 in fines and/or civil penalties up to $27,500.

From a safety and practical point of view, recreational boaters should always stay well clear of all commercial traffic, regardless of any designated security zones. If you are unsure as to whether a particular vessel falls under these requirements, assume that it does and operate accordingly. There may be certain locations where compliance with these regulations is challenging. Marinas, boat ramps, and anchorages in close proximity to naval or port facilities are often of concern, as are narrow navigation channels. When operating in these areas, always be alert for the presence of applicable vessels and operate accordingly. This may require contacting the vessel of Official Patrol on VHF Ch 13 or 16. If no VHF radio is available, slow to a minimum speed, maintain a safe course, and do not turn toward the applicable vessel. For information: 206-217-6215, www.uscg.mil/d13/units/msopuget/msopss.html

Other Restricted Areas: Do not stop or anchor near dams, power plants, and chemical or petroleum facilities as they are considered restricted areas. Likewise, do not stop or anchor under bridges or in navigable channels.

Insurance - U.S. Policy Coverage in Canada

Geographic Limits: If you are a U.S. boat insurance policy holder and plan extended cruising in Canadian waters, check on your policy's geographical limits. Navigation limits vary with each company, but many commonly designate 51 degrees North latitude as the northernmost geographical limit. Requests for alternative geographical limits may result in additional charges. Call your insurance company or broker for specifics.

Marine Trails

Washington Water Trails Association: Supports Marine Trails, including the Cascadia Marine Trail and the Lakes-To-Locks Water Trail, through education, on-site stewardship, and a number of other programs. Members receive email updates, a quarterly newsletter, and a trail guidebook with a Marine Trailhead Map that includes waypoints and driving directions to launching ramps. For information and membership details see www.wwta.org. Phone: 206-545-9161. Mail: WWTA, 4649 Sunnyside Ave. N. #305, Seattle WA 98103. Email: wwta@wwta.org.

Cascadia Marine Trail: This trail stretching from Olympia to Canada touches some of the most beautiful shorelines in Puget Sound and provides spectacular vistas of the Seattle skyline and the Cascade and Olympic Mountains. It consists of designated state, Dept. of Natural Resources (DNR), county, city, and local parks. These campsites are designed for boaters traveling by oar or wind-powered beachable watercraft. Boaters arriving by dinghy are not permitted to camp. One of the basic concepts of the Cascadia Marine Trail is that, after a day's travel, no one will be denied a place to stay. For this reason, campers should place tents compactly. Visits are intended to last one to two nights. If all campsites are full, check the registration point for information on the overflow area. w.wwta.org/trails/CMT/index.asp.

Lakes-To-Locks Water Trail: This trail includes more than 100 places to launch non-motorized boats among the Lakes (Sammamish, Washington, and Union), rivers and other waterways of the Greater Seattle area. It connects with Puget Sound and the Cascadia Marine Trail through the Hiram M. Chittenden Locks. www.wwta.org/trails/.

Cascadia Marine Trail Campsites:

South Sound: Anderson Island (available to WWTA members and guests only), Hope Island South, Jarrell Cove State Park, Joemma Beach State Park, Kopachuck State Park, Narrows Park, Penrose Point Sate Park, Walker Park.

Hood Canal: Laughlin Cove State Park, Salsbury Point Potlatch, Triton Cove State Park.

Mid-Sound/Hood Canal: Anna Smith Waterfront Park, Blake Island State Park, Fay Bainbridge State Park, Fort Ward State Park, Lisabeula, Manchester State Park, Meadowdale, Point Robinson, Port of Brownsville, Possession Point, Wingehaven.

North Sound: Ala Spit, Burrows Island State Park, Camano Island State Park, Cypress Head (DNR), Deception Pass State Park, Fort Ebey State Park, Fort Flagler State Park, Fort Worden State Park, Joseph Whidbey State Park, Kayak Point, Kinney Point, Lighthouse Park, Lummi Island (DNR), Oak Bay County Park, Oak Harbor City Park, Pelican Beach, Saddlebag Island State Park, Skagit Island State Park, Strawberry Island (DNR).

San Juan Islands: Blind Island State Park, Griffin Bay, James Island State Park, Jones Island State Park, Obstruction Pass, Odlin County Park, Point Doughty, Posey Island State Park, San Juan County Park, Shaw Island, Spencer Spit State Park, Stuart Island State Park.

Parks - Seattle

Seattle Parks and Recreation: Visit www.seattle.gov/parks/boats/default.htm for an overview of the Seattle Parks and Recreation Boating Program, including topics such as classes and programs, moorage and rental, rules and regulations, fees and charges, fishing piers, etc. For general information or to request a Park Guide call 206-684-4075 or visit www.ci.seattle.wa.us/parks. To contact the Boat Ramp Supervisor call 206-684-7249.

Seattle Boat Ramp Fees: A permit is required in order to use a motorized boat launch ramp. For active boaters, the Annual Permit ($80 or $110 with overnight parking) is the most efficient and economical. To obtain an Annual Permit download an application online, www.seattle.gov/parks/Boats/motorized.htm. Mail it or bring it in person to Frequent Boater Launching Permit, Citywide Aquatics, 860 Terry Ave. N., Seattle WA 98109. For information, call 206-684-7249. Single day launch permits ($5) can be purchased on site from yellow fee machines or kiosks. If you plan an extended stay, overnight permits, costing an additional $7 a night for up to 4 nights, can be purchased along with single day launch permits.

Parks - Washington State

Washington State Parks Headquarters: 7150 Cleanwater Lane, P.O. Box 42650, Olympia, WA 98504-2650, 360-902-8500.

Washington State Parks Reservations: You can reserve a campsite, yurt, cabin, platform tent, group camp or day use facility in more that 50 Washington State Parks. For a complete list of facilities and locations, as well as information regarding cancellations or changes to reservations, payment options and more visit www.parks.wa.gov/reserve.asp or call the Information Center at 360-902-8844 between 8am – 5pm, Monday through Friday. Before making a reservation, have the pertinent information ready (credit card number, park sites, arrival and departure dates, alternate choices, etc.). Reservations can be made up to nine months in advance by phone or online. Phone: 888-CAMPOUT or 888-226-7688. Lines are open 7am – 8pm PST daily (shorter hours on Christmas Eve and New Years Eve, closed Christmas and New Year's Days.) Online: http://www.camis.com/wa/.

Natural Investment Permits: Permits are required in state parks for vehicle parking, boat launching, and trailer dumping. Daily permits are $7 and Annual Permits are $70. Purchase Day Permits on site. Purchase Annual Permits online at www.parks.wa.gov/parking/ or in person at State Parks Headquarters, regional offices, or parks--if staff is available. Information Center: 360-902-8844.

Marine Parks Information: There are fifty marine parks in the Washington State Parks System, all offering different facilities and amenities. To locate a park by name, area, or features, visit www.parks.wa.gov/parks/. "Adventures for a Lifetime: Washington State Parks" is an excellent, free brochure containing a description of each park as well as a map showing their location. To request a copy of this publication, or for general questions, call 360-902-8844 or email infocent@parks.wa.gov. For questions regarding the boating program, launch permits or boat pump-outs call 360-586-6592.

Marine Park Moorage Fees: Mooring fees are charged at docks, floats or buoys at WA State Marine Parks between the hours of 1pm and 8am. Boaters may pay an annual or daily fee. Annual Permits fees are based on the length of the boat ($3.50 per foot), with a minimum of $50 and are valid from Jan. 1 – Dec. 31. Annual permits may be purchased online at www.parks.wa.gov/moorage/, from State Parks Headquarters, or on site. The daily fee is 50 cents per foot, with a minimum of $10. Moorage buoys cost $10 per night. These fees are paid where posted on site. Moorage is on a first come, first served basis and is limited to three consecutive nights at a facility. 360-902-8844

Marine Parks Launch Ramp Fees: The daily fee is $5 per watercraft launch. Fees are paid on site. If you plan to be gone overnight and have left a vehicle parked, an extra $10 fee is charged. Annual Natural Investment Permits may be a more economical choice for frequent users (see above). 360-902-8844, www.parks.wa.gov/launch/.

MarinePump-outs: Visit www.parks.wa.gov/moorage/pumpout/ for pump-out locations, helpful tips, and information about using specific brands of pump-outs. 360-586- 6592

Seattle Notices

Seattle Bridges: For descriptions, openings, hours, and contact information, see Chapter 3.

Seattle Police Harbor Patrol: The department operates seven vessels for patrol, fire fighting, and rescue. Personal Watercraft Operation Laws and Safety Tips are available in a brochure that can be picked up from the Harbor Patrol Office at 1717 N. Northlake Place in Seattle. For information call 206-684-4071. VHF 16, 13. www.seattle.gov/police/Units/harbor.htm.

VHF Marine Radio-United States Vessels

VHF Ship Station: United States recreational vessels under 20 meters in length, traveling only in U.S. waters, and not transmitting radio communications to a foreign station, are not required to obtain a Ship Radio Station License to operate VHF, EPIRB and marine radar. Licenses are not needed to operate GPS or LORAN receivers. Even without a license, you must follow rules specified by the FCC for calling other stations, relaying distress messages and the other operating procedures. Boaters can identify themselves over the air by using the FCC issued call sign, the state registration number, the official vessel number, or the vessel name.

United States recreational vessels which travel to Canada or any foreign port, or transmit communications to a Canadian station, must have a Ship Radio Station License. Operation of Satellite, SSB, or telegraphy transmitters require a license from the FCC. To obtain a Ship Radio Station License, file FCC forms 159 and 605 (See FCC Forms & Filing).

Restricted Radio Telephone Operators Permit: U.S. vessels equipped with a VHF Marine Band radio and that travel to a foreign port, or communicate with a foreign station, must have a person on board who holds a Restricted Radio Telephone Operator's Permit, or a higher class of operator's license issued by the FCC. However, if you navigate exclusively in domestic waters and your radio operates only within the VHF Marine Band, an operator's permit is not required.

Calling Ship To Shore: Whidbey Island VHF 87 (independently owned) is the only operating channel in Washington State.

Alaska: The ALASCOM group of public coast stations has been discontinued.

American vessels, while cruising Canadian waters: Bill calls through the Canada's Telus Marine Operator by using collect long distance, third party billing, or by charging to a calling card. From a pay phone, dial 0 to reach an operator.

Calling Marinas: In Washington State: VHF 66A is gradually becoming the channel to use for calling marinas. Many marinas in the Puget Sound area have switched to 66A on their Marine Coast Station License. Most marinas no longer monitor VHF 16 and should be called on their working frequency. See End of Chapter listings.

When calling a marina on a VHF it may be necessary to try more than once, allowing time to pass between calls. When calling through an operator, be sure the operator lets the phone ring several times since marina staff may be busy or away from the office telephone or VHF radio.

Cellular Telephones: No license is required. Coverage is good near metropolitan areas and in most open straits. The National Boating Federation, in conjunction with the Coast Guard, has published a boater's guide outlining the proper use of cell phones while boating. Individuals and boating clubs may request copies of this free brochure. Email info@rbaw.org or write the Recreational Boating Association of Washington, P.O. Box 23601, Federal Way WA 98093-0601.

Calling a vessel from shore: In Washington, dial 0 and request the Marine Operator. Your call can be billed to your long distance carrier. When in British Columbia, dial 0 and request the Telus Marine Operator.

VHF Marine Radio Digital Selective Calling (DSC) Capability: In addition to routine communications, DSC equipped radios are used for transmitting, acknowledging, and relaying distress alerts. DSC allows a vessel to automatically maintain the required watch on distress and calling channels instead of the current aural listening watch.

A DSC receiver will only respond to the vessels unique Maritime Mobile Service Identity or MMSI, similar to a telephone number or to an "all ships" call within VHF range. Once DSC has made contact, follow up communications take place on another frequency. DSC radios are fundamentally different from conventional marine radios in that; (1) You need an MMSI number, (2) DSC automatically maintains a watch on VHF channel 70, rather than you listening to channel 16, (3) You can call other stations directly using their MMSI.

All marine radios, except hand held radios, submitted to the FCC for type acceptance after June 17, 1999 must have DSC capabilities. Non-DSC marine radios approved for type acceptance prior to June 17, 1999, will continue to be sold. Vessel owners should base their purchase of DSC radios on whether there is sufficient use and coverage available to make such a purchase worthwhile.

The FCC has authorized Boat US to issue MMSI numbers, free of charge, to recreational vessels that do not require a ship station license and engage in only domestic voyages. See www.boatus.com/mmsi. If your vessel requires a Ship Station License you may request an MMSI number when you apply for, renew, or modify that license.

FCC Forms & Filings

FCC Form 160-(CORES Registration Form): This is a form that must be completed to obtain an FCC Registration Number RFN. The FCC Registration Number will be assigned by the Commission Registration System (CORES) and is required for anyone doing business with the Commission (feeable or non-feeable).

FCC Form 605 Quick- Form: Application for Authorization in the Ship, Aircraft, Amateur, Restricted and Commercial Operator, and General Mobile Radio Services: This form covers both Ship Station License and Restricted Radiotelephone Operators Permit filings with the FCC. This includes new applications, modifications or renewals.

FCC Form 159 Remittance Advice: This form must be submitted along with any kind of payment made to the FCC.

FCC Form 1070Y-Filing Fee Guide for Form 605: Use this form to determine the filing fees and fee codes. The Ship Station License fee is $205 for a new application or renewal, and the fee code is PASR. To modify a Ship Station License, the fee is $55 and the fee code is PASM. The Restricted Radiotelephone Operator Permit application fee is $55 and the fee code is PARR.

Electronic filing: All of the forms for FRN registration, new, renewal, or modification off a ship station license may be filed electronically.

All of the above forms: Are available on the internet at www.fcc.gov or by calling the FCC Forms Distribution center at 1-800-418-3676. For additional information call the FCC Consumer Assistance Branch at 1-888-225-5322.

Vessel Traffic Service

In Washington State: The Coast Guard Vessel Traffic Service (also known as Seattle Traffic) operates the TSS (Traffic Separation Scheme) along Puget Sound, the San Juan Islands, and the Strait of Juan de Fuca. Because Puget Sound is used extensively by commercial and government vessels, as well as by pleasure craft, a traffic separation plan has been adopted to increase the order and predictability of traffic flow. For a one page flyer illustrating the Traffic Scheme (TSS) in Washington State and British Columbia, call 206-217-6050 or see http://www.uscg.mil/d13/units/vts/psvts.html and www.piersystem.com/clients/uscg-13/pamphlet.pdf. Because of changes implemented in December, 2002 NOAA will issue new editions of charts 18400, 18421, 18429, 18431, 18433, 18440, 18460, 18465, 19480 and 18485. OceanGrafix Charts-on-Demand has charts available at http://oceangrafix.com or 1-877-56-CHART.

Commercial vessel "highways": These consist of a series of one way lanes and are marked by dashes on navigation charts, and, by buoys in the waterways. Pleasure craft, not using a traffic lane (travelling in it), are to avoid it by as wide a margin as possible. Pleasure boats under 66 feet, sailing vessels, or boats engaged in fishing are prohibited from impeding the safe passage of any power-driven vessel in a traffic lane, and are subject to practices of prudent seamanship, safe nav-

igation, and following the Vessel Traffic Scheme. These include moving, except when crossing, in the direction of traffic flow, crossing as much at a right angle to the lane as possible, keeping in the lanes themselves, and staying out of the "separation zone" between lanes, except when crossing, and steering clear of any ship or tug so that it does not have to change course. When in a traffic lane, a boat under sail is not a privileged vessel. Other safe navigation tips include not cutting between a tug and its tow, not trying to race vessels with the intent of crossing ahead of them, and always maintaining a sharp lookout for debris and deadheads or conditions such as fog banks or background lighting from shore which may affect safe navigation. Be aware that printed course lines often shown in marine atlases are for general guidelines only and are not intended to be used for navigation. These course lines may not be in compliance with traffic lane rules. The operator of the vessel is solely responsible for compliance with the traffic lane system. Safety note: Vessels participating with VTS are not required to monitor VHF 16.

Rosario Strait is a narrow channel with a single, 1,000 yard wide traffic lane and no separation zone. One way traffic for large commercial vessels-typically laden tankers, is imposed by VTS in this area. Due to the narrowness of the channel and the potential for a major environmental catastrophe, it is strongly recommended that recreational boaters wait to cross until the channel is cleared.

The Coast Guard encourages mariners to listen to the following frequencies while traveling in, or while crossing, a traffic lane. In most of the area, commercial traffic can be monitored on VHF 14, south of Nodule Point, or Channel 5A, to the north. On the east side of Whidbey Island, Channel 14 is used south of Possession Point, or Channel 5A north of the point, including the San Juan Archipelago, Rosario Strait, and Bellingham Bay. The secondary frequency throughout the area is VHF 13. Turn Point, on the western tip of Stuart Island is an exception. It is a Special Operating Area because the blind point restricts views of oncoming traffic. Monitor Victoria Traffic (VHF 11) when in this vicinity, or when in Haro Strait and waters north of Patos Island.

For safety reasons, mariners may call Seattle Traffic (VTS) on 5A when located east of Whidbey Island north of Possession Point or when west of Whidbey Island north of Bush Point. Use VHF 14 south of Possession Point for safety reasons involving traffic navigation. Provide radio operator with the name of your vessel (not its call sign), your vessel type (sail or power), the position (relative to a point of land or a specific buoy), and the nature of the distress or inquiry. Due to the volume of calls on the channel, transmissions should be kept as brief as possible. Channels 05A, 13, 14, 16 are monitored and recorded 24 hours a day by the PSVTS.

The Puget Sound Traffic Vessel Center: This is located at the Pier 36 Coast Guard Base on the Seattle waterfront, 1519 Alaskan Way South. Due to heightened security, tours have been discontinued. 206-217-6050. Call to request a free copy of the Recreational Boater's Informational Guide to VTS. The manual can be downloaded at www.uscg.mil/d13/units/vts/psvts.html or http://www.piersystem.com/clients/uscg-13/pamphlet.pdf.

The Vessel Traffic Scheme (TSS) continues into British Columbia waters. See description under Vessel Traffic Service at the end of the Canada Notices.

Canada Notices, Regulations, & Resources

Boating Safety

BoatSmart Canada: BoatSmart Canada Safe Boater Program provides training, testing, and resources such as a downloadable Trip Planner and Pre-Departure Checklist. www.boatsmart-canada.ca/safetyTips.cfm. 1-877-792-3926.

Transport Canada Office of Boating Safety: For locations or for boating safety information, contact 1-800-267-6687. You may also contact the Office of Boating Safety at 620 - 800 Burrard St., Vancouver B.C., Canada V6Z 2J8. 604-666-0146. Download a copy of the "Safe Boating Guide" and other publications at www.tc.gc.ca/BoatingSafety/pubs/menu.htm.

Boating Regulations: The Office of Boating Safety can answer questions regarding regulations for foreign recreational boaters. Call 800-267-6687 or visit www.tc.gc.ca/BoatingSafety/facts/foreign.htm.

Canadian National Defence

Area Whiskey Golf ("WG"): Mariners crossing or cruising in the Strait of Georgia need to be aware of the Canadian Forces Maritime Experimental and Test Ranges, Whiskey Golf (WG). Area WG can be found on Canadian charts #3512 and #3459, and U.S. #17520. The Canadian and American Armed Forces use this range year round for testing ship and aircraft systems and torpedoes. Torpedoes may be launched by a surface vessel, submarine, or aircraft. No explosives are used; however, a hazard exists due to the possibility of the torpedo homing on a vessel and striking it on its way to the surface. Testing is usually carried out from 0800 - 1730 Tuesday to Friday and occasionally on Monday or Saturday. When operations are being conducted in the area, the area is "Active". Vessels within the "Active Area" are required to clear or stop on demand from the Canadian Range Officer at "Winchelsea Island Control" or any of the range vessels or helicopters. Vessels which do not comply with such directions, in addition to having placed themselves and their craft in an extremely hazardous situation, may be charged for trespassing.

Range vessels in the area may operate outside of scheduled hours but should exhibit a flashing red light in addition to the prescribed lights and shapes. These vessels should not be approached within 3,000 yards as they may be in a three-point moor with mooring lines extending to buoys 1,500 yards away. Additionally, uncharted mooring buoys (lit and unlit) are randomly located within the area. Mariners are advised to use caution when transiting this area.

A transit area 1,000 yards north of Winchelsea Island and 1,000 yards east of South Ballenas Island has been established to enable mariners to transit safely around the active area. It also facilitates unimpeded access to marina facilities in Schooner Cove and Nanoose Bay. This transit lane is clearly depicted on charts 3512 and 3459 by means of pecked lines.

For range status information contact "Winchelsea Control" on VHF Channels 10 or 16. Call 250-756-5080 for next day information or 250-756-5002 for future plans. A notice is also broadcast on VHF Channels 21B or Weather 3 on days that the Area is "Active".

Charts-Canadian Hydrographic Service

Official Charts & Nautical Publications: Since 1883, the Canadian Hydrographic Service has been providing charts and publications. Contact: CHS 9860 W. Saanich Road, Sidney B.C. V8L 4B2. 250-363-6358. Fax 250-363-6841. Email: chartsales@pac.dfo-mpo.gc.ca. Website: www.charts.gc.ca.

Canada Coast Guard

Contact Information: Website: www.ccg-gcc.ca/. For information regarding the Pacific Region visit www.pacific.ccg-gcc.ca/index_e.htm or write Canadian Coast Guard – Pacific Region, Regional Operations Centre, 25 Huron St., Victoria BC V8V 4V9. 250-413-2800.

Canadian Notices to Mariners: www.notmar.gc.ca.

Coast Guard Boating Safety Regulations/Licensing/Education: Competency testing and licensing for Boaters is being implemented gradually and by 2009 all persons will be required to have Operator Competency Cards. Anyone born after April 1, 1983 is required to have proof of competency on-board when operating a boat fitted with a motor. Mandatory certification requirements apply for operators of pleasure crafts less than four meters in length, including dinghies with outboards. Boaters who are not Canadian Residents and plan to stay more than 45 days are required to have an operator card or proof of competency from their resident state. Contact 1-800-267-6687 or www.tc.gc.ca/pacific/marine/obs/menu.htm. The Office of Boating Safety (see above) can answer questions about Pleasure Craft Operator Cards, Vessel Licensing, and more.

Coast Guard Marine Communications & Vessel Traffic Services:
Comox: 250-339-3613
Prince Rupert: 250-627-3081
Tofino: 250-726-7777
Vancouver: 604-775-8919
Victoria: 250-363-6333

Coast Guard Marine Services On-line: See www.marineservices.gc.ca for information for recreational boaters including navigation services, regulations, marine conditions and more.

Coast Guard Notices To Shipping: www.pacific.ccg-gcc.gc.ca In bottom right hand corner there is a link to notices.

Coast Guard Search & Rescue: The Victoria Joint Rescue Coordination Centre can be reached at 1-800-567-5111 (within Canada) or 1-250-363-2333. By VHF Radio use channel 16. Some cellular telephone providers offer access at *16.

Coast Guard Towing Policy: The Coast Guard tows boats only when other towing options are not available or if waiting for a tow could be dangerous. Boaters must agree to waive all claims for damage, injury, or loss against the Coast Guard and its employees before being towed to the nearest safe haven, where the owner can arrange for repairs or a further tow.

Universal Shoreline Speed Restriction: Vessels operating within 30 meters (100 ft.) of the shore are restricted to speeds of ten kilometers per hour (5.4 knots) in inland waters (not saltwater) of British Columbia. This does not apply 1) to a vessel traveling perpendicularly away from the shore that is towing a skier, wakeboard, etc. 2) in areas which have a specified speed limit or 3) in rivers less than 100 meters (300 ft.) wide or in canals or buoyed channels.

Environment Canada

REPORT A SPILL: Marine Polluting or oil spills call 1-800-889-8852.

No Dump Zones: In an effort to protect environmentally sensitive or poorly flushed water bodies "No Dump Zones" have been established in British Columbia. The following saltwater sites (listed alphabetically) have been designated "No Dump Zones": Carrington Bay, Cortes Bay, Mansons Landing/Gorge Harbour, Montague Harbour, Pilot Bay, Prideaux Haven, Roscoe Bay, Smuggler's Cove, Squirrel Cove, and Victoria Harbour. A number of sites are under review for future inclusion on this list. No Dump Zones are part of the Federal Pleasure Craft Sewage Pollution Prevention Regulations. Within these zones, regulations require vessels with toilets to have holding tanks and permit no disposal of sewage in the water. Gray water from showers and dish washing is permitted. Check marinas and signs regarding local restrictions. For more information contact the Ministry of the Environment at 250-387-1161 or visit http://wlapwww.gov.bc.ca/epd/epdpa/mpp/boat_sewage.html. The Georgia Strait Alliance, www.georgiastrait.org/greenboating.php, provides related information and links, as well as a downloadable "Guide to Green Boating" with a map showing No Dump Zones and pump-out stations.

Weather Reporting-Environment Canada Telephone Services: Receive local forecasts and marine weather conditions for the lower mainland (Georgia, Haro, and Juan de Fuca Straits and Howe Sound) at 604-664-9010. Other Automated Telephone Answering Device, or ATAD, phone numbers are listed at the end of each chapter in this guide. On-line reports for all of Canada are available at www.weatheroffice.ec.gc.ca.

Weather Reporting Pacific Region MCTS: Information can be accessed at http://www.pacific.ccg-gcc.gc.ca/index_e.htm The B.C. marine, public, and extended forecasts, as well as the ocean buoy reports and satellite image of the northwest coast are available from this site.

Weather Reporting Program-CPS MAREP: Jointly sponsored by Environment Canada, Canada Coast Guard, and Canadian Power and Sail Squadrons, this weather reporting program is interesting, educational, and most importantly, it contributes to safe boating. MAREP reports are particularly valuable when the weather experienced by the boater varies from the forecast conditions.
All boaters are invited to participate in the program. Participants contact the nearest Coast Guard Radio Station on VHF 26 or 84 and report their ship's name, position, sky condition, present weather condition, visibility, wind direction, wind speed, and wave height. MSREP reports are re-broadcast on the Continuous Marine Broadcast weather channels. A MAREP participant should hold a Restricted Radio

Telephone Operator's Certificate (available through Canadian Power Squadron VHF course), and have a licensed VHF radio. Contact Environment Canada, Atmospheric Environmental Branch, Suite 700- 1200 West 73rd Avenue, Vancouver, British Columbia V6P 6H9. Telephone: 604-664-9188. Attention Ron McLaren. Current marine conditions can also be obtained on the Internet at www.weatheroffice.ec.gc.ca. 1-866-309-3399 (in Canada), VHF 62A.

Ferries-British Columbia

B.C. Ferries Contact Information: Call 1-888-BC FERRY (1-888-223-3779) or 250-386-3431 for information and reservations. Cell phone users on Rogers or Telus Mobility Networks, dial *223. Schedules, fares, reservations, and current conditions are available at www.bcferries.com.

B.C. Ferries Discovery Coast Passage Route: The ferry, *Queen of Chilliwack*, provides service along the mid-coast ports of call, with northbound passage beginning at Port Hardy, bound for Bella Coola, with stops at McLoughlin Bay / Shearwater, Klemtu, and Ocean Falls. Return southbound voyages leave from Bella Coola with stops at Ocean Falls, Shearwater / McLoughlin Bay. Reservations needed. For information or brochure, call 1-888-223-3779 or 250-386-3431. www.bcferries.com.

Fishing & Wildlife

Sport Fishing: Non-tidal (Freshwater) Fishing Regulations (excluding salmon) are under the jurisdiction of the Province of BC. These regulations can be accessed on-line at http://wlapwww.gov.bc.ca/fw/. Tidal Water (Saltwater) Regulations and Freshwater Salmon Regulations are governed under the jurisdiction of Fisheries and Oceans Canada. Information sources are as follows:

General Sport Fishing Regulations & Information Line, 604-666-2828.

Openings & Closures 24 hr. Line, 1-866-431-3474. (includes shellfish)

Observe, Record, & Report Line (fisheries violations), 1-800-465-4336 or in greater Vancouver 604-666-3500.

Salt Water Species Updates: Nanaimo-250-754-0230. Vancouver-604-664-9250. Victoria-250-363-3252.

Visit http://www.pac.dfo-mpo.gc.ca/recfish/default_e.htm for information, regulations, on-line licensing, special notices publications and more.

Sport Fishing Publications: Visit www.pac.dfo-mpo.gc.ca and click on "Publications and Reports" for downloadable brochures. "British Columbia Tidal Waters Sport Fishing Guide" (also available with purchase of license) contains important information for sports fishers. "Package Your Fish Properly for Transport" explains how fish should be filleted and packaged in order to conform to the rules and regulations that apply.

GST

Goods and Services Tax: Non-resident visitors can claim a refund for Goods and Services Tax

(GST) and the Harmonized Sales Tax (HST) paid on eligible goods and/or short-term accommodations while visiting Canada. Proof of export and citizenship, and original sales receipts are required. For specific information contact the Canada Revenue Agency. Phone: 902-432- 5608 (outside of Canada), 1-800-668-4748 (inside Canada). Website: www.cra-arc.gc.ca/visitors. Email: visitors@ccra-adrc.gc.ca. Mail: Visitor Rebate Program, Summerside Tax Centre, Canada Customs & Revenue Agency, 275 Pope Road, Suite 104, Summerside PC C1N 6C6 Canada. The pamphlet RC-4031 "Tax Refund" includes information, as well as an Application for Refund Form. Call 1-800-959-2221 for a copy or download from the Agency's website.

HAM Radio Net: British Columbia Boater's Net- A HAM Community Service: Volunteer net controllers broadcast information and communications for boaters during the boating season. If family or friends need to get in touch with a vessel, or if authorities need to make contact due to an emergency, HAM operators are often a successful means of communication. Some HAMS also broadcast local weather reports. From June through September HAM broadcasts air on the 2-meter band at 1700 PDT (Pacific Daylight Time). Broadcasts generally begin with a roll call for vessels that have checked in recently and include a call for new participants. Phone and fax numbers for the HAM network is given for those needing to contact boaters. Messages for boaters can also be emailed to bcboatersnet@saltsprsingisland.org. Donations are requested to help support the repeater. For information visit www.qsl.net/bcbn or contact Terrance Berscheid at 250-479-3165, email ve7tbc@rac.ca

Harbour Authorities / Fisheries & Oceans

Federal Government / Public Floats in Canada: In British Columbia, The Fisheries and Oceans Small Craft Harbour Program is divesting 65 Recreational Harbours (31 inland and 34 coastal sites). To date, 54 have been divested. In the remaining facilities (fishing harbours), the emphasis is on forming Harbour Authorities. A Harbour Authority is a non-profit, locally controlled organization whose board of directors has links with the community. It exists solely for the management and maintenance of the harbor facility that is owned and under the jurisdiction of F&O. The fishing harbours remain public and their use by a wide assortment of small vessel operators is appreciated and welcomed. For further information contact Small Craft Harbours, Fisheries and Oceans Canada, Suite 200-401 Burrard Street, Vancouver B.C. Canada V6C 3S4. Phone: 604-666-4875. Fax: 604-666-7056. www.dfo-mpo.gc.ca/sch/index.htm. For information specifically regarding Harbour Authority managed sites, www.haa.bc.ca.

Health

Paralytic Shellfish Poisoning: In British Columbia, call 1-866-431-FISH or 604-666-2828 (in the lower mainland) for Red Tide closures. Also call local Shellfish Hotlines listed on the "Essential Supplies & Services" page at the end of each chapter in this book. Website: www.pac.dfo-mpo.gc.ca/recfish/.

Licensing

Boat Licensing: All Canadian pleasure craft under 15 gross tons and powered by an engine 10 horsepower (7.5 kilowatts) or more must be licensed or registered, regardless of where they are operated in Canada. This can be done for no charge through Canada Border Services Agencies. For locations, visit www.cbsa-asfc.gc.ca/contact/rco-e.html, or call 1-800-461-9999 inside Canada.

To identify the boat properly, the license number must be displayed above the water line on both sides of the bow. The number must be block letters at least 7.5 centimeters (3 inches) in height and in a color that contrasts with the color of the boat. The original copy of the license should be on board at all times. Without correct documentation, you could be delayed or fined when clearing Canada-US Customs. If you sell the vessel, sign the transfer form on the back of the license and give it to the new owners, who should contact the Canada Border Service. For additional Pleasure Craft Licensing information see www.tc.gc.ca/BoatingSafety/pcl.htm.

Parks-British Columbia

B.C. Parks Website: http://wlapwww.gov.bc.ca/bcparks/.

Campsite Reservations: Although most campgrounds set aside some sites for use on a first-come-first-served basis, space can fill up rapidly. To secure your site, the Discover Camping Service enables campgrounds to be reserved for up to 14 days in 66 of British Columbia's Provincial Parks. Call 1-800-689-9025 or 604-689-9205 (in the Greater Vancouver area) or visit www.discovercamping.ca. Reservation agents are available daily from April 1 to September 15. (Hours: 7 am – 7 pm on weekdays, 9 am – 5 pm on weekends and holidays). Reservations can be placed up to 3 months in advance or as little as two days ahead. A non-refundable reservation service fee is due at the time of booking. The fee, which includes a 7% GST, is $6.42 Cnd per night with a maximum of $19.26 Cdn. for three or more nights per campsite. Fees can be paid with Visa or MasterCard.

Marine Park Fees: Fees are collected for moorage at designated park floats and buoys. The fees are: Floats--$2 per meter (3.28 feet) per night. Moorage buoy fees--$10 per vessel per night. Moorage is offered at a number of Provincial Coastal Marine Parks included in this guide. By order of chapter they are: Chapter 8: Sidney Spit. Chapter 9: Cabbage Island, Winter Cove. Chapter 10: Montague Harbour, Wallace Island. Chapter 11: Newcastle Island, Pirates Cove. Chapter 12: Halkett Bay, Plumper Cove, Porteau Cove. Chapter 13: Smuggler's Cove. Chapter 17: Echo Bay. Watch for updates on www.nwboat.com.

Gulf Islands National Park Reserve: This 2,500 hectares reserve was established in 2003 through the transfer of some Gulf Island Provincial Parks, Pacific Marine Heritage Legacy acquired lands, and federally acquired land on 15 islands in the Southern Gulf Islands. The National Park includes protected areas on the Pender Islands, Mayne Island, Saturna Island, Cabbage Island, Tumbo Island, Russell Island, Prevost Island, Georgeson Island, Portland Island (Princess Margaret Marine Park), Isle-de-Lis Marine Park, Sidney Spit, D'Arcy Island, and land near Sidney. Protected areas located on Galiano, Wallace and Saltspring Islands, and in the Gulf Islands north of this area, will remain as Provincial Parks under the jurisdiction of B.C. Parks. The areas south of the National Park, including Discovery Island, Trial Islands, and the Oak Bay Islets remain under the B.C. Provincial Parks system. In addition, the province contributes to the Pacific Marine Heritage Legacy toward the acquisition of new provincial park lands on Saltspring, Valdes, and Galiano Islands. A recent acquisition includes The Texada Lands on Saltspring's Burgoyne Bay. The federal, as well as provincial governments contribute toward future acquisitions to the national park.

B.C. Marine Parks Forever Society: "Buy a Marine Park...It's Easy!" This trust fund, established by the Yacht Club Council and individual boating groups, is dedicated to creating new marine parks. Over a million dollars has been raised to date for the purchase of new sites. Mail: Marine Parks Forever Society, 10 Gostick Place, North Vancouver, B.C. V7M 3G3. http://marineparks.cbcyachtclubs.ca/index.htm.

Royal Canadian Mounted Police

RCMP Westcoast Marine Service: www.members.shaw.ca/rcmpwcmd. For nonemergency calls 250-751-8845 (Nanaimo office) or 250-62-3142 (Prince Rupert office).

RCMP Coastal Watch: Help turn the tide against drug smuggling by reporting suspicious activity. For more information, call 1-888-855-6655, or the local RCMP office.

RCMP Patrol: RCMP boarding is similar to the U.S. Coast Guard boarding checks regarding fire extinguishers, PFD's, and other required equipment. If boarded, the RCMP will request your papers, documents, and customs clearance receipt or number. The RCMP monitors VHF 16.

VHF Marine Radio Canadian Vessels

A ship radio station license will not be required if you meet both of the following criteria:

(1): The vessel is not operated in the sovereign waters of a country other than Canada or the USA.

(2): The radio equipment on board the vessel is only capable of operating on frequencies that are allocated for use in the mobile marine band.

These frequencies include the mobile marine bands for VHF and radar: For a listing of these frequencies refer to Radiocommunication Information Circular 13 (RIC-13).

In Canada ALL operators of a VHF Marine Band Radio must have a Restricted Operator's Certificate – Maritime, also known as ROC(M), or a higher grade of radio operator's certificate. Candidates for a ROC(M) must successfully complete an examination. Local Canadian Power and Sail Squadrons can administer the exams for the ROC(M), as well as the new DSC and GMDSS endorsements. www.cps-ecp.ca. 1-888-277-2628 in Canada, or 416-293-2438 outside of Canada.

Canadian vessels operators may obtain their MMSI from Industry Canada at no cost. You will be required to provide the basic information for the Search and Rescue database in order to obtain a MMSI. Contact : http://sd.ic.gc.ca/eng-doc/ mmsi.jsp. Address: Industry Canada Radio Communications & Broadcasting Regulatory Branch, 300 Slater St., Ottawa Ontario K1A 0C8.

Radiocommunication Information Circulars (RIC-13) and (RIC-66) are available on the Internet at www.strategis.ic.gc.ca.

VHF Marine Radio Calls: For the correct procedure, marine operator channels, and calling etiquette, see the North Pacific Marine Radio Council's Report in the Appendix of this book. Also, the appropriate VHF marine operator channels for each area are found in the Essential Supplies & Services listings at the end of each chapter in this guide. Telus marine operators do not monitor VHF 16. Captains of Canadian vessels must establish an account with Telus Marine at 800-663-0640 (in Canada) or 604-432-2574. American vessels, while cruising Canadian waters, bill their calls through the Telus Marine operator by using collect long distance, third party billing, or by charging to a calling card. Before placing a call, the Marine Operator will request the vessel's point of registration and call sign.

VHF 16 International Distress and Calling: Canadian Coast Guard Radio requests boaters using VHF 16 to listen first to make sure no traffic is in progress and not to make any transmission when either a "SEELONCE MAYDAY" or a "SEELONCE DISTRESS" is announced. See the entire North Pacific Radio Council Guide in the Appendix of this book.

VHF New B.C. Marina Calling Channel: The official marina calling channel in British Columbia is 66A (156.325 MHz). This designation has been in effect since January 2004. Channels 68 and 73 are now intership/shipshore working channels. For questions, contact Jim Laursen at 250-363-3800, email: laursen.jim@ic.gc.ca.

Sources in Washington State predict that eventually Channel 66A will become the official marina calling channel also, however that is not in effect at this time. For updates, see www.boattravel.com.

Vessel Traffic Service

The Canadian and U.S. Coast Guards have established the *Co-operative Vessel Traffic System* (CVTS): Tofino Traffic (VHF 74) provides traffic for the offshore approaches to Juan de Fuca Strait and along Washington State's coastline from 48 degrees north. Seattle Traffic (VHF 5A) provides VTS for both the Canadian and US waters of Juan de Fuca Strait. Victoria Traffic (VHF 11) provides VTS for both Canadian and US waters of Haro Strait, Boundary Passage, and the lower Georgia Strait.

Tofino Traffic (VHF 74): Monitor the waters west of 124 40N, south to 48N, west to 127W, and then out to 50NM off the coast of Vancouver Island. Reference CHS chart 3001.

Victoria Traffic (VHF 11): When in the navigable waters of the Strait of Georgia to Merry and Ballenas Islands (excluding the areas of responsibility of Vancouver Traffic) the navigable waters of the central Strait of Juan de Fuca north and east of Race Rocks, including the Gulf Island Archipelago, Boundary Pass, and Haro Strait and

Basic Boat Maneuvering

Basic principals: Piloting a boat is not at all like driving a car. With a car, the front end moves right or left as one steers, and the back end usually follows obediently. Not so with a boat. Instead, the stern does the moving, to port or starboard, as one turns the wheel. Thus, the stern must be kept free of obstacles on either side.

As if this is not enough of a problem, the water underneath a boat is not a stable substance, like a highway. The water moves about with the current, usually either helping or hindering efforts to control the boat. Add to these variables, the unpredictable local winds inside small harbors and the close quarters that are frequently encountered, and it's no wonder that many yacht captains have Excedrin headaches.

Not that captains are the only ones who get headaches from maneuvering. Almost any first-mate, given two martinis and an opportunity to speak, can relate at least one instance when her marriage, if not her very life, was called into question by her captain shouting, "Now what did you do to make the boat do that?" It is from the frustration of such instances that even the most patient first-mate is sometimes on the verge of a nervous breakdown.

Speed: Perhaps the most frequent mistake novice boat handlers make is to use too much speed. A boat speeding about in tight quarters is almost sure to get in trouble and to do serious damage when it does. A captain proceeding slowly and cautiously can usually recover from a mistake with little more than embarrassment by simply pushing off the boat or other object into which he has been carried. There are times, of course, when wind and current require modest amounts of speed in order to maintain headway or sternway. Extreme caution is required at such time.

Observations: Take note of the direction and strength of the wind by observing flags located ashore and on boats. A boat that has a relatively flat bottom will be more affected by wind than current. With a deep V-hull, however, the current will affect the boat more than the wind. Which way the current is going to be flowing can sometimes be determined by knowing whether the tide is flooding or ebbing. Sometimes one can actually see the current in the water, or can see an object, such as a piece of drift wood, moving with the flow. Observe how the current is affecting other boats that are maneuvering in the same area. One can make a trial run and note the effect of the current on his boat. The important thing is for the skipper to take time to decide the best approach, given the present wind and current conditions. Strong preference should be given to heading into the wind or current as over against having it at the stern. When landing, it is also preferable to have the wind and current push the boat in toward the dock, rather than away from it.

Backing away from trouble: Many boaters get in trouble because they decide what they're going to do and then they keep on doing it, even though they can see that things are going wrong. It is best to abort a maneuver that is obviously getting the boat into trouble, by reversing engines and backing out into more open waters to make a change in plans or a better approach.

Continued at www.nwboat.com/meminfo/maneuver.pdf

Victoria Traffic Sector Two (VHF 74) for Fraser River, New Westminster.

Vancouver Traffic (VHF 12): Monitor when in the navigable waters north of the Iona Jetty (including Howe Sound) extending westward to a line directly south of Cape Roger Curtis, Bowen Island. The navigable waters east of Cape Roger Curtis including Burrard Inlet and Indian Arm.

Comox Traffic (VHF 71): Monitor from Ballenas Island to the north tip of Vancouver Island.

Prince Rupert Sector One (VHF 11): Monitor when in the area north of Vancouver Island through Queen Charlotte Sound and Hecate Strait, and along the mainland coast.

Prince Rupert Sector Two (VHF 71): Monitor when in the vicinity of Prince Rupert, north to Alaska on the west side of the Queen Charlottes, and along the west coast of the Queen Charlottes south to the north tip of Vancouver Island.

Basic Boat Anchoring

Today most pleasure boat anchors are patented, sophisticated devices designed to have holding power far beyond their weight. Alas, these devices are neither fool proof, nor immune to the mistakes of the un-enlightened boater! Anchoring is a simple, but precise, skill. It can lead to many satisfying experiences and good nights' sleep, or to hair-raising, ill- fated adventures well calculated to keep the boater in suspense. The following tips should help the average boater avoid trouble.

Know the bottom. A shale or soft mud bottom will not hold an anchor satisfactorily. Also, extensive grass on the bottom may prevent the anchor fluke from penetrating to the bottom. A rocky bottom requires a special anchoring technique. If the bottom has good holding material, almost anyone can anchor to it if they avoid "fouling" the anchor.

Most of the good-holding bottoms in northwest Washington and British Columbia are sand and mud or mud and clay. They are found at the heads of bays where valleys empty into the bay. Over time, rains wash soil from these valleys into the bays.

Use the proper sized anchor. In good bottom, patent anchors like Bruce and Danforth can hold up to 400 times their weight. Copies of patent anchors may not hold as well as the originals. The Bruce anchor, perhaps one size larger than speci-fied for your boat, is the best all around anchor. It will not foul, will reset itself, and will go down through sea weeds. In spite of its popularity, the Danforth anchor fails all three of these important tests.

Anchor rode: We recommend, as a minimum, enough rode to reach the bottom and allow for sufficient scope in ten to 15 fathoms. Of the more than 125 anchorages described in chapter 19, Northern British Columbia Coast, over 50% are in the ten to 15 fathom range. If Chapman's seven times depth rule were strictly followed, some 600 feet of anchor rode would be required. As a practical compromise, we use an oversized Bruce anchor with 100-feet of 5/8" galvanized chain and 200-feet of line. With this tackle, we have anchored successfully in depths up to 20-fathoms in calm weather. In bad weather, we can get a scope of three times depth in 15-fathoms, five times depth in ten fathoms, or seven times depth in

seven fathoms. Interestingly, we were unable to anchor securely in such depths with the same chain and line combination, using the more common Danforth anchor.

Watch out for the other guy's anchor. Before anchoring, try to visualize where the other boats' anchors are set.   Remember that these boats have prior claim to the territory. If unsure of how much scope or in what direction another boat's anchor lies, ask them. Then, mentally or on paper, draw a diagram of the existing anchors and boats. Plan to anchor well clear of them. Not only do they appreciate it, but, perhaps they'll return the favor in the future.

Never throw an anchor overboard. Always lower the anchor slowly from the boat, observing carefully that it is free from the following chain.

Always set your anchor properly and let out enough scope. First, use a depth sounder or lead line to determine the depth of water where you are anchoring.   Then, make a turn or two around the area in which yours will swing.   Pay special attention to any rocks or shallow points at the present tide which may give you trouble if a lower tide occurs during your stay.

Lower the anchor slowly until it is on the bottom. Gradually back the boat away from the anchor, in the same direction as the wind is expected to blow. This backing procedure is accomplished by taking the boat in and out of reverse gear.   Then, while slowly backing away from the anchor, keeping additional line from fouling it, let out enough scope to equal approximately three to four times the depth.   Grip the anchor line in your hands so as to cushion the force of the boat when the line becomes taut, or on larger boats, take a turn around the bow cleat. When the line is taut, give two or three tugs on the line to set the hook. Continue paying out line until your planned scope is reached. In a crowded anchorage on a calm night, you might reduce scope or use a stern anchor.

With the gear shift now in neutral position, the line may be tied off on the boat. If an extra high tide is expected overnight, pay out additional line to leave plenty of scope to account for the height of the tide. If an extreme low tide is expected, take in some line to keep the boat from swinging too far away from the anchor and into undesirable areas.

Putting out a stern anchor is possible using a dinghy. When reaching the desired spot for the anchor, the dinghy crew lowers the anchor slowly, hand-over-hand while more line is paid-out from the boat. In this way the anchor reaches the bottom at the location of the dinghy instead of half-way back to the boat as occurs when the anchor is thrown or dropped from the dinghy.

Anchoring with an all-chain rode. Always avoid having the chain pull full force on the anchor. Unlike nylon, chain has no give, and when drawn taut it may pull the anchor out or, if the anchor is hooked on a rock, the anchor blades (of a Danforth, for example) may actually bend.

In a wind, however, the holding power of good sized chain (3/8-inch or 5/8-inch) is effective because its weight tends to keep a sag in the line and reduce the actual pull on the anchor to as little as 5% of the wind force. Again, the chain will not have these qualities if pulled taut, thus chain of sufficient size and length is essential.

A favored way of anchoring with a chain rode is to let all or most of the chain out, letting the boat gently pull against the anchor to set it. Some of the chain may then be winched back into the locker to reduce the scope of the swing.

When weighing anchor. Should the anchor not come up easily, it may be necessary to tie off the line on the bow and push forward, against it, with the boat, in order to dislodge it. If the anchor is pushed in a direction which is exactly the reverse of the direction in which it was secured, it usually will come loose easily.

Introduction to British Columbia

Over 250,000 pleasure boats of every size and description ply the waters of Northwest Washington and British Columbia each year. The coastal waters of British Columbia provide a vast playground for exploration, relaxation, adventure, and a myriad of diversions. Although there are many designated Marine Parks, in a broader sense the entire coast is a marine park of gigantic proportion, breath-taking beauty, and bewildering variety. There are thousands of harbors (spelled harbours in Canada), bays, coves, marinas, towns, and waterways to explore.

The province covers 364,764 square miles or about 9.5 percent of Canada's surface area. British Columbia is Canada's third largest province, after Quebec and Ontario. Only one American state, Alaska, is larger in surface area. There are only 30 nations in the world that are larger in surface area than British Columbia. The province is four times the size of Great Britain. All of Japan would fit into British Columbia two-and-a-half times. Germany, France, Austria and Switzerland would all fit nicely into British Columbia. Of American states, you could fit California, Oregon and Washington into British Columbia and have enough room left over for Tennessee.

Almost 60 percent of the province is covered with forest. Huge Douglas fir and western red cedar thrive in the moist coastal regions. Vast forests of pine, spruce and hemlock are more common in the higher and drier interior. Ten percent of British Columbia is grazed by domestic animals or is under cultivation. Less than two percent, about 7,000 square miles is covered by freshwater lakes or rivers, located primarily in the trenches between the mountain ranges.

More than 90 percent of the land in British Columbia is owned by the provincial government as Crown land. (Crown is a British term which signifies the government interest.)

The climate of British Columbia varies greatly from north to south and east to west, influenced primarily by latitude, distance from the moderating effect of the Pacific Ocean and by the province's mountainous topography. The diversity results in huge variations in average hours of sunshine, rainfall, snow and temperatures, sometimes over short distances. For example, the average yearly precipitation in White Rock, a small community just south of Vancouver, is 43 inches. Less than 30 miles away in North Vancouver, the North Shore mountains force clouds to rise and release their moisture, producing yearly rainfall averaging 73 inches.

It is precisely this variation in climate that makes it possible to find the best of a wide array of outdoor activities within the same province. It is the climate, combined with suitable mountain sites, that serves up superlative skiing and heli-skiing. It is the climate of the coast that provides excellent conditions for sailing and motor cruising the inland ocean waterways of the south coastal region. It is the climate that creates the habitat which, in turn, supports the abundant and diverse wildlife of British Columbia that attract fishermen, hunters and hikers from around the globe.

In the South Coastal Region, summertime is reliably sunny, warm (not hot) and with a frequent ocean breeze. Temperatures in summer go to average highs in the mid 70° to 80° Fahrenheit, but evenings can be cool, so a sweater, even in July, is not at all out of place.

In winter, the south coastal region is the most temperate in all of British Columbia, with temperatures ranging just below 32° Fahrenheit. The weather is reliably rainy. The amount of rain varies greatly with location relative to local mountain ranges. Parts of this coast receive as much rain as the jungles of South America and they also have the lush, dense forest to match. Vancouver receives more rain than the eastern coast of Vancouver Island, including Victoria.

Winter or summer, weather here is extremely changeable. Lovers of the great outdoors should never be without rain gear and warm protection in the winter, and even in summer, for those sudden rainstorms. Most winters serve snow to the Vancouver and Vancouver Island regions at sea level. It can last from a few hours to a few weeks. The amount and duration of snow increases with the distance from the water, both horizontally and vertically above sea level. South coast ski resorts like to boast that you can ski, golf and take a swim in the ocean all on an early spring day.

Vancouver Island occupies an area about the size of Holland. A mountainous spine runs its length, breaking into long mountain fjords on its west coast that cut deeply into the island. One of them, Alberni Inlet, cuts more than halfway through the island, ending at Port Alberni. The west coast of the island is uninhabited, except for a sprinkling of small communities. The open Pacific Ocean washes its shores. Pockets of sandy beach add to a magic amalgam that attracts visitors from around the world. The island's major settlements and roads are clustered on its east coast where the ocean is protected. Lush forests of large Douglas fir and cedar thrive in the moderate, wet ocean climate. Victoria, on the southern tip of Vancouver Island, is the province's capital with more than three hundred thousand people if you include its suburban communities. Nanaimo, 62 miles north, has a population of about 78,271. The island economy is based squarely on the forest industry, with several mills located up and down the eastern coast. North of Vancouver Island lie the Queen Charlotte Islands, a scenic, mist-shrouded galapagos.

The Lower Mainland is part of the trough between the Vancouver Island mountains and the Coast Mountains on the mainland. In this trough, the Fraser River, stretching halfway up the middle of the province almost to its eastern border with Alberta, has deposited a large delta. It is on or near this delta where over 2.1 million people, close to half of the population of British Columbia, live in the city of Vancouver and its suburbs, which include Richmond, Burnaby, Delta, Surrey, North and West Vancouver, New Westminster and Coquitlam. The Lower Mainland is the commercial and transportation heart of the province. Burrard Inlet is a natural harbor with a scenic backdrop of Coast Mountains to the north.

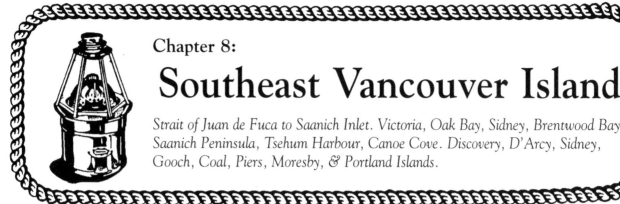

Chapter 8:
Southeast Vancouver Island

Strait of Juan de Fuca to Saanich Inlet. Victoria, Oak Bay, Sidney, Brentwood Bay, Saanich Peninsula, Tsehum Harbour, Canoe Cove. Discovery, D'Arcy, Sidney, Gooch, Coal, Piers, Moresby, & Portland Islands.

Symbols

[   ]: Numbers between [ ] are chart numbers.

{   }: Numbers & letters between { } are waypoints.

⚓: Park, ⛵: Boat Launch, ▲: Campgrounds,

⅄: Hiking Trails, ⇞: Picnic Area, ⚲: Biking

★ **Important Notice:** See "Important Notices" between Chapters 7 and 8 in this guide for specific information on boating related topics such as: Canadian & U.S. Customs, boating safety and security, navigation, weather, U.S. & Canadian Coast Guard, U.S & Canadian marine radio use, Vessel Traffic Service and traffic separation plans, security zones, and internet access. Due to new Department of Homeland Security regulations, call ahead for latest customs information and/or see Northwest Boat Travel On-line, www.nwboat.com.

★ **No Dump Zone:** Victoria Harbour

Southeast Vancouver Island

[3313, 3410, 3411, 3415, 3424, 3440, 3441, 3461]

★ **Introduction:** By sail or by motor, cruising the inland waterways of British Columbia between Vancouver Island and the mainland is a unique and superlative marine experience. The ports and places to visit on Vancouver Island, and in the neighboring Gulf Islands, are closely related in climate, topography, culture, and pleasurable experiences. There are numerous marinas and anchorages. These destinations are intimately connected by the attractive inland waterways that lead to them like highways. Boating is a way-of-life for many people who live or visit here. Shellfish, such as clams and oysters can be harvested. Fishing, observing marine and bird life, visiting sites of petroglyphs, exploring anchorages, visiting marinas, walking through Provincial Parks or towns, golfing, hiking, canoeing, kayaking, scuba diving, touring museums, dining in some very excellent restaurants,

Chart List

Canadian Hydrographic Charts:

3310, 3313, 3410, 3411, 3412, 3417, 3424, 3440, 3441, 3461, 3462, 3476, 3606, 3647

NOAA Charts:

18400, 18414-18416, 18420-18421

Marine Atlas (2005 ed.):

Pages 9, 14, 15

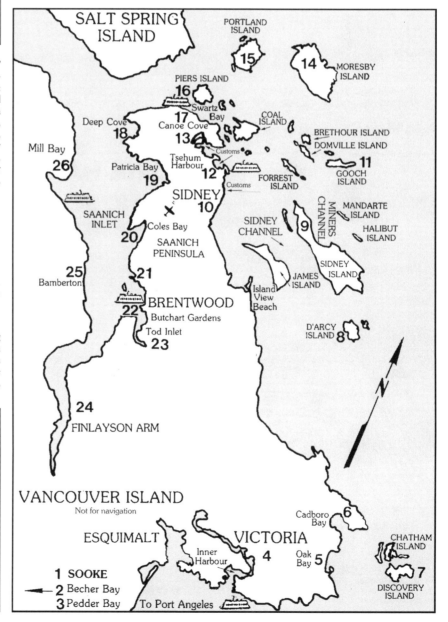

staying in fine hotels and inns, and visiting Victoria, Butchart Gardens, Oak Bay, Brentwood Bay, and Sidney are only a few of the possible vacation highlights of this area.

★ **Sooke (1):** [3410, 3411] No customs clearance available. When in the vicinity of Muir Point, near Sooke Bluffs, be aware of a hazard to navigation in the form of an Indian fish trap operated by the "T'sou-ke First Nation", Canada Department of Fisheries and Oceans, and the provincial government. The trap's design is said to allow for selective harvesting of stocks. Depending upon how you look at it, Sooke's location is either at the gateway to the west coast of Vancouver Island, or the gateway to the east coast of Vancouver Island. For description of the harbor, see Chapter 18.

Sooke Harbour Authority: Guest moorage at public floats.

Sooke Harbour Marina: Launching, moorage, power, water, showers, RV sites. 250-642-3236. VHF 16, 68.

Sunny Shores Marina: Gas, diesel, moorage, repairs, shower, lodging, campground, ramp. 250-642-5731, 1-888-805-3932. VHF 16, CB 13.

★ **Becher Bay (2):** This bay is located about ten miles from Victoria. At spring tides, currents can run to seven knots at the entrance. In Campbell Cove, anchorage can be found in Murder Bay on the north side, but note on the chart a rock that dries five feet in this cove. The east side of Becher Bay is often used for log booming.

Cheanuh Marina: Moorage, gas, water, launch ramp, Pump-out. 250-478-4880. VHF 16, CB 13.

Pacific Lions Marina: Open May-September. Limited guest moorage, cafe, campsites. 250-642-3816. VHF 16, 68.

Walk-around: East Sooke Regional Park, west of Becher Bay, contains 4500 acres with extensive hiking trails.

★ **Pedder Bay (3):** Pedder Bay indents nearly two miles, ending in mud flats. Anchorage is good near the head, however, the bay is exposed to southeast winds. A marina is located at Ash Point. The private dock east of Ash Point belongs to the college there. Orange and white buoys mark the restricted area around Williams Head Penitentiary.

Pedder Bay Marina: Moorage, gas, showers, water, launch ramp, garbage drop, laundry, 30 ampere power, limited provisions. 250-478-1771. VHF 66A.

Esquimalt: This natural harbor is home to Canada's Pacific Fleet. This is a military and industrial area. There are no good anchorages or facilities for small craft. First established by the British Navy to secure Vancouver Island for the Crown, Esquimalt received its name from the Indian word for shoaling waters. The Canadian Navy took charge in 1910.

Fleming Bay: East of the Gillingham Islands, this indentation is protected by a rock breakwater. Private floats, park, picnic area and launching ramp are found.

Victoria Harbour

★ **Victoria Harbour Traffic Scheme "Partnership In Safety":** A traffic control system applies to all vessels and seaplanes. Use Chart #3415 for reference. For the purpose of this traffic scheme, Victoria Harbour may be considered in four parts: the Outer Harbour extending from the breakwater to Shoal Point, the Middle Harbour extending from Shoal Point to Laurel Point, the Inner Harbour extending from Laurel Point to the Johnson Street Bridge, and the Upper Harbour extending north of the Johnson Street Bridge.

Two unmarked Seaplane Take-off and Landing areas, and traffic lanes for boats over 65 feet, are located in the middle of the Middle Harbour and extend out into the Outer Harbour. Located parallel to these, (on the southern portion of the Middle Harbour and extending out into the Outer Harbour) are two Inbound/Outbound Traffic Lanes for vessels to 65 feet. The southernmost lane is for inbound vessels. Four lighted yellow cautionary buoys (flashing every four seconds) are used at the eastern portion (prior to Laurel Point) to divide the inbound/outbound lanes.

All vessels entering or exiting the Inbound/Outbound Traffic Lanes should merge gradually into the appropriate traffic lane, avoiding crossing traffic lanes. If the crossing of a traffic lane is unavoidable, vessels should cross at right angles to the traffic lane.

Cautions: The vertical clearance under the Johnson Street Bridge at highwater is 5.9m (19 feet) and the width of the channel between pilings is 37m (122 ft).

White strobe lights are located at Shoal Point,

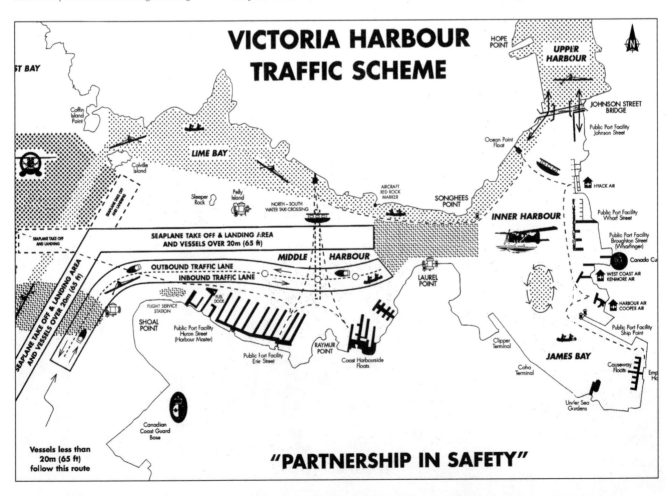

Laurel Point, and on Pelly Island and are activated by the Flight Service Station to alert mariners of the imminent take off or landing of a seaplane. When these strobe lights are activated, use extreme caution.

Three short blasts of a large ferry's whistle (the Coho) means it is in astern propulsion. Stay well clear. Never cross in front of a ferry or in its wake.

Rules and Regulations:
1. Speed Limit is five knots in the Victoria Harbour inside a line from Shoal Point to Berens Island, and seven knots outside the line.
2. Minimize wake to prevent damage.
3. No sailing is allowed in Middle, Inner and Upper Harbour. All sails must be lowered, even when under power.
4. Anchoring is prohibited without the permission of the Harbour Master.

★ **Victoria Harbour & James Bay (4):** This is a "No-dump zone." Only grey water (shower & dish water) no sewage may be released. Boats must have approved holding tank to enter a No-dump zone. Victoria Harbour is entered between Macaulay and Ogden Points. Currents run to two knots in this entrance. No sailing is allowed after rounding the breakwater, and no anchoring is permitted within the harbor. Be aware that Victoria Harbour is an aerodome, with frequent seaplane traffic. A beacon on Berens Island is activated by float plane pilots whenever they land or take-off. A dredged channel leads to West Bay. Boats arriving from the United States are to proceed to the Customs Float in the Inner Harbour. This float, identified by a large orange sign, is adjacent to the Wharf Street Float Facility. A direct line telephone is on the float. Telephone: 1-888-226-7277.

★ **Port of Victoria:** Moorage, under managment of The Greater Victoria Harbour Authority, is in several locations. While primarily on a first come-first serve basis, the staff will organize the floats for maximum use. Rafting is mandatory. The first basin, Fisherman's Wharf Floats, are to starboard upon entering the harbor. During the summer, when the fishing fleet is out, this moorage is available to pleasure craft. Because boaters have to cross open water to reach this destination, it is the policy to never turn a vessel away. The staff will attempt to find room for every visiting vessel.

Contact on VHF Channel 66A. Some areas, marked by either a yellow or red painted bull rail, are reserved. Vessels over 65' in length are requested to call ahead to give advance notice of arrival. Rafting is mandatory. Check out time is 1:00 p.m. 1-877-783-8300, 250-383-8326. Email for all facilities: moorage@victoriaharbour.org

Once in the Inner Harbour, the Empress Hotel is directly ahead, and the Parliament Buildings are to starboard. Traditionally, the favored moorage is at the city-owned Causeway Floats, directly in front of the Empress. Moorage here provides a front row view of the street scenes and the magnificent 3,300 light display on the Parliament Buildings. To the north of Causeway Floats, is Ship Point Float and Pier which offers similar views.

Farther north into the harbor, past the Customs Float, are the Wharf Street Floats. Moorage here is very convenient to shops, restaurants, and Chinatown. Continuing farther into the waterway to Upper Basin, a smaller moorage float is located adjacent to the Johnson Street Bridge (also known as Blue Bridge). The Upper Harbour, beyond the Johnson Street Bridge, is surrounded by industrial complexes. A small public float, for passenger drop-off only, is located at Banfield Park on the south shore of Selkirk Waters. Gorge Waters leads further inland, to Portage Inlet. Because of currents and restrictions, passage into the Gorge is not recommended, even by dinghy.

Customs: 1-888-226-7277 (everywhere in British Columbia).

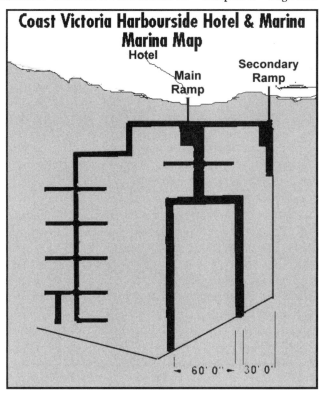

Coast Victoria Harbourside Hotel & Marina Marina Map
Hotel

Main Ramp

Secondary Ramp

60' 0"   30' 0"

★ **City of Victoria:** The capital region consists of Victoria, Oak Bay, Esquimalt, Saanich, Highlands, Sooke, Colwood, Langford, View Royal, Metchosin, Central Saanich, North Saanich and Sidney. Victoria, the *City of Gardens* is the population center of this area, and is one of the most beautiful cities in the northwest. The site was first settled in 1843 when James Douglas built a Hudson's Bay Company fort at what is now Bastion Square. Originally called Fort Albert, the name was changed to Fort Victoria. In 1852 the town site was laid out and the name shortened to Victoria. By 1864, the fort structure was demolished. It is said that, for its size, Victoria boasts more attractions catering to the interests of all ages. In addition to the Provincial Legislature Buildings and the landmark Empress Hotel, these include noted specialty shops, an aquarium, tropical indoor gardens, Maritime Museum, art galleries, miniature village, Thunderbird Park totems, Chinatown, recreation centers, Beacon Hill Park, theaters, luxury hotels, restaurants, rose gardens, heritage homes, and even a bug zoo! The Royal British Columbia Museum is probably like few others you have seen. Its *walk-through* exhibits take you to a ghost town, aboard Captain Vancouver's ship Discovery, into a native longhouse, north to the home of the grizzly bears in Khutseymateen and the mystic isles of Gwaii Haanas. Many of these attractions, and a large grocery, are within walking distance of moorage. Taxis, double-decker buses, horse drawn buggies, harbor cruises, and sight-seeing tours are available. Car ferries connect Victoria with Port Angeles year around. All year, float planes and passenger-only ferries link Victoria with Seattle, Vancouver, and Bellingham. Victoria is a center for scheduled bus service to all island communities, and buses board the ferries, taking passengers to Seattle and Vancouver.

★ **Coast Victoria Harbourside Hotel & Marina:** Daily and monthly moorage to 120' with 30 & 50 ampere power, water, and sewage pump-out. Situated on the Inner Harbour, overlooking the charming Victoria waterfront, this hotel features waterfront dining in the renowned Blue Crab Bar

Shoppers enjoy unique galleries and antique stores   Sidney Business Assoc., P. Garnham Photo

Victoria Inner Harbour   Tourism B.C. Photo

& Grill. Fitness Centre with indoor/outdoor pool, sauna and spa open to marina patrons. See our Steering Star description in this chapter. Reservations encouraged. Email: victoriamarina@coasthotels.com. Website: www.coasthotels.com. Address: 146 Kingston Street. Victoria, British Columbia, V8V 1V4. Telephone: 250-360-1211. Fax: 250-360-1418. VHF 66A.

Ocean Fuels: Gas, diesel, water, ice. 250-381-5221.

★ **Greater Victoria Harbour Authority:** Restaurants, entertainment, museums, nightlife and more await you in the charming city of Victoria...and best of all, they are all only minutes away from any of the three modern marinas located in the Inner Harbour. Permanent, guest and live-aboard moorage are available. Facilities offer power, water, security, and convenient customs clearance. For more information see advertisement in this chapter or visit www.victoriaharbour.org. Address: 202 468 Belleville St., Victoria B.C., Canada V8V 1W9. Phone: 1-877-783-8300 or 250-383-8326. VHF 66A.

★ **Fisherman's Wharf Floats:** Moorage available all year. 20 amp power, water, gas, diesel, shower, restrooms, garbage deposit. Rafting mandatory. Located east of Shoal Point. A great place to buy or eat fresh seafood. VHF 66A. 1-877-783-8300.

★ **Government Street/Ship Point:** (Causeway Moorage) Operated by the Greater Victoria Harbour Authority this moorage is located on the Inner Harbour along Government Street between Belleville and Wharf Streets and consists of the Government Street Piers and the Ship Point Wharf. Together, they provide about 2,600' of moorage on floats that accomodate boats 250 feet and less in length. Situated in James Bay, these floats are a short walk from the landmark Empress Hotel and the Tourist Information Centre. Upgraded in 2005, water and 30 amp power are available. Garbage deposit, showers, laundry, and restrooms are accessible. Open all year. First come, first served. Rafting mandatory. 1-877-783-8300. VHF 66A.

★ **Wharf Street Floats:** Open all year. Over 1,500' of moorage floats with 20, 30, 50 ampere power, water, garbage deposit. Laundry, showers, and restrooms accessible. Vessels 65-feet and over need to call ahead for arrangements. Rafting mandatory. Customs Float located nearby. 1-877-783-8300. VHF 66A.

★**Johnson Street Bridge Floats:** Approximately 100' of moorage. Open all year. Rafting mandatory, no power or water. 1-877-783-8300. VHF 66A.

West Bay Marine Village: Moorage, power, showers, laundry, RV sites, launch. 250-385-1831. VHF 66A.

Oak Bay Area

★ **Oak Bay (5):** Entrance is between Turkey Head and the breakwater projecting south from Mary Tod Island. A buoy marks the outer end of a reef extending west from Mary Tod Island. Do not pass between Tod Rock and Fiddle Reef because of shoals. The harbor has a speed limit of four knots. The Marina in Oak Bay is located here, and anchorage is possible. Named for the Garry Oaks in this vicinity, the heritage of the surrounding community dates to the days when Hudson's Bay Company personnel established summer homes and architect, Sam McClure, developed the style of English Tudor with half-timbered homes built upon native stone foundations. A contemporary architect, Francis Rattenbury, who designed the Empress and the Parliament Buildings, also had a Tudor style residence. Others who arrived from England evolved into this style of life and the heritage continues today. The area invites visitors to take a stroll and admire the fine buildings and many attractions in the vicinity. Bus and taxi service is also available to and from downtown Victoria.

The Marina in Oak Bay: Gas, diesel, moorage, power, water, launch, showers, laundry, restaurant. 250-598-3369. VHF 66A.

★ **Cadboro Bay (6):** This lovely bay is home to the Royal Victoria Yacht Club. Approach is not difficult. The recommended route from the north or east is south of Jemmy Jones Island. Anchorage is good on mud bottom near the head of the bay. A small park is within walking distance. Swimming is good, in fact Cadboro Bay is designated as a public bathing area. Launching ramps are located south of Cadboro Bay at Cattle Point. A five knot speed limit is enforced in this vicinity.

Baynes Channel: Winds are unpredictable and currents can run to six knots at the north entrance, to three knots at the south. Rips are present when wind is against the tide.

Haro Strait: See current tables for Admiralty Inlet. This strait lies between the Strait of Juan de Fuca and Boundary Bay and separates the San Juan Islands from Vancouver Island. The International Boundary between Canada and the United States lies in the center of this waterway. It is a main shipping route and traffic separation lanes are designated for large vessels. Caution advised regarding ships and the ferry which crosses the strait en route to Sidney or the San Juan Islands. The maximum velocity of tidal streams reaches four knots on the flood stream, and the strait can kick up significantly when winds are present. A local magnetic anomaly, as much as four degrees from the normal variation, has been observed in the vicinity of Bellevue Point on the east side of Haro Strait.

★⚓ **Discovery Island Marine Park (7):** [3441, 3462] This park is located two miles east of Oak Bay, where Haro Strait meets the Strait of Juan de Fuca. Enter from Plumper Passage or Hecate Passage to the west or into Rudlin Bay from the south. Because of the location and exposure to winds, there are no sheltered overnight anchorages. Temporary anchorage can be found in a niche on Chatham Island on a good bottom. Many beaches invite picnicking. No fires are permitted, use only self-contained camp stoves. Except for hiking paths, the park is undeveloped. There is a lighthouse on Seabird Point. Tide rips can be dangerous off this point as can the foul ground off Commodore Point. The southern half of the island was donated to the province by Captain E.G. Beaumont. The remainder and nearby islands are Indian Reserve. ⚲⚏

Finnerty Cove and Arbutus Cove: These coves are spots for temporary anchorage or gunkholing.

★ **Cordova Bay:** Stretching nearly four and one half miles from Gordon Head on the south to Cowichan Head on the north, this wide bay has shoal areas and some rocky patches. Kelp lines much of the shoreline. It is a popular swimming area. Anchorage can be found in the niche west of Cormorant Point. Good holding bottom. Open to north winds, however there is some protection from westerlies.

★⚓ **D'Arcy Island Marine Park (8):** [3441] This undeveloped park is surrounded by numerous shoals and reefs. Enter from the west to the south of the lighthouse. There are no sheltered anchorages. Boaters may access two mooring buoys located at the north end of the island. Call the Parks Department for a permit to go ashore. No fires are permitted, use only self contained camp stoves. Picnic tables, wilderness campsites, pit toilets, and walking paths. No water. From 1891 until 1924 this island served as a Chinese leper colony. Basic supplies were delivered by ship four times a year, but no medical attention was provided. An orchard and some ruins of buildings may be found amid the brush and undergrowth. A commemorative plaque was installed in 2001 to remember the lepers and their story. Little D'Arcy Island is privately owned. ⚏▲⚲

★⚓ **Island View Beach Park:** Island View Beach Park has a launch ramp and over four miles of sandy beach located between Cowichan Head and Cordova Spit. ⛵

★ **Saanichton Bay:** Located between Cordova Spit and Turgoose Point, this bay has good holding anchorage. A public wharf just south of Turgoose Point has a garbage drop. Mooring buoys are private.

Port Sidney Marina
Sidney Business Assoc., R. Hudson Photo

★ James Island: A conspicuous white cliff extends nearly across the south end of this thickly wooded island. Beautiful sand beaches are prevalent. Once the site of the third largest explosives plant in the world, the island has been sold and is being developed. The wharf on the east side is private. A good, all weather anchorage is located at The Gunkhole behind James Spit. The entrance is shallow, limiting sailboat access to higher tides.

★⚓ Sidney Spit Marine Park (9): This picturesque park with its long sandy beach is located on the northwest tip of Sidney Island. Shoaling has made changes in charted depths. The park is entered from Haro Strait via Miner's Channel or by Sidney Channel. There are mooring buoys, and a pier with docking facilities is available for shore access and for overnight stays. Fees charged. Boaters and park visitors will find a number of designated campsites, as well as other open, non-designated grassy field campsites. A covered picnic shelter, group camping site, picnic areas, and drinking water (rather salty!) are available. Campfires are permitted only in the designated steel fire rings provided by BC Parks. The white sand beach is irresistible to children and adults who wish to play or suntan. Several trails traverse the park—one leading to the lighthouse and one to the site where the Sidney Brick and Tile Company operated on the island in the early 1900's. Another trail leads to the lagoon, a popular spot for watching sunsets or for wildlife viewing. Look for Fallow Deer, introduced in the 1960's, and Great Blue Herons. A passenger ferry connects the park with Sidney from May 15 to September 30. ▲⛺🚶

Saanich Peninsula

[3441, 3462]

★ Saanich Peninsula: There are hundreds of things to do and see on this strip of land that stretches from Victoria north to Swartz Bay. Although Saanich Peninsula is home to Victoria International Airport, the International Ferry Terminal at Sidney, and the communities of Brentwood Bay and Sidney, there is a quiet, pas-

toral quality to the region. The word Saanich means fertile soil and there are many acres devoted to crops and dairy farms.

Visitors reach this peninsula by car ferry from Port Angeles to Victoria, Anacortes to Sidney, Tsawwassen to Swartz Bay, by passenger-only ferries from Seattle and Vancouver, by float planes, and by land plane via the Victoria International Airport. The airport, located near Sidney about 20 miles north of Victoria, serves cities around the world. Arrival by pleasure boat is to moorages in Victoria's Inner Harbour, Oak Bay, Sidney, Tsehum Harbour, Canoe Cove, and Saanich Inlet. Marinas at these locations include Port Sidney, Van Isle Marina, Canoe Cove Marina, Angler's Anchorage Marina. These are popular destinations and are courtesy telephone customs check-in sites.

Activities include touring beautiful Butchart Gardens, seeing the Model Engineer and Model Shipbuilding exhibits at the Saanich Historical Artifacts Society property near Butchart Gardens, playing golf, tennis, curling, and watching the racing at Sandown Park. Located at the airport is the British Columbia Aviation Museum. For information contact 250-655-3300. One of the world's largest telescopes is located at the Dominion Astrophysical Observatory, and the University of Victoria, located at Saanich, offers theatrical and musical performances. Local artists open their studios free to the public for the annual *Spring and Fall Studio Tours.* Major shopping localities are downtown Victoria, Royal Oak, Brentwood Bay, Saanichton, and Sidney. Saanich Inlet, which borders the peninsula's western shore, has long been known for good fishing. Launching ramps are located at Van Isle, Canoe Cove, and Angler's Anchorage Marinas, Island View Beach, Bazan Bay, Roberts Bay and Shoal Harbour.

Sidney

[3441, 3462, 3476]

★ Downtown Sidney (10): "Sidney By The Sea," is a lovely waterfront community. It is identified by the terminal for the International Ferry, a fishing pier, a wharf, and Port Sidney Marina. Sidney has the feel of a boating destination resort community. The town, and the surrounding municipality of North Saanich, are agricultural and light industrial based, but a sizeable portion is residential. Named in 1996 as the country's only "Booktown" Sidney features bookstores of every ilk. Every other May during even numbered years, Sidney hosts the *Antiquarian Book Fair.* Other shopping options include various small specialty and gift shops, pharmacies, art galleries, shopping centers, grocery stores, liquor store, hardware, marine supplies, beauty and barber shops, post office, medical services, and an array of restaurants. Services include laundry, dry cleaners, doctors, dentists.

North of downtown, the Tsehum Harbour vicinity is marine oriented with marinas, restaurants, and other attractions. See Tsehum Harbour, which follows.

Sidney is about 20 land miles from Victoria. Cyclists will enjoy the Lochside Trail, a 20-mile path to Victoria that follows the path of an old rail line. Sidney is the terminus of Washington State's International Ferry to the San Juan Islands and Anacortes, Washington. The ferry landing is about 1 mile south of the city. The Visitor's Centre is on Fifth Street, about two blocks from the ferry landing. Sidney is also connected by ferry to the Gulf Islands and to Vancouver from the Swartz Bay Ferry Terminal, north of the city, and by Victoria International Airport which is near town.

Port Sidney, the breakwater-protected moorage basin, has ample space for transient moorage with direct access to downtown Sidney. Other floats, located at the foot of Beacon Avenue in downtown Sidney, have been used for commercial vessels. Some have been removed. At this time, none are available for visitors. Customs clearance is not possible at that location. A floating Marine Ecology Centre is located at the port and is open to walk-ins. 250-655-1555. Mineral World, with interpretive centre and "scratch patch" where visitors pan for gold and excavate fossils, is located nearby. 250-655-GEMS. Beacon Avenue also hosts the *Sidney Summer Market* from June through August on Thursday evenings, featuring 170+ vendors and entertainment. The Sidney Historical Museum

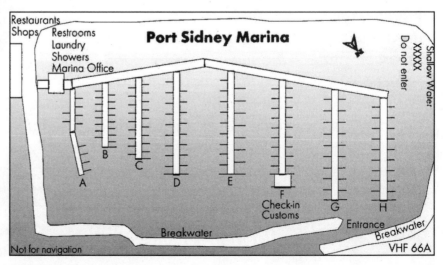

is located in the old Post Office Building, 2423 Beacon Avenue. 250-655-6355. The Mary Winspear Centre, a few blocks away, is home to the Charlie White Theatre where the Peninsula Players Community Theatre season runs from November through June. 250-656-0275. Among the city's other attractions are the Sandown Racetrack, The Institute of Ocean Sciences, and the BC Aviation Museum that holds an annual *Open House & Hangar Dance* each August. The fishing pier at the foot of Bevan has an artificial reef to attract fish. Golf enthusiasts will find several courses located nearby in North Saanich.

Port Sidney Marina: {48° 39' N, 123° 23.5' W} Open all year. Moorage, 30 & 50 ampere power, fresh potable water, laundry, showers, telephone and cablevision on certain docks. Enter via the south end of the breakwater only, where the two arms overlap. Avoid the reef extending from the north shore. Customs clearance obtainable via the courtesy telephone on the Check-in dock. 250-655-7311. VHF 66A.

Roberts Bay: This bay, with extensive shoaling at the head, lies one mile north of Sidney. Limited anchorage. Keep the day beacon on Graham Rock to port when entering.

★⚓ Ile-De-Lis Marine Park (11): Rum Island is six miles east of the Saanich Peninsula. Camping is permitted, but space is very limited. Pit toilets, but no drinking water. A trail around the island offers views of Haro Strait. Anchor temporarily in a niche on the north shore in about 30 feet of water, between the kelp patches, and tie to shore. Currents between Rum and Gooch Islands can affect boat swings. The island was named for the rum runners who frequented this area. ▲

Tsehum Harbour

[3441, 3462, 3476]

★ Tsehum Harbour (12): [3476] The harbor is easy to enter, but there are rocks along the north shore and in the approach. In season, kelp marks most of the hazards. There is courtesy telephone customs at Van Isle Marina, to port when entering, and at the Royal Victoria Yacht Club facilities. Marinas, restaurants, yacht club outstations, public floats with power, water, garbage and used oil disposal, launch ramp, telephone, charter agencies, marine supply stores, repair yards, and a shipyard are found. Named for the Indian word for clay, this is an extensive, attractive harbor located only one and one-quarter miles north of Sidney. Bus, taxi and rental cars available.

★ Van Isle Marina: Moorage for boats 20'- 300'+ in length, including a 450' section for larger vessels. Customs clearance. 110-208 volt, 15, 30, 50, 100, and 200 ampere power, telephone, cable TV hook-ups. Gas, diesel, stove oil, 50:1 outboard mix, oils, ice as well as sewage and engine oil pump-out stations, supplies, repairs,

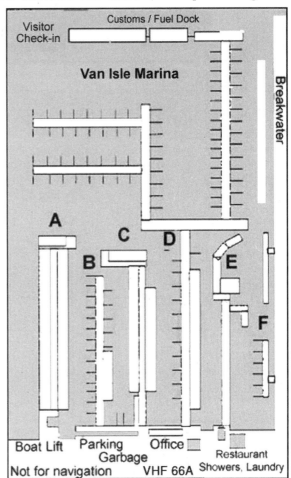

★ **Van Isle Marina:** Owned and operated by the Dickinson famiy since 1955, this full-service marina is located to port upon entering Tsehum Harbour. A 750-foot breakwater shelters an extensive moorage basin with modern concrete floats accommoding boats from 20'-300'+ in length, including a new 450' section for larger vessels added in 2002. Van Isle Marina is designated as a Port-of-Entry for courtesy telephone Canada Customs clearance. The fuel dock and the Customs float are near the harbour entrance. The fuel dock has gas,

diesel, stove oil, 50:1 outboard mix, oils, and ice as well as accessible sewage and oil pump-out stations. The fuel dock store has many supplies, from tackle to charts, mooring lines to lifejackets. Overnight, monthly, seasonal, and annual moorage is available. Shore power includes 110/208 volts, 15, 30,50, 100, and 200 amps. Telephone and cable TV services are available. A yacht brokerage, haul outs, launching, and repair facilities are part of the marina complex.

The licensed restaurant, Dock 503 Waterfront Dining, serves Sunday Brunch, lunch and dinner daily. Showers, restrooms, and a laundry building are on the premises. Garbage and recycling bins are located upland in the car parking lot. Fishing and dive charters, and whale-watching trips can be arranged. Shopping, parks, golf courses, and a recreation center are all nearby. Bus, taxi, and rental cars are available for those who would like to explore downtown Sidney or the entire Saanich Peninsula. It is also possible to headquarter here to make connections with guests who fly into nearby Victoria International Airport or who wish to arrive by ferry at the Swartz Bay – Gulf Island - Vancouver Ferry Terminal, or at the Sidney-Anacortes Ferry Terminal. Open all year. Reservations recommended. **E-mail: info@vanislemarina.com Internet site: http://www.vanislemarina.com & http://www.boattravel.com/vanisle/ Address: 2320 Harbour Road Sidney, British Columbia V8L 2P6 Telephone: 250-656-1138; Fax: 250-656-0182. VHF 66A.**

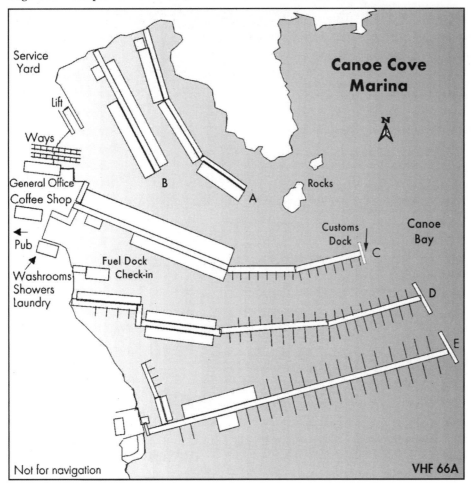

Canoe Cove Marina

Service Yard

Lift

Ways

General Office
Coffee Shop

← Pub

Washrooms
Showers
Laundry

B

A

Rocks

Fuel Dock
Check-in

Customs
Dock

C

Canoe
Bay

D

E

Not for navigation

VHF 66A

haul-outs, towing, showers, laundry, restaurant, good and helpful chandlery. VHF 66A. See our Steering Star description in this chapter. Telephone: 250-656-1138; Fax: 250-656-0182. E-mail: info@vanislemarina.com. Websites: http://www.vanislemarina.com & http://www.boattravel.com/vanisle/. Address: 2320 Harbour Road, Sidney, British Columbia V8L 2P6. VHF 66A.

The Boatyard: Complete repair faciltiy with 40 and 60 ton Travelifts. Vessels to 19' beam accommodated. Power and sail. 250-655-1511.

North Saanich Marina: Gas, diesel, water. 250-656-5558.

Philbrook's Boatyard: {48° 40' N, 123° 24' W} Yacht service, repair, and marine ways. Near Van Isle Marina. 250-656-1157.

Tsehum Harbour Authority: Transient moorage during summer months, security camera. pump-out, commercial fishing dock. Rafting mandatory. 250-655-4496.

Westport Marina: Limited moorage, power, showers, haul-outs. 250-656-2832.

Canoe Cove

[3441, 3462, 3476]

★ **Canoe Cove (13):** Iroquois Passage can be used to reach Canoe Cove from either the north or the south. If

---

★ **Canoe Cove Marina & Complete Boat Repair Centre:** Established in the early 1930's, Canoe Cove is strategically located in the sheltered waters of Canoe Bay at the northeast end of the Saanich Peninsula

on Vancouver Island. It is approximately 3 miles north of Sidney and 20 miles north of Victoria. The full service marina offers **one of the largest pleasure craft repair yards in British Columbia.** Service facilities include 65 and 35 tonne marine-ways, 35 tonne travel-lift, 40 tonne yard trailer, plus over 25,000 square feet of "inside" workshop space. Canoe Cove Marina & Blackline Marine offer most services you will require for your boat, including Yanmar Service, installation and service for heating systems, installation & service for thrusters & roll stabilizers, major & minor fibreglass work, application of Awlgrip® paint, sail boat rigging & spar building, metal fabrication, electrical, mechanical, woodwork, shipwright & brushed coatings. 50 full time staff. The dry land storage facility has a capacity for over 120 vessels. Short term and overnight moorage is available throughout the summer. On shore facilities include customs dock, laundry , showers, seaside cafe, English style pub and restaurant, marine supply store, boat brokerage, canvas & sail work, boat charters, and a full service fuel dock. **Websites: www.canoecovemarina.com,   www.boattravel.com/canoecove   Email: wharfage@canoecovemarina.com. Address: 2300 Canoe Cove Road, North Saanich, BC V8L 3X9. Telephone: 250-656-5566 or 250-656-5515. Fax: 250-655-7197. VHF 66A.**

The Empress Hotel In Victoria   *Terri Van Lith Photo*

approaching from the north, keep Goudge Island on the port and Musclow Islet on the starboard. After rounding Musclow Islet turn into the harbor. When arriving from the south, pass between Fernie Island and Goudge. After rounding Rose Rock, a passage leads into the bay.

★ **Canoe Cove Marina:** {48° 41' N, 123° 24' W} Designated as a courtesy telephone customs check-in, this full service marina and large repair facility has moorage with power and water, laundry, showers, marine parts, haul-outs, gas, diesel, propane, and chandlery. See our Steering Star description in this chapter. Website: www.canoe-covemarina.com & www.boattravel.com/canoe-cove Address: 2300 Canoe Cove Road, North Saanich, British Columbia V8L 3X9. Telephone: 250-656-5515 or 250-656-5566. Fax: 250-655-7197. VHF 66A.

★ **Moresby Island (14):** Anchorage can be found on opposite ends of this thickly wooded island in unnamed bays inside Point Fairfax and south of Reynard Point. The first gives some protection in southwest winds and the latter shelters from northeast blows. Note charts for two rocks that are hazards in this area.

★⚓ **Portland Island, Princess Margaret Marine Park (15):** Royal Cove, behind Chads Island, offers a small semi-sheltered anchorage. A dinghy dock for shore access is located at the end of the cove. A hand pump for fresh water is located ten minutes from Royal Cove by trail in the middle of an old farming field. Camping is permitted at Princess Bay, Shell Beach, and Arbutus Point. Pit toilets are located a short distance from the bay. No fires are permitted. Reefs and shoals fringe much of the shore. The principal anchorage is in Princess Bay, a fairly well protected niche at the southern end. Enter north of Tortoise Islets. Favor the islet's shore. An Information Float can be found in the bay during the summer. Black Oyster Catchers, with their red beaks and legs, feed and nest nearby. Look for fruit trees and garden plants among the native vegetation—the legacy of Hawaiian immigrants who settled here in the 1880's. In 1958, Portland Island was given to Princess Margaret when she visited British Columbia. She later returned it to the province for use as a park and today it is part of the Gulf Islands National Park Reserve. No public access is permitted onto the Brackman Island Ecological Reserve. There is temporary anchorage between Brackman Island and Portland Island.

★ **Piers Island (16):** Three, 70 foot public floats are located northwest of Wilhelm Point. Depths alongside shallow to four feet. The moorage is used primarily by island residents.

Swartz Bay (17): Located on the south side of Colburne Pass, this busy site is a major terminal for British Columbia ferries. There is ferry service to the Gulf Islands and to Tsawwassen, on the

Many communities, like Sidney, host seasonal Farmers markets.   *Sidney Business Assoc., R. Hudson Photo*

Butchart Gardens, Tod Inlet   *Tourism B.C. Photo*

mainland south of Vancouver. It is possible to use the small public float, to the left of the ferry docks, as a pick-up or departure point for guests. Two hour moorage is allowed. Minimum depths alongside the float are about two feet. Rock ledges and sand shallows are in the approach and ferry right-of-way are considerations while in this vicinity.

Saanich Inlet
[3441, 3462]

★ **Saanich Inlet:** This is a lovely and popular inlet with a reputation for good fishing and a selection of attractions, such as Butchart Gardens, Heritage Acres, Tod Inlet, Finlayson Arm, parks, restaurants, marinas, and the town of Brentwood Bay. Bluebacks are best during March and April. Chinooks and Coho are good almost anytime, with September and October the best as they migrate from the Pacific to spawn in the Goldstream River. Launching can be made at Deep Cove, Mill Bay and Brentwood Bay.

★ **Pumpty Dumpty:** The Pumpty Dumpty is a 20 foot aluminum vessel fitted with a 200 gal storage tank and suction pumps for pumping holding tanks on vessels in Saanich Inlet. 250-480-9292 or call "Pumpty Dumpty" on VHF 16, 66A.

★ **Deep Cove (18):** Entered between Moses Point and Coal Point, pass on either side of Wain Rock. If time, try a little fishing as you drift by. Deep Cove: The Canadian Hydrographic Service reports an uncharted rock, with a drying height of 0.7 meters. Ruins of a government wharf are in the south part and a marina is east of the wharf. Caution advised regarding drying rocks, marked by a day beacon and a buoy, in this area. Private buoys are often found in the bay, but limited anchorage may be possible.

Deep Cove Marina: Permanent and limited guest moorage, power, water. 250-656-0060.

Patricia Bay (19): [3462] Site of the Institute of Ocean Services and the Victoria International Airport, this bay is also used for Department of National Defense operations. Orange buoys designate the site. The breakwater is reserved for vessels of the Scientific Institute. Anchorage is not permitted within 500 feet of the operations area. Victoria International Airport is behind the bay.

★ **Coles Bay (20):** Anchorage, open to south winds, can be found near the head. There is a nice beach and a small park. Avoid shoals extending south of Yarrow Point.

Thomson Cove (21): Limited anchorage with protection from some winds.

Brentwood Bay
[3441, 3462]

★ **Brentwood Bay (22):** The community of Brentwood Bay covers the hillside and waterfront. A shopping center is located on the highway up the hill. This is the heart of the famed Saanich Inlet-Brentwood Bay fishing region. Condominiums, marinas, launch ramp, a government wharf with moorage floats, and the Brentwood Bay-Mill Bay ferry landing are located here. Bus service connects with Sidney and Victoria.

Brentwood Bay Lodge & Spa: Moorage, laundry, showers, grocery store, ice. 250-652-3151.

Anglers Anchorage Marina: Moorage, power, water, showers, laundry, pump-out, no customs clearance. 250-652-3531. VHF 68A.

★ **Tod Inlet (23):** This lovely inlet has a very narrow entrance. The first bay to the port is the boaters' entrance to Butchart Gardens. The Gardens now have a new larger float for dinghies (no boat moorage allowed) and float planes, as well as limited buoys. Do not anchor near the buoys. The bottom is foul and frequent float plane activity prohibit anchorage. For anchorage on a mud bottom, proceed father into Tod Inlet. A buoy to port, just past the entrance, marks a rock on the edge of a small gravel spit. The surrounding hillsides cradle the small basin.

★ **Finlayson Arm (24):** This is a beautiful fjord which joins Saanich Inlet with the Goldstream River. Depths can reach 600 feet. Famous for fishing and scuba diving waters.

★⚓ **Goldstream Park:** Major access is by car, however, the boundary of the park is accessible at high tides by dinghy from Goldstream Boathouse. There are about 150 campsites about a four kilometer walk from the boathouse moorage. Water is supplied as is a building which houses showers. There are picnic grounds, miles of trails, and a Nature House. ▲⚓☩

Goldstream Boathouse: Moorage, 15 & 30 ampere power, gas, diesel, water, repairs, tackle, bait, launch. 250-478-4407. VHF 66A.

Bamberton (25): Nearly 50 campsites, with wood, water, swimming, cold water shower, and picnic areas. When approaching by water, caution advised because a shelf extends about 100 feet out from shore before it makes a sharp drop-off.

Mill Bay
[3441, 3462]

★ **Mill Bay (26):** The Mill Bay-Brentwood Ferry lands at McPhail Point, south of Mill Bay. This ferry is used by those whose destination is the Saanich Peninsula and want to avoid traveling the Malahat and around to Victoria. A marina, two public launch ramps and a public float with about 75 feet of moorage are found. Four wineries are nearby and an Info Centre is in the mall convenient to the marina.

Mill Bay Marina: {48° 39' N, 123° 33' W} Gas, diesel, marine supplies, showers, and laundry are available. 250-743-4112. VHF 66A.

Victoria Inner Harbour, British Columbia Parliament Buildings   *Tourism B.C. Photo*

Essential Supplies & Services

AIR TRANSPORTATION
To & from Washington
Seattle Seaplanes **1-800-637-5553**
To & from Islands/Vancouver
Air Canada 1-888-247-2262
Baxter Air (Nanaimo) 1-800-661-5599
Harbour Air 1-800-665-0212
Tofino Air 1-800-665-2359
Vancouver Island Air . . 250-287-2433 1-877-331-2433
  (Canada only)

AMBULANCES 911

BOOKS / BOOK STORES
The Marine Atlas. **541-593-6396**

BUS TRANSPORTATION
B C Transit. 250-382-6161
Greyline (Victoria-Seattle) 800-663-8390
Island Coach Lines . . . . 250-385-4411 (US)
  . . . . 1-800-318-0818 (Cdn)
Pacific Coach Lines 1-800-661-1725
Victoria Airporter 250-386-2526

COAST GUARD
VHF 16, 26, #16
Victoria 250-480-2600
Rescue Coordination Center. 1-800-567-5111

CUSTOMS: 1-888-226-7277
See Important Notices between Chapters 7 & 8

FERRY INFORMATION
B C Ferries. 250-386-3431, 1-888-223-3779
Sidney-Anacortes 250-656-1831
Swartz Bay. 250-386-3431
Victoria Clipper (passenger only) 1-800-888-2535
  250-382-8100
Victoria-Port Angeles. 250-386-2202

FUELS
Canoe Cove: Gas, Diesel . . **250-656-5566 VHF 66A**
Cheanuh Marina: Becher Bay. Gas.
  . . . . 250-478-4880 VHF 16, CB 13
Goldstream Boathouse: Saanich Inlet. Gas, Diesel.
  250-478-4407
Mill Bay: Gas, Diesel. 250-743-4112 VHF 66A
North Saanich Marina: Tsehum Harbour. Gas, Diesel.
  250-656-5558
Oak Bay Marina: Gas, Diesel. . . 250-598-3369 VHF 66A
Pedder Bay Marina: Gas . . . . . 250-478-1771 VHF 68
Ocean Fuels: Victoria. Gas, Diesel . 250-381-5221 VHF 68
Sunny Shores: Sooke. Gas, Diesel. 250-642-5731
Van Isle Marina: Gas, Diesel.
  . . . . **250-656-1138 VHF 66A**

GOLF COURSES
These courses are accessible from moorage and have rental clubs available)
Arbutus Ridge 250-743-5000
Ardmore 250-656-4621
Glen Meadows. 250-656-3921
Gorge Vale 250-386-3401

HOSPITALS
Victoria 250-727-4212

IMMIGRATION (U.S.) / (BORDER PROTECTION)
Washington State Ferry Dock 250-656-1014
(10 a.m.-noon all year; 4-6 p.m. mid-June to mid-
  September)

Office: 812 Wharf Street, #209, Victoria, B C V8W 1T3,
  CANADA. 250-384-1821

INSURANCE
Boat Insurance Agency **206-285-1350**
Or Call **1-800-828-2446**

LIQUOR STORES
Brentwood Bay
Cowichan Bay (Pier 66)
Mill Bay
Sidney
Sooke
Victoria

LODGING
Coast Victoria Harbourside Hotel & Marina:
  Victoria. **250-360-1211**

MARINAS / MOORAGE FLOATS
Anglers Anchorage: Brentwood Bay.
  . . . . 250-652-3531 VHF 68
Brentwood Bay Lodge & Spa 250-652-3151
Canoe Cove Marina. . . . . . **250-656-5566 VHF 66A**
Cheanuh Marina: Becher Bay. 250-478-4880 VHF 16, CB 13
Coast Harbourside Hotel & Marina: Victoria.
  . . . . **250-360-1211**
Deep Cove Marina 250-656-0060
Fisherman's Wharf Floats 1-877-783-8300 VHF 66A
Goldstream Boathouse: Saanich Inlet . . . 250-478-4407
Government St/Ship Point **1-877-783-8300**
Greater Victoria Harbor Authority 1-877-783-8300,
  . . . . **250-383-8300 VHF 66A**
Johnson Street floats: . . **1-877-783-8300 VHF 66A**
Mill Bay Marina. . . . . 250-743-4112 VHF 66A
Oak Bay Marina . . . . 250-598-3369 VHF 66A
Pedder Bay Marina . . . . 250-478-1771 VHF 66A
Piers Island
Port Sidney Marina . . . . 250-655-3711, VHF 66A
Sidney Spit Marine Park
Sooke Harbour Marina:. . . . . 250-642-3236 VHF 16, 68
Sunny Shores Marina: Sooke 250-642-5731
Tsehum Harbour Authority 250-655-4496
Van Isle Marina . . . . **250-656-1138 VHF 66A**
West Bay Marina: Victoria. . . . . 250-385-1831 VHF 68
Wharf Street Floats . . . . **1-877-783-8300 VHF 66A**

MARINE SUPPLY STORES
Boathouse, The: Sidney. 250-655-3682
Oak Bay Marina . . . . 250-598-3369 VHF 66A

POISON INFORMATION
Victoria. 1-800-567-8911

PROPANE
Canoe Cove Marina. . . . . . **250-656-5566 VHF 66A**

RAMPS / HAUL-OUTS
Anglers Anchorage: Brentwood Bay 250-652-3531
Bazan Bay
Boatyard, The: Tsehum Harbour 250-655-1511
Canoe Cove Marina. . . . . . **250-656-5566 VHF 66A**
Cattle Point: Cadboro Bay
Cheanuh Marina . . . . 250-478-4880 VHF 16
Fleming Bay: Esquimalt
Goldstream Boathouse: Saanich Inlet . . . 250-478-4407
Island View Beach
Mill Bay Marina. . . . . 250-743-4112 VHF 66A
Oak Bay Marina . . . . 250-598-3369 VHF 66A
Pedder Bay Marina . . . . 250-478-1771 VHF 66A
Philbrooks Boatyard 250-656-1157
Roberts Bay

Shoal Harbour
Sunny Shores: Sooke 250-642-5731
Tsehum Harbour Authority 250-655-4496
Van Isle Marina . . . . **250-656-1138 VHF 66A**
Vector Yacht Service: Tsehum Harbour . . 250-655-3222

RED TIDE INFO 604-666-2828

REPAIRS/SERVICE
Boatyard, The: Tsehum Harbour 250-655-1511
Canoe Cove Marina. . . . . . **250-656-5566 VHF 66A**
Goldstream Boathouse: Saanich Inlet . . . 250-478-4407
Oak Bay Marina . . . . 250-598-3369 VHF 66A
Philbrooks Boatyard: Tsehum Harbour . . 250-656-1157
Sea Power Marine Centre: Sidney 250-656-4341
Van Isle Marina: Tsehum Harbour
  . . . . **250-656-1138 VHF 66A**
Vector Yacht Service: Tsehum Harbour . . 250-655-3222

RESCUE COORDINATION
Search & Rescue 1-800-567-5111
Marine Distress 250-363-2333
Cell Phone (select providers) . . . . #16

RESTAURANTS
Coast Victoria Harbourside Hotel & Marina:
  Victoria. **250-360-1211**
Van Isle Marina . . . . **250-656-1138 VHF 66A**

SEWAGE DISPOSAL
Anglers Anchorage: Brentwood Bay. Pump.
  . . . . 250-652-3531. VHF 66A
Cheanuh Marina: Becher Bay. Pump 250-478-4880
Coast Victoria Harbourside Hotel & Marina:
  Victoria. **250-360-1211**
Mill Bay: Dump. . . . . 250-743-4112 VHF 66A
Port Sidney Marina. Pump 250-655-3711
Pumpty Dumpty: Saanich Inlet. Pump.
  . . . . 250-480-9292 VHF 16, 66A
Tsehum Harbour Authority: Pump. 250-655-4496
Van Isle Marina: Pump . . . **250-656-1138 VHF 66A**

SHELLFISH HOTLINE 604-666-2828

SPORT FISHING. 250-363-3252

TAXI / RENTAL CARS
Sidney/Brentwood/Victoria 250-656-5588
  1-800-808-6881
Van Isle Marina . . . . **250-656-1138 VHF 66A**
Victoria 250-382-4235

TOWING
C-TOW. **1-888-354-5554**
Van Isle Marina: Tsehum Harbour . . **250-656-1138**
Vector Yacht Service: Tsehum Harbour . . 250-655-3222

TRAIN
Victoria-Courtenay 1-888-842-7245

VHF MARINE OPERATOR
Bellingham . . . . VHF 28, 85
Ganges . . . . VHF 27, 64
Victoria . . . . VHF 86

VISITOR INFORMATION
Mill Bay/S. Cowichan. 250-743-3566
Saanich Penin./Sidney. 250-656-0525
Sooke 250-642-6351

WEATHER:
VHF WX-1, WX-3, WX-4
Environment Canada Weather Line. 250-339-9861
Victoria (recorded) 250-363-6717

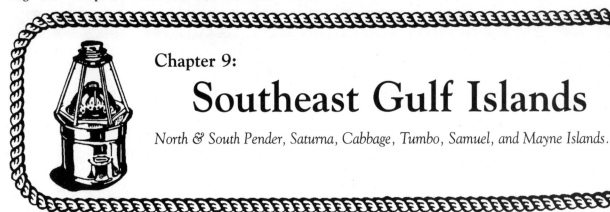

Chapter 9:
Southeast Gulf Islands

North & South Pender, Saturna, Cabbage, Tumbo, Samuel, and Mayne Islands.

Symbols

[   ]: Numbers between [ ] are chart numbers.

{   }: Numbers & letters between { } are waypoints.

⚓: Park, ⛵: Boat Launch, ▲: Campgrounds,
🥾: Hiking Trails, ⛱: Picnic Area, 🚲: Biking

★ **Important Notice:** See "Important Notices" between Chapters 7 and 8 in this guide for specific information on boating related topics such as: Canadian & U.S. Customs, boating safety and security, navigation, weather, U.S. & Canadian Coast Guard, U.S & Canadian marine radio use, Vessel Traffic Service and traffic separation plans, security zones, and internet access. Due to new Department of Homeland Security regulations, call ahead for latest customs information and/or see Northwest Boat Travel On-Line, www.nwboat.com.

Gulf Islands

[3313, 3441, 3442, 3462, 3473, 3477]

★ **Introduction:** Boating is a way-of-life for many who live and visit here. These destinations are intimately connected by the attractive waterways that lead to them like highways. The area is bordered on the south by the international boundary, on the north and east by Georgia Strait, and on the west by Vancouver Island, which provides shelter from the Pacific Ocean. Many marinas and anchorages are available. Boating visitors return again and again to these islands, discovering hide-aways and communities to explore with each visit. Chapter 9 will cover the southernmost islands. Chapters 10 and 11 will describe the

Chart List

Canadian Hydrographic Charts:

3313, 3441-42, 3473, 3477, 3478

NOAA Charts:

18400, 18421, 18432

Marine Atlas (2005 ed.):

Page 11, 12

other islands and the communities located opposite them along the east coast of Vancouver Island.

Salt Spring Island has the greatest population, with the Penders, Galiano, and Mayne following in that order. The main center of commerce is Ganges, on Salt Spring Island. Often, small communities such as Fulford Harbour, Village Bay, Sturdies Bay, and Saturna are located near a ferry landing for vessels which link the islands with Vancouver and Swartz Bay.

Shellfish harvesting of clams and oysters, fishing, observing marine and bird life, visiting sites of petroglyphs, exploring anchorages, visiting marinas, walking through parks or towns, golfing, hiking, canoeing, kayaking, scuba diving, and dining in one of the many good restaurants are only a few of the possible vacation highlights of this area.

The climate is mild with an annual rainfall of less than 30 inches, most of which falls between November and March. Summer water temperatures range from 59-63 degrees Fahrenheit. Water temperatures are higher in some coves and where the water is shallow. Normal summer air temperature range from 54-74 degrees Fahrenheit. In some locales, hot summer days of 84-90 degrees are not uncommon. The sun shines about 60 percent of the time during summer months. The summer fair weather winds are from the northwest. When these northwest winds prevail, they have a predictable pattern to them. Generally,

they will rise in mid-morning and go down in the late afternoon. As Indians observed, long before the government weather services, if these winds do not go down in the afternoon, it will likely blow for three days. These prevailing winds are modified by local on-shore winds during the afternoons and off-shore winds during the evening hours. These winds are caused by the heating and cooling of the land masses. When the wind blows from the southeast, it generally indicates a change in the weather or the approach of a storm front. The strength of southeast storm winds is difficult to predict and they can result in sea conditions that are uncomfortable or even dangerous. It is wise to spend such times in one of the well-sheltered marinas, in a very protected anchorage, or at least not on the open waters of the straits.

During summer months, higher-high tides tend to occur at night while lower-low tides occur during daylight hours. These are the tides that are treasured by shellfish collectors. Boaters, however, can be surprised by rocks and shelves that are exposed or become dangerous to navigation or anchorage. Tidal fluctuations during spring tides, when the moon is full or new, tend to be relatively large, ranging from nine feet at Victoria to seventeen feet at Comox. Tidal runs at springs are usually one to two knots, however maximums of ten knots occur in certain passes. Generally, it is best to be heading south during an ebbing tide or north during a flood tide since traveling with the current will increase speed and save fuel. The land in most of this area is composed of sedimen-

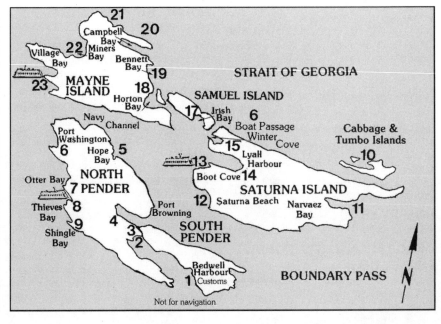

tary rock made up of sandstone, shale or conglomerate. The layers of these rocks are deposited in a northwest/southeast direction. Centuries of a process of decomposition and erosion of these materials have created ridges and valleys which generally run northwest/southeast. Where the valleys slope down to the water, there are often sheltered bays with good holding ground which has been deposited there by run-off waters from the valleys.

North and South Pender Islands

[3441, 3462, 3477]

★ **Bedwell Harbour (1):** {48° 45' N, 123° 14' W} Named for Captain Edward Bedwell, who was master of an 1860 survey ship, this harbor has several attractions. Thousands of boaters visit each year to clear customs.

★ **Peter Cove:** Private buoys limited anchorage. Open to wakes. Located to port, when entering Bedwell Harbour from the south.

★ **Egeria Bay:** This bay is to starboard upon entering Bedwell Harbour from the south, and is the site of a customs port-of-entry and a marina resort. The graffiti on the cliff by the marina dates to 1905, the work of the crew of the Royal Navy vessel *HMS Egeria*.

Customs: May 1 through September 30. Boaters arriving from the U.S. who have not cleared by CANPASS, must tie to the customs floats upon arrival. The customs staff have a boat and are often out and about. Phones on the dock connect directly to the Customs Reporting Centre. 1-888-226-7277.

Poets Cove Resort & Spa: Moorage, power, water, gas, diesel, laundromat, showers, provisions, lodge, restaurant. 250-629-2111. VHF 66A

★⚓ **Beaumont Marine Park:** Nestled against the steep hillside just northwest of Egeria Bay is this provincial park. A large number of mooring buoys are provided. A sand and gravel beach, fresh drinking water, picnic areas, and campsites are

available. ▲ ⅋

Walk Around: Walking trails lead to 890 foot high Mount Norman.

★ **Pender Canal (2):** Passage through this narrow, attractive gorge is possible at almost any tide, except for sailboats with masts that will not clear the bridge's minimum 26 feet. When leaving Bedwell Harbour through this canal, a red spar buoy is on a four foot drying rock at the south end of the canal. Passage is made between this buoy and a green spar buoy opposite it. Minimum depth in the canal is seven feet. Minimum width is 40 feet at the bridge. Maximum current at springs is four knots. The flood current sets north, ebbs south. Tidal range is 11 feet. This man-made waterway was built in 1903 to connect Shark Cove and the head of Bedwell Harbour. The bridge was built in 1955. Middens of the Coast Salish, who lived in this area more than 5,000 years ago, are still in evidence. This vicinity is designated as a provincial heritage site.

★ **Shark Cove (3):** There is temporary anchorage in this niche northwest of the bridge over Pender Canal. Two submerged rocks are visible in the emerald green water of the cove. Wakes from passing boats may be partially avoided by a stern line tied to shore, keeping the bow facing the wakes. Mortimer Spit, which lies opposite the cove, is the site of an extensive gravel beach that is a popular picnicking and swimming spot.

★ **Port Browning (4):** This is the site of the Port Browning Marina and a public float. Anchorage in the harbor is exposed to the east, but protected from prevailing westerlies. One anchoring basin is to port adjacent to Aldridge Point. Water depths are 30- 40 feet at high tide on a fairly even bottom. Hamilton Beach, with its white sand and gravel, is nearby. A very small public wharf, with tidal grid, is to starboard, and a marina resort is at the head of the bay. Within walking distance from the head of the bay is a small shopping mall with post office, liquor store, grocery, bakery, and pharmacy. On summer Saturday mornings, this becomes the site of Pender Island's Public Market. The market begins by the middle of June and takes place every Saturday until November. Because of its popularity, arrival before the 10:00 a.m. opening is suggested. **Port Browning is a**

new CANPASS only customs check-in site. (May 21, 2004)

Port Browning Marina Resort: Moorage, power, lodging, laundry, showers, launch, restaurant, beer & wine. 250-629-3493. VHF 66A.

★ **Hope Bay (5):** Tucked in behind Faine Island, this bay has a public wharf and float. Depths are shallow on the inner side of the floats at low tides. Space is limited, but good temporary anchorage can be taken a short way off in the adjacent bay. (Hope Bay Harbour Commission dock, 250-629-9990). The landmark store was destroyed by fire in 1998, but has been rebuilt to resemble the 1912 store, with modern conveniences. Navy Channel currents run to three knots, flooding to the east and ebbing to the west.

Welcome Cove & Colston Cove: These coves afford temporary anchorage, however, they are open to currents.

★ **Port Washington, Grimmer Bay (6):** Mooring floats, which extend east and west from the dock, permit temporary moorage. When approaching this public dock, note that a rock with a depth of less than six feet lies about 150 feet south of the southeast end of the dock. Grimmer Bay is divided in half by a shoal which extends to Boat Islet. Some anchorage is possible, however, the niche is open to the west and wakes of large ferries.

★ **Otter Bay (7):** The Otter Bay-Swartz Bay ferry landing is in the outer portion of the bay. There is anchorage on a mud bottom in Hyashi Cove, inland from the ferry landing. It is exposed to west winds and some ferry wash. Inquire about swimming in Roe Lake, a favorite with locals. With the development of time-share condominiums, the cove is a boating destination with docks, store, swimming pool and nearby golf course.

Otter Bay Marina: Moorage, power, water, showers, laundry, tent, provisions. 250-629-3579. VHF 66A.

Thieves Bay (8): Hidden behind a breakwater, this shallow bay is nearly filled with private moorings. A rock, marked by kelp, lies to starboard near the entrance. A launching ramp is near the head.

Shingle Bay (9): Entirely open to west winds, this bay affords only limited anchorage. The cove north of Mouat Point has adequate depths. This was once the site of a fish reduction plant. Remaining pilings are hazards.

Pender Canal

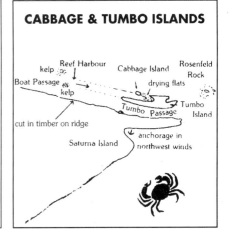

CABBAGE & TUMBO ISLANDS

Tumbo and Cabbage Islands

[3441]

★ **Tumbo & Cabbage Islands (10):** {3313, 3441} Charts are essential. These small islands lie off the southeast tip of Saturna. The area just outside of the reef line, stretching west-northwest from Tumbo and Cabbage, is a favored fishing zone. Do not attempt passage into Reef Harbour between the southeast side of Cabbage and the northeastern shore of Tumbo. A drying reef and mud flats extend between the islands at this location. No approach to Reef Harbour is without hazard. The safest approach is to locate the end of the reef that extends northwestward on a line through Tumbo and Cabbage Islands and Pine Islet. This reef is about one mile long from Cabbage Island. By avoiding the reef, it is possible to head directly toward Saturna. A turn to port is made when the vessel is on a line with Reef Harbour. Proceeding east-by-southeast on a course of about 105 degrees, it is possible to enter between the reef extending west-northwest from Cabbage and the reef extending west-northwest from the western finger of Tumbo. In season, kelp marks some of the areas to be avoided, but at other times of the year it is difficult to navigate this entry. In Reef Harbour it is necessary to consult the boat's depth sounder, the chart, and tide predictions for satisfactory overnight anchorage depths. There are drying mud flats to the east-southeast of Cabbage Island to be avoided. Although this anchorage is exposed to northwest and southeast winds and is difficult to enter, Tumbo Island at least gives protection from seas in southeast winds. Reef Harbour, between Tumbo and Cabbage, has buoys, a sandy beach on Cabbage, and good crabbing along the north shore of Tumbo near the buoys. No water is available. Anchorage is possible. Cabbage and Tumbo Islands are part of the Gulf Islands National Park Reserve established in 2003. Both are under the management of BC Parks. **Cabbage Island is a CANPASS only customs check-in site.**

★⚓ **Cabbage Island Provincial Marine Park:** Ten mooring buoys are located in Reef Harbour between Cabbage Island and the eastern tip of Tumbo. Camping is permitted on Cabbage only in designated areas. Fees are charged for campsites and mooring buoys from May 1 through September 30. Pit toilets, hiking trails, and an information shelter are available. No water available and fires are not permitted. Keep dogs on leashes at all times. Walking, swimming, fishing, scuba diving and bird watching are popular activities. Bald Eagles and Black Oystercatchers nest here. ▲⚲

Saturna Island

[3441, 3462, 3477]

★ **Saturna Island:** Although one of the largest of the Gulf Islands, Saturna is relatively undeveloped and has a permanent population of 300. Saturna is connected to the inland ferry network with the terminal located on the point of the peninsula that separates Boot Cove and Lyall Harbour. It is also accessible by chartered and scheduled float plane and water taxi. The island is home to nature trails, good biking roads, several B & B's, grocery stores, a bank, post office, a pub, restaurant, and Saturna Lodge and winery. Special events include a Pig Roast in May, a Lamb Barbecue on Canada Day (July 1), a Salmon Barbecue in August and Saturday Markets in July

Winter Cove Church   Lynn Mortensen Photo

and August. Good swimming beaches are found in Veruna Bay, Russell Reef, Thomson Park, East Point Regional Park and Lyall Harbour Beach. No public campgrounds. A fuel facility and government floats are located near the Lyall Harbour ferry landing. The island was named in 1791 after the schooner Saturnina.

East Point: An 1888 lighthouse situated here is the reference point for gathering weather conditions for the southern Georgia Strait. There is good fishing in this area. The Lighthouse Park provides views east to Mt. Baker and whales are often sighted. Beware of tidal currents running up to 5 knots around Boiling Reef, off the tip of East Point.

Narvaez Bay (11): Much of the steep sided land surrounding this bay, purchased by the Pacific Marine Heritage Program, is now a part of the Gulf Island National Park Reserve. This long bay has temporary anchorage near the head and another behind an anvil shaped peninsula off the southern shore. The bay is open to swells of passing ferries and southeast winds. Winds from the west may also funnel into the bay. Unstable bottom, watch for anchor dragging. In areas, the gravel shore allows for beaching dinghies. Hiking is possible on unmaintained trails or along old island roads. A short, but steep uphill hike leads to a meadow.

Saturna Beach (12): Mount Warburton Pike towers over 1,400 feet above this sandy beach. This is the access to Thompson Park and a winery. A dock is available for shore access. It is a 15-minute walk up the hill, through the vineyards, to the winery, gift shop, and tasting room.

Breezy Bay: This is the site of a private farm. Breezy Bay is shallow with depths less than eight feet. True to its name, it is not the best anchorage in rising winds. The float and buoys are private.

★ **Boot Cove (13):** Winds can enter this bay. Buoys at the head of the bay are private. This steep-sided cove has a narrow, but easily navigated, entrance into a basin with suitable depths for anchoring. The bottom is good holding mud. Space is limited by private docks and buoys, and aquaculture.

★ **Lyall Harbour (14):** There is plentiful and good anchorage here unless a west or northwest wind is expected. It is best to go as far into the bay as overnight depths will permit. The Saturna Island ferry landing is near the harbor entrance. A public wharf with 300 feet of float space is adjacent to the ferry dock. 250-539-2229.

Saturna Point Landing: Gas, diesel, ice, groceries, licenses, moorage. 250-539-5725.

★⚓ **Winter Cove & Winter Cove Marine Park (15):** This is a 228 acre marine park, and the site of the Dominion Day Lamb Barbecue. There are fire pits, a baseball diamond, picnic areas, pit toilets, walking trails, water, and information kiosks. No camping is allowed. There is an unpaved launching ramp, for use at half tide or higher. There are several anchorages in Winter Cove. The bottom is shallow and uneven, but holding is good. When approaching from Plumper Sound, get even with the entrance to Irish Bay, then aim toward Samuel Island until close to the shore. Avoid Minx Reef before turning to starboard and proceeding into Winter Cove. An underwater power cable crosses the west entrance. Areas close to shore are foul. The most favored anchorages are about 100 feet off shore, just southwest of the cable line, between the cables and the ruins of a concrete-supported ramp, north and east of the cable line. ⚓⛟⚲

Boat Passage (16): This narrow pass at Winter Point separates Samuel and Saturna Islands. Passage at or near high water slack is recommended. The charted location of the rock in the passage varies with the chart being used. At times the currents tend to carry boats across the rock. Maximum currents run to seven knots at springs. The favored course when going east is along the Saturna Island shore for about 150 yards on the Georgia Strait side. Then turn to port and pass through the break in the kelp beds.

Samuel Island

[3441, 3462, 3477]

★ **Irish Bay (17):** [3477, 3442, 3477] This large, scenic bay has good anchorage on a mud bottom. The bay is open to winds from the southwest and west. Samuel Island is a private estate. The beaches, uplands, and private dock are monitored all year by a caretaker. Fires are not permitted on the beaches because of the flammable growth on the island and the lack of water and facilities for fire fighting.

Mayne Island
[3441, 3442, 3462, 3477]

★ **Mayne Island:** Public floats are found at Horton and Miners Bays. These sites are CAN-PASS only locations. Marine fuel is available at Miners Bay. Regular ferry service connects the island with both Swartz Bay (to Victoria) and Tsawwassen (to Vancouver). Tranquil farms and orchards set the leisurely pace for this island's residents. Dining and accommodations. Ocean kayaking, tennis, and fishing charters are also available. There are a number of historic sites to visit, including the Mayne Museum, the Church of St. Mary Magdalene, and the Active Pass Light Station at Georgina Point. The lighthouse was originally built in 1885. In the summer, the grounds are open to the public daily from 10 a.m.- Sunset. The museum occupies what was the jail in 1896, and traces the history of Mayne Island from past to present. It is located off Fernhill Road, opposite the Agricultural Hall. Boat launching is possible at David Cove, Village Bay, and Potato Point. Annual events include the *Canada Day Celebrations* on July 1 at Dinner Bay Park, several salmon derbies in August, *Mayne Island Fall Fair* on the third Saturday in August, and the famous *Lions Club Salmon Bake* at Dinner Bay Park on Labor Day Sunday.

★ **Georgeson Passage (18):** When entering Georgeson Passage from Plumper Sound, proceed toward Irish Bay. Turn to port and continue north along the Samuel Island shore, keeping Lizard Island to port. Strong currents may be encountered in the Georgeson Passage- Bennett Bay vicinity. Currents reach four knots and maneuvering room is limited. There are reefs in the vicinity of Lizard Island. When approaching Horton Bay from the south, pass south of Curlew Island through Robson Channel. A rock, marked by kelp in season, is kept to port. A rocky ledge off Curlew Island extends to starboard. Minimum depth in this passage is seven feet. Entry to Horton Bay may also be made by proceeding farther north to the end of Georgeson Passage and rounding the north tip of Curlew Island. Rocks extend off this tip. To avoid these rocks, proceed in the direction of Bennett Bay before turning to port and entering the passage between Curlew and Mayne Islands. A private float off Curlew extends into this passage.

★ **Horton Bay (18):** Good anchorage is available in Horton Bay. A submerged rock, well marked on charts, is in the prime moorage area near the head. Check swing room depths on sounder before anchoring. Moorage may be available at the government dock located on the south shore. A CANPASS only check-in site.

★ **Bennett Bay (19):** Entry from the Strait of Georgia is made through the narrow passage between Campbell Point and Georgeson Island. Favor the Georgeson Island side. A shoal extends off Campbell Point. Anchorage is possible inside Campbell Point, but tide flats and shallow water extend to the outer end of the long wharf. A restaurant is on shore.

★ **Campbell Bay (20):** This bay is protected from northwest winds, but exposed to southeast winds. There are rocks in line with the Belle Chain and

Miners Bay   Gwen Cole Photo

extending southward from Campbell Point to beyond Georgeson Island. Anchor near the head on a mud bottom.

★ **David Cove (21):** Anchorage in this small niche with minimum depth of seven feet. Exposed to the north. Launching ramp.

Walk-around: At low tide, a shore walk can be made from this cove to the Active Pass Light Station, but the walk is rocky and slippery.

Piggott Bay: There is a good beach here, but reefs and southeast winds are hazards.

★ **Miners Bay (22):** [3473] Fuel, provisions, restaurants, and limited moorage. CANPASS check-in site (Oct. 1 to April 30 open to CAN-PASS only, May 1 to Sept. 30 open to all). Active Pass has currents to seven knots on spring tides.

See Active Pass description in Chapter 10. The northward movement of the flood tide affects the bay. On strong flood tides, with any northerly wind, rips occur from south of Mary Ann Point to Laura Point. Miners Bay is deep, so anchorage must be close to shore. Currents circle around inside the bay. There is a sunken cable west of the public floats. Ashore, there is a museum, a restaurant, and art galleries.

Active Pass Auto & Marine: Gas, diesel, propane, ice, mechanic, bait, tackle. 250-539-5411.

★ **Village Bay (23):** Terminus for the Gulf Islands-Swartz Bay and Tsawwassen ferries. Good mud bottom in 24-40 feet, but ferry wash, northwest winds, and private buoys affect anchorage. Launching ramp. Avoid Enterprise Reef. Do not pass between the reef light and the green buoy.

Bedwell Harbour

Essential Supplies & Services

AIR TRANSPORTATION
To & from Washington
Seattle Seaplanes **1-800-637-5553**
To & from Islands/Vancouver
Harbour Air: 604-274-1277
Tofino Air: 1-800-665-2359
Vancouver Island Air: 250-287-2433

BOOKS / BOOK STORES
The Marine Atlas. **541-593-6396**

COAST GUARD
VHF 16, 26, #16
Victoria 250-480-2600
Emergencies: 800-567-5111

BOAT MOVING
All Tow Boat Moving . . . .
. . . . **604-946-7899, 1-877-946-7899**

BOAT SEATS & UPHOLSTERY
Royal City Bedding **604-526-2641**

CUSTOMS
Bedwell Harbour: (May 1 -Sept. 30) 8:00 a.m.-8:00
p.m. daily, 8:00 a.m.-5:00 p.m. after Labor Day.
Closure Sept. 30 . . . . **1-888-226-7277**
Cabbage Island (CANPASS only)
Horton Bay (CANPASS only)
Miner's Bay (CANPASS only)
Port Browning (CANPASS only)
See Important Notices between Chapters 7 & 8

FERRY INFORMATION
B.C. Ferries 1-888-223-3779, 250-386-3431
Swartz Bay. 250-386-3431

FISHERIES & OCEANS . . 250-363-3252

FUELS
Active Pass. Gas, Diesel 250-539-5411
Poets Cove Resort & Spa: Bedwell Harbour.
  Gas, Diesel . . . . 250-629-3212. VHF 66A
Saturna Point Landing: Gas, Diesel 250-539-5725

GOLF COURSES
(Course accessible from moorage and have rental clubs available)
Pender Island G&CC: North Pender. 250-629-6659

INSURANCE
Boat Insurance Agency **206-285-1350**
Or Call **1-800-828-2446**

LIQUOR STORES
Miners Bay
Pender Island
Saturna Island

LODGING
Poets Cove Resort & Spa . . . . 250-629-3212. VHF 66A

MARINAS/MOORAGE FLOATS
Hope Bay
Horton Bay: Mayne Island
Lyall Harbour 250-539-5725
Miners Bay
Otter Bay Marina . . . . 250-629-3579, VHF 66A
Poets Cove Resort & Spa . . . . 250-629-3212. VHF 66A
Port Browning Harbour
Port Browning Marina . . . . 250-629-3493, VHF 66A
Port Washington

PROPANE
Active Pass 250-539-5411

RAMPS / HAULOUTS
David Cove

Lyall Harbour
Otter Bay Marina . . . . 250-629-3579 VHF 66A
Piggot Bay
Port Browning Marina . . . . 250-629-3493 VHF 66A
Potato Point:
Thieves Bay
Village Bay
Winter Cove Marine Park

REPAIRS
Active Pass . . . . 250-539-5411, VHF 66A
Boatyard, The: Tsehum Harbour 250-655-1511
Canoe Cove Marina **250-656-5566**
Cove Yachts: Maple Bay **250-748-8136**
Maple Bay Marina **250-746-8482**
Oyster Harbour: Ladysmith 250-245-8233
Philbrooks Boatyard: Tsehum Harbour . . 250-656-1157
Telegraph Harbour Marina: Thetis Is 250-246-9511
Van Isle Marina: Tsehum Harbour
. . . . **250-656-1138. VHF 66A**

RESTAURANTS / PUB
Poets Cove Resort & Spa: . . . . 250-629-3212. VHF 66A

SEARCH & RESCUE 1-800-567-5111
. . . . *311

SHELLFISH HOTLINE 604-666-2828

SPORT FISHING:
. . . . 250-363-3252

TAXI
Mayne Island 250-539-3132, 250-539-0181

TOWING
C-TOW. **1-888-354-5554**
Cove Yachts: Maple Bay. **250-748-8136**
Van Isle Marina: Tsehum Harbour
. . . . **250-656-1138 VHF 66A**
Vector Yacht Service: Tsehum Harbour . . 250-655-3222

VHF MARINE OPERATOR
Bellingham: VHF 28, 85
Ganges: VHF 27, 64
Nanaimo: VHF 87
Sechelt: VHF 86
Vancouver: VHF 23, 24, 25, 26, 86, 88
Victoria: VHF 86

VISITOR INFORMATION
All islands 250-754-3500

WEATHER
Environment Canada Weather Line. 250-339-9861
Comox (recorded) 250-339-0748
Victoria: WX-3 250-363-6717
Vancouver: WX-1, 3, 4 604-664-9010

Sea Lions in British Columbia   *Tourism B.C. Photo*

Chapter 10:
Central Gulf Islands & East Vancouver Island Coast

Cowichan Bay to Yellow Point. Ganges, Maple Bay, Crofton, Chemainus, Ladysmith. Salt Spring, Prevost, Galiano, Kuper, & Thetis Islands.

Symbols

[   ]: Numbers between [   ] are chart numbers.

{   }: Numbers & letters between {   } are waypoints.

⚓: Park, 🚤: Boat Launch, ▲: Campgrounds, ⋏: Hiking Trails, ⊼: Picnic Area, 🚲: Biking

Chart List

Canadian Hydrographic Charts:
3310, 3313, 3441-3443, 3463, 3473, 3475, 3477, 3478

NOAA Charts: 18400, 18412-18415

Marine Atlas (2005 ed.)   Pages 10, 11

★ **Important Notice:** See "Important Notices" between Chapters 7 and 8 in this guide for specific information on boating related topics such as: Canadian & U.S. Customs, boating safety and security, navigation, weather, U.S. & Canadian Coast Guard, U.S & Canadian marine radio use, Vessel Traffic Service and traffic separation plans, security zones, and internet access. Due to new Department of Homeland Security regulations, call ahead for latest customs information

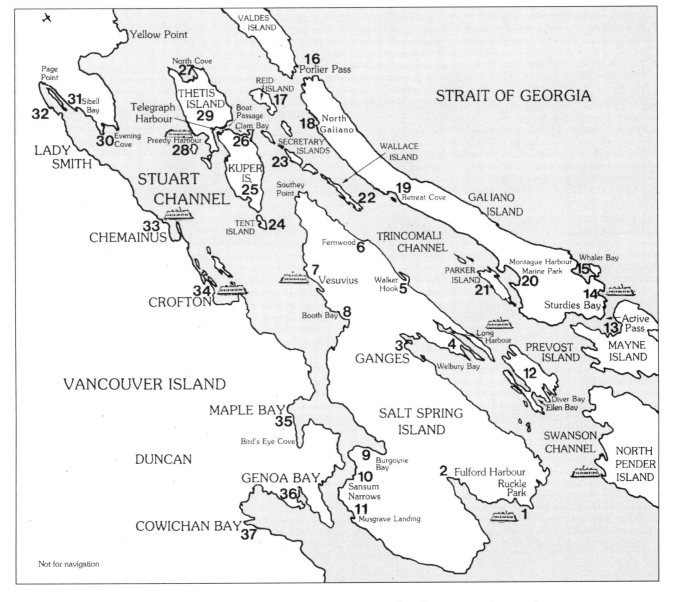

Not for navigation

and/or see Northwest Boat Travel Online, www.nwboat.com.

★ **No Dump Zones: Montague Harbour.** Dump gray water only (shower and dish water). Must have approved holding tank on board to enter No Dump Zone.

★ **Introduction to the Gulf Islands:** See the beginning of Chapter 9.

Salt Spring Island East

[3313, 3441, 3442, 3462, 3463, 3473, 3475, 3477, 3478]

★ **Salt Spring Island East:** This Island is 18 miles in length, with widths varying from two to ten miles. Its largest community, Ganges, is the main center of commerce for the Gulf Islands. Smaller ports are at Vesuvius and Fulford Harbour. There are several good bays for anchorage. The island, first settled in the 1850's was named for the brine pools at the north end of the island. "Salt Springs" is sometimes spelled as one word and other times as two, even on the same sign! Regardless of its spelling, Salt Springs is becoming synonymous with the arts. Galleries and studios are everywhere in this enclave of artisans.

Salt Spring is also a treasure trove of wildlife. Deer are prevalent, eagles soar, swans drift out in Fulford Harbour. Geese and ducks parade in Ganges Harbour and seals come to visit, especially when the herring run. But as more people come to the Island to live or visit, the habitat area of these creatures is progressively fragmented. On the north side of the island, McFadden Creek Heronry, once one of the largest heron colonies in British Columbia, is now gone. Many residents are active participants in the preservation of the natural environment and while they welcome visitors, they ask them to be respectful of the wildlife habitat. The Water Bird Watch Collective would be happy to answer questions. Write to them at 272 Beddis Road, Salt Spring Island V8K 2I1. The Island Wildlife Natural Care Centre, north of St. Mary Lake, is devoted to the care of the sick, injured or orphaned wild animals of the island. No animals are on display, nor is the facility open to the public, but you can take a virtual tour at http://sealrescue.org/. The director has written a book, *Cries of the Wild: A Wildlife Rehabilitator's Journal.* Domesticated farm animals are abundant on the island, too. Peaceful pastoral scenes are common as they graze on the rolling farmlands. In the spring, a visit during lambing season is a lasting memory. The *Fall Fair,* held the third weekend each September, celebrates the agricultural heritage of the community.

★⛺ **Ruckle Provincial Park, Beaver Point (1):** Beaver Point received its name because the Hudson's Bay Company's ship Beaver once ran aground on the point. Several small coves indent the shoreline providing temporary anchorage at this, the largest park in the Gulf Islands. A mooring buoy is often tucked in the first niche north of Beaver Point. In this bay, steamships, sailing between Victoria and Nanaimo, docked at the wharf from 1914 to 1951. This is also the terminus of Beaver Point Road. Picnic sites, pit toilets, campsites, and water, and are available. Fires are permitted in fire rings, but not on the beach. Firewood can be purchased on site. Popular recreational activities here include hiking, sea kayaking, cycling and scuba diving. King's Cove, an indentation farther north, was named for an 1880's settler, Leon King. Temporary anchorage is possible. Some of Salt Spring's largest trees still stand nearby. In 1894, gold was mined north of this cove.

The park is unique in that the Ruckle family still farms near the middle of the park acreage. Henry Ruckle immigrated to Salt Spring from Ireland in 1872 and began a prosperous farm. One hundred years later, most of the area was donated to the province, however the Ruckles have retained a lifetime tenancy on their farm, making this the oldest continuously run family farm in British Columbia. Park guests are not to use the fields or farm roads, and are asked to respect the family's privacy. Public trails are clearly marked by red metal markers nailed to trees. Dogs must be leashed. The family home of Alfred Ruckle, located near the park's entrance, is open for visitations. ⛺▲𝓀

★ **Russell Island:** Located at the entrance to Fulford Harbour, this lovely island is part of the Gulf Islands National Park Reserve. It is open to the public. A good swimming beach is on the west end. Trails lead to an old wharf and homestead. To avoid wakes from passing vessels, anchor between the island and Saltspring Island. Overnight anchorage is possible in calm weather. Kanakas (Hawaiians) settled here in the 1880's. Their ancestors had once worked for the Hudson's Bay Company.

★ **Fulford Harbour (2):** Site of the Swartz Bay-Fulford Harbour ferry, public floats, a grocery store, fuel, lodging, and a marina. Two public floats, operated by the Saltspring Harbour Authority, are available for transient moorage. Fulford Outer Harbour is small and exposed, but gives immediate access to Fulford Village and the ferry terminal. Floats at Fulford Inner Harbour have good protection, water, and 20 ampere power. However, it is often crowded. Anchorage can be found in 30-40 feet of water on a mud bottom in the center of the bay near the head. A good spot is in the small bight where the creek flows from Stowell Lake. The ferry ride to Swartz Bay, on Vancouver Island, takes 35 minutes.

Fulford Harbour Marina: Moorage, 20 and 30 ampere power, washrooms, showers. Gas and diesel available at Roamer's Landing. 250-653-4467. VHF 66A.

Fulford Inner Harbour Public Float: Saltspring Harbour Authority. Limited space, water, power.

Roamer's Landing: Moorage, gas, diesel. 250-653-4487.

Isabella Light: Located near the western entrance of Fulford Harbour, some fair weather anchorage can be found in the bay behind this light. There are rocks from the islet to shore. Approach from the south, aiming toward the pasture and a building. Anchor tucked in behind the islet. The lee of Russell Island might serve as a temporary anchorage.

Walter Bay: This shallow bay in South Ganges Harbour and the encircling spit are part of a wildlife sanctuary. Do not anchor in the area. Observe the five knot (10 km per hour) speed limit.

Ganges

[3442, 3462, 3478]

★ **Ganges (3):** Ganges (Breakwater Float) is a customs (CANPASS only) check-in location. So attractive is this picturesque community to boating families, that, more than likely, boats and float planes will be tied to moorage floats and the bay will be dotted with boats swinging at anchor. Boaters are advised to slow down when entering Ganges Harbour to five knots (10 km per hour), and are asked to slow even more to no wake speed.

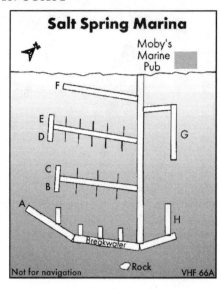

Transient moorage is available in several locations. These include two marinas and public floats. The Saltspring Harbour Authority operates public floats in the inner and outer harbors. The Government (Centennial Wharf) Boat Basin is located behind the breakwater south of Grace Peninsula. Showers, washrooms, and a garbage deposit are found here. VHF 9.

In the outer harbor, a large Breakwater Float extends into Ganges Harbour and offers protection for the visitor's floats behind it. There are spaces for float plane passenger pickup, commercial vessels, visitors, and the Coast Guard. It is the site of a waste pump-out. The Ganges Outer Harbour public float, Kanaka Visitor's Wharf, offers moorage. VHF 9.

Ganges Marina and Salt Spring Marina are located at the head of the harbor. If moorages are full, anchorage is plentiful in the harbor in depths of 24-35 feet. A dinghy dock is available for those who anchor. It is alongside the Rotary Marina Park on the water side of Thrifty Foods. Dinghies only- no larger boats.

A scenic harbor setting, park-like surroundings, and mountainous backdrop give this town an inviting, picturesque setting. The village is continuously expanding its facilities and attractions for tourists. Even with these changes the village still retains its warm, friendly, cozy atmosphere. Over 100 businesses, all within easy walking distance, radiate out from Ganges Harbour, including specialty shops, clothing stores, hardware stores, photo shops, food and meat markets, health food store, bakeries, galleries, pharmacy, liquor store, barber and beauty shops, restaurants, laundry, showers, accommodations, banks and a post office. Salt Spring is well known for its artists and crafts people, whose work can be found year around in local shops, studios, and galleries. Paintings, pottery, weaving, stained glass, woodwork, jewelry and quilts are well represented. Artcraft, highlighting the work of over 200 Gulf Island's artisans, is open daily from early June through mid-September. Located on the waterfront, Centennial Park has a playground, picnic tables and band stand. The Salt Spring Parks, Arts, and Recreation Commission also conducts a Saturday Market in the Park, from April to October. Hours: 8:00 a.m.- 4:00 p.m. Over 100 vendors exhibit arts and crafts, hand painted clothing, local fresh produce, home-baked goods, and gourmet coffees. Other island attractions include The Bittancourt Heritage House, a museum located in an 1884 house on Rainbow Road. The museum features the history of the island including the farming and pioneering families. Of special interest is the 1912 map of the island. Open June-September. Each July, the Festival of the Arts presents a wide variety of entertainment including music, theater, and dance with performances by local and international artists. ArtSpring, the long awaited performing and visual art center, is now open with on-going events, including live theater, music, and art exhibits. The much celebrated traditional country *Fall Fair* is held at the Farmer's Institute grounds in late September.

Ganges has been a commercial center since the turn-of-the-century when Mouat's Brothers Store was established in 1907. In the early days, the Ganges waterfront was the scene of high activity on *Boat Day* as eggs, butter, fruit, produce, poultry, and livestock were unloaded from farm wagons for shipment off-island, in exchange for manufactured goods. Visit Mouat's Mall to view a collection of photographs of early boating traffic in Ganges. Today, the island continues to be rich in harvests of locally produced vegetables, meats, fresh herbs, hydroponic lettuce, eggs, and flowers, and other specialty items such as honey, jams, and jellies. Very important is Salt Spring lamb, such an honored product that it was served to Queen Elizabeth II at the 1995 Commonwealth Games. The Salt Spring Cheese Co. produces goat cheese and, in summer, sheep cheese, only one of two in the province to produce this cheese. The island abounds in fruit and nut trees, some of which are growing in heritage orchards. These include apples, pears, plums, walnuts, and hazelnuts.

★ **Salt Spring Marina:** {48° 51' N, 123° 28' W} Located at Harbour's End next to Hastings House Hotel, Dining & Spa. Moorage with power, water, ice, garbage dropoff. Best views in the Harbour. Wireless internet, CLEAN NEW showers & laundry, Moby's Marine Pub reopens Dec 5th. Rogue Caffe` for healthy breakfasts & lunch-es, car, boat & scooter rentals. Fishing charters, tackle, bait, marine sales & service, chandlery. Ten minute walk or summer shuttle to village, liquor store across street. Manager Lesley Cheeseman welcomes yacht clubs, kids & dogs with well-mannered parents. See our advertisement in this chapter. E-mail: ssmarina@telus.net. Telephone 1-800-334-6629, 250-537-5810, Fax: 250-537-5809. VHF 66A.

★ **Hastings House Relais & Chateaux Hotel, Dining & Spa:** Celebrating 25th Anniversary of outstanding service and cuisine, Award-winning Chef Marcel Kauer's a la carte menus showcase the island's finest seasonal organic produce, Salt Spring lamb, and fresh local seafood. Spectacular views from all dining rooms. Wine Spectator Award of Excellence; Tour the gardens or have a cocktail on the lawn before dinner. Top Rated Canadian Resort by Zagat in 2004 with 18 luxurious suites; Reservations required 1-800-661-9255 or 520-537-2362. See our advertisement in this chapter. www.hastingshouse.com.

Breakwater Float: Moorage, pump-out, water, seaplane float. VHF 9. 250-537-5711.

Ganges Marina: Open all year. Power, fuel, washrooms, showers, laundry, garbage drop. Complimentary morning coffee. 250-537-5242.

Kanaka Visitor's Wharf: (Outer Harbour): Limited moorage, water. 250-537-5711.

Saltspring Harbour Authority: (Ganges Centennial Wharf): Moorage, power, water, showers, washrooms, launch ramp, garbage deposit. 250-537-5711. VHF 69.

Walk-around and shopping tour: If beginning from the head of Ganges Harbour, Lower Ganges Road is the main road leading into town from Salt Spring Marina. In addition to moorage, the marinas offer many services. Continue on Upper Ganges Road to Harbour House.

Walk south to reach the village center. Across the street is Mahon Hall, a heritage building and home to Artcraft since 1967. Artcraft is open seven days a week from early June- mid-September. You are now near the center of town. The Visitor Bureau, open daily, is visible from here. A map, which outlines a walking tour and contains the village directory, is available at the bureau as well as from local merchants.

If instead, you begin your walking tour of Ganges from moorage at the Government (Public) Boat Basin, you will find Centennial Park immediately adjacent. Here visitors picnic, enjoy jazz, string quartet and band concerts, dances, and Saturday's Market at the Park. There is a playground for children, and public restroom facilities are located near the Harbour Manager's office. Grace Point Square, next to Centennial Park, is a complex of retail shops and services.

A good way to learn about Ganges history is to wander through Mouat's Mall and view the exhibit of early photographs, tools and paraphernalia. Mouat's Trading Company began in 1907, when the Mouat brothers opened the first store on the island. Other stores, including a grocery store are near the mall.

At the intersection of Lower Ganges Road and Hereford Avenue is the Visitor Information Bureau. Visit the bureau and pick up a brochure outlining a Studio Tour of the Island that includes over 20 working galleries which are located in the countryside, along the pastoral roads of Salt Spring. Land transportation can be arranged.

Return to Lower Ganges Road and turn south. You will pass the Fire Hall and more shops. A drug store is located on the corner. Turn right on McPhillips and left to ArtSpring, home to live theater, music, and dance performances.

Within a mile radius of Ganges are parks, medical and dental centers, a hospital, library, the RCMP office, and several churches. Mouat Provincial Park, located to the west of the downtown core, has a nice walker's trail, frisbee golf, and picnic areas. The park, with its towering cedars, is a popular spot to stretch legs and enjoy nature. Another hike, more strenuous in nature, is the three to four hour trek to Mount Erskine. Two golf courses and tennis courts are also on the island.

Land transportation is available to all parts of Salt Spring Island. Choose from taxi service, rental cars, or charter bus and limousine service. One side trip might be to Fulford Harbour. This is the location of Fulford Marina and the Fulford Harbour-Swartz Bay ferry landing. Other trips by land might be to the Vesuvius Beach and the Vesuvius-Crofton ferry landing which are on the west side of the island. St. Mary Lake, about five miles north of Ganges, is a popular resort area with a small public beach, swimming, and fishing. To enjoy a movie, go out Lower Ganges Road toward St. Mary Lake. Cinema Central shows first run films in a 102 year old heritage building. Before each feature, cinema-goers are treated to a slide show, a virtual portrait of Salt Spring's people and beautiful places. This is also the road to a golf course and to Portlock Park's track, tennis, and outdoor pool.

★ **Salt Spring Festival of the Arts:** Celebrated in July with music, theatre, and dance performed by local and international artists. 250-537-4167.

★ **Long Harbour (4):** This lovely inlet indents into Salt Spring Island for over two miles. It is open to southeast winds. This is the terminus of the Gulf Islands - Tsawwassen ferry and the site of a yacht club outstation. Anchorage on a mud bottom is possible in several locations. A favored spot is behind the islets just inside Nose Point. Passage should not be attempted on the south side of these islets, but rather by proceeding around the red marker buoy, and then inward between the islets and the Salt Spring shore. Anchoring is also pleasant at the head of the bay in 10 to 15 feet of water. A drying lagoon extends from the head waters.

★ **Walker Hook (5):** [3442, 3463] Good anchorage is off a beautiful beach on the east side. The inlet dries. Temporary anchorage on a high tide with some protection from westerlies can be found inside Atkins Reef.

Atkins Reef: Extends northwestward and southeastward from the concrete marker. There are rocks southeast at Walker Hook extending toward the marker.

★ **Fernwood (6):** A long public pier juts into Trincomali Channel near Fernwood Point. The mooring float at the end of the dock accommodates only two to three boats. A store is at the shore end of the dock. A walk of about one mile leads to St. Mary Lake with its swimming and fishing.

Southey Point: Site of an Indian midden, the northernmost tip of Salt Spring has a white shell beach, a drying ledge marked by a light, and an adjacent bay. Southey Bay is open to the north. It is nearly filled with private buoys, thus limiting anchorage.

★ **Stonecutter's Bay:** Private homes surround this small bay. Good anchorage. Open to the northwest.

Idol Island: Reports indicate that this is to be part of a park development.

Salt Spring Island West

[3442, 3462, 3478]

★ **Vesuvius (7):** Very limited anchorage is possible south of the ferry landing, however private buoys are hazards. A small public float is located adjacent to the landing, giving shore access to an inn and food store. A road connects Vesuvius with Ganges. Good anchorage and views of sunsets can be found in Duck Cove between Dock Point and Parminter Point.

Vesuvius Bay Public Float, Saltspring Harbour Authority: No facilities, exposed to winds.

★ **Booth Bay (8):** There is anchorage, open to westerlies. Tide flats are at the head of the bay. It is possible to enter Booth Inlet at high tide in an inflatable, canoe, kayak, or dinghy. Once through the shallow entrance, there is enough water for an outboard.

★ **Burgoyne Bay (9):** Although open to southeast winds and northwest seas, this bay has anchorage and a small public float. When the drying sand at the head of the bay covers with water on summer days, it is a popular swimming area. Often used as a log sorting area, caution advised. A road leads to Burgoyne Valley and Mount Maxwell Provincial Park.

Sansum Narrows (10): Sportfishermen frequent this spot. Currents run to three knots. Erratic winds funnel through the narrows. Fishing for Springs is good June through August. The Coho season is August through October.

★ **Musgrave Landing (11):** The public wharf is seldom empty. Logging roads and trails offer good hiking. Temporary anchorage is possible north of the wharf, but it is unprotected in a south wind.

Prevost Island

[3442, 3462, 3478]

★ **Prevost Island (12):** This beautiful island has fingers of land spreading outward in a northwest-southeast direction to form six distinctly different harbors. An Irishman of noble lineage, Digby Hussey deBurge, owned the entire island in the 1920's and tended goats, sheep, and cattle. His son continued the farming tradition and raised four daughters on the isolated island. Today, the deBurge's and approximately ten other families own the property. With its tall trees, red-barked madronas, and moss covered rocks, Prevost Island displays its own special charm. Anchorage can be found in Ellen Bay, Diver Bay, Glenthorne Passage, Annette Inlet, Selby Cove, and James Bay.

★ **Ellen Bay:** Ellen Bay and Diver Bay on Swanson Channel often boast beautiful moonlight vistas on summer evenings. Anchorage on this side of Prevost Island is uncomfortable at times from the ferry wash. Ellen Bay offers good holding anchorage near the head on a mud bottom.

★ **Diver Bay:** Diver Bay, open to the southeast, offers temporary anchorage in 30-40 foot depths. Ferry wakes enter.

★ **Glenthorne Passage:** This harbor is protected by Secret Island and Glenthorne Point. The passage seems to have a south seas flavor that encourages gunkholing by dinghy. The shoreline is private. Enter between Secret Island and the outermost island or from the west along Prevost

Island. Depths average 15-25 feet.

★ **Annette Inlet:** Reflections of lingering sunsets often ripple across the water in this long indentation into Prevost Island. When entering, avoid a large kelp patch and rock directly in front of the entrance. Pass either side, then favor center channel because shoals extend from both sides. Anchorage is possible in both the inner and outer bays. In the outer bay, favor the center of the bay. There is a shallow area on the port side and shoals in the cove to starboard. A sand and grass spit extends from the port shore at the opening of the inner bay which tends to separate the inner and outer bays. In the inner bay there is extensive anchorage in the center and on the starboard side. Minimum depths average seven feet. The port side is the shallowest. Bottom is excellent holding, sticky mud. The head of the bay is a large, drying flat. A farm is located here and the shoreline is private. Entertainment is provided by large cormorants which perch in the trees along this shore. After capturing small fish they return to the stark branches to preen their feathers, spreading their wings to dry them.

★ **Selby Cove:** It is possible to go quite far into this bay and anchor over sand and mud near the head. The cove becomes shallow quickly. Anchorage far out in the center is more difficult and anchor dragging has occurred.

James Bay: Most, but not all, of the shoreline and Peile Point Peninsula is part of the Gulf Islands National Park Reserve and remains undeveloped. Early settlers planted orchards, the remains of which can still be found here. This bay is exposed to north and northwesterly winds. Temporary anchorage is possible near the head. A ledge, with sunken rocks, is off the southern shore. Walk a sheep trail from the head of the bay to Peile Point.

Active Pass (13): Active Pass separates Galiano and Mayne Islands and is the shipping channel for ferries traveling between Vancouver Island and the mainland. They navigate on a pre-determined course through the passage and have the right-of-way. Currents at springs run up to eight knots. On strong flood tides, when strong north winds are present, there are violent rips in an area that extends from mid-channel south of Mary Anne Point to Laura Point. No dangerous rips occur on ebb tides in the pass. Many fishermen recommend fishing Helen Point on the ebb and Georgina Point on the flood. Also, fish on the north sides of the reefs. This, very active, passage was not named for the water conditions or boat usage. It received its name from the United States Naval steamer USS Active which did survey work in the area in 1855.

Galiano Island

[3442, 3462, 3463, 3473, 3478]

★ **Galiano Island:** Stretching northwest by southeast along the Strait of Georgia, this long and narrow island enjoys the least rainfall of the Gulf Islands. Many of the island's permanent residents live in the southern portion bordering Montague Harbour and Active Pass. An atmosphere of relaxation and recreation prevails. Montague Harbour Marine Park, Montague Harbour Marina, Bluff Park, hiking, fishing, cycling, and restaurants are of interest. Tennis courts and a public golf course are available. Many artists live on the island and their works are on display at businesses throughout the island. Van/bus service is available for land transportation. Galiano was named for the Spanish Captain

Dionisio Alcala Galiano, who first saw the island in 1792.

★ **Sturdies Bay (14):** Toward the eastern end of Active Pass, Sturdies Bay is the site of the community of South Galiano. There are stores, accommodations, restaurant, and the landing for the Gulf Islands-Tsawwassen and Sturdies Bay - Swartz Bay ferries. A small public float, with space for two or three 20 foot boats, is tucked in behind the protection of the pilings.

Walk-around: It is a pleasant walk from Sturdies Bay to picnic grounds at Bellhouse Park.

★ **Whaler Bay (15):** Guarded from the ravages of the Strait of Georgia by shoals and Gossip Island, Whaler Bay offers anchorage. Whaler Bay was once used to harbor small whaling vessels. Enter between Galiano and Gossip Islands. Favor the west shore south of Twiss Point. A public wharf with floats is on the port side, well into the bay. Approach with caution as it is shallow. The tidal range in this bay is as much as 16 feet. Rafting is compulsory. Walk up the short hill by the dock, then wind along Cain Road for about 1/3 of a mile to South Galiano on Sturdies Bay.

Porlier Pass (16): *See current tables for Active Pass.* Porlier Pass separates Galiano Island from Valdes Island. The pass lies in a north-south direction. Currents to nine knots at springs flood northwest and ebb southeast. The ebb sets right over Romulus Rock from the direction of Virago Point. Dangerous conditions exist when the tide meets an opposing wind. Traverse the pass near slack water if possible. Blueback fishing is good in the area in April, as is Coho fishing in July. The indentations into Galiano which border Porlier Pass are protected from direct southerlies but are very susceptible to most other winds.

★⚓ **Dionisio Point Provincial Park:** Macmillan Bloedel donated 114 hectares of waterfront property to establish this park. Camping is permitted in 30 designated sites, and a hand pump offers fresh water. No fires are permitted. Use only self-contained camp stoves. Dionisio Bay offers temporary anchorage. The sandy beach at the head invites sun bathers. Hiking trails. ▲🏕🏃

★ **Lighthouse Bay:** Anchorage is found in this bay, which lies between Race Point and Virago Point. Avoid the submarine power cable near the entrance.

★ **Reid Island (17):** Fairweather anchorage is found at the southeast tip where the depth is marked "3" fathoms on the chart. Shoals, which dry five feet and three feet, and an islet enclose the basin at low tide. Since the reefs are covered at high water, the site is exposed to tidal action from Porlier Pass and southerly winds. Some anchorage may be found in an unnamed bight along the southwest shore.

★ **North Galiano (18):** A public wharf gives shore access to a store. This is about one-half mile south of Alcala Point. An unnamed indentation farther south provides limited anchorage. Ruined pilings are in the bay and the northern portion is foul.

★ **Spotlight Cove:** This tiny bight is often filled with log storage. If empty, shelter can be found by anchoring and tying to shore.

★ **Retreat Cove (19):** When entering, favor the south side. The northern part of the bay is shallow with land drying behind Retreat Island. There is barely enough room at the small public float for three or four boats. Two or three boats can usually find space to anchor. This bay offers a small, but helpful, retreat in all but westerly winds. A

road from the public wharf connects with the main island road.

★ **Montague Harbour (20):** Beautiful Montague Harbour is the site of Montague Harbour Marina, a ferry landing, and Montague Harbour Marine Park.

Montague Harbour Marina is a customs (CANPASS only) check-in location. Montague Harbour is a "No Dump Zone". Must have approved holding tank on board. Anchorage is good in several areas of the harbor. One such spot is on the shore opposite the park where Winstanley Point forms a sheltered corner. Another possible anchorage is found in Payne Bay on a sand and mud bottom. Private floats extend into this bay and anchorage can be a bit lumpy because of the numerous craft which travel en route to the park.

Montague Harbour is also known as the site of an unusual archaeological dig. Teams of researchers from Canada Yukon territories doning scuba gear, have explored the ocean floor, approximately 250 feet offshore in depths of about 20 feet, looking for artifacts to prove that the level of water has covered village sites. A harpoon, and floral organic matter under about three feet of sediment, have shown, through carbon dating, that they could be as much as 6,700 years old.

★ **Montague Harbour Marina:** {48° 53.8' N, 123° 24'W} This popular fueling and provisioning stop also has overnight moorage with power and water. Gas, diesel, oils, gifts, groceries, restaurant. See our Steering Star description in this chapter. Websites: www.montagueharbour.com & www. boattravel.com/montague/ E-mail: montaguemarina@gulfislands.com Address: S-17, C-57 Rural Route #1, Galiano Island, British Columbia V0N 1P0. Fax: 250-539-3593. Telephone: 250-539-5733. VHF 66A.

★ **Montague Harbour Marina:** Galiano Island's beautiful Montague Harbour, located in the heart of the Gulf Islands, is one of the most popular cruising destinations. The Breeze family and their friendly staff welcome you to improved facilities at Montague Harbour Marina. Annual, winter, and guest moorage, water, and 15/30 amp power available. The marina offers marine gas, diesel, fuel oils, washrooms, and a grocery store. In addition to provisions, the store carries fishing and camping accessories, fishing licences, charts, and an excellent selection of books, magazines, quality clothing, and gift items. Ice and wonderful ice cream cones are available. Relax on the licensed deck overlooking picturesque Montague Harbor and its spectacular sunset views. Enjoy excellent all day service- hot breakfasts, lunches, and dinners. Live entertainment adds great atmosphere on many evenings during the season. A Gift Shop features many Gulf Island crafts including pottery and jewelry. Moped, boat and kayak rentals are available. Fishing and sightseeing trips by arrangement. Nearby are walking trails, a safe swimming beach for children, and a golf course. Ride the famous Pub Bus to the

Hummingbird Inn. Open May to end of September. **Circle #33 on Reader Service Card at page 251. Internet sites: www.montagueharbour.com and www.boattravel.com/montague E-mail: montaguemarina@gulfislands.com Address: S-17, C-57, RR #1, Galiano Island, British Columbia V0N 1P0. Fax: 250-539-3593 Telephone: 250-539-5733 VHF 66A.**

Downtown Ganges
Salt Spring Island Chamber of Commerce Photo

Walk-around: Take a picnic lunch and head to Bluff Park with panoramic views of the western entrance to Active Pass. Because of the distance and hilly terrain, this is a rather strenuous hike and will take a few hours to make the round trip. Walk up Montague Harbour Road to Georgeson Bay Road. Turn right and continue to Bluffs Drive. Proceed on Bluffs until reaching the park and the path that leads to the edge of the bluff.

★⚓ **Montague Harbour Marine Park:** Established in 1959, this beautiful park was the first marine park in British Columbia. If approaching from the western entrance, be aware of rocks, submerged at high tide, extending off Gray Peninsula. Picnic sites, campsites, sandy beaches, hiking trails, a landing dock for dinghies, boat launch, and 35 mooring buoys are located here. Overnight moorage fees charged for docks, buoys, and camping. Water is available. A seasonal floating Nature House features hands-on displays. Swimming, fishing, kayaking and canoeing are popular aquatic activities. ⛱▲🚶

Walk-around: Walk around the saltwater marsh and the uplands with Douglas fir, red cedar, Arbutus, and hemlocks.

Parker, Wallace, and Secretary Islands
[3441, 3442, 3463]

★ **Parker Island (21):** The anvil-shaped piece of land that extends off Parker Island toward Grey

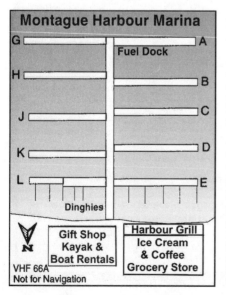

Montague Harbour Marina

G ▭▭▭▭▭▭▭▭▭▭▭ A
    Fuel Dock

H ▭▭▭▭▭▭▭▭▭▭▭ B

J ▭▭▭▭▭▭▭▭▭▭▭ C

K ▭▭▭▭▭▭▭▭▭▭▭ D

L ▭▭▭▭▭▭▭▭▭▭▭ E

Dinghies

⚓ N | **Gift Shop Kayak & Boat Rentals** | **Harbour Grill Ice Cream & Coffee Grocery Store**

VHF 66A
Not for Navigation

Ganges   *Russ Hein Photo*

Peninsula offers two unnamed bays back-to-back. These bays have anchoring possibilities. The northern bay has a fairly even bottom throughout, becoming shallow only at the head. This provides adequate anchorage, except when northwest winds are expected. The southern bay contains some ruins, dolphins, pilings, and a sometimes-present barge, that need to be considered when finding a spot to drop the hook. When proceeding north from Parker Island it is possible to use the passage between Charles and Wise Islands. Avoid the Ballingall Islets which stretch northwestward for some distance.

★⚓ **Wallace Island Provincial Marine Park (22):** This island is near mid-channel at the base of the Secretary Group in Trincomali Channel. All of the island, except two parcels on Princess Bay, is provincial park land. Caution advised off Wallace Island, when entering either Princess Bay or Conover Cove because foul ground, consisting of rocky islets and shoals, extends about 1½ miles in a southeast to northwest direction, framing the west side of the island. Trailer boats access the island by launching at Fernwood on Saltspring Island. There are campsites at Conover Cove, Cabin Bay, and Chivers Point. Fees

charged dock moorage, rings, and camping. Water must be boiled. No fires permitted. Caretakers are on the premises. Historical tours are held in summer. Sailors find the prevailing winds, which funnel between this island grouping and the steep cliffs of Galiano, excellent for a brisk afternoon sail. ▲⛱

★ **Princess Bay:** An anvil-shaped peninsula separates Princess Bay and Conover Cove. This bay provides overnight anchorage as close to the head of the bay as overnight depths will permit. Stern tie rings on shore. The bottom is even until the shallow shelf at the head. Beautiful madronas surround the cove. Two parcels on shore are private property, and not park land. No trespassing. A trail connects Princess Bay with Conover Cove.

★ **Conover Cove:** Entrance to this well protected nook is very narrow and shallow left of center when going in at low tide. Anchoring space is limited. A float that can accommodate approximately four 30' boats offers moorage. Shallow spots in the cove make it desirable to check overnight depths in the tide book and take soundings to find an appropriate position. Northwest of the float a few rings have been driven into the rocks for shore ties. Pilings near the dock can be used for stern ties. Picnic site and pit toilet on shore.

★ **Secretary Islands (23):** The two Secretary Islands are connected by a drying sand and gravel ledge. A small bight is formed north of the ledge. Anchorage is possible. Approach from Trincomali Channel, not Houston Passage.

Tent, Kuper, and Thetis Islands

[3442, 3443, 3463, 3477]

Tent Island (24): This is Indian reservation land. There is no public access. Anchorage is possible.

Kuper Island & Lamalchi Bay (25): North of Tent Island, separated by a shoal which is covered at high tide, Kuper is Indian reservation land. If the bay at Tent Island is too crowded, Lamalchi Bay provides temporary anchorage and a good swimming hole. The bay is shallow, making soundings and reference to tide charts advisable.

★ **Clam Bay (26):** This large bay is located at the eastern end of the channel separating Kuper and Thetis Islands. Rocket Shoal and Centre Reef, located in the center of the bay, are well defined by kelp and a red buoy on Centre Reef. Anchorage in 20-30 feet on a mud bottom is found south of Rocket Shoal in the southeast part of Clam Bay, bordering Kuper Island. When fresh northwesterlies are roaring on Georgia Strait, this anchorage gets rollers and is uncomfortable. Another anchorage, with more protection from northwesterlies, is on the northwest shore, avoiding the rocks and shoals to the east.

Boat Passage: [3477] This channel has been dredged since 1905. It separates Thetis and Kuper Islands and, at high tide, serves as a convenient short cut between Telegraph Harbour and Trincomali Channel. It is narrow, almost a one-way only passage, and may be used only at or near high water. The channel dries. To check the water depths in the channel before entering, read the scale shown on pilings at either end of the channel. On the west end of the channel the marker is kept to port upon entering and starboard when leaving. On the east end, passage is between the two pilings at the entrance. Approach slowly because it is important to minimize wash and to stay in the center as much as possible. There is a sharp curve near the Telegraph Harbour entrance. Use Fulford Harbour tide chart adjusted for Preedy Harbour. Current floods east, ebbs west.

★ **North Cove (27):** Completely exposed to the north, temporary anchorage is possible in the southwest corner and near the entrance to Cufra Inlet. Cufra Inlet cuts into Thetis for about one mile and, although beautiful, is useless to the boater except by dinghy.

★ **Preedy Harbour (28):** Site of the Thetis Island-Chemainus ferry landing, it is the site of a small public moorage float adjacent to the ferry wharf and anchorage. Shoal areas are marked. Anchorage on a mud bottom can be found on the north side of the harbor, north of the sunken cable.

Telegraph Harbour

[3442, 3463, 3477]

★ **Telegraph Harbour (29):** Tucked between Kuper and Thetis Islands, this attractive harbor

has two marinas, limited anchorage, and protection from most winds.

★ **Telegraph Harbour Marina:** {48° 58' N, 123° 40' W} Located in the very back of the bay in Telegraph Harbour, this excellent marina has moorage with power, gas, diesel, water, store, cafe, gifts, laundry, showers, and covered recreation building. It is within walking distance of the Thetis Island-Chemainus ferry landing. See our Steering Star description in this chapter. Fax: 250-246-2668. Websites: www.telegraphhar-

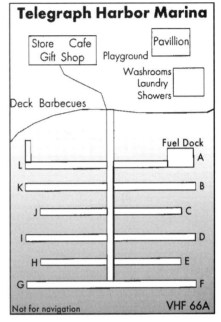

★ **Telegraph Harbour Marina:** Located at the very back of the bay, on the sunny side, this inviting marina is situated in a five acre, park-like setting which is complimented by the natural beauty of the area. The spacious grounds provide room for walking, beachcombing, secluded lounging, or group activities. There are swings, horseshoe pits, volleyball court, shuffleboard, and picnic tables with adjacent barbecues. The large, shake-roofed recreation building, equipped with a barbecue grill and electricity, provides a comfortable spot for group gatherings in any weather. Continuous improvements to the grounds and buildings provide a clean and charming atmosphere. Dock attendants welcome boaters to 3,000 feet of moorage on wide, well-maintained floats supplied with 15 and 30 ampere power and water (water is limited to 30 gals/day). The fuel dock provides gas, diesel, and oils. Washroom facilities are kept spotless. At the well stocked store, the shopper will find a selection of groceries, fresh produce, dairy products, fresh bakery goods, frozen bait and tackle, along with a variety of carefully selected B.C. gifts, native art, and books of local interest. An extensive chart selection covers waters from the San Juan Islands through the Queen Charlotte Strait. Visitors enjoy both indoor and patio seating at the cafe. The new expanded menu now includes pizza, salads, soups, and espresso drinks. This spot has become famous among boaters for its 1950's style soda fountain serving freshly baked pies, thick milk shakes, huge ice cream cones, sundaes, and banana splits. The marina's 30-year-old burgee collection, largest on the West Coast, adorns the store and cafe. Summer market on Sundays mid-May to mid-Sept. 10am to 2pm. We have wireless internet. Services limited during the winter. Individual and group reservations are welcomed and honored. Family owned and operated by Ron and Barbara Williamson. **Address: Box 7-10, Thetis Island, British Columbia V0R 2Y0. Internet Sites: www.telegraphharbour.com & www.boattravel.com/telegraph Telephones: 250-246-9511, 1-800-246-6011. Fax: 250-246-2668. VHF 66A.**

bour.com & www.boattravel.com/telegraph. Address: Box 7-10, Thetis Island, British Columbia V0R 2Y0. Telephone: 250-246-9511, 1-800-246-6011. Fax: 250-246-2668. VHF 66A.

Walk-around: From Telegraph Harbour Marina it is possible to walk to the ferry landing in Preedy Harbour and ferry to Chemainus. Check with Telegraph Harbour Marina for the ferry schedule. Walks and bike rides along the quiet roads on Thetis Island are also possible.

Thetis Island Marina: Moorage, gas, diesel, propane, power, water, laundry, showers, store, pub. 250-246-3464. VHF 66A.

Vancouver Island Central East Coast

[3313, 3441, 3442, 3443, 3462, 3463, 3475, 3478]

★ **Evening Cove (30):** Located between Sharpe Point and Coffin Point, this bay has anchorage near the head in 10-20 feet of water. It is exposed to southeast winds. Private buoys are in the inner bay.

★ **Sibell Bay (31):** Homes overlook a long crescent-shaped beach. A yacht club outstation is located on Dunsmuir Island, which frames the southwest side of Sibell Bay. Anchor in Sibell Bay itself or go around the Dunsmuir Islands and anchor off Bute Island. Log booms are prevalent and commercial oyster beds are in the vicinity. Nearby Burleigh Arm is usually filled with log booms.

Ladysmith

[3443, 3463, 3475]

★ **Ladysmith (32):** Moorage, with direct access to town, is accessible at both the Fisherman's Wharf Public Floats and the Maritime Society floats. On shore is a large concrete, no fee, launching ramp. The tidal grid alongside the wharf is available for emergencies and repairs. Repair facilities are accessible. Moorage is also available across the harbor at Page Point.

Set on the hillside, this delightful town has many attractions and special events. A call to a taxi (250-268-2114) or a walk on an up-hill path leads to downtown. Visitors discover the charm of Ladysmith as soon as they enter. Walking the streets, admiring heritage buildings, and meeting friendly people will become lasting memories. Shops and services include grocery, pharmacy, gift, jewelry, hardware, variety, liquor, wine, repair, auto supply, candy, restaurants, and bakery.

For those who enjoy a swim or sauna, the Community Center pool is on 6th Avenue. Also, Transfer Beach Park, located on the waterfront, has an excellent swimming beach, playground, kayak rentals, lessons, tours, and picnic areas. The Black Nugget Museum is a popular attraction. Exhibits include 3,500 year-old flint knives, 2,000 year old Roman glass, and an 1839 brass bed inlaid with mother-of-pearl. The Ladysmith Chamber of Commerce provides literature and information about many activities and points-of-interest at this, the *49th Parallel City*.

Ladysmith Celebration Days, held on the long weekend in August, includes a large parade and a *Saturday Soap Box Derby* down the main street. Sunday and Monday, at Transfer Beach Park, there are fireworks, live music, kayak display, and *Paddlefest* and many activities for the entire fami-

ly. Boaters usually anchor off Transfer Beach to watch the fireworks. In December, Ladysmith is known as the *Christmas Light-up Capital of Vancouver Island*. Festivities include a colorful, twinkling parade, entertainment, the arrival of Santa Claus, a spaghetti dinner, and fireworks. Over 10,000 people enjoy Ladysmith's hospitality for this event.

The town was founded in 1904, during the Boer War and named for Sir Harry Smith's wife, Lady Smith. Many of the streets were named after British Generals who served in that war. The backbone of the economy has been coal mining and later, logging. Some shops display historical information, plaques, and pictures.

LadySmith (Ivy Green) Marina: Permanent and limited guest moorage, laundry, showers, water, power. The floating building is the headquarters for Ladysmith Yacht Club. 250-245-4521. VHF 66A.

Ladysmith Fisherman's Wharf: These public floats are found in the breakwater protected boat basin right on the 49th Parallel. Look for the rip rap and pile and plank breakwaters. Moorage, power, water, garbage disposal, grid, launching ramp, and derrick. Just a short walk to town, grocery and liquor stores. The Harbour Manager's Office, with washrooms, showers, laundry, and public telephone, is located at the foot of the parking lot. 250-245-7511.

Ladysmith Maritime Society: Moorage, power, and water are available. New office with washrooms & showers to be completed by 2005. 250-245-1146. These floats lie alongside existing boathouses, between Slag Point and Fishermen's Wharf. The site is identified by a Visitors sign and a Wharfinger is often on hand to greet you. Overnight moorage is available on six floats 26' in length, and on a longer float designed for a larger boat. Fifteen and 30 ampere power and water. Harbour Tours are offered the last weekend of May through Labour Day. Weekends until mid-July, then twice a day until Labour Day, if the interest is there. Donation. Contact Ladysmith Chamber of Commerce at 250-245-2112 for information and reservations. The heritage tug, *Saravan*, and the restored water taxi, *C.A. Kirkegaard* are on display. 250-245-1146.

Page Point Inn: Moorage, power, water, laundry, showers, washrooms, lodging, restaurant, gas, diesel. 250-245-2312, 1-877-860-6866. VHF 66A.

Chemainus

[3443, 3463, 3475]

★ **Chemainus (33):** This delightful town has long been on trip itineraries of many boating families. Moorage can be found at public floats. Also, Chemainus is easily accessible by ferry from moorage at marinas in Telegraph Harbour on Thetis Island. Future plans call for Chemainus Quay with its Gateway Marina, however the construction date is uncertain. Call the Chamber of Commerce for information: 250-246-3944.

Facilities and services include a large variety of specialty shops, restaurants, gift shops, bed and breakfast inns, dinner theatre, park and picnic areas, art galleries, and a well-stocked grocery within easy distance to moorage.

Attractions appeal to the entire family. Giant murals, drawn from actual historical photographs and events, make Chemainus the world's largest outdoor art gallery. At present there are over 37 murals and 12 statues. These depict the colorful logging history of the pioneer community. For a self guided tour of the murals, follow the footprints, painted on the sidewalks. Each year, beginning in late June, the summer-long *Festival Of Murals* sponsors artists at work, parades, street entertainment, guided tours, and a myriad of other activities. Other events include *Chemainus Days* held the end of June and *Market Days* in July. The landmark Chemainus Dinner Theatre has matinee and evening performances. As you walk uptown from old town, you will see the 'band shell', trails, and theme history playground at Waterwheel Park. For picnicking there is Kin Park with a playground, swimming beach with change house, and boat ramp. Just minutes away from the town center is "Hermit's Trail." Built by a local hermit, this forest sanctuary is a refuge of stone paths, walkways, and flower gardens. Nearby are Mt. Brenton Golf Course, Fuller Lake Arena, Fresh Water Park with tennis courts and supervised swimming, bowling, and many parks and picnic areas. Overnight lodging can be

Chemainus Theatre   *Linda Schreiber Photo*

accommodated in B&B's and other inns.

The Chemainus Valley is one of the oldest European settlements on Vancouver Island. The first settlers arrived in the 1850's, and farmed the land. A small water-powered sawmill began operations in 1862, and became known for having the longest continuous period of lumber production (over 125 years) in western Canada. Chemainus' Horseshoe Bay is also the oldest deep seaport on Canada's west coast, with its major function being the center for lumber shipments. In 1980, anticipating the closing of the mill in this one industry town, the residents took advantage of Provincial assistance and established a Downtown Revitalization Project. From the belief that their history was too important to be forgotten, came the idea of bringing the community's heritage to life on the walls of the village buildings. Today, Chemainus is known as *"The Little Town That Did"*. Historic "train" ride, pulled by tractor, takes about 35 minutes.

Chemainus Public Moorage: 400' of transient moorage is available on the public floats adjacent to the Chemainus-Thetis Island ferry landing at the foot of Oak Street in Old Town Chemainus. Water and 30 ampere power on all floats, security gates. Showers and restrooms are at the head of the floats. Garbage drop. Space for loading and unloading. Limited space for day moorage is available but is to be vacated by 3:00 PM. Reservations for overnight moorage are recommended. 250-715- 8186, 250-246-4655. VHF 66A.

★ **Crofton (34):** The community of Crofton is located on the hillside behind Osborn Bay. Crofton Public Floats are tucked in behind a breakwater, adjacent to the BC ferry terminal. The ferry connects hourly with Vesuvius on Saltspring Island. A free boat launch gives quick access to good fishing grounds. A pay phone, public toilets and showers are located at the top of the dock. Pubs offer food and weekend entertainment. Two well-stocked grocery stores, some small shops, a bakery, and restaurants are nearby. Lodging is accessible. Play and picnic at Osborne Bay Park or Crofton Beach. Marine gas and diesel are available at the Shell station, not on the wharf. The Visitor InfoCentre, located in the Old School Museum, is open July and August, seven days a week. Free tours of Crofton Pulp and Paper Mill, June through August. The tour begins every week day at 1:30 p.m. 250-246-6006. Four area parks have good mountain bike and hiking trails. Crofton was founded by Henry Croft in the early days of the 1900's. Croft was a lumber and mining magnate who developed the prosperous Lenora mine at nearby Mount Sicker. He bought the land, named the townsite after himself, constructed an Opera House, and started a copper smelter on site. With copper prices plummeting in 1908, the smelter closed. In 1956, BC Forest Products developed the modern pulp and paper mill north of town.

Crofton Public Floats: Moorage, 30 ampere power, water, restrooms, showers, security gates, laundry one block away. Key available at ferry toll booth. 250-246-4655.

★ **Duncan:** While not located on the waterfront, there is easy access from Maple Bay Marina where complimentary shuttles leave twice daily. Taxi service and rental cars are also available. Duncan has a great variety of shops, restaurants, grocery stores, and liquor agency. Located in the heart of a dairy farming, market gardening, and wine producing region, it is approximately midway between Victoria and Nanaimo. There are local cheesemakers, and a selection of wineries and ciderworks are open for tours. The Visitor Info Centre has maps and more information, including descriptions of hiking trails and parks. 250-746-4636.

Duncan has the distinction of being the world's only dedicated totem city. Within the city limits stand 82 totem poles, 39 of which were sponsored by *The City of Totems* building program. Among them is *Cedar Man Holding Talking Stick*, the world's thickest totem with a circumference of 630 centimeters. It was carved from a tree estimated to be 775 years old. The Quw'utsun' Cultural and Conference Centre provides insights into the Coast Salish. Guests are treated to a feast of native dishes and a presentation of dancing and drumming. The BC Forest Discovery Centre is also located in Duncan. Visitors learn the history of the forests and lumbering by viewing working steam railways. Open May through mid October. 250-715-1113. Also, the Cowichan Valley Museum and Archives, located at Canada Avenue and Station Street, has changing exhibits housed inside a 1912 train station. 250-746-6612. On the way to or from Duncan, visit The Quamichan Inn, located on Maple Bay Road. 250-746-7028.

Maple Bay

[3442, 3462, 3478]

★ **Maple Bay (35):** Entry from the south into this lovely bay is made by rounding landmark *Paddy Mile Stone*. The bay itself may seem reminiscent of a Swiss lake. The public float directly west after entering the bay is open to winds and to wash from boats entering and leaving Bird's Eye Cove. Access to facilities which include marinas, fueling stations, provision stores, restaurants, repair facilities, charter agencies, Maple Bay Yacht Club, and walking trails to Duncan. Tidal flats and a park reserve

★ **Maple Bay Marina:** - {N 48° 47.742′ – W 123° 35.942′} CHS {Charts 3462, 3478} Maple Bay Marina is nestled in the calm south end of Maple Bay, in Bird's Eye Cove. This is a popular stop, scenic and well protected from winds and seas. The grounds are beautiful, with whimsical touches such as old marine engines, cleaned and painted red or white. This is a full service marina that offers permanent and

visitor moorage year round, power, water, gas, diesel, propane, CNG, oil, lubricants and a courtesy van. On shore facilities include ultra-clean washrooms, showers, laundromat, a covered patio for groups, internet, and fax services. The Shipyard Restaurant & Pub features an attractive menu at reasonable prices and also have beer and wine off sales. Haul out service and your chandlery needs are available through The Marine Supply store. Other businesses and services included are mechanics, shipwrights, a gift store, Passage Yacht Brokers, The Market@Maple Bay/Coffee Shop, Harbour Air, Budget Rent-A-Car, and wireless internet provided by Broadband Xpress. The Marina is 15 minutes from Duncan, the "City of Totems". Local attractions include the Quw'utsun Cultural Centre and the B.C. Forest Museum. There are four 18-hole golf courses within a 25-minute drive of the marina. Over the past decade Maple Bay Marina has established a well-deserved reputation for providing excellent service, value, and friendly atmosphere second to none. It's on your way whether you're heading North or South. Reservations recommended. **Address: 6145 Genoa Bay Road, Duncan, BC V9L 5T7. Ph: 746-8482 or 866-746-8482. Website: www.maplebaymarina.com VHF 66A**

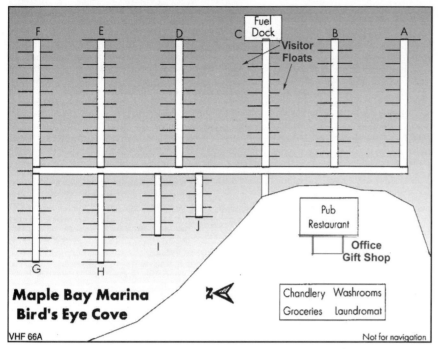

F   E   D   C   Fuel Dock   B   A

Visitor Floats

Pub
Restaurant

Office
Gift Shop

**Maple Bay Marina
Bird's Eye Cove**

N

| Chandlery | Washrooms |
| Groceries | Laundromat |

G   H
I
J

VHF 66A   Not for navigation

35.942' W} Extensive visitor's moorage with power and water available. Fuel dock dispenses gas, diesel, propane, "CNG" oils. Restaurant, pub, chandlery, groceries, clean washrooms, showers and laundromat. See our Steering Star description in this chapter. Internet: www.boattravel.com/maplebay/& www.maplebaymarina.com/. Address: 6145 Genoa Bay Road #7, Duncan, British Columbia V9L 5T7. E-mail: info@maplebaymarina.com. Fax: 250-746-8490. Telephone: Toll Free: 1-866-746-8482. VHF 66A.

★ **The Quamichan Inn:** This notable restaurant and Bed & Breakfast Inn has been a favorite stop on boater's itineraries for many years. Dinner service begins at 5:30 p.m. Open Wednesday-Sunday. Reservations recommended. Limo service from moorages. See our Steering Star description in this chapter. Websites: www.thequamichaninn.com & www.boattravel.com/thequamichaninn/. Email: thequamichaninn@shaw.ca. Address: 1478 Maple Bay Road, Duncan, British Columbia V9L 4T6. Fax: 250-746-5223. Telephone: 250-746-7028.

Bird's Eye Cove Marina: Limited overnight moorage, power, water, gas, diesel, oils, stove, ice. 250-746-0679.

Sansum Narrows: This passageway has noticeable wave action from the currents. Good fishing. Aquaculture operations are in the vicinity.

★ **Genoa Bay (36):** This bay opens off the northern shore of Cowichan Bay. Keep the red day-beacon on the starboard side and watch the green spar buoy, about 500 yards south of the charted position. There is good anchorage on a mud bottom. Exposure to southeast winds can be a problem, in which case the western shore offers the best protection. Exploring the bay by small craft, crab-

at the head of Birds Eye Cove can be explored by dinghy. Afternoon breezes of 10-20 knots are normal in summer months, providing good sailing conditions. Scuba diving is popular in the area. Diving and racing markers may be present.

Maple Bay Public Floats: Moorage (self-registration), water. 250-715-8186.

★ **Cove Yachts:** {48° 48' N, 123° 30' W} Located

in Bird's Eye Cove. Full service repair facility with limited transient moorage. Shipwrights, electricians, painters, and welders are available. Travelift, fixed crane, and marine railway. Engine repairs. See our Steering Star description in this chapter. Email: cove-y@shaw.ca Address: 6261 Genoa Bay Road, Duncan, British Columbia V9L 5Y4. Fax: 250-748-7916. Telephone: 250-748-8136.

★ **Maple Bay Marina:** {48° 47.742' N, 123°

bing, and wildlife watching are popular. Genoa Bay is connected to Duncan by road. A marina, restaurant, and aquaculture operations are located here. Old-timers will remember this bay as the site of Captain Morgan's Lodge. The lodge has been restored and is now a Bed and Breakfast Inn.

Genoa Bay Marina: Moorage, power, water, launch, laundry, bathroom & showers, provisions, café. 250-746-7621. VHF 66.

Cowichan Bay
[3441, 3462, 3478]

★ Cowichan Bay (37): Cowichan Bay is a small village, yet the activity in the harbor indicates it is a deep sea port. There are two breakwaters in the bay, a rip-rap rock breakwater and a pile and plank breakwater. Cowichan Bay is home to the Cowichan Coast Salish tribes. Known for logging, fishing, and Cowichan sweaters, the word, Cowichan, derives from the Indian term meaning *warm land*. Along the waterfront are marinas, repair facilities, shipyards, a pub, hair salon, post office, artisan's studios, convenience store, beer and wine store, restaurants, and a fresh fish market. Hotel, motel, and bed and breakfast establishments provide lodging. Of special interest to visiting families is the Maritime Centre Museum. Walk to Hecate Park for a picnic. Take in a game of tennis or golf, visit the Farmer's Market for fresh vegetables and provisions, or take a short bus ride to Duncan. Annual events include Native canoe races, *Cowichan Wooden Boat Festival* and the *Cowichan Bay Regatta*. Fishing at Sansum Narrows is three miles away.

Bluenose Marina: Moorage, power, mooring buoys, laundry, showers, restaurant. 250-748-2222.

Cherry Point Marina: Located across from Separation Point. Limited guest moorage, power, launch ramp, campsites. 250-748-0453.

Cowichan Bay Harbour Fisherman's Wharf: Inside the pile and plank breakwater. All-tide entry channel. Moorage, restaurant, power, water, garbage deposit. Rafting sometimes necessary. Office, washrooms, showers, laundry. 250-746-5911. VHF 66A.

Dungeness Marina: Moorage, power, water. 250-748-6789.

Masthead Marina: Very limited moorage, power. 250-748-3714.

Pier 66: Moorage, 15-ampere power, marine gas, diesel, pre-mix, liquor outlet, provisions. 250-748-8444.

Conover Cove, Wallace Island   Kelly O'Neil

★ **The Quamichan Inn:** For many years boaters have placed this as a "must stop" on their boating itineraries, offering outstanding food and service in the Tudor style country inn. Once at the inn, you are invited to "Take your time." Begin with a cool drink in the lounge in front of the fireplace; dine in one of the intimate dining rooms; finish with liquors and coffee on the patio while viewing a spectacular sunset. Groups are welcome to book the banquet facility. The Chef's innovative menus include Vancouver Island–Cowichan Valley produce whenever possible. You are invited to experience the wines produced from the vineyards in the area. Bed and breakfast accommodation is available. This enables guests to wine and dine and stay the night in one of the cozy rooms, each with an ensuite. Reservations are a must. The inn is open Wednesday to Sunday at 5:30 pm. Limousine service to and from Maple Bay Yacht Club and Genoa Bay is available from 5:30 p.m. **Circle #66 on the Reader Service Card. Websites: www.thequamichaninn.com and www.boattravel.com/thequamichaninn. Email: thequamichaninn@shaw.ca Address: 1478 Maple Bay Road, Duncan, British Columbia V9L 5R2 Fax: 1-250-746-5223 Phone: 250-746-7028.**

Essential Supplies & Services

AIR TRANSPORTATION
To & from Washington
Seattle Seaplanes **1-800-637-5553**
To & from Islands/Vancouver
Air Canada 1-888-247-2262
Baxter Air 1-800-661-5599
Harbour Air 604-274-1277
Tofino Air 1-800-665-2359
Vancouver Island Air 250-287-2433

AMBULANCES: 911

BOAT MOVING
All Tow Boat Moving . . . .
. . . . **604-946-7899, 1-877-946-7899**

BOAT SEATS & UPHOLSTERY
Royal City Bedding **604-526-2641**

BOOKS / BOOK STORES
The Marine Atlas. **541-593-6396**

BUS TRANSPORTATION
Cowichan Regional Transit 250-746-9899
Go Galiano Shuttle: Galiano Island 250-539-0202
Island Coach Lines 250-385-4411
Maple Bay Marina: Courtesy van to Duncan 250-746-8482

CNG CYLINDERS
Maple Bay Marina. **250-746-8482**

COAST GUARD
Comox . . . . VHF 16, 22-A, 26, 84. 250-339-3613

Emergencies. 1-800-567-5111
    From Cellphone. . . . .#16, VHF 16
Ganges. . . . . .250-537-5813, VHF 16, 22, 04
General Info . . . . 1-866-823-1110 (Canada only)

CUSTOMS
Ganges- Breakwater Float (CANPASS only)
Montague Harbour Marina (CANPASS only)

FERRY INFORMATION
B.C. Ferries . . . . 1-888-223-3779 250-386-3431 (U.S.)

FUELS
Bird's Eye Cove: Maple Bay. Gas, Diesel . 250-746-0679
Ganges Marina: Gas, Diesel . . . 250-537-5242 VHF 66A
Maple Bay Marina: Gas, Diesel
. . . . **250-746-8482 VHF 66A**
Montague Harbour Marina . 250-539-5733 VHF 66A
Page Point Inn: Gas, Diesel . . . 250-245-2312 VHF 66A
Pier 66: Cowichan Bay. Gas, Diesel. 250-748-8444
Roamer's Landing (Fulford Harbour). . . . 250-653-4487
Telegraph Harbour Marina: Gas, Diesel
. . . . **250-246-9511 VHF 66A**
Thetis Island Marina: Gas, Diesel. . 250-246-3464 VHF 66A

GOLF COURSES
These courses are accessible from moorage and have rental clubs available)
Arbutus Ridge: Cobble Hill 250-743-5000
Blackburn: Ganges. 250-537-1707
Cowichan: Duncan. 250-746-5333
Duncan Meadows 250-746-8993
Mount Breton: Chemainus. 250-246-9322
Galiano Island: From Montague Harbour. 250-539-5533

Saltspring Island: From Ganges 250-537-2121

HOSPITALS
Chemainus. 250-246-3291
Cowichan District 250-746-4141
Ganges 250-538-4800

INSURANCE
Boat Insurance Agency **206-285-1350**
  Or Call **1-800-828-2446**

LIQUOR / WINE STORES
Chemainus
Cowichan Bay (Pier 66)
Duncan
Fulford
Ganges, Saltspring Island
Harbour House, Ganges
Ladysmith
Miners Bay, Mayne Island
Sturdies Bay, Galiano Island

LODGING
Fulford Inn. 1-800-652-4432, 250-653-4331
**Hastings House Relais & Chateaux Hotel, Dining &
Spa** **800-661-9255, 520-537-2362**
Harbour House **1-888-779-5571**
Quamichan Inn: Duncan **250-746-7028**

MARINAS / MOORAGE
Bird's Eye Cove: Maple Bay. 250-746-0679
Bluenose Marina: Cowichan Bay 250-748-2222
Burgoyne Bay: Salt Spring Island
Chemainus
Conover Cove: Wallace Island
Cowichan Bay Harbour. . . . . . . 250-746-5911 VHF 66A
Dungeness Marina. 250-748-6789
Fernwood: Salt Spring Island
Fulford Harbour Marina: Salt Spring Is. . 250-653-4467
Ganges Marina . . . . 250-537-5242 VHF 66A
Genoa Bay Marina . . . . 250-746-7621 VHF 66A
Ladysmith Maritime Society 250-245-1146
Ladysmith Wharf. 250-245-7511
Lyall Harbour: Saturna Island
Maple Bay Marina . . . . . . 250-746-8482 VHF 66A
Montague Harbour Marina . 250-539-5733 VHF 66A
Musgrave Landing: Salt Spring Island
North Galiano
Page Point Inn: Ladysmith . . . . 250-245-2312 VHF 66A
Pier 66: Cowichan Bay. 250-748-8444
Preedy Harbour: Thetis Island
Retreat Cove: Galiano Island
Saltspring Harbour Authority: (Outer Harbour)
. . . . 250-537-5711 VHF 9
Saltspring Harbour Authority: (Ganges Centennial
Wharf) . . . . 250-537-5711 VHF 9
Salt Spring Marina. 250-537-5810
. . . . **1-800-334-6629 VHF 66A**
Sturdies Bay: Galiano Island
Telegraph Harbour Marina . 250-246-9511 VHF 66A
Thetis Island Marina. . . . . 250-246-3464 VHF 66A
Vesuvius: Salt Spring Island
Whaler Bay: Galiano Island

MARINE SUPPLIES & PARTS
Cove Yachts: Maple Bay. **250-748-8136**
Harbours End Marine: Ganges. 250-537-4202
Maple Bay Marina **250-746-8482**
Mouat's, Ganges **1-877-490-5593**
Pier 66: Cowichan Bay. 250-748-8444

Carl & Gloria Tenning Photo

Essential Supplies & Services — cont'd.

PARKS
B.C. Parks: South Vancouver Island 250-391-2300

PHARMACY
Pharmasave: Ganges 250-537-5534

POISON INFO: 1-800-567-8911

PROPANE
Ganges Marina 250-537-5242
Maple Bay Marina 250-746-8482
Thetis Island Marina 250-246-3464

RAMPS/HAUL-OUTS
Chemainus: Kin Park
Cowichan Bay . . . . 250-746-5911 VHF 66A
Cove Yachts: Bird's Eye Cove 250-748-8136
Crofton Ferry Landing . . . . 250-246-4655 VHF 66A
Genoa Bay Marina: 250-746-7621
Harbours End Marine: Ganges 250-537-4202 VHF 16, 66A
Ladysmith Government Float
Maple Bay Marina . . . . . . 250-746-8482 VHF 66A
Montague Harbour Marine Park . . . 250-539-5733
Oyster Harbour Marine: Ladysmith 250-245-8233
Saltspring Harbour Authority, Centennial Wharf (Ganges
  Boat Basin) . . . . 250-537-5711 VHF 9
Salt Spring Marina: Ganges 250-537-5810 VHF 66A

RECOMPRESSION: 1-800-567-5111

RED TIDE INFO: 604-666-2828

REPAIRS / SERVICE
Bayside Machine: Duncan 250-746-1952

Cove Yachts: Maple Bay 250-748-8136
Cowichan Shipyard 250-748-7285
Harbours End Marine: Ganges . 250-537-4202 VHF 66A
Maple Bay Marina . . . . . 250-746-8482 VHF 66A
Oyster Harbour Marine: Ladysmith 250-245-8233
Salt Spring Marina: Ganges

  . . . . 250-537-5810 VHF 66A

RESCUE COORDINATION
Marine Distress 250-363-2333
Search & Rescue . . . . 1-800-567-5111. VHF 16

RESTAURANTS / FOODS
Fulford Inn 1-800-652-4432, 250-653-4331
Porter's: Ganges 250-537-5571
Quamichan Inn: Duncan 250-746-7028
Hastings House Relais & Chateaux Hotel, Dining &
  Spa 800-661-9255, 520-537-2362
Shipyard Pub & Restaurant: Maple Bay
  250-746-8482
Telegraph Harbour Marina 250-246-9511

SEWAGE DISPOSAL
Saltspring Harbour Authority (Ganges Breakwater
  Float). Pump . . . . 250-537-5711 VHF 9

SHELLFISH HOTLINE: 604-666-2828
Duncan 250-746-6221

SPORTFISHING
Nanaimo 250-754-0230
Victoria 250-363-3252

TAXI / LIMO
Chemainus 250-246-4414

Genoa Bay/Duncan/Maple Bay 250-746-4444
Ganges/Salt Spring Island 250-537-3030
Ladysmith 250-245-8294

THEATER / ENTERTAINMENT
Artspring 250-537-2125
Chemainus Theatre 250-246-9800

TOWING
Bayside Machine: Duncan . . . . . 250-746-1952 VHF 16
C-TOW 1-888-354-5554
Cove Yachts: Bird's Eye Cove 250-748-8136
Harbours End Marine: Ganges 250-537-4202 VHF 16, 66A

VHF MARINE OPERATOR
Victoria: VHF 27, 86   Ganges: VHF 27, 64
Nanaimo: VHF 87   Sechelt: VHF 86
Vancouver: VHF 23, 24, 25, 26, 86, 88

VISITOR INFORMATION
Chemainus & District Chamber of Commerce & Visitor
  Information Center 250-246-3944
Cowichan Bay 250-746-4636
Crofton 250-246-2456
Duncan 888-303-3337/250-746-4636
Galiano Island 250-539-2233
Ladysmith Chamber of Commerce 250-245-2112
Maple Bay 250-746-4636
Salt Spring Island 250-537-5252, 1-866-216-2936

WEATHER:
Environment Canada Weather Line 250-339-9861
Comox 250-339-0748
Nanaimo 250-245-8899
WX-3, WX-4, 21-B

Clam Bay, Penalakut Spit   *Canadian Hydrographic*

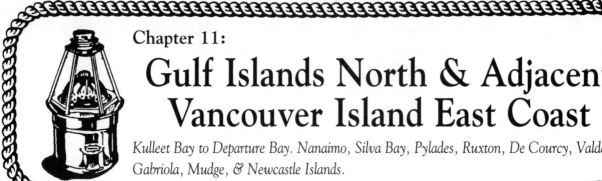

Chapter 11:
Gulf Islands North & Adjacent Vancouver Island East Coast

Kulleet Bay to Departure Bay. Nanaimo, Silva Bay, Pylades, Ruxton, De Courcy, Valdes, Gabriola, Mudge, & Newcastle Islands.

Symbols

[   ]: Numbers between [ ] are chart numbers.

{   }: Numbers & letters between { } are waypoints.

⚲: Park, ⛴: Boat Launch, ▲: Campgrounds, ⚲: Hiking Trails, ⊼: Picnic Area, ⮬: Biking

★ **Important Notice:** See "Important Notices" between Chapters 7 and 8 in this guide for specific information on boating related topics such as: Canadian & U.S. Customs, boating safety and security, navigation, weather, U.S. & Canadian Coast Guard, U.S & Canadian marine radio use, Vessel Traffic Service and traffic separation plans, security zones, and internet access. Due to new Department of Homeland Security regulations, call ahead for latest customs information and/or see Northwest Boat Travel On-line, www.nwboat.com.

★ **No Dump Zone:** Pilot Bay, Gabriola Island.

★ **Introduction to the Gulf Islands:** See the beginning of Chapter 9.

Vancouver Island South Of Nanaimo

[3443, 3463]

★ **Kulleet Bay (1):** Anchorage, with protection from northwesterlies, is found in this large bay. Anchor close in to shore on a sand and shell ledge. Shoal areas are at the extreme head of the bay, and the bottom falls away steeply from the ledges. Open to east winds. Land surrounding Kulleet Bay is Indian reservation land.

★ **Yellow Point (2):** This is a resort area, located where fish are often biting. North of Yellow Point, a shoal off-shore extends southward from the northern shore of the bay and is covered at high tide. The shoal is well marked on charts.

★ **Boat Harbour (3):** Note reefs near the entrance. Anchorage is inside Flewett Point on the south side of the harbor. This harbor is known locally as Kenary Cove after a man who made prize miniature cannons. The floats are private. Limited anchorage is possible behind Reynolds Point, farther in the harbor on the northwest side. The harbor is open to easterly winds.

De Courcy Area

[3443, 3463, 3475]

★ **Ruxton Island & Herring Bay (4):** When approaching Herring Bay on the northwest side of Ruxton, keep the day beacon to starboard. The outer limits of the bay are defined by drying reefs. Some kelp marks the reef that forms the eastern side of the entrance channel. Nearly all of the reefs are covered at high tide, making entry at that time more difficult. Entry may also be made from the southwest when the reefs are visible. Depths are 15-30 feet on a good holding sand bottom. Although partially protected by these reefs, this bay is exposed to west and northwest winds and offers little protection in a west wind. If boats shore tie, more space is available for anchorage in this relatively small cove. Seals often bask on the sandstone reefs.

★⚲ **Whaleboat Island Marine Park:** Located off the southeast tip of Ruxton Island, this park has rather unprotected anchorages. One spot is off Pylades Island in Whaleboat Passage.

★ **De Courcy Island:** Approximately 30 residents call this beautiful island home. Anchorage is found at the north end, in Pirate's Cove, and at the south tip of the island. Aside from its beauty and its location as the site of a marine park, De

Not for navigation   To Victoria

Chart List

Canadian Hydrographic Charts:

3310, 3313, 3443, 3447, 3458, 3463, 3475

NOAA Charts:

18400, 18402-03

Marine Atlas (2005 ed.):

Page 10, 22

Courcy has gained fame because it once was the 1920's compound of Edward Arthur Wilson, an English Sea Captain, who, prior to coming to De Courcy, had first settled on Vancouver Island in his Great White Lodge and House of Mystery near Cedar Point. Wilson declared himself a prophet and pronounced that a meteor was going to destroy everything in the world except this area. His ability to put himself into seemingly unbreakable trances through which he shared his visions, swayed many people into believing him and becoming followers. He later moved his operations across to De Courcy and Valdes Islands. He, and his companion, Madame Zee, were the highly unorthodox leaders of a cult community on De Courcy. It is said that over $400,000 in bank notes and gold bricks were hoarded by the pair and may still be hidden somewhere on Valdes Island. If you happen to meet an old-timer who relates these tales, or if you come upon a copy of the book, *Brother Twelve: The Incredible Story of Canada's False Prophet* by John Oliphant, you are in for an interesting story.

South Tip De Courcy Island (5): This bay is back-to-back with Pirate's Cove. The inner bay shallows. Wakes from passing boats can be uncomfortable. Private mooring buoys are in the bay to the west.

★ **Pirate's Cove Marine Park (5):** When approaching the entrance, aim for the white arrow and range marker. The arrow is painted on the shore next to a set of stairs leading to a summer cabin. Stay well off the shoal to port that extends to the Day Beacon. The reef at the entrance extends well beyond this concrete marker. There is also a shoal on the starboard side, as you enter. It is marked by a red buoy. Pass between the red buoy and the Day Beacon. Anchoring in Pirate's Cove is not as simple as its popularity might indicate. Much of the bottom is soft mud and shale. Because of the crowded conditions, it is difficult to get sufficient scope. Secondly, many a boater has dropped a hook on the shelf that lies along the southern shore of the bay only to find that the anchor will not hold because of the insufficient mud there. Thirdly, a reef extends from the northeastern shore in a westerly direction. This reef dries at low tide. Rings for stern tie-ups are embedded in the rocks. Mooring fees apply. The Parks Department requests that you not tie to trees as it damages them. Winds entering the cove have a swirling effect so boaters need to be on-the-lookout for anchor dragging. There are dinghy docks, one is to port upon entry and another lies to starboard farther into the cove. The dock to starboard upon entry is private, and the land adjacent to park property is under private ownership. Within the park are campsites, drinking water, and hiking trails. For a beautiful stroll, walk along the park land on the peninsula on the southeastern shore of the cove. Flat rocks, heated in the summer sun, offer resting spots for sun bathers. A path extends south to the cove overlooking Ruxton Passage. ▲🏃

★ **Anchorage between De Courcy and Link Islands (6):** Link Island is connected to the north end of De Courcy Island and the south end of Mudge Island by drying ridges. There is a small niche between De Courcy and Link islands for temporary anchorage. Beware of an uncharted shoal in the center with only three feet of water covering it at low water. When approaching, note that a pesky rock is off the De Courcy shore north-northwest of Pirate's Cove, about 100 yards offshore. Use caution when heading to False Narrows from Link Island or Pirate's Cove. This rock has been coined, *Brother Twelve's Rock*. See history of Brother Twelve above.

Anchorage in Pirate's Cove   *Gwen Cole Photo*

Valdes Island: This long island is separated by Gabriola Pass on the northwest side and Porlier Pass on the southeast. Steep cliffs border much of the island. Valdes is a relatively uninhabited island, not linked by ferry service. Unusual rock formations appear to have faces watching you, and a rock house, in the style of Frank Lloyd Wright, is hidden among the ledges. There are attractive beaches near Blackberry, Shingle, and Cardale Points. There is temporary shelter on either side of these points, depending on the wind direction. Much of this land is Indian Reservation land.

On the northern shore, anchorage is found in Wakes Cove near Cordero Point and in a bay formed between the three islets at Kendrick Island and the east shore of Valdes. Known locally as Dogfish Bay, it offers good sheltered anchorage and is often used by tugs awaiting favorable currents in Gabriola Pass.

★ **Wakes Cove Marine Park:** Avoid Wakes Cove in a northwest wind. Public dock & ramp to shore. Six foot minimum depths at zero tide. Walking trails. Kelp may affect anchoring. ⚓🏃

Gabriola Island
[3443, 3458, 3463, 3475]

★ **Gabriola Island:** Linked by ferry to Nanaimo, this island has many points-of-interest. These include Drumbeg Provincial Park, the Malaspina Galleries, Twin Beach Park, Silva Bay facilities, and the Gabriola Island Golf and Country Club.

★ **Degnen Bay (7):** Favor Josef Point on entry to avoid the many rocks which surround the island that is located in the center of the bay. Named after pioneer, Thomas Degnen, this bay has limited protected anchorage and a public wharf. Commercial boats have priority. A stone wall at the south end has rings for shore ties. Power is available on the floats. A five ton crane, garbage deposit, telephone, and used oil disposals, and tidal grid are available. Near the head of the bay, on a sandstone rock a few feet above the low tide line, is a petroglyph of a killer whale.

Walk-around: A road leads to Silva Bay a distance of about 1-1/2 miles. Drumbeg Park is about 1-1/2 miles southeast of Degnen Bay.

★⚓ **Drumbeg Provincial Park:** Drumbeg Provincial Park is on the north side of Gabriola Pass, east of Josef Point. Temporary anchorage for small boats only. This day use park is known for its sandstone outcroppings and nice beach. Swimming, picnicking, fishing, and hiking are possible. ⚓🏃

★ **Gabriola Passage (8):** [3475] See current tables for Active Pass. Gabriola Island received its name from the Spanish word gaviota, meaning sea gull. Currents in Gabriola Passage at spring tides reach eight knots maximum, which makes it less than pleasant for the planing hull boats to navigate at maximum runs and difficult, if not impossible, for sail boats and displacement hulls. The average velocity of both flood and ebb currents is four knots. Slack current occurs about 35 minutes before slack water at Active Pass. Flood current sets east, ebbs west. This passage is known as a "world class" dive.

★ **Silva Bay (9):** [3310, 3313] Sheltered from seas by Vance, Tugboat, and Sear Island. There are three entrances, each navigable, if you take the hazards into account. The main entrance is between Tugboat and Vance Islands. There is a drying reef which extends northward from Tugboat Island and "Shipyard Rock" lies in mid-channel. The least depth through the channel, north of the reef, is 19 feet. Silva Bay Light (Light List No. 434.3) is exhibited at an elevation of 15 feet from a white circular mast displaying a port hand daymark. Entering the bay, pass this light on the vessel's port side. Continue toward Law Point. Keep the green spar buoy U-39 to port. Do not turn too quickly to aim toward moorage facilities. The facility on Tugboat Island is a private yacht club. The south entrance is between Sear and Gabriola Islands. This channel is about 100 feet wide and has a minimum depth of four feet. It is particularly useful when heavy seas would be encountered while transiting from the south to Commodore Passage in order to reach the main entrance above. The north entrance is between Lily and Vance Islands. Enter at the north end, between Carlos Island and the shoals north of Lily Island. The minimum depth through this channel is 11 feet. An east cardinal buoy, identified as "PA" on charts, marks the drying ledges west of Carlos Island.

Once in Silva Bay, moorage is found at three marinas. On the opposite shore, on Tugboat Island, the Royal Vancouver Yacht Club main-

Dodd Narrows   Brian Watt, Canadian Hydrographic Photo

tains an out-station. Recreational activities on Gabriola Island include hiking or biking the island roads (rentals available), horseback riding, playing golf (taxi service available 250-247-0049), playing tennis, swimming in a pool or diving along shore, browsing arts and crafts shops, observing shipwrights at the Silva Bay Shipyard School, and shopping in the general store. Silva Bay is connected by road to Degnen Bay and Descanso Bay, site of the Gabriola-Nanaimo ferry terminal.

Walk-around: It is approximately one and one half miles to Drumberg Provincial Park on the north side of Gabriola Pass. Because the sun reflects off the extensive sandstone outcroppings and small beach, it is a favorite sunning, wading, and picnic spot.

Silva Bay Boatel: Moorage, 15-ampere power, mostly for small boats, groceries, pay telephone, RV parking, lodging, coffee shop, and laundromat. Fish head deposit site. 250-247-9351.

Silva Bay Resort & Marina: Moorage, 30 ampere power, limited water, repairs, marine ways, showers, laundry, bar & grill, liquor store. 250-247-8662. VHF 66A.

Pages Resort Marina: Gas, diesel, moorage, power, showers, laundry, lodging. 250-247-8931.

Notice of danger to your vessel: Before crossing the Georgia Strait to, or from, either Nanaimo or Silva Bay, read the "Notice" from the Canadian Department of National Defence, concerning area Whiskey-Golf, at the end of this chapter.

★⚓ **Gabriola Sands Provincial Park (10):** Galiano/Malaspina Galleries, a famous erosional formation in the sandstone, is located south of Malaspina Point. The galleries were noted as early as 1792 when Explorers Galiano and Valdes included drawings of them in their log. This photographer's delight is a sweeping curved roof of sandstone which resembles a giant ocean roller caught upon the point of breaking into a curve of foam. The park straddles a narrow neck of land between Pilot and Taylor Bays. Swimming is good at the sandy beaches. Picnic sites are available. Overnight camping is not permitted. 🚻

Pilot Bay: North end of Gabriola Island. Good anchorage. Protected from SE winds. No dump zone.

Entrance Island Lighthouse: Located off Orlebar Point, this is a primary weather station that reports conditions on the western side of Georgia Strait. The red and white lighthouse was built in 1875 to guide coal ships when traveling to and from Nanaimo.

Nanaimo Area

[3443, 3457, 3458, 3463, 3475]

Dodd Narrows (11): See current tables for Active Pass. Separating Vancouver Island from Mudge Island, this passage stretches in a southeast-northwest direction. Pleasure craft, tugs, barges, and small log booms pass through the opening at or near slack water. The current sets north on the flood, south on the ebb. Currents reach eight to ten knots at springs. Tide rips occur at the northwestern entrance on the flood and in the vicinity of the overhead cables on the ebb. Passage within one-half hour of slack is advised. There is a harbor speed limit.

False Narrows: Dodd Narrows is the recommended passage between the islands and Nanaimo. False Narrows is a tricky pass to navigate, so always use local charts and B.C. Pilot. The channel is very close to the shores of Gabriola Island and north of a long rocky drying ledge in the middle of the narrows. Tidal streams of four to five knots maximum are referenced at Dodd Narrows. This passage leads from the northwest end of Pylades Channel into Percy Anchorage and is navigable for small craft. When approaching from Pylades Channel, favor the Mudge Island shore to avoid a boulder-covered drying area to the north. A beacon range leads from this east end to the five to six feet deep navigable channel. Another set of beacons leads out via the west end. Keep on this west range until close to the Mudge Island shore to avoid a drying spit that extends west from the west range. Thick kelp is a hazard in summer and fall. Temporary anchorage is possible in Percy's Anchorage in 35-50 feet of water on a shell bottom.

Northumberland Channel: Leading northwest from Dodd and False Narrows between Vancouver Island and the southwest coast of Gabriola Island, boaters use this waterway en route to Nanaimo and the Strait of Georgia. Log booms are often rafted against the steep side of Gabriola Island.

Duke Point: Site of the Nanaimo-Tsawwassen Ferry Terminal and the beginning of the freeway north to Courtenay. Located south of the city, near Harmac Pacific mill. When traversing Northumberland Channel to or from Dodd Narrows, or along the northwest shore of Gabriola Island, be watchful for ferry traffic.

★ **Nanaimo (12):** [3443, 3457, 3458] Nanaimo is a customs port-of-entry. The Customs office is behind the floatplane terminal. The second largest city on Vancouver Island, Nanaimo has developed its waterfront acreage into an outstanding collection of parks, promenades, marine-oriented businesses, lodging accommodations, and parking areas. Pioneer Waterfront Plaza which provides a viewing platform overlooking Nanaimo's historic waterfront is home to retail shops and the Nanaimo Farmers' Market open Fridays from May through October. The Great Canadian Casino and Port Theatre for the Performing Arts are also notable attractions.

Area activities include fishing, golfing, hiking, scuba diving, horseback riding, indoor rock climbing, ice and roller-skating, sailing, swimming, theater attractions, and shopping. Tours of mills and hatcheries may be arranged. Trips to Bowen Park, Beban Park Sports Complex, the new Nanaimo Aquatic Centre, and Petroglyph Park require a taxi or bus ride. Bowen Park, on Comox Road, has a seasonal outdoor swimming pool, tennis courts, recreation complex, and lawn bowling. Other attractions include a duck pond, nature garden, small animal barn, and totem poles. Beban Park, further along Bowen Road, has skating and an indoor swimming pool. The Nanaimo Aquatic Centre features a 50 M pool, three slides, a lazy river, wave pool, sauna, steam room and gym facilities. Petroglyph Park, near the southern edge of the city, is the site of ancient Indian sandstone carvings believed to have been part of ancient ceremonials paying homage to a sun god. Departure Bay is the site of the Pacific Biological Research Station. The Station is not open to the general public. Another diversion is an excursion to Gabriola Island. Take the 25-minute ferry ride to the island from the landing across from Port Place Centre. Rent a car or bicycle and spend the day exploring along the road that circles the island.

Nanaimo residents enjoy celebrations. *Empire Days* are held in May, the *Dragon Boat Festival* and *Sillyboat Regatta* both occur in July. The annual *Marine Festival*, also staged in July, is when Nanaimo lives up to the nickname "Bathtub Race Capital City of the World." Entrants in bathtubs follow a route from Nanaimo Harbour around Entrance Island, head west along Georgia Strait, around Winchelsea Island, and back to Nanaimo for a thrilling finish at Departure Bay Beach. In mid-August, *Vancouver Island Exhibition* is a festival of crafts, carnival rides and games, and livestock shows.

Approaching downtown Nanaimo: The approach to the Port of Nanaimo Boat Basin is either from the northwest through Departure Bay and Newcastle Island Passage or from the east, past the southern tip of Protection Island. When entering Newcastle Passage from the north, keep the buoy near Shaft Point to port and pass in mid-channel between Shaft and Pimbury Points. The enforced speed limit in the channel is five knots. Moorage facilities, repair yards, and fuel docks line the western shore. Oregon Rock (known locally as "Rowan's Rock" for the late and legendary local mechanic, Johnny Rowan, who, prior to the rock being marked and charted, made his living salvaging and repairing boats that wandered upon it) is near mid-channel. Note the arrow that points to the correct passage on the Newcastle Island side of the rock. Continuing south, the Nanaimo Yacht Club and the Townsite Marina are located here. After passing the float-plane facility, the entrance to the Port of Nanaimo Boat Basin is at the southern end of the floating breakwater. The alternative approach to downtown Nanaimo and into Nanaimo Harbour is from the east, in the passage marked by the picturesque lighthouse on the south tip of Protection Island. Keep the red buoy to starboard and the green spar to port. Proceed around the Visiting Vessel Pier.

An aircraft radio controlled flashing white strobe light, installed on the windsock on the Central Breakwater, serves as visual warning to vessels of approaching aircraft. Aircraft trigger the strobe light, which flashes for 90 seconds prior to take-off or landing.

★ **Port of Nanaimo Boat Basin:** {49° 10' N, 123° 56' W} The Visiting Vessel Pier off the north tip of Cameron Island accommodates large pleasure or cruise vessels, and the adjacent Cameron Island Marina provides moorage for smaller pleasure craft. Moorage is on the floats in the vicinity of the fuel dock and in the Commercial Inlet Basin. Full utility services available. Sewage pump-out. Wharfinger's office and comfort station with laundry facilities and washrooms and separate washroom and showers for visiting boaters. Harbourside Walkway extends around the perimeter of the boat basin shoreline. Noon cannon firings take place beside the landmark white Hudson's Bay Bastion adjacent to the Pioneer Waterfront. Scheduled floatplane passenger service between downtown Nanaimo and Vancouver. See our Steering Star description in this chapter. Mailing address: Post Office Box 131, 104 Front Street, Nanaimo, British Columbia V9R 5K4. Fax: 250-754-4186. Telephone: 250-754-5053. Websites: www.npa.ca & www.boattravel.com/nanaimo   Email:

info@npa.ca VHF 67.

Townsite Marina: {49° 11'N, 123° 56' W} No temporary moorage available. 250-716-8801.

Brechin Point Marina: Customs port-of-entry. Gas, diesel, stove oil, ice, water, Avgas 100LL, Jet A1. 250-753-6122.

Anchorage Marina: Permanent moorage, repairs, haul-outs, water, supplies, CNG, 30-ampere power. 250-754-5585.

Moby Dick Lodge & Marina: Moorage, water, power, laundry. 250-753-7111.

Nanaimo Harbour City Marina: Long term moorage, repairs, haulout, 30 & 70 ton travel lifts. 250-754-2732.

Nanaimo Shipyard Ltd: Moorage, haul-outs, repairs. 250-753-1151.

Newcastle Marina: Power, permanent moorage, repairs, haul-outs. 250-753-1431.

Petro Canada Marine (Port of Nanaimo Basin): Gas, diesel, ice, water, oils, batteries, convenience store. 250-754-7828.

Stone's Marina: Moorage, power, water, laundry, showers, washrooms, RV park. 250-753-4232.

Nanaimo Walk-arounds: To orient yourself, remember that the streets of the city are laid out like a wheel, with the hub located at the boat basin and streets radiating out like spokes. Two self-guided tours are outlined in brochures available at the Visitor Information Centre or Wharfingers Office. The first, "A Walk Through Time," starts at Pioneer Waterfront Park. Visit the white, octagonal building located on the bluff

overlooking the harbour beside the Port Theatre. This is the Nanaimo District Museum. The museum features a coal mine exhibit, a diorama depicting pre-European Coast Salish life, and exhibits of a blacksmith shop, a Chinese gallery, and fossils. A miner's cabin, and an old locomotive are displayed in Piper Park, next to the museum. Steps lead down the wall to the Port Place Centre. The air-conditioned Centre has a Thrifty

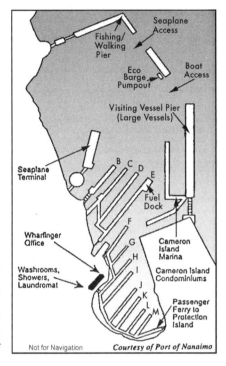

Not for Navigation   *Courtesy of Port of Nanaimo*

★ **Port of Nanaimo Boat Basin:** For many years, this sheltered yacht basin located behind the 600 foot, Visiting Vessel Pier (for cruise ships and large craft) off the north tip of Cameron Island, has been a popular rendezvous site for pleasure craft. A customs-port-of-entry, over 9,000 feet of moorage is available. Reservations are taken for the Visiting Vessel Pier and Cameron Island Marina only. When arriving to the outside of the breakwater pier, call on VHF Channel 67, or 250-754-5053, to be directed to a berth. Moorage for smaller craft is on

the floats in the vicinity of the fuel dock and in the Commercial Inlet Basin. During the summer months all of the floats are open for pleasure boats with the exception of "B" and "F" floats. 15, 30, 50, and 100 ampere shore power, fresh drinking water, water for hose-downs, and ice are available. Facilities include new showers, laundry and restrooms; 1000 pound hydraulic crane, and fuel dock where gas and diesel are available. The Eco-Barge waste pump is located alongside the floating breakwater at the marina entrance. Port of Nanaimo moorage is conveniently located in the center of the downtown area, next to a major shopping center, restaurants, hotels, theater, and casino. Mexican food and fish and chips are available on floating barges in the basin. Pioneer Waterfront Plaza, adjacent to the Commercial Inlet Basin, is a public plaza with parking and retail shops. Included are gift shops, coffee shop, ice cream/dessert shop and tea room,

and First Nations handicraft store. On Fridays there is a Farmer's Market on the Plaza and a noon cannon firing takes place every day during summer months. Bus and taxi service connects with all parts of the city and other Vancouver Island communities. Scheduled passenger service between downtown Nanaimo and Vancouver is provided by seaplane, from the Port's Seaplane Terminal which also has a restaurant and pub. Passenger-only fast ferry service between downtown Nanaimo and Vancouver is scheduled to start in summer, 2003. Wharfinger monitors VHF 67. **Circle #80 on the Reader Service Card. E-mail: info@npa.ca Websites: www.npa.ca & www.boattravel.com/nanaimo Mailing Address: Post Office Box 131, 104 Front Street, Nanaimo, British Columbia V9R 5K4. Fax: 250-754-4186. Telephone: 250-754-5053. VHF 67.**

Nanaimo

Brian Watt, Canadian Hydrographic Photo

Foods and is within easy walking distance of moorage. Exit the mall into the southeastern parking lot bordering Terminal Avenue, the location of the Great Canadian Casino and the Italian Fountain. The fountain, built in 1958 by members of the Italian Community, is decorated with colorful, inlaid tiles showing fingerlings swimming downstream to the sea. Two granite Coho salmon, each weighing four-tons, depict the fight up-river to spawn. Follow Terminal Avenue in a westerly direction. Upon reaching the busy junction of Terminal and Commercial, follow Commercial and experience the hustle and bustle of the heart of the downtown shopping district. Here construction is underway for the new Vancouver Island Conference Centre set to open in 2007, featuring a full service conference facility, expanded museum, and retail outlets. Continue on Commercial until reaching Church Street where a right turn will lead to the waterfront again.

The second tour, from the brochure "Harbourside Walkway," begins at the Commercial Inlet Boat Basin and ends two and a half miles north. Cross Front Street to the Port Theatre, an 800-seat performing arts theater. Walk up the hill to the Coast Bastion Inn. Across the street, beside Pioneer Plaza, is The Bastion, a long time Nanaimo landmark. Once a Hudson's Bay Company Fort, it was built in 1853 to protect the white settlers from hostile Haida Indians. It was later a jail and is now a museum. Here visitors view the Hepburn Stone, a large boulder carved to resemble human features. Estimates place the carving at 15,000 years old. Other artifacts of Nanaimo's maritime and coal industries occupy the three stories of the museum. Nanaimo's foundations were rooted in coal with the discovery of the large fields of the mineral in the 1850's. Coal was mined for the next 100 years. At high noon, during the summer, a bagpipe serenade, or the pomp and circumstance of the canon firing often entertain visitors. A flight of stairs near the Bastion leads to Pioneer Park. In 1854, 75 Princess Royal Pioneers landed here. The men in the party were under contract to the Hudson Bay Company. Their history is depicted on a plaque at the site. The Port of Nanaimo Float Plane Terminal is located in this vicinity. Airline offices, a restaurant, and lounge are found in the strikingly designed building. Princess Elizabeth II Promenade rims this shore. Walk along the prom-

enade in a northwesterly direction. Go up the stairs to Georgia Park with its cedar dugout canoe, drinking fountain, and fine views of the harbor. Continue on the promenade to Swy-a-Lana Lagoon and Maffeo-Sutton Park. Maffeo-Sutton Park, an extensive green belt along the waterfront, includes a saltwater lagoon with swimming beach, playgrounds, landscaped gardens, concession stands, and a small float. A passenger ferry connects with Newcastle Island Park (Information: 250-754-7893). Swy-a-Lana Lagoon is the world's only man made tidal lagoon

with the four times a day changes of tide. Tidal flows create waterfalls. Cross the bridge over the Millstream River or take a side trip under the bridge, past the hotel and follow Mill Street to Barsby Park. Back on the promenade, continue north to the Nanaimo Yacht Club. The businesses along the way have contributed by constructing and maintaining their portions of the walkway. The walkway continues to Shipyard Point, the Chinese Memorial Gardens, and to retail stores and restaurants, near the B.C. Ferry Terminal.

Located within walking distance of Nanaimo moorages, Bowen Park is a favorite of residents and visitors alike. Much of the 90-acre park is still in its natural state with a well-established trail network. The southeast section has recreational facilities including tennis courts, curling club, an outdoor lacrosse box, bowling green, swimming pools, recreation complex, and joggers' fitness circuit. The main park trail generally follows the Millstone River, a stream whose character changes with every bend. The trail starts near the Wall Street Parking lot and picnic site, meandering upstream, along the south river bank. The trail passes the Fish Ladder, waterfalls, and the Nature Centre that includes children's barnyard (summer months only), duck pond, totem poles, and interpretation center. Upstream, the trail passes through giant fir, cedar, oak, and hemlock trees and offers several beautiful views. On a quiet walk, you may encounter resident deer, beaver, otter, raccoon, grouse, pheasants and songbirds. The 30-minute stroll upstream continues around the Bowen West Playfield and across Bowen Road to Buttertubs Marsh, a migratory bird sanctuary. Returning downstream, a side trail leads toward Bowen Road past the park's recreationally developed area. This route offers several special attractions including magnificent dogwood trees that bloom in May, colorful rose gardens, and a beautiful rhododendron grove. For information and

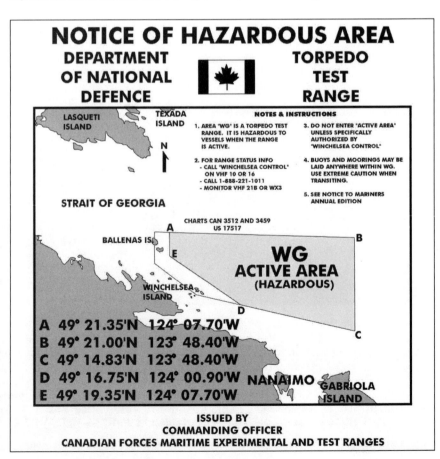

descriptive parks brochure, call the Parks and Recreation Department at 250-756-5200 or pick one up at the Visitor Information Centre on Bowen Road.

★⚓ Newcastle Island Provincial Park (13): [3457] Moorage at public floats and mooring buoys, campsites, picnic areas, and a garbage drop are available at this beautiful park. A park attendant is on duty and fees are charged for moorage and campsites. Stays at the dock are limited. Fresh water is available, as are showers and restrooms. There is a public telephone. The anchorage area is large, but often crowded. Caution is advised because of shelving off Bate Point and toward the head of Mark Bay. This island was named after Newcastle-on-Tyne, a famous coal town in England. Originally a Salish Indian camp from 1853-1883, the island was mined for coal from 1869-1932, quarried for Newcastle sandstone, and had been the site of a Japanese fishing settlement. In 1931, the island boasted an exclusive CPR resort with a dance pavilion, tea house, soccer field, and hotel where Princess Victoria once visited. The floating hotel declined after World War II, when fewer pleasure ships entered the area. The Pavilion has been restored to its 1930-vintage condition, and is used for meetings, dancing, and entertainment. Wildlife abound, including rabbits, otter, blacktail deer, and raccoons. Douglas Fir, Arbutus, Dogwood and Garry Oaks grow in abundance. Miles of paths and trails provide walking tours of the island's shoreline and to lakes in the heart of the island. Beaches are popular for swimming and sun bathing. Children enjoy the fishing wharf and playground.

A harbor ferry provides regular transportation for foot passengers between Newcastle Island Provincial Park and Nanaimo's Maffeo-Sutton Park from May until Thanksgiving. Newcastle Island ferry: 250-754-7893. ▲🏕🏃

★ Protection Island: Well named because of the shelter it provides to Nanaimo Harbour, this island is the site of a pub/restaurant. Boaters should not attempt passage between Newcastle and Protection Islands. A passenger-only ferry makes direct runs from downtown Nanaimo to Protection Island. Protection Island ferry: 250-753-8244.

Hammond Bay (14): Temporary anchorage in all except northeast winds is available. Enter north of the islets which extend from Lagoon Head. Aim straight in. Avoid foul ground off Neck Point. A submarine pipeline runs down the center of the bay, affecting anchorage position. A launching ramp is on shore.

Snake Island: On June 14th, 1997, the community of Nanaimo, in cooperation with the Nanaimo Dive Association, the Artificial Reef Society of British Columbia, and the Cousteau Society, sank the retired Navy-class destroyer *HMCS Saskatchewan* as an artificial reef. Located just east of Snake Island, the artificial reef is expected to enhance fish habitat and recreational diving opportunities.

Essential Supplies & Services

AIR TRANSPORTATION
To & from Washington
Seattle Sea Planes 1-800-637-5553
To & from Islands/Vancouver
Air Canada 1-888-247-2262
Baxter Air 1-800-661-5599
Harbour Air 604-274-1277
Tofino Air 1-800-665-2359
Vancouver Island Air 250-287-2433

AMBULANCES: 911

BOAT MOVING
All Tow Boat Moving . . . .
. . . . 604-946-7899, 1-877-946-7899

BOOKS / BOOK STORES
The Marine Atlas. 541-593-6396

BOAT SEATS & UPHOLSTERY
Royal City Bedding 604-526-2641

BUS TRANSPORTATION
Metro Transit: 250-390-4531
Island Coach Lines: 250-753-4371

COAST GUARD:
Comox: VHF 16, 22-A, 26, 84. 250-339-3613
Emergencies: 1-800-567-5111, VHF 16
Cell Phones: #16

CNG CYLINDERS
Anchorage Marina: Nanaimo 250-754-5585

CUSTOMS: 1-888-226-7277
See Important Notices between Chapters 7 & 8

FERRY INFORMATION
British Columbia Reservations:1-888-724-5223,
604-444-2890; Schedules & Fares: 1-888-223-3779
Newcastle Island: 250-754-7893
Protection Island: 250-753-8244

FUELS
Brechin Point: Nanaimo. Gas, Diesel 250-753-6122
Port of Nanaimo: Gas, Diesel 250-754-7828
Page's Marina: Silva Bay. Gas, Diesel . . . 250-247-8931

GOLF COURSES
(These courses are accessible from moorage and have rental clubs available)

Gabriola Island 250-247-8822
Nanaimo 250-758-6332
Pryde Vista 250-753-6188
Fairwinds: Schooner Cove 250-468-7666

HOSPITALS: NANAIMO . . 250-754-2141

INSURANCE
`The Boat Insurance Agency 206-285-1350
Or Call 1-800-828-2446

LIQUOR STORES
Gabriola Island
Nanaimo: Harbour Park Mall & Terminal Park Plaza

LODGING
Coast Bastion Inn: Nanaimo 250-753-6601

MARINAS / MOORAGE FLOATS
Degnen Bay: Gabriola Island
Nanaimo, Port of . . . . 250-754-5053, VHF 67
Nanaimo Harbour City Marina 250-754-2732
Nanaimo Shipyard Ltd. 250-753-1151
Newcastle Island Provincial Park. 250-754-7893
Pages Marina: Silva Bay 250-247-8931
Silva Bay Inn & Store 250-247-9351
Silva Bay Resort & Marina 250-247-8662
Stone's: Nanaimo. 250-753-4232
Townsite Marina: Nanaimo . . . . 250-716-8801 VHF 66A

POISON INFORMATION
1-800-567-8911
Nanaimo 250-754-2141

RAMPS / HAUL-OUTS
Anchorage Marina: Nanaimo 250-754-5585
Brechin Point Ramps
Degnen Bay: Gabriola Island
Hammond Bay
Hub City Boatyard: Nanaimo 250-755-2000
Nanaimo Harbour City Marina 250-754-2732
Nanaimo Shipyard 250-753-1151
Silva Bay Resort & Marina 250-247-8662

RECOMPRESSION 1-800-567-5111

RED TIDE INFO 604-666-2828

REPAIRS / SERVICE
Anchorage Marina 250-754-5585
Blue Peter Boatyard. 250-754-7887

Nanaimo Harbour City. 250-754-2732
Nanaimo Shipyard 250-753-1151
Newcastle Marina: Nanaimo 250-753-1431
Silva Bay Resort & Marina 250-247-8662

RESCUE & SEARCH:
. . . . 1-800-567-5111, Cell Phones: *16

SEWAGE DISPOSAL
Port of Nanaimo 250-754-5053

SCUBA AIR
Page's Marina: Silva Bay 250-247-8931
Sundown Diving: Nanaimo 250-753-1880

SHELLFISH HOTLINE
. . . . 250-754-0325, 604-666-2828
Nanaimo 250-754-0230

SPORT FISHING INFO . . . 250-754-0325

TAXI
Gabriola Island 250-247-0049
Nanaimo 250-753-8911, 250-753-1231

TOWING
C-TOW. 1-888-354-5554
VESSEL ASSIST South Gulf Islands . . 250-539-3644
Georgia Strait 250-247-8934

VHF MARINE OPERATOR
Bowen Island: VHF 84
Ganges: VHF 27, 64
Sechelt: VHF 86
Nanaimo: VHF 87
Parksville: VHF 28
Vancouver: VHF 23, 24, 25, 26, 86, 88
West Vancouver: VHF 85

VISITOR INFORMATION
Nanaimo 250-756-0106, 1-800-663-7337
B.C. 1-800-663-6000
Gabriola Island 250-247-9332

WEATHER
Environment Canada Weather Line 250-339-9861
Comox: VHF WX-1 161.35, 250-339-0748
Vancouver: VHF WX-2 162.40, 604-664-9010
Vancouver: VHF 21 161.65
Nanaimo: 250-245-8899

Chapter 12:
Fraser River, Vancouver & Howe Sound

Tsawwassen, Delta, Richmond, New Westminster, Vancouver, North & West Vancouver, Squamish. False Creek, Burrard Inlet, Indian Arm, Bowen, Gambier, Keats, & Anvil Islands.

Symbols

[   ]: Numbers between [ ] are chart numbers.

{   }: Numbers & letters between { } are waypoints.

⚲: Park, ⛵: Boat Launch, ▲: Campgrounds, 𝕩: Hiking Trails, ⌒: Picnic Area, ⬥⬥: Biking

★ **Important Notice:** See "Important Notices" between Chapters 7 and 8 in this guide for specific information on boating related topics such as: Canadian & U.S. Customs, boating safety and security, navigation, weather, U.S. & Canadian Coast Guard, U.S & Canadian marine radio use, Vessel Traffic Service and traffic separation plans, security zones, and internet access. Due to new Department of Homeland Security regulations, call ahead for latest customs information and/or see Northwest Boat Travel On-line, www.nwboat.com.

Boundary Bay

[3463]

★ **Point Roberts:** For additional information, see Chapter 6.

Point Roberts Marina Resort: Moorage, power, water, showers, gas, diesel, propane, repairs, pump-out, laundry, 35-ton lift, sling, provisions. 360-945-2255.

Crescent Beach & White Rock: For additional information see Chapter 6.

Chart List

Canadian Hydrographic Charts:

3061, 3062, 3311, 3463, 3481, 3488, 3489, 3490, 3491, 3492-3495, 3512 3526, 3534

NOAA Charts:

17517-19, 18400, 18405-09, 18412

Marine Atlas (2005 ed.):

Page 12, 20, 21, 25

★ **Crescent Beach Marina:** Located in historic Crescent Beach, this marina is the Customs port-of-entry. Moorage from 20' - 50' (year round), transient moorage, 15 & 30 amp power, water, fuel- diesel, regular & premium, full chandlery store, washrooms, laundromat, showers, repairs, parts, haul-outs, dry storage compound, launch ramp. Close to shopping, fine dining, golfing. Thirty minutes to Vancouver. Address: 12555 Crescent Rd, Surrey, B.C. V4A 2V4. Website: www.crescentbeachmarina.com. Telephone: 604-538-9666. Fax: 604-538-7724. VHF 66A

Ward's Marina: Very limited moorage. 604-535-6426.

Tsawwassen (1): [3463, 3492, 3499] Site of a large ferry terminal with service to Swartz Bay, the Gulf Islands, and Nanaimo. The super port has been expanded to include a Container Terminal (Deltaport). Small boats should be aware of increased deep sea and tug movements in this area. For boaters, there is a dredged channel parallel to the south side of the long ferry causeway that leads to a mooring basin for temporary

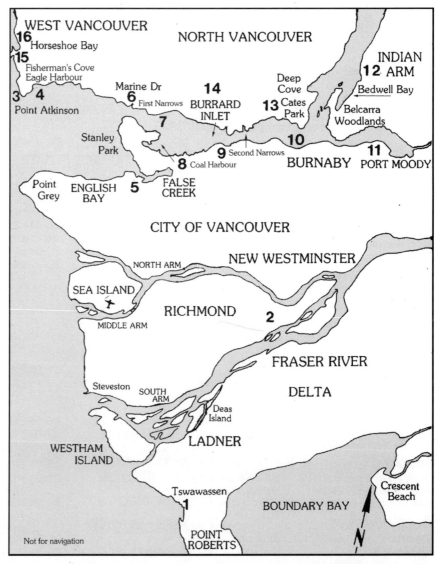

Not for navigation

anchorage. Temporary anchorage is also possible north of the terminal. Watch depth sounder. There is good fishing between the terminal and the Roberts Bank Superport. A launching spot is a rough ramp on the beach along the south side of the causeway going out to the terminal. Often there are Great Blue Herons walking in the shallows between the spit and the coalport. Shallow mudflats extend some distance.

Fraser River

[3488, 3489, 3490, 3491, 3492]

★ **Fraser River:** This waterway is the largest river in British Columbia. Over 2,000,000 people live in close proximity to its waters which flow past Vancouver, Richmond, Delta, Ladner, New Westminster, Surrey, Burnaby, Coquitlam, Port Coquitlam, Mission, Steveston, and many other small communities. Two strip charts cover the Fraser River from Harrison Mills to the Pattulo Bridge. They are #3488 and #3489. Other charts are #3062 for Pitt Lake and #3061 to Harrison Lake.

Travel on the Fraser requires extra care. Launching can also be tricky. The current is strong, and the water is very murky. Commercial areas are dredged regularly but, further upstream, a guide with local knowledge may be needed in order to safely navigate between the sandbars. Debris from log handling is always present. Skippers need to keep a sharp lookout, not only for debris, but also for the many commercial vessels that ply the waters, and, at times, the pods of killer whales that visit. Water level is lowest during January, February, and March. It begins to rise with the first melting snows and is at its highest near the end of June. Currents run to five knots during the summer, with higher rates of flow in

narrow places. Waters begin to subside toward the end of August. September to November are good months for river navigation because the water is still high enough for small vessels to reach Hope, but the current reduces to three or four knots. The river runs downstream at all times, however, there may be reversal at large flood tides. Turns of the tide are later than those on Georgia Strait. Tide and current tables and detailed charts are a necessity. A northwest wind opposing the flood tide or a southwest wind blowing against the current cause dangerous waves. When entering from the strait, all can buoys to port are green, with odd numbers. Buoys on the starboard are red with even numbers. Lighted buoys to port flash green and those to starboard are red. The mouth of the river has several entry channels and arms.

The Fraser and its tributaries have the largest natural salmon runs in the world, and produce over one quarter of the salmon caught off the coast of Canada. Since each salmon tries to return to its birthplace to spawn, in some years more than ten million salmon enter the mouth of the river. Before they begin their arduous journey, they gather at the mouth of the river to rest and feed. This is one of the best opportunities to catch one of these world famous delica-

cies. The mouth of the North Arm and the Main Arm are popular fishing spots and each channel has a boat launching ramp near its mouth. Because of conservation efforts, the mouth of the Fraser is only open to salmon fishing from July 1 to December 31. Chinook (Spring salmon) fishing is closed all year.

★ **North Arm:** [3491] This arm is used extensively by tugs and barges, as well as pleasure craft. When entering, give the tidal flats at Wreck Beach a wide berth. There is a park on Iona Island with sand dunes and picnic sites. A launching ramp with picnic facilities and restrooms is found at McDonald Beach. Fraser River Park is in Vancouver at the south end of Angus Street at 75th Avenue. It is a fine picnic spot and has a large playing field. There is a boardwalk through a tidal marsh for enjoyment and education. Beach area depends on the amount of tide. Also on the

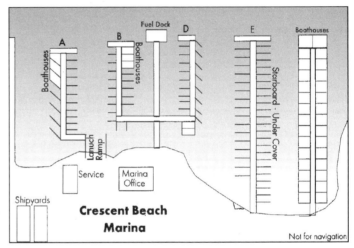

North Arm is Fraser Foreshore Park in Burnaby. It is at the south end of Byrne Road. It has a walkway along the river, picnic and barbecue areas, and fishing.

★ **Middle Arm:** [3491] Entered south of Sea Island, this is the arm used mainly by pleasure craft. Sea Island is the site of Vancouver International Airport. A boat launch is on the southeast side of Sea Island.

★ **South Arm:** [3490] Avoid approaching when northwest winds oppose a flood tide. This is the main channel of the Fraser. It is entered at Sand Heads. Since the river is a major transportation link for industry and commerce as well as pleasure craft, every effort must be taken to avoid hindering the commercial traffic. From July to November, large numbers of gillnetters may be encountered in South Arm, presenting a hazard to navigation.

★ **Steveston:** [3490, 3492] Customs check-in site. This town lies on the north side of the Main Channel at the southwest corner of Lulu Island, and is the center of the salmon processing industry. A cannery, wharves, fueling stations, and boatyards line the north side of Cannery Channel. Restaurants, groceries, fresh water, ice, Post Office, and stores. This town is a blend of historic fishing village, quaint tourist destination, and fashionable enterprise. Stores, with rolls of netting, bins of lures, and weights of all sizes, speak of the town's close connection to the fishing industry, while fashionable boutiques tell the rest of the story. The interesting museum, located on Moncton Street, occupies a 1906 prefab former bank building and houses displays of the local fishing industry. Self-guided walking tour brochures are available here.   604-271-6868. Visit the Gulf of Georgia Cannery, a restored

National Historic Site open April through October. For hours and information, 604-664-9009.

Wampler Marine: Gas, diesel, stove oil, ice, showers. 604-277-5211.

Steveston: Chevron Marine, gas, diesel, water, ice, showers, laundry, bait, lubricants. 604-277-4712.

Steveston Harbour Authority: Cannery Channel. Moorage, power, water, garbage drop, showers, haul-out, repairs. The fishing fleet uses the wharves and floats, but pleasure boats may use them when there is space available. 604-272-5539.

South of Steveston: There are at least three launch ramp sites on the main arm. Two are on Lulu Island, southeast of Steveston and at the foot of Nelson Road. The third is under the Port Mann Bridge in Coquitlam. Also south of Steveston is Westham Island, winter home to over 200 species of waterfowl, shore birds, and birds of prey. The George C. Reifel Bird Sanctuary includes 850 acres. The best times of the year to visit are during the fall and spring migrations. There are large numbers of Snow Geese and Trumpeter Swans. It is possible to walk through two miles of marsh and managed habitat. In the summer, numerous waterfowl and their offspring make this their home. Pets are not allowed. Canoe Passage is another small arm of the Fraser. With an up-to-date chart (3492), and a little local knowledge, Canoe Pass is navigable by small craft. The Westham Island Bridge, with a vertical clearance of only 36', is manned 24 hours a day. Five blasts on the horn will alert the attendant to open the bridge. A launch ramp is on the island, southwest of the bridge.

★⚓ **Deas Island Regional Park:** This large park has tree-lined dikes, tidal marshes, and trails. Two historic buildings, a turn-of-the-century residence, and a heritage schoolhouse are open for exploration. Picnicking, canoeing, nature studies, and bar fishing are popular activities. ⚓🚶

★ **RiverHouse Marina Restaurant & Pub:** Relax and enjoy the spectacular waterfront views from the restaurant, pub and heated patio of this newly renovated facility. Choose from an extensive menu featuring West Coast Cuisine, tasty pub fare and great monthly features-all which are prepared with the freshest ingredients. Guests are offered an impressive selection of wines, draught beers, martinis and cocktails designed to compliment any meal. Located on the banks of the Deas Slough, at the south end of the Deas Tunnel behind the Town & Country Inn. Reservations recommended. Open daily from 11 am to 11 pm. Sunday Brunch is served from 11 am to 2 pm. See our Steering Star description in this chapter. Website: www.riverhousegroup.com. Telephone: 604-946-7545.

Richmond
[3490]

★ **Richmond (2):** This thriving community is on the Main Arm of the Fraser River. There are extensive yachting and travel activities and services, including marinas, charter agencies, boat repairs and services, fueling facilities, stores, restaurants, and accommodations.

★ **All-Tow Boat Moving Ltd:** Situated in Delta, All-Tow Boat Moving will celebrate their 35th year of service in 2006. Owned and operated by Tom Plain and long time employee Mike Craft

★ **All-Tow Boat Moving Ltd:** All-Tow Boat Moving Ltd. is situated in Delta and will celebrate their 35th year of service in the year 2006. Owned & operated by Tom Plain and long time employee Mike Craft of 27 years. The company relocates boats of 16' to 140' and has moved weights of up to 235 Ton. We operate in B.C., Alberta, and Washington State. Boats are lifted or pulled from various ramps onto trailers which are built to be able to off load at the location you have chosen. **Our address is #400 – 6165 Hwy 17, Delta, B.C. V4K 4B5. Email: alltow@dccnet.com. Web: www.alltowboatmoving.com. Phone: 604-946-7899. Fax: 604-940-4531.**

★ **Shelter Island Marina & Boat Yard:** Use Chart #3490. Located at Richmond, 14 miles upriver from Sand Heads, this well known facility offers expanded permanent and guest moorage, an extensive list of repair services, a pub, and a beer and wine store. When approaching, do not go between Don and Lion Island. Since its establishment in 1978, Shelter Island has continuously modernized its facilities and services to include attractions of interest to the pleasure boater. Over 1100 linear feet of fresh water moorage is reserved for guests. Telephone, water, cablevision, and metered 20, 30 and 50 ampere power are available. *Tugboat Annie's,* the pub and restaurant, specializes in a menu selection of great pub fare enjoyed while watching the views of the river. Pool tables add to the entertainment. Transportation by bus and/or taxi opens the door to Richmond, Lulu Island, the Vancouver International

Airport, and downtown Vancouver. The marine supply store is fully stocked with parts, electronic items, rope, paint, chain, anchors, charts, and other marine gear. The 20,000 square foot *Marine Services Building* houses businesses specializing in such services as welding, fiberglassing, and painting. Do-it-Yourself Yard. Two of the largest Travelifts on the coast lift vessels from 20' to 130'. U.S. boaters visit Shelter Island to save money. Bank rate given on U.S. funds. Open all year. **Circle #44 on Reader Service Card. Websites: www.shelterislandmarina.com & www.boattravel.com/shelterisland Email: infodesk@shelterislandmarina.com Address: 6911 Graybar Road, Richmond, British Columbia V6W 1H3. Fax: 604-273-6282. Telephone: Toll-free 1-877-270-6272, 604-270-6272. VHF 66A.**

(27 years), the company relocates boats of 16' to 140' and has moved weights of up to 235 tons. The operation covers B.C., Alberta and Washington State. Boats are lifted or pulled from various ramps onto trailers which are built to be able to off load at the location you have chosen. See our Steering Star description in this chapter. Address: #400-6165 Hwy 17, Delta, B.C. V4K4B5. Email:alltow@dccnet.com. Website:www.alltowboatmoving.com. Telehone: 604-946-7899, Fax: 604-940-4531.

★ **Shelter Island Marina:** {49° 09.08' N, 122° 59.03' W} Come to this marina, not only for moorage with power and water and repairs, but also to visit the restaurant, pub, beer and wine store, and chandlery. Haul-out and pump-out available. 400 lineal feet of moorage has been added. Connected by bus to downtown Vancouver and surrounding areas. See our Steering Star description in this chapter. Websites: www.shelterislandmarina.com & www.boattravel.com/shelter Email: infodesk@shelterislandmarina.com Address: 6911 Graybar Road, Richmond, British Columbia V6W 1H3. Fax: 604-273-6282. Telephone: 604-270-6272. VHF 66A.

Bridgeport Marina: Moorage, water, power, showers, laundry, phones. 604-273-8560 or 604-328-1694.

Captain's Cove Marina: Moorage, power, water, gas, diesel, showers, laundry, haul-outs, launch ramp nearby. 604-946-1244.

Delta Marina: Moorage, power, water, repairs, lift, customs clearance. 604-273-4211.

Richmond: Gas, water, diesel, lubricants. 604-278-2181.

Skyline Marina: Moorage, water, power, repairs, haul-outs to 30-tons. New management is extending the boat yard and providing improvements including laundry, showers and washrooms. 604-273-3977.

Vancouver Marina: Gas, diesel, water, power. Limited moorage, call ahead. 604-278-9787. VHF 66A. Haul-out, mechanical services call 604-273-7544.

★ **New Westminster:** Located 12 miles east of Vancouver, this site was the capital of British Columbia from 1866 to 1868. Because it was named by Queen Victoria, it is known as The Royal City. There is a modern Skytrain to downtown Vancouver. For information call 604-953-3333. Westminster Quay Public Market features fresh foods, shops, and restaurants. Moorage is available. The *Samson V Maritime Museum* is a 1937 sternwheeler. Also, the *M.V. Expo Tugger* is a unique attraction for children.

★ **Royal City Bedding:** Over a half a century of quality craftsmanship and customer satisfaction

has earned RCB a solid reputation as one of the best in the business. Regardless of the size, space or configuration of your boat, RCB can meet all of your marine seating and bedding needs. See our full page ad in the A Pages. Website: www.rcb.ca. Email: hardeep@rcb.ca. Address: 131 East Columbia St. New Westminster BC, Canada V3L 3V9. Telephone: 1-877-887-6887 or within Greater Vancouver 604-526-2641. Fax: 604-526-6340.

★ **New Westminster to Pitt River:** It is possible, and can be enjoyable, to cruise up the Fraser River beyond New Westminster. Strip charts #3488 and #3489 describe the river from Pattullo Bridge to Harrison Bridge. An unmarked channel is maintained with channel depths of 11.8 feet below low-low water line (LLWL) to Whonnock, and 8.2 feet below LLWL from Whonnock to Hope. Because of changing sandbars and dead-heads, it is advisable to have someone with local knowledge on board or to hire a tug or towing captain as a guide. There is considerable commercial vessel activity along with pleasure craft and sports fishermen. To starboard are the Fraser Surrey Docks. The Skytrain Bridge connects Westminster and Surrey. Approaching the Pattullo Bridge, keep the red buoys to starboard. Further upstream is the Port Mann Bridge. Douglas Island marks the gateway to Pitt River and Lake.

★ **Pitt River:** [3062] This navigable, 14 mile-long river connects with the Fraser River. It is possible to transit the river and explore expansive Pitt Lake. Port Coquitlam City is on the river's west bank. Several uncharted sloughs empty into the river. There are tidal flats, usually marked by grass. There is a marina at the mouth of the Alouette River, where it joins the Pitt. Several bridges cross the river. Log rafts are frequently stored along the river. Transit Grant Narrows and Grant Channel through a buoy-marked channel, through the flats at the southern part of Pitt Lake. There is a public boat launch at Pitt Polder near the mouth of Pitt Lake. Some canoes are available for rent. Much of this area is best explored by canoe. It is possible to paddle behind Siwash Island and up Widgeon Creek. This is a wildlife Preserve. It takes 90 minutes by canoe to reach Widgeon Creek Park, with picnic area, campsites, and Forest Service trails.

Pitt River Boat Club: Gas, water, ice, restrooms. 604-942-7371.

Pitt Meadows Marina: Mid-grade gas, ice, water, power, moorage, launch. 604-465-7713.

★ **Pitt Lake:** A voyage to Pitt Lake, the world's largest freshwater tidal lake, is an interesting day trip. This lake is considered by many to be a beautiful, relatively untouched gem of a boating destination. The large lake is deep with picturesque islands. Because of the topography, wind funnels through the vicinity in unpredictable patterns. The lake may be choppy at times, even though

nearby waters are calm. There are anchorage possibilities off the islands. The Burke-Pinecone Provincial Park is on the west shore.

★ **Pitt River to Fort Langley and Mission:** Abreast of Douglas Island, heading east, keep to the port side of the Fraser, staying about one third of the breadth of the river from its northern boundaries. The channel is not adequately marked, but the above course is the best choice available for reducing the risk of grounding. Barnston Island is peaceful agricultural land suitable for bicycling or walking. No usable beaches. A ferry runs on demand from Surrey to the island. A boat launch is at the ferry dock. Derby Reach Regional Park is on the site of the first Fort Langley, built in 1827. The marshy ground was not easily defended, so the fort was later moved. The park has overnight campsites along the river. Seasonally, costumed interpreters describe the early days of the 1850's when the fort was active. 604-530-4983. Fishing is the main attraction, especially in fall when the salmon are running. The Fraser and its tributaries have the largest natural salmon runs in the world, and produce over one quarter of the salmon caught off Canada's west coast.

Upstream, past Derby Reach, is McMillan Island. Here, a ferry connects Maple Ridge and Fort Langley. The around-the-clock ferries have the right of way. Go past McMillan Island and then turn west into Bedford Channel to visit Fort Langley. The Fort Langley Marina Park and boat launch is to port. Just past the park is a small dock. It may have one or two spots to tie up. There is no other public float. Antique and craft shops, two museums, washrooms, and the restored Hudson's Bay Company Fort, circa 1858, are in the vicinity.

When coming abreast of Crescent Island, keep to the port side of the island. The Stave River flows into the Fraser. Do not pass under the railroad bridge. Keep a third of the way out from the north bank of the Fraser. Pass Benson and Matsqui Islands and have the Mission Bridge in your sights. This bridge connects Mission with Abbotsford and Clearbrook. Immediately up-river from the traffic bridge is the railway bridge. If more than 12 to 15 feet clearance is required, contact the bridge tender on VHF Channel 69 and request opening the bridge. Just past the Railway Bridge, on the port side, is the Mission dock.

★ **Mission:** Visitor moorage is on the outside of the community dock.

Mission Harbour Authority: Limited moorage (call ahead), power, security gate, water taxi. River pilots can be arranged to travel to Harrison Lake. 24-hour message center. 604-826-4414.

Catherwood Towing: Gas, diesel, assistance with bridge opening, information, water taxi and pilots for river travel. 604-462-9221, 604-826-9221. Fuel: 604-826-9257. VHF 69.

★ **Mission to Harrison River and Lake:** [3061] It is a necessity that a guide or pilot be hired for this trip. The channels of the upper Fraser are ever changing. The natural beauty and abundant wildlife make traveling this area highly recommended. The journey on the Fraser will come to an end at Billy Smith Rock. The Harrison River used to run into the Fraser, but around 1976, the Fraser cut itself a new channel, and it now runs into the last quarter of a mile of the Harrison River. Here, at Billy Smith Rock, the Harrison and Fraser Rivers come together in a spectacular, powerful array of swirling, frothing multi-colored waters. Further on, waits may be necessary at the CPR Railway Bridge and the Harrison Mills

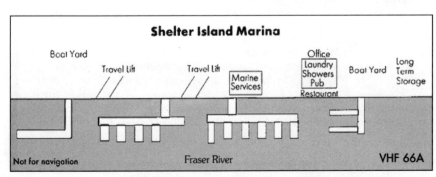

Shelter Island Marina

Boat Yard — Travel Lift — Travel Lift — Marine Services — Office Laundry Showers Pub Restaurant — Boat Yard — Long Term Storage

Not for navigation   Fraser River   VHF 66A

Bridge. After passing the Harrison Rapids, there is an Indian Reserve to port.

★ **Harrison Hot Springs and Harrison Lake:** [3061] After entering the cold, clear waters of Harrison Lake, pilots will keep a safe distance from the village's shores to starboard, and tie up at the docks of the hotel. Beautiful sites include Rainbow Falls, where, if the angle of the sun is just right, a myriad of rainbows surround the cascading waters of the falls as they tumble into the waters below.

Harrison Resort Adventure Park Marina: Moorage, power, water. 1-800-663-2266, 604-796-2244.

Killer's Cove Marina: Moorage, gas, water, power, water taxi. 604-796-3856.

Vancouver

[3481, 3493, 3494, 3495]

★ **Vancouver:** Moorage is available at marinas in False Creek and Burrard Inlet. This beautiful city, the third largest in the country, is *Canada's Gateway to the Pacific.* To the east and north, the majestic Coast Mountains overlook this metropolis. To the south, are the lush, green farmlands of the Fraser Valley. To the west, the waters of Burrard Inlet, Vancouver Harbour, False Creek, English Bay, and the Strait of Georgia all embrace Vancouver City's shores. Much of Vancouver's economy and recreation are intimately involved with the sea. One in four Vancouver families owns a boat. Because Vancouver is blessed with a mild climate, the port is ice free all year. Even fair weather boaters can enjoy a long boating season, beginning in March and continuing well into October. The miles of commercial wharves that line the shores are used for shipping coal, potash, sulfur, mineral concentrates, wheat, forest and petroleum products, and general cargo. Storage warehouses and grain elevators are conspicuous along the waterfront. In English Bay, the *International Fireworks* events are spectacular. Early arrival is recommended.

Vancouver, with its unique cultural and ethnic history, offers hundreds of shopping opportunities. Long known for its British influence and treasures, there is an abundance of typical motherland wares, teas, and foods, such as fish and chips wrapped in newspapers with the typical dash of vinegar. Chinatown, the third largest in North America, is a bustling community with hundreds of shops and curios where merchants sell authentic Chinese crafts and artifacts. Vancouver also offers high fashion clothing and jewelry boutiques on Robson Street, representing some of the world's most famous designers. For an alternative shopping experience, there are six public markets. Granville Island Market and Westminster Quay have waterfront access and offer local fresh produce, seafood caught only minutes away, and crafts fashioned by local artisans. Visitors to the Steveston docks in Richmond can purchase fresh sea food straight off the fishing boats. Native west coast Indian arts and crafts are among the wares available, including carved jade sculptures and jewelry, whalebone scrimshaw, and native made sweaters.

There is always something going on in Vancouver. For cultural enthusiasts the *Bard on the Beach Shakespeare Festival* runs from June through September. June is also the month for the *Vancouver International Jazz Festival.* July's festivities include *Canada Day Celebrations* and the *Vancouver Folk Music Festival.* For more information about the attractions and events in the Vancouver area, contact the Vancouver Tourist Info Centre. 604-683--2000.

Vancouver received its name from Captain Vancouver who sailed through First Narrows and along the waters of the inlet in 1792. Later, Port Moody became a site for the Royal Navy. In 1863, a lumber mill and shipping port was opened on the north shore. In the 1880's, Gastown became the terminal for the Canadian Pacific Railway. With trains connecting with ships to provide both land and sea transportation, the future of Burrard Inlet as a world trade center was assured. The city was incorporated in 1886. Then came the Klondike Gold Rush and the growth of steamship lines traveling to and from Vancouver to all corners of the globe.

Port of Vancouver: The Vancouver Port Authority has navigational jurisdiction over a water area of 214 square miles, including Burrard Inlet and Indian Arm, English Bay bounded by an imaginary line running from Point Atkinson to Point Grey, and a narrow coastal strip that includes the approaches to the Fraser River, Sturgeon Bank, Roberts Banks, and Boundary Bay.

Burrard Inlet

[3481, 3493]

Point Atkinson: Site of a landmark lighthouse. The fog signal has been discontinued.

Caulfeild Cove: This is a small indentation east of Point Atkinson. It offers a spot for a lunch hook. A small, often crowded, public float extends from the starboard shore. A green meadow provides a blanket for shoreside picnics.

Burrard Inlet (3): The four mile opening of the inlet extends from Point Atkinson on the north to Point Grey on the south. This extensive inlet penetrates eastward over 12 miles where it divides into Indian Arm and Port Moody.

English Bay (4): This bay stretches three miles between Spanish Bank and Stanley Park. Shallow, shifting ledges of sand gradually moving into the southern part of the bay have extended beyond the existing markers. Yacht clubs maintain facilities on this shoreline. There is a launching ramp west of the Kitsilano Coast Guard station. Often large freighters lie at anchorage in the bay.

False Creek

[3311, 3481, 3493]

★ **False Creek (5):** Customs check-in sites are no longer found at False Creek facilities. Proceed to Coal Harbour to the new Canada Parks Welcome Float.

Pass under Burrard Street and Granville Street Bridges at entrance to False Creek. These have 90' and 92' clearances respectively. Speed limit is five knots. No sailing is permitted, west of Granville Street Bridge. Tidal streams run to three knots here. At low tide, the channel is half as wide as it is at high tide. This can make maneuvering among pleasure yachts and commercial tugs and barges, difficult. Vanier Park, the Pacific Space Centre, and the Maritime Museum are to starboard as you leave English Bay. A breakwater shelters historic ships. Among the Maritime Museum attractions is the St. Roch, the schooner which traversed the Northwest Passage. After entering False Creek, Granville Island and Fisherman's Terminal are to starboard.

There is moorage, with a maximum stay of three hours, at the Public Market floats on Granville Island. This island hosts marine businesses, boat brokerages, repair yards, and charter agencies.

False Creek, Granville Island   Tourism Vancouver Photo

The Expo '86 site, now the Plaza of Nations, is to port. B.C. Place Stadium and the British Columbia Pavilion, renamed *Enterprise Centre,* are used for sports, cultural programs, pubs, eateries, and exhibitions. The Cambie Bridge spans False Creek. Vertical clearance is 46 feet above the high tide line. A condominium marina is at the northwest end of Cambie Street Bridge. Within walking distance of the eastern edge of the grounds is an authentic classical Chinese garden, Sun Yat Sen Classical Chinese Garden. On Carroll Street, in Chinatown, three acres are designed in the tradition of the Ming Dynasty of 2,500 years ago. It is of special interest because the artisans used old techniques and tools to create the garden.

★ **Granville Island:** Moorage can be found at Pelican Bay Marina and may be available at Fisherman's Terminal, when the fishing fleet is out. Formerly an industrial area, the buildings of Granville Island have been converted to house marine-oriented businesses, restaurants, book and gift shops, a hotel, theaters with live performances, galleries, the Granville Island Brewery, a large public seafood and produce market, and a waterpark for children. Additions include a Model Ship Museum featuring replicas of miltary, working tugs, and steam vessels, and a Sport Fishing Museum, with a unique collection of tackle and trophy fish from around the world. Passenger service by False Creek Ferries. 604-684-7781 makes downtown, Yaletown, Chinatown, sports venues, and theaters very accessible. Park lands with picnic facilities and trails are plentiful. Kayak and small boat rentals are available, as are scenic cruises.

False Creek Marine Esso: Gas, diesel, oil, ice, CNG, water, moorage, nearby showers. 604-733-6731.

Burrard Bridge Civic Marina: Limited moorage, power, pump-out, launch ramp, garbage deposit, grid. 604-733-5833, 604-505-5833.

False Creek Fishermen's Wharf: Moorage, call ahead. 20 & 30-ampere power, water, washrooms, showers, laundry, restaurant, waste oil disposal. 604-733-3625. VHF 66A.

False Creek Yacht Club: Limited moorage, power, washrooms, showers, laundry, pump-out. Call ahead. 604-868-4275.

Heather Civic Marina: Permanent moorage, water, power, showers, laundry, free pump-out. 604-874-2814.

Pelican Bay Marina: Moorage, power, water, washrooms, cable, phone hook-ups. 604-729-1442.

Plaza of Nations Marina (Vancouver Yacht Charters & Marina): Moorage, 30 & 50 ampere power, water. No showers or laundry. 604-682-

2070, 604-818-3366.

Quayside Marina: New, first strata ownership marina to be developed in an urban centre along the west coast of North America. Limited temp moorage for boats up to 120'. Water, 30, 50, 100 amp power, laundry, showers, ice, sewage pumps. Close to all amenities. Call ahead 604-681-9115, 604-209-6456. VHF 66A.

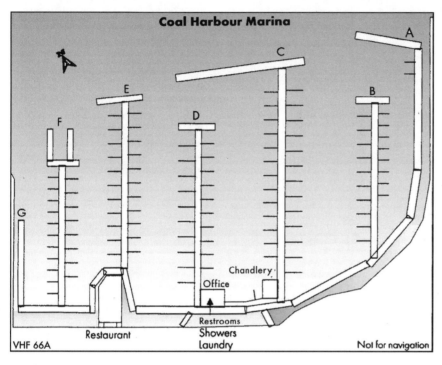

Coal Harbour Marina

Not for navigation

VHF 66A

First Narrows to Coal Harbour

[3481, 3493]

First Narrows (6): Freighters, tugs, barges, ferries, and small craft traverse the channel between English Bay and Vancouver Harbour. First Narrows, which offers a boat's-eye-view of Stanley Park and the Lions Gate Bridge, is the first of three narrows in Burrard Inlet. Incoming traffic must stay close to Stanley Park. No fishing, sailing, or cross traffic is allowed. Listen to VHF 12 to hear commercial traffic information. When a strong northwest wind meets a large ebbing tide, the turbulence can be dangerous in the narrows. Boats must be under power between the entry to First Narrows and mid-harbor in Vancouver Harbour. Caution advised in regard to strong currents near Prospect Point at the mouth of the Capilano River. The Prospect Point Fog Horn has been permanently discontinued. Currents in the narrows run to six knots. Before the channel was dredged and widened, currents ran to ten knots through this narrow opening.

★ **Vancouver Harbour (7):** Vancouver Harbour is the portion of Burrard Inlet east of First Narrows. The north shore outlines North Vancouver terminus of the Vancouver SeaBus which connects with downtown Vancouver. The west portion of Vancouver Harbour contains Coal Harbour and the shoreline of downtown Vancouver. Sailing is permitted in a designated area shown on the Port of Vancouver map. No scuba diving, water-skiing, or personal watercraft allowed between First and Second Narrows. Vancouver Harbour is a security zone.

Coal Harbour

[3481, 3493]

★⚓ **Stanley Park:** Although there is no direct boater access, beautiful Stanley Park, a 1,000 acre peninsula, borders Coal Harbour. A seawall, with walking path, lines the shore. Activities and facilities include cycle paths, cricket playing, a miniature railway, children's farmyard, pitch and putt course, tennis, concessions, swimming, dancing, rose gardens, aquarium, and the world's most viewed totem site. Each year at least eight million people view the collection of eight Kwakwaka'wakw and Haida totems. The park was dedicated in 1889.

★ **Coal Harbour (8):** After traversing First Narrows and rounding Stanley Park's Brockton Point, one enters Coal Harbour, where a five knot speed limit is enforced. The fog signal on the point has been discontinued. Moorage is available at marinas. Anchorage is not permitted. Since this area is a seaplane aerodome, a good look-out should be kept while in the area because hundreds of floatplanes land daily. Royal Vancouver Yacht Club and the Vancouver Rowing Club are headquartered here. The new customs dock at the foot of Bute Street is named The Parks Canada Welcome Dock.

★ **Coal Harbour Marina:** Located at 1525 Coal Harbour Quay, Vancouver, BC, V6G 3E7; Telephone: 604-681-2628; Fax: 604-681-4666; email: info@coalharbourmarina.com;. Website: www.coalharbourmarina.com / www.boattravel.com/coalharbour. Monitoring VHF Channel 66A. N°49 17.500' W°123 07.0600'. Located in the heart of downtown Vancouver, Coal Harbour Marina is within walking distance of Vancouver's beautiful sites and attractions including Stanley Park, Robson Street, Vancouver Aquarium, Canada Place, Gastown and English Bay. See our advertisement in this chapter.

Coal Harbour Fuel: Gas, diesel, ice, water, showers, waste oil disposal, marine supplies. 604-681-3841. VHF 16, 12.

Coal Harbour Chevron Station: Gas, diesel, water, washrooms, ice, waste oil disposal. 604-681-7725.

Harbour Cruises Marina: Limited guest moorage, power, water. 604-687-9558.

Westin Bayshore Marina: Permanent moorage, 30-100 ampere power, water, cable TV hook-up. 604-691-6936.

Second Narrows (9): See current tables for Burrard Inlet. The Seymour River flows into Burrard Inlet here. This site is four miles from First Narrows. Conditions are similar to those at First Narrows. The Second Narrows Highway Bridge is a landmark. No sailing is permitted through the narrows. A large marina is between Second Narrows and the Lynterm wharves. There are parks on both banks, nearly opposite each other. Picnic sites, playground, and swimming pool are attractions. No anchoring is allowed.

Burnaby & Port Moody
[3494, 3495]

★⚓ **Barnet Marine Park (10):** This Burnaby park is the site of the old Kapoor sawmill. There are athletic fields, a swimming beach, and fishing pier. Anchor east of the pier or in the small niche.

★ **Port Moody (11):** Port Moody ends in drying flats. For environmental reasons, the City of Port Moody prohibits vessels east of a line drawn from the first day beacon and projected north to the shore at Old Orchard Park. Be aware that the area along the North Shore from Old Orchard Park to the west is the subject of many waterlot leases. Boats anchoring there could be liable for trespass. A dredged channel, marked with day beacons, leads to Rocky Point Park. A wide launching ramp, floats for small boats, a museum, a long lighted pier with benches, and two covered pavilions are provided. The grassed park area has a concession, a swimming and wading pools, sandbox, playground, picnic tables, and restrooms.

Reed Point Marina: Permanent & limited guest moorage, 20 ampere power, gas, diesel, water, washrooms, showers, moorage, haul-outs, repairs, pump-out. 604-937-1600.

Indian Arm
[3495]

★ **Indian Arm (12):** This three-mile-wide, ten-mile-long fjord offers a convenient day cruise in generally calm, easily navigated waters. Thermal drafts can create down-slope winds and choppy waters. The arm's deep green waters lie at the base of peaks which rise to heights of 5,000 feet. Much of the shoreline is undeveloped. Waterfalls plunge down the cliffs in spring and early summer, making the surface water nearly fresh. Speed limits of five knots are in effect in the channel between Twin Island and the mainland, in Belcarra Bay near the floats, in the south end of Bedwell Bay, and between Jug Island and peninsula at the entrance. Ling cod and rockfish are found in this

deep water. Three yacht clubs have outstations and there is anchorage near the head of the arm. Caution advised regarding snags in the area. Boats can be beached on the sand flats of the river estuary. Wilderness camping is available at Bishop Creek and Granite Falls, near the head of Indian Arm.

★⚓ **Indian Arm Park:** Located adjacent to Mount Seymour Provincial Park in North Vancouver, the park is situated on the east and west sides of Indian Arm. Park designation protects the shores, old-growth forests, several alpine lakes, a waterfall 50 metres high, numerous creeks, and the Indian River estuary. The Indian River supports five species of salmon and the estuary is vital habitat for prawns, crabs, waterfowl, and harbor seals. Park beaches are popular with boaters, especially kayakers and scuba divers. Park areas are primarily accessed by water. No facilities are provided. The park is a wilderness area. Please practice the "no trace" policy. Dinghies, kayaks, and canoes may enter the river at the head, however shoaling makes this difficult. A small beach, east of the river, can be used for shore access.

Belcarra: Floats with wheelchair access are for loading and unloading only. No overnight moorage. Anchorage is possible south of the long wharf or in Belcarra Bay. Drying flats extend from shore.

Walk-around: Belcarra Regional Park has been expanded to include Buntzen Ridge. Hike to the viewpoint that overlooks Burrard Inlet and Buntzen Lake.

Deep Cove: This is a residential area with a marina and public float. Moorage for loading and unloading only at the public float. No waterskiing. A five knot speed limit is enforced. Nearby Panorama Park has a diving raft and swimming beach.

Deep Cove North Shore Marina: Moorage, showers, laundry, mechanic, gas, diesel, boat rentals. 604-929-1251. 66A.

★ **Bedwell Bay:** Located at the southeast end of the arm. Good anchorage. There is an access road to Vancouver.

Woodlands: No marine services. A municipal float has a 24 hour limit. A rock, southwest of the float, is covered five feet at high water.

★ **Racoon and Twin Islands:** These three islands comprise Indian Arm Marine Park. Temporary anchorage is found near the northwest side of Racoon. Two rocks which dry are approximately 200' off shore. Other shoals extend off the islands. The waters around these islands are deep. A small public pier is on one of the islands. A limited trail system is provided. Good scuba diving. Limited wilderness camping is permitted only on the Twin Islands. Visitors are asked to observe the "no trace" policy.

Granite Falls: The 165' high falls are the largest in Indian Arm. No public access.

★⚓ **Cates Park (13):** This 58 acre park is one mile northwest of Roche Point. Picnic sites, playground, a swimming beach, trails, and a garbage deposit are available. Temporary anchorage is possible and there are floats for small boats. There is a launching ramp at Roche Point. ⚓⛵

North Vancouver
[3481, 3493, 3494]

★ **North Vancouver (14):** Connected to Vancouver by the Lions Gate Bridge, North Vancouver is home to marinas, waterfront restaurants, repair yards, chandleries, and tourist attractions. These include Presentation House public art gallery and theater; The Ecology Centre which features natural history, fauna, and flora; Maplewood Farm; the William Griffin Rose Garden; the Capilano Suspension Bridge; and Grouse Mountain. Visit Lonsdale Quay Market on the waterfront and take the Sea Bus ride to downtown Vancouver. There are marine businesses along Vancouver Harbour from First Narrows through and beyond Second Narrows.

Fraser Fibreglass: Extensive repair and boat building. 604-985-1098.

Lynwood Marina: No guest moorage, haul-outs to 60 feet, repairs, supplies, restaurant. 604-985-1533.

Mosquito Creek Marine Basin: Permanent moorage, power, water, haul-outs, repairs. 604-987-4113.

West Vancouver
[3481, 3526]

Point Atkinson: [3481] Passage around this point was recorded by Captain George Vancouver in 1792. The first lighthouse was built in 1874. The present building was constructed in 1912. It was declared a national historic site in 1994 and is now an automated station. The fog signal has been permanently discontinued. The 185 acre Lighthouse Park, with road access from Marine Drive, has old growth conifers and five miles of trails. No access from the water. For tide here, refer to Atkinson Point, Burrard Inlet.

★ **Eagle Harbour-Fisherman's Cove (15):** This vicinity is about one and one half miles north of Point Atkinson. Look for the highway cut into the hillside directly above Fisherman's Cove. Entrances to Eagle Harbour and Fisherman's Cove are south and north of Eagle Island. In Eagle Harbour, extensive permanent moorage and repair facilities predominate with little or no transient moorage available. There is limited anchorage in Eagle Harbour, close in near the head. Fisherman's Cove is the site of a yacht club and fuel facilities. No anchorage is possible.

ESSO Marine Station-Fisherman's Cove: Gas, diesel, propane, kerosene, CNG, ice, water. 604-921-7333. VHF 16.

Thunderbird Marina: Permanent and limited guest moorage, power, water, repairs, haul-outs, chandlery, showers, washrooms. 604-921-7434.

Bachelor Cove: Enter between Bird Islet and Whyte Islet. There is anchorage, open to winds from the south, at the head.

Whyte Cove: This is the site of Whytecliff Park. Activities and facilities include swimming, scuba diving in the underwater marine sanctuary, and a low tide walk to scenic Whyte Islet.

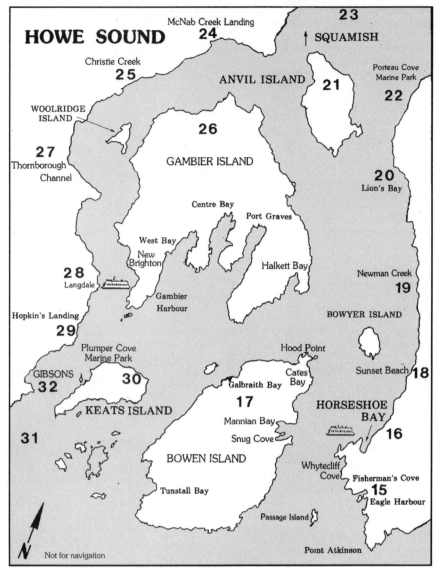

HOWE SOUND

McNab Creek Landing
24

23
↑ SQUAMISH

Christie Creek
25

ANVIL ISLAND

21

Porteau Cove
Marine Park
22

WOOLRIDGE
ISLAND

26

27
Thornborough
Channel

GAMBIER ISLAND

20
Lion's Bay

Centre Bay

Port Graves

West Bay

New
Brighton

28
Langdale

Gambier
Harbour

Halkett Bay

Newman Creek
19

BOWYER ISLAND

Hopkin's Landing
29

Plumper Cove
Marine Park

Hood Point

Sunset Beach
18

GIBSONS
32

30

Galbraith Bay

Cates
Bay

17

HORSESHOE
BAY

KEATS ISLAND

Mannian Bay

Snug Cove

16

31

BOWEN ISLAND

Whytecliff
Cove

Fisherman's Cove
15
Eagle Harbour

Tunstall Bay

Passage Island

N

Not for navigation

Point Atkinson

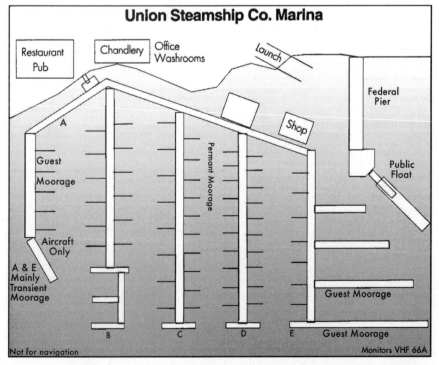

Union Steamship Co. Marina

Restaurant
Pub

Chandlery

Office
Washrooms

Launch

Federal
Pier

Shop

A

Guest

Moorage

Permant Moorage

Public
Float

Aircraft
Only

A & E
Mainly
Transient
Moorage

Guest Moorage

B   C   D   E   Guest Moorage

Not for navigation

Monitors VHF 66A

Howe Sound

[3526, 3524]

★ **Howe Sound:** This extensive body of water northwest of Vancouver is entered through one of the four main channels. The steep-sided shores are mountainous and heavily forested. Ferries from Horseshoe Bay cross to Bowen Island, Langdale on the mainland, and Nanaimo on Vancouver Island. Howe Sound is surprisingly undeveloped. Anchorage here is limited because of deep waters. Log tie-ups are often necessary. There are marina facilities in Horseshoe Bay, Snug Cove, Lion's Bay, Sunset Beach, and Gibsons. Porteau Cove and Plumper Cove are marine parks. Upper Howe Sound is closed for fishing from June 1-September 30. All of Howe Sound is closed to shellfish harvesting because of chemical contamination.

Horseshoe Bay

[3481, 3526, 3534]

★ **Horseshoe Bay (16):** A breakwater extends from the starboard shore on entry, providing protection for the public floats. Transient moorage is available, however, commercial boats have priority. Provisions, repairs, and restaurants are in the vicinity. There is frequent bus service to downtown Vancouver. This is the busy arrival-departure center for ferry traffic linking Vancouver and Bowen Islands and the Sunshine Coast.

Sewell's Marina: Gas, diesel, moorage, ice, power, provisions, launch. 604-921-3474. VHF 81A.

Bowen Island

[3526, 3534]

★ **Bowen Island (17):** This beautiful island lies about eight nautical miles northwest of Vancouver. The island is about 20 square miles in size, with a ragged 23 mile coastline. It is connected to Horseshoe Bay by year-round daily scheduled ferry service. Many of the 3,500 residents who live here attend school or work off island and commonly make the 20 minute commute by ferry. In its early history, the island and surrounding waters were rich hunting and fishing grounds for the Salish, Squamish and other Native tribes. In the 1800's settlers came to work in the logging mills and camps harvesting local timber. Other industries through the years have included fishing, a dynamite factory located in Tunstall Bay, and a brickyard that produced bricks from the clay at Deep Bay. Today tourism is the mainstay of the island economy.

★ **Snug Cove:** Site of the Bowen Island-Horseshoe Bay ferry landing, marinas and public floats, this is the shopping center for Bowen Island residents. A variety of restaurants, shops, and galleries featuring the work of local artists are fun to browse. A seasonal weekend market is held here offering local products, as well. A community museum is open daily during the summer. Located near the Snug Cove dock is the restored Union Steamship General Store which houses an information center for Crippen Park. Groceries and liquor are available. The park is built on what was once Union Steamship Co. Resort. Swimming at local beaches, hiking and biking trails, fishing, scuba diving, and kayaking are possible activities. Rent kayaks and bikes locally. Bus (604-947-0229) and taxi (604-947-0000) service are available. Various B&B's offer accommodations.

★ **Union Steamship Co. Marina:** {49° 23' N, 123° 19' W}ʼ Excellent moorage, with power, water, and fishing supplies is found on large, stable floats at this first-class, year around facility adjacent to Snug Cove's parks, village, and boutiques. See our Steering Star description in this chapter and advertisement on back cover. Internet: www.boattravel.com/bowen & www.steamship-marina.bc.ca. E-mail: ussc@shaw.ca. Mailing Address: Post Office Box 250, Snug Cove, Bowen Island, British Columbia V0N 1G0. Fax: 604-947-0708. Telephone: 604-947-0707. Please check in on VHF 66A for berth assignment.

Bowen Island Marina: Limited moorage, garbage drop, power. 604-947-9710.

Galbraith Bay: This bay, east of Hutt Island, has a public float and a road connection to Snug Cove.

Hood Point: The beaches near Hood Point and Finisterre Island have attracted summer vacationers for many years. Permanent homes and summer cabins line the timbered shore. Anchorage is possible in Smuggler's Cove, Encanta, Columbine, or Cates Bays. Avoid the drying rock in the center of Encanta Bay.

Mannion Bay: For many years this bay, which lies directly opposite Horseshoe Bay, was known as Deep Bay. Southeast swells enter. There is temporary settled weather anchorage off the head favoring the southwest side. The water tends to be warm in this bay. Charted hazards are sunken and drying rocks.

Seymour Landing: This landing, in the southwest corner of Seymour Bay, does not have a public wharf. There is anchorage, but it is open to Horseshoe Bay Ferry wakes.

Apodoca Cove: This is a little haven in westerlies. Apodoca Provincial Park, a nature reserve, borders the north side.

East Howe Sound

[3526]

Sunset Beach (18): Site of a marina.

Sunset Marina: Gas, water, ice, limited moorage to 30', washrooms, repairs, marine ways to 26', launch ramp, bait, tackle. 604-921-7476.

Newman Creek (19): Housing development; no marine facilities.

Lion's Bay (20): Launching ramp and marina.

Lion's Bay Marina: Moorage, water, gas, haul-out to 30', propane, repairs. 604-921- 7510.

Alberta Bay: Brunswick Beach, Alberta Bay, is one mile north of Lion's Bay. There is temporary anchorage and a swimming beach.

Anvil Island (21): It isn't hard to imagine how Captain Vancouver chose this island's name in 1792. The 2,500 foot peak on Anvil Island resembles the horn of an anvil pointed upward. A peninsula, which is also shaped like an anvil, juts into Montague Channel on the eastern side of the island. The beach along the northern side of this peninsula is a popular picnic and barbecue site. Unpredictable *Squamish Winds* can roar down the inlet in the Anvil vicinity.

★⚓ **Porteau Cove Park (22):** A point of land curves to form a small bight. Anchorage for small craft is possible here. No mooring buoys.

Fees charged for moorage and anchoring. Many campsites, vehicle and walk-in, are scattered up the coastline of the 11 acre park. It has a natural swimming pool, a concrete double width launching ramp, boat trailer parking, pay phone, water, showers, toilets, sani station, change house for divers, fish cleaning station and a detached dock for scuba divers. There are sunken ships and man made reefs in the vicinity. Walking trails overlook the cove. 604-898-3678.⚓▲☂

Britannia Beach (22): Home of the BC Museum of Mining. Visitors can ride underground through a 1912 mining tunnel, pan for gold, enjoy live mining demonstrations and museum displays, peek into the historic 1923 concentrator mill, and marvel at the 235 ton Super Haul Truck. 604-896-2233

★ **Squamish (23):** There is a dredged channel and boat harbor, with public floats and a launching ramp, on the west bank of the east arm of the Squamish River. The channel has a five foot minimum depth. When entering, put the old Can Oxy Plant to port, then line up the amber range lights. Logging and forestry, plus a rapidly expanding tourist industry, are the backbones of the economy. Shops, restaurants, large supermarkets, a liquor store, and public telephones available. The West Coast Heritage Park houses the largest collection of vintage railway rolling stock, locomotives, and artifacts in Western Canada. Open daily all year from 10 to 5 with special events, a gift shop, and a miniature railway on site. 604-898-9336. *Squamish Days Loggers Sports* are held the first week in August. Another interesting mode of transportation to access Squamish, in addition to pleasure boat, Harbour Ferries, and car, is by the Royal Hudson Steam Train from Vancouver. Beside ocean frontage, there are five rivers with steelhead,

salmon, and giant sturgeon to tempt the angler. The Squamish River is the winter home of the Bald Eagle with record numbers congregating in the area. The "spit" in Squamish where Howe Sound and the Squamish River meet is a popular windsurfing destination.

Squamish Harbour Authority: Moorage, water, power. Diesel, gas, stove oil, water nearby, pump-out, showers. 604-892-3725, 604-898-5477.

West Howe Sound

[3526]

Zorro Bay: This niche is marked by a small peninsula of land that extends out to form a headland. Avoid the charted rock to the south. Anchorage is possible, but it is open to the north.

McNab Creek Landing (24): A dredged basin is on the east side of the creek mouth. Anchorage is possible off the flats. Potlatch Creek, farther into the sound, has anchorage off the delta.

Christie Creek (25): This tiny bight is south of Stolterfoht Creek. Anchor off south shore with stern tie. Do not block entrance.

Gambier Island

[3526]

★ **Gambier Island (26):** Gambier Island is the largest island in Howe Sound. It is connected by water taxi to nearby communities. New Brighton and Gambier Harbour are connected by road. Four bays indent the island from the south. These are West Bay, Centre Bay, Port Graves, and Halkett Bay. These bays are deep and afford little anchorage.

Gambier Harbour: There is temporary anchorage here when winds are not from the south or east quadrants. There is a public wharf with floats for moorage, however they are exposed to winds.

Brigade Bay: Anchorage in calm weather in this bight on the east side of Gambier Island.

★ **New Brighton:** At the head of Thornbrough Bay, New Brighton has a public wharf and mooring floats attached to it. A store is nearby. Water taxi service may be arranged to Langdale and Gibsons. Of interest in this area is Mariner's Rest. This site on Steamboat Rock is the only official sea burial marker in British Columbia waters. Steamboat Rock was renamed in honor of 31 who lost their lives here.

★ **West Bay:** A public float is on the west shore. Favor this shore to avoid drying rocks a short distance within the entrance. Anchorage is difficult because of the depths and sunken logs on the bottom. Summer homes dot the western shore.

★ **Centre Bay:** There is protection between the peninsula that juts out from the western shore of Gambier Island. Two yacht clubs maintain outstations here, one on Alexandra Island and one in a niche on the eastern side of the bay.

★ **Port Graves:** Inside Potts Point is the largest anchorage in Howe Sound. A spit of foul ground extends 300 feet off the point. Log booms are often tied near the head of the bay. There is a public wharf with a five-ton crane and a float. Minimum depths at the float are seven feet. No garbage deposit. The land above the wharf is private. The floats to the east of the wharf belong to the camp.

★⚓ **Halkett Bay Marine Park:** A public float is in the cove southwest of the west side near the entrance. Fees charged for moorage. Rocks are near shore and in the center of the bay. Avoid private buoys. Log booms are common. Campsites and picnic tables. ⛺

Walk-around: A trail leads to Mt. Artaban, a 10 km round trip hike for experienced hikers.

Port Mellon (27): This is the site of a pulp mill.

Langdale (28): This is the site of the large British Columbia Ferries landing. Ferries connect with Horseshoe Bay.

★ **Hopkins Landing (29):** There is a 60' public float at the end of the wharf. Look for the landmark row of oil tanks one mile to the north when locating the site.

Keats Island

[3526]

★ **Keats Island (30):** This island, named to honor Captain Richard Keats, a British naval officer, is a popular recreation island for Vancouverites. It is the site of Plumper Cove Marine Park.

Eastbourne: Eastbourne, 1/2 mile from Cotton Point, has a wharf and float. The mooring buoys are private.

Keats Island Settlement: Many summer homes are in this area. A public float, primarily used by residents, has fresh water available.

★⚓ **Plumper Cove Marine Park:** Anchorage, mooring buoys, and floats located in the basin behind the Shelter Islets. Fees charged for moorage. Enter north of the islets. These islets are joined by a drying ledge. A buoy marks a shoal in the vicinity of the floats. A display board at the head of the wharf shows the trail routes and campsites. Water and pit toilets available. The beaches are small gravel, so portable boats can be beached. There is exposure to winds from the south or southwest. A park ranger is on duty in summer. ⛺🏕🚶

Walk-around : A trail encompasses the park and may be walked in 1 1/4 hours. Observatory Point offers memorable views of Shoal Channel. A 3-kilometre trail leads to the Keats Landing Foot Ferry Terminal.

Shoal Channel (31): [3534] This channel separates Keats Island from the mainland. A sand and rock bar extends across mid-channel. Minimum depth is five feet. A rock lies 1/4 mile southwest of Steep Bluff. Fishing can be good in this area. Seas break when the wind and tide clash.

★ **Gibsons (32):** This is the southern gateway to the Sunshine Coast. See Chapter 13.

Essential Supplies & Services

AIR TRANSPORTATION
To & from Washington
Seattle Seaplanes **1-800-637-5553**
To & from Islands/Vancouver
Air Canada 1-888-247-2262
Baxter Air 1-800-661-5599
Harbour Air 604-274-1277
Tofino Air 1-800-665-2359
Vancouver Island Air 250-287-2433

AMBULANCE: All 911

BOAT MOVING
All Tow Boat Moving . . . .
. . . . 604-946-7899, 1-877-946-7899

BOAT SEATS & UPHOLSTERY
Royal City Bedding 604-526-2641

BOOKS / BOOK STORES
The Marine Atlas 541-593-6396

BUS TRANSPORTATION
Bus Info 604-953-3333

Greyhound 800-231-2222, 604-482-8747
Pacific Coach Lines 604-662-8074

CNG CYLINDERS
False Creek Fuel Dock 604-733-6731
Fisherman's Cove Marina 604-921-7333
River Marine: Richmond 604-324-9454

COAST GUARD:
Comox . . . . VHF 16, 22-A, 26, 84. 250-339-3613
Emergencies . . . . 1-800-567-5111, VHF 16
Kitsilano C G 604-666-1840
Vancouver Boating Safety 604-666-0146
Cell Phone: #16

CUSTOMS: See Notices between Chapters 7 & 8
Vancouver 1-888-226-7277

FERRY INFORMATION
B. C.. . . . . 1-888-223-3779, 250-386-3431
Granville Island 604-684-7781
Nanaimo: 1-888-724-5223 (B.C.), 604-444-2890 (Res.)
Sea Bus 604-953-3333

FUELS
Captain's Cove Marina: Ladner. Gas, Diesel.
. . . . 604-946-1244
Catherwood Towing: Mission. Gas, Diesel.
. . . . 604-462-9221, 604-826-9257. VHF 69
Coal Harbour Chevron: Gas, Diesel.
. . . . 604-681-7725 VHF 16
Coal Harbour Esso: Gas, Dielsel.
. . . . 604-681-3841 VHF 16, 12
Crescent Beach Marina: Gas, Diesel.
. . . . **604-538-9666 VHF 66A**
Deep Cove North Shore Marina: Deep Cove. Gas, Diesel.
. . . . 604-929-1251
False Creek ESSO: Gas, Diesel 604-733-6731
Fisherman's Cove: W. Van. Gas, Diesel.
. . . . 604-921-7333 VHF 16
Lion's Bay Marina: Howe Sound. Gas . . . 604-921-7510
Pitt Meadows Marina: Mid-Grade Gas. . . 604-465-7713
Reed Point Marina: Port Moody. Gas, Diesel.
. . . . 604-937-1600
Richmond Chevron: Diesel 604-278-2181
Sewell's Marina: Horseshoe Bay. Gas, Diesel.
. . . . 604-921-3474 VHF 81A

Please tell our advertisers that you found them in Northwest Boat Travel® & Northwest Boat Travel On-Line®

Essential Supplies & Services — cont'd.

Steveston Chevron: Gas, Diesel........ 604-277-4712
Steveston ESSO: Gas, Diesel......... 604-277-5211
Sunset Marina: Howe Sound. Gas..... 604-921-7476
Vancouver Marina: Richmond. Gas, Diesel.
.... 604-278-3300

INSURANCE
Boat Insurance Agency 206-285-1350
Or Call 1-800-828-2446

LODGING
Union Steamship: Bowen Island.
.... **604-947-0707 VHF 66A**

MARINAS / MOORAGE
Barbary Coast: Coal Harbour......... 604-669-0088
Bowen Island....................... 604-947-9710
Burrard Bridge Civic.... 604-733-5833, 604-505-5833
Captain's Cove: Ladner 604-946-1244
Caulfeild Cove: W. Vancouver
Coal Harbour Marina..... 604-681-2628 VHF 66A
Crescent Beach Marina... 604-538-9666 VHF 66A
Deep Cove North Shore Marina: Deep Cove.
.... 604-929-1251
Delta Marina. Richmond 604-273-4211
Eastbourne: Keats Island
False Creek Harbour .... 604-733-3625 VHF 16, 68
Galbraith Bay: Bowen Island
Gambier Harbour: Howe Sound
Great Canadian Marina: Richmond 604-273-8560
Halkett Bay: Gambier Island
Heather Civic: False Creek 604-874-2814
Hopkins Landing: Howe Sound
Horseshoe Bay
Keats Island Settlement
Lion's Bay: Howe Sound 604-921-7510
Lynwood Marina: Second Narrows 604-985-1533
Mission
New Brighton: Gambier Island
Pelican Bay Marina: False Creek 604-729-1442
Plumper Cove Marine Park: Keats Island
Port Graves: Gambier Island
Quayside Marina 604-681-9115
Reed Point: Port Moody 604-937-1600
Sewell's: Horseshoe Bay 604-921-3474
Shelter Island Marina: Richmond.
.... **604-270-6272 VHF 66A**
Skyline: Richmond................. 604-273-3977
Snug Cove: Bowen Island
Squamish Harbour Authority:
.... 604-892-3725, 604-898-5477
Steveston...................... 604-272-5539
Sunset: Howe Sound............... 604-921-7476
Union Steamship Marina: Bowen Island.
.... **604-947-0707 VHF 66A**
Vancouver: Richmond............. 604-278-9787
West Bay: Gambier Island

MARINE SUPPLY STORES
Shelter Island: Richmond........ 604-270-6272
Wright Mariner Coal Harbour 604-682-3785

PARKS
B.C. Parks..................... 604-898-3678

POISON INFO: 1-800-567-8911
Vancouver...................... 604-682-5050

PROPANE
Fisherman's Cove 604-921-7333
Lion's Bay Marina: Howe Sound 604-921-7510

RAMPS / HAUL-OUTS
Burrard Bridge Civic 604-733-5833
Captain's Cove Marina: Ladner 604-946-1244
Cates Park: Burrard Inlet
Crescent Beach Marina 604-538-9666
Deep Cove North Shore Marina....... 604-929-1251
Fort Langley: Fraser River
Kitsilano Beach: English Bay
Lion's Bay Marina: Howe Sound 604-921-7510
Lulu Island: Main Arm Fraser River
Lynwood Marina: Second Narrows..... 604-985-1533
McDonald Beach: N. Arm Fraser River
Mosquito Creek Marina: N. Vancouver... 604-987-4113
Pitt Meadows Marina................ 604-465-7713
Pitt Polder: Pitt Lake
Port Mann Bridge: Port Coquitlam
Porteau Cove Provincial Park
Reed Point Marina: Port Moody 604-937-1600
Rocky Point Park: Port Moody
Sea Island: Middle Arm Fraser River
Shelter Island: Richmond.. 604-270-6272 VHF 66A
Skyline Marina: Richmond........... 604-273-3977
Squamish River
Steveston
Sunset Marina: Howe Sound......... 604-921-7476
Surrey
Thunderbird Marina: W. Vancouver..... 604-921-7434
Tsawwassen
Westham Island: Fraser River

RED TIDE: 604-666-2828

REPAIRS / SERVICE
Fraser Fibreglass: North Van 604-985-1098
Granville Island Boat Lift 604-685-6924
Lynnwood Marina: North Vancouver 604-985-1533
Reed Point Marina.................. 604-937-1600
Shelter Island Marina: Richmond... 604-270-6272
Thunderbird Marina: West Van 604-921-7434

RESCUE COORDINATION
Emergencies.................... 1-800-567-5111

RESTAURANTS
False Creek Harbour .... 604-733-3625 VHF 16, 68
Lynwood Marina: Second Narrows 604-985-1533
Riverhouse Marina Restaurant & Pub 604-946-7545
Shelter Island Marina: Richmond.
.... **604-270-6272 VHF 66A**

SEWAGE DISPOSAL
Burrard Bridge Civic Marina: Pump.
.... 604-733-5833, 604-505-5833
Coal Harbour Marina: Pump 604-681-2628
False Creek Yacht Club 604-682-3292
Heather Civic Marina: Pump 604-874-2814
Point Roberts: Pump................. 360-945-2255
Reed Point Marina.................. 604-937-1600
Shelter Island Marina: Pump...... 604-270-6272
Squamish Harbour Authority.......... 604-892-3725
Union Steamship: Pump 604-947-0707

SHELLFISH HOTLINE: 604-666-2828

SPORTFISHING: 604-666-2828

Local Fisheries Canada Offices: Mission 604-814-1055,
Squamish 604-892-3230, Steveston ... 604-664-9250
Vancouver 604-666-0384

TAXI: 604-871-1111

TOWING
C-TOW................... 1-888-354-5554

VHF MARINE OPERATOR
Bellingham: VHF 28, 85
Fraser River: VHF 23, 86
Lulu Island (Fraser River): VHF 26
Pender Harbour: VHF 25
Nanaimo: VHF 87
Sechelt: VHF 86
Vancouver: VHF 23, 24, 25, 86
West Vancouver: VHF 85

VISITOR INFORMATION
Tourism Vancouver 604-683-2000
Tourism B.C. 1-800-663-6000

WEATHER
Environment Canada Weather Line 250-339-9861
Comox:VHF WX-1 162.55 250-339-0748
Bowen Island: VHF WX-3
Vancouver: VHF WX-2 162.40
Vancouver: VHF 21 161.65
Vancouver........... 604-664-9010, 604-666-3655

Horseshoe Bay, West Vancouver   *Linda Schreiber Photo*

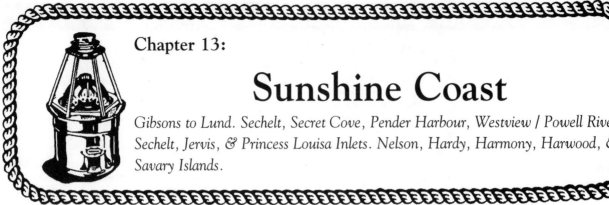

Chapter 13:

Sunshine Coast

Gibsons to Lund. Sechelt, Secret Cove, Pender Harbour, Westview / Powell River. Sechelt, Jervis, & Princess Louisa Inlets. Nelson, Hardy, Harmony, Harwood, & Savary Islands.

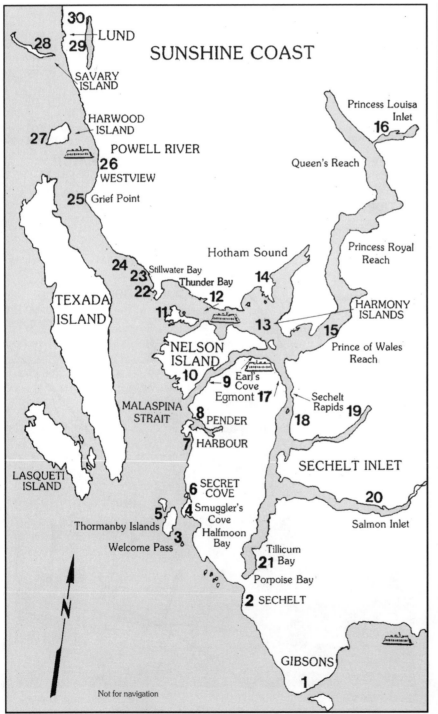

SUNSHINE COAST

30 — LUND
28   29
SAVARY ISLAND
HARWOOD ISLAND
27
POWELL RIVER
26
WESTVIEW
25   Grief Point
24   23   Stillwater Bay
22   Thunder Bay
12
TEXADA ISLAND
11   13
NELSON ISLAND
10
9   Earl's Cove
Egmont   17
8   PENDER
7   HARBOUR
MALASPINA STRAIT
LASQUETI ISLAND
5
4   Smuggler's Cove
6   SECRET COVE
3   Halfmoon Bay
Thormanby Islands
Welcome Pass
21   Tillicum Bay
Porpoise Bay
2   SECHELT
GIBSONS
1
N
Not for navigation

Princess Louisa Inlet
16
Queen's Reach
Hotham Sound
14
Princess Royal Reach
HARMONY ISLANDS
15
Prince of Wales Reach
Sechelt Rapids
18   19
SECHELT INLET
20
Salmon Inlet

Symbols

[   ]: Numbers between [ ] are chart numbers.

{   }: Numbers & letters between { } are waypoints.

⚲: Park, ⛵: Boat Launch, ▲: Campgrounds, 𝝹: Hiking Trails, ⊼: Picnic Area, ⚲: Biking

★ **Important Notice:** See "Important Notices" between Chapters 7 and 8 in this guide for specific information on boating related topics such as: Canadian & U.S. Customs, boating safety and security, navigation, weather, U.S. & Canadian Coast Guard, U.S & Canadian marine radio use, Vessel Traffic Service and traffic separation plans, security zones, and internet access. Due to new Department of Homeland Security regulations, call ahead for latest customs information and/or see Northwest Boat Travel On-line, www.nwboat.com.

Introduction

★ **The Sunshine Coast:** Well named because of the amount of annual sunshine that warms this area, residents along the Sunshine Coast report that the sun shines 300 days each year. No wonder this stretch of mainland is a popular playground for boaters! They come from near and far, plying the waters to and from Desolation Sound, Discovery Passage, and destinations farther northwest. The coast provides delightful miles of scenic views, inviting coves, sandy beaches, and picturesque fjord-like inlets offering outdoor exploration, fishing, kayaking, swimming, dining, diving, and destination resort comfort. Boaters who have made the cruise through the reaches of Jervis Inlet and traversed Malibu Rapids will never forget the spectacular beauty of the Yosemite Valley-like Princess Louisa Inlet, with its breath-taking Chatterbox Falls. Gibsons, Sechelt, Secret

Chart List

Canadian Hydrographic Charts:

3311, 3312, 3514, 3534, 3535

Marine Atlas (2005 ed.):

Page 22, 26-30

Cove, Pender Harbour, Egmont, and Powell River each offer their own unique variety of scenic wonderland, vacation attractions, facilities, and activities. The entire coast seems rather isolated, yet it is within easy reach of Vancouver by boat, automobile, bus, or air. If traveling by car or RV, two rather short ferry rides add variety to the scenic roadway that permits exploration of the entire length of the coast, ending at Lund. The first ferry is a 40 minute ride and departs from West Vancouver at Horseshoe Bay, taking you to Langdale on the other side of Howe Sound. There are sailings every two hours, seven days per week. At Earls Cove, near Egmont, the next ferry is a 50 minute ride, landing at Saltery Bay, on the northwest side of Jervis Inlet.

Gibsons to Welcome Pass

[3311, 3526, 3534]

★ **Gibsons (1):** [3534] Named after George Gibsons, a British Officer who landed here in 1886, this hillside city offers good, breakwater protected, moorage at the strategic Gateway to Howe Sound and the Sunshine Coast. If approaching from the Strait of Georgia, pass Gower Point and enter Shoal Channel, otherwise known as The Gap. Gibsons is a friendly place to visit. Both permanent and overnight moorage is available. The downtown is known for being the home of the CBC's former television series "Beachcombers." The waterfront Landing area is a collection of intriguing stores, including a grocery store, book store, clothing shops, art gallery and studios, and antique stores. Restaurants, pubs, lodging, and the Tourist Information Centre are also found here. Of the nearly 4,000 residents who live in Gibsons, 10% are artists or craftsmen. Look for purple banners hung outside of studios, a welcome signal for drop-in visitors. Uphill from the downtown area is a large shopping mall housing a variety of businesses. Sunshine Coast Museum & Archives, one block west of the harbor, focuses on Howe Sound to Jervis Inlet and features marine and shell collections, along with Coast Salish artifacts. 604-886-8232. Stroll through beautiful Winegarden Waterfront Park overlooking the harbor. Annual community events include the *Gibsons Jazz Festival* in June, the *Sea Cavalcade Festival* held during the last week in July, the internationally recognized *Howe Sound Outrigger Canoe Race* also held in July, and the *Fibre Arts Festival & Workshop* in August. The city also hosts *"Music in the Landing,"* a popular weekend summer concert series.

Gibsons Marina: Power, water, porta pump-out, washrooms, showers, laundromat, chandlery, fishing gear, marine supplies. Telephone: 604-886-8686. VHF 66A.

Hyak Marine Ltd: Gas, diesel, ice, water, repairs, ways, haul-outs. 604-886-9011.

Gibsons Landing Harbour Authority: Moorage, 15 & 30 ampere power, water, pump-out, laundry and shower facilities, pedestrian promenade and park areas. 604-886-8017. VHF 66A & 68.

Roberts Creek: Residential area, parks, restaurants, shops, art studios, lodging, golf course and launching ramp.

Port Stalashen, Wilson Creek: Moorage to 50', water, power. Entrance channel aligns with breakwaters and has two-feet of water at zero tide. 604-885-4884, 604-740-0174.

Sechelt (2): Sechelt is unusual in that the community stretches across land which fronts on both the Strait of Georgia and the inland fjord of Sechelt Inlet. There is limited, exposed anchorage in the northeast corner of Trail Bay. The rip-rap breakwater at Selma Park encloses an Indian Reservation harbor and shelter is found in the lee of the breakwater. Sechelt is a thriving town with all conveniences, a hospital, a mall as well as various small shops, galleries with local crafts and carvings, a liquor store, motels, marine repairs, marinas (on the Sechelt Inlet shore), and restaurants. Arts and crafts fairs are held in August and December. The magnificent Raven's Cry Theater, with its museum and gift shop, is a popular attraction. Built by the Shishalh Natives around the theme of the salmon people, the theater features live performances by theater groups, and films five nights a week. Tourist activities include kayaking, skim-boarding, fishing, diving, golf, beachcombing, and visiting Chapman Creek Hatchery. A pedestrian pier is located in Trail Bay, off of Wharf Street in downtown Sechelt. In Sechelt Inlet, The Inland Sea, moorage is available at Porpoise Bay. There is also a lovely, sandy beach in Porpoise Bay. See Sechelt Inlet in this chapter.

★⚓ **Sargeant Bay & Sargeant Bay Provincial Park:** Located west of Sechelt, this bay is open to the south. Anchorage in settled weather only because strong northwest winds also have a way of entering. Anchor off the beach or behind the rock at the north end of the bay. Caution advised regarding a drying rock some distance southwest of the large rock. The provincial park includes 30 acres of land and is a bird sanctuary with extensive marshlands. Picnic area, trails, no camping. Colvin Creek, a 300 meter walk from the bay, has a fish ladder.🏃⛩

Walk-around: Hike from Sargeant Bay to Trout Lake.

Trail Islands: Limited shelter suitable for temporary anchorage.

Welcome Pass
to Secret Cove

[3311, 3535]

★ **Welcome Pass (3):** Merry Island, marked by a white and red lighthouse, lies in the middle of the southern end of Welcome Pass. This passage is used extensively by boaters traveling between Nanaimo, Silva Bay, Gibsons, or Vancouver and the Sunshine Coast. There are two unmarked rocks in the pass. Frazer Rock, near Lemberg Point, has about seven feet of water covering it at low tide. Egerton Rock lies south of Lemberg Point. Currents in the pass run to three knots at springs, setting north on flood and south on ebb tides. Merry Island Lighthouse has a fog horn of three long blasts per minute. Pirate Rock has a black, white and green day beacon on it. The pass, and some of its surrounding landmarks, were named over 100 years ago when Mr. Merry's horse, Thormanby, won a race over the favored horse, Buccaneer. There is a public wharf and float in Halfmoon Bay.

★ **Halfmoon Bay (3):** This is a large and attractive bay that can be a welcome refuge to travelers headed toward, or coming from, the strait. A public wharf is at Priestland Cove at the northeast portion of the bay with a small public float adjacent to it. A public boat launch site is nearby. The irregular shoreline invites exploration

by dinghy or small boat. Of interest is the historic Redroofs Trail and Bridge.

★ **Frenchman's Cove:** It is easy to believe that a smuggler could disappear into the entrance and hide unnoticed in this cove. Note that Frenchman's Cove is actually one arm of a horseshoe-shaped passage. This secluded anchorage is perfect for adventurous boaters who desire a hidden retreat, are willing to go cautiously "gunkholing" to find the entrance, and can accept the risk of making a mistake. Numerous unmarked drying and submerged rocks, some charted and some not charted, lie offshore, between the entrance to the cove and Welcome Pass. Although the editors have been in this anchorage many times, each return is a renewed challenge to find the opening. The entrance is so well hidden, that perhaps the only advantage we have is that we believe the hole is there, because we have been through it so often. The entrance is an elusive cut in the high-bank northwest shore of Halfmoon Bay. As you near this shore, locate the houses on the bank at the other end of the horseshoe passage. Then, move your eyes, or field glasses, to the left and examine the shoreline for a large rock that guards the entrance. Even now, you cannot see an opening. Head slowly for that large rock. As you near the rock, the hole in the wall will begin to open in front of you. The width of the passage is about 40 feet, although it seems much narrower. Once through the entrance, the cove widens, giving ample room for one boat, or a small raft of boats, to swing at anchor. There is good holding mud in the cove, with minimum depths of about five feet on a zero tide at Atkinson Point, Burrard Inlet (See current tables for Vancouver, British Columbia). Boaters have commonly ridden out many a high wind, snuggled in this little cove. Locate a rocky area and shoals which extend from shore before setting anchor. Entry can also be made through a narrow pass at the other end of the horseshoe-shaped passage leading into a small basin. Private docks are found here, but very limited anchorage might be available. A drying inlet is at the extreme head of the cove. Drying rocks separate this northern vicinity from the preferred anchorage described above. If traversing the entire passage, do so only at high water and with a shallow draft vessel.

★⚓ **Smuggler Cove Marine Park (4):** A narrow entrance with reefs on both sides leads into this popular stopover. Low tide is the optimum time to avoid reef and rocks. Favor the port side (Isle Capri). There is extensive anchorage with fair-to-good holding bottom in two main bays. On the south side of the first bay, there is an uncharted rock about 50 feet out from the house on shore. This rock is covered about five feet at high tide. When entering the inner bay, the reef in the passage, marked by a wooden pointer, extends farther into the passage than one might expect. Rings for shore ties have been driven into the rocks on both sides of the inner cove. Fees charged. A courteous tie to shore makes room for additional boats. It is possible to walk to a lookout into Frenchman's Cove.

★ **Thormanby Islands (5):** North and South Thormanby Islands are noted for sandy beaches, good swimming, and good fishing grounds.

★ **Buccaneer Bay:** Located between North and South Thormanby, the entrance to the bay is obstructed by a long ridge of rocks on Tottenham Ledge that extend to the buoy some distance off shore. Silting conditions cause depth variations in the bay. A public wharf, for loading and unloading only, is at Vaucroft

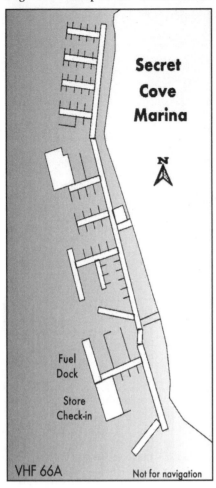

Secret
Cove
Marina

N

Fuel
Dock

Store
Check-in

VHF 66A   Not for navigation

Beach on the bay's west side. A telephone is accessible. No garbage drop. Observe private property regulations. Fine, white sand beaches rim much of the bay. On the southern tip of North Thoramby Island, is Buccaneer Bay Provincial Park. Grassy Point and Gill Beach offer temporary, daytime anchorage and good swimming. This vicinity is unprotected from northwest winds, which usually start after dusk. Anchor behind the Surrey Islands for some protection from the southeast and northwest winds, or in Water Bay behind the reef in the center of the bay. Seals and sea lions are common sights.

★ Farm Bay: Also on South Thormanby Island are two coves, both suitable for anchorage in settled weather. Farm Bay is the site of Simson Marine Park and a park sign identifies the location. When anchoring, pay close attention to the chart and identify shoal areas. A second anchorage is in a cove adjacent to Farm Bay. It is also open to the south.

Walk-around: Farm Bay is a good place for a shore walk through unusual rock formations and along old logging roads. Begin at the head of the bay and walk to an old orchard.

Secret Cove

[3311, 3535]

★ Secret Cove (6): A marker sits atop a rock at the entrance to this cove. Keep this marker to starboard during entry. The topography makes reducing speed at the entry marker important, both for courtesy and safety. This is the site of marinas with protected moorage and a repair facility. Anchorage is possible, however dragging anchor often occurs in winds. Many sports

fishermen headquarter in Secret Cove because of good fishing grounds nearby.

There are three arms that extend east, northeast, and northwest: (1) The northwest arm lies to port and leads to Secret Cove Marina, the major destination moorage in Secret Cove, and a public float. Daily bus service connects with points north, and Vancouver. The anchoring bottom is tricky in this arm. In a wind, dragging is not uncommon. (2) The middle (northeast arm) lies almost directly ahead. Marina, fuel and repair facilities are in this arm. (3) The arm to starboard (east arm) has a narrow entrance and is of limited interest to travelers, since all docks in this arm are private. If entering this east arm, keep the channel marker to port and be aware that there are rocks to starboard. At the head of the arm is an extensive drying flat.

★ Secret Cove Marina: {49° 32' N, 123° 58' W} This is a popular moorage and traveling boater's headquarters. Gas, diesel, moorage with power, water, store, restaurant, fish cleaning tables, a garbage deposit, picnic tables, showers, liquor, groceries. Annual moorage and boat sitting are also available. See our Steering Star description in this chapter. Internet sites: www.boattravel.com/secretcove & www.secretcovemarina.com. Email: mailto:info@secretcovemarina.com. Mailing address: Box 1118, Sechelt, British Columbia V0N 3A0. Fax: 604-885-6037. Telephone: 1-866-885-3533. VHF 66A.

★ Rock Water Secret Cove Resort (formerly Lord Jim's Resort Hotel): Located in the spectacular Sunshine Coast, Rock Water Secret Cove Resort, offers a wide variety of amenities including ocean views from all lodge rooms and cabins, cocktail bar and lounge, fine dining,

patio dining, outdoor heated pool, wonderful spa facilities and more. Enjoy the conference and banquet facilities or a round of golf at any of the three fine courses in the area. Other activities include hiking, fishng, kayaking and scenic coastal excursions. Chef Alan Edginton and his team have prepared a wonderful menu of West Coast offerings focusing on freshness and using the finest ingredients from the land and ocean. See our advertisement in this chapter. Website: www.lordjims.com. Address: 5356 Ole's Cove Road, Halfmoon Bay, BC, Canada V0N 1Y2. Telephone 1-877-296-4593, 604-885-7038.

Buccaneer Marina: Gas, diesel, propane, haul-outs, repairs, water. 604-885-7888, 1-877- 885-7888.

Jolly Roger Marina: Moorage, power, water, laundry, showers, restaurant. 604-885-7860.

Secret Cove to Pender Harbour
[3311, 3535]

Wood Bay: Anchorage is possible with some protection from both northwesterly and south-easterly winds. There is aquaculture in the area.

Harness Island: There is anchorage behind the island. Reefs extend between islets. Pass between the tallest islet and Harness Island. A kelp marked rock is a hazard.

★ **Bargain Bay (7):** Access to this anchorage is from Malaspina Strait between Francis Peninsula and Edgecombe Island. The entrance is wide enough to allow easy passage. There are two rocks with less than six feet of water over them, one on each side of the passage. A channel, about 100 yards in width, is between the rocks. Once past the rocks, the head of the bay offers good anchorage in depths of 20-30 feet. Bargain Narrows, known locally as Canoe Pass, connects the head of Bargain Bay with Gerrans Bay. However, the pass is obstructed by a drying bank and is navigable only at high tide and by very small, flat bottomed boats. A bridge with a 13 foot vertical clearance crosses the passage.

Pender Harbour
[3311, 3535]

★ **Pender Harbour (8):** The main entrance is between Henry Point and Williams Island. Inside the entrance, a speed limit of seven knots is enforced. This well-protected and beautiful harbor attracts golfing, recreational boating, dining, diving, and fishing enthusiasts. The public wharves within Pender Harbour (Hospital Bay, Welbourn Cove, Gerrans Bay) are now operated by the Harbour Authority of Pender Harbour. The distinctive red wharf railing and policies remain the same. After entering the harbor, a marina is to port. Heading farther into the harbor to port is Hospital Bay, site of a marina, store, liquor, post office, fuel, and a public float. Returning to the main channel and continuing east into the harbor, Garden Bay, to port, is the site of the Garden Bay Restaurant, Pub, & Marina, and Garden Bay Marine Park. Outside Garden Bay, the main harbor narrows near the head, at the entrance to Gunboat Bay, named for Her Majesty's gunboats stationed nearby in the 1860's. There are oyster beds nearby. Between Gunboat Bay and Madeira Park is a

protected niche, home of Sunshine Coast Resort.

Madeira Park in Welbourn Cove, is the primary shopping site, and is home port for Madeira Pharmacy, a liquor store, restaurants, shops, the IGA Super Market, bank (including ATM), repair services, Music Hall, and Cultural Center. Headed west from Madeira Park, along the south shore, is the entrance to Gerrans Bay.

Visitors can explore the different communities in Pender Harbour by means of the 12 passenger, Pender Harbour Ferry - Stops: Irvines Landing, Hospital Bay, Garden Bay, Madeira Park, Gerrans Bay.

Activities in, and near, Pender Harbour include golfing, fishing for salmon (with excellent catches of Coho up to 20 pounds and Chinook up to 40 pounds), fishing for cod, sole, or hake, harvesting shellfish, or scuba diving in the clear and clean waters nearby. Annual events include *May Day*, celebrated on the Saturday before the 24th of May, *Happy Days* held in August, and the *Pender Harbour Jazz Festival* the third weekend in September.

Joe Bay: This bay is to port upon entry to Pender Harbour.

Irvine's Landing: Moorage, power, water, launch, pub. 604-883-1145.

Duncan Cove: This cove is to port after Farrington Cove. It is the site of a resort.

Duncan Cove Marina: Moorage, showers, laundry, lodging, RV sites. 604-883-2424.

★ **Hospital Bay:** As the name implies, there was once a hospital here. This is the site of a public float complex, resort-marina, store, fuel

dock, liquor agency, post office, and restaurants. It is a short walk to Garden Bay, home of Garden Bay Hotel and Marina.

★ **Fisherman's Resort & Marina Ltd:** Located in Pender Harbour's Hospital Bay. Deep water moorage, 20 & 30 amp power, showers, laundry, garbage & recycling. Ice, tackle, books, charts, launch ramp & secure parking. Kayak & power-boat rentals. Waterfront cottages, RV & camp sites. See our advertisement in this chapter. Address: 4890 Pool Rd., Garden Bay, BC. Email: fishermans@dccnet.com. Telephone: 604-883-2336. VHF 66A.

Hospital Bay Public Floats: (Operated by the Harbour Authority of Pender Harbour). Moorage, power, water, new deck, newly renovated. 604-883-2234. VHF 66A.

★ **John Henry's Marina:** Only fuel dock in Pender Harbour. Propane, bait, tackle, fishing & hunting licenses, ice, liquor store, charts, lotto, groceries, office services & Post Office. See our advertisement in this Chapter. Address: 4907 Pool Lane, Garden Bay, BC V0N 1S0. Telephone: 604-883-2253, Fax: 604-883-2147.

★ **Garden Bay:** This bay is to port, near the head of Pender Harbour. At the site are marinas, a marine park, a yacht club outstation, and a restaurant and pub.

★ **Garden Bay Restaurant, Pub & Marina:** {49° 37.8' N, 124° 01' W} Moorage is available directly in front of this fully-licensed restaurant and pub. Fifteen and 30 amp power. See our Steering Star description in this chapter. Websites: www.gardenbaypub.com & www.boat-

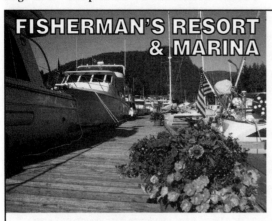

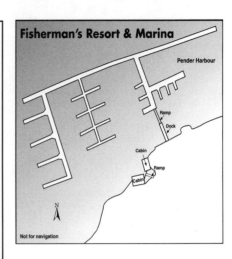
travel.com/gardenbay. E-mail: gbhm@dccnet.com. Address: Post Office Box 90, Garden Bay, British Columbia V0N 1S0. Telephone: Marina / Pub / Fax: 604-883-2674, Dining: 604-883-9919.

Sportsman Marina & Resort: Permanent and guest moorage, power, laundry, showers. 604-883-2479.

★⚓ **Garden Bay Marine Park:** Anchorage is possible off this park. A dinghy dock with ramp and three finger floats provide shore access. The park land includes Mount Daniel, of historical importance to the local Sechelt Indians. Road access from Highway 101.

★ **Gunboat Bay:** Entered through the narrow channel at the head of Pender Harbour. The entry channel is charted to have a drying rock and a minimum depth of four feet. The upper reaches of Gunboat Bay dry at low tide.

Headwater Marina: Limited moorage, power, shower, washrooms, RV sites. 604-883-2406.

Sunshine Coast Resort: Nanaimo Yacht Club out-station. Moorage, 30 amp power, showers, washrooms, laundry, wireless internet, lodging. 604-883-9177.

★⚓ **Madeira Park:** {49° 37' N, 124° 01' W} This is Pender Harbour's largest community. Modernized and expanded public floats offer access. A large grocery store, pharmacy, bank, liquor store, restaurant, post office, beauty parlor, marina and Visitor Infocentre are some of

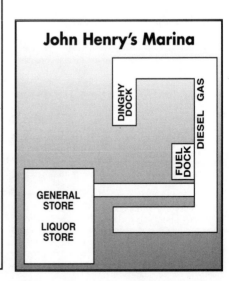

Ballet Bay   Canadian Hydrographic Photo

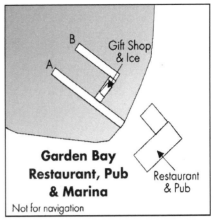

Garden Bay
Restaurant, Pub
& Marina

Gift Shop
& Ice

Restaurant
& Pub

Not for navigation

the many attractions. The Department of Fisheries operates a spawning creek for Coho salmon and trout. An early pioneer, born in Portugal, named the site after the Island of Madeira.

The main wharf fronting Madeira Park and surrounding property has been redeveloped. Seafarer's Millennium Park features picnic areas, a boardwalk, and gazebo over the water. Residents raised funds and volunteered in every aspect of this endeavor. Examples include an artist's sculpture for the gazebo, wood carvings, rockwork, and flowers donated by local gardeners. Showers and washrooms are in the Office Building.

★ **Madeira Marina:** Pender Harbour's complete marine supplies & services store. Services include trailer haulout to 35 feet, welding & fabrication, light machining & dry storage. Sales and service for Honda Outboards,

★ **Garden Bay Restaurant, Pub & Marina:** After rounding beautiful Garden Peninsula and entering Garden Bay, the floats of Garden Bay Restaurant and Pub will come into view at the head of the bay. Visitors to this calm, protected bay will find 1500' of guest moorage with 15 and 30 ampere power and water. On shore, vaca-

tioners are, most likely, relaxing under a patio umbrella with a beverage and pub fare, or are in the dining room experiencing the gourmet cuisine that began when the new chef arrived from Whistler. Visitors have described the food as "five-star". Pub hours are from 11:00 a.m. daily and the restaurant is open for dinner from 5:00 p.m. daily. To add to the festivities, live entertainment (from the long weekend in March though mid-September) is another weekend ingredient on the menu. Nearby diversions include hiking trails, fresh water swimming, and golf. For those who would like to learn the inner secrets of the Pender Harbour vicinity and its legendary fishing grounds, fishing and dive charters can be arranged. Garden Bay Marina is a good place to meet friends who arrive by car, bus, or float plane. Charter flights can be arranged. Their slogan is "A Lot of Everything!" Open year around, seven days a week. **Circle #41 on Reader Service Card at page 251.** Websites: www.gardenbaypub.com & www.boattravel.com/gardenbay   Email: gbhm@dccnet.com Address: Box 90. Garden Bay, British Columbia V0N 1S0. Telephones: Pub & Moorage: 604-883-2674 (phone & fax), Restaurant: 604-883-9919.

Mercruiser, John Deere Marine, Volvo Penta and other major brands. See our advertisement in this chapter. Address: 12930 Madeira Park Rd., Madeira Park, BC, Canada V0N 2H0. Telephone: 604-883-2266.

★ **Madeira Park Marketplace IGA:** Full service supermarket with bakery and deli, convenient to the public floats. *Maderia Park Marketplace IGA is Hometown Proud.* See our Steering Star description in this chapter. Address: Post Office Box 155, Madeira Park, British Columbia V0N 2H0. Telephone: 604-883-9100. Fax: 604-883-9145.

Harbour Authority of Pender Harbour, Madeira Park: Moorage, 15, 30, and 50 ampere power, launching ramp, garbage deposit, showers, washrooms, pump-out. 604-883-2234. VHF66A.

★ **Gerrans Bay:** Locally known as Whiskey Slough, this bay is near Madeira Park, on the south side of Pender Harbour. Enter either side of Mary Islet, but avoid Griffin Ledge which lies between Mary Islet and Welbourn Cove. Anchorage is found in this bay, between Francis Peninsula and Dusenbury and Alder Islands, and also at the head of the bay. There is a public float.

Whiskey Slough Government Dock: Harbour Authority of Pender Harbour. Moorage, power water. 604-883-2234. VHF 66A.

Coho Marina: Limited guest moorage 20' & under, power, water, launch, showers. 604-883-2248.

Lowe's Resort: Limited moorage, campsites, diver's air, showers, laundry, lodging, RV sites. 604-883-2456, 1-877-883-2456.

Agamemnon Channel

[3311, 3312, 3512, 3514]

Agamemnon Channel (9): This is the shortest route when headed for Egmont, Princess Louisa, Sechelt Inlet or Hotham Sound. It also provides a place to run when Malaspina Strait is choppy. If a storm is brewing, the Hotham Sound vicinity can be a nice place to spend time until calmer weather arrives. Agamemnon Channel stretches in a north and northeast direction for about eight miles and is about a half mile wide. Depths range from 20-140 fathoms. There is no place for anchorage except Green Bay. Tidal streams attain rates of one to two knots with the flood tide headed northward and the ebb tide south. This waterway was named for the *HMS Agamemnon*, a 64 gun battleship commanded by Nelson. Just below Green Bay, on the west side of Agamemnon Channel, a small lagoon with a narrow entrance opens up. This can be entered by shallow draft, small craft. The steep-sided fjord walls of Agamemnon Channel and Jervis Inlet provide superb wall diving on vertical cliffs that plunge several hundred feet straight down. Six foot cloud sponges and enormous fans of gorgonian corals live in the clear waters, where wintertime visibility frequently exceeds 80 feet.

★ **Green Bay:** Green Bay provides well-sheltered anchorage in depths of five to seven fathoms. Rocks near the center and the head of the bay dry at half tide. This bight is often used as a booming ground for logs. The west side forms a nook that offers the most protection. Booming rings that can be used for stern tying are found in the southern side of the nook. On the north side of the bay anchorage is found near the remains of a wharf and cabins.

Agamemnon Bay & Earl's Cove: This is the terminus of the Earl's Cove-Saltery Bay ferry which connects the main highway from Vancouver north to the highway's terminus at Lund. Limited anchorage is possible, staying away from the ferry landing. This is the site of a small private marina.

Nelson Island

[3311, 3312, 3512, 3514]

★ **Nelson Island (10):** This Island borders Blind Bay. There are oyster culture beds and popular anchorages nearby. Quarry Bay, Cockburn Bay and Hidden Basin are entered from Malaspina Strait, Ballet Bay from Blind Bay. Vanguard Bay is on the south side of Jervis Inlet.

★ **Quarry Bay:** Use Chart #3512. There is anchorage in the western arm. Watch for a drying rock. There is also good anchorage in the cove in the eastern end, south of the old granite quarry. The quarry site is nearly buried in brush and vegetation. A rock is 200 yards north of the south shore. Watch for drying reefs and rocks. Do not anchor in the northern section of the easternmost arm because of the telephone cable. There is shelter from southeasterlies in the bight to starboard in the entrance. Because of limited swinging room, a shore tie is recommended.

★ **Cockburn Bay:** The narrow entrance to this bay is obstructed by foul ground. Small vessels can enter and leave near high water. Stay mid-channel in the entrance. Favor the north shore for the next 200 feet. Depths inside are around 18 feet at high tide. When anchoring, note the location of the telephone cable.

Billings Bay: An unmaintained public float offers protection from winds.

★ **Hidden Basin:** Entrance to this secluded anchorage is through a narrow entrance in Billings Bay. Pass to starboard of the islet at the entrance. There is about four feet of water in this passage at a ten-foot tide at Atkinson Point, Burrard Inlet. Currents run strong, requiring entry at or near high water slack. Because of the constricted passage, slack water tends to occur about five minutes per foot of change later than the slack outside. There is anchorage in the northeastern portion of this mile-long basin. An uncharted drying rock is in the easternmost end of the cove. Aquaculture operations are along the western shore.

★ **Blind Bay:** Use Charts #3514, #3512 or Chartbook #3312. This bay lies between the northwest side of Nelson Island and the southeast side of Hardy Island. The deep entrance channel is bordered by islets on each side and a sharp lookout for reefs is advised. When winds are kicking up in Malaspina Strait, at the time of an ebb tide in Jervis Inlet, the seas can be rough in the entrance to Blind Bay. Aquaculture operations are prevalent in several areas, and booming grounds are located north of Fox Island and along the south shore of Hardy Island. Anchorage can be found in the indentations along the Hardy Island shore and in Ballet Bay, on the southeast shore of Blind Bay. A popular anchorage is behind Fox Island. Often crowded conditions, and a rocky bottom, call for shore ties.

★ **Ballet Bay:** Numerous islands shelter this bay, on the southeast shore of Blind Bay. Aquaculture operations are along some of the shoreline. Range markers assist navigation when approaching from the northeast. Recommended entry is from the west. You will be in the correct channel if you see a sign posted on an island to port saying "Clio Island." When approaching from the west, watch for uncharted rocks. There is good anchorage in the outer bay in 30 to 40 feet of water. There is more protected anchorage in the inner bay in 25-30 feet of water at high tide. Much of the bottom near shore is rock. Good holding mud has accumulated in the center of the bay. A path leads from Ballet Bay to Hidden Basin. It is said the bay was named by a ballerina who believed the water flow and motions to be similar to the flowing motions of the dance.

★ **Vanguard Bay:** This is a log booming center. Limited anchorage is north of the islets off the east shore. A rock, which is covered at high tide, lies behind the innermost islet.

★ **Hardy Island (11):** This island is part of the Marine Provincial Park System. Several niches along the Blind Bay shore offer good one or two boat anchorages close in and with a tie to shore. Log booms often provide tie-ups and are breakwaters sheltering some coves. A narrow fjord-like indention into Hardy Island, north of the wider bay, is deep enough for anchorage. For scuba divers, wall dives are made where Ball Point drops vertically to depths of 200 feet.

★ **Fox Island Anchorage:** There is a popular anchorage in the bay that is opposite Fox Island. The bottom tends to be rocky. Anchorage is best close in with a tie to shore to secure the hook and to make room for others.

★⚓ **Musket Island Marine Park:** The small island in Blind Bay, just off the south shore of Hardy Island, northwest of Fox Island, is now a provincial park. Good anchorage.

Telescope Passage (12): Picturesque, this narrow channel between the small islands off Hardy and Nelson Islands leads from Blind Bay to Jervis Inlet. A sprawling rock covered by a few feet of water at high tide, lies in this passage. The rock is near mid-channel and spreads out toward the Hardy Island side. Pass close to Nelson Island.

Jervis Inlet

[3311, 3312, 3512, 3514]

★ **Jervis Inlet (13):** High, rugged mountains rim this 46 mile inlet. Currents are weak, however dangerous rips occur at the mouth of the inlet when the wind is against the tide that is exiting the inlet. The summer wind pattern is up inlet winds during the day and light or down inlet winds at night. Winds are strongest during clear weather.

★ **Thunder Bay:** Thunder Bay, and adjacent Maude Bay near the mouth of Jervis Inlet, are two of the few anchorages available in Jervis Inlet. There is anchorage near the sandy beach tucked in behind the point. When entering, stay off the western shore to avoid an unmarked rock. Several summer homes dot the shore.

★⚓ **Saltery Bay & Saltery Bay Park:** Public floats are adjacent to the Saltery Bay-Earls Cove ferry landing. A ramp for the disabled and a garbage drop are provided. Boat launching is possible at Saltery Bay Park. There are many camp and picnic sites. This park is accessible from Highway 101 as well as by water. Underwater, scuba divers search for a nine foot bronze statue of a mermaid. At the turn-of-the century, a Japanese owned and operated fish saltery was near the vicinity of the ferry terminus. ▲⛵🚶

Walk-around: A relaxing walk on a well maintained trail around the park's eastern portion ends at Park Creek. Look for salal, hanging moss, 100 year-old stumps in the forest comprised of Douglas Fir and cedar. When you get to the rinse area for divers, take the path east and have a picnic at the tables.

St. Vincent Bay: This is a center of oyster culture operations. There is limited anchorage in the bays on both sides of Sykes Island.

Whiskey November (WN): The area between St. Vincent Bay, Captain Island, and the entrance to Hotham Sound is a Canadian Armed Forces National Defence military exercise zone for air to surface and torpedo firing. Buoys are present. Caution is advised if active operations are in evidence. Interestingly, the deepest "holes" on the Pacific Coast are within this area.

Hotham Sound

[3311, 3312, 3512, 3514]

★ **Hotham Sound (14):** This is a deep, six mile long sound surrounded by high mountains. There is temporary anchorage in a niche on the west shore. Temporary anchorage is possible in Granville Bay off flats where Lapan Creek enters. Friel Falls, a lovely, tiered waterfall cascades into the sound. The head of the sound has anchorage close to shore in Baker Bay and in the niche to the southeast.

★⚓ **Harmony Islands & Marine Park:** Long a favorite of boaters, please be aware that some of these islands are private and some are included in a provincial park. As with many marine parks, the boundaries between park and private lands are sometimes difficult to discern. According to the B.C. Provincial Park System description, "the park is situated on the east side of Hotham Island, north of Granville Bay and consists of the southernmost island." The two central islands are posted: "Private Island, No trespassing, No stern ties, No kayakers, No fires". Property owners in the vicinity have to struggle to protect their lands from public encroachment. The delicate relationship between the land owners and the thousands of visitors can be enhanced and "harmony" maintained in the Harmony Islands by a little care, thoughtfulness, and respect by all parties.

Anchorage is possible in all areas covered by saltwater, **except those areas leased for private buoys, aquaculture, and other purposes.** Anchoring may be difficult and take patience because much of the bottom is rock. **Shore ties allowed only to the two Marine Park Islands, not to private lands.**

Satisfactory anchorage is possible in the passage between the islands and the mainland shore. Be prepared for mosquitoes when taking a dinghy to the mainland or when anchoring close to shore. **Great care needs to be taken to avoid the danger of fires in the area.**

Prince of Wales Reach

[3311, 3312, 3514]

★ **Prince of Wales Reach (15):** Prince of Wales, Princess Royal Reach, and Queen's Reach form one long, about 30 mile, waterway leading to Princess Louisa Inlet. Because of great depths, anchorages are few.

★ **Egmont and Bathgate Marinas & Egmont Village:** See section on Sechelt Inlet.

Dark Cove: Anchorage is close to shore west of Sydney Island. Winds tend to enter the bay and the bottom is not dependable. Goliath Bay to the north is too deep for anchorage.

Killam Bay: There is a small sand beach and limited anchorage.

Vancouver Bay: The shoreline shoals and then drops off rapidly, thus limiting anchorage.

★ **McMurray Bay:** Limited anchorage is found here, also in the bight just north.

★ **Deserted Bay:** Anchorage is possible in this bay on Princess Royal Reach. A shelf on the southeast corner, marked "Indian Village Abandoned" on the chart, provides excellent bottom for anchorage. Parts of the shelf are very shallow at low tide.

Princess Louisa Inlet

[3311, 3312, 3514]

★ **Princess Louisa Inlet (16):** This beautiful inlet was named after the mother of Queen Victoria. The existing park at Chatterbox Falls was recently increased fifty-fold when 2,221 acres of pristine property surrounding the park was deeded to the Province of British Columbia by the Nature Conservancy of Canada and the Princess Louisa International Society. Plans to acquire the three district lots on the south shore are pending funding. New quarters for the Park Ranger are being constructed by BC Parks.

★ **Malibu Rapids:** Malibu is 32 miles from Egmont. No fuel is available after Egmont.

Currents in the rapids attain rates to nine knots at springs. Because of strong currents and overfalls, the rapids should be entered at or near slack water. High-water slack is preferable because of the added room for navigation in the narrow passage. When waiting for slack, waterfalls located a short distance up the Reach and on the same shoreline, provide diversion. Slack water calculations can be made using standard tide tables. Refer to the time of slack water at Atkinson Point, Burrard Inlet. Slack times vary with the height of the tide. Slack water occurs about 24 minutes after high water and 36 minutes after low water at Atkinson Point. Following a large tidal change the actual slack may be delayed several minutes while pent-up waters move through the rapids. Years of boating experience have proven that while the strip of white water is still visible, looking like a tread across the passage, it is not advisable to go through the rapids, even though one might be anxious to get a spot at the floats. The overfall is caused by the backing-up of water on one side of the narrow, shallow constriction. This results in a different level of water inside and outside the rapids. From the time of the appearance of the overfall until after it disappears, the rapids will be running at full force. Thus, entry is preferable after the slack occurs, as the tidal current actually changes direction, and before the next overfall, rather than just before the slack water. These principles apply during large tidal changes. Following a small change, only a slight current will be encountered a few minutes before and after the current reverses. The maximum rate of the current is nine knots. Because of limited visibility of boats entering at the other end of the rapids, use of VHF 16 to announce your approach is recommended.

The lodge, which is situated at the rapids, was built in the 1940's by a millionaire to be used as an exclusive retreat. It is now operated by a religious organization which uses it for a summer camp. Tours may be given. No overnight moorage.

★⚓ **Princess Louisa Provincial Marine Park:** Known to many as the *Eighth Wonder of the World*, this four mile valley with a boomerang-like curve to port near the head, rivals Yosemite Valley in California for its picturesque 5,000 to 8,000 foot mountain sides and its many seasonal cascading waterfalls. Chatterbox Falls roars at the head of the inlet. Visitors are asked to respect the calm stillness of this remote location and, in order to prevent wash, there is a speed limit of four knots. The park is staffed from May to mid-October.

Stern-tie mooring eyes have been placed in the land in a niche to port after entering from Malibu Rapids, on and opposite Macdonald Island. In places where the rock wall shoreline is very steep, two rings or "eyes", one above the other, have been placed to make them reachable at any tide. Check for empty mooring buoys located between Macdonald Island and the mainland. Good anchorage is possible, with depths to 60', in the channel near the island, using at least 200 feet of anchor rode. Another two and one-half miles into the inlet, floats provide moorage with a spectacular view and sounds of Chatterbox Falls. Maximum stay on the floats is 72 hours. Because of popularity, dock space may not be available. One strategy is to moor at MacDonald Island, or anchor in front of the falls and move to the floats when boats depart for the morning slack. There are shore-tie rings on the starboard shore, before reaching the float area. These rings are difficult to use as shore ties for anchorage, because of the depth of the adjacent waters. There are also rings to the left of the falls. Anchorage with stern ties to these rings is possible. Our favorite anchorage is found off the base of the 120 foot-high falls. Set the hook in the silt shallows, very close in, at the

foot of the falls (in five to ten feet of water). Put the boat in reverse at low throttle to set the anchor. The ledge drops quickly. Once the anchor catches properly, the current from the falls will keep a constant pull on the anchor and keep the boat facing the beautiful falls. A viewing platform with a bronze plaque and the ashes of "Mac" Macdonald, Father of the Inlet, are in a granite wall near the falls. Wildlife is abundant. Mountain goats maneuvering on the 3,000-foot cliffs opposite the floats are a sight to see. Trails, pit toilets, and a picnic shelter at the falls are available. Floats and facilities are provided and maintained by The Princess Louisa Society through memberships and donations.

Major fund raising efforts are underway to secure monies to purchase some, if not all, of the lands surrounding the inlet.⚲⚘

★ **Princess Louisa International Society:** The Princess Louisa International Society is a charitable society and can issue Canadian tax receipts for donations. Its companion Princess Louisa International Foundation is registered with the IRS as a 501(c) (3) charitable organization for US donors. Membership fees and donations contribute to the costs of maintaining these facilities and acquiring additional lands for the Park. Nearly 40 yacht clubs support the society. For information contact the Princess Louisa Society, PO Box 17279, Seattle, Washington 98127, or PO Box 33918, Station D, Vancouver, British Columbia   V6J   4L7.   Email: info@princesslouisa.bc.ca   Website: www.princesslouisa.bc.ca   Telephone: 604-737-8361 Fax: 604-737-8343.

Walk-around: The society reports that more and more hikers are climbing the blazed trail to the Trapper's Cabin. The trail is relatively safe, but the steep climb will take nearly two hours. The views of Princess Louisa Inlet, the upper reaches of Jervis Inlet, and of Mount Albert are memorable.

Sechelt Inlet

[3311, 3312, 3512]

★ **Sechelt Inlet (17):** This large, lovely inlet is actually an arm of Jervis Inlet. It has been called an Inland Sea. Here you will find the Skookumchuck Narrows. Skookumchuck, the Chinook word for "strong waters", aptly describes the turbulent whirlpools and rapid tidal currents, often reaching 14 knots, that ocurr at change of tide. The Skookumchuck Narrows and Sechelt Rapids form the first three miles of the inlet. Following this, the indentation stretches 16 miles and ends in Porpoise Bay. Narrows Inlet and Salmon Inlet branch toward the interior. Beginning in early morning, winds blow up Salmon and Narrows Inlets. Down inlet winds often come at night. Maximum tidal range within the inlet is ten feet. Undeveloped park lands and anchorages are available. Moorage and supplies are found at Egmont, Tillicum Bay, and Porpoise Bay. Gas and diesel are available at Egmont Marina and at Bathgate General Store and in Egmont Village. Gas is available at Midcoast Air in Porpoise Bay. Logging operations are prevalent and tugs are a frequent sight. There is a launching ramp at Four Mile Point and at Porpoise Bay. Undeveloped marine parks are at Halfway Islet, Skaiakos Point, Tuwanek Point, Nine Mile Point, and Piper Point.

★ **Egmont Marina:** {49° 48' N, 123° 56' W} Located to starboard in Sechelt Narrows, near Agamemnon Channel,. 900' of transient moorage with 115 and 220 volt, 15 and 30 ampere power.

Gas, diesel, stove oil, fresh drinking water, showers, laundry, RV Park, and launch ramp. Pub restaurant, provision store, retail liquor store, repairs, guide service, water taxi and emergency towing. Representative for C-Tow. New lodging. Currents can be strong at the fuel float. BoatUS Participating Marina. See our Steering Star description in this chapter. Internet Site: www.egmont-marina.com and www.boattravel.com/egmont. Address: Egmont, British Columbia V0N 1N0. Telephones: 604-883-2298, 800-626-0599. VHF 66A.

★ Egmont Village (17): Located at Secret Bay. Watch for the landmark Bathgate store building. Moorage floats, fuel, a liquor agency, post office, rental accommodations, and store. The reef in Secret Bay is not difficult to get around. There are

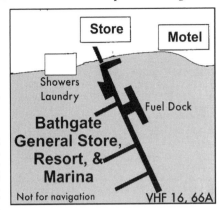

three markers in the bay. The center marker is labeled "Caution" and sits on the reef. Do not go between the two beacons. Remember "Red Right Returning." Keep the red day beacon well to starboard. If approaching the public floats, note that the reef also extends off the green day beacon toward the public floats. Egmont was named by Captain Richards after the H.M.S. Egmont which plied the waters around 1860.

★ Bathgate General Store, Resort, & Marina: {49° 48' N, 123° 56' W} Located on the Secret Bay hillside, this facility offers moorage, gas, diesel, power, water, excellent ice, laundry, showers, new motel. Groceries, fresh meat, dairy and bakery products, vegetables, liquor agency, charts, bait, repairs and water taxi. New lodging. See our Steering Star description in this chapter. E-mail: bathgate@lincsat.com. Internet: www.boattravel.com/bathgate. Address: 6781 Bathgate Road, Egmont, British Columbia V0N 1N0. Fax: 604-883-2750. Telephone: 604-883-2222. VHF 66A.

Sechelt Rapids (18): [3514, 3512] Use Volume 5 of the Canadian Tide and Current Tables. Under the heading of Sechelt Rapids are the turns, maximum times, and knots. Because there is no problem going through these narrows at slack water, plan to go through at time of turn. Proper planning is essential to avoid dangerous runs. At spring tides these rapids attain a rate of 15 knots. The preferred route is west of Boom Islet and Sechelt Isle Light. Give Roland Point a wide berth, especially on a flood tide. There can be a spectacular over fall of eight to ten feet. If mooring at Egmont Village and walking in to view the rapids, plan to do so at a maximum time and knots. - means ebb, + means flood.

Walk-around: The viewpoint at Skookumchuck Narrows Provincial Park is a three mile hike from

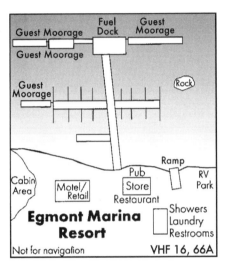

Egmont. The path, a quarter mile from the public floats, is marked by a sign. Along the trail there are information signs and restrooms. Visitors viewing from shore, can best see the incoming current from Rowland Point and the flow of the outgoing current can be spectacular when viewed from North Point. Surf kayakers riding the waves can often be seen. A unique variety of creatures have adapted to life in the raging water flow. Tapestries of dahlia anemones, giant barnacles, encrusting sponges, blue mussels and plumose anemones cling tightly to the rocks and can be seen by scuba divers during the short intervals between the incoming and outgoing currents. Within the inlet itself, a premiere diving site is the sunken naval vessel HMCS Chaudiere, a 365 foot destroyer given over to the diversity of sea life and to the divers who explore the artificial reef.

★ Narrows Inlet & Tzoozie Narrows (19): In this inlet are Storm Bay, Tzoozie Narrows, a

★ **Egmont Marina:** Located to starboard in Sechelt Narrows near Agamemnon Channel, Egmont Marina is a well-known stop and the last service center when cruising to Princess Louisa Inlet. It is also near beautiful Harmony Islands and Sechelt Inlet, the Inland Sea. The owners invite you to come to see the expansion and new services. In addition to moorage, other facilities include the *Backeddy Marine Pub*, liquor retail store, an RV park and campground, light housekeeping cabins, motel, and a provision store. When approaching the floats, head into the current and be aware that moderate to strong currents are constant in the vicinity. The dock attendant monitors VHF Channels 16 and 66A. Expanded floats with 900' of transient moorage, equipped with 115 volt, 15 and 30 ampere power, accommodate boats to 90'. Permanent moorage is available. Gas, diesel, stove oil, fresh drinking water, hose down water, showers, laundry, and launch ramp are accessible. Major renovations are being made to the pub and restaurant. The pub's Skookum Burger, said to be the largest burger on the B.C. coast, is a popular favorite. Other house specialties include fish and chips and fresh local prawns and oysters (in season). Open for breakfast, lunch, and dinner. The store stocks the goods most requested by boaters including ice, fresh dairy products, frozen foods, canned goods, drugstore items, housewares, clothing, and books. Fishing licenses, bait, tackle, charters, and guide service are available. Boat rentals, and a dive shop are on site. Tradesmen and divers are on call for repairs, including welding. Water taxi and emergency towing. Representative for C-Tow. By car, the resort is a two hour drive from the Langdale ferry landing on Highway 101. The RV Park and campground, located overlooking the scenic narrows, is equipped with RV hook-ups (AC only). Open all year, seven days a week. Summer hours 8:00 a.m.-8:00 p.m. Winter 9:00 a.m. to 5:00 p.m. **BoatUS Participating Marina. Internet Sites: www.boattravel.com/egmont & www.egmont-marina.com E-mail: info@egmont-marina.com Address: Egmont, British Columbia V0N 1N0. Telephone: 604-883-2298, 1-800-626-0599. VHF 16, 66A.**

marine park, a recreation preserve, coves for anchorage, the fishing grounds of the Tzoonie, and logging operations. Anchorage is good in Storm Bay, inside the islets east of Cowley Point or behind the point that extends into the middle of the bay. Currents run to four knots in Tzoonie Narrows. Park land is on both sides and there is a nice beach. The recreation reserve is another mile into the inlet.

★ **Salmon Inlet (20):** Power plants and logging operations are at the head. Avoid low hanging power lines. North of Kunechin Point, there is anchorage and park land. Anchor off the north-eastern shore near a log float. No fires are allowed at Kunechin Park. An artificial reef, created by the sinking of the Canadian destroyer, Chaudiere, attracts marine life (and scuba divers, as well!). An undeveloped park is at Thornhill Creek. North of Thornhill Point is scenic Misery Creek Falls. There is anchorage at the west end of Misery Bay.

★ **Porpoise Bay (21):** See Sechelt description near the beginning of this chapter. Close to the town of Sechelt, this bay has moorage and a launching ramp. There is limited anchorage west of Porpoise Island and off the wharf. Drying shoals, located about three miles from the head of Sechelt Inlet, are shallower than marked on the chart.

Harbour Authority of Sechelt Inlet: Moorage, 15 & 30 ampere power, water, pump-out, tidal grid. 604-885-8063.

MacKenzie Marina: Permanent moorage. 604-885-7851.

Poise Cove Marina: Limited moorage, power, launch. 604-885-2895. VHF 16, 70.

Royal Reach Motel: Moorage, limited power, water, pub, restaurant. 604-885-7844.

Tofino Air Services: Limited moorage, power, water, mid-grade gas, washrooms, repairs. 1-888-436-7776, 604-740-8889.

Walk-around: Porpoise Bay Provincial Park has a one-half mile sandy beach with campsites, showers, and good swimming. Walk along Angus Creek into the woodlands and forest. In the fall, spawning salmon can be seen in the creek.

Malaspina Strait

[3311, 3512, 3513]

McRae Cove (22): Although open to south winds, this cove is sheltered from the prevailing westerlies of the Malaspina Strait. Rocks and drying shoals are in the entrance. The head is a drying flat and the bottom is uneven with shallow spots. The Scotch Fir Point vicinity can be dangerous when strong westerly or southerly winds meet an opposing outgoing tide from Jervis Inlet.

Stillwater Bay (23): There is temporary protection from southeasterlies in this bay which lies about 2½ miles northwest of Scotch Fir Point. Booming operations occur frequently. The bay is open to the west. A conspicuous water tower can be used as a landmark.

Lang Bay (24): White sandy beaches line this open, shallow bay at the delta of the Lois River. There is a rock breakwater and often there are log booms. The old public wharf is used by large ships as a fueling station. Good swimming and a visit to the public park are fair weather recreations here.

Powell River

[3311, 3536]

Grief Point (25): {49° 48.3' N, 124° 31.5' W} This point lies two miles south of Powell River. It is marked by a light and homes fronting on the beach. A large rip rap breakwater, housing a marina, is south of the point. When there are wind warnings for this area, rough seas may be encounted off the point.

★ **Beach Gardens Motel & Marina:** {49° 48.3' N, 124° 31.5' W} Transient moorage, with 15, and 30 amp power and fresh water available. Gas & Diesel (in season), and lube oil, ice, showers, laundromat, pay garbage deposit and motel accommodations with new ocean view rooms. Liquor Store and Lounge. See our Steering Star description in this chapter. Websites: www.beachgardens.com & www.boattravel.com/beach. Address: 7074 Westminster Avenue, Powell River, British Columbia. V8A 1C5. E-mail to: beachgardens@shaw.ca. Telephones: Motel: 604-485-6267, 1-800-663-7070. Marina: 604-485-7734. Fax: 604-485-2343.

★ **Westview & Powell River (26):** The Powell River, for which the community is named, is only about one quarter mile in length, running from Powell Lake to the strait. The boat basins at Westview, a residential suburb adjacent to Powell River's Historic Townsite, are surrounded by a large rock breakwater which forms into two basins. This is also the terminus of the Powell River-Texada Island-Little River ferries. The northern basin is used primarily for permanent moorage. Transient pleasure craft utilize the moorage on city-owned floats in the southern basin. Moorage is on a first come first served

---

★ **Bathgate General Store, Resort, & Marina:** This is an old-time country general store and marina with fuel dock, laundromat, showers, and lodging, celebrating over 50-years at Secret Bay. The facility has established a reputation for cleanliness, an extremely well stocked store, and friendly service. A new waterfront motel, featuring a deluxe honeymoon/wheelchair accessible suite has been completed. A government float is adjacent, providing additional boat and float plane access. For directions regarding

entering Secret Bay, see description under Egmont Village in this chapter. Gas, diesel, oils, camp fuel, marine stove alcohol, and fresh water are available. Guest moorage, with 15 and 30 amp power, is limited. Reservations advised. The skipper will find an excellent selection of groceries, including prawns, fresh produce, meat, and dairy products, ice cream, bakery goods and liquor. Frozen bait, tackle, fishing licenses, boat rentals, batteries, gifts, books, marine charts, tide books, clear cube and block ice, movie rentals, public phones, internet connection, post office, and fax service are found. Propane cylinders filled. Marine ways to 40 tons. On-site mechanic. Water taxi service is available. When visiting, hike to Skookumchuck Provincial Park to view one of the world's fastest tidal rapids. Open year around, seven days a week, including liquor sales. Hours: 9:00 a.m.- 6:00 p.m. year round. This is a great provisioning stop before cruising to Harmony Islands and Princess Louisa Inlets and is the last fueling location for Sechelt Inlet. Family owned and operated by Doug and Vicky Martin. **Internet: www.bathgate.com & www.boattravel.com/bathgate E-mail: bathgate@lincsat.com Address: 6781 Bathgate Road, Egmont, British Columbia. V0N 1N0. Fax: 604-883-2750. Telephone: 604-883-2222. VHF 16, 66A.**

basis. Within walking distance of the public wharf are a grocery, pub, laundromat, marine supply store, restaurant, and several hardware, drug, and other retail stores. Three shopping malls are a taxi ride away. There is also a courtesy bus which makes scheduled runs Monday through Saturday to the Town Centre Mall where the Town Centre Hotel and a liquor store are located. The waterfront is currently being redeveloped with a sea walk now completed and additional shops opening in 2006.

Onshore diversions include guided tours of the paper mill, ice skating and swimming at the recreation convention center, golf at the Myrtle Point Golf Course. The Powell River vicinity is known as the hot spot for scuba diving. There are 19 dives in the immediate vicinity. These include the reefs of Vivian Island and Rebecca Rock and the sheer drop-off at the Iron Mines. Diving is excellent in the winter when the water is especially clear. Free, and very informative tours are available at the Catalyst Paper Mill in June, July and August. Paper was first produced here in 1912. In the off season the Mill Lookout provides a scenic view, photos and information. Wear good walking shoes. Powell River has a good city bus line. Its stops include the historic townsite, malls, the museum, pottery shops, and art galleries. Located at Willingdon Park, the Powell River Historical Museum's displays include Billy Goat Smith's cabin, the development of the pulp mill, ship and train replicas, native baskets and masks. Open year round.

There are an estimated 2,400 hours of annual sunshine in the Powell River area of the "Sunshine Coast," making outdoor activities and events, such as the *Canada Day Celebration* July 1, the *Seafair Festival* also in July, the *B.C. Day Celebration* the first weekend in August, the *Blackberry Festival* in late August, and the *Sunshine Folkfest* over Labour Day weekend which is popular with visitors. Kayaking, canoeing, hiking, mini-golf, diving, swimming, and visiting salmon hatcheries are also possible activities. The Farmers Market each Saturday and Sunday is a weekly treat. By road, the town of Powell River is about 80 miles north of Vancouver. Two ferry trips are required, so allow at least three to four hours travel time in order to coordinate ferry departure schedules. Daily bus and air service also connect Powell River with Vancouver. For additional information : Powell River Visitor Info Centre, 604-485-4701, 1-877-817-8669, www.discoverpowellriver.com.

Westview Harbour Master: Moorage, power, water, showers, garbage & oil deposit, credit card telephone. Free shuttle bus to Town Centre Mall in July and August. 604-485-5244. VHF 68.

Westview Fuel Dock: Gas, diesel, lube oils, water, ice. 604-485-2867. VHF 66A.

★ **Harwood Island (27):** This Island, part of the Sliammon Reservation's land, has rock and shoals rimming its shores. A small cove at the south end provides anchorage. Beautiful sandy beaches are noteworthy.

★ **Savary Island & Keefer Bay (28):** Known for beautiful beaches and Sand Golf, this island is noted for its resemblance to islands in the South Seas. There are private homes, a small public float, a B&B, and restaurant. The Royal Savary Hotel once thrived on this island. There is limited anchorage in Keefer Bay, inside Mace Point. This is a tricky anchorage because of drying sand beaches, which drop off quickly, poor holding sand bottom, and winds that enter through Manson Passage. Overnight anchorage is not recommended.

Lund

[3311, 3538]

★ **Lund (29):** This small village lies at the most northerly point of Hwy 101, the northernmost end of the Pan American Highway. Moorage, hotel, RV Park, fuel, store, bakery, restaurant, Post Office, Lund Auto & Outboard sales and repairs. Bus to Powell River. Water taxi service to Savary and Hernando Islands. The Thulin brothers built a hotel here in 1899 and named the site Lund after their Swedish home site.

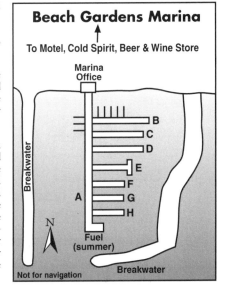

★ **Beach Gardens Motel & Marina:** This port-of-call is a favorite of many boating families. Breakwater-protected moorage is strategically located just south of the Grief Point Lighthouse south of Westview. This is approximately halfway between Jervis Inlet and Desolation Sound. Summer marina hours are dawn to dusk, seven days a week. The Wharfinger greets arrivals and assigns slips.

Transient moorage, with 15 and 30 amp power and fresh water, gas & diesel (in season), lube oil, ice, laundromat, as well as pay garbage deposit are available. Courtesy tie-ups for short visits. New ocean view motel rooms with a liquor store and lounge are nestled into the trees above the Marina and has a unsurpassed view of Malaspina Strait with the snowcapped peaks of Vancouver Island in the distance. Fishing and sightseeing charters on site. Marine repair service operates on call. A small grocery store is located nearby and free transportation to the mall (in season). A championship golf course welcomes out of town guests. **Circle #15 on Reader Service Card. Websites: www.beachgardens.com & www.boattravel.com/beach Address: 7074 Westminster Avenue, Powell River, British Columbia V8A 1C5. Email: beachgardens@shaw.ca. Fax: 604-485-2343. Telephone: 604-485-6267. Marina: 604-485-7734. Toll free reservations for both marina and motel: 1-800-663-7070.**

★ **Lund Auto & Outboard:** Service calls to Stuart Island, Savary Island, and Desolation Sound. Boat storage. Yanmar Diesels, MerCruiser Sterndrive sales and service. Smokercraft. See our advertisement in this chapter. Email: lundauto@lincsat.com Website: quicksilverparts.com Address: 1520 Lund Hwy, Lund, British Columbia V0N 2G0. Telephone: 604-483-4612, Fax: 604-483-9356. VHF 66A.

Lund Harbour Authority: Entry to the public boat basin can be made around either end of the breakwater. A can buoy marks a rock between the water taxi and the wharf. Moorage floats, power, water, expanded launch ramp, showers, washrooms. Additional moorage inside breakwater. No reservations. 604-483-4711. VHF 73.

★ **The Historic Lund Hotel:** Built in 1905, this beautifully restored hotel is located in the heart of Lund. View rooms offer modern amenities and unique custom touches like one-of-a-kind hand painted murals in every room. The hotel restaurant features westcoast and international cuisine, highlighting fresh, local seafood. The pub offers a delicious menu as well, with outdoor dining oportunities on the waterfront patio. Guests enjoy a wide array of onsite facilities and services including a hot tub, laundromat, bakery, conference meeting room, tour and activity packages, general and liquor store, ATM, Internet, postal station, and marina and fuel dock. See our advertisement in this chapter. Website: www.lundhotel.com. Email: info@lundhotel.com. Phone numbers: Hotel 604-414-0474, 1-877-569-3999. Restaurant 604-414-0479. Pub 604-414-0478. Store 604-414-0471.

Nancy's Bakery: Located near Lund Hotel. Breakfast served from 7am with lots of indoor seating. Cinnamon buns, etc., all baked fresh. Liquor license, live music & tapas on weekends. 604-483-4180.

★ **Finn Bay (30):** Located north of Lund, this bay has anchorage and protection from westerlies. A public float, not connected to shore, is in the bay. Floats for an aquaculture project are hazards.

★ **Jack's Boat Yard:** {49:59.112N 124:46.05W} Located in Finn Bay, just north of Lund, this haul-out, storage, and repair facility has a Travel Lift for all types of boats to 30 tons, 55 feet in length, 18 feet in width. Do-it-yourself Yard, propeller and shaft repairs, painting, zincs, and welding. Jack has excellent contacts for any other type of repair or renovation. Extensive boat storage available with power and water. Garbage deposit. Ask about long-term storage discounts, marine shelters, and computer services. A rental vehicle is available for clients. Request their brochure for rates and pictures. Owners Jack and Gerry Elsworth. Address: 9907 Finn Bay Road, Post Office Box 138, Lund, British Columbia V0N 2G0. E-mail: jack@twincomm.ca. Website: www.jacksboat-yard.com. Telephone: 604-483-3566. VHF 66A.

Thulin Passage: This narrow waterway separates the mainland and Copeland Islands. The courteous skipper will lower his speed and watch his wake for safety and to avoid causing havoc with other vessels. The fuel barge has been moved to the Lund facility.

Essential Supplies & Services

AIR TRANSPORTATION
To & from Washington
Seattle Seaplanes 1-800-637-5553
To & from Islands/Vancouver
Air Canada 1-888-247-2262
Baxter Air 1-800-661-5599
Harbour Air 1-800-665-0212
Tofino Air, Sechelt 604-740-8889, 1-888-436-7776
Vancouver Island Air 250-287-2433,
. . . . 877-331-2433 (B.C.)

AMBULANCES: 911

BOAT MOVING
All Tow Boat Moving . . . .
. . . . 604-946-7899, 1-877-946-7899

BOAT SEATS & UPHOLSTERY
Royal City Bedding 604-526-2641

BOOKS / BOOK STORES
The Marine Atlas. 541-593-6396

BUS TRANSPORTATION
Grayhound. 604-482-8747
Powell River 604-485-4287
Sechelt. 604-885-3234

COAST GUARD
Comox: VHF 16, 22-A, 26, 84 . . . . . 250-339-3613, #16
Emergencies. . . . . 1-800-567-5111, VHF 16

FERRY INFORMATION
. . . . 1-888-223-3779, 250-386-3431

FUELS
Bathgate General Store: Gas, Diesel.
. . . . 604-883-2222 VHF 16, 66A
Beach Gardens Motel & Marina: Gas, Diesel.
. . . . 604-485-7734
Buccaneer Marina: Secret Cove. Gas, Diesel.
. . . . 604-885-7888
Egmont Marina: Gas, Diesel.
. . . . 800-626-0599 VHF 16, 66A
Hyak Marine: Gibsons. Gas, Diesel. . . . . 604-886-9011.
John Henry's Marina: Gas, Diesel . . 604-883-2253
Lund: Gas, Diesel 604-414-0474
Secret Cove Marina: Gas, Diesel.
. . . . 604-885-3533 VHF 66A
Tofino Air, (mid-grade gas) Sechelt. . . . 604-740-8889
Westview: Gas, Diesel 604-485-2867

GOLF COURSES
(These courses are accessible from moorage and have rental clubs available)
Sechelt G&CC. 1-800-882-6177
Sunshine Coast 604-885-9212
Pender Harbour. 604-883-9541
Myrtle Point. 604-487-4653

GROCERY STORES
Bathgate General Store
. . . . 604-883-2222 VHF 16, 66A
Egmont Marina . . . . 1-800-626-0599 VHF 16, 66A
Madeira Park Marketplace IGA 604-883-9100
John Henry's Marina: 604-883-2253
Secret Cove Marina . . . . . 604-885-3533 VHF 66A
The Historic Lund Hotel 604-414-0471

HOSPITALS/CLINICS
Gibsons. 604-886-2870
Pender Harbour Clinic. 604-883-2764
Powell River 604-485-3211
Sechelt. 604-885-2224

INSURANCE
Boat Insurance Agency 206-285-1350
Or Call 1-800-828-2446

LIQUOR STORES
Bathgate General Store . . 604-883-2222 VHF 16, 66A
Egmont Marina . . . . 1-800-626-0599 VHF 16, 66A
Gibsons
Garden Bay
Halfmoon Bay
John Henry's Marina: 604-883-2253
Lund
Madeira Park
Powell River/Westview
Sechelt
Secret Cove Marina . . . . . 604-885-3533 VHF 66A

LODGING
Bathgate General Store: Egmont.
. . . . 604-883-2222 VHF 16, 66A
Beach Gardens Motel & Marina: Powell River.
. . . . 604-485-6267
Egmont Marina . . . . . . 800-626-0599 VHF 16, 66A
Fisherman's Resort & Marina, Pender Harbour.
. . . . 604-883-2336
The Historic Lund Hotel 604-414-0474
Rock Water Secret Cove Resort. . 1-877-296-4593,
. . . . 604-885-7038
Sunshine Coast Resort: Madeira Park. . . 604-883-9177

MARINAS / MOORAGE
Bathgate General Store
. . . . 604-883-2222 VHF 16, 66A
Beach Gardens Motel & Marina . . . 604-485-7734
Buccaneer Marina: Secret Cove. 604-885-7888
Coho Marina: Pender Harbour. 604-883-2248
Duncan Cove Marina: Pender Harbour . . 604-883-2424
Egmont Village

Egmont Marina . . . . . 800-626-0599 VHF 16, 66A
Finn Bay
Fisherman's Resort & Marina, Pender Harbour.
. . . . 604-883-2336
Garden Bay Restaurant, Pub, & Marina.
. . . . 604-883-9919
Gerrans Bay-Whiskey Slough Public Float.
. . . . 604-883-2234
Gibsons Landing Harbour Authority 604-886-8017
Gibsons Marina . . . . 604-886-8686 VHF 66A
Halfmoon Bay
Harbour Authority of Sechelt. 604-885-8063
Headwater Marina: Pender Harbour 604-883-2406
Hospital Bay: Pender Harbour
Irvine's Landing: Pender Harbour 604-883-1145
John Henry's Marina: Gas, Diesel . . 604-883-2253
Lund Harbour Authority. 604-483-4711
Lund Hotel Fuel Dock. 604-414-0474
Madeira Marina Ltd. 604-883-2266
Madeira Park: Harbour Authority of Pender Harbour.
. . . . 604-883-2234
Princess Louisa Marine Park
Saltery Bay
Savary Island
Secret Cove
Secret Cove Marina . . . . . 604-885-3533 VHF 66A
Sportsman Marina/Resort: Garden Bay. . 604-883-2479
Tofino Air, Sechelt 604-740-8889
Westview. 604-485-5244

PHARMACY
Marina Pharmacy: Madeira Park 604-883-2888

POISON INFO: 800-567-8911

PROPANE
Bathgate General Store: Egmont
. . . . 604-883-2222 VHF 16, 66A

Harmony Islands   Brian Watt, Canadian Hydrographic Photo

Essential Supplies & Services — Cont'd.

Buccaneer Marina: Secret Cove....... 604-885-7888
John Henry's Marina: Gas, Diesel . . 604-883-2253
Lund Hotel 604-414-0474
Vandercamp's: Westview............ 604-485-9774

RAMPS / HAUL-OUTS

Bathgate General Store, Resort, & Marina:
  Egmont. . . . . 604-883-2222 VHF 16, 66A
Buccaneer Marina: Secret Cove....... 604-885-7888
Coho Marina: Pender Harbour........ 604-883-2248
Egmont Marina. . . . . 800-626-0599 VHF 66A
Fisherman's Resort & Marina, Pender Harbour.
  . . . . 604-883-2336 VHF 66A
Four Mile Pt.: Sechelt Inlet
Gibsons
Halfmoon Bay
Hospital Bay, Pender Harbour
Hyak Marine: Gibsons 604-886-9011
Irvine's Landing: Pender Harbour 604-883-1145
Jack's Boat Yard: Finn Bay. 604-483-3566 VHF 66A
Lund Hotel 604-414-0474
Madeira Marina 604-883-2266
Porpoise Bay: Sechelt Inlet
Roberts Creek
Saltery Bay

RED TIDE INFO: 604-666-2828

REPAIRS

Bathgate General Store, Resort, & Marina:
  Egmont. . . . . 604-883-2222 VHF 16, 66A
Buccaneer Marina: Secret Cove....... 604-885-7888
Cole's Marine Diesel: Gibsons........ 604-886-2875
Jack's Boat Yard: Finn Bay. 604-483-3566 VHF 66A
John Henry's Marina: Pender Harbour . . 604-883-2253
Lund Auto & Outboard: Mobile
  . . . . 604-483-4612 VHF 66A
Madeira Marina: Pender Harbour. . . 604-883-2266
Tofino Air: Sechelt Inlet 1-888-436-7776

RESCUE COORD:

  . . . . 800-567-5111, Cell phone *16

RESORTS:

See Sportfishing & Resorts

RESTAURANTS / PUBS

Egmont Marina . . . . . . 800-626-0599 VHF 16, 66A
Garden Bay Restaurant, Pub, & Marina:
  Pender Harbour . . . . 604-883-9919 VHF 66A
Nancy's Bakery 604-483-4180
Rock Water Secret Cove Resort. . 1-877-296-4593,
  604-885-7038
The Historic Lund Hotel 604-414-0479

RV PARKS

Egmont Marina Resort . 800-626-0599 VHF 16, 66A
Headwater Marina 604-883-2406
Lund Auto & Outboard: Mobile.
  . . . . 604-483-4612 VHF 16
Lund 604-414-0474

SEWAGE DISPOSAL:

Gibson's Landing Harbour Authority.... 604-886-8017
Gibson's Marina 604-886-8686
Harbour Authority of Sechelt Inlet.
  . . . . 604-885-8063, 604-885-1986

SHELLFISH HOTLINE: 604-666-2828

SPORT FISHING INFO: 604-666-2828

Local Fisheries Canada Office--Powell River . . . .

. . . . 604-485-7963

SPORTFISHING & RESORTS

Bathgate General Store, Resort, & Marina:
  Egmont. 604-883-2222
Beach Gardens Motel & Marina . . . 604-485-6267
Egmont Marina: Egmont.
  . . . . 800-626-0599 VHF 16, 66A
Lord Im's Resort & Hotel 604-885-7038

STORAGE

Jack's Boat Yard: Finn Bay. 604-483-3566 VHF 66A
Lund Auto & Outboard 604-483-4612

TAXI SERVICE/RENTAL CARS

Egmont/Bathgate 604-883-2222
Egmont Water Taxi 604-883-2092
Gibsons 604-886-7337
Powell River 604-483-3666
Sechelt. 604-885-3666

TOWING

Bathgate General Store, Resort, & Marina:
  Egmont . . . . 604-883-2222 VHF 16, 66A
C-TOW. 1-888-354-5554

Egmont Marina: 604-883-2298 VHF 16, 66A
Pender Harbour Water Taxi 604-740-2486

VHF MARINE OPERATOR

Jervis Inlet: VHF 24
Nanaimo: VHF 87
Patrick Point: VHF 24
Pender Harbour: VHF 25
Powell River: VHF 85
Sechelt: VHF 86
Vancouver: VHF 23, 24, 25, 26, 86, 88
West Vancouver: VHF 85

VISITOR INFORMATION

Gibsons 604-886-2325
Pender Harbour 604-883-2561
Powell River 604-485-4701
Sechelt. 877-633-2963

WEATHER

Environment Canada Weather Line 250-339-9861
Comox: VHF WX-1. 250-339-0748
Sechelt. 604-885-4100
Vancouver: VHF WX-4, 21-B
Vancouver 604-664-9010

Princess Louisa Provincial Marine Park   *Jim Duncan Photo*

Sechelt Rapids, Skookumchuck Narrows

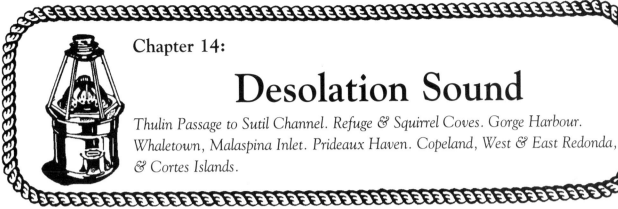

Chapter 14:

Desolation Sound

Thulin Passage to Sutil Channel. Refuge & Squirrel Coves. Gorge Harbour. Whaletown, Malaspina Inlet. Prideaux Haven. Copeland, West & East Redonda, & Cortes Islands.

Symbols

[   ]: Numbers between [   ] are chart numbers.

{   }: Numbers & letters between {   } are waypoints.

⚓: Park, ⛵: Boat Launch, ▲: Campgrounds, 🥾: Hiking Trails, ⛱: Picnic Area, 🚲: Biking

★ **Important Notice:** See "Important Notices" between Chapters 7 and 8 in this guide for specific information on boating related topics such as: Canadian & U.S. Customs, boating safety and security, navigation, weather, U.S. & Canadian Coast Guard, U.S & Canadian marine radio use, Vessel Traffic Service and traffic separation plans, security zones, and internet access. Due to new Department of Homeland Security regulations, call ahead for latest customs information and/or see Northwest Boat Travel On-line, www.nwboat.com.

★ **No Dump Zones: Carrington Bay, Cortes Bay, Gorge Harbour, Manson's Landing, Prideaux Haven, Roscoe Bay, Squirrel Cove.** Dump gray water only (shower and dish water).

Must have approved holding tank on board to enter No Dump Zone.

Thulin Passage

[3311, 3538]

Thulin Passage: This narrow waterway separates the mainland and Copeland Islands. The courteous skipper will lower his speed and watch his wake for safety and to avoid causing havoc with other vessels. The fuel barge has been moved to Lund.

★⚓ **Copeland Islands Marine Park (1):** Known locally as the Ragged Islands, a prominent marine park sign welcomes visitors to this collection of small islands. Four larger islands and islets make up the undeveloped marine park. Although there are several indents and bights, protection is limited because of boat wash from Thulin Passage and west side exposure to the Strait of Georgia. A popular anchorage is on the Thulin Passage side about halfway through the passage. Anchorage on the rock bottom is tricky. If the anchor will not hold in the center of the bay, try it close to the shore. Another small bay, with anchoring possibilities, is between two of the northern islets. Another anchorage is in a southerly notch on the west side of the 87 meter island.

Desolation Sound

[3312, 3538, 3541, 3555]

★ **Desolation Sound:** The name alone has intrigued boaters for many years, and once they round Sarah Point and see Mt. Denman in the distance, what Captain George Vancouver described as desolate in 1792, is wide open for interpretation today. Still desolate in terms of development, most boaters experience a feeling of awe when entering this sound. A time period of several days is recommended for exploring the variety of bays and facilities in the Desolation Sound vicinity. Anchorages, fuel, moorages, groceries, liquor, and other provisions are available. During the peak season from July 1 through August, many anchorages and moorage floats become crowded. Reservations at marina facilities are essential. The lush scenery, warm bays for swimming, tasty shellfish, and bountiful catches of sport salmon, combine to make this one of the top conversation spots for both Canadians and Americans. There is fishing along Mary Point, the shore of Cortes, off Sarah Point past Zephine Head, in Roscoe Bay and in Homfray Channel. Eagles often sit in the trees to watch for fish to eat. Thus, locations with eagles in the trees may be good fishing grounds. The flood streams from north and south meet near Squirrel Cove. Currents from Johnstone Strait meet those from the Strait of Juan de Fuca and Georgia Strait. There is little current, but the area is affected by winds.

★⚓ **Desolation Sound Marine Park:** This is one of the largest and most visited parks in the British Columbia Marine Park system. It includes much of Gifford Peninsula, Grace Harbour, Tenedos Bay, Prideaux Haven, Copeland Islands, and Squirrel Cove. However, as with most marine parks, the boundaries between park and private lands are sometimes difficult to discern. Property owners in the vicinity have a struggle to protect their lands from public encroachment. Many private lands are posted. The delicate relationship between the owners of these parcels and the thousands of visitors can be enhanced by a little care,

Cassel Falls, Teakerne Arm Marine Park   *Howard Eskildsen Photo*

Chart List

Canadian Hydrographic Charts:

3311, 3312, 3538, 3541, 3555, 3559

Marine Atlas (2005 ed.):

Page 29-32, 34

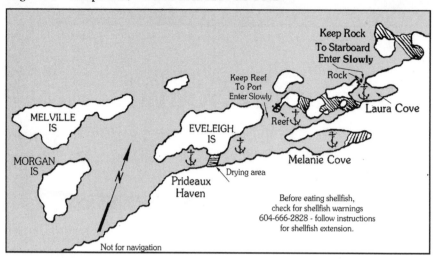

MELVILLE IS

MORGAN IS

EVELEIGH IS

Prideaux Haven

Drying area

Keep Reef
To Port
Enter Slowly

Reef

Keep Rock
To Starboard
Enter Slowly

Rock

Laura Cove

Melanie Cove

Before eating shellfish,
check for shellfish warnings
604-666-2828 - follow instructions
for shellfish extension.

Not for navigation

thoughtfulness, and respect by all parties concerned. Anchorages (on the water side) are all open to the public, since all areas covered by saltwater are public. However, the government has leased certain areas for private buoys, aquaculture, or other purposes. In regard to the shore side, if not sure, it would be well to attempt to ascertain the proper status and, if privately owned, to obtain permission for tying to shore or other planned usage, or to avoid trespassing. Whether on public or private lands, great care must be taken to avoid the danger of fires. ▲⚓

★ Sarah Point (2): This is a popular salmon fishing area. If trolling close in along the shore to Myrmidon Point, avoid Stacey Rock, which is covered at high tide.

Malaspina Inlet

[3312, 3538, 3559]

★ Malaspina Inlet (3): Several good anchorages, places to explore, and delicious shellfish delights are found in this lovely and extensive inlet. Much of the inlet is now part of Desolation Sound Marine Park, however, many of the oyster beds are private. Although there are rocks and shoal areas, large kelp beds often mark their location during summer months. Tidal streams in the entrance reach four knots. The entrance channel is not difficult to chart and navigate. The water is warm, shellfish are harvested, and jellyfish can be a nuisance.

★ Parker Harbour: Two anchorages are in Parker Harbour. One is tucked behind Beulah Island and the other is at the south end behind Thorp Island. Enter north of drying reefs, north of Thorp Island. Give the island a wide berth to avoid shoals. Aquaculture operations are marked by buoys.

★ Cochrane Islands: A drying ledge connects these two islands. Watch for rocks. There are anchorages behind the islands. Aquaculture operations are along the shoreline.

★ Grace Harbour (4): This large bay is a popular anchorage. The first anchorage is in a bight at Kakaekae Point just before entering Grace Harbour. When passing Jean Island, a Desolation Sound Park sign welcomes boaters. An area behind Jean Island also has anchorage. Shoals are visible. Farther into the entrance, the bay opens into a heart-shaped basin. Anchorage is good both near shore or in the center. Dinghies can be beached at the site of a park information board which illustrates the surroundings. A trail leads to

a lake where swimming is possible. The water is quite brown and marshy with several beaver dams. There are many loons in the area.

Trevenen Bay: This bay is formed between the Coode Peninsula and Malaspina Peninsula. Aquaculture operations marked by large buoys tend to block the bay. If possible to enter, there is anchorage and shelter in southeasterly winds. Log booms may be in the bay.

★ Okeover Inlet (5): Along the western shore are public floats, provincial park. There is a natural launching ramp next to the public floats. Okeover Arm Provincial Park, north of the wharf, has picnic and camping sites. Anchorage is possible in Penrose Bay and also at Freke Anchorage, near the head of the inlet. The latter offers protection in southeast winds. A rockfill causeway, ramp, float, and buildings about one mile north of the public wharf at Freke Anchorage are the property of an Indian seafood company. A water pipeline runs across Freke Anchorage from the plant. The warm, sheltered waters in this area make this a prolific place for marine life. Much of the area is leased as oyster beds. Scuba divers know the secrets of submarine cave formations found in Okeover Inlet.

★ Penrose Bay: This bay is open to the south. There is anchorage at the head of the bay. Oyster beds are privately owned.

Okeover Arm Marina: Closed indefinitely.

Okeover Harbour Authority: 400' of moorage, most of which is used by oyster farming boats. Power, no water, pay phone on the wharf head. Boat launching is a simple task, though boats over 24 feet may find the access restrictive. Covered outdoor dining. 604-483-9775.

★ Lancelot Inlet (6): Anchorage is possible in Isabel Bay, Thors Cove, Wooton Bay, and behind Susan Islets. Enter the inlet between Edith Island and Hillingdon Point. There is much aquaculture in this inlet.

★ Isabel Bay: Isabel Bay is entered from Lancelot Inlet. Pass between Polly Island and Madge Island. A drying rock lies about 100 yards northeast of Polly Island, and drying ledges extend north and northeast from Madge Island. Despite the fact that aquaculture operations are in the bay, anchorage can be found. West of Madge Island, anchors have fouled on a section of sunken bull dozer track lying at the location marked "4.2m" depth on the large scale chart. The other section of track can be seen high and dry on the nearby rock.

★ Thors Cove (7): There is anchorage at the south end of the bay behind the small islet. Enter from the north to avoid hazards. At certain times of the year, the intensity of the green on the surrounding hills and shores of this cove is like something out of a picture book. Aquaculture operations are along some of the shoreline.

★ Theodosia Inlet (8): [3559]. The narrow entrance channel has depths of six feet even at low water. Stay in center channel. The head of Theodosia Inlet dries and is used for log storage. Good anchorage is possible in several places on a sticky mud bottom. A favorite spot is behind the islet to port on entering the inlet. Outside the inlet, anchorage is possible near Grail Point behind Susan Islet. An old orchard is a landmark.

★ Susan Islets Anchorage: When entering Theodosia Inlet, the Susan Islets will be to port. Good anchorage is found. Locate the rock which dries and a shoal north of the islets before setting the anchor.

★ Wooten Bay (9): Located near the head of Lancelot Inlet, anchorage is open to south and southeast winds, but offers some protection from

Prideaux Haven   Brian Watt, Canadian Hydrographic Photo

westerlies. Property at nearby Portage Cove is posted as private and is not included in Desolation Sound Marine Park.

★ **Galley Bay (10):** Good anchorage is found, however this harbor is open to the north. Two large drying rocks are shown on charts. The one near the center dries three feet and the one farther in dries 15 feet. Anchorage is possible in the western area and behind the drying shoals and islet in the eastern portion in 30-35 feet of water. Private ramps with floats extend from shore. A stern tie to shore is recommended. Once the site of a commune.

★ **Mink Island (11):** This island is private property, but there is a favorite anchorage on its southeastern side. The outer area of the bay is open to east winds. There is more protected anchorage farther in where the bay turns to the north. Depths are 10-20 feet. A drying lagoon is at the head.

Curme Islands: This cluster of islands stretches along the north-northeast shore of Mink Island. Anchorage, in settled weather, is possible in the passage between the two largest islands in the northernmost group of three islands. The channel is shallow and narrow in spots.

★ **Tenedos Bay (12):** A rock off Bold Head hides its ugly head and has caught many unwary boaters entering or leaving Tenedos Bay. Depths range 200-350 feet in the center. There are coves and niches suitable for anchorage. High, steep cliffs surround the bay. When entering, favor mid channel, aiming straight ahead to the niche that is marked with a 40 on Chart #3312 metric. When adequately past the rock that is to port, turn to port and find anchorage behind the two small, bare islets in the south corner of Tenedos. Farther in on that side is an island that is connected to shore by a drying ledge. Many boaters choose to anchor behind the island in a narrow channel between the island and the mainland. The bottom is mostly rock and quite fickle. A stern line to shore can provide additional room for others, as well as keeping the anchored boat from turning and pulling the anchor out from under the rock where it may be lodged. When a westerly wind arises, it whistles through this area. Unmarked rocks extend from this island in several places. A more popular anchorage is in the area where a stream flows down the bank from nearby Unwin Lake. Anchorage with stern ties to shore is required. Fresh water swims in the lake are popular on hot summer days.

★ **Otter Island (13):** A navigable, very narrow, passage separates Otter Island from the mainland. There is a tiny bight in this passage which provides anchoring room for one or two boats. Sky Pilot Rock, one of the most dangerous hazards in the area, lies north of Otter Island. It waits menacingly out in mid-channel only a few feet under water at high tide. To avoid the rock, favor the Otter Island shore when traveling to and from Prideaux Haven.

★ **Eveleigh Island Anchorage:** [3555] Anchorage is possible in 40 feet on the southeast side of Eveleigh Island.

Prideaux Haven

[3312, 3538, 3555]

★ **Prideaux Haven (14):** No dump zone. This is the most popular spot in Desolation Sound. Prideaux Haven consists of several sheltered harbors. When approaching, avoid the shelf about 100 yards south of Lucy Point and the three-foot drying rock close to Lucy Point on Eveleigh Island. Approach the narrow entry from the passage between Eveleigh Island and Scobell Island. Kelp may be encountered off the Eveleigh Island shore, but this side, or preferably a mid channel course, is necessary to avoid Oriel Rocks. In the narrow entrance, the white areas that show through the green clear water at some tides are shoals and rocky extensions of the shore. Fires are not permitted on shore. Majestic mountain peaks rise to heights of 4,590 feet. The tidal range is one of the largest in the area. A change of as much as 18 feet on a large tide is not uncommon. Use depth sounder and Chart #3555 or Chart #3312 metric, page 11. Once inside Prideaux Haven, anchorage is possible in the south part, in the center, in the larger bay east of William Islands, and in the approach to the indentation that separates Copplestone Island from the mainland.

★ **Melanie Cove:** This is an extremely popular, often crowded anchorage. There may be room for a few boats to swing at anchor in the center, however, most boaters anchor, back off toward shore, and tie a shore line. The land surrounding Melanie Cove is deeded to the University of British Columbia. A small stream of fresh water empties into the bay near the head of Melanie Cove. On a quiet evening the sound of the bubbling brook may be heard. A hike of about 1/2 mile from the head of Melanie Cove will lead to Laura Cove. A trail follows an old logging road and a stream, and leads around old fallen trees, through soggy patches, through a patch of cedar and hemlock seedlings, across a rotting cedar log that bridges the creek, through a field of huge ferns, among rows of alders, and finally through a patch of ivy to the old cabin at the head of Laura Cove.

★ **Laura Cove:** Enter Laura Cove at half tide or better. Do not go west of the charted rock because the passage is blocked from the rock to Copplestone Island. Correct passage is between the rock and Copplestone Point. Shoals also extend from Copplestone Point, making this a narrow entry passage. At peak times during the summer season it is necessary to anchor and tie a stern line to shore to avoid swinging. The land at the head of Laura Cove is an ecological reserve.

★ **Roffey Island:** Drying ledges extend from this island and from the opposite shore on the mainland. A settled weather anchorage can be found behind Roffey Island. The passage behind the island has one particular shoal which stretches nearly across from the island to the mainland. Anchorage is possible both north and south of this shoal. Do not attempt to anchor here unless a detailed chart is used and the captain takes a good cruise around the anchorage with the help of the depth sounder. Two rocks are also hazards.

★ **Homfray Channel:** This channel extends 12 miles from Horace Head on the south end of East Redonda Island to Hepburn Point on the north end of the same island. Unless the clouds are too low and obscuring the mountains, this is some of the best scenery on the south coast of British Columbia. Red snapper fishing is often excellent in Homfray Channel. For the description of the northern region of Homfray Channel and the extension of Toba Inlet, see chapter 16.

★ **Forbes Bay (15):** This wide bay off Homfray Channel is open to the northwest. Temporary anchorage is possible close in near the head.

Attwood Bay (16): Swimming is good in the small bight at the extreme head of this bay. The bay is deep and is too open to southerly winds for good anchorage.

East Redonda Island

[3312, 3541, 3555]

★ **Pendrell Sound (17):** This six mile indentation into East Redonda Island nearly splits the island in two. High mountains surround the sound. Water temperatures are uncommonly warm, as high as 78 degrees in the summer. Wind patterns vary in different locations. West winds in summer may be strong near the head of the sound. This is one of the largest oyster producing regions in Canada. Posted signs indicate oyster preserves and restrict speeds to four knots to protect oyster spat collecting and propagating equipment. The spat is especially vulnerable to disturbances in July and August. Anchorage is possible near the north end behind the islets, in a niche at the northwest point at the entrance, and on the western shore between the island and shore in the bay in front of the lagoon.

West Redonda Island

[3312, 3541, 3555]

Waddington Channel: This waterway separates East and West Redonda Islands and connects Desolation Sound with Pryce Channel. Currents are negligible. Floods north. Anchorage is found in Roscoe Bay, behind the unnamed island north of Church Point (often called Oyster Island), and in Walsh Cove.

★⚓ **Roscoe Bay Marine Park (18):** No dump zone. Use Chart #3312 metric. North of Marylebone Point, Roscoe Bay indents into West Redonda Island. This very protected inlet is the site of a marine park. There is a drying shoal across the entrance, and entry just before or at high water slack is necessary. Plan to stay until the next high tide. Black Lake is within walking distance. For best fishing, carry a light-weight dinghy and fish out in the lake. Swimming is good. Water from a small spring drizzles down the rocks, creating a refreshing waterfall sound on a quiet evening. ⚓⚲

Squirrel Cove, Cortes Island   Brian Watt, Canadian Hydrographic Photo

★ **Oyster Island (19):** This small island is unnamed on the charts. Because of the many oysters in the vicinity, it is named Oyster Island by those who frequent the area. Also known as Alfred Island, Elworthy Island, and, most recently, as Cougar Island, this island is north of Church Point. There is good holding ground for anchoring in the passage between the island and West Redonda Island. Enter either side of the island. If approaching from, or exiting to, the north, favor the Oyster Island shore. A rock is in the bay on the north side of the island. There are 20 foot depths in the southern end of the passage and 40 foot depths in the northern end of the passage. Aquaculture operations affect anchoring sites.

★ **Allies Island (20):** Only a short distance north of Oyster Island is Allies Island. There is limited anchorage on the south side in a small indentation. This is open to winds from the southeast. A far better harbor is on the northwest side. Aquaculture operations may be along the shore. There are rocks to port. Maintain a mid-channel course when entering. The bay is deep in the center (110 feet). Anchorage may be obtained close to the Allies Island side by snuggling near the steep rock shore. Venturing north a mile or so from Allies, one will find good anchorage in the shelter of an appendix of land extending from West Redonda Island. A tie ashore is a must.

★ **Doctor Bay (21):** A salmon aquaculture farm may occupy nearly all of the bay. Efforts are being made by the Council of B.C. Yacht Clubs to re-open the bay to pleasure craft. The inlet is open to winds from the southwest but is very protected by the massive hills from any disturbance from the northwest. Some foul ground is near the island on the port side when entering. Anchorage area is very limited and may be closed.

★⚓ **Walsh Cove Marine Park (22):** This cove is about one mile from the junction of Waddington and Pryce Channels. Enter from the south and not through False Passage between West Redonda and the Gorges Islands. Look for seven pictographs of red ocher in the granite cliff. This Salish ancient burial site is a marine

park. There are several nooks and crannies along the West Redonda shore on the port side when entering. There is good anchorage in the center of the bay if prepared to anchor in 15 fathoms. Anchorage is complicated by the rocky bottom in most of the cove. The first anchorage is an arrowhead-shaped indentation. Five or six boats could tie ashore and raft up with little difficulty. A second bight on the port offers good anchorage. Shoals are easily visible. An uncharted rock has been reported at the entrance to the nook west of Butler Point. The Gorges Islands might well be named the Gorgeous Islands as the rock formations and stately evergreens cast a spell and intrigue the visitor into exploration by dinghy. ⚲

★ **Redonda Bay (23):** Settled weather anchorage only because it is exposed to the west and north. The bottom is rock. The old public wharf and float are beyond use. This bay was once a center for logging operations and the site of a busy cannery and a store. Today the bay is deserted, with the possible exception of a small forestry camp. Ruined pilings extend from shore over shoal areas. Rocks in the bay are shown on charts.

★⚓ **Teakerne Arm Marine Park (24):** A dinghy float is found at the site of the marine park. Anchoring is difficult in unsettled weather conditions, and is not recommended in this arm because of exposure to northwest winds and the difficulty of securing a proper anchorage. There are often log booms in Teakerne Arm and boom ties may be possible. A lovely waterfall cascades down the bluff from Cassel Lake. There is deep anchorage in the second hollow west of the falls. Look for oysters on the vertical rock faces. Activities might include a walk and refreshing swim in the lake. While his men fought battles with insects and took showers in the falls, Captain Vancouver became depressed with the excessive rain and named the area Desolation. ⚲

★ **Refuge Cove (25):** {50° 07' N, 124° 51' W} On the east side of the cove are more than 1,000 feet of public floats with moorage, fuel, water, and access to Refuge Cove Store. Seaplanes make scheduled stops and this refuge is a popular rendezvous and provisioning location during summer months. An island lies in the center of the cove. A year round aquaculture operation is anchored alongside the island at the northwestern entrance to the cove, and a summer garbage scow is anchored by the island at the southeastern entrance to the cove. You will find your welcome much more friendly if you slow down well before entering the cove. Wakes from approaching boats can play havoc with boats moored at public floats as well as the private floats around the cove shoreline. If the floats are full, usually during the mid-day period, it is safe to anchor out anywhere in the cove. Before 1930 there were over 200 residents here. At that time, logging, fur farming, and agriculture were the major economic pursuits.

★ **Refuge Cove Store:** When entering Refuge Cove, look for the hillside store, with floats and fuel dock. This popular stop is the main provi-

sioning center for the entire area. See our Steering Star description in this chapter. Websites: www.refugecove.com www.boattravel.com/refuge. E-mail: crobert@oberon.ark.com Mailing Address: Refuge Cove, British Columbia V0P 1P0. Telephones: Store: 250-935-6659. Residence: Telephone & Fax: 250-935-6549.

Cortes Island Vicinity
[3312, 3538, 3555]

★ **Squirrel Cove (26):** No dump zone. The Indian church and public wharf are landmarks when locating the entrance to Squirrel Cove. When approaching, avoid the long string of rocks off Boulder Point. These are now marked by a beacon. Squirrel Cove often contains more anchored craft than any other harbor in Desolation Sound. Several fingers offer good anchorage. Some of these have mud bottoms. Others are rocky, requiring care in anchoring and a tie to shore for stability. This prevents swinging and provides room for additional boats. Sunken logs and cables can foul anchors. In the northeast corner, drying rapids lead to a saltwater lagoon.

Squirrel Cove Public Float: New launch ramp. At high water a small day-use dock is available. Larger boats should anchor out and take the dinghy to the float. Moorage, showers, laundry, garbage drop, telephone, no water.

Squirrel Cove Store: High water dock, boat launch, hand carried gas, diesel, propane, provisions, marine supplies, liquor, postage, showers & laundry. Open 7 days. 250-935-6327. Restaurant with large patio seating. 250-935-6350.

Walk-arounds: After anchoring in the inner bays of Squirrel Cove, dinghy to the logging skids near the cove entrance. A logging road here joins with the main island road. Turn left and walk about one and one half miles to the store. A second hike is on a trail that connects Squirrel Cove with Von Donop Inlet. The beginning of this trail is on the beach farther in from the cove entrance. Dinghy to the first indentation that shows a wreck (not the wreck by the public wharf) on chart 3538. The hike on the trail takes about 20 minutes.

Seaford: No facilities. To the south, a private float is near Mary Point. There is anchorage in the niche on the north side of Mary Point.

★ **Robertson Cove (27):** This unnamed bay lies at the outlet to Robertson Lake just north of Von Donop Inlet. Robertson Lake, about ¼-mile away, is a good swimming spot, as well as a place for trout fishing. A painted rock marks the start of the trail. The bottom of the bay is not dependable for holding.

★⚓ **Von Donop Inlet & Provincial Marine Park/Hathayim (28):** The inlet and surrounding lands which comprise this park are part of the traditional territory of Klahoose First Nation who knew it as Hathayim. Some private land remains at the south end and north of the lagoon. There is good anchorage and protection from winds in this three-mile-long, narrow inlet. A large rock marked by kelp at low water is in the center of the narrows. Pass either side, but the starboard (west) side upon entry is recommended. The first anchorage is to port in a bight near the outlet of a lagoon. Rocks restrict the lagoon entrance and currents are encountered from the water flowing to or from this lagoon. At low water, there is as much as a six foot overfall.

★ **Refuge Cove Store:** When in the Desolation Sound vicinity, join your friends at this popular provisioning and fueling centre. Moorage and power are available, along with unlimited water. Water faucets installed on the floats enable boaters to take on water while moored thus enabling the fuel float to operate more efficiently. Gas, diesel and lube oils are available at the fuel float, whilst propane is dispensed midway

to the airplane dock. An ample supply of block and party ice is available at the store. Real ice. Open from June through September, the store is known for its friendly service and great variety of attractions including fresh vegetables; deli meats and cheeses; dairy products; a large inventory of canned and packaged goods; fresh cut steaks and frozen meats; charts; fishing tackle; fishing licenses; housewares and hardware; marine batteries; and post office. Ice cream cones are scooped during July/August. The liquor agency offers a good cross section of wine listings and the adjacent book section carries a large selection of local interest titles, pocketbooks, magazines, t-shirts and hats. The laundromat; a hamburger

stand and a coffee shop are adjacent to the store. A garbage service is located on a barge anchored off the Centel Island as you approach Refuge Cove. Interac, Visa and Mastercard accepted. Store hours are 9:00 a.m.-5:00 p.m. in June and September and 9:00 a.m.- 6:00 p.m. in July and August. **Email to:** **crobert@oberon.ark.com Websites: www.refugecove.com & www.boattravel.com/refuge Mailing address: Refuge Cove, British Columbia V0P 1P0. Telephone: 250-935-6659.**

Gorge Harbour   *Brian Watt, Canadian Hydrographic Photo*

Farther into the inlet two indentations in the western shore are anchorage possibilities. The most popular overnight anchorages are near the head. A favorite is behind the point which is to port as one turns into the final nook. There is excellent holding bottom of thick, sticky mud in this bay. Depths are 25-30 feet at high water. A rock, which dries at nine feet, is off the eastern shore, almost on a line across the entrance to the bay, opposite the point. Two picnic areas are located on the adjoining peninsula. Another anchorage is in the wide area near the head of the bay. ⛺🏕

Walk-around: A trailhead is on the southeast side of the bay where the 4-6' depths show on chart 3535. Look for an outhouse that marks the trail to Squirrel Cove. In season, you can enjoy the huckleberries on the way. Robertson and Wiley Lakes, which may be reached by rough trail, are popular for swimming and fishing.

★ **Quartz Bay (29):** Excellent anchorage is available in 30-40 feet of water in the inner harbor. Aquaculture operations are present as are private homes.

★ **Carrington Bay (30):** No dump zone. The lagoon at the head may be visited at high tide by portaging a dinghy over the entrance. Currents, caused by the force of the water entering and draining from the lagoon, must be considered when anchoring. Bottom is rock. Several boats were observed dragging anchor in westerly winds. A recreation area includes 130 acres.

★ **Coulter Bay (31):** Good anchorage is possible with fair protection from westerlies. Tuck in close to Coulter Island. Before anchoring, watch for signs indicating a private water line.

★ **Subtle Islands (32):** These two are connected by a sand and gravel ledge. The northern larger island has a bay for anchorage. The bottom shoals gradually from 60 feet in the middle to 25 feet and then to a shallow ledge fringing the rocky shore. Huge bleached tree stumps are on the beach. There is protection from the south. It is exposed to northwest winds. A sandy, small gravel beach on the Plunger Passage shore has anchorage off the beach in 20-30 feet of water.

★ **Whaletown (33):** This is the terminus of the Cortes-Quadra Island ferry. A public float has a capacity of eight to ten boats. When entering, keep the green-banded white towers on the rocks to port and the red spar Q-10 buoy to starboard. The buoy is on a rock. Shoals extend from shore near the float. Provisions are available. No fuel.

Whaletown Store: Post office, groceries, propane, telephone, library (Fridays). 250-935-6562.

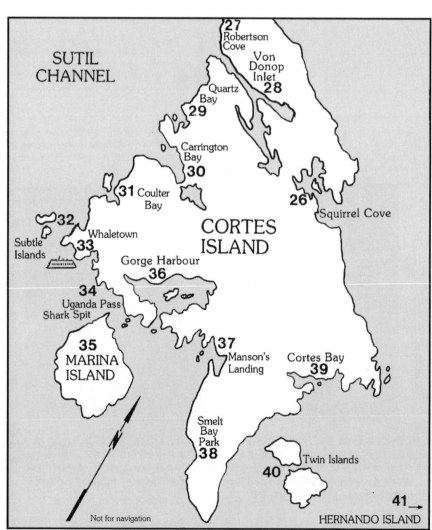

SUTIL
CHANNEL

27
Robertson
Cove

Von
Donop
Inlet
28

Quartz
Bay
29

Carrington
Bay
30

31 Coulter
Bay

32

Subtle
Islands

Whaletown
33

Gorge Harbour
36

34
Uganda Pass
Shark Spit

35
MARINA
ISLAND

26

Squirrel Cove

CORTES
ISLAND

37

Manson's
Landing

Cortes Bay
39

Smelt
Bay
Park
38

Twin Islands
40

41

Not for navigation   HERNANDO ISLAND

Pendrell Sound   Brian Watt, Canadian Hydrographic Photo

★ **Uganda Passage (34):** This well-marked passage between Marina Island and Cortes is not difficult to navigate. Consult tide chart and sounder. When west bound, keep green Q-11 and Q-13 markers to port at the tip of the spit. Green markers are small and may be difficult to see. The red buoy and light are to starboard. Stay inside the channel marked by buoys. The markers are on rocky areas. Temporary anchorage is possible inside Shark Spit. Currents in the passage run two to three knots, flooding north, ebbing south.

★ **Marina Island & Shark Spit (35):** A dangerous reef, studded with boulders, extends a mile from the south end of the island. A red buoy marks the end of the reef. Shark Spit has a good beach and anchorage. Contrary to the name, there are no marinas on this island. The island was named for Marina, Hernando Cortes' mistress who, in 1519, acted as interpreter for the Spaniards when they attacked Mexico.

★ **Gorge Harbour (36):** No dump zone. The gorge that forms the entrance to the harbor is a half mile long and only 200 feet wide in places. Currents at springs run to four knots in the passage. Least depth is 36 feet. Good anchorage is possible in many areas of the harbor. Passage between the two small islands inside the entrance is blocked by a shoal. Squalls occur because of the harbor's enclosed topography. In strong winds, try the bay on the extreme northwest corner. A rock is in the bay. The Salish Indians, who once inhabited this harbor, used the caverns on the east side of the entrance for burial caves. They protected their harbor from raiding canoes of enemies by rolling rocks onto the canoes from atop the gorge. The harbor is the site of anchorage and Gorge Harbour Marina Resort.

Gorge Harbour Marina & Resort: Moorage, power, water, laundry, showers, gas, diesel, propane, restaurant, store, liquor, lodging. RV sites. New Owners. 250-935-6433. VHF 66A.

Walk-around: Gorge Harbour Park is on the northwest side of the harbor, near the site of the resort. There are trails and picnic tables. It is a half-hour walk to Whaletown on a good hiking road. An attraction is a huge fir, nine feet in diameter, that was a sapling 2,000 years ago.

★⚓ **Manson's Landing (37):** No dump zone. This is the site of a Provincial Marine Park. Fronting both Hague Lake and Manson Bay, this 100 hectares park offers swimming, marine wildlife viewing, pit toilet, day use picnic sites, fresh/saltwater fishing, and trails. No fresh water available. Exposed anchorage is possible in the bay, northwest of the wharf. Avoid the drying bank that extends from the lagoon entrance. There is some protection from southwesterlies between Cat and Sheep Islet and behind Cat Islet. About one half mile up the road from the public float is a museum. Visitors welcome. Admission by donation. A grocery store, restaurant, coffee shop, post office and library are also found in Manson's Landing. ⛺🚶

Manson's Landing Public Floats: 400 ft. of moorage float. Power, no water, garbage drop, telephone.

Walk-around: It is a short walk to a lagoon above the landing. In 1887, John Manson established a trading post on the sand spit which separates the bay from the lagoon. In 1973, this entire 117 acres was designated as a marine park. There is a substantial stretch of sandy beach, suitable for picnicking or beachcombing. Walk

south for about 3/4 mile on the paved road, then left about 1/3 mile on another paved road to a trail down to Hague Lake. Hague Lake is noted for its excellent swimming and sunbathing beaches.

★⚓ **Smelt Bay Park (38):** This bay is named because of the smelt that spawn on the sandy beach when there's the light of a full moon. There is a 40 acre park about half way between Manson's Landing and Sutil Point which may be used by small craft. Approach straight in and anchor close to the beach. There are 25 campsites and several picnic areas. An RV sewage pump-out is located near here. ⛺▲🛏

Sutil Point: For many, rounding this point seems as if it takes forever. The Sutil Point light and bell buoy is almost a mile off shore near the southwest extremity of the rocks and shoals which extend off Cortes Island.

★ **Cortes Bay (39):** No dump zone. Many boaters have found themselves aground if not careful in the vicinity of the Three Islets. These are in the approach to Cortes Bay. The picturesque entrance to the bay itself has a rock with a beacon which flashes after dusk. Keep this marker to starboard when entering and to port when leaving. There is a 196-foot public float on the west shore of the bay. The former marina is now a yacht club outstation. The bay is uniformly 20 to 40 feet deep with a soft mud bottom. Since the mud is very soft, additional anchor rode may be necessary. Northwest winds funnel in from the head of the bay. Southeast seas enter and ricochet off the shore, thus sending waves sideways across the harbor. Anchor dragging is common. Coast Guard Rescue Boat 509 is stationed in Cortes Bay.

★ **Walk-around:** The main road from Cortes Bay has good walking opportunities which lead past picturesque fields and farms.

★ **Twin Islands (40):** These islands are really two humps of a single island connected by a drying ledge. They are owned by a German prince, a cousin to the Queen of England. A resident caretaker lives on the premises. Anchorage is possible in Echo Bay. This offers protection from westerly winds. The bay is exposed to the south. A recommended anchorage is on the northwest shore of the northernmost island between the islet and the shore. Depths are 15-20 feet. Central Rock, a hazard off the northwest corner of Twin Islands, dries at low tide.

★ **Hernando Island (41):**   Named after Hernando Cortez, Spanish conqueror of Mexico in the early 1500's, this island has many shoal areas containing uncharted rocks. Manson Passage, between Hernando and Savary Islands is not recommended. There is protection from southeasterlies along the beach by Spilsbury Point and in Stag Bay. There is a long, private wharf in the bay.

Uganda Pass separates Marina and Cortes Islands   *Canadian Hydrographic Photo*

Essential Supplies & Services

AIR TRANSPORTATION
To & from Washington
Kenmore Air: 1-800-543-9595
Seattle Seaplanes **1-800-637-5553**
To & from Islands/Vancouver
Air Canada 1-888-247-2262
Baxter Air 1-800-661-5599
Harbour Air 1-800-665-0212
Helijet (BC) 1-800-664-4354
Tofino Air 1-800-665-2359
Vancouver Island Air . . 250-287-2433, 1-877-331-2433

AMBULANCES: 911

BOAT MOVING
All Tow Boat Moving . . . .
604-946-7899, 1-877-946-7899

BOOKS / BOOK STORES
The Marine Atlas **541-593-6396**

BUS TRANSPORTATION
Campbell River 250-287-RIDE
Laidlaw Coach 250-287-7151
Powell River 604-485-4287

COAST GUARD:
Comox: VHF 16, 22-A, 26, 84 . . . . . 250-339-3613, #16
Emergencies . . . . 1-800-567-5111, VHF 16

FUELS
Gorge Harbour Marina: Gas, Diesel . . . .
. . . . 250-935-6433 VHF66A
Refuge Cove Store: Gas, Diesel   250-935-6659

GROCERY STORES
Gorge Harbour Marina Resort . . 250-935-6433 VHF 66A
Refuge Cove Store **250-935-6659**
Squirrel Cove 250-935-6327
Whaletown Store 250-935-6562

HOSPITALS
Campbell River 250-287-7111
Powell River 604-485-3211

INSURANCE
Boat Insurance Agency **206-285-1350**
    Or Call **1-800-828-2446**

LIQUOR STORES
Gorge Harbour Marina . . . . 250-935-6433 VHF 66A
Refuge Cove Store **250-935-6659**
Squirrel Cove Store 250-935-6327

LODGING
Gorge Harbour Marina Resort 250-935-6433

MARINAS / MOORAGE
Cortes Bay Public Floats
Gorge Harbour Marina . . . . 250-935-6433 VHF 66A
Manson's Landing Public Floats
Okeover Arm Public Floats
Refuge Cove Store **250-935-6659**
Squirrel Cove Public Floats
Whaletown Public Floats

MARINE SUPPLY STORES
Ocean Pacific Marine Supply: Campbell River.
. . . . **250-286-1011**

POISON INFO: 250-287-7111

PROPANE
Gorge Harbour Marina Resort . . 250-935-6433 VHF 66A
Refuge Cove Store: 250-935-6659
Squirrel Cove 250-935-6327
Whaletown Store 250-935-6562

RAMPS / HAUL-OUTS
Gorge Harbour Marina Resort 250-935-6433
Jack's Boat Yard: Finn Bay. 604-483-3566 VHF 66A
Ocean Pacific Marine Supply: Campbell River.
. . . . **250-286-1011**
Okeover Arm Public Floats

RED TIDE HOT-LINE: 604-666-2828

REPAIRS
Altech Diesel: Campbell River 250-286-0055

Carmac Diesel: Campbell River 250-287-2171
Jack's Boat Yard: Finn Bay.
. . . . **604-483-3566 VHF 66A**
Lund Auto & Outboard: + Mobile.
. . . . **604-483-4612 VHF 66A**
Ocean Pacific Marine: Campbell River.
. . . . **250-286-1011**
Refuge Cove Store **250-935-6659**

RESCUE: 800-567-5111

RV SITES
Gorge Harbour Resort & Marina 250-935-6433

SHELLFISH HOTLINE: 604-666-2828

SPORT FISHING: 604-666-2828
Cambell River 250-850-5701
Comox 250-339-2031

STORAGE:
Jack's Boat Yard: Finn Bay 604-483-3566 VHF 66A
Lund Auto & Outboard . . . . **604-483-4612 VHF 66A**

TOWING
C-TOW **1-888-354-5554**
Carmac Diesel: Campbell River 250-287-2171

VHF MARINE OPERATOR
Campbell River: VHF 27, 64
East Thurlow Island: VHF 24
Powell River: VHF 85
Sayward: VHF 28

VISITOR INFORMATION
Campbell River 250-287-4636, 1-800-463-4386
Powell River 604-485-4701

WEATHER
Environment Canada Weather Line 250-339-9861
Comox: 250-339-0748 (recorded)
Comox: VHF WX-1
Vancouver: 604-664-9010

Chapter 15:

Northwest Georgia Strait

Nanoose Harbour to Oyster River. Schooner Cove, French Creek, Comox, Courtenay.
Ballenas, Hornby, Denman, Lasqueti, & Texada Islands.

Symbols

[   ]: Numbers between [   ] are chart numbers.

{   }: Numbers & letters between {   } are waypoints.

♠: Park, ⬛: Boat Launch, ▲: Campgrounds,
⋏: Hiking Trails, ⋒: Picnic Area, ⊶: Biking

★ **Important Notice:** See "Important Notices" between Chapters 7 and 8 in this guide for specific information on boating related topics such as: Canadian & U.S. Customs, boating safety and security, navigation, weather, U.S. & Canadian Coast Guard, U.S & Canadian

marine radio use, Vessel Traffic Service and traffic separation plans, security zones, and internet access. Due to new Department of Homeland Security regulations, call ahead for latest customs information and/or see Northwest Boat Travel On-line, www.nwboat.com.

★ **Area Whiskey Golf:** Mariners crossing or cruising in the Strait of Georgia should be aware of Canadian Forces Experimental and Test Ranges near Nanaimo. When active, this area poses a life-threatening danger to yachtsmen and their vessels. An official notice issued by the Canadian Department of Defence concerning the activities and dangers in this area, designated as "WG" on charts, appears near the end of Chapter 11.

Vancouver Island Side

[3459, 3512, 3513, 3527]

★ **Nanoose Harbour (1):** Nanoose Harbour is between Blunden and Wallis Points. This bay can be an important refuge during a blow on the

Chart List

Canadian Hydrographic Charts:

3458, 3459, 3512-13, 3527, 3536

Marine Atlas (2005 ed.):

Page 23-24, 27, 29

★ **Fairwinds Schooner Cove Hotel and Marina:** Visitors arrive by land, sea, and air to enjoy the facilities at one of Vancouver Island's most popular destination resorts. Stay to port when entering through the breakwater. A rock on the starboard side, marked by an orange float, is submerged at high tide. Moorage available for boats to 150'. Fifteen, 30 and 50 ampere power is available at a nominal charge, along with gas and diesel fuel. The hotel-marina complex, coupled with the Fairwinds development, has something for everyone. The hotel offers 32 rooms, outdoor pool, hot tub, exercise room, free showers, coin-operated laundromat, mail

and fax services. Facilities for weddings, anniversaries, conferences, business meetings, and seminars are available to marina patrons. A launching ramp, shallow and deep grids for low tide hull maintenance, tackle and boating supplies, bait, fishing licenses, ice, garbage drop, bike rentals, fishing and sailing charters, and a yacht club are available onsite. Other area recreational facilities available to hotel and marina guests include kayaking, tennis, scuba diving, horseback riding, nature walks, hiking, and golfing at the spectacular and challenging 18-hole Fairwinds course. BCPGA 1999 facility of the year. Pump out at end of G dock. Complimentary

shuttle service operates between the hotel-marina and the golf course. Rental cars may be ordered from nearby Parksville. Enjoy the incredible view of Georgia Strait, which acts as a backdrop to the marina and enhances the enjoyment of dining in the Laughing Gull Pub. For early morning fisher-folk and late evening boaters alike, The Dockside Cafe serves satisfying short order snacks. The cold beer and wine store rounds out the array of amenities available to the discriminating boater. The coordinates of Area Whiskey Golf test range have been reduced to one-half mile north of Winchelsea Island and one-half mile east of Ballenas Island, allowing for easy access to Schooner Cove. **Circle #11 on the Reader Service Card. Websites: www.fairwinds.ca/ & www.boattravel.com/fairwinds/ Email: marina@fairwinds.ca Address: 3521 Dolphin Drive, Nanoose Bay, British Columbia V9P 9J7. Hotel: 250-468-7691. Hotel Reservations: 1-800-663-7060; Marina: 250-468-5364. Fax (all departments): 250-468-5744. VHF 16, 66A.**

strait. Snaw-naw-as Marina is in the harbor. A marked entrance leads behind a sandspit and breakwater extending from the southern shore. The two summits of Nanoose Hill rise above the northern side of the harbor. Ranch Point, on the north side of the harbor, is an Armed Forces Base. Mooring buoys belong to the Canadian Department of Defence. Anchorages are along the northwestern shore, below Nanoose Hill, and along the southern shore, near the marina, behind the breakwater at Fleet Point. Neither camping nor picnicking is permitted on much of the shore. Arbutus Grove Provincial Park is on the south shore. Pilings sit on a mud flat, some of which are hazards because they are covered at high tide.

Snaw-naw-as Marina: Closed for renovation. Launch ramp usable.

Winchelsea Island: Canadian Armed Forces station. Trespassing is not permitted. Winchelsea Control is in charge of Whiskey Golf operations and all vessels traversing the area. See Canadian Department of Defence Notice at the end of Chapter 11. Winchelsea Control monitors VHF 10, 16.

★ **Schooner Cove (2):** A large rip rap breakwater protects this marina basin. Enter north of the lighted breakwater. Fairwinds Schooner Cove Resort Hotel & Marina is located in the cove.

★ **Fairwinds Schooner Cove Hotel & Marina:** Truly a destination resort and marina. 360 permanent and visitor berths, 30 and 50 ampere power, water, gas & diesel fuel, complimentary use of showers. Pump-out at end of "G" dock. Pool, sauna, tennis, and a shuttle to Fairwinds Golf Course available. The hotel has 32 spacious guest rooms, pub, cold beer and wine store, cafe, tackle, ice, and marine store. Tee times may be booked with moorage reservations. Golf club and cart rentals available. See our Steering Star description in this chapter. Websites: www.fairwinds.ca& www.boattravel.com/fairwinds. E-mail: marina@fairwinds.ca. Address: 3521 Dolphin Drive, Nanoose, British Columbia V9P 9J7. Telephones: Hotel: 250-468-7691. Hotel & Marina Reservations: 1-800-663-7060. Marina: 250-468-5364. Fax (all departments): 250-468-5744. VHF 66A.

Walk-around: Walk or bike through the 1,300-acre Fairwinds community.

Ballenas Islands (3): [3512] Limited shelter is possible in the bay that indents the southernmost island. Navigating the narrow channel between the two islands is tricky. Enter at high water, avoiding rocks in center channel. Anchorage is prohibited because of cables on the bottom of the bay. The north shore has a sand beach. The northern island is the site of an old and picturesque lighthouse and weather reporting station.

★ **Northwest Bay (4):** Pass between the green and red buoys. Avoid the rocky area marked by a red spar buoy. There is anchorage, exposed to northwest winds, near the head of the bay. A breakwater on the eastern shore shelters a public float complex.

Beachcomber Marina: Limited moorage, gas, diesel, power, water, showers, launch, repairs. 250-468-7222. VHF 66A.

Parksville: A sand beach extending a quarter mile from shore offers sunbathing opportunities and sandcastle architects claim this beach is one of the best for building such structures. Anchor offshore in settled weather only. The town was named for pioneer and postmaster, Nelson Parks.

★⚓ **Rathtrevor Beach Park:** A gem of the provincial parks. Rathtrevor has 136 campsites, sani-station for RV's, showers, picnic areas, and a lovely sand beach. No marine facilities. 🚶🚲⛺🏕

★ **French Creek (5):** [3512] A dredged channel, with a minimum depth of 15 feet at mean low tide, leads to a public wharf and floats. Groceries, fresh seafood, marine supplies, and a restaurant are available. This is the western terminal of the Lasqueti Island Ferry. Designated moorage for Coast Guard Search & Rescue and Fisheries & Oceans officers.

Harbour Authority of French Creek: Moorage (between docks D & E or 2 & 3 - Register at Harbour Office 8 a.m.- 5:30 p.m., any day), power, water, restrooms, showers, waste oil deposit, garbage drop, pump-out, dump, security cameras. 250-248-5051.

French Creek Seafoods: Gas, diesel, ice, retail store, fresh water with fuel purchase. 250-248-7100.

French Creek-Lasqueti Island Foot Passenger Ferry: Daily except Tuesdays. For information call 604-681-5199.

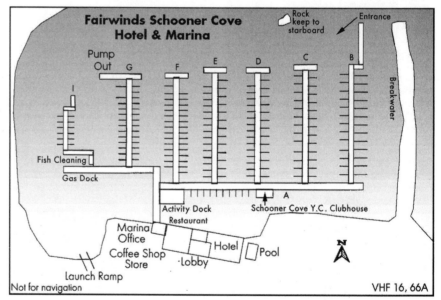

Not for navigation   VHF 16, 66A

Qualicum Beach (6): Miles of beautiful sand beaches with gentle surf and sparkling-clear waters comprise the Qualicum Beach shoreline. There are no marine facilities or sheltered coves. Anchor in settled weather only.

Qualicum Bay: Located eight miles north of Qualicum Beach, this wide bay has good holding bottom for anchoring and offers a limited amount of protection in northwesterly winds. The Qualicum wind blows offshore and results in local choppy waters.

★ **Hornby Island (7):** Hornby offers anchorages, provincial parks, and a public float complex at Ford Cove. Anchorage is possible in Tribune Bay with its Hawaiian-like white sand beaches. Nash Bank, outside the bay, is a popular fishing spot. Anchorage is also possible south of Shingle Spit in Lambert Channel, however, northwest winds funnel through the channel. A ferry connects Hornby with Denman Island at Shingle Spit. A rock breakwater shelters the landing from southeasterly winds. No fresh water available in the vicinity.

★ **Tribune Bay:** Good anchorage on a sand bottom in depths of about 40 feet is available, with shelter from north and west winds. While the bay is protected from northwesterlies, southeasterlies cause havoc. Tribune Bay Provincial Park is undeveloped. Take a picnic lunch and walk to Helliwell Provincial Park at St. John Point.

★⚓ **Helliwell Provincial Park:** Located by road from Tribune Bay anchorage, this relatively undeveloped park also includes the channel south of Hornby Island and up into Lambert Channel where there is an underwater cave and a shipwreck for diving. Also, six gill sharks, normally a deep sea shark rarely found in shallow waters in Canada, are found off Hornby and are attractions for divers. ⛱⚲

★ **Ford Cove:** Entry to Ford Cove is between the green spar buoy and the breakwater. The basin is dredged to minimum eight foot depths. Three floats are in the basin, behind the breakwater. Launching ramp. Anchorage is possible.

Walk-around: A path along the shore from Ford Cove to Shingle Spit makes a good hike.

Ford Cove Harbour Authority: Call ahead for moorage. Power, no water. 250-335-2141.

Ford Cove Marina: Store, fishing gear, bait, cottages & camping. 250-335-2169.

★ **Denman Island & Henry Bay (8):** Temporary anchorage, open to the west, is found in Henry Bay inside Longbeak Point. Anchor well off the oyster beds. On Baynes Sound, about half way down the island, there is a public float and launch ramp at the site of the Denman-Vancouver Island (Buckley Bay) ferry. A moorage float is adjacent to the landing. Nearby, on the hillside, stands a post office, telephone, and store. There is no garbage drop. There is also a launch ramp at Gravelly Bay. The museum in the Seniors Community Hall contains fossils, shells, butterflies, and items used by the original European settlers. 250-335-2809.

★⚓ **Fillongley Provincial Park:** Ten campsites, picnic facilities, lovely beach, and trails are attractions. Accessible by car ferry from Buckley Bay. No drinking water. ▲⛱⚲

Baynes Sound
[3513, 3527]

★ **Baynes Sound (9):** This is one of the largest oyster producing regions on the coast. Tidelands are leased. Public harvesting is prohibited. Baynes Sound stretches about 12 miles along the shore of Vancouver Island, and ranges in width between one and two miles. Currents can run to three knots in the southern entrance. This waterway is convenient for those visiting Comox and Courtenay.

Deep Bay: Site of a public float complex, this bay is near the southern entrance to Baynes Sound. A sandy shoal extends outward from Mapleguard Point. The point was named for the maple trees that once flourished here. Anchorage is behind the point in 30-50' depths. Poor holding bottom. Large aquaculter operations restrict anchorage. Wide tidal fluctuations affect depths in the anchorage.

Deep Bay Harbour Authority: Moorage, power, water, garbage deposit, tidal grids, ramp, pumpout, washrooms, showers, campgrounds, oil disposal. 250-757-9331. VHF 66.

Fanny Bay: This is a camper and RV area. A wharf with moorage float is private, for the use of the residents only. Very limited anchorage near the float, however it is tricky because of the shoals. The beached coastal freighter is a landmark. In an emergency, a nearby store has gasoline.

Buckley Bay: Site of the Denman Island ferry landing.

Union Bay: Site of a once active coal loading wharf, this facility was closed in 1959. Ruins of pilings are hazards. There is anchorage close to shore and a launching ramp to the north, near a rock breakwater.

Comox Vicinity
[3513, 3527]

★⚓ **Sandy Islands Marine Park (10):** Accessible from the water only, this marine park lies northwest of Denman Island. Locals call this Tree Island. The park includes the Seal Islets. Anchorage is on the south side of the island, in 30-50 feet of water and in nearby Henry Bay. ▲⚲

★ **Comox Harbour (11):** When crossing the Comox Bar from the north, keep the three red buoys to starboard and line up with the range markers on the mainland. The day markers of the range are white with a red stripe. After passing the last red buoy, continue on a bit before turning to starboard. To port, a green can buoy marks the end of the shallows off Gartley Point. Proceed into the harbor with the green can well to port. Anchor avoiding mud flats near Royston.

The Courtenay River empties into the harbor. Eddies are caused by the freshwater currents flowing in different directions from the salt water underneath. The north side of the harbor has drying flats nearly to the head of the pier. Anchorage is considered good. Boats with a draft of less than four feet can travel farther up the river to Courtenay [3527]. The channel seldom, if ever, completely dries because of the water flowing down from the river. Least depth is about five feet up to the Courtenay Bridge, south of Lewis Park. Stay in the marked channel on line with the range lights.

Departing Comox to head north in the Strait of Georgia, it is first necessary to cross the Comox Bar. From the light on Goose Spit, at the entrance to the harbor, head for Sandy Island. Proceed about two miles on that course until you can see the three red buoys that should be lined up to indicate the proper course, as shown on Chart 3527. The range markers shown on this chart are lights only, so they are of no benefit during daylight hours. Keeping the red buoys to port, the smoke from the Powell River Pulp Mill, across the Strait of Georgia, should be dead ahead, more or less. The chart shows a least depth of over two meters, so even on a low tide, most boats should have plenty of water. Continuing on the same course about two more miles, you must first round East Cardinal Buoy "PJ" (black with a yellow band) to clear the shoals around Cape Lazo. It is about 22 miles from Cape Lazo to the lighthouse on Cape Mudge.

★ **Comox:** The town of Comox has four marinas sheltered by a rock breakwater. A promenade with pier, garbage drop, used oil dump, and public telephone are accessible. A shopping center, golf course, restaurants, and pubs are within a short walk. Marina Park, adjacent to the Municipal Marina has restrooms, play area and boat launch.

The name Comox originally came from the native word "Komuckway," meaning plenty or abundance. Considering that Comox is situated amid the rich agricultural lands of the Comox Valley, the name makes perfect sense. Comox's first wharf was built in 1876, the same year the navy established a base at Goose Spit. Today, the Canadian Armed Forces still operates a base at the spit. The base's airfield is the site of a popular bi-annual air show. Visitors are welcome to picnic on the public part of the spit. Comox is home to about 12,000 people and boasts an array of services and facilities, including a large hospital. History buffs will enjoy the Comox Museum 250-339-2882 and the Comox Air Force Museum 250-339-8162. The Filberg Heritage Lodge and Park hosts the *Filberg Festival*, an annual arts & crafts festival. 250-339-2715. Comox is accessible by land, sea, or air. Daily ferries from Powell River land a bit north, at Little River. The Comox Valley Airport, north of Cape Lazo, features daily flights to Vancouver. Highway 19 connects Comox with communities from Victoria to Port Hardy.

Blackfin Marina: Moorage, showers, laundry, gas, diesel, power, water, provisions. Telephones: Pub 250-339-5030, Marina 250-339-4664. VHF 66A.

Comox Bay Marina: Moorage, 15 & 30 ampere power, water, showers, laundry, haul-out. 250-339-2930. VHF 66A.

Comox Municipal Marina: Call ahead for very limited moorage, power, water, garbage deposit, launch ramp. 250-339-2202.

Comox Valley Fisherman's Wharf: Guest moorage available on the east side of the harbor. Water, power, waste oil deposit, garbage drop, telephone, laundry, restrooms, showers, pumpout. No reservations. 250-339-6041. VHF 68.

Courtenay: [3527] The Courtenay River is navigable by very shallow draft boats. Follow range markers, and check local conditions and water level. The entrance to the slough may be more shallow than the channel itself. Courtenay is a trading center for the mid-Vancouver Island area and features shops, lodging, restaurants, and services. Daily Train service connects Courtenay with Victoria. 888-842-7245. Visit the Comox Valley Farmer's Market from June through September. The Courtenay & District Museum highlights Valley history and offers fossil tours. 250-334-0686. The *Comox Valley Fall Fair*, held in late August attracts over 15,000 visitors annually.

Cape Lazo: See current tables for Seymour Narrows, British Columbia. Interestingly shaped, Cape Lazo has a flat summit and headland with yellow cliffs. It appears to be an island. Hazards extend to the east and southeast. Buoys mark the rock hazard from the cliffs of the cape and from Kye Bay. The lighthouse is a landmark. This is Lighthouse Country with lights on Hornby, Denman, Lasqueti, Chrome, and Sisters Islands.

Coast Westerly Hotel: Located in the Comox Valley, close to five golf courses and easy distance by taxi from Comox Marinas. Guest rooms and suites, dining in the GreenHouse Restaurant, Gulliver's Pub or Snooker's Lounge. 250-338-7741.

Little River & Kuhushan Point: This stretch of shoreline north of Cape Lazo has settlements and resorts near the river deltas. Little River is identified by the ferry landing. It is the western terminus of the Vancouver Island-Westview/Powell River ferry. In nor'westers, there is shelter for small boats south of the ferry landing. A launching ramp is next to the resort at the ferry landing.

Miracle Beach: A lovely white sand beach marks the spot of Miracle Beach Provincial Park. There are over 175 campsites. A launching ramp is provided.

Oyster River: Oyster River has a dredged channel into an inland boat basin. The channel has a slight curve in it. At zero tide there is a minimum depth of two feet of water in the channel and eight feet of water in the basin. Enter between the two lighted markers. If possible, approach not quite at high tide, so that it is possible to discern the sides of the channel, which are covered at high water.

Pacific Playgrounds Resort & Marina: Moorage, power, water, showers, laundry, gas, diesel, grid, provisions. Internet access in store. 250-337-5600.

Kuhushan Point: North of Kuhushan Point is another dredged small boat basin. The entrance channel is straight, shallow, and narrow. Orange signs are range markers. Enter between the pilings. Incoming boats have the right-of-way.

Salmon Point Resort: Day use moorage for boats to 26', gas, RV park, lodging, ice. Entry channel 5' minimum depth. 250-923-6605. VHF 14.

Sunshine Coast Side
[3312, 3512, 3536]

Sisters Islets: These two islets are the site of a light tower, fog signal, and weather reporting station.

Sangster Island: Anchor only in settled weather. The anchorage is northwest of the light. Avoid a drying rock in the entrance to this bight.

★ **Lasqueti Island:** [3512, 3513, 3536] Lasqueti Island is a quiet hideaway for relaxation with fishing and gunkholing spots. The island is about 13 miles in length and the irregular shoreline

invites exploration. Logging and fishing are active pursuits here. False Bay is the center of activity and home to a public float and the Lasqueti Island Store and Marine. Lasqueti is connected by passenger only ferry with French Creek on Vancouver Island.

★ **Squitty Bay (12):** This marine park has a public float with moorage for three to four 20 foot boats. Maneuvering room is limited. There is no space for anchorage. Several rocks obstruct the entrance. The safest passage is along the south shore when entering. The bay is dredged to depths of eight feet.

Walk-around: A road from the public float leads to other settlements on the island. A walk up the dirt road and up the hillside can provide spectacular view sites.

★ **Boat Cove (13):** This niche in the southwestern shore offers anchorage on a good bottom. Avoid rocks in the southeast entrance. The cove is protected from westerlies, but is wide open to southeast winds.

★ **Old House Bay:** There is anchorage with protection from northwest winds off the head. Watch for shoals when locating a spot.

★ **Richardson Cove:** There is anchorage at the head.

★ **False Bay (14):** [3536] The settlement of Lasqueti is in Mud Bay on the east side of this bay. There is a public float. At times evening westerlies and Qualicum winds enter, and moorage at the float is bumpy. A passenger-only ferry runs to Frenchman's Creek on Vancouver Island. Anchorage is on the north side of the bay in three niches in the shoreline. Try east of Higgins Island. There is a good holding bottom. Beware of a drying rock when crossing from the public float. A lagoon has protected anchorage however the entrance, east of Prowse Point, dries in the middle at about half tide. At high water, near slack. A three to four knot current occurs in the channel. Favor the north side, but watch for rock ledges extending from shore and a drying rock in the middle of the channel.

Lasqueti Moorage Float and Hotel: Limited moorage. Lodging, restaurant, store across the street. Under renovation. 250-333-8503.

★ **Spring Bay:** This wide bay has anchorage off the head. Good protection in southerly winds.

★ **Scottie Bay (15):** This small lovely bay provides excellent protection from winds. Enter south of Lindbergh Island. Keep hard to port to avoid a reef off Lindberg Island. There is a private wharf here and a few homes. A road runs about a mile and one half across the island to False Bay.

★ **Tucker Bay:** Anchorage for small craft is possible south of Larson Islet adjacent to Potter Point. Allow at least a 300 foot clearance off the west point of Larson Islet when approaching. Charted Tuck Rock is a hazard in the bay. Much of the bay is open to northwest and north winds.

Jervis Island: There is anchorage between Bunny and Jervis Islands.

★ **Boho Bay (16):** There is anchorage in the harbor between the southern shore of Boho Island and Lasqueti. It is the site of an undeveloped marine park. At times, there are strong currents here. Aquaculture.

★ **Skerry Bay:** There is good protection in this bay on the north side of Lasqueti, in all but northwest winds. Rocks, one of which dries five feet, are in the north entrance. Aquaculture is in the north portion.

★▲ **Jedediah Island & Deep Bay (17):** This beautiful 640 acre island park has anchorage in several places. Bull Passage, between Lasqueti and Jedediah has several rocky patches, but provides shelter. Jedediah Bay, a small indentation shaped like a dock cleat, offers limited anchorage. An unnamed bay on the southeast end has anchorage and some protection from Rabbit Island. An extremely steep bluff is a landmark.

Deep Bay, on the northwest side, has anchorage. Winds, which tend to swirl around the bay, and the deep bottom, affect anchoring. A tie to shore is advised once the anchor is set. Rings, somewhat difficult to reach at lower tides, are installed on both the south and north shores. Pit toilet, trails, wilderness camping. Anchorage is also found in the passage between Paul Island and Jedediah. ▲⚲

Walk-around: A cleared trail at the head of Deep Bay leads through forest to a meadow, and eventually, Home Bay. Beaches, grazing land, and old growth Douglas Fir are on the island.

★ **Texada Island:** This 27-mile-long, mountainous, forested island stretches from Point Atwood on the south to Grilse Point on the north and forms the western boundary of the Malaspina Strait. The population of the island is about 1,200. Texada's wealth of limestone, marble, gold, iron, and copper have all played a part in the economy of the island. Limestone has been quarried here since 1897. Two marine parks are located on South Texada, South Texada Park on the southwest side, and Anderson Bay on the southeast side. Mountain bikers will enjoy exploring the old road crisscrossing South Texada.

★ **Anderson Bay (18):** Many boaters have sought shelter in westerlies in this narrow bay located on South Texada Island's eastern shore near the southeast point. Anchorage is possible near the head in 10-20 feet of water. When entering north of the island at the entrance, stay south of the rocks that are in the center. These rocks are covered at high water.

★ **Northeast Bay (19):** Although constricted with an island in the center, there is sufficient room for anchorage when seeking shelter from west and southeast winds.

★ **Pocahontas Bay (20):** Although only a small bight, there is shelter here from southeasterlies.

★ **Gillies Bay (21):** This bay has some protection in north winds. An extensive drying flat is at the head. Its sandy beaches invite exploration by small boat. This is the site of the only settlement on the west side of Texada. Also accessible by car from Vananda and Blubber Bay. An airport is nearby. There is a park, resort, store, liquor store, restaurant, and medical clinic in Gillies Bay.

★▲ **Harwood Point Provincial Park (21):** Anchorage, launching ramp, campsites, picnic tables, hiking trails, and fresh water. ⚲🚤🏕️▲

Limekiln Bay (22): There is temporary anchorage in this shallow bight along the northwestern shore. The beach is white sand. An explosives company is on the east side. No docking is permitted near the company.

Blubber Bay (23): This wide indentation is on the north shore between Blubber Point and Grilse Point. A ferry landing and public float are on the west side of the bay. The ferry connects Texada with the mainland at Westview/Powell River. Up from the ferry terminal it is an easy walk to the Visitor Centre, museum, and art gallery. Anchorage on sand and mud is possible, but space is limited and the bay is open to north and northwest winds. Favored salmon fishing waters are from Grilse Point south to Hodgson Point and Eagle Cove. About 100 years ago, this was the site for whale rendering operations.

★ **Vananda & Sturt Bay (24):** Moorage is

found and limited anchorage is possible. This end of the island has a rock bottom. Consequently, pilings are difficult to sink adequately and heavy weights with cables are used to secure the floats. The Texada Island Yacht Club has good, sheltered moorage. There are no posted vessel length restrictions, however, vessels larger than 40 feet may put an undue strain on the unusual float installation. Water is provided, no power. There is some mud toward the low bank of the shoreline, however there is little protection from wind at this location.

A variety of businesses are a short five minute walk away. These include a grocery store, liquor store, bank, a Legion where all retired military are welcome, a hardware store, bakery, coffee shop, fax service, flower shop, and a hotel with a restaurant, pub and take-out pizza. In season, fresh produce is sold on a farm uphill from the yacht club.

Essential Supplies & Services

AIR TRANSPORTATION
To & from Washington
Seattle Seaplanes 1-800-637-5553
To & from Islands/Vancouver
Air Canada 1-888-247-2262
Baxter Air 1-800-661-5599
Harbour Air 604-274-1277, 1-800-665-0212
Helijet. . . . . 1-800-665-4354 (B.C.)
Tofino Air 1-800-665-2359
Vancouver Island Air 250-287-2433
. . . . 1-877-331-2433 (B.C.)

AMBULANCES: 911

BOAT MOVING
All Tow Boat Moving . . . .
. . . . 604-946-7899, 1-877-946-7899

BOOKS / BOOK STORES
The Marine Atlas. 541-593-6396

BUS TRANSPORTATION
Courtenay 250-334-2475,
. . . . 1-800-318-0818

COAST GUARD
Comox: VHF 16, 22-A, 26, 84.
. . . . 250-339-3613, 250-339-1053, #16
Emergencies. . . . . 1-800-567-5111, VHF 16
Texada Rescue: VHF 16 or CB 9

FERRY INFORMATION
B.C. 250-386-3431, 1-888-223-3779
Nanaimo 888-223-3779
Denman Island 250-335-0323
Fr. Creek-Lasqueti 604-681-5199
Little R-Texada-Powell R 250-339-3310
Hornby Island 250-335-0323

FUELS
Beachcomber Resort . . . . . . Gas, Diesel. 250-468-7222
Black Fin Marina: Gas, Diesel . . . 250-339-4664 VHF 68
Fairwinds Schooner Cove: Gas, Diesel.
. 250-468-5364
Ford Cove: Gas, Diesel . . . . . 250-335-2169 (call ahead)
French Creek Seafoods: Gas, Diesel 250-248-7100
Pacific Playgrounds: Gas, Diesel. 250-337-5600
Salmon Point: Gas. 250-923-6605

GOLF COURSES
(These courses are accessible from moorage and have rental clubs available)
Comox 250-339-4444
Fairwinds Schooner Cove 1-800-663-7060
Glacier Greens (Comox) 250-339-6515
Saratoga Beach 250-337-8212

HOSPITALS
Comox. 250-339-2242
Courtenay 250-339-2242
Deep Bay 250-339-2242
Powell River 604-485-3211
Texada Health Centre. 604-486-7525

INSURANCE
Boat Insurance Agency 206-285-1350
Or Call 1-800-828-2446

LIQUOR STORES
Comox
Courtenay
Denman Island
Gillies Bay Store
Qualicum Beach
Vananda

LODGING
Coast Westerly Hotel 250-338-7741
Fairwinds Schooner Cove 1-800-663-7060

MARINAS / MOORAGE FLOATS
Blackfin Marina: Comox . . . . . 250-339-4664. VHF 66A
Blubber Bay: Texada Island
Comox Bay . . . . 250-339-2930, VHF 66A
Comox Municipal. 250-339-3141
Comox Valley Harbour Authority. . 250-339-6041, VHF 68
Deep Bay Harbour Authority . . . 250-757-9331, VHF 66
Denman Island
Fairwinds Schooner Cove 250-468-5364
False Bay: Lasqueti Island
Ford Cove: Hornby Island
French Creek 250-248-5051
Pacific Playgrounds:Resort & Marina . . . 250-337-5600
Salmon Point: Kuhushan Point 250-923-6605
Squitty Bay: Lasqueti Island
Vananda/Sturt Bay: Texada Island

POISON INFORMATION
Comox/Courtenay 250-339-2242
Powell River 604-485-3211

PROPANE
Gillies Bay Store: Texada Island

RAMPS / HAUL-OUTS
Comox
Comox Bay Marina 250-339-2930
Deep Bay
Denman Island
Fairwinds Schooner Cove 250-468-5364
Fanny Bay
Ford Cove, Hornby Island
French Creek
Gillies Bay, Texada Island

Gravelly Bay: Denman Island
Little River
Miracle Beach
Pacific Playgrounds: Oyster River 250-337-5600
Snaw-naw-as: Nanoose Bay.
Union Bay

RED TIDE INFO: 604-666-2828

REPAIRS (All Campbell River area)
Altech Diesel 250-286-0055
Carmac Diesel 250-287-2171
Island Outboard. 250-287-9248
Ocean Pacific. 800-663-2294

RESTAURANTS
Fairwinds Schooner Cove. 1-800-663-7060

SEWAGE DISPOSAL
Comox Valley Harbour Authority: Pump . 250-339-6041
Deep Bay Harbour Authority: Pump 250-757-9331
Fairwinds Schooner Cove: Pump . . . 250-468-5364
French Creek Harbour Authority: Pump, dump.
. . . . 250-248-5051

SHELLFISH HOTLINE: 604-666-2828

SPORTSFISHING
Local Canada Fisheries Offices: Comox 250-339-2031,
Parksville 250-954-1354

TOWING:
C-TOW. 1-888-354-5554
Carmac Diesel 250-287-2171
VESSEL ASSIST . . . . Georgia Strait 250-247-8934

VHF MARINE OPERATOR
Nanaimo: VHF 87
Parksville: VHF 28
Powell River: VHF 85
Vancouver: 23, 24, 25, 26, 86, 88
West Vancouver: 85

VISITOR INFORMATION
Campbell River Chamber/Info Centre.
. . . . 250-287-4636 Ext. 1, 1-866-830-1113
Courtenay-Comox 250-334-3234, 1-888-357-4471
Parksville. 250-248-3613
Powell River 604-485-4701

WEATHER
Environment Canada Weather Line 250-339-9861
Comox: VHF WX-1
Comox: Recorded 250-339-0748
Discovery Mt.: VHF WX-4
Texada Island: WX-1
Vancouver: VHF WX-3

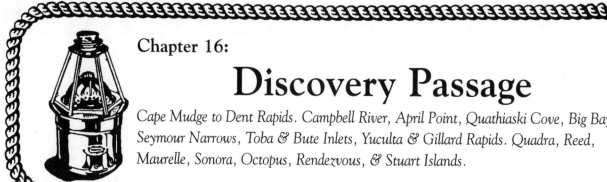

Chapter 16:
Discovery Passage

Cape Mudge to Dent Rapids. Campbell River, April Point, Quathiaski Cove, Big Bay, Seymour Narrows, Toba & Bute Inlets, Yuculta & Gillard Rapids. Quadra, Reed, Maurelle, Sonora, Octopus, Rendezvous, & Stuart Islands.

Symbols

[   ]: Numbers between [   ] are chart numbers.

{   }: Numbers & letters between {   } are waypoints.

⚓: Park, ⛵: Boat Launch, ▲: Campgrounds, ⚲: Hiking Trails, ☂: Picnic Area, ☂: Biking

Chart List

Canadian Hydrographic Charts:

3312, 3513, 3537-3543

NOAA:

17503

Marine Atlas (2005 ed.):

Pages 30, 32-35

★ **Important Notice:** See "Important Notices" between Chapters 7 and 8 in this guide for specific information on boating related topics such as: Canadian & U.S. Customs, boating safety and security, navigation, weather, U.S. & Canadian Coast Guard, U.S & Canadian marine radio use, Vessel Traffic Service and traffic separation plans, security zones, and internet access. Due to new Department of Homeland Security regulations, call ahead for latest customs information and/or see Northwest Boat Travel On-line, www.nwboat.com.

Discovery Passage

[3312, 3513, 3539, 3540]

Discovery Passage: Named for Captain Vancouver's ship, this passage separates Quadra and Sonora Islands from Vancouver Island. It is the main shipping channel leading northwest from the north end of the Strait of Georgia and is used by tugs, freighters, cruise ships, and fish boats as well as by pleasure craft. Entry on the south is at Cape Mudge and it is exited on the north at Chatham Point. The flood stream sets south and the ebb north, attaining velocities of five to seven knots on big tides. When the current is strong in mid-channel, try closer to shore where back currents can be helpful to move you

against the flood. (See Seymour Narrows, British Columbia current tables). Dangerous rips can form at Cape Mudge where tidal streams can run 7-9 knots. Avoid this area if a southeast wind is blowing on a flood tide. The vicinity of Menzies Bay also gets bad rips. Seymour Narrows, where tidal currents attain speeds of 15 knots, should be transited at or near slack water. Discovery Passage is a designated Vessel Traffic Service Zone and boaters are advised to monitor traffic on Channel 71. A

ferry service crosses the passage from downtown Campbell River to Quathiaski Cove on Quadra Island.

★ **Mitlenatch Island (1):** The Island is home to the Mitlenatch Island Nature Provincial Park where the areas largest seabird colony is found. Park access is through Northwest and East Bay, but most of the island is closed to visitors. There is temporary shelter on this rocky, windswept island. Northwest Bay has a fair anchorage that would be treacherous overnight. Camp Bay, on the southeast, is small and is not sheltered in southeast winds. Legend tells that this island is an Indian princess turned to stone and placed there to remind the Cape Mudge Indians to be less boastful. The island was once used by the Manson family of Cortes Island as a sheep farm. Wild flowers and cactus grow profusely, as do many species of birds. Please stay on trails, no pets onshore. One pit toilet available.

Cape Mudge (2): Located on Quadra Island, a cluster of sparkling white, red-roofed, lighthouse buildings are landmarks for this cape which is famous for salmon fishing. Chinooks to 30 pounds are caught from early June through mid-September. Coho run from mid-June to mid-October. See current tables for Seymour Narrows, British Columbia. The tidal streams in the area run five to seven knots. The flood current flows south, down Discovery Passage, and the ebb flows north. Do not be surprised to see boats going backwards at strong tides. A back eddy close in to Quadra Island makes for easier going when heading up Discovery Passage against the current. When there is a flood tide and southeast winds, dangerous rips occur off Cape Mudge. When rounding the cape be sure to clear the black can and red spar buoys that mark the end of the Wilby Shoals.

Cape Mudge Village: This Indian settlement is home to a museum and lodge. The Kwakiutl Museum building, whose builders were inspired by the shape of a sea snail, houses part of a potlatch collection with totem poles and ceremonial regalia. A path, behind the lighthouse, leads to Indian petroglyphs on the tide flats and eastward around Francisco Point.

★ **Campbell River (3):** The Campbell River

waterfront has changed dramatically in recent years. As you approach, identify the three breakwater-protected moorage basins. Riprap breakwaters extend from shore at each site.

The southernmost basin is the Campbell River Harbour Authority's Small Boat Harbour which contains public floats used primarily by commercial vessels. There is also room for transient moorage, and more emphasis is being placed on accommodating visiting pleasurecraft. Ocean Pacific Marine Supply and Shipyard is adjacent to this basin. A public fishing and recreation pier is a landmark nearby. This basin is within walking distance to downtown.

To the north, a breakwater protects the Coast Marina, located in the heart of downtown.

The Coast Discovery Inn is across the street. Tyee Plaza Shopping Centre, with a variety of shops and grocery is in the immediate area.

The northernmost basin encircles the Discovery Harbour Marina and Shopping Centre and the Campbell River Harbour Authority's North Floats. An ESSO fuel dock is located here. On shore is the large, modern Discovery Harbour Shopping Centre. A second Ocean Pacific Marine supply store is conveniently located in this large center as well as a bank, liquor store, grocery, department store, restaurant, and other specialty shops.

Coined *A Place For All Seasons* and *The Salmon Capital of the World*, Campbell River is more than a fishing destination. It offers a vari-

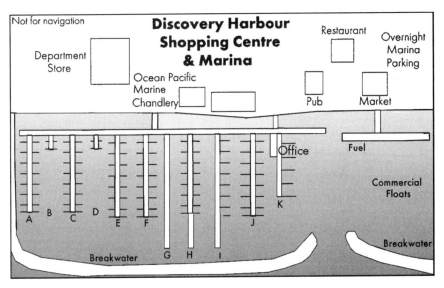

★ **Discovery HARBOUR Marina:** Look for the massive rock breakwater and the ESSO sign located north of the Campbell River-Quadra Island ferry landing. Check-in at the head of "K" dock. This large, well protected marina has 100 guest berths with power and water, and 200 permanent berths with power and water for boats from 18' to 100' in length. Plus 2400' of side moorage, with 20, 30, 50, and 100 Single Phase Service. Power is also available for boats over 100'. There are showers and laundry facilities on-site. The ESSO fuel dock has gas, diesel, oils, stove oil ice, bait, and offers oil changing. The marina is a stop away from Desolation Sound and North Island communities. Visitors comment that Discovery Harbour is a wonderful place for dock walking and talking with other guests and local residents. The shopping center, adjacent to the marina, contains restau-

rants, a pub, liquor store, drug store, gift shops, banks, Zellers, Super Store, Spinner's Sports, and Ocean Pacific Marine Supply. The marina is within walking distance to downtown and taxi service is also available. **Address: #392-1434 Island Hwy, Campbell River, British Columbia V9W 8C9. Circle #06 on Reader Service Card. Websites: www.discoveryharbourmarina.com & www.boattravel.com/discovery Email: tara@discoveryharbourmarina.com Fax: 250-287-8939. Telephone: 250-287-2614. VHF 66A.**

ety of facilities for year around vacationing. This is the largest Vancouver Island city north of Nanaimo and is the center of commerce for the northern island, Discovery Passage, and the adjacent islands northward to Queen Charlotte Strait. The city is centrally located 175 miles from both Victoria to the south and from Cape Scott on the northern end of Vancouver Island, making it the center of the Strathcona Park Wilderness. Logging, mining, fishing, and tourism are major industries in the area. There are also eight parks, several golf courses, hunting, tennis, skating, curling, scuba diving, beachcombing, clam digging, oyster gathering, berry picking, water sports, and shopping to entice visitors looking for diversions. Try a visit to the Campbell River Museum, with its collection of Indian artifacts. Summer activities include a *Summer Festival, Logger's Sports,* and *Fishing Derby.* The Wei Wai Kum House of Treasures is located in the Discovery Harbour Shopping Centre adjacent to the Discovery Harbour Marina. This cultural Centre contains first Nations exhibits and some live performances at the Gildas, Box of Treasure Theatre which is located in the same building. The Visitor Centre, operated by the Chamber of Commerce, is open all year and is within walking distance of moorage. 250-287-4636 ext. 1.

★ **Discovery HARBOUR Marina:** {50° 02.15' N, 125° 14.40' W} Look for the large riprap breakwater and the ESSO sign north of the ferry landing. Moorage, gas, diesel, oils, stove oil, ice, showers, and oil changing are available. See our Steering Star description in this chapter and the full page advertisement on the inside front cover. Websites: www.discoveryharbourmarina.com & www.boattravel.com/discovery. E-mail: tara@discoveryharbourmarina.com. Address: #392-1434 Island Hwy, Campbell

River, British Columbia V9W 8C9. Fax: 250-287-8939. Telephone: 250-287-2614. VHF 66A.

★ **Ocean Pacific Marine Supply & Shipyard:** {50° 01.50' N, 125° 14.20' W} Location at Campbell River Harbour Authority's South Basin has marine supply store and shipyard. Complete inventory of marine parts. Marine ways, repairs. Second location has complete marine supply store at Discovery Harbour Marina. See our Steering Star description in this chapter. Websites: www.oceanpacificmarine.com & www.boattravel.com/oceanpacific. Email: sales@oceanpacific-marine.com Addresses: Main Store - 871 A Island Highway Campbell River, British Columbia V9W 2C2. Fax: 250-286-6254. Telephone: 250-286-1011, 1-800-663-2294. Discovery Harbour Marina Site: Telephone: 250-286-9600. Open seven days-a-week.

Coast Discovery Marina: {50° 01.81' N, 125° 14.20' W} Moorage to 150', 30, 50, 100 amp. power, water, sewage pump-out. 250-287-7155, 250-287-7455. VHF 66A.

ESSO Marine Station - Seaway Marine Sales at Discovery Harbour Marina: Gas, diesel, stove oil, ice, oil changing, moorage, showers, laundry, groceries and liquor nearby. 250-287-3456. VHF 66A.

Campbell River Public Wharf: Behind Discovery Harbour Marina Breakwater. Small boat harbour: South Basin. Commercial vessels, limited transient pleasure moorage. New pump-out on Dock C in area marked "Loading Zone". 20, 30, 50 amp power, water, restrooms, showers. 250-287-7931. VHF 66A.

Freshwater Marina on Campbell River: Moorage, power, water, washrooms. 250-286-0701.

Quadra Island

[3312, 3539, 3540,3543]

★ **Quadra Island:** Quadra Island is on the east side of Discovery Passage. Several days could be spent circumnavigating and exploring this island, visiting numerous anchorages, parks, and the shore facilities at Quathiaski Cove, Heriot Bay, and April Point. Of five parks on Quadra Island, the Main Lakes Chain is of special significance. For a different experience, it is possible to launch a hand carried craft into this lake chain and enjoy peaceful, lily studded waterways that meander through the country side. Quadra was named for the Spanish explorer, Quadra, who researched the coast at the same time as Vancouver. They became good friends, and Vancouver originally named Vancouver Island, Quadra and Vancouver Island, but this was changed by the British Admiralty after deciding that the name was too long and unwieldy. Quadra had to settle on having his name on the neighboring island, the largest in the Discovery Passage group.

★ **Quathiaski Cove (4):** Known as Q Cove, this harbor is located opposite Campbell River on the eastern side of Discovery Passage. Enter north or south of Grouse Island. This is the site of public floats, pub, boat yards, and the terminus of the Quadra Island-Campbell River ferry. The public wharf has power on the floats and garbage and oil disposal. A small shopping center, lodging, showers, groceries, bait, herring are all within one kilometer of the public floats.

★ **April Point & April Point Cove (5):** This point of Quadra Island forms a protective windbreak for an appendix-shaped cove which lies south-southwest of Gowlland Island. Here is a

Please tell our advertisers that you found them in Northwest Boat Travel® & Northwest Boat Travel On-Line®

Dent Island Vicinity   *Jack Schreiber Photo*

beautiful, quiet moorage with wharfage available at April Point Lodge or good anchorage on a mud bottom.

April Point Marina & Resort: The marina is in a sheltered bay around the point from the lodge. 20, 30 and 50 amp power, water, laundry, showers, lodging, restaurant. Advance reservations: 1-800-663-7090. Marina: 250-285-2222 VHF 10.

★ **Gowlland Harbour (6):** There is peaceful and secure anchorage in several places within this large harbor. Enter from the north by passing north-northeast of Gowlland Island. Currents here can reach five knots outside the entrance, but no noticeable current is felt inside. Avoid Entrance Rock to port upon entering. Entry through the narrow passage from April Point at or near the head is not recommended as the passage is rock strewn. Anchorage is good east of Crow Islet, south of Stag Island and Doe Islet, and in the large basin at the head. Log booms fringe the shore. Tie-ups are not recommended because the area is actively used as a booming ground. Several private floats extend from shore.

Seymour Narrows (7): Use the *Seymour Narrows, British Columbia* current tables. Powerful currents run to 16 knots at springs, causing overfalls. Travel is advised within a half hour of slack water. The narrows is about two miles long and has high, rugged shorelines on each side. Watch for drift in the waterway. Flood current sets south, while the ebb current sets north. When either stream is running at strength, the eddies and swirls are extremely heavy, and if opposed by a wind, can create very dangerous conditions for mariners. The duration of absolute slack water can range from 12 to 15 minutes, but when there is a large range of tide, the interval of change is less. If weather conditions are extreme, they affect the change also. Race Point, to the south, has strong back eddies on a flood tide. This causes rips, especially if there is wind. Passage at these times is best closer to Quadra Island. When approaching from the south, there is temporary anchorage between Maud Island and the Quadra Island shore. Menzies Bay is also used for anchorage, behind Defender Shoal, marked with an anchor on the

charts. When approaching from the north, Deepwater Bay, while open to northwesterlies, does provide temporary shelter. There is a charted rock near Separation Point. Ripple Rock was located only about a fathom below the surface and near mid-channel until its destruction by explosives in 1958. It was the cause of several tragic accidents. The three million dollar explosion was the largest non-nuclear explosion to that time. Seymour Narrows was named for Rear Admiral Sir Francis Seymour who was in command of a station here in the 1840's.

★ **Maud Island:** Temporary anchorage is found in the channel between the island and the Quadra shore. The *HMCS Columbia*, 366 feet in length, was purposely sunk by the Artificial Reef Society of British Columbia to serve as an artificial reef.

Brown's Bay Marina: Moorage, gas, diesel, 15, 30, 50 amp power, water, showers, laundry, provisions, launch, RV, restaurant. 250-286-3135. VHF 66A.

★ **Kanish Bay (8):** This bay indents about two miles into Quadra Island. The Chained Islands, which lie along the southern border of the bay, provide protection and anchorage between the islands and shore. There are rocks and a drying shelf.

★ **Granite Bay (9):** This bay extends southeast off Kanish Bay. The entrance is narrow. A rock is to port near the entrance. Depths within the bay average 30 feet, mud bottom. This was once the site of a community of some 500 residents who were engaged in logging, farming, and mining at the Lucky Jim Gold and Copper Mine. Today, there are few residents. A tiny bay between Granite Bay and Small Inlet has some protection from west winds. A road leads to Heriot Bay, Quathiaski Cove, and April Point.

★ **Small Inlet (10):** Small Inlet has, at least, two good anchorages. After negotiating the narrow entrance, the inlet opens up to reveal high mountains and an abundance of greenery. Enter in mid-channel to avoid kelp patches off both shores. Entrance depths at half tide average 18 feet. There is good anchorage far into the bay.

★ **Otter Cove (11):** Shelter is found from westerlies, and this is also a spot for awaiting favorable current conditions at Seymour Narrows. Enter north of Limestone Island and go close in to the head. Kelp marks dangers near the small island. The southern approach is blocked by extensive kelp and foul ground. The bottom is rock.

Chatham Point: White buildings with red roofs mark the lighthouse at this weather reporting station. Dangerous conditions can exist from tide rips caused when a strong west wind meets an ebbing tide. See current tables for Seymour Narrows, British Columbia.

Rock Bay: Ruins of a wharf are on the west side. An old road connects with Hwy 19. Site of Rock Bay Marine Park. The park land is strictly along the shore, other area is privately owned. It is possible to trailer a boat to this site using an old logging road that is passable during the dry months. Activities include scuba diving, fishing, paddling, and wildlife viewing.

Okisollo Channel
[3312, 3537, 3539]

★ **Okisollo Channel:** This picturesque 12 mile channel runs along the north shore of Quadra Island. There may be fresh water on the Sonora Island shore, opposite Metcalf Island. A spring usually cascades down the cliff behind the trees to the water below. It is possible to edge up to the bank to fill containers. To locate the spring, look for an especially green spot on the bank. In settled weather, there is anchorage behind Metcalf Island. It is possible to avoid much of the current at Lower Rapids and Gypsy Shoal by passing north of the Okis Islands toward Barnes Bay. Gypsy Shoal, with depths of less than six feet, nearly blocks Lower Rapids. Passage is made south of the shoal at slack water only. Heavy overfalls occur on an ebb tide at Upper Rapids, off Cooper Point. Passage in this area is recommended at or near slack. Slack occurs at Lower Rapids, Upper Rapids, and Hole-In-The-Wall close to the same time (About 55 minutes before slack water at *Seymour Narrows*. Use the Seymour Narrows current tables or see the current tables for Seymour Narrows, British Columbia.). Hazards are Bentley Rock off Quadra Island, and a reef off Cooper Point. Okisollo Channel continues in a southeasterly direction past the Octopus Islands and Yeatman Bay to Surge Narrows. Opposite Bentley Rock, the sign on the dock on the Sonora Island shore marks the site of a gift shop.

★ **Chonat Bay:** Chonat Bay is used primarily for log storage, but anchorage is possible.

Walk-around: A trail leading from the head of the bay crosses over a concrete dam and leads to Chonat Lake. Another small road to starboard, before the bay shallows, leads to Ashlar Lake.

Barnes Bay: Often there are extensive logging operations in this Bay. Anchorage is tricky because the bottom is rock.

★ **Owen Bay (12):** This bay has good anchorage. Enter north of Grant Island. Rocks extend off Walters Point. Another approach can be made south of Grant Island. Rocks and narrow channels make this entrance less inviting. Strong currents are frequent. There is a public float. A lagoon, south of the floats, can be explored by dinghy.

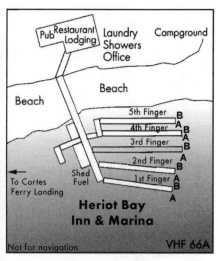

East Quadra Island

[3312, 3538, 3539]

★ **Crescent Channel (17):** Enter from Hoskyn Channel keeping Bold Island to starboard. There are rocks lying along the Bold Island shoreline. The land in this harbor is private. Anchorage is recommended about halfway into the southwestern channel in five fathoms.

★ **Village Bay (18):** In settled weather, there is fair anchorage near shore, straight in or to the right of the islet near the head.

Walk-around: A trail leads to Village Bay Lake. This lake connects with both Main Lake and Upper Main Lake, making it the longest freshwater passage in the Gulf or Discovery Islands. Good canoeing and bird watching.

★ **Mould's Bay (19):** This bay is tucked in at the northwestern end of the Breton Islands. Anchorage is fair in 25-35 feet of water on a rocky bottom. It is open to southerly winds. Old timers know the bay as once home to a lady who put great store in the readings from her crystal ball.

★ **Heriot Bay (20):** At Heriot Bay there is a public wharf with moorage, garbage drop, power, and water and, on the shore to port when entering, lies historic Heriot Bay Inn Marina. Nearby, Island Market offers free delivery to moorages. Anchorage is found west of the public float. This bay is terminus for the Quadra Island-Cortes Island ferry.

★ **Heriot Bay Inn & Marina:** Over one hundred years of old fashioned charm and hospitality with a face lift due to new ownership. 1,800' of moorage (reservations suggested): water, wireless internet, 15 & 30 amp power, gas, diesel, propane, fish cleaning station, showers, laundry, nearby grocery store with dockside delivery. Casual seaside dining in Herons, serving delectable West Coast inspired meals; HBI pub with gourmet grill & weekly live music. Island Adventure Centre offering orca whale watching, fishing charters, kayak tours & rentals, bike rentals, grizzly bear expeditions in season, & sightseeing tours! Also at the Heriot Bay Inn: local artisans gift shop, newly renovated rooms, cabins, and tent / RV park with full hook ups. See our advertisement in this chapter. Websites: www.heriotbayinn.com & www.islandadventure-centre.com. E-mail to: info@heriotbayinn.com. Mailing Address: Box 100, Heriot Bay, British

★ **Hole In The Wall:** See current tables for Seymour Narrows, British Columbia. The western end of this channel has rapids which run up to 12 knots at springs. Floods northeast, ebbs southwest. Florence Cove, about halfway through the passage, may provide limited anchorage, but winds funnel into the cove. The eastern end of the passageway is a popular fishing hole.

★⚓ **Octopus Islands Marine Park (13):** This marine park, west of Hole In The Wall, is a popular anchorage. Small islets protect larger anchoring basins. One favored entry is from Bodega Anchorage through the narrow northern cut between Quadra and the Octopus Islands. Depths of 15-20 feet are in mid-channel. At the western end of the channel, rocks sitting just below the surface show bright green through the clear water. Anchorage is possible in the first bay to starboard. Avoid a large, sprawling rock to port on entering. Several boats can be accommodated with ties to shore. A second bay, also to starboard, provides more anchorage. The west end is a drying flat. The park includes foreshore on Quadra Island and numerous small islands. The two largest islands are private. Swimming, scuba diving, hiking and fishing are possible recreational pastimes. ⚲

★ **Waiatt Bay (14):** The safest entry to this bay is the same as the entry to Octopus Islands Marine Park as described above. It is possible to enter from the south, but caution is advised because the fairway is strewn with rocks and kelp. The bottom of Waiatt Bay has depths of 25-40 feet. There is good anchorage near the head of the bay in 15-25 feet of water. Because this bay is protected from prevailing summer westerlies, this anchorage is often mirror smooth. Rock formations along the shoreline, reflecting in the still water, are called floating totems. Aquaculture operations are on the southeast side.

Walk-around: A small beach at the head of Waiatt Bay is the site of a path which leads up the hill and offers a vista of Small Inlet, the narrow bay which indents Quadra from Kanish Bay on the other side of the island.

★ **Yeatman Bay:** Anchorage is found while awaiting slack at Surge Narrows. A trail from the bay leads to Main Lake.

★ **Surge Narrows (15):** See current tables for Seymour Narrows, British Columbia. This maze of islands and islets is best traversed within a few minutes of slack water. Duration of slack is about 11 minutes. Beazley Pass, between Stuart and Peck Islands, is the navigable passage. Tidal currents run as high as 12 knots at spring floods and 10 knots at spring ebbs. Floods east, ebbs northwest. Charted Tusko Rock lies in the passage. Drying at low water, Tusko Rock is just west of Sturt Island, in line with the ebb current from the pass. Favor the west side of the pass. There are wild mountain goats on Sturt Island. The small community of Surge Narrows on Read Island has a public float. See (23).

★ **Whiterock Passage (16):** Whiterock Passage is a shortcut from Hoskyn Channel to Calm Channel. It lacks the strong currents found at nearby Surge Narrows. This dredged passage has a least depth of six feet and currents of only two knots. There are rocky patches at the southern entrance. These are easily identified in the clear water. Two sets of range markers mark the passage. Foul ground and shoals are easily avoided if the boat is lined up correctly to match the targets. Passage at half tide or a bit more is recommended. If traversed before actual high water, the shoals are easier to identify.

Columbia V0P 1H0. Telephone: Toll Free: 1-888-605-4545, 250-285-3322.   Fax: 250-285-2708. VHF 66A.

★ **Heriot Bay Tru-Value Foods:** For over 50 years this grocery store has served both the local and boating communities. Large selection of fresh organic and conventional produce, meat, deli, and instore bakery products. A full line of groceries, frozen products, whole and organic foods, bulk items, magazines, videos, hardware and fishing licenses.   Will cater to all your needs. A well stocked liquor agency, full service post office, craft store and cafe` are all available for your one stop shopping. Open seven days a week 8:00 a.m. - 8:00 p.m. Sun-Thurs and 8:00 a.m. - 9:00 p.m. Friday and Saturday. Free dock delivery to Heriot Bay Inn & Marina, Government Dock and Rebecca Spit.   See our advertisement in this chapter. Mailing Address: Box 200, Heriot Bay, British Columbia, V0P 1H0. Street Address: 1536 Heriot Bay Rd. Telephone: 250-285-2436. Fax: 250-285-2430.

★ **Drew Harbour & Rebecca Spit Marine Park (20):** This beautiful area, on the eastern side of Quadra Island, contains many attractions. Drew Harbour and Rebecca Spit Marine Park are southeast of Heriot Bay. Many artists have found this spit, with its white sand and picturesque trees, the perfect subject for paintings and photographs. Park acreage is the strand that stretches from the tip of the spit to its base. A sandy beach invites sunbathers. There is also a road for walking, a launching ramp, and picnic sites on the spit. Water is available from pump at park entrance. Anchorage is good in the bight near the tip of the spit, as close to shore as depths will permit. Anchorage is also possible near the head of the bay in 25-35 feet of water on a mud bottom. Beachcombing and picnicking are popular on the spit. Buoys and facilities at the head of the bay are private.

Read Island

[3312, 3537, 3538, 3539, 3541]

★ **Read Island:** Anchorages are in Hjorth Bay, behind the King Islets, Boulton Bay, Evans Bay and Burdwood Bay. The sites of Surge Narrows and Evans Bay have small public floats.

Lake Bay: Once the site of old timer Charlie Rosen's homestead, this bay is deep and offers only limited anchorage with some shelter from northwesterlies.

★ **Hjorth Bay (21):** This picturesque bight and islet, on the west side of Read Island, has anchorage in five fathoms near the head. It is open to west winds, but provides protection in a southerly.

★ **Boulton Bay (22):** This narrow indentation adjacent to Sheer Point has lovely, but limited anchorage near the head. A steep bluff to port cuts off westerly winds, however, the spot is open to the south.

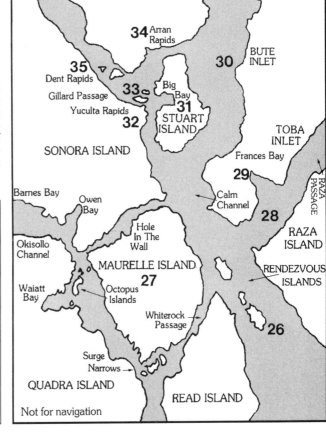

Discovery Harbour Shopping Centre   *Linda Schreiber Photo*

Surge Narrows (23) (15): [3537] This is the site of a public float, store, post office, and a few homes.

Surge Narrows Store: 240' transient moorage. Provisions, ice, hardware, marine supplies, 250-287-6962. VHF 12, 66.

★ **Evans Bay (24):** Several indents form anchorages. North winds hit the southern portion of the bay, near the public float. The float has about 100 feet of moorage. When approaching the float, keep the spar buoy to port. The buoy sits on a shoal. South and east winds enter the central portion of the bay. Bird Cove has some anchorage. Many of the nooks have shallow, drying flats at the heads. The niche farther into Evans Bay has anchorage behind the islets. The unnamed arm of Evans Bay that extends farthest north is the preferred anchorage although it is open to southerly winds. Anchor in the center opposite an old wharf in 30-40 feet of water, or near the steep bluffs in 50 feet of water. This second anchorage provides a haven of early shade when hot summer suns bake the bay. This bay is shallow. Swimming is recommended as the water is clear and warm.

★ **Burdwood Bay (25):** Protection in northwesterlies is possible here. Prior to 1900, in the days of the pioneer logging families, Burdwood Bay was the site of Wylie's Hotel and a murder. Anchor in small basin behind chain of islands in southern part of the bay.

Hill Island: Private. Closed to the public.

North of Read Island

[3312, 3539, 3541]

★ **Rendezvous Islands (26):** Temporary anchorage is possible in a small bight on the southernmost island, behind a small islet and in an unnamed bay on the west side of the middle island. The latter niche has a private float and dolphins extending from shore, restricting space. Lodge on NE Rendezvous Island.

★ **Maurelle Island (27):** Anchorages are not obvious along much of the shore as the hillsides are steep and rocks hide the tiny bights. The vicinity west of Antonio Point is recreational reserve land and includes two small anchorages. Florence Cove, about halfway up Hole In The Wall also offers anchorage.

★ **Toba Inlet (28):** This 20 mile inlet is very deep and the mountains rise 8,000 feet above the water. The turquoise blue glacier-fed waters make underwater visibility difficult. The fjord ends at the estuary of the Toba River. There are numerous waterfalls in the spring and early summer. Water is available from a spring that empties into the inlet about two and one half miles south of Brem Bay. There is a road beyond Snout Point that can provide a walking place. Near Brem River, Cutthroat fishing is reported to be excellent during May, June, and July, and the Coho runs are September to October. There is a resort on the mainland, north of Double Island.

Toba Wildernest Resort & Marina: Moorage, water, showers, provisions, lodging. 250-202-0478. VHF 66A.

Snow Bay: Known locally as Blue Ice Bay, this spot provides glacial ice for summer boaters. This bay is in a niche marked 13 fathoms on the chart, on the south side of the inlet. Some

Campbell River   Linda Schreiber Photo

anchorage is possible at the head of the bay in the northwest corner; not much protection from winds. Large horse flies may be pests.

★ **Frances Bay (29):** Lying off Raza Passage, there is clear water and good swimming in this bay, also known as Fanny Bay. Anchorage in 10 fathoms or less is good at the head, but very exposed to east winds coming down Toba Inlet. The view of Pryce Channel to Toba Inlet is memorable. Two miles southwest of Frances Bay is Church House, with its landmark church.

★ **Bute Inlet (30):** [3542] Milky, glacier fed waters flow in this inlet. The green water is caused by the mineral content of the glacier runoff. The inlet is deep, but the bottom often shoals rapidly near shore. There are drying flats at the mouths of rivers. Lines ashore may be helpful when anchoring. It may be possible to tie to log booms. Temporary anchorages, close to the drying flats, in Waddington Harbour, Orford Bay, and the bights below Purcell Point and Fawn Bluff. The niche below Leask Lake has a 14 fathom reef near the entrance. Locals boast about the cod fishing over this reef. A stream empties from Leask Lake. Log booms may provide tie-ups. Winds are unpredictable and may rise suddenly. The prevailing summer wind pattern is an inflow during the afternoon and an outflow at night and early morning.

Stuart Island

[3312, 3541, 3543]

Yuculta Rapids (32): [3543] See current tables for Seymour Narrows, British Columbia. These rapids are in the narrows north of Kellsey Point. The currents are strong and quick to rise. Floods south, ebbs north. The best time to traverse is within one-half hour of slack at Gillard Passage. If planning to continue on west through the passage, arrive before high water slack in order to coordinate times with slack waters at Gillard and Dent Rapids. The *British Columbia Sailing*

Directions recommends that low powered small craft headed northwest should approach Yuculta Rapids about one hour before turning to ebb in order to take advantage of a back eddy along the Stuart Island shore until off Kellsey Point. Then cross to the Sonora Island side where there is a prevailing northerly current. This should allow time to transit Gillard and Dent Rapids before the ebb current reaches full force.

Gillard Passage (33): Recommended passage is south of Jimmy Judd Island, between Jimmy Judd and Gillard Islands. Flood currents reach eight knots; ebb ten knots, at springs.

★ **Stuart Island & Big Bay (31):** This attractive island hosts hundreds of fishing vacationers each

Big Bay   Gwen Cole Photo

season. It is the home of a post office and public wharf. A large kelp patch is a hazard on approach. The public wharf lies behind the pile and plank breakwater, to the right of the old Big Bay Marina when entering the bay. Surges and tidal currents in the bay amplify boat wakes. A courteous throttle-down upon entry is advisable. The other settlement on Stuart Island is at the southwest tip of the island, next to Harbott Point Light. The floats there are privately owned.

★ **Stuart Island Community Dock:** The dock motto is "WATCH US GROW!" Community dock has 650 lineal feet with airplane float and will expand to 1050 lineal feet in 2006. Accommodates boats over 100'. Fresh water, showers, laundry, post office, small general store, ice, fresh crab & prawn sales, espresso bar & ice cream counter, fishing licenses, fishing gear. Also find sport fishing guides for hire with 15 to 20 years experience. Tidal and Eagle Eco-tours. Walking trail to Eagle Lake. Future plans include liquor store, expanded moorage, gift shop, bakery and pizzeria. Reservations are suggested. Profits will go towards salmon enhancement and other community initiative programs. See our advertisement at A-1 in the front of the book. Email: stuartislandca@aol.com. Telephone: 250-202-3625. VHF 66A.

Big Bay Marina Resort: Closed. Property is now private.

Morgan's Landing Resort: Expanded docks and facilities with overnight moorage. Lodge, restaurant. 250-287-0237.

Stuart Island Resort: Private facility located at Harbott Point.

Arran Rapids (34): These occur where Cordero Channel joins Bute Inlet. See current tables for

Octopus Islands   *Carl & Gloria Tenning Photo*

Seymour Narrows, British Columbia. Floods east, ebbs west. Flood and ebb tides can both reach nine knots.

Dent Rapids (35): [3543] The flood current flows east (095 degrees) and ebbs west (290 degrees). The time of slack water at Dent is identical with that at Arran Rapids. A whirlpool, called the Devil's Hole, is created at peak flow south of the south point of Little Dent Island. Maximum flood is nine knots, ebb is eight.

★ **Dent Island Lodge:** Come in to the area slowly and, after landing, check in at the lodge. If calling ahead, cell phone coverage is functional. Moorage, power, cabins, full service dining room. Open May through September. See our Steering Star description in this chapter. Internet: www.dentisland.com, www.boattravel.com/dentisland. E-mail henry@dentisland.com. Mailing address: Dent Island, British Columbia V0P 1V0. Fax: 250-203-1041. Telephone: 250-203-2553. VHF 66A.

★ **The Dent Island Lodge:** This hidden treasure is nestled on the islets between Dent Island and the mainland, just a few minutes west of Big Bay. Look for the cedar shake-roofed lodge with dark green trim.

Enter from the southeast end of Dent Island and tie to the floats adjacent to the reversing tidal rapids of Canoe Pass. Water, 15, 30 & 50 ampere power are available on site. A hot tub and sauna are available to all our boating guests – free of charge. Visitors are captivated by the beautiful, clear turquoise waters that surround our two islets. The Dent Island Lodge is a destination resort for boaters, a fishing lodge for the discriminating angler, and a choice location for those planning conferences, seminars, reunions, or retreats. The dining room menu includes a selection of unique northwest cuisine and fine wine, all served in a showcase setting that overlooks Canoe Pass and Cordero Strait. Please drop in for lunch, or call ahead for dinner reservations. **Circle #45 on the Reader Service Card. Internet: www.dentisland.com or www.boattravel.com/dentisland/ E-Mail: henry@dentisland.com Mailing address: Dent Island, British Columbia V0P 1V0. Telephone: 250-203-2553. Fax: 250-203-1041. We Monitor VHF 66A.**

Essential Supplies & Services

AIR TRANSPORTATION
To & from Washington
Seattle Seaplanes 1-800-637-5553
To & from Islands/Vancouver
Air Canada 1-888-247-2262
Baxter Air 1-800-661-5599
Coril Air 250-287-8371, 1-888-287-8366
Harbour Air 604-274-1277, 1-800-665-0212
Helijet 1-800-665-4354
Tofino Air 1-800-665-2359
Vancouver Island Air . . 250-287-2433, 1-877-331-2433

AMBULANCE: 911

BOOKS / BOOK STORES
The Marine Atlas. 541-593-6396

BUS TRANSPORTATION
Campbell River Metro 250-287-7433
Greyhound Coach Lines 250-287-7151

COAST GUARD: #16
Comox: VHF 16, 22-A, 26, 84 250-339-3613
Emergencies. . . . . 1-800-567-5111, VHF 16
Campbell River . . . . 250-287-8612, VHF 16, 22, 61, 71

FERRY INFORMATION
B.C. Ferries: 250-386-3431, 1-888-223-3779 (B.C.)
Campbell R-Quadra, Cortes: 250-286-1412

FUELS
Brown's Bay: Gas, Diesel . . . . . 250-286-3135 VHF 66A
Campbell River Seaway ESSO: Gas, Diesel.
. . . . **250-287-3456 VHF 66A**
Heriot Bay Inn: Gas, Diesel. 250-285-3322 VHF 66A

GOLF COURSES
(These courses are accessible from moorage and have rental clubs available)
Sequoia Springs 250-287-4970
Storey Creek 250-923-FORE

GROCERY STORES
Heriot Bay Tru-Value Foods. 250-285-2436
Stuart Island Community Dock 250-202-3625

HOSPITALS
Campbell River 250-287-7111
Powell River 604-485-3211

INSURANCE
Boat Insurance Agency 206-285-1350
Or Call 1-800-828-2446

LIQUOR STORES
Heriot Bay Tru-Value Foods. 250-285-2436
Quathiaski Cove

LODGING
April Point Resort & Marina.
. . . . 1-800-663-7090, 250-285-2222 VHF 10
Dent Island Lodge: Dent Island 250-203-2553
Heriot Bay Inn: Quadra Island 250-285-3322

MARINAS / MOORAGE
April Point Resort & Marina . . . . 250-285-2222 VHF 10
Brown's Bay Marina . . . . 250-286-3135 VHF 66A
Campbell River Harbour Authority. 250-287-7931
Coast Marina . . . . 250-287-7155 VHF 66A
Dent Island Lodge 250-203-2553
Discovery Harbour Marina . 250-287-2614 VHF 66A
Evans Bay: Read Island
Freshwater Marina. 250-286-0701
Heriot Bay Inn: Quadra Island 250-285-3322
Heriot Bay: Public floats
Owen Bay: Sonora Island
Quathiaski Cove
Stuart Island Community Dock 250-202-3625
. . . . **VHF 66A**
Surge Narrows Settlement: Read Island
Toba Wildernest. VHF 66A

MARINE SUPPLY
Ocean Pacific: Campbell River 800-663-2294

PROPANE
Heriot Bay Inn: Quadra Island 250-285-3322

RAMPS / HAUL-OUTS
April Point Resort & Marina: Quadra Island.
. . . . 250-285-2222

Brown's Bay Marina. 250-286-3135
Cape Mudge Boatworks:
. . . . 1-866-452-6950 (Toll free), 250-285-2155
Freshwater Marina. 250-286-0701
Jack's Boat Yard: Finn Bay 604-483-3566
Ocean Pacific Marine Supply: Campbell R.
. . . . **800-663-2294**
Quadra Island: Quathiaski Cove, Heriot Bay, Rebecca
Spit

RED TIDE INFO: 604-666-2828

REPAIRS
Altech Diesel 250-286-0055
Cape Mudge Boatworks: 1-866-452-6950
. . . . 250-285-2155. 250-285-3167 (8 a.m. – 10.pm.)
Carmac Diesel: Campbell R. Mobile: 250-287-2171
Jack's Boat Yard: Finn Bay 604-483-3566
Ocean Pacific Marine: Campbell R . 250-286-1011

RESTAURANTS
April Point Resort. 1-800-663-7090
Dent Island Lodge 250-203-2553
Heriot Bay Inn: Quadra Island 250-285-3322

RV SITES / TRAILER PARKING
Brown's Bay Marina . . . . 250-286-3135 VHF 66A
Heriot Bay Inn: Quadra Island 250-285-3322

SEWAGE DISPOSAL
Campbell River Harbour Authority: Pump.
. . . . 250-287-7931, VHF 66A
Coast Marina: Pump. 250-287-7455
Year round general info 250-287-7155
Fairwinds Schooner Cove: Pump. . . 250-468-5364

SHELLFISH HOTLINE:
. . . . 250-850-5701, 604-666-2828

SPORT FISHING:
April Point Resort: Quadra Island 250-285-2222
Dent Island Lodge 250-203-2553
Fishing Information 250-850-5701
Government Information 604-666-2828
Heriot Bay Inn: Quadra Island 250-285-3322

STORAGE:
Jack's Boat Yard: Finn Bay 604-483-3566

TAXI
Campbell River 250-287-8294
Quadra Island 250-205-0505

TOWING
C-TOW. 1-888-354-5554
Carmac Diesel 250-287-2171

VHF MARINE OPERATOR
Campbell River: VHF 27, 64
East Thurlow: VHF 87
Sayward: VHF 28

VISITOR INFORMATION
Campbell River 250-287-4636, 1-866-830-1113

WEATHER
WX-1, 162.55
Environment Canada Weather Line. 250-339-9861
Alert Bay 250-974-5305
Campbell River. 1-866-830-1113
Comox. 250-339-0748
Port Hardy. 250-949-7148

Dent Rapids   *Linda Schreiber Photo*

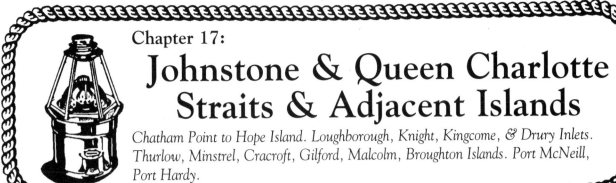

Chapter 17:
Johnstone & Queen Charlotte Straits & Adjacent Islands

Chatham Point to Hope Island. Loughborough, Knight, Kingcome, & Drury Inlets. Thurlow, Minstrel, Cracroft, Gilford, Malcolm, Broughton Islands. Port McNeill, Port Hardy.

Symbols

[   ]: Numbers between [ ] are chart numbers.

{   }: Numbers & letters between { } are waypoints.

⚓: Park, ⛵: Boat Launch, ▲: Campgrounds,
⚲: Hiking Trails, ⚏: Picnic Area, ⚲: Biking

★ **Important Notice:** See "Important Notices" between Chapters 7 and 8 in this guide for specific information on boating related topics such as: Canadian & U.S. Customs, boating safety and security, navigation, weather, U.S. & Canadian Coast Guard, U.S & Canadian marine radio use, Vessel Traffic Service and traffic separation plans, security zones, and internet access. Due to new Department of Homeland Security regulations, call ahead for latest customs information and/or see Northwest Boat Travel On-line, www.nwboat.com.

Seasonal Changes: Many resorts in this area are seasonal or have seasonal hours. May to September is high season. During the off season it is wise to call ahead to check on availability of fuel, provisions, and other services.

Introduction

★ North to Johnstone and Queen Charlotte Straits: Adjacent to the Johnstone and Queen Charlotte Straits are some of the most beautiful and secluded anchorages south of Alaska, and some of the best salmon, cod, halibut, snapper, and prawn fishing anywhere. These are the waters of adventure and exploration. Each year more boaters are lured northwestward, beyond Desolation Sound and Discovery Passage, to the Johnstone Strait and adjacent waters. Here, it is still possible to experience the solitude of having the only boat anchored in one of the hundreds of

bays. People who enjoy a leisurely pace-of-life and who are pleased to share a story about the islands, past and present, await It is impossible to spend much time here without coming away with memories of beautiful scenery, and with a respect for the spirit and perseverance of those who live here and those who provide facilities and services for visiting boaters.

★ **Facilities:** Each year more facilities are adding power and conveniences. It must be understood that, for the marinas and resorts, bringing in provisions and holding them, especially cold items, is an expensive and troublesome task in these out-of-the-way places. Power is generated by the user, at a much higher cost than power purchased in more populated areas. The season is extremely short. Whenever it is possible to pay for overnight moorage by choosing a privately owned float, to buy groceries or fuel from these remote provisioners, or to have a memorable dinner out, prepared

by skillful and dedicated chefs, it is an opportunity to participate in the continuance of these "trading-post" style operations.

Weather Patterns: The most common climate from Minstrel Island northward is low clouds and fog in the morning, with clearing in the afternoon. The climate is often refreshingly cooler than the extreme heat of Desolation Sound. The weather is a bit more uncertain than it is to the south. There are more overcast and rainy days. Fog often wraps itself in angel-hair-like chains and patches, around the islands and into the fjords. Radar is a significant advantage.

Currents, Winds, & Larger Tidal Changes: A number of the waters in this section are in, or near, passages where current and turbulence can be strong. There is no reason to fear these passages, provided they are traversed with a knowledge of the currents and a respect for the force of

Chart List

Canadian Hydrographic Charts:

3312, 3515, 3543-3548, 3549, 3564

Marine Atlas (2005 ed.):

Pages 33, 35-41

VANCOUVER ISLAND
Not for navigation

the waters. Passage at, or near, slack water is prudent. Tide and current tables list the rate and direction of flow, as well as the slack water times for most navigable passages in the region. Some of the more notable rapids and maximum runs are: Yuculta Rapids, six-seven knots; Dent Rapids, eight-nine knots; Green Point Rapids, seven knots; and Whirlpool Rapids, seven knots. If adequate planning is done, overfalls and whirlpools can be avoided completely. When in the vicinity of a whirlpool, pass on the side which is moving in the same direction as the boat. This will usually push the boat away from the pool, rather than into it. Even with a faster boat, the speed of the water itself is not the problem, but the overfalls and whirlpools caused by that speed.

Both currents and winds must be considered. The ebbing tide flows northwest; the flooding tide southeast. However, when there is wind, the current that opposes the wind will greatly increase the seas. Since the ebb currents are stronger than the floods (because of residual water), the seas will be the worst with a northwest wind opposing an ebbing tide. For an example of strategic planning, see Wellbore Channel (12) below. Because of tidal ranges of up to 20 feet at springs, additional allowances for overnight or low tide depths must be made.

★ Insurance Coverage: Many United States boat policies designate Malcolm Island as the northernmost geographical limit. Generally, a telephone call to the broker or company will result in an endorsement for extended cruising. There is sometimes a nominal charge. Since Minstrel Island is at about the same latitude as Malcolm Island, it is wise to obtain the endorsement before continuing northward beyond that point.

Johnstone Strait

[3312, 3543, 3544, 3545, 3546]

★ Johnstone Strait: This 54 mile long body of water stretches from Chatham Point to Blinkhorn Peninsula. The flood current sets east and ebbs west. A residual westerly current causes the ebb to be stronger than the flood. See current tables for Seymour Narrows, British Columbia. If possible when traversing this strait, go with the wind and the current. Tide rips are often off Needham Point, Ripple Point, in Race and Current Passages, and between Kelsey Bay and Port Neville. When there is a west, northwest, or southwest wind in Current Passage, rips can be amplified and become dangerous. For shipping lane information, see the Canadian Hydrographic publication, Sailing Directions, PAC 203, and VHF 71.

Lower Johnstone Strait: This is the narrowest portion of Johnstone Strait. Uncomfortable conditions can occur when westerly winds are against even a minimal tide. The old timers' adage is, "Never go to Kelsey Bay on any westerly wind." Perhaps even better would be to avoid the Chatham Point to Kelsey Bay route entirely, and go the inside route, staying in the more protected waters of inside channels whenever possible. If traversing Johnstone Strait, after Ripple Point, the waterway narrows to a width of one mile, for the next nine miles. Emergency anchorage can be found at Turn Island, between Turn and the East Thurlow Island shore. Currents and winds can enter, but it provides shelter and an indication of conditions on the strait. Another emergency anchorage is in the Walkem Island group, in about four fathoms of water, in the bight on the south side of the larger island and between the two islands. Avoid the bare rock. Little Bear Bay, on the Vancouver Island shore, opposite the Walkems, ends in a drying flat, with limited pro-

tection in southeast winds. Past the Walkem Islands, Mayne Passage joins Johnstone Strait, and provides a route to the more protected waters. Continuing northwest in Johnstone, Knox Bay on West Thurlow Island has some protection as a temporary anchorage. Logging operations may be present in the area. On the Vancouver Island shore, limited protection can be found behind the islet in Bear Bight, in Humpback Bay, and in Palmer Bay, the narrow indentation west of Humpback Bay. Don't be surprised to find logs filling Bear Bight. A drying flat extends from the mouth of the creek in Humpback Bay. Currents become stronger near Camp Point and can reach six knots with heavy tide-rips. Check the Tide and Current tables for Race Passage and Current Passage. See current tables for Seymour Narrows, British Columbia. Tidal streams run strongly through these passages, attaining five knots on the ebb and flood in Current Passage and six knots on the ebb and flood in Race Passage. Eddies and swirls are numerous. Do not traverse this vicinity when an ebb (westerly flowing) current meets a west wind. Steep-sided Vere Cove, on the west end of West Thurlow is wide open to the west, however shelter is found in a southeast wind. Anchorage is deep (60' plus), but it is also out of the current.

A Vessel Traffic Separation Scheme is in effect. Using Ripple Shoal and Helmcken Island as natural obstacles to divide eastbound from westbound traffic, it is recommended that eastbound traffic use Race Passage and westbound traffic use Current Passage. Boats finding it necessary to do otherwise are asked to notify others in the area by using VHF 71. Caution advised in the area of Ripple Shoal, east of Helmcken Island. Pass north of the shoal. For more on the Helmcken Island vicinity, see (14).

Nodales Channel

[3312, 3543]

Nodales Channel (1): This waterway runs north and south, connecting Discovery Passage to Cordero Channel. The flood flows north. Rips can form off Johns Point at the north end where flood streams meet. Aquaculture operations are on the west shore. Good anchorages are found in bays on both sides of the channel.

★ Cameleon Harbour: Although open to northwest winds, anchorage is possible in this harbor. Marshy land extends from the port side at the head. Anchor favoring the starboard side near the head.

★ Handfield Bay: This small bay in the northern part of Cameleon Harbour is picturesque and offers anchorage in depths of 15-25 feet. There is a drying shoal to port in the entrance and a small islet to starboard. The bay shallows quickly. The head is a drying flat. Handfield Bay is part of Thurston Bay Provincial Marine Park.

Walk-around: Ashore, the old orchard can be explored. A path, west of the creek, leads to Anchorage Cove at the south end of Thurston Bay.

★⚓ Thurston Bay Provincial Marine Park: Avoid the rocks near the entrance. This undeveloped marine park includes land at the north and south ends of Thurston Bay. Anchorage Cove, at the south end of the bay, is a lovely, lagoon-like spot, with trees down to the water's edge. Depths are adequate for overnight. At the head, there is a marshland, with a drying flat. Other anchorage spots are in the northern portion of Thurston Bay, behind Block Island. ⚓⚓

Walk-around: For nearly 30 years Thurston Bay was the headquarters for the British Columbia Forest Service. It is possible to walk to the site of the old station and to follow trails and old roads in the vicinity. A trail leads to Florence Lake, about one and one half miles inland. A stream provides fresh water. The lake offers great trout fishing.

★ Hemming Bay (2): This bay is across Nodales Channel from Cameleon Harbour. Entry is made between a point on the south and the Lee Islands. Favor the Pinhorn Islet side to avoid Menace Rock that lies in the center of the outer bay. The indentation continues inland, past shoals and islets to port. Anchorage is possible in an area tucked behind the islets, but the bottom is rocky and holding is insecure. The extreme inner bay may be explored by dinghy.

Cordero Channel

[3312, 3543]

Cordero Channel: Beginning in the vicinity of Gillard Pass, this waterway extends in a westerly direction approximately 20 miles until it meets Chancellor Channel.

★ Frederick Arm (3): There is good anchorage in ten fathoms at the northwest corner of the head of this arm. Open to south winds. It is possible to enter scenic, four mile long, Estero Basin at or near high slack tide in a skiff or dinghy. It is uncharted. The entrance is blocked at low tide. Locate Estero Peak, over 5,000' in height, and let your imagination work to see what it resembles.

★ Phillips Arm (4): Anchorage is possible in Fanny Bay or in ten fathoms near the head. The arm shoals quickly and the bottom is hard to see because it is covered with weeds. Fanny Bay is a center for logging operations and booms are present. A log boom tie up may be possible.

★ Shoal Bay (5): This bay is on the northeast shore of East Thurlow Island. There is public moorage with water available. Anchorage can be found off the wharf's end. The head of the bay shoals and anchorage is not possible. The frame building on the wharf was once a store. Before World War II, Thurlow was the site of three saloons and two gold mines. Miners from two other mines up Phillip's Arm and hand-loggers frequented the site, thus making Thurlow a jumping town.

Shoal Bay Lodge & Pub: Pub and cafe open. Lodge, cabins, laundry, showers. Moorage available at public wharf. New freshwater system. 250-287-6818. VHF 66A

★ Bickley Bay (6): This bay is on the north shore of East Thurlow Island. There is anchorage on a mud bottom in 20-35 feet of water near the head. Peel Rocks are charted. Favor the port side when entering. The bay is open to northwest winds and currents invade the area. Anchor dragging has been noted. There may be aquaculture in the bay.

Cordero Lodge & Pub: Located on Lorte Island, accessible only by boat or seaplane. Charming getaway with German style food and hospitality. Moorage, lodging, restaurant (reservations required). 250-287-0917. VHF 66A.

Walk-around: A good trail leads to an old logging road, and eventually to a lake.

Tallac Bay (7): Three rocks lie to starboard near

the entrance. Pass either side of the rocks and then favor the western portion of this small niche. Set the hook as the boat is aimed toward the logging road on the hillside and then reverse. Tie to shore for overnight stability.

★ **Cordero Islands Anchorage (8):** There is anchorage behind this picturesque group of islets.

Crawford Anchorage (8): The bottom of this anchorage is rock and anchoring is difficult. Rocks lie southeast of Mink Island and in the passage off Erasmus Island. In the niche on Erasmus Island, marked by a "2" on the chart, there is fair anchorage on the west side. A taut tie to shore may add to the security of the ground tackle. There are shoals in the bay. It is possible to walk along the logging road.

West Thurlow Island

[3312, 3543]

★ **Mayne Passage (9):** Floods north, ebbs south with currents to five knots at springs. See current tables for Seymour Narrows, British Columbia. Mayne Passage connects Johnstone Strait with Cordero Channel. This is the site of Blind Channel Resort.

★ **Blind Channel Resort:** {50° 24.50' N, 125° 30.03' W} This family owned and operated resort is located in a lovely area. Moorage, power, water, gas, diesel, propane, lodging, provisions, seaside cottage available, wireless internet, liquor, showers, laundry, restaurant, and credit card telephone. See our Steering Star description in this chapter. Email: info@blindchannel.com. Internet sites: www.blindchannel.com & www.boattravel.com/blindchannel. Address: Blind Channel Post

Office, Blind Channel, British Columbia V0P 1B0. Telephone: 250-949-1420. 1-888-329-0475. VHF 66A.

Walk-around: Maps are available at the store. Walk the Big Cedar or the Viewpoint Trails. The Big Cedar Trail rises to an elevation of 200 feet over a length of about 1/3 mile. It can be walked in a 45 minute round trip. The Viewpoint Trail is shorter and easily walked in a 30 minute round trip.

Knox Bay: This indent into West Thurlow has given shelter from northwesterlies to many boaters. Favor the port side near the head. Although much of the shore is foul, the ledge drops quickly and there is good holding bottom in 45-50 feet of water.

Greene Point Rapids (10): See current tables for Seymour Narrows, British Columbia. These rapids run to seven knots at springs. Slack water is predicted to occur about one hour and 30 minutes before slack water at Seymour Narrows. Slower boats will want to plan passage within about one-half hour before or after slack. When east bound on a strong flood current, avoid heading toward Erasmus Island.

★ **Loughborough Inlet (11):** [3543, 3555] This inlet stretches inland for 18 miles. A stream cascades down the bank making fresh water accessible near the entrance to the inlet about one-half mile in from Styles Point. Depths are too great for anchorage in most of the inlet. There are no public floats. There are anchorages in Beaver Inlet and Sidney Bay. Log boom tie-ups may be possible in Heydon Bay.

★ **Beaver Inlet:** This inlet lies to port, a short distance in from the entrance to Loughborough Inlet. It is open to northwesterlies because the

wind funnels through the draw at the head. There is anchorage at the head, southwest of Dickson Point. Large tidal changes occur in this vicinity. Beware of sunken logs that can foul your anchor when going too far toward the head of the inlet.

★ **Sidney Bay:** Adjacent to Beaver Inlet, Sidney Bay has anchorage at the head in 30-40 feet of water.

Shorter Point: A tiny bight into West Thurlow Island, on the east side of the point, opposite the entrance to Wellbore Channel, has some shelter when there are winds and rips on Chancellor Channel. Anchor close in to the head. The bottom drops quickly to 50 feet.

Wellbore Channel (12): This is the inside passage to the northwestern end of Hardwicke

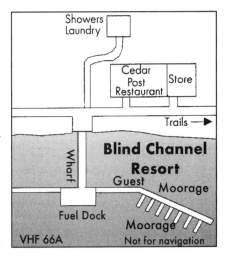

★ **Blind Channel Resort:** As you approach the moorage floats of this popular resort, you are first greeted by the colorful flags flying in the breeze above the wharf, and then by the flower boxes and stone mosaics which seem to extend a "Welcome Home" message to the visiting family. Since 1970, the Richter family has welcomed

boaters to their home and facilities, located on the gently sloping hillside along the protected harbor on Mayne Passage. Modern concrete floats have widely spaced berths with convenient power outlets, and water spigots for the pure spring water. A quiet generator, located away from the water, provides excellent shore power for the floats. Be aware of a large eddy in the bay with the current usually running south to north off the fingers, and north to south at the fingers. Gas, diesel, oils, and propane are accessible. Wireless internet available. On shore, Annemarie Richter's beautiful tapestries and quilts decorate the Cedar Post Inn, the fully-licensed restaurant and lounge. A seaside cottage is also available. Food and beverage service is provided on the patio overlooking the marina. The well stocked store provides groceries, liquor, frozen meats, block and cube ice, tackle, dairy products, a post office, gifts, a large selection of charts and an Internet Station. Jennifer's delicious bread and other baked goods are made fresh daily during the season. A path leading to the Thurlow Cedar, a humbling giant measuring 20 feet across, has been extended to the bluffs overlooking the channel. Logging roads make long walks across the island possible. Its central location and south coast climate (summer fog is rare) have made Blind Channel a favorite rendezvous spot for boaters meeting fly-in guests. Scheduled flights to Campbell River and Vancouver. Kenmore Air makes daily scheduled flights from Seattle. **Address: Blind Channel Post Office, British Columbia V0P 1B0. E-mail:info@blindchannel.com Internet: http://www.blindchannel.com & www.boattravel.com/blindchannel/ Telephone: 250-949-1420. 1-888-329-0475. Call "Blind Channel" on VHF 66A.**

Island. The advantage of using this and Sunderland Channel is that it avoids both Race and Current Passages in Johnstone Strait, where an ebbing tide and northwest wind can cause heavy chop near Helmcken Island and Earl Ledge. If you pass through Greene Point Rapids near high slack when traveling north, you will have the ebbing tide behind you all of the way through Wellbore Channel and Whirlpool Rapids. In this way one has the aid of the northbound, ebbing current for several hours. If winds are from the west, however, the wind will be against the ebbing tide and produce heavy rips, especially in Chancellor Channel. For Greene Point Rapids, see current tables for Seymour Narrows, British Columbia.

Whirlpool Rapids: Currents do not exceed seven knots. The whirlpools form south of Carterer Point on flooding tides and north of this point on ebbing tides. Heading south, if you pass Whirlpool at low water slack, you can cruise 30 miles to Stuart Island with the flood tide pushing you. You will probably have to wait at Dent Rapids until one half hour before high water before starting through. For Whirlpool Rapids, see current tables for Seymour Narrows, British Columbia.

★ Forward Harbour & Douglas Bay (13): [3544] A narrow entrance off Wellbore Channel leads to a long, wide indentation with high mountains and a snowy peak as a backdrop. A small bight to port in the entry, near a grassy knoll, is large enough for one or two boats. Douglas Bay, within Forward Harbour, is the popular anchorage. The crescent-shaped beach encircles an anchorage area that can accommodate 10-15 boats. Rocky shelves extend from shore. Depths average 30-40 feet before a quick drop to 50-60 foot depths. Holding bottom is only fair close in and anchor dragging is not uncommon. The one boat to one anchor rule is prudent here. The holding bottom appears to be better farther out, in the deeper water. Bears are often seen walking the beach.

Walk-around: Hike across to Bessborough Bay and suntan on the beautiful white sand beach. Tied-on plastic bottles mark the trail. It might be prudent to bring along a cowbell or pan and large spoon to use as a noisemaker to ward off the bears.

Sunderland Channel: Eight miles in length, this passageway leads west-southwest to join Johnstone Strait. When rounding Althorp Point at the head of Wellbore Channel, it is possible to judge sea conditions on Johnstone Strait. If conditions are choppy entering Sunderland Channel, the chop on Johnstone can be expected to be heavier. Bessborough Bay, at the east end, has anchorage and a lovely white sand beach, however, this is open to the west. Jackson Bay on the north side of Topaze Harbour has anchorage and is the site of a logging camp. A bay, east of Gunner Point, has temporary shelter in strong westerlies.

Yorke Island: If passing on the south side, look up the hillside to see remnants of two large gun batteries that were built in 1939 as an armed look-out point to guard against any enemy ship which would, by necessity, have to transit this strategic area.

Helmcken Island (14): This island divides the waters of Johnstone Strait. Current Passage and Race Passage border the island. Anchorage is possible on an undependable bottom in the northern cove near the west side and in Billy Goat Bay (unnamed on the chart) on the north

side at the east end on a mud bottom. Enter in the passage northwest of the island that has the antennae. Anchor close in. A shore tie might be necessary. The bay is marked with a three on the chart. Comox Coast Guard broadcasts local weather conditions for the area from information gathered by an automated weather station on this island.

Race and Current Passages: Currents near Earl Ledge run three to six knots in Race Passage and three to five knots in Current Passage. See current tables for Seymour Narrows, British Columbia.

Kelsey Bay (15): When entering Kelsey Bay from the south, keep the sunken freighter breakwater on your port side. A nearly 200 foot long public wharf has a 150 foot float adjacent to it. A breakwater gives some protection, except in gale force southeast winds. Floats in the small craft harbor, located south of the wharf, have better moorage. The Salmon River Logging Company bought the land from the Kelsey family in 1937 and much of it is used for log storage. Heavy rips form off Kelsey Bay in the vicinity of Earl Ledge. The admonition, "never go to Kelsey Bay on an ebb tide in any westerly wind", may be worth noting. East of Kelsey Bay, a small bight behind Peterson Islet provides some shelter in westerlies. Visit the Salmon River Wildlife Reserve. Whale watching charter boats are common and the tour companies claim this area is the number one spot in the world for sighting Killer Whales.

Kelsey Bay Harbour: The only small craft harbour located between Campbell River & Port McNeill on Johnstone Straits. Moorage, power, water, launch ramp, gas, garbage deposit.

Sayward: This is a small community inland from Kelsey Bay, on Sayward River. Hotels, stores, restaurants; buses connect with other island communities. Time your visit for *Harvest Fall Fair* the 1st week-end in October or *Art in the Park* during 2nd week-end in July. Logging and tourism are the main industries.

Central Johnstone Strait
[3544, 3545, 3564]

McLeod Bay (16): This bay provides temporary anchorage when escape from a west wind is desired. Head in toward the logging road and equipment storage.

Tuna Point (17): A small bay tucked in behind Mary Island provides temporary protection during westerlies. Logs may be stored here.

Blenkinsop Bay (18): Blenkinsop Bay has a shallow flat at the head, preventing moorage close enough to shore to find protection from winds.

★ Port Neville (19): This seven mile long inlet is used when westerlies invade Johnstone Strait. Anchorage is possible along the west shore opposite the public float, however, strong tidal currents swirl through this area. The public wharf has a float with some moorage. No store or marine facilities are available. An Art Gallery & Museum holds impromptu potluck dinners for boaters. A Post Office is on site. Mail delivered on Wednesdays. Holds mail for traveling public. Call "Ransom Pt." on VHF 06. 250-949-1535. For those who go exploring farther into the inlet, Robber's Nob is the site of Indian petroglyphs. Look on the northwest side.

Anchorage is possible southwest of the point. Logging operations are prevalent in the area. There is abalone at Cuthbert Rock, near Collingwood Point. Baresides Bay is recommended for temporary anchorage only.

Broken Islands (20): These islands lie at the entrance to Havannah Channel. See current tables for Seymour Narrows, British Columbia. Many boaters know of the Broken Islands because, after rounding them, heading northwest, the waters are more sheltered from sea and winds on the Johnstone Strait. Not to be confused with the Broken Islands of Barkley Sound, on the west coast of Vancouver Island.

Forward Bay & Boat Bay: These indentations, between the Broken Islands and Growler Cove, across from Robson Bight, have some protection in west winds. In Forward Bay, anchor north of the Bush Islets. If attempting to enter Boat Bay, watch for the foul area near the entrance. You can listen to Captains of whale watching cruises talking to each other on VHF 77.

Havannah Channel Vicinity
[3312, 3545, 3564]

★ Port Harvey (21): It is possible to anchor north-northwest of the Mist Islets and near the head, north of Range Island. The bottom is mud. Depths range from 15-35 feet. This harbor has some protection from southerly winds and northwesterly winds near Tidepole Islet. Good "gunkholing" by dinghy to site of a meadow. A drying gorge separates Port Harvey from Cracroft Inlet.

Boughey Bay (22): Anchorage, open to north winds, is in 30-40 feet of water on a mud bottom. Strong southeast winds also tend to "funnel" into the bay.

★ Matilpi (23): Anchor behind the Indian Islands, off the white shell beach, which marks the site of a midden and an abandoned Indian village. Approach from the north, around Indian Islands. Outside, in Chatham Channel, lies Tom Islet, with its fluffy green underbrush and feather-like cedar trees, which have earned Tom Islet the nickname of *Irishman's Hat*.

★ Burial Cove (24): There is good anchorage in this bay on the east side of East Cracroft Island. Round Island offers some protection. Anchor near the center in 25-40 foot depths. The head of the bay is a drying flat. This cove was once used as an Indian burial ground. There may be aquaculture both in, and nearby, the bay.

★ Call Inlet (25): Steep-sided and deep, Call Inlet extends ten miles into the mainland. A 50' float is reported to be near the head on the north side. Winds tend to funnel down the inlet. The Warren Islands, near the entrance, are reminiscent of the lovely Harmony Islands in Hotham Sound. Anchorage in settled weather is possible in small bights and in the channel, with a tie to shore, in depths of 25-40 feet of water. Streams enter the channel separating the islands at two green grass beach sites. Across the inlet at Squire Point, there is an anchorage in 35-50 feet of water. This bay is open to south winds.

Chatham Channel (26): [3545, 3564]. This five mile long waterway is easier to navigate than the charts indicate. Line up with the range markers. Targets are lighted at night. See current tide table for Sitka, Alaska and current tables for Seymour Narrows, British Columbia. Kelp extends from both shores. If traversing at a low tide, the kelp will branch out to mid channel and it will be necessary to go through some of it. This should not restrict passage. Strongest current is at Root Point. Flood currents flow to the southeast and ebb to the northwest. Currents do not exceed 5 knots at springs. High water slack is 45 minutes before high water slack at Seymour Narrows. Low water slack is one hour and 25 minutes before slack at Seymour.

★ **Cutter Cove (27):** There is good anchorage in this long, shallow cove. Favor the north shore in westerly winds and the south during easterly winds. The bottom is good holding mud. The head of the cove is a drying flat. At high tide it is possible to explore a series of swamp-like channels which indent inland.

The Blow Hole (28): Separating Minstrel Island from East Cracroft Island, this passage is named for the wind which sometimes funnels through it. Rocks are marked by kelp in summer months. Favor mid-channel, slightly on the Minstrel Island side.

★ **Minstrel Island (29):** When the Union Steamships made regular stops, Minstrel Island was the entertainment center for the region. The island is said to have received its name because traveling minstrel shows once played here. Several other such names nearby, such as, Sambo Point, Bones Bay, and Negro Rock attest to this theory. At one time, the now demolished hotel with its pub, sold more take out beer than any other pub in British Columbia.

Minstrel Island Resort: Closed

★ **Cracroft Inlet (30):** This inlet contains anchorages, a marina, lagoon, and a drying gorge that leads to Port Harvey. Anchorages are in Lagoon Cove and behind Dorman and Farquharson Islands in the channel that separates West Cracroft Island from these islands. Note the covered rocks on the chart. The inner cove may be explored by dinghy.

Lagoon Cove Marina: Gas, diesel, moorage, water, power, showers, propane, fishing supplies, oil, charts, haul-outs, open all year. VHF 66A.

Knight Inlet

[3515, 3545]

★ **Knight Inlet (31):** Over 70 miles in length, this narrow, steep-sided fjord is one of the longest indentations into mainland British Columbia. The waters are deep and anchorages are few and far between. Winds are frequently strong, funneling down or up the inlet. It can be difficult to find a nearby place to hide. There is no lack of beautiful scenery, waterfalls, and good fishing and prawning. There are anchorages near the mouths of such streams. Stern ties to shore are necessary to maintain position if anchored on a rocky bottom or if anchored in a narrow niche where swinging is not desired. The bottom is difficult to see in the milky water. A great amount of fresh water from the Klinaklini and Franklin Rivers at the head flows well into the inlet. Much of the surface water is fresh. South and west winds blow up the inlet

and, if strong, the rate of the current may also be affected as much as two knots. There are logging camps in the inlet. Generally speaking, the camp operations do not welcome visitors, except in an emergency.

★ **Port Elizabeth:** Anchorages in Maple and Duck Coves provide shelter. The head of Duck Cove is a drying flat. There is another anchorage next to an islet north of Duck Cove. Avoid rocks which extend from shore. They show as a single rock on the chart, but are really a chain of rocks. Log storage occupies much of the anchorage.

Tsakonu Cove: Anchorage is fair with some protection from west winds. Hills behind the head are low. Since the bottom is hard and rocky, some dragging is possible.

★ **Sargeaunt Passage:** High hills border each side of this narrow channel. There is anchorage on both sides of the narrows. Favor the east side when anchoring. Fishing boats often use this passage.

Hoeya Sound: Anchorage at the head is possible, but questionable.

★ **Siwash Bay:** Anchorage is along the east shore.

★ **Glendale Cove:** This cove has anchorage near the head and is the site of a private fishing resort. Also home to one of the largest concentration of grizzly bears in B.C. See current table for Sitka, Alaska.

Knight Inlet Lodge: No services for boaters. 250-337-1953.

Ahnuhati Point: A niche has anchorage and views of waterfalls. There is limited anchorage near the valley, next to the point.

Wahshihlas Bay: Logging operations are located here. Limited anchorage.

Clio Channel Vicinity

[3545, 3546]

Clio Channel: Clio Channel runs from Minstrel Island to Nicholas Point on Turnour Island where it splits into Beware Passage and Baronet Passage. Possible anchorage.

★ **Bones Bay:** This large bay is the site of an abandoned cannery. The ruins here are dangerous, trespassing is not permitted. Anchorage is found near islets on the south shore.

★ **Bend Island:** This island is connected to West Cracroft Island by a drying ledge. There is anchorage behind the island on either side of the ledge. The northern basin is deeper and has protection in westerlies.

★ **Potts Lagoon (32):** This inlet offers anchorage on a mud bottom. The inner bay is somewhat shallow. Large tidal changes must be considered for overnight depths. A lagoon and meadow may be visited by dinghy at high tide. A cove on the east side near the entrance to Potts Lagoon is a bit deeper and also has good anchorage. A grassy patch at the head identifies this anchorage. When proceeding to the inner harbor, the channel is to starboard of the island that is connected to shore by a drying ledge. In the inner harbor, the anchorage basin is opposite the picturesque ruins of a pier in 25-30 feet

of water at high tide. There is a logging camp and caretaker on the shore. The island gives some protection in winds. Strong winds can enter this area.

Baronet Passage: Baronet Passage is often used to and from Blackfish Sound and Alert Bay. Tidal currents flood to the west and reach three knots. The vicinity of Walden Island should be navigated cautiously. Preferred passage is the West Cracroft Island side, keeping an eye out for the kelp-marked rock located off the island's southwest tip. Zigzag to pass west and around the kelp. Bell Rocks and strong currents are hazards at the west end, however, the passage is not difficult.

Beware Passage: [3545] Beware Passage is what its name implies. It separates Turnour and Harbledown Islands. Good visibility is necessary to navigate this passage. Do not attempt in fog. There are rocky patches and shoals extend from some of the islets. If traversed at slack on a low tide, with a rising tide, it is not difficult to see the hazards. Approach very slowly. Use depth finder. Tide floods east, ebbs west attaining two-three knots.

Karlukwees: A pier is in ruins and the old float has been removed at this abandoned Indian village. There is a steep shell midden and a nice beach. No-see-ums are prevalent, and bears may be a hazard.

Caution Cove: There is anchorage on Turnour Island. Caution Rock dries four feet and marks the entrance. Two other rocks are farther in off the head. The cove is open to northwest winds and logging operations are often present.

★ **Beware Cove:** Also off Beware Passage, Beware Cove has more protection in northwest winds and has anchorage over a mud bottom. It is open to the southeast.

Canoe Passage: This drying passage separates Village Island from Turnour Island. Winds will funnel through the narrow pass.

★ **Native Anchorage:** There is anchorage that is open to westerlies at the west end of Canoe Passage. East winds can also funnel into the bay. It is a large, attractive basin with anchorage depths of 25-50 feet of water. One anchorage is in the northwest corner. Note shoaling at the head.

★ **Mamalilaculla, Village Island (33):** This site belongs to the First Nations people. No permission is needed to visit. There is anchorage in the bay, near the ruined wharf, behind the rock islets, in about 25 feet of water. There is a breakwater, dock access to the beach, and six mooring buoys which can be reserved. All dogs should be on leash. Gift shop, food, if arranged. The outside of the float is reserved for commercial vessels. In season there are wild roses, rhubarb, onions, and mint. Guided tours are run by Tom Sewid of Village Island Tours, 250-282-3338, 1-877-282-8294. M. Wylie Blanchet, in her book *Curve of Time*, devotes an intriguing chapter to the Native life at Mamalilicula. This was the site of the last big Potlatch, held during Christmas week, 1921. In later years, the structures housed a village school and TB hospital. In season call "Village Island" on VHF 79A. www.villageisland.com.

★ **Compton Island:** This is Indian Reserve land with hiking trails. Inquire at Village Island. VHF 79A.

Mamalilakulla   Stephanie Satter Photo

★ **Crease Island:** Anchorage, with protection from west winds, can be found in the bay between the southeast corner of Crease Island and Goat Island. Use chart 3546. Enter north of Goat Island.

★ **Farewell Harbour, Berry Island:** Good anchorage is found in six fathoms on a soft bottom. A private facility, Farewell Harbor Resort, is located here. Pre-arranged meals may sometimes be available. 250-974-8105.

★ **Harbledown Island:** Anchorage (and aquaculture operations) can be found between Harbledown and Mound Islands and in the niche behind Dead Point. Parson Bay is wide and open to west winds. Temporary anchorage near the head in settled weather only.

Blackfish Sound & Blackney Passage (34): Blackfish Sound, famous for good fishing grounds, connects the southeast portion of Queen Charlotte Strait with Blackney Passage and Johnstone Strait. Currents run to five knots, flooding east, ebbing west. The flood flows north and south of Hanson Island and meets near the south end of Blackney Passage causing a strong tidal race in mid-channel. Strong rips occur near Egeria Shoal and Cracroft Point. Fishing is good off Bold Head and Cracroft Point. Blackney Passage is a very busy shipping channel, with large tows and cruise ships. Traffic on VHF 16 and 21.

★ **Hanson Island (35):** This island is on the north side of the western extremity of Johnstone Strait. There are anchorages in Double Bay. Enter on the west side of the bay to avoid the rock and reef at the entrance. Anchorage is also found in six fathoms in the adjacent bay, inside Sprout Islet. These bays offer protection in summer westerlies and south winds.

Walk-around: A trail leads through the island's rain forest.

Double Bay Resort: Private fishing resort. 250-949-1911, 780-467-6893.

★ **Growler Cove:** Fishing boats flock to this haven on the western tip of West Cracroft Island. It is known as Pig Ranch Cove by the fishermen. Limited shelter for pleasure craft. The head dries, and rocks are off both shores. Depths are 30-45 feet.

Queen Charlotte Strait
[3547, 3548]

Queen Charlotte Strait: This strait connects Johnstone and Broughton Straits with Queen Charlotte Sound. It is about 15 miles wide, if traveling from Wells Passage to Port McNeill. Although most of the time Johnstone and Queen Charlotte Straits have similar weather conditions, listen carefully when different weather reports are given for the two straits. There may be small craft warnings on one, while the other may be calm. Flood tides set east-southeast and ebb west-northwest. See current tables for Seymour Narrows, British Columbia. The prevailing summer wind pattern on a clear morning, is a rising breeze from the northwest, rising in the afternoon and calming just before dark. When checking Alert Bay, WX 1 for the wind reports, take note of Alert Bay, Pulteney Point, Scarlett Point and Pine Island readings.

Retreat Passage
[3515, 3546, 3547]

Retreat Passage: Retreat Passage separates Bonwick from Gilford Islands. There is an unusual magnetic disturbance near Meade Bay which can throw off a compass as much as 18 degrees.

★⚓ **Broughton Archipelago Marine Park:** This park acreage is a rich, scenic wilderness area with more than 300 islands and abundant marine and bird life. Totaling more than 11,500 hectares, much of the designated park land is water. Park boundaries stretch from Fife Sound on the north to Indian Channel on the south, and from Blackfish Sound on the west to Baker Island/Bonwick Island on the east. The boundary lines are uneven because they dodge in and around some islands, while excluding others. Included are many small islands which have nooks and crannies perfect for secluded anchor-

ages, making it a haven for canoeists and kayakers. There are no moorage buoys & fresh water is difficult to find.

★ **Bonwick Island (36):** There are several anchorages in indentations off Retreat Passage. The first, Carrie Bay, has anchorage in 25-35 feet of water. Grebe Cove, farther north, shoals gradually to a depth of about 20 feet near the head. This is good anchorage, however the head is rather low and winds can enter. Dusky Cove and Betty Cove have tricky anchorages in settled weather only.

★ **Waddington Bay:** This bay deserves special mention because it is an outstanding anchorage with views of wildlife. Approach through the northern channel that passes through the Fox Group. The bottom is thick mud and depths are 30-40 feet. Anchorage is good in the bay to starboard upon entry. An uncharted rock is reported in this bay - watch for kelp. There is good anchorage along the southeast shore east of the island that is connected by a drying ledge. This bay is especially good for exploration by dinghy.

★ **False Cove:** There is anchorage at the extreme head of the cove where water flows in from a mountain lake. Open to west winds.

★ **Health Bay:** This bay on Gilford Island has small islets in the entrance and a brilliant green backdrop. There is good protection from southerly winds, but not from westerlies. The best anchorage is at the five fathom mark on the chart, in toward the head. Health Lagoon dries, except for an entrance channel. The brightly painted houses, about 1/2 mile northwest of the bay, are part of an Indian village.

★ **Crib Island & Sunday Harbour (37):** The small bay on the north side has anchorage with protection in most winds. Sunday Harbour, bordering the southern shore, has been described beautifully in M. Wylie Blanchet's book, *The Curve Of Time.* Sunday Anchorage is a shallow, wide harbor that is open to winds. Anchor in settled weather only. The thick kelp on the bottom makes anchoring questionable, if at all. An indentation into the north shore of Crib Island is more protected.

Tracey Island & Monday Anchorage (37): Monday Anchorage separates Tracey and Mars Islands. It is a large bay with anchorage in several locations. Since it is open to the west, both west and southeast winds will affect anchorage. Anchor in 35-45 feet of water off the northern or southern shores, depending on wind conditions.

Fife Sound
[3515, 3547]

★ **Blackfish Archipelago:** Some refer to this area as Blackfish Archipelago, although no official charts show such a designation at present. We have used the official chart names throughout the area.

★ **Eden Island & Joe Cove (38):** There is anchorage in several unnamed bays behind Fly Island. The larger, thumb-shaped bay is the best. It is protected from winds and, although shallow, can accommodate several boats. Depths are 15-30 feet on a sticky mud, seaweed covered bottom. Adjacent to this bay is another cove that offers anchorage. The head is a drying shelf and large drying rocks restrict too deep an entry into the bay. Joe Cove, on the southeast side of Eden Island, nearly back-to-back with the other bays, has anchorage in about 30-50 feet over mud. Another anchorage, with protection in westerlies, is in an unnamed bay on the south side of Eden Island. Avoid rocks which extend off the port shore at the entrance. The head is a drying flat. The best anchorage is off those flats, but is open to the east.

★ **Cullen Harbour (39):** The most protected anchorage is northeast of Olden Island, in six fathoms. Anchorage in a second cove, on the east side, is open to swells from Queen Charlotte Strait.

★ **Booker Lagoon (39):** Enter through Cullen Harbour and round the tip of Long Island. Avoid the reef off the northeast side of Long Island. The channel narrows and minimum depths are 21 feet in mid channel. Because of strong currents which run in excess of four knots, entry is recommended near slack water. Strong flood current with back eddies along shore create conditions where boats swing a lot at anchor. There is good sheltered anchorage on mud in each of the four arms.

★ **Fife Sound (40):** Fife Sound opens into Queen Charlotte Strait and is frequently used when traveling to and from Port McNeill, Sointula, and Alert Bay. Hazards are few in this deep waterway. There is deep anchorage, with fair protection from west winds, behind

Wicklow Point. Farther in, a bight behind Pemberton Point can be used for anchorage.

Indian Passage (40): This narrow, deep passage is nearly parallel to Fife Sound. It is often used as a short cut from Echo Bay and outer islands. Current floods east, ebbs west. There are anchorages in a small bight on the southeast shore of John Island and in the narrow indentation into Davies Island. Old Passage, separating Insect and Baker Islands, is passable and scenic. At times the currents are stronger in this passage than in alternative waterways.

★ **Deep Harbour (40):** Pass either side of Jumper Island when entering this long harbor. Aquaculture pens obstruct the central part of the bay. The extreme head, which looks on the chart to have anchorage, is, unfortunately, blocked by a string of logs attached to shore by cables. An old log skid marks the site of the blockage. Therefore, anchorage is limited. There is a niche on the south shore east of a rock shown on the chart. Check depth and overnight tide when anchoring.

Baker Island: When cruising in the Ragged Island vicinity off northern Baker Island, be on the lookout for Pym Rocks. They are barely under the surface and are hazardous.

★ **Shoal Harbour (41):** There is anchorage on a good holding mud bottom to the right or left of the entry passage. Depths are about 50 feet. To starboard, there is anchorage behind the small islet at the location shown by a three fathom designation on the chart, or temporary anchorage in the inner bay marked by one fathom on the chart. This inner bay is too shallow to be a recommended overnight anchorage. In addition, the entrance to this inner cove is restricted by a drying shoal at a 5.6' tide at Alert Bay. Swamp water often colors the water a dark brown.

Bill Proctor's Museum: Between Shoal Bay and Echo Bay. Excellent to visit. Admission by donation. Hours are 10am-5pm.

★ **Echo Bay (42):** This attractive bay is on the northwest side of Gilford Island off Cramer Passage. Anchorage is not recommended, because the holding bottom is fickle. Amenities include a post office, grocery store & gift store.

★ **Echo Bay Resort:** {50° 44.60'N, 126° 29.85' W} Located in the heart of good fishing grounds, this popular resort has moorage, power, water, gas, diesel, propane, laundry, showers, lodging, and provisions. Full facilities from late April to October, with the store and gas dock open Monday, Wednesday and Friday off season. Internet access for boaters. See our Steering Star description in this chapter. Cell phone

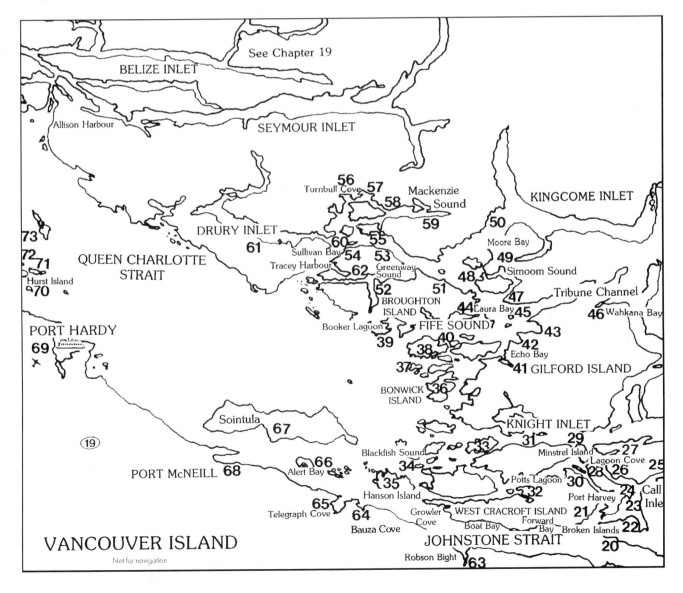

Not for navigation

reception is good past Fife Channel and Cramer Pass. Address: Simoom Sound Post Office, British Columbia V0P 1S0. Fax & Telephone: 250-956-2121. VHF 66A.

★▲ **Echo Bay Marine Park:** This small, usually crowded public float is limited to boats less than 24 feet. Larger vessels must anchor or use the neighboring dock located at Echo Bay Resort. Unstable pilings make the restriction necessary. Repairs to the dock begin late summer 2005 which will restrict access. Space is reserved for the school boat. The school house is just beyond the park boundary. Day use picnic area, pit toilet, no water, wilderness camping. ⛺🚶▲

Walk-around: We get many questions about how to get to Scenic View. Take a lunch and a hand held VHF, if you have one. Walking at "legal speed" (not in any hurry), it takes about

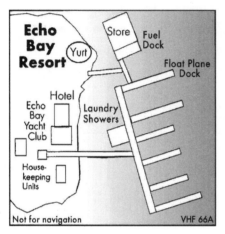

Echo Bay Resort

Store Fuel Dock

Yurt

Float Plane Dock

Hotel

Echo Bay Yacht Club

Laundry Showers

House-keeping Units

Not for navigation   VHF 66A

45 minutes to the logging road and another 40 minutes to the look out. Behind the school are water lines that run up the hill. Follow them to a dam. Continue almost to the top, where there are four small trees, two on each side of the path. They have fluorescent flags attached. Turn left between the flags and follow flags still going up the hill. You will come to a logging road which is edged by a stoned slope. You will have to climb over to get up onto the logging road. Turn left and follow the road up another hill to the end of the road. There are lots of alder growing on the road. Spring of 2005 a few kids cut some of the alder down the middle of the road. Now it looks like a tunnel. From the look out you can see from Cramer Pass to the Burdwood Group, including Fife Sound and Penphase Pass. It's worth the walk! Local knowledge from Nancy Richter, Echo Bay Resort.

Windsong Sea Village Resort of Echo Bay: Moorage, lodging, showers, art gallery, and bakery in July and August. 250-974-5004. VHF 66A.

★ **Scott Cove:** [3515] Site of a logging camp and marina. When entering, check the chart and avoid Powell Rock off Powell Point.

Pierre's Bay Lodge & Marina: Moorage, limited water, showers, laundry, lodging, dining room by reservation, bakery, power. 250-949-2503, 250-247-9704. VHF 66A.

★ **Viner Sound (43):** There is anchorage, open to west winds, in indentations on either side near the head.

★ **Laura Bay (44):** When approaching this lovely cove, avoid the long shoal which extends from Hayle Point. Tucked behind Trivett Island,

this bay has adequate anchorage for three to four boats. There is a small islet with a shoal out from it. Enter to port of the islet. An anchorage is north of the islet in 30 feet of water on a zero tide at Alert Bay. This bay is protected from north winds. An uncharted rock lies near the passage that separates Trivett Island.

Burdwood Group (45): This large group of islands lies near the western entrance to Tribune Channel. Anchorage is a matter of gunkholing and is not recommended, except in very settled weather. Salmon farm has been removed.

Tribune Channel (46): Tribune Channel extends along the entire northern and eastern border of Gilford Island to join Knight Inlet. It is used by those who wish to take the inland route from Minstrel Island to Fife Sound.

★ **Watson Cove:** This bay lies off Tribune Channel. A rock lies to starboard at the entrance. Favor the steep hillside to port. Inside, the cove is well protected, except in strong westerlies. Anchoring depths are 40-50 feet at high tide. The shallower anchorage might have room for one or two boats. Anchorage depths vary widely near the head.

★ **Wahkana Bay:** High hills overshadow the entrance channel. The bay is narrow and winds in toward a cut at the head. Descending mountain heights create the cut. Anchorage is possible along the shore at the spot marked with a "5" on the chart. The indentation to port at the head has shoals for some distance off the creek and then a quick drop. The cove to starboard at the head has anchorage in depths of 60-70 feet of water on a 13 foot tide at Alert Bay. It is difficult to get close to shore because of shoaling.

★ **Kwatsi Bay:** [3515] When a westerly is affecting Watson Cove, this bay has protected moorage. If anchoring, because of the depths, it is necessary to anchor close to shore in the corners of the bay and a shore tie might be advised. Waterfalls and a stream provide background music.

Kwatsi Bay Marina: Moorage, showers, water. Small gift shop. 250-949-1384, VHF 66A.

Kingcome Inlet & Vicinity

[3515, 3547]

★ **Simoom Sound (47):** Named after her Majesty's Ship *Simoom*, this inlet, entered between Deep Sea Bluff and Pollard Point, has several anchorages in McIntosh and O'Brien Bays. Deep Sea Bluff is noted as a good fishing ground. Buoys marking commercial prawn fisherman traps may be hazards in the vicinity of Louisa Islet. Aquaculture operations may be present to port, after rounding Esther Point.

★ **McIntosh Bay:** After passing Hannant Point, good anchorage is found in McIntosh Bay. Caution advised regarding shoals and drying rocks which, at low tide, offer platforms for those swimming in the warm water. Anchorage is also found in other indentations into the shoreline.

★ **O'Brien Bay:** Located at the head of Simoom Sound, well protected anchorage with plenty of room to swing is found.

★ **Shawl Bay (48):** This popular bay is on Wishart Peninsula, west of Simoom Sound. It is the site of some float houses and a marina.

Shawl Bay Marina: Moorage, 15 and 30 ampere power, water, lodging, ice, laundry, showers, provisions, internet, satellite system. 250-483-4169. VHF 66A.

★⚓ **Moore Bay (49):** A shallow, narrow, but navigable passage separates outer Shawl Bay from Moore Bay. Two rocky areas off Gregory Island dictate favoring the mainland side of the passage. Minimum depth is zero at a three foot tide at Port Hardy. Two bright orange buoys are located near shore at the site of the former dock. There is a ramp ashore, with a 15-foot float. The sign reads: "B.C. Forest Service Recreation Site. No vessels over 14-feet in length". Walking trails, four picnic tables, several benches, a outhouse, and a fire-wood lean-to. The improvements have been crafted from the huge trees felled during storms. The bay in the southeast corner behind the small island offers protected anchorage in eight fathoms of water, soft bottom. 🚶🚶🏕️

★ **Gregory Island:** Views looking up Kingcome Inlet and across Thief Island to the 2,500 foot high Mount Plumridge are spectacular. Coves on the north side have good views and provide anchorage. Milky green waters make it difficult to see the shoaling near shore. Favor the center of either bay in 30-40 feet of water at a five foot tide at Port Hardy. These bights are open to north-northeast winds.

★ **Kingcome Inlet (50):** Long and deep, this inlet stretches 17 miles to the Kingcome River delta. Most of the inlet is too deep for anchorage. Anchorage Cove on the southeast shore, and a small bight to port and inside the entrance to Belle Isle Sound, offer anchorage. If the wind is blowing down Belle Isle Sound from

Bear along the Port McNeill - Port Hardy Road　　　　*Linda Schreiber Photo*

the west, the small bight behind the point, one half mile south of the entrance offers protected anchorage in ten fathoms on a soft bottom. Another anchorage is in an unnamed bay adjacent to Reid Bay. This bay has a rocky bottom with depths of 20-30 feet. A ridge at the head cuts off northwest winds, but the bay is open to the southeast. There are some uncharted rocky patches off the Magin Islets, near the entrance to this bay. Wakeman Sound is a center for logging operations in the region. There is no satisfactory anchorage in Wakeman Sound. There is a small float on the north side of Kingcome Inlet, one half mile past Petley Point. This serves the Indian village and the logging camp at Petley Point. It is available for temporary moorage. It is possible to dinghy up the river to the Indian village that is described in the book, *I Heard The Owl Call My Name*, by Margaret Craven.

Sir Edmund Bay: A drying rock is a hazard off Hayes Point. Preferred entrance is the channel east of Nicholls Island. Anchorage is possible off a grassy flat in the western corner and behind drying rocks in the southeast corner. Aquaculture operations may be present.

★ **Cypress Harbour (51):** This is one of the prettiest spots on Broughton Island. It is located near the popular fishing areas of Sutlej Channel. Approach with caution, because of Fox Rock and the drying shoal which extends to mid-channel from Woods Point. Enter favoring port. The best shelters are in Miller Bay on the east shore, Berry Cove, and in the niche between Harbour Point and Blount Point. Bottom fishing is good off the tip of Fox Rock. Farther into the bay, after Roffey Point, there is anchorage in the center. Shoals and aquaculture operations are hazards. BC Forest Service Recreation Site Cypress Harbour is located on Cawston Point. There are campsites with picnic tables, firepits, and a pit toilet. Old logging roads provide a chance to get in some walking.

Greenway Sound

[3547]

★ **Greenway Sound (52):** This boot-shaped sound between North Broughton and

Broughton Islands has a number of anchorages. The first anchorages are in the vicinity of Cecil Island. Pass either side of Cecil. The innermost site is behind a small islet with a shoal. A basin with depths of 50 feet is between the islet and the grassy head. There are two rocks near the head. One is covered with yellow seaweed in season. Anchor in the center giving berth to the shoal off the eastern shore. This anchorage is shown by a "5" on the charts. Several boats can be accommodated with shore ties. An outlet from Broughton Lagoon empties into the bay. Another anchorage is close to Cecil Island where a wider passage enters the lagoon. Currents are noticeable making more than temporary anchorage a questionable course of action.

A dinghy trip into the lagoon is possible. Broughton Lagoon: This local knowledge is from Tom Taylor of the former Greenway Sound Marine Resort. "This lagoon is fun to enter and explore in a substantial dinghy. The North entrance is a reversing rapids that allows about 20-30 minutes inside the lagoon to see it. It has a beautiful setting. The trick is to go in about an hour and fifteen minutes after high tide at Alert Bay. At full high tide, the lagoon is filling very rapidly, but as the tide lowers, the rapids slow down. Typically, the rapids reverse and the lagoon flows out about an hour and a half after high tide. Your time inside is usually from 1:15 after high tide to 1:45 after high tide. As soon as you enter, note the location of the passage for your return exit passage. It is hard to find from inside the lagoon. The North passage is quite deep. Do not try to go through the South passage. It dries. Continuing into the Sound, the former Greenway Sound Marine Resort lies to port, in the large bay around the next point. Whether passing or approaching slow down and watch your wake. Because of the contour of the cove, wakes can damage the floats, shore-tied facilities, and docked boats. Some charts still show the words "float" and "oil tanks" at this site, but they no longer exist. There is also an anchorage opposite the marina, in a bight marked by an "8" fathoms mark on charts.

If traveling farther into the sound, refer to chart 3447 to locate the rock near the center of the waterway, just northwest of Greenway Point. It dries one foot and kelp may not be present to mark it. Shrimp pots may also be hazards in this area. On the west shore at the bend, there is anchorage in the nich marked on the chart as "2" fathoms. Turning the corner of Broughton Point into Carter Passage leads to another anchorage behind the lovely islet at the entrance. There are two other anchorages within this eastern section of Carter Passage. When entering Carter Passage proceed in the narrow, but deep, channel to port of the islet. Continuing into the sound, there is anchorage to starboard prior to reaching Simpson Island. It is marked as seven fathoms. Pass to port of Simpson Island. There is anchorage in a bay straight ahead on the southeast shore, or go around the islet, and continue to the head of the sound. There is good anchorage in 40-50 feet, tucked behind the little peninsula at the head, opposite an old logging road. The extreme head is an active logging operation, unsuitable for anchorage. Protect forest from fire while walking or hiking in the area.

★ **Greenway Sound Marine Resort:** At this time resort is for sale. For up to date information check their webiste at www.green-waysound.com or call 360-466-4751.

Walk-around: A dinghy float nearby provides access to shore for a walk in Broughton Island Forest Service Park to Broughton Lake.

Sutlej Channel & Sullivan Bay
[3547]

★ **Cartwright Bay (53):** This indent into North Broughton Island provides good anchorage. Depths are 15-30 feet. There is a small swampy beach near the head. There is shelter from both south and west winds, however, it is open to easterlies.

Boyer Point: Good fishing grounds.

★ **Sullivan Bay (54):** Site of Sullivan Bay Resort.

Sullivan Bay Marine Resort: Moorage, power, water, propane, gas, diesel, provisions, restaurant, liquor, showers, laundry, post office, privately owned float homes in "floathouse subdivision." Sullivan Bay Post Office, Sullivan Bay, B.C. Canada V0N 3H0. 403-997-0111. VHF 66A.

★ **Hopetown Point (55):** Anchorage in 35-45 feet of water over a mud bottom is found in Hoy Bay, east of Hopetown Point. Hopetown Passage may be traversed by shallow draft small craft at high water slack only.

★ **Burley Bay:** Good anchorage, mud bottom.

Mackenzie Sound
[3547]

Watson Point: Seals often frolic in kelp beds off abandoned sawmill site on Watson Point.

★ **Turnbull Cove (56):** This large bay is located off Kenneth Passage. The muddy bottom is very flat with depths of about 30 feet at a 14 foot tide at Alert Bay. Anchorage is possible almost anywhere. The bottom has excellent holding power. There is room here for a large number of boats without any feeling of overcrowding. Forest Ministry has a dinghy dock. Strong southeast winds have been known to

swirl around the bay. It is possible to walk to Huaskin Lake. There are often commercial prawn traps near the entry.

Roaringhole Rapids & Nepah Lagoon (57): [3547] The truly adventurous may run the Roaringhole Rapids at high slack water in a shallow draft boat and enter Nepah Lagoon (3-ft' draft at low water). Since slack lasts five minutes, tight entrance is dangerous and the visit may have to be a short one. Depths in the bay discourage or prohibit anchoring. High water slack occurs two hours after high water at Alert Bay. Current run to eight knots. See current tide table for Sitka, Alaska.

Kenneth Passage: [3547] This passage links Grappler Sound with Mackenzie Sound. Indian petroglyphs can be seen on the steep cliffs in the area. Pass clear of Kenneth Point and proceed around the islet. Passage is made between the unnamed island in the center and Jessie Point. There is a rock marked by kelp off Jessie Point. Currents swirl through the area causing whirlpools at times. Passage is not restricted and may be made at any tide. It is easiest to go in and out with the tide.

★ **Steamboat Bay:** There is anchorage on a mud bottom. A bright green grassy beach and swampy area are in the background. A shallow area is in mid-bay and a drying rock is to port near the head.

★ **Mackenzie Sound (59):** This is a lovely and isolated area. Heavy moss hangs from the trees along the shoreline. Anchorage is possible. Burly Bay, near the entry to the sound, has anchorage spots near its head and inside Blair Island. Proceeding into the sound, there is a small rock about 100 yards northwest of Turner Island. This rock is especially dangerous because it is covered at high tide. Nimmo Bay and Little Nimmo Bay lie about five miles into the sound. Another anchorage area is at the extreme head of Mackenzie Sound in six to seven fathoms. It is protected from all but west winds. Carvings in the solid rock at the head are believed to be Spanish. The geometric designs, cut with great precision, are of a different nature from those of Indian origin.

Nimmo Bay & Little Nimmo Bay: Nimmo Bay is shallow with a drying head. The drying rocks in the entry make it appear uninviting. Little Nimmo's entrance has depths sufficient for passage. Near the entrance is a grass and gravel spit. The spit extends about half way across the passage, and is partially covered at high water. A fishing lodge is located here. The remainder of the bay is open for anchorage.

Nimmo Bay Resort: This resort features 'Heli-venture" day-trips for boaters, gift shop, restaurant (dinner with reservations) 250-956-4000, 800-837-4354.

Grappler Sound
[3547]

★ **Grappler Sound (60):** Many anchorages are found in this vicinity. Embley Lagoon and Overflow Basin may be explored by dinghy.

Embley Lagoon: The lagoon is fed by Embley Creek. The water is shallow and there are several rocks to avoid. It is possible to go ashore by dinghy to explore the fish ladder. Land at high water on the west side near the ruins. Logs are tied together at the trail head. Beware of bears.

Take a ten minute hike to the left, past a shack, uphill. Check to see if the rotting bridge is still safe to cross. Once across the bridge, uphill and to the right, the fish ladder is in sight. This can be spectacular when the pink salmon are climbing the ladder. The lagoon seems to boil with the jumping salmon during runs. The confined, shallow entry to the lagoon prohibits overnight anchorage.

★ **Woods Bay:** Anchor off the south shore in 30-40 feet of water.

★ **Claydon Bay:** One of the most popular anchorages in the area, shelter is found in either the northern or southern section depending on wind direction. Drying patches in the entrance are clearly marked on charts. Favor the south shore when entering. An islet has reefs extending from it. A sharp rock sits atop the westerly reef. Pass west of this rock when entering the northern basin. Anchorage is possible.

★ **Carriden Bay:** Large, with a curving shoreline and fairly even bottom, this bay offers excellent holding on hard mud. The shore is skirted with drying flats. Anchor near the center in 25-35 feet of water. Adequate protection for south and west winds is possible.

Stuart Narrows (61): This passageway extends from Morris Islet to Leche Islet. Since currents run to seven knots, flooding west, ebbing east, plan to enter or exit at slack water. Depths are adequate for low water entry. High and low water slack are ten and 15 minutes respectively after high and low water slack at Alert Bay. Welde Rock, a large drying, nearly flat rock is a hazard in the center of the narrows. Covered at high water, it dries eight feet and has kelp to help identify it. Pass either side.

★ **Drury Inlet (61):** This inlet is surrounded by low, rolling hills.

Richmond Bay: Turning into the bay, pass to the north of Leche Islet, and give a wide berth to rocks in the center of the bay. One anchorage site, on the east shore, is marked with "4" fathoms on the chart. It is open to westerlies. The other, with more protection, is at the extreme southern head, marked by a "3" fathoms on the chart.

Tancred Bay: Open to northwesterly winds.

Davis Bay: There is anchorage on the north side, marked "2" fathoms on the chart. Beware of sunken pilings.

Jennis Bay: This bay, across the inlet from Davis Bay, has a small community. There is anchorage far in the bay, opposite the peninsula.

★ **Sutherland Bay:** This bay is large and shallow. There is good anchorage, with protection from most winds.

Actress Passage, leading to Actaeon Sound: This pass is rock strewn and hazardous. Passage at slack water is recommended. Pass west of Dove Island. Avoid Skene Point by favoring the Bond Peninsula shore.

★ **Bond Lagoon:** Good anchorage, however, the entrance dries three feet, leaving you landlocked at lower tides. Anchorage can also be found in Hand and Creasy Bays and behind the islet in the niche formed by England Point.

Tsibass Lagoon: The narrow entrance has least depths of two feet and should be explored only by dinghy at high water slack which occurs two hours and 20 minutes after high water slack at Alert Bay.

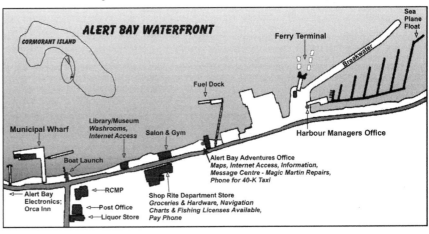

Wells Passage Vicinity

[3547]

★ **Tracey Harbour (62):** Tracey Harbour was once a major center for logging operations. Remnants of booms may still be in Napier Bay. Trailers, trucks, and a few boats remain active at the camp site. Anchorage is excellent in six fathoms mud bottom, at Napier Bay opposite the camp. In addition, a pleasant anchorage is in the inlet next to Carter Point. The bottom is rock until near the head, however, good anchorage is found in 30 feet of water at a 16 foot tide at Alert Bay. A shoal extends from shore.

★ **Carter Passage (62):** Since this passage is blocked by a boulder-covered drying shelf two and a half miles from its western entrance, it may be better to describe the passage as two inlets, separated by the drying obstruction. Anchorage is found at both ends of the passage. When approaching the western entry, pass either side of the cluster of rocks and islets just outside the entrance. Currents in the narrow pass run to seven knots, ebbing west, flooding east. Plan to enter or leave at high water slack. There is 17 feet of water on a 12 foot tide at Alert Bay. The starboard shore on entering has kelp covered rocks. Favor the left center of the fairway. Inside are three unnamed anchoring sites. The two to port are sheltered from the north with anchorage in 30-40 feet of water. The bay to starboard, while open to northwest winds, is smaller, with anchorage in 35-45 feet on a good mud bottom. A shoal, covered at high water, is to port near the entrance to this bay. The head of this bay is a drying flat. The eastern portion of Carter Passage is reached from Greenway Sound. Keep to port when passing the islet off Broughton Point. Adequate depths for passage are found in this narrow channel. Anchorage can be found in the bay to starboard, behind the islet and in niches on both sides farther into the waterway. Survey the area to check out small reefs protruding from shore.

Wells Passage: This well traversed waterway opens from and to Queen Charlotte Strait. It is a primary passage for those heading to or from Port Hardy or Port McNeill to the islands and for those heading to or from Northern British Columbia and Alaska. Numas Islands are offshore, providing a landmark when locating the entrance. When approaching Wells Passage from the southeast, the opening is wide. Polkinhorne Islands, Vincent, and Percy Islands dot the starboard side but provide little shelter. Any anchorages in the Polkinhornes are open to the northwest, thus open to prevailing winds. When approaching from the west, avoid Lewis Rocks which extend southeastward far off the peninsula that borders Lewis Cove. It is possible to pass between the rocks and the peninsula, then to give a wide berth when rounding Boyles Point. Once in the pass, the waterway narrows and Ommaney Islet is to starboard. Pass to port between the islet and the famous fishing grounds off James Point. The nearest anchorages adjacent to Wells Passage are adjacent to Popplewell Point (temporary anchorage), in the bay on the northeast side of Dickson Island, Carter Passage, and Tracey Harbour.

★ **Dickson Island:** Good anchorage is found in the bay on the northeast side. Kelp patches mark a rock and shoals off the small island. The extreme head is shallow, however anchorage can be found. Depths in the main anchoring basin are 40-55 feet. The low hills do not block strong westerlies.

Vancouver Island Side

[3545, 3546, 3548, 3549]

Robson Bight (63): Named after Lieutenant Commander Charles Robson, this reserve is at the mouth of the Tsitika River, directly opposite the West Cracroft light. The vicinity is a major gathering site for pods of killer whales who like to rub barnacles off their stomachs on the shallow beaches. By way of interest, a pod consists of five to 20 whales. Nineteen of about 30 pods that travel between Washington State and British Columbia are found in the Johnstone Strait area. Female whales live to be 100 while bulls live half that long. Killer whales travel between six-eight knots. Boaters are required by law to stay more than one half mile off from shore and give the whales a wide berth.

★ **Bauza Cove (64):** Entry is made either side of Bauza Islet. This picturesque, deep cove provides anchorage and protection in westerlies.

★ **Telegraph Cove (65) [#3546]:** Located in the sheltered niche just southwest of Ella Point at the entrance to Beaver Cove, this picturesque harbor is the location of an RV park and marina-launch ramp facility - resort development. There is a gallery and restaurant. Many of the old buildings, connected by boardwalks, sit on stilts above the water. As the site of a 1911 telephone station, a 1920's fish packing operation and the Broughton Sawmill (to make boxes for the fish packer), a 1940's telegraph installation, and a stop for Union Steamship Company vessels. A visit to today's Telegraph Cove is like experiencing the past and looking ahead to the future at the same time.

Telegraph Cove Marina : Moorage to 100 feet in length, power, water, handicapped accessible restrooms, showers, and laundry. Launch ramp, RV park, lodging. 250-928-3163, 1-877-835-2683. VHF 66A.

Telegraph Cove Resort: Gas, moorage to 25' on inside of docks - phone ahead for larger boats. Water, showers, provisions, liquor, laundry, lodging, ramp, RV park. 250-928-3131.

Beaver Cove (65): Enter between Ella and Lewis Points. This is the site of an old ferry landing and log storage. There is deep, temporary anchorage here. An area called Englewood is in the extreme head of Beaver Cove. Log booms often provide tie-ups. There is protection in westerlies. There was once a sawmill here, and sunken logs may foul the anchor line.

Broughton Strait Area

[3546]

★⚓ **Cormorant Channel Provincial Park:** This park encompasses the Pearse and Plumper Island groups, including Stubbs Island, a well-known diving destination. The 740 hectare, mostly water park, offers opportunities to view killer whales, sea lions, otters, porpoises, and other marine life. The park does not have protected anchorages. Strong tidal currents occur in the area, fog is common, and even in the summer the wind can whip up rough seas.

Broughton Strait: This channel lies between Johnstone Strait and Queen Charlotte Strait, separating the Pearse Islands, Cormorant Island, Haddington Island, and Malcolm Island from Vancouver Island. A rock, which dries six feet, is located one half mile west-northwest of Pearse Reefs. If crossing between eastern Malcolm Island and eastern Cormorant Island, a course must be set to miss it. The reference point for weather conditions is Pulteney Point. Currents can reach four knots. While currents do not greatly affect Port McNeill, moorings in Sointula and Alert Bay may be affected. A 27 car, 293 passenger ferry connects Port McNeill, Alert Bay, and Sointula.

★ **Alert Bay (66):** The Alert Bay Boat Harbour is sheltered by a rock breakwater and has moorage (3,487' total berthage), garbage, power, water, and daily fuel delivery. Southwest of the rock breakwater, good anchorage can be found on the sandy bottom at depths of 40-50 feet. In the center of the bay, Government Wharf offers a temporary moorage for six to eight boats with water, but no power. There is no breakwater at this location and boaters should be aware of strong currents. Comox Coast Guard Radio covers this area. Alert Bay takes it name from H.M.S. Alert, a British ship that surveyed the area in the mid-1800's. Together, the Municipality of Alert Bay and The "Namgis First Nation" have about 1,100 residents. An historic Native fishing village, Alert Bay, *Home of the Killer Whale*, featues a number of interesting sites like the century old Anglican Church. Other attractions include the Library/Museum, "Namgis First Nation" burial grounds, the world's tallest totem pole, Gator Gardens Ecological Park, and the "Namgis Big-House. www.namgis.org. A must see, the U'mista cultural Centre is open May Day to Labor Day, seven days a week, 9am to 5pm. During July and August traditional dances are performed in the Big-House Thursday through Saturday at 1pm.   250-974-5403.   www.umista.org. Downtown Alert Bay, within walking distance of the harbour, offers a Post Office, credit union (ATM), liquor, groceries, laundromat, pharmacy, hardware, shops, hospital, restaurants, and lodging.   The Library/Museum offers free Internet access (1/2 hour, donations accepted). July and August hours are 1pm to 4pm Monday-Saturday. 250-974-5721. Daily ferries connect Alert Bay to Port McNeil and Sointual. 888-BC FERRY.

Alert Bay Boat Harbour: Moorage, water, 20 & 30 ampere power, 110 volt power, garbage drop. 250-974-5727. VHF 66A.

Alert Bay Electronics: Repairs radios, radars, other electronics. 250-974-5737.

Alert Bay Shipyard: Engine, hull repairs, welding, marine ways to 60 tons, supplies. 250-974-5446.

Alert Bay Visitors Information Center: 250-974-5024. http://alertbay.ca.

SaveOn Fuels: Gas, diesel, oils, water. 250-974-5411.

★ Sointula (67): Malcolm Island has breakwater protected moorage in Rough Bay, at the north side of Sointula, one mile north of town. Sointula is also reached by car and passenger ferry from Port McNeill and Alert Bay. Fishing is the main source of livelihood for the 1,000 residents. Sointula, meaning harmony, was settled by Finnish immigrants at the turn-of-the-century as a utopian colony. The museum houses displays depicting how, at the turn-of-the-century, Matti Kurikka and Matti Halminen acquired the land. 250-973-6683. The Finnish influence lends charm to the community. The Co-op, founded in 1909, is the oldest and largest on the west coast. It has groceries, dry goods, marine hardware, credit union, and liquor. The town has a post office, medical center, gift shop, hotel, pub, bank, campgrounds, restaurants, beauty shops. Hiking trails, dive shop, and bike and kayak rentals all provide wonderful opportunities to explore the area. www.island.net/~sointula/services.

Sointula Boat Harbour: Lighted moorage, power, garbage drop, water, showers, phone, laundry. Repairs and provisions nearby. 250-973-6544, VHF 66A.

Mitchell Bay: Located near Donegal Head, there is a public wharf and anchorage in the bay. Fishing and scuba diving are popular in the area.

Pulteney Point: See current tables for Seymour Narrows, British Columbia. Site of lighthouse, fog signal, and weather reporting station. Avoid a kelp patch 1 1/2 miles northwest of the point.

Port McNeill
[3546]

★ **Port McNeill (68):** The town is well known as a convenient supply center for boaters. The small craft harbor is north of the ferry landing. Protected moorage, most with power, is available. Moorage is on a first come, first serve basis. Anchorage is also possible. When strolling the waterfront, the vintage 1938 steam engine is an impressive landmark. It was once used to haul logs in the surrounding forests. The commercial center is within a block or two of the waterfront. Medical, dental, hospital, and banking services are available. A well-stocked grocery, beauty shop, galleries, gift shops, marine repair & supply, sports center, bank, lodging, restaurants, liquor store, post office, laundromat, and the Heritage Museum are within easy walking distance. There is a 24 hour banking machine and a Visitor Infocentre. Inquire about forestry tours. There is an outdoor public swimming pool, tennis, nearby golf course, artificial running track, ice and roller skating, and an airport limo. Special events include *Orca Fest* held the second Saturday in August, with salmon barbecue, parade, chowder cook-off, float plane rides, and dance. Chartered float planes and helicopters are available. Visit Port McNeill & District Museum which houses both the museum and chamber of commerce. For more information call 250-956-9898. Ferry service connects Port McNeill with Alert Bay and Sointula. Port McNeill was named for Captain McNeill, skipper of the famed SS Beaver, the first steam-powered vessel to ply the waters of the west coast.

★ **IGA "Hometown Proud":** Located two blocks south of the municipal marina, this modern supermarket features fresh meat and produce as well as a full service delicatessen. Pizza Hut on site. Fresh goods are baked daily. The store is well stocked and offers speedy service by friendly, helpful cashiers. Master Card, Visa, American Express, and Interac Direct Payment accepted. See our advertisement in this chapter. Web: www.marketplaceiga.com.   Email: iga044@igabc.com. Address: 1705 Campbell Way, Post Office Box 549, Port McNeill, British Columbia V0N 2R0. Fax: 250-956-3822. Telephone: 250-956-4404.

★ **Mackay Whale Watching Ltd.** Join the Mackay family, pioneers in the killer whale watching industry, for an educational and entertaining cruise departing daily (June-Oct.) from Port McNeill. Lunch included. Located one block south of the fuel dock. See our advertisement in this chapter. Web: www.whaletime.com.   Email: mackaybd@island.net. Mailing Address: Post Office Box 66, Port McNeill, British Columbia V0N 2R0. Fax: 250-956-9864. Telephones: 250-956-9865, 1-877-663-6722 (toll free in BC).

★ **Port McNeill Marine Fuels:** Because this marine and aviation fuel facility is operated in conjunction with an automotive and marine supply company and Radio Shack, it offers the boater everything from a battery for the cell phone to a bilge pump. Propane, repairs, supplies, laundromat and internet services are available. Float planes land at the site. Inquire about the availability of a courtesy car. See our advertisement in this chapter. Mailing address: Post Office Box 488, Port McNeill, British Columbia V0N 2R0. Telephone: 250-956-3336. VHF 66A, fuel dock: VHF 7. After hours: 250-956-4475.

★ **Timberland Sport Centre Ltd.:** The friendly staff at this popular store will be more than happy to share local fishing information and answer any questions you might have about cruising in the area. Stocked with everything a fisherman would need, such as licenses, tackle, bait, downriggers, weights, lures, and knives. Complete lines of sport clothes and footwear. Located at Pioneer Mall. #2 - 1705 Campbell Way. See our advertisement in this chapter. Mailing address: Post Office Box 163, Port McNeill, British Columbia V0N 2R0. Email: tscentre@island.net. Telephone: 250-956-3544, 250-956-3205.

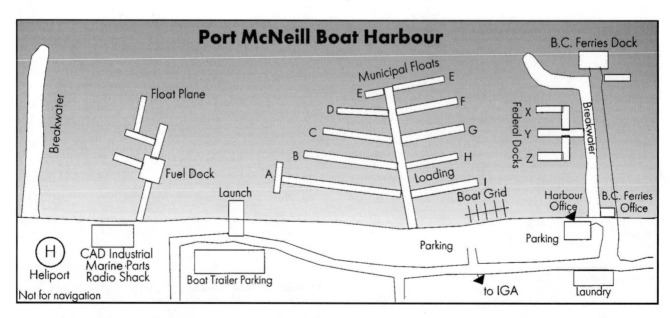

Port McNeill Boat Harbour

Port McNeill Boat Harbour: Anchorage, about 3,000 feet of moorage on outer docks (D, E, F, G), 20, 30, 50, 100 (208 volts) ampere power, launching, grid to 50', gas, diesel, aviation fuel, garbage, oil disposal, water, showers, washrooms, new laundromat, waste pumpout. 250-956-3881. No reservations, but call upon approaching breakwater: New loading dock with 2 hours courtesy time. VHF 66A.

★ **Beaver Harbour:** There are three entrances to this harbor. One is through Daedalus Passage to the north on the west side of Peel Island. The second is to the south of Peel Island, watching out for Twin Rocks on the south side of the passage. The third entrance is to the south between

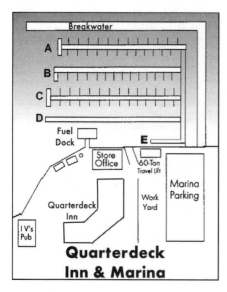

Quarterdeck Inn & Marina

Deer Island and Thomas Point. One anchorage is on a soft bottom on the west side of the southernmost tip of the Cattle Islands in five to seven fathoms of water. Shell Islands, to the south of the Beaver Harbour anchorage, have several large Indian middens on them.

★ **Patrician Cove:** Lying in the northwest corner of Beaver Harbour, there is anchorage in seven fathoms, on a soft bottom. On shore at Fort Rupert, former site of a Hudson's Bay Company Fort (1839), there is a gift shop where resident native artists' work is on display.

Port Hardy

[3548]

★ **Hardy Bay (69):** Hardy Bay is a long indentation culminating in the drying flats of the Quatse and Glen Lyon Rivers. Shoals extend from shore in several places. Use charts and keep the red markers well to starboard when entering Hardy Bay.

Bear Cove: This cove, located in Hardy Bay, is the site of ferries to Prince Rupert and the mid-coast, and a marine fuel dock.

★ **B.C. Ferries Discovery Coast Passage Route:** The ferry, *Queen of Chilliwack*, provides seasonal service along the mid-coast ports of call, with northbound passage beginning at Port Hardy (Bear Cove), bound for either Ocean Falls and Bella Coola or Klemtu, with stops at McLoughlin Bay / Shearwater. Southbound voyages leave from Bella Coola. For the schedule call 1-888-223-3779 (BC). To receive a brochure, call 250-386-3431. www.bcferries.bc.ca/ferries.

★ **B.C. Ferries Prince Rupert & the North Coast Route:** The ferry, *Queen Of The North*, provides passenger and vehicle transportation to Prince Rupert every other day May-September and weekly during October-April. 250-386-3431 or 1-888-223-3779 (BC).

Petro Canada-Bear Cove: Gas, diesel, lubricants, propane, filters, showers, waste oil disposal, water, lodging. 250-949-9988. VHF 9.

★ **Port Hardy:** This community is to starboard when entering Hardy Bay. All city amenities are found here including a hospital, museum, hotels, shopping centers, restaurants, bakeries, laundromat, clothing, hardware, and liquor stores. Visitor attractions include an indoor swimming pool, ice arena, tennis courts, racquet ball club, bowling alley, gift shops, shallow and wreck diving sites, and a nearby golf course. The museum on Market Street features exhibits depicting the early days of white settlement on Vancouver Island. Special summer programs instruct about where to find good walks and how to view the whales in Robson Bight. Points of interest include the remains of the old chimney at Fort Rupert and the whaling station at Coal Harbour. Vanishing Cave, the Cave of the Eternal Fountain, the Cave of the Devil's Bath, and Minizill Caves are all part of an underground system that is within thirty miles of Port Hardy. The Quatse River Fish Hatchery is also open for tours. Hours: M-F 8am-4pm, 250-949-9022. Logging companies host public tours showing the logging process from falling to reseeding.

Daily bus service is available to and from all points south, including Victoria and Vancouver. Chartered float and land plane and helicopter service is accessible. The Port Hardy Airport is about eight kilometers southeast of the city.

★ **Quarterdeck Inn & Marina:** Situated in the inner harbor of Hardy Bay, over 150 slips accommodate vessels to 140'. Fifteen, 30, and 50 ampere power and fresh water are on the floats. Showers and laundry facilities are conveniently located. The fuel dock dispenses gas, diesel, propane, lubricants, and CNG. A 60 Ton Travelift and a full service work yard are on the premises. In the marine supply store and chandlery, the large selection of items includes tackle, licenses, charts, parts, galleyware, clothing, and ice. Beer and wine Store. Fishing and Eco charters and boat rentals are also available. Overlooking the harbor is the beautiful, modern Quarterdeck Inn. Relax in one of 40 deluxe oceanview rooms and suites, enjoy a complimentary Continental Breakfast, and experience a luxurious soak in the hot tub. Meeting room and conference facilities make this an ideal site for a rendezvous, seminar, or yacht club gathering. For memorable afternoons and evenings, visit I.V.'s Quarterdeck Pub and Restaurant. Pub fare features fresh halibut and chips, homemade hamburgers, oyster burgers, and a great selection of appetizers. An extensive dinner menu includes daily specials. All items available to go, plus there are off-sales. Pub hours 11:00 a.m.-midnight daily. **Circle #55 on the Reader Service Card. Websites: www.quarterdeckresort.net & www.boattravel.com/quarterdeck Email: info@quarterdeckresort.net Address: 6555 Hardy Bay Road, Post Office Box 910, Port Hardy, British Columbia V0N 2P0 Fax: Marina: 250-949-7777 Quarterdeck Inn: 250-902-0454. Telephones: Quarterdeck Inn: 1-877-902-0459 (toll free), 250-902-0455. Marina: 250-949-6551. VHF 66A.**

There are scheduled flights to and from Vancouver. Special events include *Filomi Days*, which incorporates fishing, logging, and mining interests, held the third weekend in July. Festivities include a parade, demolition derby, salmon barbecue, and dancing. Copper mining, fishing, logging, and tourism are local industries.

The Coast Guard Rescue Boat is stationed at Port Hardy.

ESSO Ridor Fuels: Located in front of the old cannery in inner Hardy Bay. Gas, diesel, lubricants, stove oil, charts, filters, parts, water, ice. 250-949-9986, 250-902-1199.

Port Hardy Berthage: A large public wharf, with floats attached, extends from shore directly in front of downtown. A larger basin is farther into Hardy Bay. This inner vicinity has log storage, a cannery with a float complex, and moorage protected by a breakwater. One portion, identified by the red railings, contains public floats, primarily for commercial vessels. The left portion of the basin has both permanent and transient moorage at floats which belong to Quarterdeck Marina. There is a boat launching ramp, grid, fuel, marine hardware, repair services, RV park, pub, hotel, and restaurant located at the boat basin.

★ **Quarterdeck Inn & Marina:** lodging on site. Moorage floats with 15, 30, & 50 ampere power, gas, diesel, lubricants, outboard oil, stove oil, propane, CNG, marine supplies, laundry, and showers. Beer & wine Store. Moorage for vessels to 140'. Call for reservations. See our Steering Star description in this chapter. Internet sites: www.boattravel.com/quarterdeck & www.quarterdeckresort.net/. Email to: info@quarterdeckresort.net. Address: 6555 Hardy Bay Road, Post Office Box 910, Port Hardy, British Columbia V0N 2P0. Fax Marina: 250-949-7777, Inn: 250-902-0454. Telephone Marina: 250-949-6551, Inn: 250-902-0455, 1-877-902-0459 (toll free). I.V.'s: 250-949-6922. VHF 66A.

★ **I.V.'s Quarterdeck Pub:** Located at Quarterdeck Marina, this popular pub serves a variety of pub fare and dinner entrees. See our Steering Star description in this chapter. Internet sites: www.quarterdeckresort.net and www.boattravel.com/quarterdeck. Email: info@quarterdeckresort.net. Mailing address:

End of the Trail in Blind Channel   *Carl & Gloria Tenning Photo*

Box 670, Port Hardy, British Columbia V0N 2P0 Fax: 250-949-7777. Telephone: 250-949-6922.

Fisherman's Wharf Small Craft Harbour: Limited moorage (no reservations), 20, 30 amp power, water, sewage pump-out, washrooms, grid, garbage, boat ramp. 250-949-6332, 250-949-0336. VHF 66A.

Port Hardy Marine Hardware: Boating supplies, fishing tackle and licenses. 250-949-6461.

Walk-around: A sidewalk leads to downtown from the moorage basin. Taxi and limousine service is also available to downtown, the ferry terminal, airport, or points-of-interest. Visit the waterfront at the north end of Market Street for walks along the seawall and views of the bay. The seawalk passes famous "Carrot Park" and ends at Gwa'Sala-'Nakwax'xw Park and Playground. There are beaches at Beaver Harbour Park and Stories Beach.

★ **Bell Island (70):** [3549] There are good protected anchorages on the south side of Bell Island and between Bell Island and Heard Island. These islands lie between Goletas Channel and Gordon Channel, about four miles north of Duval Point or seven miles north of Port Hardy moorages. Depths vary from seven to 11 fathoms. There is limited anchorage in the passage between Bell and the two islands directly south. Be aware of the hazards on both sides. These are marked with kelp in season. There is a large Indian midden on the south side of Bell Island in this passage.

★⚓ **God's Pocket Marine Park:** Located on the north side of Goletas Channel, the park is a group of small islands at the entrance to Queen Charlotte Strait, including Hurst, Bell, Boyle and Crane Islands. The focus of the 2,025-hectare park is habitat protection for wildlife.

★ **Hurst Island (71):** God's Pocket is frequently used by boaters, which offers welcome relief from foul weather when conditions in the strait deteriorate. Mooring buoys, resort.

God's Pocket Resort: Lodge, moorage, coffee shop, diver's air. 250-949-1755. VHF 66A.

★ **Nigei Island (72):** Anchorage is found where rocks and islets form a line at the entrance to an unnamed bay across from Cardigan Rocks off Browning Passage. Entry is possible between the southeastern end of the chain of islets. Anchor in the middle of the main channel, not in the lower basin. Port Alexander, a steep-sided, wide, long bay is open to the southeast. Pass Fraser Island and anchor near the head. Anchor in settled or northwest wind weather only. Loquililla Cove, on Goletas Channel, has anchorage and protection from west winds. Avoid kelp covered rocks at the southern entrance.

★ **Hope Island & Bull Harbour (73):** There is a three knot speed limit in the harbor. Pass to the right of the island in the entrance. Anchorage is possible between the two docks in mid-bay. Do not go too close to the head because it shoals rapidly. The public float is not connected to shore. The former Coast Guard Station is no longer in operation. All of Hope Island, including Bull Harbour at the west end of Goletas Channel, is property of the Tlatalsikwala Native Band, who are slowly resettling the island.

Kingcome Inlet from Moore Bay   *Linda Schreiber Photo*

Essential Supplies & Services

AIR TRANSPORTATION
To & from Washington
Seattle Seaplanes **1-800-637-5553**
To & from Islands/Vancouver
Air Canada 1-888-247-2262
Baxter Air 1-800-661-5599
Helijet. 1-800-665-4354
Pacific Coastal Airlines. 1-800-343-5963, 250-949-6353
Pacific Eagle Aviation. 250-956-3339
Tofino Air 1-800-665-2359
Vancouver Island Air 250-287-2433

BOOKS / BOOK STORES
The Marine Atlas. **541-593-6396**

BUS TRANSPORTATION
Port Hardy. 250-949-7532
Port McNeill. 250-956-3556

CNG CYLINDERS
Quarterdeck Marina . . . . . **250-949-6551 VHF 66A**

COAST GUARD:
Comox: VHF 16, 22-A, 26, 84.
. . . . 250-339-3613, 250-339-1053, #16
Emergencies. . . . . 1-800-567-5111, VHF 16
Port Hardy: Rescue Boat 250-949-9099

DIVER'S AIR:
God's Pocket Resort 250-949-1755

FERRY INFORMATION
Port McNeill-Alert Bay.
. . . . 250-956-4533, 1-888-223-3779 (B.C.)
Port Hardy-Prince Rupert 250-949-6722

FUELS
Alert Bay: Gas, Diesel 250-974-5411
Bear Cove Petro Canada: Gas, Diesel.
. . . . 250-949-9988, VHF 9
Blind Channel Resort: Gas, Diesel.
. . . . **250-949-1420 VHF 66A**
Echo Bay Resort: Gas, Diesel.
. . . . **250-956-2121 VHF 66A**
ESSO Ridor Fuels: Port Hardy. Gas, Diesel.
. . . . 250-949-9986, 250-902-1199
Lagoon Cove Marina: Gas, Diesel. VHF 66A
Quarterdeck Marina: Gas, Diesel. . . 250-949-6551
Port McNeill Marine Fuels. Gas, Diesel.
. . . . **250-956-3336, 250-956-4475 VHF 7**
Sullivan Bay Resort: Gas, Diesel. . 403-997-0111 VHF 66A
Telegraph Cove Resort: Gas 250-928-3131

GOLF COURSES:
Seven Hills. 250-949-9818

GROCERY STORES
Blind Channel Resort . . . . **250-949-1420 VHF 66A**
Echo Bay Resort . . . . **250-956-2121 VHF 66A**
IGA Plus: Port McNeill Foods **250-956-4404**
Shawl Bay Marina: . . . . 250-483-4169, VHF 66A
Sullivan Bay Marine Resort . . . 250-949-2550 VHF 66A
Telegraph Cove Resort. 250-928-3131

HARDWARE:
Port Hardy Marine Hardware 250-949-6461
Quarterdeck Marine. **250-949-6551**

HOSPITALS
Alert Bay 250-974-5585
Port Hardy. 250-949-6161
Port McNeill. 250-956-4461
Campbell River 250-287-7111

INSURANCE
Boat Insurance Agency **206-285-1350**
Or Call **1-800-828-2446**

LIQUOR STORES
Alert Bay 250-974-5450
Blind Channel Resort . . . . **250-949-1420 VHF 66A**
Port Hardy
Port McNeill
Sointula
Sullivan Bay Marina Resort 403-997-0111 VHF 16, 66A
Telegraph Cove Resort. 250-928-3131

LODGING
Blind Channel Resort . . . . **250-949-1420 VHF 66A**
Cordero Lodge . . . . 250-287-0917 VHF 66A
Echo Bay Resort . . . . **250-956-2121 VHF 66A**
Pierre's Bay Lodge: VHF 66A
Quarterdeck Inn **250-902-0455**
Shawl Bay Marina: . . . . 250-483-4169, VHF 66A
Telegraph Cove Resort. 250-928-3131

MARINAS / MOORAGE
Alert Bay Boat Harbour: 250-974-5727
Blind Channel Resort . . . . **250-949-1420 VHF 66A**
Bull Harbour
Cordero Lodge . . . . 250-287-0917, VHF 66A
Double Bay Resort: Hanson Island.
. . . . 250-949-1911 VHF 66A
Echo Bay Park
Echo Bay Resort . . . . **250-956-2121 VHF 66A**
God's Pocket: Hurst Island. 250-949-1755 VHF 16
Kelsey Bay
Kingcome Inlet: Float
Kwatsi Bay Marina . . . . 250-949-1384 VHF 66A
Lagoon Cove Marina: VHF 66A
Minstrel Island . . . . 250-949-0215 VHF 6, 66A
Mitchell Bay: Malcolm Island
Pierre's Bay Marina: Scott Cove 250-949-2503 VHF 66A
Port Hardy Public Harbour . . . . 250-949-6332 VHF 66A
Port McNeill . . . . 250-956-3881 VHF 66A
Port Neville
Quarterdeck Inn & Marina: Port Hardy
. . . . **250-949-6551 VHF 66A**
Shawl Bay Marina. . . . . 250-483-4169 VHF 66A
Shoal Bay
Sointula 250-973-6544
Sullivan Bay Marine Resort
. . . . 403-997-0111 VHF 66A
Telegraph Cove Marina 250-928-3163

MARINE SUPPLIES
Port Hardy Marine Hardware 250-949-6461
Quarterdeck Marina . . . **Port Hardy. 250-949-6551**

POISON INFORMATION
Campbell River Hospital 250-287-7111

PROPANE
Alert Bay Propane-Shoprite 250-974-2777
Bear Cove Petro: Port Hardy 250-949-9988
Blind Channel Resort **250-949-1420**
Echo Bay Resort . . . . **250-956-2121 VHF 66A**
Lagoon Cove Marina: VHF 66A
Quarterdeck Marina: Port Hardy . . **250-949-6551**
Port McNeill Marine Fuels **250-956-3336**
Sointula
Sullivan Bay Marine Resort 403-997-0111
Telegraph Cove Marina 250-928-3163

RAMPS / HAUL-OUTS
Alert Bay Shipyards, Bear Cove, Beaver Harbour Park,
Lagoon Cove, Port Hardy, Port McNeill, Telegraph
Cove.
Quarterdeck Marina: Port Hardy . . . **250-949-6551**

RCMP (POLICE)
Port Hardy. 250-949-6335
Port McNeill. 250-956-4441
Alert Bay 250-974-5544

RED TIDE: 250-949-6422
. . . . 1-866-431-3474

REPAIRS
Alert Bay Electronics 250-974-5737
Alert Bay Shipyards: Cormorant Island . . 250-974-5446
Lagoon Cove Marina: VHF 66A
Port McNeill Marine Fuels **250-956-3336**
Quarterdeck Marina: Port Hardy . . . **250-949-6551**
Shawl Bay Marina: . . . . 250-483-4169, VHF 66A
Telegraph Cove Marina 250-928-3163

RESTAURANTS
Blind Channel Resort **250-830-8620**
Cordero Lodge . . . . 250-287-0917 VHF 66A
V'S Pub: Port Hardy **250-949-6922**
Nimmo Bay Resort 250-956-4000

RV PARKS
Telegraph Cove Marina 250-928-3163
Telegraph Cove Resort. 250-928-3131

SEWAGE DISPOSAL
Port Hardy Fisherman's Wharf: Pump. VHF 66A
Port McNeill Boat Harbour: Pump. 250-956-3881
Telegraph Cove Marina: Dump 250-928-3163

SHELLFISH: 250-949-6422
. . . . 1-866-431-3474

SPORTFISH: 250-949-6422
. . . . 1-866-431-3474

SPORTING GOODS
Timberland Sport Centre **250-956-3544**

TAXI
Alert Bay 250-974-5525
North Island Taxi 250-949-8800
Port McNeill Rainbow Taxi. 250-956-8294

TOURS
Mackay Whale Watching **250-956-9865**

TOWING
C-TOW. **1-888-354-5554**

VHF MARINE OPERATOR
Alert Bay: VHF 26, 86   Port Hardy: VHF 24, 84
Cape Caution: VHF 02   Sayward: VHF 28
East Thurlow: VHF 23

VISITOR INFORMATION
Port Hardy. 250-949-7622
Port McNeill. 250-956-3131
Alert Bay 250-974-5024

WEATHER
Environment Canada Weather Line 250-339-9861
Alert Bay: 250-974-5305 (recorded)
Comox: VHF WX-1, 2, 21-B. 250-339-0748
Discovery: WX-4, 21-B
Port Hardy. 250-949-7148

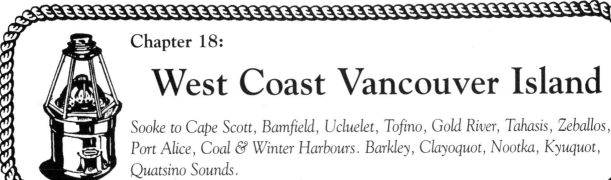

Chapter 18:

West Coast Vancouver Island

Sooke to Cape Scott, Bamfield, Ucluelet, Tofino, Gold River, Tahasis, Zeballos, Port Alice, Coal & Winter Harbours. Barkley, Clayoquot, Nootka, Kyuquot, Quatsino Sounds.

Symbols

[   ]: Numbers between [ ] are chart numbers.

{   }: Numbers & letters between { } are waypoints.

♠: Park, ⛵: Boat Launch, ▲: Campgrounds,
🅇: Hiking Trails, ⊼: Picnic Area, ⛲: Biking

★ **Important Notice:** See "Important Notices" between Chapters 7 and 8 in this guide for specific information on boating related topics such as: Canadian & U.S. Customs, boating safety and security, navigation, weather, U.S. & Canadian Coast Guard, U.S & Canadian marine radio use, Vessel Traffic Service and traffic separation plans, security zones, and internet access. Due to new Department of Homeland Security regulations, call ahead for latest customs information and/or see Northwest Boat Travel On-line, www.nwboat.com.

Vancouver Island

★ **Vancouver Island:** This heavily forested island is the largest pacific island of North America, extending half the length of the B.C. coast and about half the distance from Washington to Alaska. It is 282 miles long, about 70 miles across at its widest point. About 90 percent of the population lives along a narrow coastal strip, between Sooke and Victoria, on the south, and Campbell

Chart List

Canadian Hydrographic Charts:

3410, 3411, 3602-06, 3623-25, 3638, 3641, 3646-47, 3651-52, 3668, 3670-71, 3673-76, 3679-83

NOAA Charts:

17541-46, 17548-50, 17489, 17491, 17495, 18400, 18460, 18465, 18480, 18484-85

Marine Atlas Volume 1 (2005 ed.):

Pages 13-14

Marine Atlas Volume 2 (2005 ed.):

Pages 1-12

River, on the north. About half of this population lives in the greater Victoria area. The remainder of the island, including about 75 percent of the coast line, is very sparsely settled. Several chapters in this publication cover the waterways along the eastern shoreline of the island from Victoria to Port Hardy. This chapter deals only with the outer coast.

★ **Circumnavigating Vancouver Island:** A cruise around Vancouver Island, a complete circumnavigation, is a challenge that lures many Northwest mariners, both sail and power. It is a shorter trip than the Inside Passage to Skagway or Glacier Bay, but is in several ways more difficult and more dangerous. The western Vancouver Island Coast is remote and beautiful, with many inviting sounds and inlets. The winds and water conditions along this coast can be extremely dangerous, and have been responsible for more than their share of shipwrecks, both large and small. There are enough villages to provide fuel, water, supplies, and ice, if proper travel plans are made. For this trip, the boat needs to be better equipped, and the captain more experienced, than for cruises in the more sheltered waters of the Inside Passage.

★ **A cruise of Vancouver Island's west coast:** This is most often done as a circumnavigation of the whole island. Otherwise, unless continuing on from the north, one would be retracing his steps—which is not all bad because there is much to see and do on that beautiful coast! This direction of the circumnavigation is typically in a counterclockwise direction. That is because most of the population and repair facilities are found on the inside of the island where they're more likely to be required during the first part of the voyage. This route is also preferred because of the protection afforded on the inside of the island. One of the biggest advantages for the counter clockwise route is the prevailing wind. The typical summer afternoon westerlies are much easier to run with, than against. Once on the outside of the island, the typical northwest wind of late summer, along with the big ocean waves, would all be going in the direction of travel. Unfortunately however, this is not always the case. Winds on the west coast can shift to southerly, bringing rough seas. It is during these rough seas that our vessels are challenged most and when boat equipment or structural failures are most likely to occur. Sailing this long stretch, though, can be one of the highlights of a circumnavigation.

The only community of any size on the west coast is Port Alberni, at the end of a 40 mile inlet from the Pacific Ocean, and 15 miles overland from the Georgia Strait. The only others are a dozen or so small fishing and logging villages, some with no land access at all. Paved roads cross the island to Ucluelet, Tofino, Port Renfrew,

Gold River in Nootka Sound, Coal Harbour, and Port Alice. Gravel logging roads, most of which are open at all times to the public, lead to Bamfield, Tahsis, Zeballos, Fair Harbour, Holberg, and Winter Harbour. Traveling these logging roads can be hazardous and it is imperative to inquire locally about access before using them. The longest stretches of open water are the two approaches at the north and south ends of the island. One can avoid these by trailering to Port Alberni, Ucluelet, or Tofino and then cruising Barkley and Clayoquot Sounds or even Nootka Sound. In the north, one can trailer to Coal Harbour and cruise Quatsino and adjoining sounds. There are good ramps, serviced by paved roads. If it is preferable not to trailer or if the boat is large, there are commercial haulers available.

Fog: From June to October, the surface of the ocean is frequently warmer offshore than immediately along the west coast of Vancouver Island. This is the primary cause of sea-fog, when the wind is blowing onshore. These fogs may come and go several times a day, or last for many days. They do not necessarily follow the typical pattern one would expect with this type of fog, where morning fog dissipates by afternoon. In fact, the afternoon westerlies can even blow in more fog. This can cause some real problems when trying to locate an entrance to one of the inlets. Radar is recommended equipment for this voyage. Even with radar, approaching a narrow entrance in fog can be hazardous. Because electronic equipment can fail, basic navigation is still essential. In these waters, the use of dead reckoning, using time, distance and speed to determine boat position, can be important to fall back upon. The problem is not so much in the fog itself, but the rocks. Hitting a rock in the protected waters of the San Juan Islands, for instance, is one thing, but coming down a big Pacific Ocean wave onto one is quite another. Even for an experienced boater, it's surprising how fast an object can burst out of the murky surroundings. On the other hand, fog is so common on this coast that it's hard to avoid and with some experience, it's not such a problem. Radar is not as important as a good depth sounder, compass and loran or GPS. A radar reflector and horn are also musts. Most important, however, is to slow the boat down in fog, listen, at least through an open window, and watch carefully in all directions. With these basics, most of the open inlets along this coast can be safely approached in fog.

Storms: While traversing the coastline, the mariner is fully exposed to any adverse weather on the Pacific Ocean. Large swells are often encountered in the outer waters of some inlets, even during calm wind conditions. Although there are numerous sounds and inlets offering protection, the mariner must be especially alert to weather forecasts and able to interpret storm signs in time to run for cover. The numbers of large ships that have been lost along this coast confirm that it is no playground for the unwary.

"Roughness" of the sea, however, is not usually the problem one would think here. Even on the open ocean, there's usually hardly enough wind for a sailboat to sail effectively. In fact, the distances between ports often makes such leisurely sailing impractical. On the other hand, storms with gale-force winds are common along this coast. During one recent summer, there were two storms with winds of actual hurricane force. Plan some extra time for such a voyage because of the likelihood of being holed up for an extra day or two.

Rain too varies greatly, even between early and late summer. During one recent June in Tofino, right in the middle of this coast, there was rain every single day and in Uchucklesit Inlet the average annual rainfall is 300 inches. For this reason, the best time to plan for such a trip is mid to late summer. The drawback to this time of year is that statistically, parts of this coast have roughly twice the number of foggy days in July as June and twice again as many in August.

Rocky coast: Not only is the coastline itself rocky, but there are many offshore rocks, making careful navigation important. Many of the sounds and inlets also have numerous underwater rocks present. A good fathometer and a complete set of charts are absolute necessities. Nothing can substitute for an alert and knowledgeable navigator

aboard.

Points: The points of land along this coast can be particularly rough. This can be a problem for both power and sailboats. The repeated heavy seas can loosen debris in fuel tanks, clog filters, stop a motor, or break a traveler or mast step on a sailboat. With such breakdowns, a great deal of time may be required to make repairs.

Winds: Calm mornings are often the rule. Prevailing summer wind is from the southwest and west, with winds rising in late afternoon.

Anchoring: Knowing, and adhering to, correct principals of anchoring is more important along the West Coast than in more protected inland waters. First, because there are so few docks, a mariner is forced to anchor most of the time. Secondly, this area is more exposed and subject to storms. Winds can funnel into the inlets, as well as down mountains. The primary anchor should be heavy, and an even heavier auxiliary anchor should be available in case the primary is lost or doesn't hold. It's best that the auxiliary anchor be of a different type than the primary one, so that, if one doesn't hold on the particular bottom, the other may. Both anchors should have at least 30' of chain and 200' of line. Using, two or three times the depth for the anchor scope may work for protected areas, but much more rode is sure to be needed on this trip. The main thing to do is to back away from the anchor, after it is set, using plenty of power, although beginning slowly so as

not to dislodge the anchor when the line is made abruptly taut. Once anchored, watching the shore off the side of the vessel, a range between a near tree and far hilltop beyond it, should not change. Using a stern anchor or a stern line to shore may not work here, because such a tie does not allow the boat to swing freely with the wind, and may hold the boat broadside to wind and/or waves. Two anchors, both set from the bow, can help. Prior to anchoring it is wise to not only circle the perimeter of probable swing during the night, but the adjacent area as well.

Important Items For This Trip
1. A reliable and seaworthy boat
2. All Canadian Hydrographic charts for the area
3. An accurate, compensated compass
4. A fathometer
5. A marine VHF two-way radio, with weather and emergency channels
6. A radar
7. RDF, Loran, or GPS
8. The British Columbia Small Craft Guide, Volume 1
9. Sailing Directions British Columbia Coast, PAC 204 (Vancouver Island, West Coast and Coastal Inlets)
10. A captain experienced in boat handling and navigation
11. Ample time for the cruise to allow for weather changes
12. Inflatable dinghy
    This last item can be invaluable for a voyage

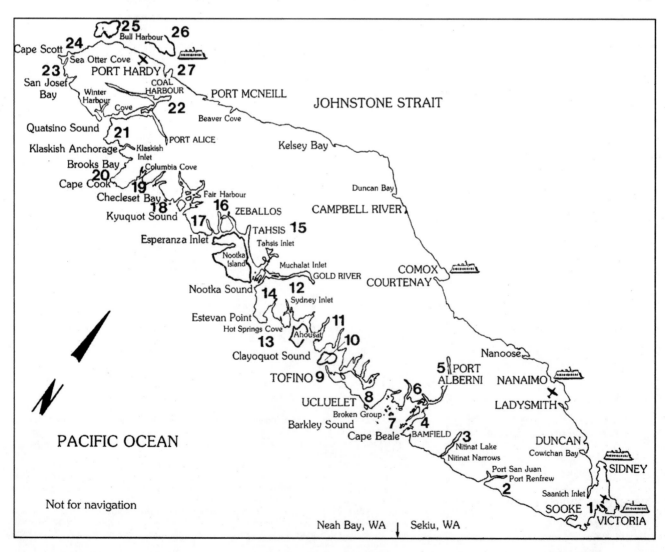

Not for navigation

PACIFIC OCEAN

Neah Bay, WA | Sekiu, WA

on the West Coast. A quality inflatable, with an outboard powerful enough to plane, vastly expands the exploring possibilities. A dinghy is the best way to get around in many of these coastal towns, some of which are built right along the water or are divided by bodies of water. Dinghies often provide the most direct route, avoiding a long distance trek. Planing at two or three times the speed of a main boat, inflatables can quickly get to and into tight little spots that are otherwise inaccessible to a larger boat, even via "gunkholing". For scouting shorelines, even in open waters, an inflatable can be safer than the main boat, because it can bounce off rocks and ride big seas. These inflatables also work well in the open ocean.

Strait Of Juan de Fuca To Barkley Sound

[3461, 3602, 3606]

★ **Sekiu, Washington:** See information near the end of Chapter 4. Sekiu is 39 nautical miles west of Port Angeles, located in the northwest corner of Clallam Bay. The small craft basin has a curved, stone breakwater on the west shore of Clallam Bay. There is a marina with moorage, gasoline, water, ice, and a good launching ramp. Grocery, motels, and restaurants are 1/8 mile from the marina. Anchorage is open to the north.

★ **Neah Bay, Washington:** This customs port-of-entry is 14 nautical miles from Sekiu. The well protected harbor houses marinas with diesel, gas, water, ice and ramps. See Chapter 4.

Crossing Juan de Fuca Strait: It is 40 nautical miles across the mouth of Juan de Fuca Strait to Cape Beale.

Traveling from the Puget Sound to Barkley Sound, Juan de Fuca Strait must sooner or later be crossed. Crossing early and following the Canadian coastline is more scenic and less populated. After Port San Juan, there are no communities or safe harbors over this 37 mile distance to Barkley Sound. The only places seen here are those hiking the West Coast Trail, established in 1909 after 126 survivors from the shipwrecked Valentia were unable to make it out by foot. Miles of this shoreline are composed of multicolored, tilted sandstone with caves, arches, blow holes and waterfalls. One waterfall is 80 feet high.

The best time of day to traverse this long section is morning. This avoids much of the typical afternoon westerlies, but means leaving very early in the morning. The summer westerlies are created by the daily heating of the mainland, and often result in strong winds funneling down the strait. Compounding that, the stronger ebb currents, flowing against the wind, can cause severely choppy seas, which not only require hours longer to travel, but can be a danger, even capsizing a smaller boat caught abeam steep breaking waves. These conditions must be anticipated and avoided because, once in them, it's too late to simply speed up and run the long distances for cover.

Traveling in the other direction, from Barkley Sound eastward, can be quite a contrast and reason enough, if circumnavigating the island, to do so in a counterclockwise direction. Traveling eastward, with the combination of the westerly wind and a flood current, a boat can double its normal ground speed for many miles. For the sailor, this can also provide one of the best and longest sails of a circumnavigation.

Fog is common in the strait and it can last all day. An advantage of traveling this coastline when fog is present is that there are no obstacles within one mile of land. This distance can be

maintained, with a depth sounder and chart, by following between a 15 and 30 fathom curve. Although land may never be seen, this way the distance from it will always be known.

Current: Juan de Fuca Strait funnels a lot of water, like the neck of an hourglass between the ocean and two inland seas—Puget Sound and the Strait of Georgia. This causes significant currents. Also, the "mixed tides" in this area result in a great variation between every other high and low tide. That's because, especially in early summers when the moon is high in the Northwest, it exerts a direct gravitational pull on the water, causing an extreme high and low tide along with their correspondingly strong currents. Then, by the time the next high and low tides come, the earth has rotated to another position, such that these are much less and the corresponding currents are less too.

The places this current is most dramatic on the routes to Barkley Sound are at the points of land. The primary such points are Point Wilson, near Port Townsend, Discovery Island, near Victoria and Race Rocks, near Sooke. Where different currents meet each other, especially at places like this, they result in tide rips. While tide rips can be only areas of swirling water in places like the San Juan Islands, in the above three areas, they can be hazardous and even flip a smaller boat. Such severe tide rips can be avoided by carefully studying the following the U.S. *Pilot*, the *British Columbia Coast Sailing Directions*, the *Pacific Coast Current Tables*, the *Canadian Tide and Current Tables*, and the fine print on the large-scale charts. The main precaution is to either try to wait out the times of these worst rips or skirt them widely. As an example of how currents can vary widely within a general area, at two specific places near Point Wilson only five miles apart, the difference in the times of the same slack current is 3 1/2 hours and the difference in strength is ten times.

Traveling from Juan de Fuca Strait, the current usually does not present a problem. In fact, contrary to the inside of Vancouver Island, where the transits of many waterways may have to be timed around the slack current, there are no such problems on the entire West Coast of Vancouver Island, with the possible exception of Quatsino Narrows, near Coal Harbour.

Race Rocks: Now automated, this 89 foot tall lighthouse is made of granite blocks which were shipped around The Horn from Scotland in 1860. Other landmarks are the keepers white house with its red roof and grass lawn. The light transmits in Morse Code. The fog signal is three blasts every 60 seconds. When this station was manned, the keeper on duty climbed the 114 steps each day to check the light.

Sooke

[3461, 3606, 3647]

★ **Sooke (1):** Sooke is at the gateway to the west coast of Vancouver Island. It is the site of government float moorage and fuel. Sooke is a major fishing center. Much of the harbor is used by commercial and sport fishermen and by tugs and barges engaged in logging operations. When entering, line up the outer range before crossing the bar. The bar extends from Parsons to Simpson Points and has a least depth of 14 feet of water. When approaching the tip of Whiffin Spit, favor the Simpson Point side. Foul ground, marked by kelp, extends for some distance from the western shore to port. Currents run to four knots and the streams set toward that shore. When rounding Whiffin Spit, stay about 100 feet offshore and keep Grant Rocks to starboard. Grant Rocks con-

sist of three rocks--one that dries and two that are covered. Strong currents tend to push toward the rocks. The harbor has shallow areas, usually marked by kelp in summer. When proceeding to the marine businesses, public floats, and the community of Sooke, give Woodward Point a wide berth and follow the channel marked by red spar buoys. Keep these to starboard. If the range light is your marker, the white sector shows the preferred channel.

A public wharf, with finger floats, is located on the western shore. Power, fresh water, and garbage disposal facilities are accessible. Hardware, liquor, grocery, pharmacy and other stores are within walking distance of the public wharf. Hosting a population of over 10,000, this is among the oldest settlements on the coast. Exhibits at the outstanding Sooke Region Museum and Visitor Infocentre (250-642-6351) reconstruct the history of the southwest coast of Vancouver Island. These consist of logging and fishing artifacts and Coast Salish artifacts, Historic Triangle Island Lighthouse, Moss Cottage (built in 1870) and Vancouver Island's only remaining Tidewater House. Tours available for lighthouse & Moss Cottage. 250-642-6351. The *Sooke Fall Fair*, held every September since 1913 is a perennial favorite with both locals and visitors.

Sooke Harbour Marina: Marina has been sold, look for changes in 2005. 250-642-3236. VHF 16, 68.

Sunny Shores Resort & Marina: Gas, diesel, moorage, launch, repairs, showers, lodging, campground, pool & minigolf. 250-642-5731, 1-888-805-3932. CB 13, VHF 16.

Vacations West Resort: Moorage, power, water. 250-642-5644.

Sheringham Point: Eight nautical miles from entrance to Sooke Inlet, a lighthouse and fog signal are located here.

Port San Juan (2): [3647] Port San Juan can be identified by a huge gap between two mountain ranges. A light and fog signal are on San Juan Point. The fog signal is one blast every 30 seconds. The entrance is 49 nautical miles from Victoria, 35 miles from Sooke. The inlet extends three and one-half miles inland. It is exposed to southwest winds and a gale from that direction may produce large swells in the inlet. Some anchorage can be found in six fathoms about one mile from the head, in a small niche on the south side, off the west shore north of Quartertide Rocks, offshore from the mouth of Hobbs Creek, or behind the breakwater near the fuel dock at Port Renfrew.

★ **Port Renfrew:** The best anchorage is in Mill Bay in San Juan Harbour. A public float in Snuggery Cove provides shore access, but no stable moorage because of swells. The Community Dock has been expanded for a few transient boats. Gas and diesel can be delivered by truck. Port Renfrew is connected to Victoria by Highway 14. It is the southern terminus of the West Coast Lifesaving Trail. A hotel, pub, and pay telephone are nearby. Limited groceries are available. There is a marina across the harbor at the northern corner of the entrance to the Gordon River. It is necessary to go up the river to get to the marina. Because of shallow water, this is not recommended for sailboats. Power boats, with over three-four foot draft, should cross the entrance only at high tide. VHF 66A.

Port Renfrew Marina & RV Park: Moorage, launching, fuel. Opposite Port Renfrew at entrance to Gordon River. 250-647-0002. VHF 16, 68.

Bonilla Point: This point is marked by a light from June-December. Reefs extend south and west of the point.

Carmanah Point: Light and fog signal. This is the northwest entrance point to Juan de Fuca Strait. A Canadian troller fisherman passed on the tip that there are often reverse currents close to the Vancouver Island shore during strong tides. Ebb tides are the strongest.

Nitinat Narrows and Nitinat Lake (3): [3647] Very hazardous during adverse weather conditions. Under these circumstances no vessel should attempt to enter. Even with good weather, an ebb tide meeting incoming swells on the entrance bar will make for very hazardous conditions. There are no marine facilities. This is the site of an abandoned Indian village.

Cape Beale: [3671] This is 86 nautical miles from Victoria. A light and fog signal are located here, at the entrance to Barkley Sound. The temptation, once Barkley Sound is in sight, is to cut right in toward it. However, this desire must be resisted, because Cape Beale is the worst obstacle encountered so far along this route. Rocks surround it for about one-third of a mile in all directions. Give it plenty of leeway.

Barkley Sound

[3602, 3646, 3646, 3668, 3670, 3671]

★ **Barkley Sound:** There are three main entrance channels, Trevor, Imperial Eagle, and Loudoun Channels. The sound is 15 miles wide and indents about 25 miles into the island. This body of water, with all of its small and large islands and numerous channels, has great attraction for both the sailor and the power boater. Once behind the outer islands, the waters are relatively protected, as witnessed by the number of kayaks and canoes seen in Pacific Rim National Park. However, the sound is exposed to the full sweep of the Pacific Ocean, resulting in heavy swells during stormy conditions. Even during calm weather, swells may be present. Thus, quiet and safe anchorages can be found only in the inner protected areas. In recent years, primarily due to a successful salmon enhancement program, Barkley Sound has become well known for its excellent chinook salmon fishing. There are also many cohos and sockeye in these waters. Fishing peaks about Labor Day. Barkley Sound, with all of its rocks and reefs, also offers some of the best bottom fishing to be found anywhere. While searching for trading partners for sea otters in 1787, Captain Charles Barkley entered this intriguing sound and named it.

Entering Barkley Sound by way of the first channel, Trevor Channel, the ocean waves usually quickly subside; however, don't be lulled. Barkley Sound is a sea of rocks and many are pyramid shaped. Because of the shape of these rocks, a depth sounder doesn't help much, because the top of the rocks emerge too fast. Charts must be carefully followed.

★ **Deer Group:** This small group of islands has anchorage in Dodger Channel. The scenery quickly improves as soon as Trevor Channel is entered. The Deer Group of islands to the west are thickly forested and to the east are several long sand beaches separated by rugged headlands. There are sculptured rock towers with tortuous Sitka spruce on their crests. Anchorage is possible in some of these bays, but watch for rocks and kelp. Anchor securely because the near-by ocean waves can swing in. Much of this area is Indian reserve and permission to go ashore should first be obtained. The beaches are nice for walking and most of the headland can be scaled.

Another way to these beaches is by a trail at the head of Bamfield Inlet, but the wharf there is only usable at higher tides. A second trail in the Bamfield vicinity leads four miles to the Cape Beale lighthouse, however this trail is un-maintained and in poor condition.

★ **Bamfield (4):** [3646] Bamfield straddles Bamfield Inlet. There are four public floats here and mooring buoys in both Bamfield and Grappler Inlets. Anchorage is possible near Burlo Island and in Grappler Inlet. Mean depths are 50', good holding bottom. Entering the harbor, the Canadian Coast Guard Station is on your starboard side, immediately followed by the West Public Wharf. A general store, with liquor agency, lodging and restaurant are located in the vicinity of the West Public Wharf, as well as several locations on the west side. Many lodges have their own floats for easy access. Midway down the harbor there is another public float. Post office, school, and Red Cross Outpost Hospital are also on the west side. Prominent on your port side is the Bamfield Marine Station. The East Side Government Wharf provides access to a motel, pub, general store with liquor agency, restaurant, deli, and additional lodging. Marine repairs are also available on the east side at Breaker's Marine, located 1/8 mile from the dock. There are no banks in Bamfield, however both groceries have debit card machines.

Bamfield is connected to Port Alberni by an industrial logging road, as well as year-long steamer and water taxi service. Bamfield is also the northern end of the West Coast Life Saving Trail. The 45 mile trail was originally cleared in 1907 to help those stranded by coast wrecks. The trail has been rebuilt and attracts thousands of hikers each year. (See update information under Pacific Rim below). Brady's Beach, about a 20-30 minute easy walk, has spectacular views, with swimming and picnicking nearby. Keeha and Pachena Beaches are accessible by trail and are equally spectacular.

Bamfield, lying 92 nautical miles from Victoria, was the eastern terminus of the Trans-Pacific Cable from 1902 to 1959. The 4,000 mile cable connected Fanning Island near the Equator. A newer cable has since been laid from Port Alberni to Hawaii and the old Cable Station on the hillside is now the home of the West Canadian Universities Marine Biological Station. The town has been referred to as, "The Venice Of Vancouver Island".

Kingfisher Marina: Gas, diesel, oils, limited moorage, water, ice, lodging, tackle. 250-728-3228.

★ **Pacific Rim National Park:** The park contains three sections: Long Beach, the Broken Islands, and the West Coast Trail from Pachena Bay near Bamfield to Port Renfrew. Attractions include sandy beaches, camping, kayaking, diving, fishing and hiking. Because 10,000 people hiked the trail last year, a limit of 52 hikers per day has been set. Twenty-six hikers leave from each end of the trail, at Port Renfrew and at Pachena Bay. There will also be a six month closure from November to April. Reservations will be necessary. A user fee has been instigated to help pay maintenance costs. Address: Superintendent, Pacific Rim National Park, Box 280, Ucluelet, BC, Canada V0R 3A0. ▲⊼人

★ **Grappler Inlet:** This inlet is entered from the east side of Bamfield Inlet about one-quarter mile from the entrance. Port Desire, one-half mile inside Grappler Inlet, has a small public float and launching ramp. Two campgrounds are within walking distance of the public float. Anchorage is possible, but the depth is shallow.

★ **Poett Nook:** Good, protected anchorage, in three fathoms of water. A logging road connects with Port Alberni and Bamfield.

Poett Nook Marina: Gas, moorage to 26 feet with larger boats by prior arrangement, showers, water, campsites, some provisions, lodging, launch. Telephone: 250-758-4440, 250-720-9572.

★ **San Mateo Bay:** Anchorage is found in Ritherdon Bay at the entrance to San Mateo Bay. A public float is moored on the south side of Bernard Point. Aquaculture operations are in the vicinity.

★⊼ **China Creek Provincial Park:** Fresh water, picnic sites. ⊼

China Creek Marina: Moorage limited, 15 ampere power, diesel, gas, propane, water, showers, campsite, laundry, launching ramp. Located nine miles southwest of Port Alberni. 250-723-9812. VHF 16.

★ **Port Alberni (5):** [3668] Port Alberni is located at the head of Alberni Inlet, 30 nautical miles from Cape Beale. Supplies, equipment, parts, marine ways, fuel floats with diesel, gasoline and water. Marinas are located in the harbor, on the Somass River, and at China Creek (five miles south into the inlet). The latter two have multiple lane, concrete launching ramps. The Port Alberni Yacht Club has facilities located at the north end of Fleming Island in Robbers Pass. Port Alberni is a shipping center for lumber products and has a population of about 20,000. Commercial fishing is a big industry, as well as fish farming in Alberni Inlet. Activities for visitors include swimming, roller skating, golfing, racquet ball, wind surfing, horseback riding, and hiking. Camping is also popular and numerous sites are found throughout the Alberni Valley. The Alberni Harbour Quay is the site of a view tower, shops and Farmers Market on Saturdays 10am-1pm year round. The Maritime Discovery Centre, a unique hands-on maritime museum, housed in the heritage lighthouse is also found here. It is open June 25 - September 5, 10am to 5pm daily. 250-723-5910. The museum at Port Alberni's Echo Center features Alberni Valley and West Coast history, with unusual exhibitions of logging and machinery. Examine the first paper made on the Canadian Coast, use an old fashioned telephone switchboard and telegraph, see native masks, baskets, & canoes. Tours available. Annual events such as *Forest Fest, Fall Fair*, "*Funshine*", *Folkfest Parade*, and *Port Alberni Salmon Festival* are enjoyed by residents and visitors alike. *Forest Fest* is staged at the McLean Mill National Historic Site, accessed by steam train from the station at Harbour Quay. Every three years, the community hosts the *Tall Ships Festival*, the next one planned in 2008. In 1891, Port Alberni was the site of the first paper mill in British Columbia.

Columbia Fuels-Shell: Gas, diesel. 250-724-7286.

Port Alberni Fisherman's Harbour: Moorage, power, water, garbage, washroom, pumpout. 250-723-2533. VHF 68, 16.

Port Alberni Harbour Quay: Breakwater protected moorage to 50-feet, side ties for larger vessels, 15 & 30 ampere power, showers, washrooms, laundry. 250-723-1413. VHF 66A.

Clutesi Haven Marina: Moorage to 32', gas, power, water, ice, washrooms, launching ramp. Located at head of the inlet at the mouth of the Somass River. 250-724-6837. VHF 66 A.

Petro Canada, Port Alberni: Located across the street from marina. Gas, diesel, marine fuel, propane, oils available, (must be hand carried to boat), ice, restrooms. 250-724-2626.

★ Trailering to Port Alberni: It is possible to trailer a boat to Port Alberni, avoiding the exposed waters of Juan de Fuca Strait. This can be accomplished from French Creek or Nanaimo. The ramp at Nanaimo, located at the north end of the channel, between Vancouver Island and Newcastle Island, makes an excellent loading spot. The distance from Nanaimo is only 54 miles. The road is good, but there are steep hills, even though the actual summit is relatively low. For boaters who do not have a trailer or prefer not to use it, several commercial haulers are available at reasonable prices. Most of them are equipped to haul large boats, both sail and power, up to 40 feet.

★ Nahmint Bay: Temporary anchorage is found close to shore, near ruins of a former wharf. A 100 foot float for the emergency use of small craft is moored in a bay 7/10 mile northeast of Nahmint Bay. Depth is about seven feet.

★ Limestone Bay: Sheltered anchorage is available in four to five fathoms of water.

★ Uchucklesit Inlet (6): Kildonan, once a fish cannery, is currently the home for a number of retired people, families, and small businesses. There is a post office but no other services are available. Anchorages can be found in the inlet. Green Cove lies just inside the entrance, with anchorage in five to ten fathoms of water. The bottom is rock and sand. Snug Basin, at the head of the inlet, has completely protected anchorage in eight to ten fathoms of water, mud bottom.

★ Sproat Bay: Anchorage with fair protection can be found in the southern portion in two to three fathoms of water.

★ Roquefoil Bay: Fairly sheltered anchorage is available in eight to ten fathoms.

★Robbers Passage: Use Charts #3668, 3671.This passage is shallow and rock studded. A day beacon is on a drying rock in the eastern entrance. The preferred channel is to the right.

Port Alberni Yacht Club Outstation: Moorage, water, emergency power, showers, restrooms, and hiking trails. Post Office Box 37, Port Alberni, British Columbia V9Y 7M6.

Satellite Passage: Anchoring is prohibited because of submarine cables.

Imperial Eagle Channel: During south or southwest gales there is a very heavy sea in this channel. Use Charts #3670 and #3671.

Ecoole: Ecoole is in Junction Passage, which connects Trevor and Imperial Eagle Channels. It is located in a small bay on the southeast side of Seddall Island.

★ Useless Inlet: The entrance to Useless Inlet is rocky but attainable by small craft. Fatty Basin, near the head of Useless Bay, is best explored by dinghy.

Vernon Bay: Entrance is between Palmer and Allen Points. The shore is high and rugged. Depths prohibit anchorage. Jane Island, at the head of the bay, is in the entrance to a deep, sheltered basin, Jane Bay.

Jane Bay: Entrance is about 100 yards wide.

Eagle Nook (Jane Bay): Limited moorage, limited power, lodging, restaurant. 250-728-2370. VHF 73.

★ Alma Russell Islands: Sheltered anchorage for small craft is found in Julia Passage. The periphery of Barkley Sound along with some of these inlets are partially inhabited with houseboats; however they can become part of the interest of the exploring.

★ Julia Passage: This passage can be entered at its north end, but it's tight and the trees on either side must be watched.

★ Pinkerton Group: Continuing counterclockwise around Barkley Sound, the small, low Pinkerton Group of islands are particularly scenic. Rocks, however, are numerous here and very slow boat speed is recommended.

★ Pipestem Inlet: Located on the northwest side of Barkley Sound, Pipestem Inlet is a four and one-half-mile-long fjord. It is steep sided, fairly easy to navigate, and worth the side trip. Anchorages are at the entrance, east of Refuge Island, and east and southeast of Bazett Island. The latter have mud bottom, abundant oysters, and room for several boats. Check the Shellfish Hotline 250-720-4440. Travel to the end of Pipestem Inlet at ebb tide to gather larger oysters. Use your dinghy because depths at the head are too deep for anchorage. Temporary anchorage can be found in 20 meters on the northwest end. See description of Lucky Creek below.

Lucky Creek: This is located at the west end of Pipestem Inlet, north of Bazett Island. With a flat bottom dinghy, go to three tiered Lucky Creek Falls at any time. Watch the depth finder closely and have someone on the bow watching for rocks. The channels run on the outside of the curves. With a deeper draft dinghy, go about an hour before flood and leave about an hour after flood. Tie up to a tree on the east side, close to the wall. Climb the trail leading to the left of the first level of falls. A beautiful secluded place to sun, picnic, swim (cold). Especially good for children. Oysters are abundant in Lucky Creek Bay.

Stopper Islands: Just beyond Pipestem Inlet, this group of two primary islands offers only provisional anchorage because it is open to Loudoun Channel. Anchor in 18 meters between Larken Island and South Stopper Island. Enter from the north.

★ Broken Islands (7): [3670] On chart 3670, remove the freshwater symbol from Benson, Clarke, Effingham, Turret, Willis, Dodd, and Hand Islands. This interesting group of islands, about 100 in all, is part of the Pacific Rim National Park. The group consists of a number of islands, islets and rocks, lying between Imperial Eagle and Loudoun Channels. There are several passages through the group, but only two, Sechart and Coaster Channels, are marked by lights. All other channels are hazardous, and unless in possession of local knowledge, should be approached very cautiously. The term rock pile certainly is fitting for this group. The Park Service has a float and primitive campground with water on the north side of Gibraltar Island, behind a small island. It is not connected to shore, and is used by the M.V. Lady Rose, from Port Alberni. Primitive camping areas are on the islands. There are few good anchorages in the Broken Group. Effingham

Bay, Island Harbour, and an anchorage made by Walsh, Turtle, Dodd, and Willis Islands are the most sheltered. Three Indian reserves on the islands are not open to the public.

★ Effingham Island & Effingham Bay: The bay is on the northwest side of the island. Good anchorage, on a mud bottom, and room for a number of boats. Many kayakers and canoeists are in the area and the designated campsites are only for their use. From the head of Effingham Bay's southwest bight, a short trail leads across the island to one of about 100 Indian village sites where a total of about ten thousand natives once lived. Just up from the shore is a 300' terrace which is actually a 30' deep midden, where for centuries, natives ate shellfish beside their fires. On close examination, some of the logs in this zone are seen to be squared rather than rounded, identifying them as round house beams.

★ Walk-around: Walking the beach toward the ocean, the seascape is rugged but the scenery and caves make the walk worthwhile. One cave is 100' deep and can be entered at lower tides. When exploring such caves great caution is required to avoid being trapped inside by a rising tide. Likewise, caution is also needed when beach walking along the West Coast, because in places the dense underbrush along the shoreline is so impenetrable, one can be trapped by an incoming tide.

Jaques Island: The Jaques Island lagoon is intriguing for gunkholing. However, because it is very rocky and shallow, for most boats it is only accessible at higher tides.

Wouwer Island: This is one of the best examples of a rugged out-island on the coast. This close to the ocean, anchoring is precarious; however, in reasonable weather, there is provisional anchorage on the inside of the island. Entering this area from the west, the seas breaking all around on the nearby rocks can be intimidating. Entering from the east, there is an unlikely approach which is smoother but the extreme of gunkholing. Although this is not recommended, on higher tides and in mild weather, the tiny slit between Batley and Wouwer Islands is barely passable for most boats. Once inside, there are tight anchorages in the next two bays of Wouwer Island. Another way here is by dinghy from a more protected inland anchorage.

After taking the dinghy ashore, there's a short trail from the deepest bay to the other side of the island, directly facing the ocean. The beach here is jam-packed with drift logs. Walking the beach and logs and south, around the teeming tide pools and climbing around headland here can be a highlight of the trip. There are thick carpets of mussels, dozens of roaring sea lions and eagles clinging to shreds of storm-torn trees. For any such walk, it's important to allow plenty of time because the walking is slow. Also take a flashlight because some of the trails like this are actually tunnels of dense salal and after dark they're absolutely black.

★ Loudoun Channel: Most of this channel is too open for good anchoring, but there are some locations at the north end. The southeast corner of Mayne Bay, off David Channel, is one. Another anchorage is in Pipestem Inlet, behind Bazett Island. The latter is more sheltered, but caution should be used because of rocks on both sides of the entrance. During fair weather, Toquart Bay offers sufficient shelter for anchoring in several small bays and coves. There is access to Toquart Bay by logging roads. Camping and launching facilities are very primitive.

Zeballos Wharf   Linda Schreiber Photo

★ **Ucluelet (8):** Pronounced You-cloo-let, meaning *safe landing place.* This fishing and logging village is located at the west entrance to Barkley Sound, 22 miles from Bamfield. It is connected to Port Alberni by a paved road. There are several public floats in the inlet, as well as two fuel floats with diesel, gas and water. Scuba diving here is excellent. A small boat harbor is entered two tenths of a mile west of the north end of Lyche Island. A launching ramp is just west of the Trans-Pacific Fish Wharf. An Indian reserve with two public floats is on the starboard side of the inlet upon entering. A large general store has a complete line of groceries, fresh and frozen meats, and produce. A liquor store, drugstore, bakery and post office are located in the village. There are several motels, laundry facilities, one hotel, restaurants, and lounges. Marine and electronic repair facilities are accessible. A medical clinic is operated in conjunction with the hospital in Tofino. M.V. *Lady Rose* and M.V. *Francis Barkley* connect Ucluelet with Port Alberni from June through September. In 1870 Ucluelet was a fur trading post. During the war, a seaplane base was located here.

Ucluelet Small Craft Harbour: Located west of the north tip of Lyche Island. Moorage, power, water, washroom. 250-726-4241.

Eagle Marine: Gas, diesel, water, supplies, ice, bait. 250-726-4262.

Island West Fishing Resort: Moorage, RV sites, lodging, fishing gear, launch ramp, water, (showers, laundry, sani-dump (for guests only), restaurant/pub, internet cafe nearby. 250-726-7515, VHF 66A.

Barkley Sound To Clayoquot Sound

[3603, 3646, 3671, 3673, 3674, 3685]

★ **Carolina Channel:** Carolina Channel is the most direct route between Barkley and Clayoquot Sounds. Because of this and because

it's also the most direct route to the fishing grounds, this fairly narrow channel is often crowded with fishing boats. Ordinarily none of this is a problem except in fog, which however, is often thick here. Then, between all the boats here and the reefs surrounding the channel, navigation is critical.

Long Beach: There is no moorage or shore access, but from land, this is a popular part of Pacific Rim National Park. The 12 miles of sand and surf, numerous picnic areas and 1,000 campsites are located near motels and restaurants. From late June to September, park service naturalists present programs. A large airport, established during the war, is still in use today.

★ **Tofino (9):** [3685] When approaching, watch for shoal areas in the harbor. Tofino is a fishing village with many supplies and services. The harbor office is on the 4th Street dock, VHF 6. There are several public floats. The most westerly moorage is at the First Street Public Dock. The next moorage, headed eastward, is for the fishing fleet. Next comes the Weigh West Marine Resort floats. About a mile from town there is moorage at the Crab Dock. Note that getting sea weed in your propeller is a hazard at this site. All the moorages can be hectic, when the fishing fleet is in. Mooring buoys southwest of Beck Island have been removed. Facilities include a hospital, hotel, motels, resorts, liquor store, general store, bakery, drug and pharmacy store, and post office. The population of the combined Ucluelet-Tofino area is about 3500. It is the site of a Coast Guard Life Boat Station. Visit the West Coast Maritime Museum, which features artifacts from fur trading and pioneer days. These include artifacts from sunken ships. Open June-August. By boat you can visit nearby Fort Defiance, on Meares Island. A good paved road connects Tofino and Ucluelet, with access to Long Beach. Scenic float plane flights to Hot Springs Cove can be arranged.

Method Marine Supply: Gas, diesel, stove oil, propane, limited moorage, power, water, ice, hydraulic repairs, divers air, restrooms, chandlery, laundry, fishing supplies. 250-725-3251. VHF 6.

Stubbs Island: Private wildlife reserve. No services for boaters. A fur trading post was established here in 1875.

★ **Yarksis:** Anchorage in the bay is possible in nine to 15 feet of water. Ruins of a former Indian village are situated on Father Charles Channel on the southeast side of Vargas Island.

★ **Tofino Inlet:** Tofino Inlet is a dead end. Because of this, fewer boats are found, yet the area contains some of the best and most secluded anchorages in Clayoquot Sound. Many of these areas have been logged. While this may not be as scenic, it does offer the advantage of providing miles of logging roads to walk. There are some spectacular views. Before departing on such a walk, be sure to tie the dinghy high and dry, or, with the tidal range in this area, you could return to find the anchor under water. Many of the logging roads appear to be close to the water. However, these areas often turn out to be a nearly impossible to penetrate, maze of slash. The logging roads are usually lined with bear attracting berry bushes. Even though bears are numerous along the coast, they are rarely a problem, but take along some pots and pans to bang together in case you want to scare them away. Wolves are often heard howling at night, even on a beach.

Entering Tofino Inlet from Tofino, there's more of a challenge than one would think from a glance at the chart. Traveling east from the main part of town, the channel becomes narrower and at the last dock, the Crab Dock, there's not enough room to easily turn a boat around between the dock and a sand bar to the north. Furthermore, the flood current is strong enough here to sweep a boat into a reef just beyond the dock. Instead, a sharp left turn is required between two tight buoys. Also there's an uncharted rock right off the Weigh West Marina dock. To avoid all this, especially on a flood tide, it is safest to use one of two more preferred but more indirect routes. One is through Heynen Channel and west of Morpheus Island and the other is through Duffin Passage and between Strawberry and Riley Islands. Because of these problems in the vicinity of the Crab Dock, the preferred dock, which is accessible unless full with fishing boats, is the large public dock just inside buoy Y29.

Grice Bay: There is a good paved ramp, parking, and a small campground here, but no floats. The bay is very shallow. This is a favorite spot for park naturalists who lead canoe and kayaking groups through this area.

★ **Island Cove:** At entrance to Tofino Inlet, there is protected anchorage in eight to nine fathoms of water. Use the passage north of the island in the entrance.

★ **Gunner Inlet:** Just north of Island Cove, this inlet has several protected anchorages.

★ **Kennedy Cove:** Found at the entrance to Kennedy River. Anchorage is possible in two to four fathoms of water in either the north or south side of the cove.

★ **Meares Island (10):** Mosquito Bay, in the northeast corner of Meares Island, has good anchorage in two to six fathoms of water. The passage west of Kirshaw and Wood Islets has the fewest obstructions. Also, Ritchie Bay, in the northwest corner, has good anchorage in four to five fathoms of water.

Clayoquot Sound to Nootka Sound

[3603, 3673, 3674, 3675, 3676]

★ **Hecate Bay and Cypress Bay:** These are opposite the northwest corner of Meares Island. Several very good anchorages are available.

★ **Matilda Inlet:** This niche is in the southeast corner of Flores Island and has several attractions. Anchorage is in the inlet at several points. Ahousat, a settlement on the west side of the inlet, has public floats, restaurant, and a store that carries local artwork for sale. The harbor approach is very hazardous and not recommended. Anchorage is possible in the portion of the inlet marked hot spring. It is possible to take a skiff to Marktosis, an Indian village on the east side.

Ahousat General Store: Gas, diesel, stove oil, water, groceries, ways, very limited moorage. 250-670-9575. VHF 68.

★⚓ **Gibson Marine Park (11):** This British Columbia Provincial Marine Park is located on the north shore of Whitesand Cove. Enter from Russell Channel. Ahousat Hot Springs are found in the park. No marine facilities. A primitive hiking trail goes from Ahousat through the park to the broad, sandy beaches of White Sand Cove. ⛺🧍

★ **Cow Bay:** This is the local name for the bay just north of Russell Channel, into which Cow Creek flows. This is the most likely place to see gray whales.

★ **Whitepine Cove:** Although this cove is open and exposed, just to its west is a portion of the cove which is fully protected. It is entered through the channel west of the charted 310 foot island and continuing south of the 240 foot island. At this point, the water is very shallow, however even at a fairly low tide, traveling slowly, the rocks can be seen and avoided. Inside, there's a wide area for anchorage.

Bawden Bay: The inner side of Bawden Bay has several little nooks to explore, however the whole bay is exposed to the north and the nooks are too small for proper anchoring.

★ **Ross Passage:** On the south side of Ross Passage there is presently a fish farm, but the north side is uninhabited and scenic. Inside the charted 200 foot island, there is anchorage and the channel there is passable.

★ **Gibson Cove:** This cove, on the east side of Herbert Inlet, offers good anchorage in six fathoms of water in the southeast corner.

★ **Sulphur Passage, East of Obstruction Island:** The bay in the southwest corner of the passage offers anchorage in seven to nine fathoms of water. The north end of this passage has many rocks and is not recommended.

★ **Riley Cove (12):** Located at the junction of Shelter Inlet and Sydney Inlet, this area has good shelter for anchoring. There is a mud bank in the harbor that should be located while looking for an anchoring location. A tie to shore might be a good idea.

★ **Sydney Inlet:** [3674] Sydney Inlet is a classic example of a fjord. It is an extensive, inviting waterway, enclosed with tall cones. The dense foliage is "trimmed", by the salt water, precisely to the high-water line, forming a horizontal line as far as the eye can see. Though Sydney Inlet is spectacular to see, typical of such fjords, it is too deep for good anchorage. A branching fjord, Stewardson Inlet, is also good for exploring. It has a logging site at its end.

★ **Young Bay:** This bay, located in Sydney Inlet, two miles north of Starling Point, offers secure anchorage in six to nine fathoms. A short walk to freshwater Cecelia Lake rewards the explorer with clean water and swimming. The trail has become nearly obliterated in places and is not an easy walk. The ruins, at the north side of the entrance, is that of a pilchard plant. Bays like this one offer about as much beauty as one could desire. Bear can be seen and heard ashore as they leisurely grind mussels. Thrushes sing fluting spirals back and forth to each other across the bay. In places aligned for viewing it, the setting sun forms a tall picket fence of black shadows between the brilliantly lighted trees. The lacy summer clouds change suddenly to gray, then black,and the sky changes from dark blue to bright yellow, then pink. On some nights, the moon rises above a near horizon, like an immense flashlight, illuminating the trees an eerie snow-gray.

★ **Holmes Inlet:** Holmes Inlet, an eastern branch of Sydney Inlet, offers some especially good gunkholing and some unusual anchorages. The first unnamed bay entering Holmes Inlet on the east has been called "Still Cove" because of its quiet serenity. It is entered through a bottleneck entrance with two narrow but passable constrictions and inside the bay there's ample room for a good choice of anchorages.

Continuing north and east of a charted 225 foot island is another anchorage adjacent to the remains of a recently abandoned oyster farm. North of that, through a very narrow passage, is a tiny bay to the east with more remnants of the oyster farm. This bay is just large enough for one boat to anchor, with minimal scope in what feels like a mountain lake. From here there are two of the narrowest passages possible for gunkholing. The one leading west and north of the 225 foot island, has underwater rock shelves extending out from its sides. The other passage, to the north, is hardly discernible through the trees, but at higher tide, is barely negotiable, staying between the trees in mid-channel.

Pretty Girl Cove: The name alone makes this bay irresistible to see. The bay is scenic and the tidal grass at its head looks like an immense lawn. The anchorage, however, is not good because the bay is wide open and typical of the heads of some of these bays with streams entering them, the delta formed the stream ends suddenly and drops like a cliff, here to 80 feet.

Exiting Sydney Inlet, toward the ocean, there are some tempting little bays along the western shore. These can be entered, but with the swells here, close navigation is necessary, because of the typical rocks. The largest of these bays is behind a charted 190 foot island, where there is reasonably secure anchorage. This island is an example of places with forests of original growth.

★ **Hot Springs Cove (13):** Part of the Maquinna Provincial Park, this cove is located at the northern entrance to Clayoquot Sound. About two-thirds of the way into the bay on the north side is an Indian Village. There is good anchorage available here, as well as public floats, mooring buoys, fuel, and, as the name suggests, hot springs. To the east of the harbor entrance on Sharp Point are a light and fog signal. On the west side is the Mate Island light. Favor a mid-channel course when entering the harbor. Approaching Hot Springs Cove from the north, there's a contrast between the way things look on a chart and how they actually are on the water. The narrow entrance is barely discernible until one is almost there, when finally, the two points forming its entrance separate. Many years ago there was a store at Hot Springs, but it was eventually abandoned. Since then several floating stores have operated out of the cove at one time or another, illustrating how things can change at these coastal settlements. A well maintained boardwalk trail, about one mile in length, leads from the public wharf to the hot springs. Anchoring near the springs to avoid the walk is not recommended. Landing there by dinghy in the surf requires jumping frantically ashore in a sort of semi-controlled crash. The Indian word for the site is Mok-seh-kla-chuck, meaning smoking water, and during the peak months of July and August it draws up to 300 visitors daily. A $3.00 user fee (per person, per day) was instituted in 2004. At the hot springs, water streams over a falls, through some pools cut into the black rock, and then into the ocean surf. This is a good place to sit among the rocks and watch the ocean sparkling below. If you like hot baths, try the higher pools. Bubbling out of the earth at about 117 degrees Fahrenheit, the water continues to cool gradually as it cascades to the pools below. Despite park regulations to the contrary, don't be surprised if you find yourself conversing casually with a nude bather, especially earlier or later in the day when most of the regular tourists are not present. The natural beauty of this whole area is spectacular. For an interesting side trip take a dinghy into the slit inside inner Mate Island. This requires about a mid-tide and you will need to secure the dinghy to the Vancouver Island side to protect it from the ocean. The beach that stretches to the northwest is some of the most rugged and scenic of the coast.

★ **Nootka Sound (14):** [3675] It is about 28 nautical miles from Hot Springs Cove to Friendly Cove, allowing for plenty of clearance for Estevan Point and Perez Rocks on the Hesquiat Peninsula. With reasonable weather and good visibility, most of the first part of this coastline between Mate Island and Hesquiat Point can be taken close enough to see the large caves. It is possible, in good weather to land on some of these beaches and even in the entrances to the caves; however there are some important precautions. Because many of these caves were native burial sites, permission from Hesquiat band members should first be obtained. Also, when landing a dinghy on beaches exposed to the ocean like this, even when the waves are low, they usually still break on the beach. Be prepared for an unexpected swamping by trying to land the dinghy straight in, requiring that you protect valuables from the salt water and jump quickly ashore with the painter. When landing on the beach of such a cave, there's another precaution. It is possible that the waves breaking on the beach may not allow for an exit and the steep sides of the cave may not allow for an escape. This is a real advantage for taking a portable VHF radio when doing such dinghy exploring.

A light and fog signal are on Estevan Point. Shoals extend a great distance. It would be possible to enter Hesquiat Harbour about seven nautical miles from the entrance to Hot Springs Cove. There are several good anchorages, but the Hesquiat Bar stretches across the entrance to this bay. There are rocks with kelp and shoals. Do not cross in rough weather. The most protected anchorage is Roe Basin at the head of the bay. When entering Hesquiat Harbour, the bar shallows to eighteen feet and is covered with kelp. Once inside, the remaining waves still make for a rolling anchorage, especially in the outer portions of the harbor. Extensive beaches, covered with clam shells, line most of the harbor. In the vicinity of Hisnet Lake there are some smaller caves which, with a little rock climbing, can be explored. Nootka Sound has historical importance because it was the first place where Europeans landed on the coast of British Columbia.

★ **Friendly Cove:** This spot, on the southeast corner of Nootka Island, just north of the light on San Rafael Island, was where Captain James Cook first landed in 1778. There is a public pier and a float available during the summer. No services. An Indian village, Yuquot, is in the cove. Once lined with long houses, now only one family lives in Friendly Cove. Ray and Terry Williams were born and raised here, and are descendants of those early longhouse natives. Ask their permission when going ashore. The Spanish had a settlement here after taking it from the British in 1789. A war almost resulted, but a 1792 treaty returned the cove to Britain. A church here is adorned with native carvings and stained glass windows commemorating the meeting of Captains Vancouver and Quadra, averting this war between England and Spain. The lighthouse is probably the most accessible on this coast to visit. Lighthouse keeper Ed Kippert, who's been here over twenty years, will show visitors to the top of the tower. A small fee is charged by the Williams' for people to moor and come ashore. The fee helps to pay for the upkeep of the church.

★ **Santa Gertrudis Cove:** Protected anchorage is found in this secluded, small bay that is about one mile from Friendly Cove. The very narrow entrance has rocks in the center and northern side. Even shallow draft boats should use extreme caution and enter only at high tide.

★ **Nootka:** About one and one half miles north of Friendly Cove is the site of an abandoned cannery. Caution is advised here because there are many underwater objects such as broken piles. Protected anchorage is available here, as well as a public wharf.

★ **McKay Passage:** Between Saavedra Islands and Nootka Island is the location of a fishing resort.

★ **Plumper Harbour:** Good sheltered anchorage can be found on the west side of Kendrick Inlet.

★ **Bligh Island:** [3675] Bligh Island, now a provincial marine park, fills the center portion of Nootka Sound. It is here where Captain Cook, accompanied by the infamous Bligh and after which the island is named, cut spars from the tall trees for their ships, Resolute and Discovery. At the extreme end and western bight of Ewin Inlet of Bligh Island is one of the most secluded anchorages anywhere.

Gold River: [3675] This is a logging port at the head of Muchalat Inlet. The town itself is eight miles inland, and is connected by paved highway to Campbell River.

Gold River Public Dock: Very limited moorage, no amenities, rough paved ramp.

Tuta Marine: Showers, ice, freezers, bait, kayak launching, moorage, camp ground. 250-283-7550.

★ **Tlupana Inlet:** North of Bligh Island, this inlet has several anchorages in its bays and coves. Near its head is a box canyon which wings into the end of Tlupana Inlet to the west and Nesook Bay to the east. Perpendicular Bluff at this junction is well named. It is so steep that a boat passing

alongside would bump the inlet's sides before touching bottom. Because this vicinity is so steep anchorage is difficult.

★ **Hisnit Inlet:** This Inlet, branching west from lower Tlupana Inlet, has fair anchorage near its head and better anchorage in Valdez Bay. Watching closely along the western shore near the head of the inlet, some weathered piles of gigantic marble slabs are visible. Ashore is the swimming pool-sized pit from where marble was quarried. Small marble samples are easy pickings. In this, and many other places along the coast, oysters are plentiful; however, because the vastness of the coast makes monitoring impractical, the entire coast is closed to shellfish harvesting. Such red tide poisoning can be fatal, and contrary to common opinion, there is no good way for a boater to test for it. Eating one as a test for lip numbness doesn't work, because only one in a hundred may be toxic.

Critter Cove: Located approximately one mile south of Argonaut Point. This unnamed cove is now known as Critter Cove. There is anchorage.

Critter Cove Marina: Moorage, gas, lodging, restaurant, showers, ice, bait, tackle. 250-283-7364. VHF 7.

★ **Tahsis Inlet:** [3604, 3675, 3676] Because of the wind that is commonly funneled up or down this long fjord, it can provide a sailor with one of the best spinnaker runs of the whole voyage. Gunkholing through Princesa Channel and behind Bodega Island, some protected anchorage is attainable.

★ **Tahsis (15):** Located at the head of Tahsis Inlet. Tahsis was the winter village of Nootka Chief, Maquinna, who hosted Vancouver and Quadra in 1792. It is now a sawmill town and port for overseas shipments of forest products. Public floats, marinas, fuels, repairs, water, ramp, laundry, showers, liquor, post office, groceries, sporting goods, marine hardware, medical clinic, RV park, restaurants, hotel, motel, bed & breakfasts, modern recreation center with pool and exercise facilities, fishing charters. 40 miles of good gravel road connect the town to the paved road at Gold River.

British Columbia Chamber of Commerce: 1201-750 West Pender Street, Vancouver, BC, V6C 2T8. 604-683-0700, 1-800-435-5622.

North Island Information: http://north-island.ca/.

Tahsis Village Information: www.villageoftahsis.com.

Westview Marina: Moorage, gas, diesel, water, showers, provisions, ice, laundry, restrooms, restaurant, fishing supplies. Propane, internet access. 250-934-7672. VHF 6, 66A.

★ **Esperanza:** [3663, 3676] There is a village on the north side of Hecate Channel with a small public dock.

Esperanza Marine Service: Gas, diesel, water, moorage, laundry, showers. No moorage, showers, or laundry during month of July. 250-934-7792. VHF 6.

★ **Ceepeecee:** This old cannery site is one mile northeast of Esperanza. Private floats, water and some repairs available.

★ **Zeballos (16):** This community is a logging village that was, in the 1930's, the scene of a gold rush. The village was named after a 1791 Spanish

Lieutenant, Ciriaco Cevallos. Zeballos is a throwback to a quaint, little, no-nonsense community, where a store may stay open late for a visitor and a shower in the pub is paid for by throwing some money in a pot for an up-coming celebration. Don't mind the people walking by while you shower. A stretch of 26 miles of logging roads connect the town to paved Island Highway. Village Office: 250-761-4229. www.zeballos.com.

Zeballos Facilities: Small craft harbor with 400 feet floats, power, water, concrete boat launch, parking, hotel, restaurant, general store, sport shop, convenience store, museum, library, campsite, RV sites, motels, laundry, showers, post office, repairs, medical clinic. Harbour Manager: 250-761-4238. VHF 6.

Weston Enterprises: Gas, diesel, oils, propane, water. 250-761-4201. VHF 68.

★ **Queen Cove:** In Port Eliza, this cove has good anchorage in six fathoms on a mud bottom. Excellent for a relaxing stop over. Very protected. The entrance to the channel is narrow.

★ **Nuchatlitz Inlet:** Although this inlet is somewhat out of the way for boats traveling in or out of Esperanza Inlet, with an extra day or two, its remoteness and beauty are worth the side trip. Its entrance is particularly rocky and right off the ocean like this, careful navigation is required. Once inside the rocks, there are several choices of secluded anchorages. The most protected of these is Mary Basin, near the end of Nuchatlitz Inlet and behind Lord Island. This basin is large with a choice of anchorage sites.

★ **Inner Basin:** Beyond Mary Basin is the almost irresistible three mile Inner Basin. Its entrance, however, is not only extremely narrow and rocky, but it has strong currents. The current here is not listed in the tables, so the only safe way to enter is by waiting for a near slack current and, because of the shallow rocky entrance, this should preferably be the slack high water. This also means that either a quick trip must be made, exiting again with the same slack current, or spending the night in the basin and returning with the next day's high slack. Anchorage in the basin is possible along some of the shorelines, perhaps with a stern line ashore.

Nuchatlitz: This Indian village is in another part of the bay, not so far out of the way from Esperanza Inlet. The village itself is nearly abandoned now and the entrance is tricky and more easily accomplished by anchoring farther out and going by dinghy.

★⚓ **Catala Island Marine Park:** [3676] This island is accessible from anchorage in Queen Cove. It has an unusual beach on its southeast side, composed of mid-sized rocks and steep enough so that they roll downhill with the beach walker. On the northeast side of the island, accessible at lower tides, is a series of interconnected caves. Toward the east end of the island are some spires and arches and a beach with an unusual accumulation of chip-sized drift. Rough trails lead to a lake and marshy area at the Island's center.
▲

★ **Esperanza Inlet (17):** [3676] This is the northern access to the inlets of Nootka Sound. Gillam Channel is the preferred approach because it is marked by navigational aids.

Rolling Roadstead: Traveling to or from the northwest, Rolling Roadstead is a shortcut from the preferred Gillam Channel route. This shortcut not only saves a few miles but also avoids the usually rough ocean here. The portion of this route between Obstruction Reef and High Rocks, however, is reasonably close to some rocks which break heavily.

Nootka Sound to Kyuquot Sound

[3603, 3623, 3651, 3675, 3676]

★ **Clear Passage:** Traveling north, this passage is another shortcut which is easier to negotiate than Rolling Roadstead. Immediately before McQuarrie Islets, there is a break in the inner reef, through which a nearly direct inward turn can be made. Then stay in the middle of Clear Passage and turn back out just after Grogan Rock, a jagged 23 foot spire.

★ **Kyuquot Sound (18):** The distance from the outer marker in Gillam Channel to the outer marker for Kyuquot Channel is 13 nautical miles. Kyuquot Sound is the smallest of the five large sounds on the West Coast of Vancouver Island. Surrounded by fairly high mountains, Kyuquot Sound has two main inlets, Kashutl and Tahsis, and many islands and islets.

Fair Harbour: Entering through Kyuquot Channel, the first good anchorage is about ten miles in, on the east side.

Dixie Cove: This cove, on Hohoae Island, is small, but has protected anchorage, with no swells. A second anchorage is adjacent to Dixie Cove. Enter through the narrow channel to reach it. There is 20 feet of water here, even on a minus tide.

Walk-around: Inside Rugged Point, at least provisional anchorage is satisfactory for a short walk across the isthmus of this marine park and a beach walk on a wide, sand beach.

★ **Kyuquot & Walters Cove:** This fishing village is located in Walters Cove on the north side of Walters Island. Public dock with two floats and power. There is a general store, post office, marine hardware store, lodging and seasonal restaurant. The Red Cross Outpost Hospital with a resident nurse can be reached at 250-332-5289. Help is also available on VHF 6. Be prepared for the store to open after the noon hour. It is well stocked and includes ice, fishing gear, bait, tackle, groceries, hardware, produce, baked goods. 250-332-5211. Rose bushes line some very pretty lanes and the walkway resembles that of an English country village. The entrance to Kyuquot is intricate and precise navigation is required because this entire area is a garden of rocks. First Nations Band Office: 250-332-5259. Boaters are to check in at the Band Office when visiting. VHF 14.

★ **Fair Harbour:** Fair Harbour is connected to Zeballos by 20 miles of logging roads. This is the only land access to Kyuquot Sound. A small campground is located about one-half mile from the wharf. There are no services and no habitations. Some anchorage on a mud bottom can be found in either the east or west end. A public dock with a float and a primitive ramp are also in the harbor. During north gales the wind may funnel into the harbor, but the holding ground is good.

★ **Kashutl Inlet:** Anchorages can be found in Hankin Cove, on the east side of the inlet in 40-60 feet of water. The cove is a booming ground with logging operations. There are no anchorages in Tahsis Inlet. Easy Inlet, on the west side of Kashutl Inlet, is another anchorage with good holding ground. Small craft anchorage is also available in Wood Cove.

★ **Crowther Channel:** Heading north from Kyuquot Sound, the route through this channel is much shorter than the more preferred Kyuquot Channel route. There is a narrow but deep exit between Amos Island and a charted 26 foot rock to the south.

Kyuquot Sound to Quatsino Sound

[3604, 3623, 3624, 3651, 3679, 3680, 3683, 3686]

Checleset Bay (19): The 56 mile stretch from Kyuquot Sound to Winter Harbour is one of the longer runs on the West Coast. One must cross Checleset Bay and round Cape Cook on Brooks Peninsula. There are three smaller inlets in Checleset Bay that offer shelter (Malksope, Ououkinsh, Nasparti), but the approaches to them have many hazards, especially during poor weather conditions. The coast along the southeast side of Brooks Peninsula, northeast of Clerke Point is locally known as Shelter Shed and is used by fishermen in northwest winds. Columbia Cove, inside Jackobson Point in Nasparti Inlet has good shelter and two mooring buoys. A drying rock spit extends from Jackobson Point. Very large swells can be encountered rounding Cape Cook, even for those traveling a good two miles outside of Solander Island.

★ **Bunsby Islands:** The rugged Bunsby Islands offer some of the best of gunkholing as well as dinghy exploring. Some of the better anchorages are along both sides of Gay Passage. Getting to the Bunsby Island from Kyuquot, there is a protected passage inside the Barrier Islands. Entering this passage at St. Paul's Dome, use careful navigation between the inner and outer set of reefs.

Battle Bay: Battle bay is very rocky, but has some areas offering reasonable anchorage. From here, either by foot or dinghy, there is a site charted as an Indian village, on the southeast side of Acous Peninsula, where by scouting around, a large midden area can be found, and, partially hidden in the brush, the collapsed remains of a longhouse and two totems, one prone and the other leaning. In another area there is a burial ground, with partially intact dugouts and moss-covered skulls. Without realizing it, it is possible to be treading on sacred ground.

★ **Nasparti Inlet:** The Inlet area has several choices of interesting anchorages. Dinghy exploring into lagoons, like Johnson Lagoon, with a narrow entrance, however, holds a risk. The entrance must be carefully sized up for current before approaching. Unless the entire entrance way can be seen, it is possible to be sucked into a torrent of rapids and the danger of being capsized is present.

Cape Cook: Exiting the interior of Checleset Bay in any direction, navigation is especially important. The reefs here are probably the most extensive and difficult to identify than any along the coast. With the constant ocean swells breaking over their exposed and unexposed rocks, these kinds of reefs are the most dangerous. Rounding Cape Cook from this direction, another hazard is the first prominence of Brooks Peninsula, Clerke Point. Surrounded by kelp one-and-one-half miles out, this broad shallow

grounds must be given a wide berth. Cape Cook, along with the entire Brooks Peninsula, juts farther out into the ocean than any other prominence of the coast. Because of this, the wind is accelerated here and it is likely to be the roughest part of a circumnavigation. That's why it's commonly called the "Cape of Storms." On the other hand, surfing with the wind in a sailboat here, can be one of the most thrilling parts of the voyage. There are no adequate anchorages all the way around the end of the peninsula. The route often taken by local fishing boats inside of Solander Island is tricky to navigate, doesn't save much distance and is not recommended. Because the outside of Solander Island is deep, the island can be taken close enough for a good view of the extensive population of sea birds and sea lions on this barren monarch of an island. This general area of Vancouver Island is particularly desolate and other mariners are less frequent. Yet in these waters, the boat often parts tens of thousands of common murrs, rhinoceros auklets, sooty shearwaters and tufted puffins.

★ **Brooks Bay (20):** [3624, 3651, 3680] This is the most remote major bay along the coast. Even during the peak of the summer, a mariner is likely to be the only one here.

★ **Klaskish Inlet & Klaskino Inlet:** These inlets indent into Vancouver Island north of Brooks Peninsula. Klaskish Inlet is deep. The basin at the head has protected anchorage from the seas, however, strong winds can blow down from the mountains. There are public mooring buoys in the basin. Klaskino Inlet, farther north, is entered north of Heater Point. There is an anchorage southeast of Anchorage Island and a few public mooring buoys are east of the island. A fresh water stream exits the delta south of there, with a three foot deep pool of water about 100 yards upstream.

★ **Lawn Point:** The entire reef surrounded prominence of Lawn and Kwakiutl Point are examples of why it is a good rule to give most of the west coast of Vancouver Island a two mile berth.

★ **Quatsino Sound (21):** [3605, 3624, 3679, 3686] This is one of the largest sounds on the west coast of Vancouver Island. It has several communities in it, all but one connected by road to Port Hardy. There are strong tidal currents in parts of the sound, especially in Quatsino Narrows, where the maximum is usually five knots, but can reach eight at springs. Heavy tiderips are also encountered at times.

★ **Winter Harbour:** This harbor is an interesting fishing community, with a boardwalk running its length. It is at the head of Forward Inlet, 15 miles from Holberg and 47 miles from Port Hardy by logging roads. There is a public dock with moorage floats, public telephone, launch ramp, post office, and general store. The store is open all year. Fresh meats and produce in the summer. Liquor and fishing supplies. Gas, diesel, water. There is sheltered anchorage in eight fathoms of water over mud. Try crabbing in the bay across from town. Harbour Master 250-969-4313.

The Outpost at Winter Harbour Grant Sales Limited: Moorage, gas, diesel, campsites, groceries, liquor, laundry, showers, ice, fishing supplies, lodging. Reservations: 250-969-4333.

★ **North Harbour:** On the west side of Forward Inlet, North Harbour also offers sheltered anchorage in seven fathoms of water. Mooring buoys.

Ucluelet   *Tourism B.C. Photo*

★⚓ **Koprino Harbour & Quatsino Marine Park:** Anchorages are west and north of Schloss Island. The marine park has campsites and a small dock.
⚓

★ **Pamphlet Cove:** Land around this cove has been purchased as a recreational reserve. It is on the north side of Drake Island and has sheltered anchorage.

★ **Julian Cove:** Southeast of Banter Point in Buchholz Channel is small but has anchorage for small craft.

Quatsino: This is a small village with a public dock. No fuel (Fuel is found in Coal Harbour).

Jeune Landing, Neroutsos Inlet: A small settlement with a public dock and float. Highway to Port Hardy. No services.

★ **Rumble Beach & Port Alice:** [3679, 3681] Connected to Port Hardy by paved highway, these two places are really one community, population about 750. There is currently a pulp mill at Port Alice but it may be closing soon. The only facilities for boaters in Neroutsos Inlet are the floats of the Port Alice Yacht Club and an excellent paved ramp with parking adjoining. For information concerning Port Alice Yacht Club, 250-284-3253. There are overnight accommodations, RV sites, a golf course, restaurants, taxis, banks, a liquor store, and a hospital. For information about the village call 250-284-3391.

★ **Coal Harbour (22):** This harbor is 12 miles from Port Hardy by paved road. There is a public dock with several mooring floats, power, water, fuel, a post office, and a good paved ramp with adequate parking. This is the best access to Quatsino Sound for trailer boaters. Mechanical and hull repairs are available. Other amenities in Coal Harbour include fishing charter, water taxi, seaplane, and tours to view local caves. Originally a coal-mining site, Coal Harbour became a seaplane base for Catalinas in the 1930's. The infrastructures that remained were later used for the whaling industry. This village was a whaling station through 1967 where whales were brought ashore for processing. One hanger where whale blubber was rendered still exists and is home to a floatplane company. The rings to which cables were fixed for hauling the whales ashore can still be seen adjacent to the boat ramp. Jaw bones of whales are also visible in the side street by the post office.

D H Timber Towing: Operates tugs, water taxi. 250-949-6358. VHF 10.

★ **Holberg:** This logging community is at the head of Holberg Inlet. There is a pub, coffee shop, store, launch ramp, and post office. Propane can be obtained from a resident's home. Danish settlers came at the turn of the century, and by 1916 only a few were left at the Cape Scott area.

★ **Varney Bay, Rupert Inlet:** There is anchorage in this bay, near the inlet entrance. There is a large drying flat at the head of the bay. From Varney Bay, a dinghy trip can be made at higher tides right into the box canyon of near-by Marble River, with its overhanging caves. Utah Copper Mines, on the north side of the inlet, has an ore loading facility for large ships.

Quatsino Sound to Port Hardy

[3549, 3605, 3624, 3679]

★ **Kains Island:** Leaving Quatsino Sound, fishing boats are often seen taking the route inside Kains Island; however, without local knowledge, the route outside the island is the safest.

★ **Sea Otter Cove (23):** Heading north from the entrance to Quatsino Sound, it is 56 nautical miles to the first secure anchorage at Bull Harbour. Sea Otter Cove is a possible stop along the way. Use Chart #3624. The cove lies east of Cape Russell and is marked by a light. Kelp covers most rocks and reefs. The cove is used by small craft during the summer. The entrance is very shallow and should be approached cautiously. There are mooring buoys in the cove. There is a fresh water stream on the north shore.

★ **Hansen Bay:** Although Hansen Bay is exposed, in reasonably calm weather, provisional anchorage is possible for a brief dinghy trip into Hansen Lagoon. In lagoons like this, however, being caught in a dropping tide can mean a long muddy wait for the next high tide.

Cape Scott: This cape is the northwest corner of Vancouver Island. The weather is often windy and tidal currents of up to three knots can cause heavy tide-rips and overfalls on both sides of Scott Channel, between the Cape and the Scott Islands. When the wind is against the tide these areas can be dangerous. This is now a Provincial Park. Rounding Cape Scott is probably the highlight of a Vancouver Island voyage. It is the point where the mariner turns the boat clear around, heading back the other way. The radio beaken has been permanently discontinued. Cape Scott is connected to the mainland of Vancouver Island by a half mile sand isthmus. Access to this isthmus can be gained from either its north side in Experiment Bight, when the weather is from the south or from its south side in Guise Bay, when the weather is from the north. Either of these bays can likewise be used for protection and provisional anchorage in the case of storms. Experiment Bight is open, but Guise Bay takes some navigating to get between a reef in the middle of its entrance and rocks on either side. Once ashore, this extensive and desolate isthmus can easily be crossed for some beautiful beach walking on both sides. Also a trail from here leads to the Cape Scott Lighthouse.

Scott Islands: The five Scott Islands extend 25 miles west from Cape Scott. None of them offer very protected anchorage and they are so exposed, venturing there can be risky. On Triangle Island, a storm 80 years ago, blew down a lighthouse which was braced and cabled to the island.

Nahwitti Bar (24): See current tables for Seymour Narrows, British Columbia. This bar stretches across the west entrance to Goletas Channel. It is best crossed at times of slack. Because of shallowing depths as low as six fathoms, waves break over the bar. If traveling from north Vancouver Island around Cape Scott, it is possible to cross Nahwitti Bar at high slack and ride the ebb tide out. With a west wind opposing a falling tide, there can be very heavy breaking and dangerous seas. The alternative is to go around Hope Island.

★ **Bull Harbour (25):** [3549] This harbor, on the south side of Hope Island, is marked by an entrance light. Enter east (right side) of mid-channel island. The speed limit is three knots. There is anchorage exposed to winds. The south part of the bay is foul anchorage. Try anchoring above Norman Island or in the middle of the bay, not too close to the head. There is a public float that is not connected to shore.

★ **Goletas Channel:** See current tables for Seymour Narrows, British Columbia. Inside Nahwitti Bar extends east southeast from Godkin Point, the entrance to Bull Harbour, to Duval Point, the northwest entrance to Port Hardy. It is deep and free from obstructions. This is a good place to troll for silvers. Try Buzz Bombs near the surface while traveling at three knots.

★ **Loquillia Cove:** This cove can be used for anchorage in settled weather or in northwest winds. Open to the southeast. Avoid kelp covered rocks at southern entrance.

★ **Shushartie Bay:** Open to the northwest. There is anchorage in five fathoms of water on the east shore near the entry.

★ **Port Alexander:** There is anchorage at the southeast corner of Nigei Island.

★ **God's Pocket (26):** This niche on Christie Passage has been a favorite shelter for fishermen for many years. Two mooring buoys are placed in the bay. Anchorage can be found on the west side of Hurst Island. God's Pocket Resort is on shore. See information in Chapter 19. The waters around God's Pocket are among the world's best cold water diving areas.

★ **Port Hardy (27):** This area is described in Chapter 17.

Essential Supplies & Services

AIR TRANSPORTATION
To & from Washington
Seattle Seaplanes 1-800-637-5553

To & from Islands/Vancouver
Air Canada 1-888-247-2262
Baxter Air 1-800-661-5599
Harbour Air 1-800-665-0212
Tofino Air 1-866-486-3247
Vancouver Island Air . . 250-287-2433, 1-877-331-2433

AMBULANCES: 911

BOOKS / BOOK STORES
The Marine Atlas 541-593-6396

BUS TRANSPORTATION
Greyhound 250-724-1266
Port Alberni Western Bus Lines 250-723-3341
Tofino 250-725-3431
Ucluelet 250-726-4337
West Coast Trail Bus 250-477-8700

COAST GUARD: VHF 16, 22A, 26, 84
Emergency Rescue 1-800-567-5111
Emergency Cell Phones *16
Bamfield Lifeboat Station 250-728-3322
Tofino Lifeboat Station 250-725-3231
Ucluelet 250-726-7312

CUSTOMS: 1-888-226-7277

FERRY INFORMATION
Gold River/Nootka/Kuyquot/Esperanza (Passenger,
 freight only) 250-283-2515
Bamfield / Port Alberni/Ucluelet (Passenger only) . . . . .
 . . . . 250-723-8313, 1-800-663-7192

FUELS
Ahousat General Store: Gas, Diesel. 250-670-9575 VHF 68
China Creek: Port Alberni. Gas, Diesel. . . 250-723-9812
Clutesi Haven: Port Alberni. Gas. . 250-724-6837 VHF 66A
Columbia Fuels-Shell: Port Alberni. Gas, Diesel.
 250-724-7286
Critter Cove: Gas . . . . 250-283-7364 VHF 7
D.H. Timber: Coal Harbour. Gas, Diesel.
 . . . . 250-949-6358 VHF 10
Eagle Marine-Petro: Ucluelet. Gas, Diesel.
 . . . . 250-726-4262 VHF 8
Esperanza: Gas, Diesel . . . . 250-934-7792 VHF 6
Hot Springs Cove (Indian Village)
Kingfisher: Bamfield. Gas, Diesel. 250-728-3228
Method Marine Supply: Tofino. Gas, Diesel.
 . . . . 250-725-3251 VHF 6
Neah Bay: Washington. Gas, Diesel 360-645-2374
Petro Canada: Port Alberni. Gas, Diesel, Marine Fuel.
 Must Hand Carry to Boat 250-724-2626
Poett Nook: Gas . . . . 250-720-9572 VHF 6
Olson's Resort: Sekiu. Gas, Diesel 360-963-2311
Sunny Shores Marina: Sooke. Gas, Diesel.
 . . . . 250-642-5731 VHF 16
Weston Enterprises: Zeballos. Gas, Diesel.
 . . . . 250-761-4201 VHF 68
Westview Marina: Tahsis. Gas, Diesel. . . . . VHF 6, 66A
Winter Harbour: Gas, Diesel 250-969-4333

HOSPITALS
Bamfield 250-728-3312
Kyuquot . . . . 250-332-5289 (Nurse) VHF 6
Port Alberni 250-723-2135
Port Alice 250-284-3555
Tofino 250-725-3212

INSURANCE
Boat Insurance Agency 206-285-1350
Or Call 1-800-828-2446

LIQUOR STORES
Bamfield   Tahsis
Gold River   Tofino
Port Alberni   Ucluelet
Port Alice   Winter Harbour
Sooke   Zeballos

MARINAS / MOORAGE FLOATS
Ahousat
Bamfield
China Creek Marina . . . . 250-723-9812 VHF 16
Clutesi Haven: Port Alberni . . . . 250-724-6837 VHF 66A
Critter Cove 250-283-7364
Esperanza . . . . 250-934-7792 VHF 6
Fisherman's Harbour: Port Alberni . 250-723-2533 VHF 68,16
Harbour Quay: Port Alberni. 250-723-1413 VHF 16, 66A
Island West: Ucluelet . . . . 250-726-7515 VHF 66A
Kingfisher Marine: Bamfield. (limited) . . . 250-728-3228
Kyuquot
Makah Marina: Neah Bay . . . 360-645-3015 VHF 16, 66
Method Marine Supply:Tofino . . . . 250-725-3251 VHF 6
Olson's Resort: Sekiu 360-963-2311
Poett Nook Marina 250-758-4440
Port Alice Yacht Club 250-284-6249
Port Renfrew Marina: (limited) 250-647-0002
Sooke Harbour Marina 250-642-3236
Sunny Shores Resort & Marina: Sooke 250-642-5731 VHF 16
Tofino: VHF 6
Tuta Marina: Gold River 250-283-7550
Ucluelet 250-726-4241
Westview Marina: Tahsis . . . 250-934-7622 VHF 6, 66A
Winter Harbour 250-969-4313
Zeballos 250-761-4238

POISON INFO: See Hospitals

PROPANE
Breakers Marine: Bamfield 250-728-3281
China Creek, Port Alberni 250-723-9812
Holberg
Method Marine: Tofino . . . . 250-725-3251 VHF 6
Petro Canada: Port Alberni 250-724-2626
Port Alice
Westview Marina: Tahsis . . . 250-934-7622 VHF 6, 66A
Weston Enterprises: Zeballos . . . 250-761-4201 VHF 68

RAMPS / HAUL-OUTS
Alberni Engineering: Port Alberni 250-723-0111
Bamfield
China Creek Provincial Park
China Creek: Port Alberni 250-723-9812
Clutesi Haven: Port Alberni . . . . 250-724-6837 VHF 66A
Coal Harbour
Fair Harbour
Gold River
Grappler Inlet: Bamfield
Holberg
Island West Fishing Resort: Ucluelet
 . . . . 250-726-7515 VHF 66A
Neah Bay: Washington 360-645-2374
Poett Nook
Port Alberni
Port Renfrew Marina 250-647-0002
Sekiu: Washington
Sooke Harbour Marina 250-642-3236
Sunny Shores: Sooke . . . . 250-642-5731 VHF 16
Tahsis

Tofino
Ucluelet
Winter Harbour
Zeballos 250-761-4238

RECOMPRESSION: 1-800-567-5111

REPAIRS
Alberni Engineering: Port Alberni 250-723-0111
Breakers Marine: Bamfield 250-728-3281
Ceepeecee
Coal Harbour
Sunny Shores Marina: Sooke . . . 250-642-5731 VHF 16
Tahsis
Ucluelet
Zeballos

RESCUE: 800-567-5111

RESTAURANTS
Coast Hospitality Inn: Port Alberni . 250-723-8111

SEWAGE DISPOSAL:
Port Alberni Fisherman's Harbour: Pump.250-723-2533
Ucluelet: Island West. Dump. VHF 66A

SHELLFISH HOTLINE:
Gold River 250-283-9075
Port Alberni 250-720-4440
Port Hardy 250-949-6422
Tofino 250-725-3500
 Recorded message updated daily 250-723-0417

TAXI
Kyuquot Sound Water Taxi 250-332-5232
Port Hardy 250-949-8800
Port Alberni 250-723-2121, 250-723-3511
Port McNeill 250-956-8294

TOWING
C-TOW 1-888-354-5554
D H Timber: Coal Harbour . . . . . 250-949-6358 VHF 10

VHF MARINE OPERATOR
Bamfield: VHF 27
Brooks Peninsula: VHF 87
Estevan Point: VHF 23
Holberg: VHF 60
Jordan River: VHF 23
Kyuquot: VHF 01
Pachena Point: VHF 87
Port Angeles: VHF 25
Ucluelet: VHF 28
Tofino: VHF 24
Victoria: VHF 86
Winter Harbour: VHF 27

VISITOR INFORMATION
Bamfield 250-728-3006
Port Alberni 250-724-6535
Sooke 250-642-6351
Tofino 250-725-3414

WEATHER
VHF WX-1, 2, 4
VHF 21
Environment Canada Weather Line 250-339-9861
Alert Bay . . . . 250-974-5305 (recorded)
Comox 250-339-0748
Gold River 250-283-2652
Port Alberni . . . . 250-724-1333 (recorded)
Port Hardy . . . . 250-949-7148 (recorded)
Tofino 250-726-3415

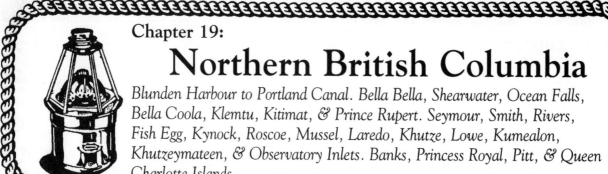

Chapter 19:
Northern British Columbia

Blunden Harbour to Portland Canal. Bella Bella, Shearwater, Ocean Falls, Bella Coola, Klemtu, Kitimat, & Prince Rupert. Seymour, Smith, Rivers, Fish Egg, Kynock, Roscoe, Mussel, Laredo, Khutze, Lowe, Kumealon, Khutzeymateen, & Observatory Inlets. Banks, Princess Royal, Pitt, & Queen Charlotte Islands.

Symbols

[   ]: Numbers between [ ] are chart numbers.

{   }: Numbers & letters between { } are waypoints.

⚑: Park, ⛵: Boat Launch, ▲: Campgrounds,
⚲: Hiking Trails, ⊼: Picnic Area, ⚙: Biking

Important Notices

★ **Important Notice:** See "Important Notices" between Chapters 7 and 8 in this guide for specific information on boating related topics such as: Canadian & U.S. Customs, boating safety and security, navigation, weather, U.S. & Canadian Coast Guard, U.S & Canadian marine radio use, Vessel Traffic Service and traffic separation plans, security zones, and internet access. Due to new Department of Homeland Security regulations, call ahead for latest customs information and/or see Northwest Boat Travel On-line, www.nwboat.com.

Fuel, Supplies, & Services Availability: Because of the ever and rapid changes in facilities in the area covered by this chapter, it is always advisable to call ahead to determine the availability of needed fuel, supplies, and services. Telephone numbers and VHF frequencies are provided in this book wherever they are available and known at publication time. See "Fuel" at the end of this chapter.

British Columbia Marine Parks: Several Provincial Marine Parks and protected areas

have been established in recent years. These include Penrose Island, Green Inlet, Codville Lagoon, Oliver Cove, Jackson Narrows, Union Passage, Lowe Inlet, Kitson Island, and Klewnuggit Inlet, Gilttoyees Inlet, Bishop Bay, Weewaniee Hot Springs, and Sue Channel. These join Hakai Pass Conservation Study Area, Fiordland Recreation Area, and Sir Alexander Mackenzie Provincial Park in the park system. These are remote wilderness parks and do not have facilities of any kind. Access by boat or float plane only.

Seasonal Changes: Many resorts in this area are seasonal or have seasonal hours. May to September is high season. At other times, it is wise to call ahead to check on availability of fuel, provisions, and other services.

Telus Standby Location Service: Incoming traffic service may be available for this area during the summer months for vessels whose locations are listed with the Telusmarine operator. Incoming calls are kept on a traffic list. Contact Telus for information.

Insurance Coverage: Many United States boat policies designate Malcolm Island or latitude 52.0 as the northernmost geographical limit. Verify your policy limits wth your insurance broker/company. An endorsement for extended cruising may be required.

B.C. Ferries Discovery Coast Passage Route: The ferry, *Queen of Chilliwack*, provides service along the mid-coast ports of call, with north-bound passage beginning at Port Hardy, bound for either Ocean Falls and Bella Coola, with stops at McLoughlin Bay / Shearwater. Return southbound voyages leave from Bella Coola retracing the routes and stops. Reservations required. www.bcferries.bc.ca. 1-888-223-3779.

comprise the most difficult waters of the entire Inside Passage. While these waters should be treated with caution, a safe and enjoyable passage is possible if one is well prepared and willing to wait for good weather. Good ground tackle, reliable electronic gear, a complete spare parts kit, VHF radio, and if possible, radar, are basic equipment. An extensive collection of charts is advised. The Canadian Hydrographic Service publishes two volumes of Sailing Directions, PAC 205 and PAC 206 that are an invaluable resource. Call 250-363-6358 or visit www.charts.gc.ca.

Each summer many trailer boats are launched at Port Hardy, bound for Rivers Inlet for the salmon fishing. Many boaters who venture past Cape Caution are intent on getting to Southeast Alaska as soon as possible and hurry single-mindedly through the waters to Prince Rupert without taking the time to cruise into the various inlets along the North Coast of British Columbia. They are missing the boat (so to speak)! These waters are some of the best on the entire Inside Passage. The scenery in such places as Roscoe Inlet, Kynoch Inlet and Gardner Canal is equal to any in Southeast Alaska. The only thing missing might be a tide water glacier calving icebergs into the salt water. British Columbia's glaciers have retreated up the valleys and mountains, but they are still visible.

Anchoring and Tie-up: Adequate ground tackle and log tie-up equipment are essential when traveling these waters. Recommended, as a minimum, is enough rode to reach the bottom and allow for sufficient scope in 10 to 15 fathoms. Over 50% of the anchorages described in this chapter are in the 10 to 15 fathom range. Please refer to "Basic Boat Anchoring" at the end of the Important Notices section of this guide. Read the "Anchor Rode" entry for specific information.

Log tie-up fenders: Tie only to the extreme outside of a log boom. Booms are often unstable and move with the wind and tide. A tie to a side or the inside could result in the boat being trapped against the shore. To protect the boat, cylindrical-shaped fenders with an eye on each end and a few ten pound lead weights tied to the bottom ends of the fenders, are handy. The old fashioned window sash weights are excellent and inexpensive at a house wrecking junk yard. Lower the fenders to the proper depth, keeping them between the log and the boat. Tie them off in the usual manner. Regular fenders will float out of place and fail to give protection from the log.

Fuel Availability: The lack of available fuel between Port Hardy and Prince Rupert can present a problem for gasoline powered boats. From south to north: Rivers Inlet: Gas and diesel at Dawsons Landing and Duncanby Landing. Namu: Gas, 250-949-4090. Shearwater: Gas and diesel.

Chart List

Canadian Hydrographic Charts:

3549, 3550, 3551, 3552, 3598, 3570, 3711, 3719, 3720, 3721, 3724, 3726-3730, 3734, 3737, 3741-3743, 3745, 3753, 3772, 3778, 3779, 3785, 3793, 3802, 3807, 3808, 3811, 3853, 3854, 3868, 3869, 3890-3892, 3894, 3895, 3902, 3921, 3925, 3927, 3931,3933, 3935, 3936, 3937, 3940, 3955, 3960, 3962, 3963, 3964, 3994

Marine Atlas Volume 2 (2005 ed.):

Pages 13-28

Introduction

The Lure of the North Coast: For most boaters, the North Coast of British Columbia starts in the Port Hardy/Wells Passage area, even though it technically does not begin until Cape Caution, some 40 miles farther northwest. There are thousands of miles of island-studded channels stretching northwest all the way into southeast Alaska, waiting to be explored by those who love natural surroundings, quietude, and being away from city amenities. Facilities are more primitive and farther apart. Except for Prince Rupert, there are no roads north of Port Hardy, unless one counts the out-of-the-way roads to Bella Coola and Kitimat, and one to Stuart, British Columbia and Hyder, Alaska.

Queen Charlotte Sound and Cape Caution

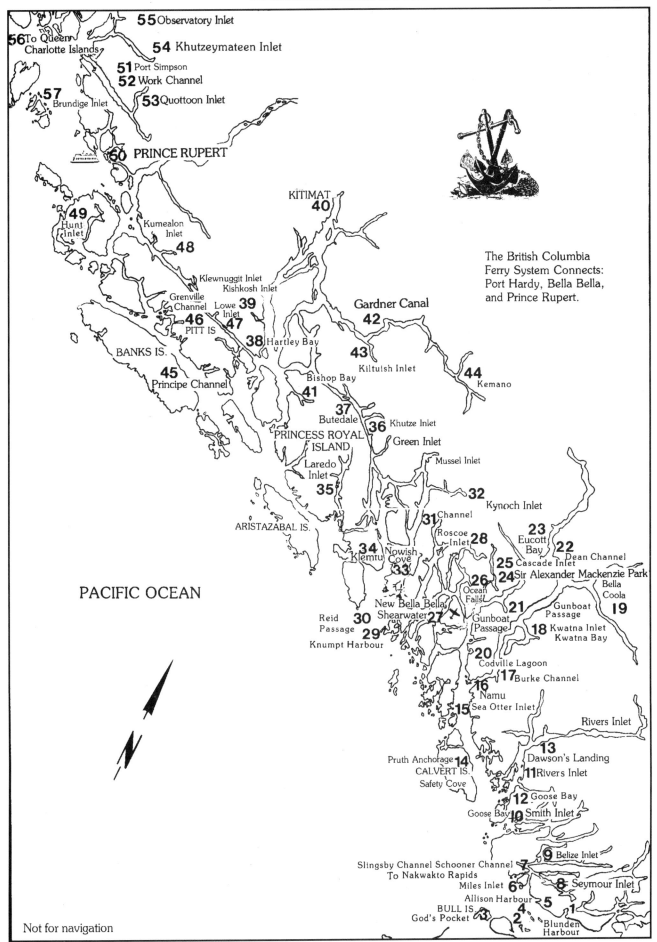

55 Observatory Inlet

56 To Queen Charlotte Islands

54 Khutzeymateen Inlet

51 Port Simpson
52 Work Channel

57 Brundige Inlet

53 Quottoon Inlet

50 PRINCE RUPERT

KITIMAT
40

49 Hunt Inlet

Kumealon Inlet

48

The British Columbia Ferry System Connects: Port Hardy, Bella Bella, and Prince Rupert.

Klewnuggit Inlet
Kishkosh Inlet

Grenville Channel

Lowe Inlet 39

46

47

PITT IS

Gardner Canal
42

BANKS IS.

38 Hartley Bay

45 Principe Channel

43 Kiltuish Inlet

44 Kemano

Bishop Bay

41

37 Butedale

36 Khutze Inlet

PRINCESS ROYAL ISLAND

Green Inlet

Laredo Inlet

Mussel Inlet

35

32 Kynoch Inlet

ARISTAZABAL IS.

31

Channel

Roscoe Inlet 28

23 Eucott Bay 22

Dean Channel

34 Klemtu

Nowish Cove

33

25 Cascade Inlet

24 Sir Alexander Mackenzie Park

PACIFIC OCEAN

26 Ocean Falls

Bella Coola

New Bella Bella Shearwater 27 ✕

21

Gunboat Passage

19

Reid Passage 30

29

Gunboat Passage

18 Kwatna Inlet
Kwatna Bay

Knumpt Harbour

20 Codville Lagoon

17 Burke Channel

16 Namu
Sea Otter Inlet

15

Rivers Inlet

13 Dawson's Landing

Pruth Anchorage 14
CALVERT IS.
Safety Cove

11 Rivers Inlet

12 Goose Bay

Goose Bay 10 Smith Inlet

9 Belize Inlet

Slingsby Channel Schooner Channel 7
To Nakwakto Rapids

Miles Inlet 6

8 Seymour Inlet

Allison Harbour

5

BULL IS.
God's Pocket 3

4

2

1 Blunden Harbour

Not for navigation

Bella Bella: Gas and diesel. Klemtu: Gas and diesel. Hartley Bay: Gas and diesel. Fuel is also available at Bella Coola and Kitimat, however these are a considerable distance off the beaten track. Since many dispensors depend upon fuel being barged to them, it is always wise to call ahead to check availability at any of the above locations. See the telephone numbers listed under "Fuel" at the end of this chapter.

Approaches to Cape Caution

[3547, 3548, 3550, 3552, 3797, 3921]

★ **Blunden Harbour (1):** [3548] This chart is necessary because of hazards in the entrance. Good anchorage can be found on a mud bottom in depths of 40-55 feet of water. Secure anchorage is found over mud in front of the beach. Posted signs instruct that the Canadian Heritage Law prohibits digging in abandoned Nakwoktak Indian shell middens and cairns. The anchorage in the outer basin is equidistant between Edgell Island, Brandon Point and Augustine Island. Byrnes Island, with its burial boxes, is an abandoned Indian burial ground where trespassing is forbidden. Bradley Lagoon is extensive and may be explored by dinghy. The entrance dries more than ten feet. Tidal currents become strong in the shallow entrance. Kelp may make entry difficult. Rockfish and ling cod are found near kelp patches outside.

Jeanette Island Light: Temporary anchorage is possible east of Robertson Island in seven to eight fathoms. It is somewhat exposed, and currents run through the passage.

★ **God's Pocket (2):** Here is a good jumping off point if going across Queen Charlotte Sound by way of Pine Island. This little cove, on the west side of Hurst Island, is not named on charts, but is much used by fishing boats. It is off Christie Pass, about 1 1/2 mile southwest of Scarlett Point Light. Good shelter. Two mooring buoys are in the cove. Several marked trails for hiking and a helicopter pad are at the site.

God's Pocket Resort: Divers air, lodge, moorage, coffee shop. 250-949-1755. VHF 16.

★ **Bull Harbour (3):** See the reference at the end of Chapter 18. This is another useful anchorage if going directly across Queen Charlotte Sound.

★ **Walker Group (4):** This island group lies approximately 11 miles north of Port Hardy. Anchorage is between Kent Island and Staples Island in three fathoms, soft bottom. Good protection. Access is from the west or east entrances.

Deserters Group: There are no good anchorages in this group of islands. There is good fishing for salmon and bottom fish on both sides of Castle Point and on the south and east side of Echo Islands.

★ **Allison Harbour (5):** There are no facilities here and only ruins remain of the former community. Anchorage is possible in the small bay by the ruins. Avoid the reef off the east shore and drying rock farther in on the east side. Depths in the upper harbor are about 28 feet. The bottom is very soft mud and is difficult to hold at times. This anchorage is in a good position for an early morning crossing of the sound.

★ **Skull Cove:** There is good anchorage here on a good, sticky mud bottom. Very sheltered anchorage is possible in the first basin in 25 foot depths, equidistant from the three nearest points. It is possible to observe sea conditions outside while in the shelter of this anchorage. If going in to the back or northernmost basin, keep to the west side to avoid the two drying rocks shown on the chart.

★ **Miles Inlet (6):** A small, sheltered anchorage is in about three fathoms of water on a mud bottom. The best spot is right in the cross of the "T" shaped inlet. It is possible to take a skiff into the lagoon at the north end, but only at high slack. There are overfalls at both ebb and flood. This is the closest anchorage to Cape Caution. It is hard to see the entrance at first, but McEwan Rock is a good landmark.

Slingsby & Schooner Channels to Nakwakto Rapids (7): [3552] Nakwakto Rapids are included in the Canada Tide & Currents Tables, Volume 6.

★ **Schooner Channel:** [3797, 3921] This channel has moderate currents, but is narrow with several hazards. The least width is 200 feet and the least depth about two fathoms. The northern approach, via Slingsby Channel, can have extremely strong tide rips in its western entrance, caused by strong ebb tides meeting the swells that are usually present in Queen Charlotte Sound. The entrance is wide and deep, but should be approached with caution on even a moderate ebb tide.

★ **Treadwell Bay:** Sheltered anchorage is in the inside of Slingsby Channel in 45 feet of water, mud bottom. Seymour Inlet Lodge. VHF 16.

★ **Nakwakto Rapids:** Tide and current tables are necessities for entering these rapids and are not included in this book. Use Canada Tide and Current Tables, Volume 6. These rapids are among the fastest in the world and should be approached with caution. The maximum currents are 16 knots on the ebb and 14 knots on the flood, caused by the six inlets drawing through this one narrow passage. In the inlets inside the rapids, the average tidal range is just four feet while outside the average range is 12 feet. Fortunately not all tides are large spring tides, and in most months, and certain phases of the moon, the maximum rate will not reach four knots on the smallest tide of the day. It is best to make the transit as close to slack water as possible. Passage is possible on either side of Turret Rock (or Tremble Island as it is sometimes called) but the west passage is the preferred one. The passage is short, straight, relatively wide, and deep, if one avoids the shoal southwest of Turret Rock.

Inside of Nakwakto Rapids are two large inlets, Seymour and Belize, 35 miles and 24 miles in length respectively. There are also four smaller sounds, Nugent, Mereworth, and Alison, each about ten miles in length, and Frederick Sound about six miles in length. Each of these waterways is surrounded by mountains, and offers beautiful scenic attractions. There are several good anchorages in each of these inlets, but there are no facilities of any sort for boaters. The only habitations are an occasional floathouse or logging camp. There is good radio reception, including VHF, so getting weather reports is no problem. On warm, clear days expect some fairly strong afternoon up channel breezes, as in most coastal inlets.

Seymour Inlet

[3552, 3921]

★ **Charlotte Bay (8):** This bay, five miles from the rapids, is the first good, protected anchorage. Anchor in four to five fathoms, mud bottom. Look out for the charted rocks in the northern part of the bay.

★ **Harriet Point:** At Harriet Point, Seymour Inlet narrows and makes a dog leg turn to the north. Anchorage is possible in the small bay directly across from Harriet Point, behind the

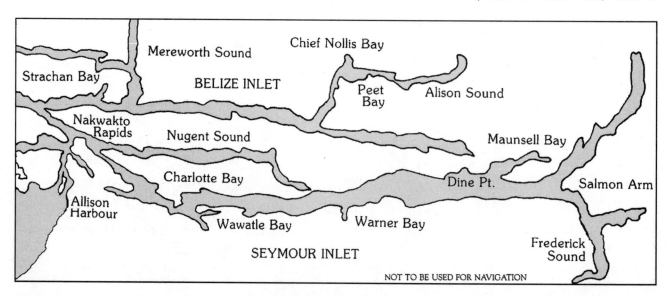

NOT TO BE USED FOR NAVIGATION

small 26 meter island on the chart, in two to three fathoms. There is some kelp in this bay.

★ **Wawatle Bay:** Anchorage is found at the head of this bay.

★ **Frederick Bay:** As Seymour Inlet continues to the east it becomes wider, and the shores more mountainous. Anchorage is possible in a small nook at the west end of Frederick Bay in about five fathoms, soft bottom.

Warner Bay: Some anchorage is found here. Beware of the drying rock in the center of the bay.

★ **Dine Point Vicinity:** Proceeding east there are two anchorages about seven miles from Warner Bay. The cove on the north side, about one mile west of Dine Point, is not named on the chart, but is known as, Jesus' Pocket. There is room for only one or two boats, in four fathoms, with protection.

★ **Towry Point Vicinity:** Directly across the inlet, on the south side there is good anchorage on the east side of Towry Point in ten fathoms, mud bottom, with protection from all but east winds.

Maunsell Bay: Located on the north side of Seymour, this bay is large and too deep for anchorage. A cove at the east end does offer sheltered anchorage in 12 fathoms, mud and gravel bottom.

To the Head of Seymour Inlet: Another three miles to the east of Martin Point is Eclipse Narrows, the entrance to Frederick Sound. Seymour Inlet turns northeast here, and continues for another eight miles to its head where there may be a logging camp on the east side. The only possible anchorage would be at the very head of the inlet. The bottom is steep-to and there is no shelter from prevailing winds blowing in the inlet. Temporary anchorage in ten fathoms of water is possible if one wishes to explore the Seymour River. The river is large and may be explored by dinghy for about two miles where there are some big falls.

Frederick Sound

★ **Frederick Sound:** Currents in Eclipse Narrows, at the entrance to the sound, run four to five knots. Changes are about $1/2$ hour after tide changes at Nakwakto Rapids. This sound is about six miles long. Anchorage is possible in ten fathoms at the head of Frederick Sound, or at about the same depth in the northeast corner of Salmon Arm, which lies on the east side of this sound. The Salmon Arm anchorage is the more scenic of the two anchorages, but don't anchor in less than ten fathoms because there is a drying deadhead farther into the cove.

Nugent Sound

★ **Nugent Sound:** Entered $1^1/2$ miles southeast of Nakwakto Rapids, this sound is ten miles long and very attractive. The best anchorage is three miles from the entrance in the bay on the north side, across from Nugent Creek on the south side. Depths are eight fathoms, good holding on a sand bottom. The anchorage is well protected with room for several boats. Anchorage is also possible at the head of the sound in 8-12 fathoms, mud and sand bottom, open to the southwest. The entrance to Schwartzenberg Lagoon is less than three feet deep with currents to five knots and is passable only by dinghy.

Belize Inlet

★ **Belize Inlet (9):** The entrance is at Mignon Point, about two miles northeast of Nakwakto Rapids. There is good, relatively protected anchorage at the very head of Rowley Bay, two miles west of Mignon Point, in ten fathoms, soft bottom. Some exposure to east winds. Better anchorage can be found at the head of Westerman Bay, on the north side of the inlet four miles northwest of Mignon Point in the cove at the north end in three fathoms on mud with good protection. Belize Inlet stretches 24 miles to the east from Mignon Point. It is straight, lined by mountain ranges on both sides. The only possible anchorage appears to be at the very head of the inlet, in the southeast corner in about 15 fathoms, but with no shelter from frequent, up inlet winds. Good anchorages, however, are found in Mereworth Sound and Alison Sound, which branch off to the north of Belize. These sounds are also very scenic.

Mereworth Sound

★ **Mereworth Sound:** Excellent anchorage is found in the cove at the southwest corner of Strachan Bay in seven fathoms, mud bottom. There is plenty of room, and good protection from all directions. Village Cove, about two miles into the sound, has anchorage in seven to eight fathoms on mud. There is good protection if one anchors in the northwest corner of the cove. Another good anchorage is in the cove southwest of Rock Island on the south side of the sound. There is good protection and plenty of room in eight to ten fathoms, mud bottom.

Alison Sound

★ **Alison Sound:** This sound is the most scenic of the six sounds. The entrance is about 18 miles east of Mignon Point. Beware of the three meter shoal on the west side of the entrance. Obstruction Island lies in the narrows about $1^1/2$ miles inside the sound. Currents run to five or six knots, and the preferred channel on the west side is about 300 feet wide and 30 feet deep. Current changes seem to follow closely to those at Nakwakto Rapids. The passage offers no problems. The best anchorage in this sound is in Peet Bay about $1^1/2$ miles past the narrows in five to six fathoms, soft bottom. The bay is small, but has good protection. Other possible anchorages are in the cove about one mile north of Obstruction Island in 15 fathoms, mud and sand bottom, good protection. Chief Nollis Bay has anchorage in 12-13 fathoms and Summers Bay has anchorage in 13-15 fathoms. The last two have limited protection.

Smith Sound & Smith Inlet
[3776, 3931, 3934]

★ **Smith Sound and Egg Island (10):** There are three entrances to Smith Sound. One is Alexandra Passage, just south of Egg Island, between North Iron Rock to the south and Egg Rocks to the north. The clearest passage, and the best one to use, if visibility is minimal, is Loran Passage between Egg Island to the south and Table Island to the north. The last, and northernmost passage, has three possible entries, Radar

Passage, Irving Passage, or the innermost, between False Egg Island and Tie Island, often used by commercial fishermen going from Smith Sound to Rivers Inlet. There are no facilities for boaters in Smith Sound or Smith Inlet. Egg Island is the site of a manned lighthouse. When passing Egg Island, you can call "Egg Yolk" to say hello to the caretakers. Fog horn discontinued.

★ **Millbrook Cove:** [3934] Anchorage is available in Millbrook Cove on the north side of the sound, near the entrance. The cove is marked by red spar buoy "E-6", with a radar reflector on it. Best anchorage is at the north end of the cove, behind the island marked 30 meters on chart #3934 and 100 feet on the older charts. It may be passed on either side. If using the wider eastern entrance, give the island plenty of clearance. Anchorage is in four fathoms on mud.

★ **Jones Cove:** Southeast of Macnicol Point is a little cove with fair protection, that provides an emergency anchorage. Avoid the reef 600 feet southwest of Turner Islands. At Jones Cove entry is around the east point with a minimum of 300 foot clearance.

★ **Fly Basin, Takush Harbour:** The entrance to Takush is rock strewn, first to the east, then to the west. But the chart shows the hazards. A huge landlocked basin provides protected anchorage with flat shallow anchorage in four to six fathoms on good holding sticky mud.

★ **McBride Bay:** This bay has anchorage in about 12 fathoms.

★ **Margaret Bay:** This bay is located on the north side of the inlet and has anchorage in eight to 12 fathoms.

★ **Ethel Cove:** Adjacent to Margaret Bay, this cove offers protection in six to eight fathoms with good holding mud and sand bottom. Anchor mid-channel to avoid dumped logs and snags. Watch for grizzlies on shore.

★ **Finis Nook:** This nook is off Boswell Inlet. Protected anchorage in depths of three or four fathoms.

★ **Anchor Cove & Quascilla Bay:** This cove, on the south side of Smith Inlet, is about nine miles east of the entrance to Smith Sound. There is anchorage in ten fathoms.

★ **Smith Inlet:** [3931] This chart made exploration possible for the first time. The inlet is about 18 miles long, from the entrance at Ripon Point to the head in Walkum Bay. The mountain scenery is beautiful, but anchorages are scarce. Anchorage might be possible off the flats in Walkum Bay, but the shoaling is very steep-to, and there is exposure to up-inlet winds. A temporary anchorage is possible off the Nekite River flats, in the cove on the east side of Jap Island.

★ **Boswell Inlet:** This eight mile long inlet is entered north of Denison Island. The ruins of the former settlement of Boswell are on the north shore of the inlet. Security Bay appears to be a good anchorage. The narrows, about one and $1/2$ mile farther east, are wide and deep and present no problems. An excellent, protected anchorage is $1/2$-mile above the narrows in the unnamed cove to the west, in five fathoms, soft bottom. Anchorage is possible at the head of Boswell Inlet in ten to 13 fathoms. Beware of very rapid shoaling. The head of Boswell is very scenic.

Turret Rock, Nakwakto Rapids   *Linda Schreiber Photo*

Rivers Inlet

[3932, 3934, 3994]

★ **Rivers Inlet (11):** This is an active fishing resort area during summer season. The welcome of pleasure craft at fishing camps is uncertain at best and sometimes less than friendly. Commercial salmon fishing began here in 1882. At one time there were as many as 17 operating canneries located in this inlet.

★ **Goose Bay (12):** Islets and drying rocks are in the entrance. Pass either east or west. A store and marina have been located on the east side of the entrance to Goose Bay.

Duncanby Lodge & Marina: New Ownership. Moorage, gas, diesel, propane, water, 30 ampere power, provisions showers, laundry, restaurant, lodging. 403-997-8516. VHF 6.

Wadhams: This is the site of an abandoned cannery. No facilities.

★ **Finn Bay:** Sheltered, but deep anchorage can be found here. Private floats are in the bay. Beware of a rock, covered less than six feet, two tenths of a mile inside the entrance on the north shore.

Klaquaek Channel: [3994] This channel leads north from Rivers Inlet between Ripon and Walbran Islands to the east and Penrose Island to the west. There are several possible entrances from the south. The northern entrances are rocky, and the western-most, next to Penrose Island, is probably the best. Darby Channel is at the north end of the channel. There are several good anchorages in 10 to 15 fathoms on either side of Klaquaek Channel. Penrose Island's, Frypan Bay, on the west side of Klaquaek Channel, is a nice, small indentation. Anchorage is possible in seven fathoms, mud bottom.

★⚓ **Penrose Island Marine Park:** [3921] This is a very scenic park with anchorage and a network of narrow channels. There are inviting beaches and good diving sites. The southwestern shore of the island offers sandy, shell strewn beaches, lagoons, and islets. On the east side are two deep inlets which provide excellent anchorages pro-

tected by a steep wooded shoreline. Clamming is prohibited.

★ **Schooner Retreat:** [3934] Located on the southwest side of Penrose Island, Schooner Retreat is composed of three anchorages: Frigate Bay to the southeast, Exposed Anchorage to the northwest and Secure Anchorage in between. Anchorages are in ten to 15 fathoms, much of it on mud, but rather exposed to southeast and southwest winds. The entrances and anchorages have many rocks requiring close attention to the chart.

★ **Fury Island:** There is a bay between Fury Island and Penrose Island that can be entered through the channel north of Heathcoat Island. Although not well protected from winds, anchorage is otherwise excellent and it is possible to note sea conditions on Queen Charlotte Sound.

★ **Dawsons Landing (13):** The very small public float is for government fisheries vessels.

★ **Dawsons Landing General Store:** Secure moorage, water, gas and diesel, showers, laundry facilities, a well stocked general store with frozen foods, fresh vegetables, dairy products, gifts, souvenirs, chandlery, cube ice, and Post Office. Liquor Store. See our Steering Star description in this chapter. Email: dawsonslanding@ hotmail.com. Address: Dawsons Landing, British Columbia V0N 1M0. Fax: 250-949-2111. Phone: 403-987-9058. VHF 6.

Darby Channel: [3934] This channel runs from Fitz Hugh Sound to Dawsons Landing, and saves several miles of travel. There are several hazards, but, with caution, passage is easy.

★ **Sandell Bay:** Located about five miles north of Dawsons Landing, Sandell Bay offers relatively protected anchorage in five fathoms, soft bottom, open to the south.

★ **Taylor Bay:** On the east side of Walbran Island, Taylor Bay offers a small, but secure, anchorage in 11 fathoms of water over mud.

★ **Johnston Bay:** Traditionally, there has been good, well protected anchorage in this bay just south of the lodge and at the head of the bay in ten to twelve fathoms, mud bottom. Avoid the

reef in the outer bay and other hazards by keeping to the west side all of the way in. Some old abandoned net floats are at the head of the bay. This is a delightful place.

★ **Weeolk Passage:** An unnamed cove on the east side of the passage provides good, relatively sheltered anchorage in 50 feet of water over a mud bottom. A rocky ridge on the north side is a hazard. The charted rock in the entrance is best passed on the south side.

Rivers Inlet Continued: Rivers Inlet proper culminates in the big, two mile wide bay ending in the Wannock River flats to the east and Kilbella Bay and its flats to the north. The waters are always discolored, either by mud after a rain, or glacial silt at other times. There are no facilities for boaters. Logging camps and native villages are located on the river flats. The only anchorage, other than those off the river flats, is in a small bight behind McAllister Point in six to eight fathoms, good holding bottom, protected from all but east winds.

Moses Inlet: Moses Inlet runs 14 miles north from McAllister Point to the drying flats at its head. Half way up it has a dog-leg to starboard, and is constricted by Nelson Narrows. The island in the center can be passed on either side. A day beacon marks a shoal to be avoided on the port side. Depths are adequate and currents are negligible. The only signs of human activity are two logging camps in the lower half of the inlet and four in the upper half. Three to four thousand foot mountains line the sides of the inlet. Depths are great throughout, and there are no good anchorages. The only possibilities are off the steep-to Clyak River flats at the head of the inlet, or in the northeast corner of Inrig Bay, both exposed.

★ **Hardy Inlet:** Six mile Hardy Inlet takes off to the west from Moses Inlet, two miles north of McAllister Point. Mountains range to 2,500 feet on both sides, and again the inlet is deep. Two coves at the very head of the inlet offer the best anchorages. The cove straight ahead is the best, with a soft bottom and anchorage in eight fathoms, protected from all but east winds. The scenery looking back down the inlet is wonderful. If the wind is up the inlet from the east, the bight on the south side affords some protection in about the same depths.

Draney Inlet

[3931]

★ **Draney Inlet:** [3931] This chart, on a scale of 1:40,000, covers this inlet for the first time. Draney is an 11 mile long inlet, on the east side of Rivers Inlet. It is entered through Draney Narrows. The narrows is shown on an inset to the chart. Currents run to ten knots. The narrows are best entered at or near slack tide. The narrows is known for good Chinook and Coho fishing.

★ **Fishhook Bay:** This bay is one mile past the narrows. Anchorage is in two to four fathoms, with good protection.

★ **Robert Arm:** There is very good anchorage in this arm, in about seven fathoms, mud bottom and good protection from all but east winds.

★ **Allard Bay:** At high tide, there is anchorage in six to nine fathoms in the entrance. There is more room than might be apparent on the chart and the bottom is mud. Several boats could snuggle here, but check overnight tidal depths vs present depths. The head of Draney Inlet has an excellent, protected anchorage in 15 fathoms, mud bottom.

Fish Egg Inlet

[3921]

★ **Fish Egg Inlet:** These interesting waters are entered to the east of Addenbroke Island, and its lighthouse. The first chart published for these waters came out in July 1991, so they are relatively unexplored by pleasure boaters. They present excellent waters for "gunkholing" and there are numerous good anchorages. Entry is either by Convoy Passage to the south, or Patrol Passage and Fairmile Passage to the north.

★ **Green Island Anchorage:** [3921] This lies at the entrance to Illahie Inlet. Protected anchorage is in seven fathoms, mud bottom off the island that gives the cove its name. The southeast entrance is the safest one. This chart shows Fish Egg Inlet and Allison Harbour, metric, scale 1:20,000.

★ **Illahie Inlet:** Anchor in the cove at the head , mud bottom. When weighing anchor, be ready with hose or bucket water to clean chain. The area has been logged recently, but there is good protection.

★ **Joes Bay:** This bay, located at the entrance to Elizabeth Lagoon, has protected anchorage in ten fathoms. The entrance to the lagoon has tidal rapids and many obstructions and is best avoided.

★ **Waterfall Inlet:** This inlet has a nice protected anchorage at its head, in the northeast corner, in ten fathoms, mud bottom. An uncharted rock lies just off the east shore, about 200 yards south of the head of the inlet. It is clearly visible at lower tides.

★ **Mantrap Inlet:** A well protected anchorage is found at the southern end in ten fathoms. Because of the very shallow, rocky entrance, it is better to enter or exit on the top half of the tide. Currents are weak in the entrance.

Gildersleeve Bay: Open to the north. Two anchorages in the southwest corner are not good. The northernmost is too shallow, and the southern one has a rocky bottom.

★ **Eastern Section of Fish Egg Inlet:** East of The Narrows are some nice anchorages. The farthest eastern cove has a good, protected anchorage in 6½ fathoms on a mud bottom. Oyster Bay has a well protected anchorage in four fathoms, mud bottom. Fish Trap Bay has an anchorage in its very small cove.

Hakai Pass & Fitz Hugh Sound

[3727, 3784, 3785, 3921, 3934, 3936, 3937]

★ **Hakai Pass Conservation Study Area:** Located about 130km north of Port Hardy and 115km southwest of Bella Coola, Hakai Pass Conservation Study Area is almost 15 times the size of Desolation Sound Marine Park and is the largest marine park on British Columbia's west coast. Popular fishing spots are Odlum Point, The Gap, and Nalau Passage. The park boundaries stretch from Fitz Hugh Channel on the east, the top half of Calvert Island to the south, Goose Island on the west, to the northern half of Hunter Island. Major anchorages include Pruth Bay on Calvert Island, Crab Cove in Sea Otter Inlet, the north end of Triquet Island near Spider Anchorage, Spider Anchorage southeast of Spider Island and Bremner Bay on Hunter Island. No developed facilities. Chart 3937. Respect "First Nations Cultural Heritage Sites".

★ **Safety Cove (14):** Located just above Calvert Island's southernmost tip, this cove offers good anchorage in 8 to 15 fathoms of water on mud. This is the first anchorage on Calvert Island, after crossing Queen Charlotte Sound.

Addenbroke Island Lighthouse: Located four miles north of Safety Cove on Calvert Island. At the time of this writing, the principal lightkeepers appreciated receiving VHF calls and mail from old and new friends. They say the coffee is always on! In settled weather, anchoring is possible in 60', sand bottom, near the lighthouse boat launch. New road, derrick pad, hydraulic engines, and lights. Do not anchor in too closely to the old cannery site. Call on VHF 09, 82, or VHF 16 to be met. During winter months 82A is used exclusively. Call "Addenbroke Lighthouse" on either channel or, on VHF 82, you can also use "Late for Supper". Address: Addenbroke Lighthouse, Canadian Coast Guard Bag 3670, Prince Rupert, British Columbia V8J 3R1 Canada.

★ **Pruth Bay & Kwakshua Inlet:** [3921] The call sign for the marine park ranger vessel stationed near the entry to the anchorage during the summer is "Hakai Ranger." This well-protected inlet has good anchorage in 40-50 feet near mid channel, sand and mud bottom. The bottom is hard along the south shore. A dinghy float is at the sports fishing lodge and visitors are welcome to visit their lodge and restaurant. A landmark carved mask is in the cedar tree behind the gift

★ **Dawsons Landing General Store:** Serving boaters and fishermen for the past 45 years, this store and fueling facility is located on the west shore of Rivers Inlet, opposite the northeast end of Walbran Island. Secure moorage, with fresh water on floats that rim the front of the buildings. Gas and diesel are now available on a regular basis and stove oil is accessible. New showers and laundry facilities have been added. The well stocked store carries a large selection of canned and frozen goods, fresh vegetables and dairy products, liquor, gifts, souvenirs, chandlery items, block & cube ice, and is the site of the post office. Bait, tackle, and fishing licenses are sold. Accommodations are available with reservations advised. Located in the heart of the fabulous fishing grounds of Rivers Inlet, Dawsons is headquarters for the sports fisherman, as well as commercial and pleasure craft. Daily scheduled float plane service links with several communities along the coast, both large and small. Proprietors Nola and Robert Bachen. **Email: dawsonslanding@hotmail.com. Circle #50 on Reader Service Card. Address: Dawsons Landing, British Columbia V0N 1M0. Fax: 250-949-2111. Phone: 403-987-9058. VHF 06.**

Ocean Falls   *Linda Schreiber Photo*

shop. There is a trail to West Beach. Fishing is good at the junction of the two arms of Kwakshua Channel.

Hakai Beach Resort: Boaters are welcome to tie their dinghies to the dock and go ashore. Dining is available, but reservations must be made by noon of the day they wish to eat. A mask, which was carved into a tree years ago, still attracts visitors. Boaters can walk through the premises for ocean beach access. Numerous hiking trails across the area, lodging, fishing. 250-847-9300, 800-668-3474. VHF 16, 23, 09.

Hakai Passage: This open passage to the Pacific lies at the north end of Kwakshua Channel and Hecate Island. This is a famous sport salmon fishing area, especially around Odlum Point, but beware of strong swells and currents. Anchorage is possible at the north end of Choked Passage in nine to ten fathoms, between the north end of Calvert Island and Odlum and Starfish Islands. While there is protection from the seas, there is not much protection from strong west and southwest winds.

★ **Goldstream Harbour:** Anchorage can be found here in depths of 40-60 feet on a mud and sand bottom. Evening Rock is located in the center of the bay. It dries four feet and fishermen often mark it. Favor the Hat Island side unless Evening Rock is showing so it can be avoided easily. Kelpie Point, at the northernmost tip of Hecate Island and Hakai Passage are noted for good salmon fishing.

Kwakume Inlet: [3784] On the east side of Fitz Hugh Sound, about six miles north of Addenbroke Island Light, Kwakume Inlet offers protected anchorage in seven to ten fathoms with almost unlimited room. Use caution in the entrance. The small treed island that appears to be in the center of the entrance should be passed on the north side. There is a least depth of 25' in this 250' wide northern channel. There is a rock one tenth of one mile west of the entrance.

★ **Koeye Point:** This bay is at the mouth of the Koeye River. An uncharted rock is near the entrance to the narrow boat channel. There is anchorage off the point to starboard after entering. Trout fishing is said to be good in the river.

The river may be traversed by dinghy for some distance. The ruins of an old mine wharf and a cabin are about 1/2 mile up the river. There is a white sandy beach. Note the white quartz and the pockets in the marble made by water action. In fishing season this small harbor may be crowded with commercial fishermen.

★ **Lewall Inlet:** [3784] Indenting Sterling Island, this shallow, narrow, L-shaped inlet has good anchorage. Very isolated, pretty, many jellyfish. Avoid shallow spot to starboard, near the end of the entrance passage.

★ **Hunter Island & Sea Otter Inlet (15):** On the west side of Fitz Hugh Sound, Sea Otter Inlet offers anchorage with excellent protection near the head of the south arm in ten fathoms, or in five fathoms in the north arm, called Crab Bay - a misnomer for us, because we caught no crabs.

Warrior Cove: This is a pretty spot, south of Namu. Anchor in the back of the cove, behind a small peninsula.

Namu: (16): [3784, 3785, 3936] Beware of Loo Rock. There is an orange bobber on this charted rock. Site of a former B.C. Packers facility, now a marina with lodging. Ferry flag stop.

Namu: Moorage floats. 15 ampere power, water, showers, laundry, lodging (reservations requested), gas, diesel, ice, garbage. 250-949-4090 (may be changing). VHF 10.

Burke Channel

[3729, 3730]

★ **Burke Channel (17):** Burke Channel leads off to the northeast from Fitz Hugh Sound about two miles north of Namu, at Edmund Point. It continues in a northeast direction for 55 miles to the village of Bella Coola, which is connected to the town of Williams Lake in the interior by a 300 mile long road, largely unpaved. This is some of the best scenery on the British Columbia coast, if the weather cooperates. Strong winds often blow up and down this inlet. Caution advised at Mesachie Nose. Known locally as Dancing Waters, dangerous tide rips form at this location.

★ **Fougner Bay:** Anchorage is possible in the outer part of the bay in seven to ten fathoms.

★ **Restoration Bay:** This anchorage was first used by George Vancouver in 1793 to overhaul his ships. It has good holding in 55 feet of water. The Bay is exposed to the southwest. Caution must be used when approaching the head because the bay shoals very rapidly.

★ **Cathedral Point:** Anchorage is possible in the small cove right on the point in 25 feet of water over a mud bottom. There is not much room, but it is satisfactory in settled weather. If an east wind is blowing down Burke Channel, the anchorage will be uncomfortable.

★ **Kwatna Inlet & Kwatna Bay (18):** This scenic inlet lies to the south of Burke Channel. The entrance is between Mapalaklenk Point and Cathedral Point. It extends 12 miles southwest from the latter point and is very scenic and uncrowded. There is excellent anchorage in ten fathoms at the head of the inlet. Be cautious, because there is much shoal water at the head, but there is plenty of room to anchor before reaching the shallows. This is a very nice anchorage, with beaches to explore. Kwatna Bay, on the east side, about four miles south of Cathedral Point, is too deep for anchorage, and the mud flat at the head is steep. There is a logging camp at the head of Kwatna Bay.

★ **South Bentinck Arm:** This 19 mile inlet has some of the most beautiful scenery on the British Columbia coast. Spectacular mountains on either side are covered with glaciers and snow. Anchorages are in Larso Bay in ten fathoms, or at the head of the inlet in the southwest corner in 11 fathoms. About six miles in from the entrance of South Bentinck Arm, hot springs warm a pool created with rocks and man-made structures.

★ **Bella Coola (19):** [3730] The public floats are located in a sheltered small boat harbor located about 1 1/2 miles from the center of town. There is an easy access float for boats over 45 feet. Rafting must be expected. Water, power, garbage, waste pump-out, gas, diesel available, as well as laundry, washrooms, and showers. The downtown area has shopping facilities, post office, telephone, liquor store, restaurants, motels, laundry, showers, and a hospital. Taxi service and car rentals are available. A road connects to Bella Coola with Williams Lake, 300 miles to the east. Scheduled air service to Vancouver. Alexander Mackenzie ended his trip across Canada, the first land crossing of the North American Continent, in 1793 at this point. A monument commemorating this event is on the north shore of Dean Channel, about two miles west of Cascade Inlet. This is the point where Mackenzie was forced to turn around by hostile Bella Bella Indians. The Bella Coola Valley was settled by Norwegian immigrants from Minnesota in 1894. Visit the museum which is located in a school house and a land surveyor's cabin. It features items brought from Norway. Open June-September. Bella Coola and the surrounding area have a population of about 2,200. This is a stop on the B.C. Ferries *Discovery Coast Passage* route from Port Hardy. www.bellacoola.ca. Bella Coola Harbour Master: 250-799-5633.

Tallheo: On the north shore of North Bentinck Arm, across from Bella Coola, is the site of a former cannery. There are no longer any facilities here for boaters, except one small float.

Fisher Channel

[3720, 3785]

★ **Kisameet Bay:** Passing Burke Channel and Humchit Island in Fitz Hugh Sound, tuck to the northeast behind Kipling Island. Proceed northeast behind Kisameet Island, carefully avoiding charted rocks. Kisameet Bay offers sheltered anchorage in six to ten fathoms on good holding mud bottom. Remains of a cabin are on shore on the small island with a rock shelf baring at very low tide. This "window to Fitz Hugh Sound" at the anchorage site shows rocks which block transit at low tide. On the chart, note Kisameet Lake to the northeast.

★⚓ **Codville Lagoon Marine Park (20):** The entrance to Codville Lagoon is located off Fisher Channel at the head of Lagoon Bay. The narrow, tree-lined entrance off the channel gives protection to this lovely area. There are obstructions, including a rock just north of mid-channel, but they are easily avoided. There is good, all weather anchorage in six to seven fathoms in the cove behind Codville Island. NOTE: B.C. Parks reports that a large landslide on the southeast side of the lagoon has produced numerous logs and deadheads. Also, marine chart information may no longer be accurate, so use caution. Wildlife is plentiful in this small park. A sign on shore at the north end of the lagoon indicates an unmaintained trail to Sagar Lake. The trail is steep, rugged, and usually very wet. The 20-minute walk ends at the lake where there is a nice, reddish colored sand beach and swimming possibilities. ⚡

★ **Evans Inlet:** Good anchorage in 12 fathoms is found at the head of this four mile inlet. The head of the inlet shoals rapidly.

Port John: Port John, about 1 ¹/₂ miles north of the entrance to Evans Inlet, has a temporary anchorage in its northeast corner in seven fathoms, soft bottom. Open to the southwest. If traveling from Evans Inlet to Port John via Matthew Passage, beware of Peril Rock in the center of the passage.

★ **Gunboat Passage (21):** [3720] This narrow, rocky, but well marked passage is the shortest route between Dean Channel/Ocean Falls and Shearwater/Bella Bella. This chart and the Canada Hydrographic Services' PAC 205 *Sailing Directions: Inner Passage, Queen Charlotte Sound to Chatham Sound* should be consulted. Gosse Bay, on the north side of the passage, offers good, protected anchorage in eight fathoms. Anchorage is also possible in the bay lying northwest of Stokes Island, at the east end of Gunboat. Anchor in 15 fathoms next to Stokes Island near the head of the bay. The bottom is hard, but held when tried in settled weather.

Dean Channel

[3720, 3729, 3730, 3781, 3789]

★ **Dean Channel (22):** This channel is about 53 miles long, extending northeast from Rattenbury Point, where it meets Fisher Channel to its head at the Kimsquit River flats. The scenery is wonderful, especially in the upper sections, past Edward Point, where it meets Labouchere Channel, which connects it to Burke Channel. Mountain peaks reach 6,000 and 7,000 feet on both sides of the channel.

★ **Eucott Bay (23):** Twenty-five miles from Bella Coola by way of North Bentinck Arm and Labouchere Channel, this bay has a hidden surprise at every turn. High stony mountains, several waterfalls that cascade down hundreds of feet, hot springs, marshes on shore, skunk cabbage, and bears, Arctic loons, mallards, and Canada Geese. Anchorage in this bay is good, and well sheltered, though quite shallow. Depths are greatest near the east side of the bay, two to 2° fathoms, and good mud.

★ **Carlson Inlet:** This is a deep anchorage in 20 fathoms at the very head, but well sheltered. The current from the stream will probably keep the boat headed toward it at all times.

Kimsquit Bay: Deep anchorage is possible here, at least 20 fathoms, and there is a private float. Anchorage might be possible in front of the ruins across the channel, just north of Kimsquit Narrows. The head of the inlet is very deep, and the flats steep.

★⚓ **Sir Alexander Mackenzie Park (24):** [3720] Located just east of Elcho Point, on the north shore of Dean Channel. A 43' high monument commemorates the first land crossing of the North American continent in 1793 by Sir Alexander Mackenzie. A trail from a small, light gravel nook near the monument may be passable. Dinghy to this nook. However, because of the steep bank, it might be easiest to use binoculars to view the chiseled inscription. Look directly below the cairn, high on the rock face, to read: "Alex Mackenzie from Canada by land 22d July 1793". The original writing by Mackenzie was done with red pigmented grease.

★ **Elcho Harbour:** Good, protected anchorage in about 11 fathoms, soft bottom, is available in the northeast corner. In August one could see salmon going up the river and bears and eagles in pursuit.

★ **Cascade Inlet (25):** [3729] This 13 mile long inlet is well worth exploring because of its numerous waterfalls. Anchorage is possible in the northeast side at the head in ten fathoms, soft bottom, even though the flats are very steep-to.

Nascall Hot Springs: The old hot tubs have been removed. A bathhouse charging a fee is on private land. Anchorage is possible, however it is exposed to southeast winds.

★ **Ocean Falls (26):** [3720] This abandoned paper mill town, whose heyday was in the 1960's and 1970's, is experiencing new life through tourism. The remote community, located at the head of Cousins Inlet, has no road access. It is available by pleasure craft and is a stop on the B.C. Ferries Discovery Coast Passage route from Port Hardy. It is a lovely place and well worth the visit.

The shack on the public docks is now open for everyone to use as a covered facility (no water, kitchen facilities, or reservations). A gift shop at the Ocean Falls Ways building offering Cowichan pattern hand knit sweaters, handcrafted footstools, and many small keepsakes. Fresh herbs and greens are available at Audrey's Greenhouse, just a mile from the dock. There are also some interesting places to eat. Eva's Holy Grille is open for lunch and dinner at the church rectory, while Ocean Falls Lodge, in the old bank building provides breakfast/brunch and dinner. Check for summer hours and menu selections on the information board in The Shack.

Once a populated settlement prior to the closure of the pulp mill, many local buildings serve a new purpose. The former hospital, now the Coast Lodge, offers a coin-op laundry, with ice available, as well as showers, a café, rooms to rent and a licensed lounge. The former Court House is home to the Post Office, public library, the Town Directory Board, and a part time medical clinic.

Most residents live at the end of the one mile paved road to Martin Valley. The valley is also the location of the area's one grocery store, The Rain Country Store. When heading that direction, stop by popular Saggo's Saloon, located in a nicely restored building that was previously a home. 250-289-3823. Renovation of older homes in the valley is becoming more common and attractive to summer residents.

Ocean Falls is a great place for hiking and short walks, but be aware that black bears and porcupines may share the trails and town site. Historical tours of the old town site and sightseeing on the 18 mile long Link Lake can be

Ocean Falls   *Linda Schreiber Photo*

Seal Rocks West of River's Inlet   *Linda Schreiber Photo*

arranged. Check the information board in The Shack or inquire at the Post Office for tour contact information. Salt and/or fresh water fishing charters are also available.

Ocean Falls Public Dock: New main float has 20 & 30 ampere power. Moorage, haul-outs to 20 tons. Water is available. New water purification system. Washroom at the top of the ramp and garbage deposit is available. No fuel on-site, however gas and diesel available across the harbor on scheduled days. Harbormaster: 250-289-3859. Wharfinger: 250-289-3211. VHF 06, 09.

Jenny Inlet: On the south side of the channel, anchorage is possible at the head in 11 fathoms, mud bottom. The logging camp burned.

Bella Bella & Shearwater Area

[3720, 3785]

★ **Bella Bella & Shearwater Area (27):** These two communities, a few miles apart, provide a good base for exploring some of the most beautiful waters on the west coast. There is scheduled land plane service to each community from Port Hardy, Bella Coola, and Vancouver.

★ **B.C. Ferries Discovery Coast Passage route:** The ferry, *Queen of Chilliwack*, provides service along the Mid-Coast ports of call, with northbound passage beginning at Port Hardy, bound for either Ocean Falls and Bella Coola, with stops at McLoughlin Bay / Shearwater. Return southbound voyages leave from Bella Coola. Reservations required. 1-888-223-3779. www.bcferries.bc.ca.

★ **New Bella Bella & Waglisla:** Facilities are located at this native Indian settlement on the west shore of Lama Passage. These include a general store with groceries, meat, dairy products and produce, liquor store, hospital, and telephone. Fuel dock dispenses gas, diesel, stove oil, kerosene, naptha, oils, and water. Floats provide moorage adjacent to the fuel dock, in front of the general store. Additional fuel storage and a water separation system are recent improvements. The R.C.M.P. facility located here services Ocean Falls, Shearwater, Klemtu, and Namu areas. In recent years, non Indians have been welcome in New Bella Bella. Garbage may be left at the head of the fuel dock ramp.

Bella Bella Fuels: Gas, diesel, stove oil, lubricants, good water. 250-957-2440. VHF 6, 78A.

Bella Bella: The British Columbia Packers sold all the facilities at Old Bella Bella on the eastern shore of Lama Passage to the Indian Tribe several years ago. Although there are no facilities, there is some moorage and the fisheries office is here.

★ **Shearwater:** This settlement is on the west side of Kliktsoatli Harbour, about two miles southeast of New Bella Bella. It is connected to New Bella Bella by water taxi service. Moorage and anchorage are found - mooring buoys have been removed. Anchor in ten to 12 fathoms throughout this large bay. The Bella Bella Post Office is located here. There is scheduled daily air service to and from Vancouver, Bella Coola, and Port Hardy. Now on the B.C. Ferries Discovery Coast Passage route from Port Hardy. A sunken vessel in Shearwater Harbor is popular with scuba divers.

Shearwater Resort Hotel & Marina: Denny Island. Gas, diesel, propane, water, moorage, 15, 30, 50 amp. power, repairs, haul-outs, 60 ton travel lift, laundromat, showers, restrooms, restaurant, pub, provisions, marine store and internet. 250-957-2305. Resort: 250-957-2366. VHF 6, 66A.

★ **Kakushdish Harbour:** This well protected harbor, one and ½ miles east of Shearwater, offers anchorage in seven fathoms, mud bottom. There are shoals in the entrance and on the south side near the head. There is adequate room for anchoring in the channel. An Indian reservation, with some inhabited cabins, is at the head.

★ **Campbell Island:** This harbor's entrance, about ½ mile north of New Bella Bella, is marked by a green spar buoy. Keep well north of the buoy because of shoals. There are several floats behind the rock breakwater, rafting is often necessary. In addition to the public floats there is a marine repair facility with a marine railway.

★ **Troup Passage & Troup Narrows:** [3720] This passage, northeast of Shearwater between Cunningham and Chatfield Islands, has no problems except at Troup Narrows at the northeast end. The Narrows is shallow and rocky, and must be navigated with caution. Tidal information is given in the Tide Tables, Volume 6. A nice, protected anchorage is found in the unnamed bay ½ mile west of the south end of Troup Narrows. Depth is six fathoms, soft bottom. An even more protected anchorage is in the bay to the east on the north end of the narrows, on mud in four to five fathoms. When approaching Troup Narrows from the north, the best course is along the east side of the bay.

★ **Roscoe Inlet (28):** [3729, 3940] This spectacular inlet extends north and east for 21 miles from its entrance, at the junction of Johnson and Return Channels, about ten miles northeast of New Bella Bella. At one point, just southwest of

Hansen Point, there is a sheer cliff 1,200 feet high rising from the water. The inlet is quite narrow and crooked, and if the weather is good, there is some really beautiful scenery to be seen. Good anchorages in ten to 15 fathoms can be found in Clatse Bay, Boukind Bay, and at the head of the inlet. Quartcha Bay is too deep for anchoring for most boaters.

★ **Kynumpt Harbour (29):** This harbor, located on Campbell Island, on the south shore of Seaforth Channel, offers secluded, sheltered anchorage. Anchorage is good in 45-60 feet of water on a sandy mud bottom. A wild mint patch is on the south shore. Big, white butter clams and little neck steamers are found here. Wild blackberries grow in profusion.

★ **Dundivan Inlet & Lockhard Bay:** Located one mile east of Idol Point, this inlet has several possible anchorages. The best are in Lockhart Bay's two arms in eight to ten fathoms, soft bottom and good protection. The West Arm is especially protected. Idol Point is a favorite salmon fishing area.

St. John Harbour: [3711, 3787] This is an excellent, well protected anchorage six miles south-southwest of Ivory Island Lighthouse. There is a red spar buoy marking the reefs on the starboard side on the approach. Raby Islet may be passed on either side. Anchorage is in Dyer Cove in ten fathoms of water on a mud bottom.

Reid Passage Mathieson Channel

[3710, 3711, 3728, 3734, 3962]

Reid Passage (30): [3710] This route offers a more sheltered alternative to going out into Milbanke Sound at Ivory Island and then continuing north in Finlayson Channel. The entrance, which lies just east of Ivory Island, and its lighthouse, marked by starboard and port markers, is 13 miles west of Dryad Point Light. Carne Rock, the main hazard in the passage, is now marked by a beacon. There is ample room for safe passage on the east side.

Mathieson Channel (31): [3728, 3710, 3711, 3734, 3962] This 35 mile channel extends north from Milbanke Sound to Sheep Passage. It is off the regularly traveled route, and offers beautiful scenery.

Perceval Narrows: [3710] Located at the south end of Mathieson Channel. Currents run to five knots ebbing south and flooding north. Listed in *Canadian tide and current tables* Volume 6. Strong tide rips can be encountered south of the narrows on an ebb tide when there are swells coming in from Milbanke Sound.

★⚓ **Oliver Cove Marine Park:** This is a popular anchorage in Reid Passage about one mile north of the light on Carne Rock. There is a charted rock in the entrance and a ledge on the north side of the entrance. Good protected anchorage in the center of the bay in six fathoms with a soft bottom.

★ **Boat Inlet:** On the west side of Reid Passage, anchorage is possible in two to three fathoms, soft bottoms.

★ **Cockle Bay:** Anchorage in ten to fifteen fathoms, soft bottom, but open to winds from the northeast. Beautiful sand beach.

★ **Tom Bay:** [3728] Well protected anchorage in five fathoms, mud bottom is available. If the hook won't hold, it is probably because of kelp on the bottom. Try ten fathoms in the center of the bay.

★ **Arthur Island:** A well protected anchorage in the eastern most of two coves on Dowager Island is just north of Arthur Island. Ten fathoms, soft bottom.

Salmon Bay: If the wind is not from the west, this is a nice anchorage with a soft bottom, in ten to twelve fathoms. A favored spot for eagle watching.

★ **Rescue Bay:** This is an excellent, large, protected anchorage at the east end of Jackson Passage. Depths of eight to ten fathoms, over a soft bottom. Log rafts may have the prime anchorage site.

Oscar Passage: This is the easiest passage west to Finlayson Channel and Klemtu.

★⚓ **Jackson Passage & Jackson Narrows Marine Park:** [3711, 3734] The narrows is now designated as a marine park. It is a picturesque passage, but narrow at the east end and obstructed by rocks and drying reefs. The passage should be navigated only at high slack. On the ebb, current in Jackson Passage flows east.

★ **James Bay:** [3962] Located on the west side of Mathieson Channel, James Bay offers good anchorage in eight to ten fathoms, soft bottom. Beware of shoaling on west side at head of bay. Good crabbing. There is no protection from south winds.

Railway Station Museum in Prince Rupert

Fiordland Recreational Area

[3738, 3962]

★ **Fiordland Recreational Area:** This includes Mussel and Kynoch Inlets and Pooley Island. The topography of this 225,000 acre (91,000 hectares) park is similar to the fjords of Norway and New Zealand.

★ **Kynoch Inlet (32):** This eight and a ¹/₂-mile inlet is near the north end of Mathieson Channel. A scenic waterfall near the entrance of the inlet cascades from Lessum Creek. Here is found some of British Columbia's most spectacular scenery. Goats range on the cliffs, grizzly bears feed on fish in the streams, and dozens of falls spill off the mountains rising steeply off the shores. When ashore be watchful for grizzlies which were moved here from Kitimat a few years ago. Because these bears had become accustomed to people, their behavior is unpredictable and they may be more dangerous than a bear that has known only the wilderness. Hiking is not recommended. Anchorage is possible at the head of the inlet, off the drying flat, in about ten fathoms of water. The best anchorages are on the north side, but beware because it shoals very rapidly at the head. This can be a rough anchorage when the wind blows up the inlet, but it is worth it. Fishing for trout and salmon is possible in the creek entering the inlet.

★ **Culpepper Lagoon:** Culpepper Lagoon, to the east, should be entered only at or near high slack tide. Tides are said to run to eight knots in the narrows and can develop small rapids. Use Bella Bella tide information. The only anchorage is off the flats at the head of the lagoon, in about 15 fathoms at high tide. It will not be possible to see the flats when anchoring because you will be

coming in at high tide. The chart does not show the true location of the flats on the north side. They extend very far out, drying at low tide. This anchorage is usually better protected than those at the head of Kynoch Inlet, but strong wind gusts have been known to enter. The lagoon has great scenic beauty, when the clouds allow you to see the mountains.

★ **Desbrisay Bay:** Deep and exposed, this bay on the north side of Kynoch Inlet does have anchorage in the northwest corner in ten fathoms, soft bottom. Great scenery.

Sheep Passage: Connecting Mathieson Narrows and Mussel Inlet, Sheep Passage is free from dangers. South and west, the passage leads to Finlayson Channel and north and east to Poison Cove and Mussel Inlet.

Griffin Pass: [3962] Newly charted, not recommended. The narrows at the south entrance and at another spot in the northern part, are dangerous.

Mussel Inlet: There are several waterfalls in this inlet, one from McAlpin Lake, and two which enter Oatswish Bay. Because of the depths, anchoring is difficult.

David Bay: Too deep for good anchorage.

★ **Mussel Bay:** Anchorage is possible in this bay at the head of Mussel Inlet. Anchor in nine fathoms, in front of the river. Beware of rapid shoaling, and, if going on shore, watch out for grizzly bears. (See information under Kynoch Inlet.)

Oatswish Bay: Oatswish Bay is deep, but a temporary anchorage is in ten fathoms near its head, on the west side. It may be too exposed to up-inlet winds for overnight. Lizette Creek Falls may be the most beautiful on the British Columbia Coast.

Poison Cove: Named by Captain Vancouver, whose crew members were poisoned by eating shellfish, probably mussels. The cove is too deep to be a good anchorage.

★ **Bolin Bay:** The mountains rise to 3,000' around this little bay. This makes a spectacular anchorage in 11 fathoms, mud bottom. Protected

in all but east winds. Beware of the drying flats at the head of the bay.

★ **Windy Bay:** There is plenty of anchorage here in 10 to 20 fathoms. The best protected anchorage is behind the island at the east side of the entrance.

Finlayson & Tolmie Channels

[3711, 3734, 3902]

★ **Nowish Cove & Nowish Narrows (33):** This lovely cove in Susan Island is protected by Nowish Island. Entry must be made from the west, north of Nowish Island. The deep cove requires anchorage in 70-80 feet of water. Use plenty of scope because an eddy current sweeps the cove. Bottom is coarse sand. Nowish Narrows, south of the cove, has currents to six knots. Charles Narrows is strewn with rocks and should not be used. These narrows lead into Nowish Inlet. Exploration into the inlet by dinghy is possible, however, currents are strong.

★ **Klemtu:** (34): Klemtu is home to the Kitasoo and Xai'xais Bands. This native Indian village is located on Swindle Island, three miles south of the Boat Bluff Lighthouse (Boat Bluff Fog Horn has been permanently discontinued). "First Nations Fuel". Gas, diesel, water, stove oil, propane, propane for Coleman stoves, ice, potable water, store, coffee shop, wharf, floats, restrooms, and fish processing. Moorage is exposed to the wakes of passing boats. 250-839-1233. VHF 6. Now on the B. C. Ferries route, Discovery Coast Passage, from Port Hardy, this has been one of the most isolated communities on the British Columbia coast. Call ahead to verify current availability and hours. 250-386-3431, 888-223-3779. Klemtu Tourism Info: 877-644-2346.

★ **Alexander Inlet:** [3734] This five mile inlet off Meyers Passage, six miles north of Klemtu, seems to be overlooked by many boaters. It is very scenic, especially the first part, and offers an excellent, protected anchorage in the cove at the head in five fathoms, soft mud.

★ **Bottleneck Inlet:** A good, protected anchorage in six fathoms, mud bottom. No problems at the entrance. Beautiful reflections when the water is smooth.

★ **Goat Cove:** Entrance is ¹/₂ mile east of Goat Bluff. Good anchorage in 6¹/₂ to ten fathoms in the inner basin, east of the stream at the head. Well protected and good holding in gravel and sand.

★ **Cougar Bay:** Cougar Bay is located ten miles north of Klemtu on Tolmie Channel. Anchor in the bight on the east side of the bay. Depths are ten fathoms on the east and south sides.

★ **Work Bay:** Located on the east side of Sarah Island. Good anchorage can be found at the far northeast end of the bay in seven fathoms. Well protected from all but south winds.

★ **Carter Bay:** This bay, at the junction of Sheep Passage, offers anchorage in 12-15 fathoms, near the wreck of the Ohio, but it is fully exposed to the south. The most interesting thing about the bay is the bow section of the steamer Ohio, still visible where she was beached in 1909 after striking Ohio Rock in Finlayson Channel, about three miles southeast of where she now lies.

Hiekish Narrows: These narrows extend 5 miles north northwest from Finlayson Head to Sarah Head at the north end of Sarah Island. The narrows floods to the north at a maximum rate of four knots and ebbs south a maximum rate of 4¹/₂ knots. Most days the maximum current run is between 2¹/₂ and 3¹/₂ knots. The best course is on the east side of the buoy on the reef at Hewitt Rock which is marked for passage on either side. If you are here at slack water, there can be excellent fishing on this reef.

Graham Reach to Fraser Reach

[3739, 3740, 3902]

★⚓ **Green Inlet Marine Park:** Sheltered anchorage is in Horsefly Cove. The cove is just off Graham Reach at the entrance to Green Inlet, 196 kilometers south of Prince Rupert. Anchor in about 13 fathoms of water. It is a beautiful, tiny anchorage.

★ **Khutze Inlet (36):** [3739] Just off Graham Reach, Khutze lies near the most cruising boats take beyond Klemtu. This four mile, deep inlet ends in a drying mud flat where anchorage is possible. Anchor to starboard (facing falls) of the largest waterfall and stream in 11 fathoms. This clears the mud flats plus the wreck at the southwest extremity of the mud flats. Commercial crabbers may have traps which will limit the anchorage area. Watch for eagles feeding on salmon at the stream southeast of the flats and deer swimming the channel. Anchorage is also possible on the east side of the kelp area, marked Green Spit on the chart, in about 15 fathoms. Tide and currents need to be considered. This anchorage can be rough when south winds blow up Graham Reach and bounce off the mountains on the north side of the inlet. The valley at the head has deer, Canada geese, and mink. Salmon, flounder, and small cod are caught. A three mile hike up the river valley leads to an abandoned gold mine.

Aaltanhash Inlet: Anchorage at the head of the inlet is possible, but the bottom is very rocky. There are strong currents from the two rivers, and

there is exposure to the wind. Good halibut fishing and beautiful scenery.

Butedale (37): Located on beautiful Princess Royal Island. Anchorage is possible, however it is open to winds. Caretaker is on the premises. Volunteers have established 500-feet of moorage floats, small store, showers. Rooms and meals may be available. Picturesque Butedale Lake is located here. Lake waters abound with Kamloops Rainbow and Dolly Varden Trout. Butedale Creek exits the lake via the magnificent ¹/₄-mile cascade of Butedale Falls The falls can be viewed from the channel below the falls. Established in the early 1900's, Butedale was then a prosperous fishing, mining, and lumbering community. The cannery and reduction plant buildings still stand, but they have been inoperable since the mid-1950's.

★ **Klekane Inlet:** This inlet, across from Butedale, offers anchorage in 12 fathoms of water off Scow Bay, with some protection. Open to the south. Anchorage is also found at the northwest corner, in ten to 14 fathoms, at the head of the inlet.

Douglas Channel & Gardner Canal

[3743, 3745, 3902]

★ **Hartley Bay (38):** Four public floats are behind the breakwater and one mooring buoy is in Stewart Narrows. Limited provisions, gas, diesel. As with most fuel facilities in this area, it is wise to call ahead to determine availability on the day you are planning to fuel. Towing, minor engine repairs, water at end of ramp, no liquor. Major credit cards accepted. Carving shed for Tsimshian First Nation Art (totems and bentwood boxes). New Community Hall. Scheduled flights connect to Prince Rupert for supplies or passengers. Indian Band Office is open Monday-Friday. 250-841-2500. CB 14. VHF 6, 60.

Walk Around: Inquire about walking to a lake.

★ **Curlew Bay:** On the northeast corner of Fin Island, there is anchorage in eight fathoms, soft bottom, protected.

★ **Kiskosh Inlet (39):** On the west side of Douglas Channel, anchorage is less than ideal in this five and ¹/₂ mile inlet. Just inside the narrow, shallow entrance lies a mud flat. Crabs, clams, scallops, cod and flounder are visible. This inlet is worth exploring for these delights, and for the startling luminescence of the water at night.

★ **Gilttoyees Inlet & Foch Lagoon:** Douglas Channel adjoins Foch Lagoon and Gilttoyees Inlet protected areas. The government plans to include such areas in a marine protected area system which will eventually extend from the south coast to the north coast and establish an international system of marine parks. Foch/Gilttoyees will tie Kitimat into this system, and provide tourism benefits to the local community. The Gitnadoix and Foch-Gilttoyees area encompasses over 118,000 hectares of pristine wilderness, creating more than a 50 kilometer corridor stretching from Douglas Channel, south of Kitimat, to the Skeena River, west of Terrace. This includes anchorages, hotsprings, waterfalls, beaches, fishing opportunities and a Scuba diving site. Boaters can explore six mile-long Foch Lagoon and seven mile-long Gilttoyees Inlet, both of which have exceptional natural features. These include wet alpine meadows, forests of coastal western hemlock and western red cedar, and a number of tarns

in dramatic cirque basins bordered by receding glaciers on their upper sides. Highly productive tidal estuaries are known for good Chinook, Chum, Pink Salmon, Steelhead, and especially Coho salmon. Wildlife includes Grizzly bear, wolverine, hawks, Peregrine Falcon, Trumpeter Swan, Short Eared Owl, and even the Coastal Tailed Frog.

The entrance to this inlet is on the north side of Douglas Channel, about 16 miles southwest of Kitimat. The scenery in this seven mile narrow inlet is spectacular, when the cloud cover does not prevent seeing the tops of the tall mountains on both sides. The best anchorage is in the small bay on the east side, 2¹/₂ miles south of the drying flats at the head. Anchorage is in eight fathoms, mud bottom, with excellent protection. No crabs, just huge starfish.

★ **Kitimat (40):** [3736, 3743] When traveling up the inlet, the prevailing winds are calm in the mornings with rising inland winds in the afternoon. This city is located at the head of Kitimat Arm, an extension of Douglas Channel. Moorage is at M K Bay Marina, about 11 km from town, and at Moon Bay Marina, opposite each other in Kitimat Harbour. Cab service to town is available. There are supermarkets, as well as shops, a bakery, post office, banks, drug stores, liquor store, hospital, and restaurants. Points of interest include the Centennial Museum, Hirsch Creek Golf & Winter Club, and Riverlodge Recreational Complex, and B.C.'s longest living Sitka Spruce. Racquetball and tennis are available and there is good fresh and salt water fishing. Only 160 years ago the Kitimat Valley was covered by a shallow sea. Since then the area became a missionary village and then an industrial town. Visit the Kitimat Centennial Museum. 250-632-8950. Kitimat, population 12,000, is connected to the interior by good paved roads and scheduled air service from the Terrace-Kitimat Airport 35 miles north. The town was developed by The Aluminum Company of Canada when they built the huge smelter in the 1950's. Industrial tours are available as are tours of the fish hatchery. 250-639-8000. Kitimat Info Centre: 250-632-6294, 800-664-6554.

M K Bay Marina: Moorage, power, water, gas, diesel, oils, laundry, showers, provisions, marine supplies, bait, tackle, ice, launch, repairs, haulout. A RV campground is adjacent. 250-632-6401. VHF 66A.

Moon Bay Marina: Moorage, gas, diesel, water, camping, 25-ton marine railway, launch, washroom, showers. 250-632-4655. VHF 16.

★ **Bishop Bay (41):** Located off Ursula Channel, Bishop Bay is the site of a well known hot springs. The mooring buoys and floats have been removed, but there is fair anchorage, in ten to 15 fathoms, around the head of the bay. Salmon fishing is often good in early June.

★ **Kitsaway Anchorage:** Situated on the east side of Hawkesbury Island, this spot offers excellent protected anchorage in six to 13 fathoms on mud. Good crabbing.

★ **Weewanie Hot Springs:** These are located in Devastation Channel, about 2¹/₂ miles Northeast of Dorothy Island Light, and about 17 miles south of Kitimat. The Kitimat Yacht Club has erected a metal sided bath house with separate areas for soaping and soaking. There are two mooring buoys and anchorage is in eight fathoms or more.

Sue Channel: Anchorage is available here in the bight on the north side of Hawkesbury Island, about two miles west of Gaudin Point, in ten fath-

Kitlope Anchorage, Gardner Canal

Hugo Anderson Photo

oms. This site is not well protected from the wind. A bay on the south side of Loretta Island, while better protected, is deep, but does offer potential anchorage.

★ **Gardner Canal (42):** [3745] This is one of the most beautiful spots on the whole coast, and one of the least visited. The canal is 45 miles long, narrow and winding, with snow covered mountains over 6000 feet high on either side. The entrance is at Staniforth Point, about 26 miles south of Kitimat.

★ **Triumph Bay:** Protected anchorage is in the bight on the east side of the bay, about one mile south of Walkem Point in 70 feet of water, mud bottom.

★ **Kiltuish Inlet (43):** [3745] Anchorage is in 12 fathoms in the bay just west of the entrance to the inlet. The inlet itself is about three miles long after going through the very rocky narrow entrance. Least depth in the entrance is six feet, but because of swift currents, entrance should be near high slack. This passage is hazardous and should be approached very cautiously. The scenery inside is very good, with 4,000 and 5,000 foot peaks on either side. There is plenty of room to anchor inside with reasonable depths. This is the only chart available for this area.

★ **Europa Point:** Site of lovely hot springs. It is possible to soak and cast a line into the water at the same time.

★ **Kemano Bay (44):** [3736, 3745] A century-old Indian graveyard and fishing village is on Kemano Spit. The old ALCAN wharf is located in Kemano Bay. Protected anchorage is possible in the bay at under 20 fathoms depth, but use caution. The bay shoals suddenly near the tidal flats.

This was the traditional home of the Haisla until, after a 1940's smallpox epidemic, the survivors from the Kitlope and Kemano areas moved to Kitimat (Kitamaat).

★ **Kemano (44):** In summer, 2000, the ALCAN town of Kemano, located about seven miles from Kemano Bay, was closed. The residential area is being returned to nature. No services are available. ALCAN operations continue at their electric generating plant. 250-639-8000. The entire plant, including offices, is inside a mountain. The source of the water is Nechako Reservoir on the east side of the Coast Range. It is brought to the turbine by means of a tunnel. The vertical head of water, or drop, is 2,600 feet, so it reaches the turbines at a very high pressure. The electricity that is generated is transmitted 50 miles to the smelter at Kitimat by high power transmission lines. No tours.

★ **Chief Mathews Bay:** This bay, about seven miles south of Kemano, is said to be too deep for anchorage, but is worth exploring because of the huge glaciers that can be seen on the mountains at the head of the inlet. Anchorage may be possible off the drying flats at the head, but they are very steep-to.

★ **Kitlope Heritage Conservancy:** This region is described as *the world's largest undisturbed coastal temperate rain forest.* The scenery is very beautiful-in fact, one of the loveliest places on the coast. Within its 883,000 acres are hanging glaciers, waterfalls cascading down 2,000' granite cliffs, and thermal springs. This is a haven for the photographer. You will see black bears, harbor seals, beaver, eagles, mountain goats, caribou, moose, and various waterfowl. The land is protected under the supervision of the B.C. Department of Environment, Parks, and Lands, and the Haisla

First Nations, whose main village is at Kitimaat. For more information about the region and permission to visit, contact Na na kila Institute in Kitimaat Village, Haisla Post Office Box 1039, V0T 2B0. Telephone 250-632-3308. Na na kila administers the Kitlope Heritage Conservancy Watchmen's Program and conducts studies of the area. www.nanakila.ca.

★ **Kitlope Anchorage:** Good anchorage. Very few boaters reach these waters. While at Kitlope Anchorage, dinghy the Kitlope River Estuary and river. As the mountains diminish, a wide valley containing sandbars and grassy knolls spreads before you. River current can be strong and difficult to travel, because the milky-blue water makes depths difficult to determine. About a half-mile up river, look for the Na na kila watchmen's cabin. Please report. About one-mile up river, look for a cave in a cliff that was the site for Haisla to hide from enemy raids of the Haidas. Another 1$^1/_2$ miles takes you to an old logging camp that now is a base for the Haisla Rediscovery Program. It is possible to go all the way up the river (nearly six miles) to Kitlope Lake.

Principe Channel, Banks, Princess Royal, & Pitt Islands

[3710, 3711, 3719, 3721, 3737, 3741, 3742, 3902, 3927]

Meyers Passage: [3710, 3719, 3721, 3753] See current table for Wrangell Narrows. This is the southern entry to the west side of Princess Royal

Prince Rupert

Shutter Shack Photo

Island. The route along the west sides of Princess Royal and Pitt Islands is an alternative for travel from Klemtu to Prince Rupert. The distance is about the same, there are many anchorages and less traffic, but there is more exposure to storms. Passage should be made at or near high tide. The least depth, at zero tide, is only three feet. The inset on Chart #3710 shows the course to be followed. The passage is choked with kelp and it is important to stay on the designated course, plowing through the kelp when necessary.

★ **Parsons Anchorage:** Located at the south end of Kitasu Bay on the northwest corner of Swindle Island, this bay has anchorage in six fathoms, soft bottom. Open to northwest winds.

★ **Laredo Inlet (45):** [3737] Eighteen mile Laredo Inlet is the longest of the dozen or so inlets that are encountered between here and Prince Rupert. Laredo Inlet is very scenic, with high mountains on both sides. There are a half dozen good anchorages in the inlet.

★ **Alston Cove:** Anchorage is possible in six fathoms, mud bottom with good protection.

★ **Fifer Cove:** This cove is eight miles farther north on the east side of the inlet. An excellent, beautiful anchorage in ten fathoms, mud bottom, and good protection in front of the large stream at the head of the cove.

Brew Island: Located at the head of Laredo Inlet. The inlet has a temporary anchorage on its northwest corner in ten fathoms, soft bottom. Limited protection from up-inlet winds.

★ **Weld Cove:** Located on the west side of Pocock Island, this cove offers anchorage in ten to 12 fathoms, mud bottom, with entry on either side of Kohl Island. The entrances are rocky, and caution must be used when entering or departing.

★ **Bay of Plenty:** Good, scenic and well protected anchorage in nine fathoms is on the southwest side at the head of the bay, mud bottom.

★ **Mellis Inlet:** Anchorage in 12 fathoms in the cove at the head, soft bottom. Open to winds from the south. Beautiful scenery with high mountains on both sides.

★ **Trahey Inlet:** [3737] Lying just west of the entrance to Laredo Inlet, there is well protected anchorage at the head of its west arm in six to

seven fathoms, mud bottom. Entry is possible on either side of Jessop Island, but because of many hazards, extreme caution is necessary. This chart, scale 1:77,429, is the only chart available, and it isn't very helpful.

Kent, Helmcken, Commando, & Evinrude Inlets: [3719] These inlets indent Princess Royal Island on the east side of Laredo Channel. The chart above is essential for entering any of these waters. Kent and Commando have strong tidal currents and should be entered only at slack water, preferably high slack. Evinrude Inlet has a shoal on the north side of its entrance. Anchoring depths are fairly deep. Helmcken Inlet should be entered south of Smithers Island. Anchorages are also deep in this inlet. The best choice is in the small bight on the east side of Smithers Island, in 11 fathoms, on a soft bottom. There is good protection from winds. The cove on the southwest side of Smithers Island is too exposed to west and southwest winds to be a good anchorage.

★ **Surf Inlet:** [3737] This 11 mile inlet is the most beautiful of all the inlets on the west sides of Princess Royal and Pitt Islands, with steep sides, and a relatively narrow channel. Anchorage is possible at the head of the inlet in eight to ten fathoms, but very little protection from winds up or down the inlet. The mountain scenery is beautiful and the dam and abandoned power house at Port Belmont, remaining from the days when the large Belmont gold mine was operating up the valley, are still visible.

★ **Penn Harbour:** This harbor, four miles from the head of Surf Inlet, is by far the best anchorage. Anchorage is in nine to ten fathoms, soft bottom, and excellent protection. Some nice waterfalls are at the head of the bay.

★ **Cameron Cove:** Located in Barnard Harbour on the northwest corner of Princess Royal Island, the head of this cove has well protected anchorage in seven fathoms, soft bottom.

★ **Monckton Inlet:** [3721] Located on the west side of Pitt Island. The first anchorage is near the head of the large cove on the north side of the inlet, about ¹/₂ mile north of Roy Island in nine fathoms, mud bottom, and good protection. Additional anchorages are in the cove to the northwest of Monckton Point in nine to ten fathoms, and near the head of the inlet in six to ten fathoms. Entrance to Monckton Inlet is easy.

★ **Port Stephen:** Good, well protected anchorage in the first cove to the northeast of Littlejohn Point. Anchorage is in ten fathoms, soft bottom. Another anchorage is in the cove to the north of the west entrance to Stephen Narrows in 11-12 fathoms, soft bottom, fair protection.

★ **Buchan Inlet:** [3721] This inlet, five miles north of Monckton Inlet, is entered north of Tweedsmuir Point. Both the inlet and the point are named for the author, John Buchan, Lord Tweedsmuir, the former Governor General of Canada. The inlet offers sheltered anchorage in nine to ten fathoms just north of Elsfield Point, and for the more adventurous, several anchorages in the inner basin. Don't try this without the above chart. Least depths of six feet are reported in the narrows.

★ **Patterson Inlet:** This inlet is about six miles north of Buchan Inlet. Anchorage is possible in either of the two coves at the head of the inlet, in six fathoms in the north cove and ten to 12 fathoms in the southern one.

Mink Trap Bay: [3721] The best anchorage is in Moolock Cove, in the basin on the far south end, in ten fathoms with a mud bottom. Good protection from seas, but there is limited shelter from south and west winds. Wind can come in over the low ground around the cove. Because of numerous shoals and rocks, caution must be exercised when entering. Both of the anchorages in Patterson Inlet are more secure and easier to enter.

Petrel Channel: [3746, 3927] This channel is entered at Foul Point on Anger Island. It runs 23 miles north and west to Comrie Head, where it meets Ogden Channel. Tidal currents can run to three knots in Petrel Channel. Petrel Channel continues northwest from Foul Point. Three excellent anchorages lie off of Petrel Channel.

★ **Hevenor Inlet:** This inlet is five miles long and has a well protected anchorage in six to eight fathoms, soft bottom, at the very head of the inlet.

★ **Newcombe Harbour:** [3753] This harbor is four miles north of Hevenor Point. It is a large, scenic, well protected anchorage in nine fathoms, mud bottom, just south of the prominent point on the west side at the head of the bay.

★ **Captain Cove:** The best protected anchorage is near the head of the cove, on the south side, just east of the islets, in ten to 12 fathoms, mud bottom.

Principe Channel (45): Not many pleasure boaters venture into Principe Channel. Most prefer Grenville Channel, en route to Alaska. If crossing to the Queen Charlotte Islands, however, one can use this route.

Larson Harbour: On the northern tip of Banks Island, this protected anchorage is often used by boats waiting to cross Hecate Strait to the Queen Charlotte Islands. Two lights mark the entrance. One must sail directly through thick kelp beds to approach it. Inside are six mooring buoys and space to anchor.

Grenville Channel to Prince Rupert

[3772, 3773]

Grenville Channel (46): See current table for Wrangell Narrows. This trench-like channel is very narrow, deep and straight, and extends northwest 45 miles from Sainty Point to Gibson Island. From Gibson Island it is another 27 miles to Prince Rupert Harbour. The tidal currents in the channel can reach two knots on springs, flooding from each end, meeting near Evening Point, just south of Klewnuggit Inlet.

★⚓ **Lowe Inlet Provincial Marine Park & Nettle Basin (47):** Anchorage is possible in Nettle Basin in front of beautiful Verney Falls. Anchor in or on either side of the stream, depending on the tide and wind. Strong currents can lead to dragging anchor. Our favored anchorage is south of the stream on a sandy mud bottom. Anchorage is in 70-90 foot depths. It is possible to approach the foot of the falls where "leaping" salmon put on a show while awaiting high tide and the chance to jump the falls leading to the lake above. Bears and seals are also seen here. A short trail to the left of the falls leads to the lake where anglers will find good trout fishing. Much of the shoreline is undeveloped parkland. The falls and the trail to the lake is First Nations Reserve land. On the north side of Nettle Basin, on private land, stand the remnants of an old cannery.

★⚓ **Klewnuggit Inlet Provincial Marine Park:** This undeveloped park consists of East Inlet and the two lakes above. Good anchorage is at the north end of East Inlet in nine fathoms over a good bottom. Crabbing is good here. Brodie Lake is separated from the inlet by a small rock step.

Kxngeal Inlet: Anchorage in ten to 14 fathoms near the inlet's head. Although exposed to south winds, this provides welcome shelter when strong north winds catch you out in Grenville Channel.

★ **Baker Inlet:** [3772] Enter north of Griffon Point by way of 200 foot wide Watts Narrows. Be aware of strong currents in Watts Narrows. A light marks the entrance to this four-mile long inlet. The entrance is not as difficult as it looks. There is plenty of water. Use the chart inset and go through near slack water. Slack water is about the same as the turn at Prince Rupert. Drying reefs and shoals are on the south side. Anchorage is found in 11 fathoms at the head of the inlet, south of the small island. It has good holding bottom, and is very well protected. A family of seven wolves was once observed on shore.

★ **Kumealon Inlet (48):** An attractive anchorage in six fathoms is found inside the island near the entrance of this inlet located 28 miles from Lowe Inlet and 37 miles from Prince Rupert. Anchorage is also possible in 15 fathoms, mud bottom, behind the small island at the head of the inlet. Pass to the north side of this island when entering.

★ **Lewis Island Anchorage:** [3927] Bloxam Pass lies between Lewis Island and McMicking Island. Enter from Arthur Passage just north of the light on Herbert Reefs. Relatively protected anchorages in five to ten fathoms, soft bottom, are available in several locations in the passages on the northeast side of Porcher Island. The most protected is off the west side of Lewis Island in five to six fathoms, good bottom. Entrance or exit is also possible to the north via Chismore Passage. Kelp Passage, to the south, is not recommended because of obstructing reefs. These anchorages are about 18 miles south of Prince Rupert.

Porcher Island

[3927]

★ **Porcher Island:** See current tide table for Ketchikan, Alaska.

★ **Hunt Inlet (49):** This bay, located on the northwest side of Porcher Island, has shelter in all winds. A dangerous rock ledge is near the entrance. A public float is on the west side. There are no marine facilities.

Kinahan Islands: Anchorage is in seven fathoms over a mud bottom in the bay between the two islands with exposure to southeast winds.

★ **Port Edward:** Named for King Edward VII this community is located about six miles south of Prince Rupert. Port Edward has greatly enlarged small boat facilities in recent years. The Porpoise Harbor Boat Launch has temporary moorage, washrooms, and fish cleaning table with no fees. It is convenient to Chatham Sound and popular fishing grounds. The North Pacific Fishing Village, a major tourist attraction is located in Port Edward. Twenty-eight historic buildings, some dating to 1889, house a restaurant and inn, art studio, and museum. Visitors enjoy tours, performances, exhibits and displays illustrating the historic importance of these canneries and the workers who kept them running. Museum is open daily 9am – 6pm from May 15 – Sept. 30. 250-628-3538.

Port Edward Public Moorage: Power, potable water on main float, showers, laundry, 15-ton Travel Lift. Harbor Authority: 250-628-9220. VHF 72.

★⚓ **Kitson Island Provincial Marine Park:** Kitson Island and adjacent Kitson Islet at the southern entrance to Prince Rupert Harbour, northeast of Smith Island and south of Ridley Island, comprise this undeveloped park. Enter from Chatham Sound, and be alert for shoals. When the wind blows against the current, expect choppy conditions around the island. Sandy beaches with landing areas for kayaks. No sheltered anchorages.

Prince Rupert

[3955, 3958]

★ **Prince Rupert (50):** All vessels transiting Prince Rupert Harbour, Venn Pass, and Porpoise Harbour are requested to observe the five knot speed limit and minimize wakes. Exercise extreme caution in the vicinity of the Digby Island Ferry Landing and within three cables of the harbor shoreline.

Prince Rupert lies at the heart of the traditional territory of the Tsimshian First Nation. Their ancestors traded with the early Europeans and later the Hudson's Bay Company. Early on the focus was the fur trade, but soon newcomers saw potential in the rich salmon runs of the Skeena and Nass rivers. By the end of the 19th century dozens of cannery villages were scattered throughout this area.

Modern day Prince Rupert began with the coming of the Grand Trunk Pacific Railroad. Prince Rupert grew from a railroad town to a thriving fishing and port community in the early 1900's. Canadian and American troops flooded in during World War II, when Prince Rupert was an American sub-port and staging area for troops and munitions.

Many buildings from Prince Rupert's early days still stand in the Historic Downtown Shopping District. In fact, a statue of the Grand Trunk Pacific Railway's first president stands with totem poles beside City Hall on Third Avenue, representing the city's twin foundations. Visitors will find a variety of grocery and department stores, and an array of shops and galleries, in a scenic setting with fountains, gardens and totem poles sprinkled among the historic architecture.

Prince Rupert's fishing heritage is recalled in Cow Bay. During the heyday of the canneries when so much fresh halibut was shipped from Prince Rupert it was famous as the "Halibut Capital of the World," this was the home of the "Mosquito Fleet" of small boats. Today Cow Bay is a waterfront area of historic buildings, many of them built on pilings. This trendy shopping district offers a variety of boutiques, souvenir and gift shops, several restaurants and coffee shops, and local tour companies.

Prince Rupert is a vibrant port city, home to cultures from all over the globe. It has become a centre for commerce and transportation, a meeting point for British Columbia and Alaska ferries, terminus of the Queen Charlotte Islands ferry, and the place where the Yellowhead Highway and VIA Rail meet the sea. Visitors come to this cosmopolitan city to experience 10,000 years of living culture, world-class sport fishing, or spectacular wildlife viewing. In the summer, the city hosts nearly 100,000 cruise ship passengers.

Your first glimmer of what you will experience unfolds as you cruise into the harbour. Immense tidal changes create continually changing landscapes, sometimes linking isolated islands with clam-filled sandbars. The rugged coastline hosts a variety of wildlife including bears, moose, wolves and deer and the sky is often filled with eagles and ravens. In every district of Prince Rupert, nature plays a vital role in life on the Northwest Coast. This is Canada's northern rainforest. Spend a quiet moment along the waterfront and you may be rewarded by a glimpse of a harbor seal or one of many species of seabirds, and on rare occasions even humpback or killer whales. Here nature and history are vital to daily life. You can share the culture and people, the forest and wildlife, and the many moods of British Columbia's Northwest Coast.

Prince Rupert has a variety of shore excursions available, many focusing on nature, wildlife and the outdoors. Kayaking, whale watching, nature hikes, bike tours, sport fishing, floatplane and helicopter tours, and bear watching at the Khutzeymateen Grizzly Bear Sanctuary are a few. Prince Rupert is also home to the world class Museum of Northern British Columbia. 250-624-3207. The Performing Arts Centre, the Jim Ciconne Recreation Centre, and the Prince Rupert Golf Club offer visitors alternate activities. For information about the city and activities, visit www.tourismprincerupert.com or call the Visitor Information Centre, 250-624-5637 or 1-800-667-1994.

Banks, restaurants, hotels, bed and breakfasts, retail centres, grocery and liquor stores, as well as marine supply stores, charts, fishing equipment and licenses, and repairs are all easily located in the area.

Customs check-in: Customs service is available 24 hours. 1-888-226-7277, or 1-888--CANPASS. Prince Rupert Customs: 250-627-3003.

Prince Rupert Berthage: Pleasure craft moorage is available at Cow Bay (at the public floats and the Prince Rupert Yacht Club), Atlin Terminal, and Rushbrooke Harbour. Fairview Harbour is primarily designed for commercial craft, with moorage available only when the fleet is out. The public floats are protected by breakwaters. For general port information: Port Edward Harbour

Authority 250-628-9220. Prince Rupert Port Authority (Atlin and Fairview Terminals) 250-627-8899.

★ **Cow Bay:** Local lore attests that in 1906 the first dairy herd arrived via ship. With no dock to unload the cargo, the cows were unceremoniously dumped overboard and swam ashore. Today a harbor front walk leads to dining, shopping, and historic buildings. In July *Cow Bay Days* are celebrated and the *Udder Fest Theatre Festival* occurs each August.

Public floats are the closest public floats to town, and, because of lack of amenities, are usually used by boaters for come and go stops while visiting the town to shop. Overnight moorage is possible with fees paid at Rushbrooke Harbour. There is a garbage drop, but no power or water.

New facilities for transiting pleasure craft are available at the Atlin Terminal located adjacent to the Cow Bay floats and Prince Rupert Yacht and Rowing Club in Cow Bay.

Atlin Cruise Terminal (pocket Cruise ship facility): Prince Rupert Port Authority owned and operated. This facility consists of 340' of concrete floats along with a 60' x 40' lightering float for vessels at anchor; a 65' aluminum ramp/walkway with secure access to the floats. Small transiting vessels may tie-up directly to the floats while large vessels tie-up to the bollards located on the dock itself. The maximum length of vessels is 328' with a draft up to 18'. On-site amenities include water, garbage, provisions, one ton hydraulic lift, and Canadian Customs facilities. 250-627-8899. www.rupertport.com.

Petro Canada-Cow Bay: Gas, diesel, stove oil, lubricants, showers, water, garbage, ice, bait & tackle. 250-624-4106. VHF 78.

Other Services: Laundry: 250-624-6811. Propane: 250-624-4301

Prince Rupert Rowing and Yacht Club: Customs clearance. Public moorage (reservations recommended), 15 & 30 ampere power, showers, water, telephone, bait, wireless internet. 250-624-4317. VHF 73.

★ **Rushbrooke Harbour:** This basin is the primary harbor for pleasure craft moorage. Enter through the northern breakwater entrance. The main float and seven finger floats have accommodated as many as 400 boats on a busy summer night. Rafting is common. No reservations. Fifteen amp power and water are available. There is a boat launching ramp and garbage deposit. The Harbour Manager's office has washroom and showers. A warm welcome is extended which includes a selection of brochures and literature describing what to do and see in Prince Rupert. Telephones are found at the Harbour Manager's office. When mooring at either the Rushbrooke or the Yacht Club floats, be aware of strong currents which may affect maneuverability. It is about a 15 minute walk to town. Harbour Manager: 250-624-9400, 250-628-9220.

Wampler Marine: Gas, diesel, stove oil, supplies, showers, laundry, fishing tackle. 250-624-5000.

Fairview Harbour: Floats are sheltered by two breakwaters--a rock breakwater on the south and a floating pipe on the west. Moorage is primarily for fishing vessels, but they will accommodate pleasure craft if space is available. Short layovers (few hours) permitted for clearing customs and provisioning. Power and water available in loading areas. Garbage drop. Located at the bottom of Park Avenue, 1.5 kilometers from downtown Prince Rupert. 250-624-3127. VHF 16, 9.

★ **Venn Passage:** [3955, 3957, 3959, 3985] Both northbound and southbound approaches to Prince Rupert may be shortened by about ten miles by traversing this passage, known locally as Metlakatla Pass. The twisting channel is reef infested, and requires extreme caution. It is well marked with buoys and segmented lights. Currents run to three knots. Coast Guard approved charts and a sounder are musts. The large Tsimshian native village of Metlakatla is on the north side of the passage. Traffic should slow down when passing the floats in front of this village.

There is a short cut to the north, about ³/₄ of a mile west of Metlakatla, that is about three miles shorter than following the old route around Enfield Rock. It goes east of Tugwell Island into Duncan Bay, and then northwest to pass on either side of Hodgson Reefs. Pay close attention to the channel markers to avoid numerous shoals.

The four public mooring buoys between Isabel Islet and Auriol Point have been permanently discontinued by the Coast Guard.

★ **Tuck Inlet & Tuck Narrows:** [3964] This inlet is a continuation of Prince Rupert Harbour. It is entered at Tuck Point, five miles north of Rushbrooke Harbour. This is a convenient anchorage, if everything is full in Prince Rupert or you want a quieter place. Anchorage is in the bight 3/8 of a mile west of Tuck Point in eight to ten fathoms on a mud bottom with protection from all except down-inlet winds. Another spot is at the head of the inlet in 16 fathoms on a mud bottom. There is protection from all but up-inlet winds. Be aware that the head shoals rapidly, especially to port. Currents at Tuck Narrows run to six knots, but the channel is short, wide and deep. See current tide table for Wrangell Narrows.

Prince Rupert to Alaska Border

[3802, 3933, 3960, 3963]

★ **Port Simpson (51):** [3933] Port Simpson may be approached by Cunningham Passage from the south or Inskip Passage from the north. This harbor offers good anchorage. There are no tidal streams and approach is unobstructed. It is sheltered from all but west winds. Port Simpson was established in 1834 as a Hudson's Bay Company trading post. Today it is populated by Natives who are mainly engaged in the fishing industry. Fuel is available during the fishing season and there is a store. Moorage floats are on the east side of Village Island. This is a good jumping off place for crossing Dixon entrance.

There are several large inlets in British Columbia, north and east of Port Simpson, that are passed up by most boaters, but are worth exploring. They are surrounded by beautiful, high mountains, some with glaciers, have abundant wildlife, and there are three ghost towns. These waterways are Work Channel, Quottoon, Khutzeymateen, Observatory, and Portland Inlets, and Portland and Pearse Canals. The latter three are covered in Chapter 20.

Brundige Inlet

[3980]

★ **Brundige Inlet & Dundas Island (57):** This excellent anchorage is on the north end of Dundas Island, and 35 miles north of Prince Rupert via Venn Passage. It is a good jumping off place for crossing Dixon Entrance. The best

anchorage is in the far south end of the inlet, in seven fathoms of water, or in the bay on the port side, in about halfway, in five fathoms of water. Good holding bottoms. To anchor near Fitch Island, to port after entry, pass Fitch Island, then slowly turn in, keeping it to port and use a depth finder to ease between Fitch Island and the baring mound, labeled "18" on the chart. Keep the mound to starboard and go into the head of the cove for secure holding bottom in four fathoms. At low tide, observe the baring mound and record the location for future use. Ketchikan, the first port in Alaska, is about 55 miles from here.

Work Channel

[3963]

★ **Work Channel & Trail Bay (52):** Enter at Maskelyne Point on the north end of Maskelyne Island. Dudevoir Pass, south of this island, has a least depth of three feet, and, though used by some commercial fishermen, is not recommended. Paradise Passage, two miles inside Work Channel on the north side, is not recommended for the same reason. Work Channel is about 28 miles long, is bordered by high mountains, and is very scenic, especially Quottoon Inlet. Anchorages are rare, but there are a few good ones. The first anchorage is in Trail Bay, six miles southeast of Maskelyne Point. Anchor either at the head of Trail Bay in about ten fathoms, sand and gravel bottom, or at a better more protected anchorage in Zumtela Bay, on the west side of Trail Bay, in eight fathoms, sand bottom. Legace Bay, about five miles southeast of Trail Bay could be used as an anchorage, but it is deep, about 15 fathoms, and not too well protected.

★ **Quottoon Inlet & Quottoon Narrows (53):** Also known as the North Arm, this inlet branches off to the north about 19 miles from the entrance of Work Channel. Good, protected anchorage in Quottoon Inlet is in the unnamed cove just north of Quottoon Narrows, in ten to 11 fathoms, well protected. Quottoon Inlet is surrounded by 3,000' to 4,000' mountains, and is the main reason for exploring Work Channel. Tidal currents are strong in Quottoon Narrows, but it is wide, 450 feet. Favor the east side of the narrows when making the passage. The three miles remaining to the head of the inlet offer spectacular scenery, with snow capped peaks and beautiful waterfalls, in June. The inlet is too deep and the flats at the head too steep, to offer any anchorages. From Quottoon Point, Work Channel continues another nine miles to its head in Davies Bay.

★ **Davies Bay:** Well protected anchorage is possible in about eight to ten fathoms of water on gravel on the east side at the head of Davies Bay. Davies Lagoon dries nine feet, according to the chart, and may be entered by small craft at or near high water.

★ **Union Inlet:** This inlet is entered at John Point about two miles northeast of Maskelyne Point. Anchorage is possible near the head in 15 to 17 fathoms, on a mud bottom.

Khutzeymateen Inlet

[3980]

★ **Khutzeymateen Inlet (54):** Khutzeymateen Inlet is 13 miles long and is entered between Keemein and Welgeegenk Points. The entrance is nine miles northeast of Maskelyne Point, up Steamer Passage. The best anchorages are either at the head of the inlet, or in Tsamspanakuck Bay. At the head, the most protected anchorage is in the northeast corner in 15 to 17 fathoms, soft bottom. There is good crabbing, and a very large seal population. We have been told that on occasions Killer Whales come here to hunt for these seals. The scenery at the head of Khutzeymateen Inlet is very beautiful. Khutzemateen Inlet has a good sized Grizzly Bear population, and, for that reason, was designated as a Grizzly Bear Sanctuary several years ago. The Khutzemateen Valley is a British Columbia Class A Provincial Park. Visitors must register at the Khutzemateen Grizzly Bear Sanctuary Guardian Station upon entering the sanctuary. The Khytzemateen Guardians will explain regulations and guidelines. Entry into the estuary is restricted to those with permitted guides only. Limited guided trips must be reserved in advance. No land based access is permitted in the sanctuary. Fishing on the Khutzemateen River is closed. Review the Tidal Waters Sport Fishing Guide for fishing regulations within the tidal waters of the sanctuary. Hunting of wildlife is prohibited below 1000m. Check the latest regulations at the district office 250-798-2277. District Manager, Skeena District, 3790 Alfred Avenue, Bag 5000, Smithers, British Columbia V0J 2N0. http://wlapwww.gov.bc.ca/bcparks

★ **Sommerville Bay:** This bay, on the north end of Sommerville Island, offers good anchorage in 11 fathoms, sand bottom, with protection from all but northeast winds.

Observatory Inlet

[3793, 3933]

★ **Observatory Inlet & Perry Bay (55):** This inlet begins at Nass Point at the north end of Portland Inlet. The Kincolith native village is about one mile southeast of Nass Point. The public boat harbor is protected by a rock breakwater, but it is shallow and very small. When the local gill netters are in, the harbor will probably be full. There is an unprotected small float just west of the breakwater that could be used temporarily. The public wharf in front of the village can only be reached at high water. It is about a 20 minute walk to town from the harbor. There are grocery stores, but no fuel or water are available. The first 22 miles up Observatory Inlet are bounded by 4,000 foot mountains. All of these waters are very deep, and anchorages are rare. Salmon Cove, 16¹/₂ miles north of Nass Point, has a possible anchorage in 11-12 fathoms, but there is very little protection from winds blowing up or down the inlet. Brooke Point is 22 miles northeast of Nass Point. Continuing up Paddy Passage and Liddle Channel for four miles brings one to the entrance of Perry Bay, the best anchorage in the area. There is well protected anchorage in nine to ten fathoms, mud bottom. This is a good base from which to explore the surrounding waters. There are black bears around the bay, and good crabbing. Caution must be exercised at the entrance to Perry Bay because there are shoals on both sides.

★ **Alice Arm:** Extends northeast nine miles from Liddle Island in its entrance. There are no suitable anchorages, but mooring is possible at Alice Arm float located at the head of the inlet. One can walk into the ghost town of Alice Arm, a former gold mining community, a distance of about ¹/₂-mile by road. The town is still inhabited and even has air service from Prince Rupert. There is no road connection.

Kitsault: This abandoned molybdenum mining town lies across the arm. This large establishment was built by AMAX, a United States mining firm, in the 1970's and shut down in 1983 when the world market for this mineral, used as an alloy in steel manufacturing, collapsed from over production. There is a private gravel road connecting the town to Terrace, British Columbia. A security staff remains on the premises.

★ **Hastings Arm:** [3793, 3933]This scenic inlet extends 13 miles north from Davies Point, and has high mountains on both sides. At the head of the inlet one is about 20 miles north of Prince Rupert and about 65 miles southwest of Ketchikan, Alaska. Anchorage might be possible at the head of the inlet. There is an abandoned cabin and a buoy on the east side, and the flats are steep-to. There is temporary anchorage 4¹/₂ miles south of the head of Hastings Arm, in nine to ten fathoms, off the mouth of the creek. The bottom is soft. No protection from winds blowing up or down the inlet.

★ **Granby Bay & Anyox:** The dominant feature in this bay on the west side of Observatory Inlet is the abandoned copper mining town of Anyox and its smelter. The copper smelter was built in 1915, and the town and copper mines precede that date. A fire in 1923 exploded the plant's powder magazines and destroyed the town. No one was hurt, and since much copper remained, the town was soon rebuilt. It continued to operate until 1935, when, because of low copper prices, it was shut down. In 1942 forest fires burned the town down, and the brick buildings and smoke stacks are all that remain. Granby Bay is very deep, and the best anchorage is in the bay on the west side of Granby Peninsula in about ten fathoms, with good protection. The barren landscape around the town is the result of the fumes once emitted by the smelters.

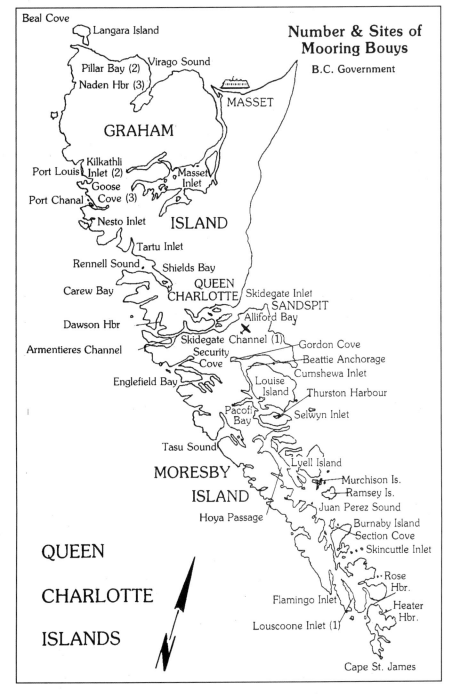

Number & Sites of Mooring Bouys

B.C. Government

Beal Cove
Langara Island
Pillar Bay (2)
Virago Sound
Naden Hbr (3)
MASSET
GRAHAM
Kilkathli
Port Louis Inlet (2)
Goose
Masset
Port Chanal Cove (3)
Inlet
Nesto Inlet
ISLAND
Tartu Inlet
Rennell Sound
Shields Bay
QUEEN
Carew Bay
CHARLOTTE
Skidegate Inlet
SANDSPIT
Dawson Hbr
Alliford Bay
Skidegate Channel (1)
Gordon Cove
Armentieres Channel
Security
Beattie Anchorage
Cove
Cumshewa Inlet
Englefield Bay
Louise
Island
Thurston Harbour
Pacofi
Bay
Selwyn Inlet
Tasu Sound
MORESBY
Lyell Island
ISLAND
Murchison Is.
Ramsey Is.
Hoya Passage
Juan Perez Sound
Burnaby Island
Section Cove
Skincuttle Inlet
QUEEN
Rose
Hbr.
CHARLOTTE
Flamingo Inlet
Heater
Hbr.
ISLANDS
Louscoone Inlet (1)
Cape St. James

Whale Watching

Queen Charlotte Islands

[3802, 3807, 3808, 3809, 3811, 3825, 3853, 3859, 3868, 3869, 3890, 3891, 3892, 3894, 3895]

★ **Queen Charlotte Islands (56):** In this island 190 mile chain there are some 150 islands and islets that are isolated from the British Columbia's mainland by the 60 miles of Hecate Strait. These islands lie roughly in a triangle about 65 miles across the top and tapering to a point at the south end. Graham, Moresby, and Kunghit are the three largest islands. There are numerous narrow and intriguing passages. The north end of Graham Island is about 45 miles from the Alaskan border.

The climate of the Charlottes is considered to be mild. The mean annual temperature is 46 degrees. Summer temperatures are similar to those in northern and central British Columbia and winter temperatures are moderated by the Japanese current. It was this climate that encouraged homesteaders to establish large farms, hopeful of successful crops because of the long growing season. The total population of the Charlottes is about 6,000. The Charlottes have a reputation for rain. Actually, the eastern side is in a rain shadow, created by mountains on the west. West coast rainfall does average 180 inches, and there are huge cedars dripping with moss. July is the driest month, October the wettest. There are miles of sand dunes on Graham Island. Industries include fishing, logging, and argillite and silver carvings by the Haidas. The larger communities are Masset, Queen Charlotte City, and Skidegate Landing on Graham Island and Sandspit on Moresby Island. Many advise that Graham lends itself to exploration by car, while Moresby is best explored by boat. Boaters are wise to carry extra fuel, water, oil, stove fuel, charts, and a spare anchor. Most nights are spent anchored or tied to a buoy. A good dinghy, capable of carrying several persons, is valuable. The islands are not monitored for paralytic shellfish poisoning. Do not eat clams, mussels, oysters, and other bivalves. The Parks Service has upgraded some facilities on South Moresby, including the watering station west of Shuttle Island, on the east side of Hoya Passage. There is a 70 foot long concrete float, with abundant fresh water. Tasu, a former supply stop on the West Coast, is closed. Nothing is available here except good water.

B.C. Ferries Corporation operates a ferry between Prince Rupert and Skidegate Landing. During June-September it sails often. For information call 1-888-223-3779. The two largest islands are then connected by a ferry between Alliford Bay and Skidegate. Bus and rental car transportation is possible. Logging roads are controlled by MacMillan Bloedel and are available for car use. There are boat launches at Alliford Bay, Sandspit, Copper Bay, and Masset. Several

charter agencies run tours through the islands. Car rentals are possible in Masset, Queen Charlotte City and Sandspit. Queen Charlotte City visitor information 250-559-8316. There is daily scheduled airline service to Sandspit, on Moresby Island, from Vancouver and Prince Rupert. Reservations are highly recommended between July and late September.

This is home to the Haida Nation. Five sites are operated by the Haida Gwaii Watchmen Program 250-559-8225. Skidegate Band Council 250-559-4496. These islands were first sighted by Juan Perez in 1774. They were named in 1787 after Queen Charlotte, wife of King George III. Recommended are the charts noted above and *Sailing Directions for the British Columbia Coast* PAC 206 and *A Guide To The Queen Charlotte Islands* by Neil Carey.

★ **Gwaii Haanas:** The southern half of Moresby Island, and adjacent smaller islands, are designated as Gwaii Haanas National Park Reserve/Haida Heritage Site. All visitors must have a reservation (1-800-HELLO-BC) and register before entering the protected area. Internet: http://parkscan.harbour.com/gwaii. PO Box 37, Dept. NW, Queen Charlotte, British Columbia V0T 1S0. To register call 250-559-8818.

★ **Masset & Graham Island:** [3895] Packers Cannery, the Canadian Forces Base, and facilities for the fishing fleet combine to make Masset the largest island community. The Canadian Forces Station is continuing a major down-sizing from about 600-700 personnel to 50. The buildings are being sold to the village for residences. Attractions are totems, *Beach Buggy Days* in September, and a wildlife sanctuary. You can hike to the Blow Hole, climb Tow Hill, or collect agates, glass balls, driftwood, and shells at Agate and North Beach, see standing poles, or buy Haida arts and crafts. There are rivers that can be fished or the Dixon Entrance Golf Course that can be played. At the Delkatla Wild Life Sanctuary, more than 140 species of water fowl and shore birds have been seen. There is a viewing tower, and bird watching walks are available. In Old Massett you can view the totem carving shed: 250-626-3985. For the old village sites in the northern area of Graham Island, contact the Massett Band Council at 250-626-3337.There is an aircraft landing strip, laundry, liquor store, restaurant, hotel, hardware, retail shops, car rentals, and boat launching. Masset is connected by road to Queen Charlotte City.

North Arm Transportation Ltd.: Gas, diesel, lubricants, water. 250-626-3328. VHF 18A.

★ **Queen Charlotte City:** [3890] The public floats are well protected. Rafting is usually neces-

Mother Grey Whale Statue, Prince Rupert   *Curt Johnson Photo*

sary. Fresh water and propane are available. This is the site of a Royal Canadian Mounted Police Station. Restaurants and coffee shops, a Credit Union, bank machine, many bed and breakfasts, laundry, liquor, clothing, and hardware stores are accessible. Artwork by local artists can be found in many of the shops. If you visit on the Saturday closest to June 21st, you can join in the fun during *Hospital Day*. A parade, games, races, and music are part of this annual event. Sleeping Beauty Mountain offers alpine hiking west of the city and a number of less challenging trails are located nearby. Scuba charters are available for exploring the area's crystal clear waters. Bike and kayak rentals are also popular. There is fishing in the Yakoun River and Yakoun Lake is a senic spot to explore. A boat launch is located halfway between the town and Skidegate Landing. Rennel Sound, on the west coast, can be accessed from this location. The road to Port Clements passes through the town of Tlell.

Tlell: This tiny community of artisans inlcudes shops, animal clinic, and restaurant. Beaches and sand dunes are lovely along the Tlell River. A good hike is to the shipwreck of the barge *Pezuta*. Site of the annual *Edge of the World Music Festival* in July.

★ **Port Clements:** An old Golden Spruce is located 3¹/₂ miles from the city. Lodging, restaurants, heritage museum, logging tours and groceries are available. Mayer Lake has fishing, boating, and picnic sites.

★ **Skidegate:** [3890] Ferry landing, lodging, restaurants, stores, and the Haida Gwaii Museum are located here. There are longhouses, the Bill

Reid Pole at the museum, Loo Taas Canoe at the Watchmen Office, and Haida arts and crafts shops.

Walk-around: The Spirit Lake trail makes a good family hike.

Skidgate Fueling: It is possible to have gas and diesel trucked to the government dock in Queen Charlotte City. Call the day before of the desired delivery day to make arrangements for fuel delivery at 250-559-4611 or VHF 6.

Skidgate Narrows: This passage is narrow, rocky, shallow, and well marked. If possible, follow a local boat through at high water slack. There is anchorage in Dawson Harbour, in five fathoms, behind the small island on the south side. There is a buoy at the east end of the narrows, on the south side.

★ **Sandspit & Moresby Island:** [3890, 3894] There is a basin for small craft. The majority of approaches to Sandspit Harbour are made from the east crossing Hecate Strait, over Dogfish Banks, into Skidegate Inlet, and direct to Sandspit. While the crossing can be "lumpy" at times, the prudent mariner with an eye on the weather and tides will have no problems with the well charted and marked channel. Lit ranges and other aids to navigation are waiting to guide you. Monitor weather channel VHF 3 for up-to-date information. Use Charts #3890 and #3894 and the North Coast Sailing Directions. This is the site of the airport and air transportation to, and from, Vancouver, Prince Rupert, and the Charlottes. There is lodging, provisions, a golf course, camping, swimming, and beachcombing at Gray Bay, or you can take a helicopter tour of the area. Groceries and rental cars can be delivered to the marina. A community visitor center, open May 1 to Labor Day, is located in the airport terminal. There is also a two man detachment of the R.C.M.P. in Sandspit, as well as a Coast Guard Marine Emergency Center. Sandspit Visitor Info: 250-637-5362.

★ **Sandspit Harbour:** {58° 14.3' N, 131° 51.8' W} Located just east of Haans Creek on Moresby Island. Moorage, gas, diesel, 15, 30, 50, & 100 ampere power, fresh water, waste pump-out, showers, launch ramp. Taxi and grocery delivery to moorage. Fishing and tour charters. Recreational activities nearby. See our Steering Star description in this chapter. Internet: www.sandspitqci.com/harbour & www.boattravel.com/sandspit/. E-mail: sandspit@island.net. Address: Post Office Box 477, Sandspit, British Columbia V0T IT0. Office: 250-637-2466. Harbour: 250-637-5700. Fax: 250-637-2460.

Sandspit and Sandspit Harbour   Sandspit / North Moresby Chamber of Commerce Photo

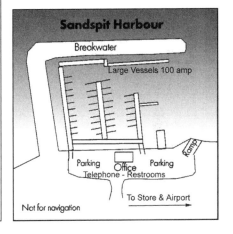

Sandspit Harbour

Breakwater

Large Vessels 100 amp

Parking   Office   Parking
Telephone - Restrooms

Ramp

To Store & Airport

Not for navigation

★ **Sandspit Harbour:** [3890, 3894] The gateway marina to the Gwaii Haanas National Park Reserve / Haida Heritage Site is a brand new, state-of-the-art facility. (53 14.3 N, 131 51.8 W , NAD 27) Situated in the heart of the picturesque Queen Charlotte Islands, Sandspit Harbour is ideally located for exploring the islands and Gwaii Haanas. Visitors take away fond memories of the natural beauty of the area and the

breathtaking island sunsets reflecting off the water around the harbour. Eighty-four slips are available for permanent and transient moorage, accommodating vessels up to 100' in length. Fuel: regular, premium gas & diesel are dispensed at the fuel dock; potable water, dockside electricity (15, 30, 50, 100 ampere), 2.5 ton lift, storage yard, seaplane float, restrooms, showers, garbage bins, waste pump-out, public phone and launching ramp are all located in this quiet, well-protected harbour. Spacious fairways allow for safe and easy maneuverability. Recreational activities such as deep sea and fresh water fishing, kayaking, canoeing, photography, scuba diving, hiking, mountain biking, sightseeing, whale or bird watching, golfing, beachcombing, helicopter tours, and many others are available right in Sandspit. Groceries, restaurants, pub, post office, liquor store, hair salon, cappuccino bar, propane, fishing supplies and licenses, marine supplies, airport, and lodging accommodations are located within two miles. Free grocery and rental car delivery to the harbour. When travelling the north coast of British Columbia, a stay at this modern, well equipped harbour is a must. **Circle #81 on Reader Service Card. Call ahead on VHF 73 to contact the Wharfinger. Internet: www.sandspitqci.com/harbour & www.boattravel.com/sandspit/ E-mail: sandspit@island.net or Address: Post Office Box 477, Sandspit, British Columbia V0T 1T0 Office: 250-637-2466. Fax: 250-637-2460. Harbour: 250-637-5700**

Essential Supplies & Services

AIR TRANSPORTATION
To & from Washington
Seattle Seaplanes **1-800-637-5553**
To & from Islands/Vancouver
Air Canada 1-888-247-2262
Pacific Coastal 1-800-663-2872
Vancouver Island Air . . 250-287-2433, 1-877-331-2433

AMBULANCES: 1-800-461-9911
Prince Rupert: 911

BOOKS / BOOK STORES
The Marine Atlas **541-593-6396**

BUS TRANSPORTATION
Kitimat (Coastal Buslines) 250-632-3333
Prince Rupert 250-624-5090, 250-624-3343
Queen Charlotte 250-559-4461, 1-877-747-4461

COAST GUARD
Emergencies . . . . 1-800-567-5111, VHF 16
Prince Rupert . . . . 250-627-3081, VHF 16, 22A
Cellphone: *16

CUSTOMS
Ketkchikan 907-225-2380, 907-225-2254
Prince Rupert 250-627-3003, 1-888-226-7277

DIVERS AIR:
God's Pocket: Hurst Is. . . . . . . 250-949-1755, VHF 73

FERRY INFORMATION
Alaska (U.S.) 800-642-0066
Alaska Ferries: (Call a.m.) 250-627-1744
B.C. Ferries . . . . 250-386-3431, 1-888-223-3779 (B.C.)
Prince Rupert-B.C. Ferries 250-624-9627

FUELS
Bella Bella Fuels: Gas, Diesel. 250-957-2440 VHF 6, 78A
Bella Coola: Gas, Diesel
Cow Bay Petro: P.R. Gas, Diesel. 250-624-4106 VHF 78
Dawsons Landing: Gas, Diesel.
. . . . **403-987-9058. VHF 6**
Duncanby Landing: Gas, Diesel . . 403-997-8516 VHF 6
Hartley Bay: Gas, Diesel. . . . 250-841-2675 VHF 6 (call)
Klemtu: Gas, Diesel . . . . 250-839-1233 VHF 6 (call)
M K Bay Marina: Kitimat. . . . . . 250-632-6401 VHF 66A
Masset: Gas, Diesel . . . . 250-626-3328 VHF 18A
Namu: Gas. . . . . 250-949-4090 VHF 10
Moon Bay: Kitimat. Gas, Diesel. . 250-632-4655 VHF 16
Ocean Fall: Gas, Diesel.
Prince Rupert ESSO: Gas, Diesel. 250-624-5000
Queen Charlotte City: Skidegate Esso delivers gas &
   diesel by truck . . . . 250-559-4611 VHF 6
Sandspit Harbour, Moresby Island: Gas, Diesel.
. . . . **250-637-5700**
Shearwater Marine Resort & Marine Centre: Gas.
   Diesel. AV fuel, jet fuel. . . . . . . 250-957-2305 VHF 6

GOLF COURSES
Hirsch Creek: 250-632-4653
Prince Rupert Centennial: 250-624-2000

HOSPITALS
Bella Coola 250-799-5311
Kitimat 250-632-2121
Prince Rupert 250-624-2171
Queen Charlotte 250-559-4300
   Emergency 250-559-4506

INSURANCE
Boat Insurance Agency **206-285-1350**
   Or Call **1-800-828-2446**

LIQUOR STORES
Bella Coola
Dawsons Landing
Duncanby Landing
Kemano
Kitimat
Masset
New Bella Bella
Prince Rupert
Queen Charlotte City
Stewart

LODGING
Dawsons Landing . . . . **403-987-9058 VHF 6**

MARINAS / MOORAGE FLOATS
Alice Arm
Alliford Bay: Moresby Island
Bella Bella Public Dock 250-957-2440
Bella Coola 250-799-5633
Cow Bay: P.R. 250-628-9220
Dawsons Landing . . . . **403-987-9058 VHF 6**
Duncanby Landing: . . . . 403-997-8516 VHF 6
Fairview Harbour: P.R. . . . . . 250-624-3127 VHF 16, 9
Hartley Bay: 250-841-2675
Hunt Inlet
Kincolith
Klemtu 250-839-1233
M K Bay Marina: Kitimat . . . . . . 250-632-6401 VHF 66A
Masset: Graham Island
Moon Bay Marina: Kitimat . . . . 250-632-4655 VHF 16
Namu . . . . 250-949-4090 VHF 10
New Bella Bella
Ocean Falls Public Dock . . . . . . 250-289-3859 VHF 9
Port Clements Village 250-557-4295
Port Edward 250-628-9220
Port Simpson
Prince Rupert Yacht Club . . . . . . 250-624-4317 VHF 72
Queen Charlotte City 250-559-4650
Rushbrooke: P.R. 250-624-9400
Sandspit Harbour: Moresby Island . . **250-637-5700**
Shearwater Resort Hotel/Marina
. . . . 250-957-2305 VHF 6, 66A
Skidegate: Moresby Island

POISON INFO: 250-624-2171

PROPANE
Duncanby Landing: . . . . 403-997-8516 VHF 6
K & K: Queen Charlotte City
Klemtu 250-839-1233
Masset . . . . 250-626-3328 VHF 18A
Prince Rupert Deltech Propane/Welding . 250-624-4301
Sandspit Harbour, Moresby Island . . **250-637-5700**
Shearwater Resort Hotel/Marina
. . . . 250-957-2305 VHF 6, 66A

RAMPS / HAUL-OUTS
Alliford Bay
Copper Bay
M K Bay Marina: Kitimat 250-632-6401
Masset North Arm Trans. 250-626-3328
Moon Bay Marina: Kitimat . . . . 250-632-4655 VHF 16
Ocean Falls
P.R. Deltech 250-624-4301
Rushbrooke: P.R. 250-624-9400
Sandspit
Shearwater Resort Hotel & Marina
. . . . 250-957-2305 VHF 6, 66A

REPAIRS
Apex Marine: P.R. . . . . 250-627-7978 VHF 16
Bytown Diesel: P.R. 250-627-1304
Command Marine: Kitimat. . . . . 250-632-6676 VHF 74
Don's Marine: Sandspit 250-637-5432
McLean's Shipyard: P.R. 250-624-3142
R G's Marine: Kitimat. 250-632-7722
Rocky's Equipment Sales: Queen Charlotte City
. . . . 250-559-8311
Sea Sport: PR. 250-624-5337
Shearwater Marine Ltd. . . . . 250-957-2305 VHF 6, 66A

RESCUE: 800-567-5111

SEWAGE DISPOSAL
Bella Coola
Sandspit Harbour, Moresby Island . . **250-637-5700**

SHELLFISH HOTLINE
Bella Bella 250-957-2363
Bella Coola. 250-799-5345
Masset. 250-626-3316
Prince Rupert 250-627-3499
Queen Charlotte City 250-559-4413

TAXI
Prince Rupert Skeena Taxi . . . . . . 250-624-2185 VHF 8

TOWING
C-TOW **1-888-354-5554**
Hartley Bay . . . . 250-841-2675 VHF 6, 60
Shearwater Marine Ltd . . . . . 250-957-2305 VHF 6, 66A

VHF MARINE OPERATOR
Barry Inlet: VHF 26   Bella Bella: VHF 25
Bella Coola: VHF 24   Burnaby Island: VHF 3
Calvert Island: VHF 23   Cape Caution: VHF 2
Cape St. James: VHF 24   Cumshewa: VHF 84
Denny Island: VHF 01   Dundas Island: VHF 85
Gil Island: VHF 60   Grenville Channel: VHF 24
Griffin Point: VHF 85   Hopkins Point: VHF 24
King Island: VHF 28   Klemtu: VHF 84
Langara: VHF 3   Louise Island: VHF 64
Masset: VHF 24   Mount Dent: VHF 84
Mount Gill: VHF 26   Mount Hays: VHF 84
Naden Harbour: VHF 84   Namu: VHF 60
Noble Mountain: VHF 2   Pearse Island: VHF 60
Prince Rupert: VHF 25, 27   Rennell Sound: VHF 86
River's Inlet: VHF 3   Smith Sound: VHF 85
Swindle Island: VHF 87   Tasu: VHF 25
Trutch Island: VHF 86   Van Inlet: VHF 26

VISITOR INFORMATION
Gwaii Haanas 250-559-8818
Kitimat 800-664-6554
Klemtu 877-644-2346,250-839-2346
Prince Rupert 250-624-5637, 800-667-1994
Queen Charlotte City 250-559-8316
Sandspit 250-637-5362

WEATHER
Barry Island, Calvert Island: VHF WX-2
Cumshewa: VHF WX-4, Dundas Island: VHF WX-2
Kitimat: VHF WX-4, (Recorded) 250-632-7864
Klemtu: VHF WX-1
Langara Island, Mt. Gil: VHF WX-2
Prince Rupert: VHF 21, WX-2 (Recorded) 250-624-9009
Sandspit, Morsby Island: VHF 3
Swindle Island, Van Inlet: VHF WX-1

Chapter 20:

Southeast Alaska

Portland Canal to Lynn Canal, Ketchikan, Wrangell, Petersburg, Juneau, Haines, Skagway, Sitka, Craig, Misty Fjords, Ford's Terror, Glacier Bay. Prince of Wales, Kupreanof, Admiralty, & Baranof Islands.

Symbols

[   ]: Numbers between [ ] are chart numbers.

{   }: Numbers & letters between { } are waypoints.

⚓: Park, ⛴: Boat Launch, ▲: Campgrounds, 🅇: Hiking Trails, ⛱: Picnic Area, 🚲: Biking

Important Notices

★ **Important Notice:** See "Important Notices" between Chapters 7 and 8 in this guide for specific information on boating related topics such as: Canadian & U.S. Customs, boating safety and security, navigation, weather, U.S. & Canadian Coast Guard, U.S & Canadian marine radio use, Vessel Traffic Service and traffic separation plans, security zones, and internet access. Due to new Department of Homeland Security regulations, call ahead for latest customs information and/or see Northwest Boat Travel On-line, www.nwboat.com.

We recommend the following NOAA publications, now published by International Marine: *Tide Tables West Coast of North and South America* and *Tidal Current Tables Pacific Coast of North America and Asia.*

Airline Connections: There is passenger and cargo plane service by jet to six airports in Southeast Alaska: Ketchikan, Wrangell, Petersburg, Sitka, Juneau, & Gustavus.

Chart List

Canadian Hydrographic Charts:

3779

NOAA Charts:

17300, 17301, 17303, 17314-17318, 17320-17324, 17331, 17333, 17336-17339, 17360, 17362, 17363, 17367, 17375, 17378, 17384, 17385, 17387, 17400, 17403-17405, 17407, 17408, 17420, 17422-17424, 17426, 17428, 17430-17438

Marine Atlas Volume 2 (2005 ed.):

Pages 29-66

Alaska Department of Fish & Game/Sportfish: Headquarters: 907-465-4180, Craig: 907-826-2498, Douglas: 907-465-4270, Ketchikan: 907-225-2859, Petersburg: 907-772-3801, Juneau: 907-465-4180, Haines: 907-766-2625, Sitka: 907-747-5355, Klawock: 907-826-2498, Yakutat: 907-784-3222. Website: www.adfg.state.ak.us.

Alaska State Parks: 907-465-4563. Website: www. dnr.state.ak.us/parks/.

Charts and publications: In addition to the charts for the waters in which one intends to cruise, three publications from the National Oceanic and Atmospheric Administration (NOAA) are absolute necessities. They are: (1) the latest edition of the United States Coast Pilot 8; (2) Tidal Tables, West Coast of North and South America; and (3) Tidal Current Tables, Pacific Coast of North America and Asia. It is best to obtain all of these, including the charts, before leaving your home port, although they may be purchased in Ketchikan at Tongass Trading Company and in Thorne Bay at the Thorne Bay Company.

Crossing the border: The border between British Columbia and Alaska is about two miles north of the north end of Dundas Island, in Dixon Entrance. The exposure to the Pacific Ocean continues until one is behind Duke Island, a distance of about 20 miles. The United States Coast Pilot 8 gives the mileage from Seattle to the border as 615 miles. The distance between Seattle and Juneau is 900 miles. A few years ago Alaska changed from the Pacific time zone to Alaska time zone, and they are now one hour behind British Columbia and the rest of the west coast. The Customs Port-of-Entry is Ketchikan (907-225-2254) Have passports or birth certificates ready to show.

Fishing licenses: Everyone who fishes in salt or fresh water in Alaska must purchase a license sold at sporting goods stores. There are four different types of licenses depending on the length of time desired. These range from one to 14 days, or an annual license. Fees are from $10-$100. If fishing for King salmon, the King Salmon Stamp Program is in effect and an extra charge is collected. A hunting license is required and hunters will need locking tags, and the required permits. 907-465-2376. To obtain fishing licenses on-line, go to: www.state.ak.us.

Glacier Bay Information: Glacier Bay National Park Superintendent, Post Office Box 140, Gustavus, Alaska 99826. Telephone: 907-697-2230, 907-697-2627, VHF 16. Request entry permits or publication *Glacier Bay Park Handbook.* Emergency (after hours): 907-697-2651. Website: www.nps.gov/glba/.

Health and Safety Guides For Alaska Visitors: *Help Along the Way*—*"Emergency Medical Services for Alaska Travelers"* (which provides information for travelers on the road system, along with some marine highway contact information) and *Basic Medical Resources*—*"A Guide to the Medical Resources of Ports Served by Cruise Line Vessels".* Both are available on the Internet at www.chems.alaska.gov. Go to EMS site, click on EMS downloads, then Misc. Contact the Division of Public Health, Section of Community Health and EMS, PO Box 110616, Juneau, Alaska 99811-0616. Telephone: 907-465-3027.

Misty Fjords Information: *Misty Fjords National Wilderness Map R-10-RG-11.* This publication contains a wealth of information regarding specific buoy and float locations, geology, climate, ecosystems, special features, history, volcanic activity, picturesque areas, and more. Call Alaska Natural History Association for informative and educational materials 907-228-6233. Call Alaska Discovery Center for general information on Alaska public lands. 907-228-6220.

Paralytic Shellfish Poisoning Information: There is no designated hotline number to call in regard to which beaches are closed to shellfish harvesting. The Environmental Health Department warns that although Alaska has a significant problem with poisonous shellfish, beaches are not monitored or tested. DO NOT eat shellfish in S.E. Alaska, except cleaned and properly cooked crabs. For more information, contact the Environmental Conservation Department in Anchorage: 907-269-7501, 907-269-7638.

United States Forest Service Cabins: Tongass National Forest has more than 130 public recreation cabins. Many of them have salt water, as well as float plane access. They are available for a very reasonable fee per night, and are very popular. The cabins must be reserved in advance. Using a cabin without having the required permit for the day of use can result in a large fine and six months in jail. Application for cabin reservations may be submitted up to 180 days in advance by calling 1-877-444-6777 or visiting any Forest Service office in Alaska. Use is limited to seven days April 1-October 31 and ten days at other times.

Weather Information: See information at the end of this chapter under Essential Supplies and Services. If you are in a location where you cannot receive any of these stations, you can call NOAA Juneau 907-586-3997 and receive a continuous tape about weather conditions in Southeast Alaska. National Weather Service Weather Line: 1-800-472-0391; press 4 for Southeast Alaska; press 2 for marine weather & observations.

Wildlife: Humpback whales, Orca whales, Stellar sea lions, harbor seals, Dall porpoises, harbor porpoises, sea otters, river otters, black bears, brown bears, and bald eagles, and many other varieties of birds are found in the region. Bring along guide books to use when identifying the abundant marine and bird life.

Introduction

★ **Southeast Alaskan Panhandle:** [17300, 17320, 17360, 17400, 17420] Hundreds of islands and inlets are found among the more than 11,000 miles of coastline contained in southeast Alaska. The entire territory is over 400 miles long and about 125 miles wide. The majority of channels are wide and deep. Hundreds of freighters, ferries, cruise ships, tugs and barges, fishing boats, and pleasure craft ply this marine highway each year. Sixty percent of the region consists of hundreds of islands covered with dense deep-green forests of spruce, hemlock and cedar. Above the timberline on the mainland are snow-capped peaks and glaciers moving slowly down the valleys to the sea. Southeastern Alaska lies at the same latitude as Scotland, Denmark, and southern Sweden. Warmed by ocean currents, this region experiences relatively mild, warm summers with July temperatures averaging about 60 degrees. An occasional heat wave may go into the 80's. Winters are cool but not severely cold, sub-zero temperatures being uncommon. The region experiences considerable rainfall, averaging more than 160 inches annually with the heaviest in late fall and a lighter average in summer. Almost all of Southeast Alaska lies within the 16 million acre Tongass National Forest, the largest National Forest in the United States. The forests of the region provide one of Southeastern's three major industries, timber harvesting. Fishing and fish processing are the second major industry. Government is the third. Tourism is also a major contributor to the economy. Seventy five percent of the population lives in the five major communities of Juneau, Ketchikan, Petersburg, Sitka and Wrangell. More than 20 percent of the population are native Indians. The Forget-Me-Not is the state flower and the Sitka Spruce is the state tree. By way of interest, the Sitka Spruce can grow to 49 feet in circumference and 213 feet in height. The state flag, a deep blue with stars in the pattern of the Big Dipper was designed by a 13 year old boy. The Big Dipper, part of the constellation Ursa Major or the "Big Bear" connotes strength and the North Star represents the most northern state and its bright future. Alaska was purchased from Russia in 1867 for only $7.2 million (a bargain at two cents an acre!). Sitka was the first capital city. Juneau is the capital today.

Portland Inlet, Canal, & Pearse Canal
[17420, 17425, 17427]

Portland Inlet & Portland Canal: This inlet begins five miles north of Port Simpson and continues for 90 miles north to the Ports of Stewart, British Columbia and Hyder, Alaska. The scenery at the head of Portland Canal is beautiful, with mountain peaks over 7,000 feet, covered by glaciers and large snow fields. A problem facing any boater going to the head of the canal is the wind that often blows up or down, the waterway with considerable force. When the wind blows against the tide it can create very uncomfortable condi-

tions. Good anchorages are rare in Portland Canal. The international boundary more or less follows the center of the canal. If planning to fish both sides of Portland Canal for salmon, you'll need both Alaskan and British Columbia fishing licenses.

★ **Halibut Bay (Alaska):** This is the best anchorage in Portland Canal. It is 47 miles north of Port Simpson and 46 miles south of Stewart. Anchorage is possible in seven fathoms, good holding bottom, on the west side of the bay. However, if the wind is blowing up the canal, as it often does, seas will come right into the anchorage.

★ **Whiskey Bay (British Columbia):** This little cove at the north end of Pearse Island offers anchorage in five to seven fathoms, soft bottom when the wind is blowing in Pearse and Portland Canals. There is protection from all but north winds. In a north wind, go down Pearse Canal, with the seas behind you, to Winter Inlet, also on Pearse Island.

Pearse Canal: Lies between Pearse Island, British Columbia, and the Alaska mainland. The international boundary runs down the canal. These waters are more protected than those of Portland Canal and Inlet.

Hidden Inlet (Alaska): Ruins of a former cannery are on the north shore of the canal west of Hidden Inlet. The currents in and out of Hidden Inlet are very strong.

★ **Winter Inlet (British Columbia):** This inlet, at the west end of Pearse Island, offers good, protected anchorage in seven fathoms, on mud bottom.

★ **Wales Island (British Columbia):** Anchorage can be found in Wales Harbour and near Swaine Point.

★ **Wales Harbor (British Columbia):** On the north side of Wales Island. Good anchorage in eleven fathoms, on mud, at the head of the harbor.

★ **Swaine Point (British Columbia):** Anchorage in seven fathoms of water with fair shelter is possible in the small bight immediately west of this point on the east side of Wales Island. Good salmon fishing may be found at Swaine Point.

★ **Regina Cove (Alaska):** Offers protected anchorage in ten fathoms, on the north side of Pearse Canal.

★ **Nakat Harbor (Alaska):** Finding the entrance to the harbor can be tricky. This bay, on the east side of Nakat Bay, has anchorage in 12 fathoms, mud bottom, at the head of the north arm. It has some protection, but not from south or southwest winds. Anchorage is also possible in the southwest arm, between the mainland and the island to the west in ten fathoms just short of the rock that bares four feet. It is well protected with a good holding bottom.

★ **Hyder, Alaska:** Located at the head of Portland Canal, this town once bustled with the business of mining. By the mid-1950's most of the major mines had closed. Today, tourism is the mainstay of this community known as the "Friendliest Ghost Town in Alaska." Recreational fishing and hunting, heliskiing, snowmobiling, camping, and hiking are among the possible activities. Hyder has a post office, library, museum, restaurants and bars, and motels. Moorage is available. While the ferry no

longer stops here, bus service to Terrace and float plane service to Ketchikan are available.

★ **Stewart, British Columbia:** Moorage, lodging, restaurants, and groceries. This is a place of natural beauty and friendly people. This community is connected to the rest of British Columbia by paved road. Highway 37 to Cassiar goes near the Grand Canyon of Stikine, regarded as spectacular land formations in British Columbia. Dease Lake or Iskut are day trips. Another picnic site is Bear Glacier, which laps into a turquoise blue lake between Stewart and Meziadin Lake. It is a 60-minute drive to Salmon Glacier, the 5th largest glacier in the world that is accessible by road. The films *Bear Island*, and *The Thing From Planet X* were photographed here. Around 1910, settlers came here dreaming of gold and furs. Chamber of Commerce: 250-636-9224, 888-366-5999.

Dixon Entrance To Wrangell
[17420, 17434]

★ **Foggy Bay, Very Inlet (1):** [17434] Use United States Coast Pilot when entering Foggy Bay. Hundreds of gill netters fish the Tree Point area. Stretched nets are a hazard. The bay, a mile south of Very Inlet, has a tiny, narrow, but deep entrance. Anchorage is possible in 30-40 feet on a sticky mud bottom. Favored anchorage is behind an islet on the east side. The north entrance is the deepest. The south entrance bares at half-tide and should not be attempted. There is good protection from seas in Revillagigedo Channel. A Fish and Game Warden is stationed here most of the summer. It is possible to explore Very Inlet.

★ **Kah Shakes Cove (2):** [17434] This anchorage, named for a Tlingit Chief, is about 30 miles south of Ketchikan. Several rocky islets extend in a westerly direction off the north side of the cove. The entrance is narrow, but the chart is an adequate guide. Favored anchorage is eastward of the two inner points. Some swells may come in from the south in the area farther westward and closer to the entrance. Excellent clamming beds near the entrance uncover at a plus five foot tide. Anchorage depths are 35-45 feet on a sandy mud bottom. Good holding in winds. Loons, eagles, minks, and seals frequent this area. A smokehouse is available for use. The user must provide his own alder.

★ **Boca de Quadra:** This is off the beaten path. The 25 mile long inlet, and its five smaller inlets, provide intriguing cruising waters and several good anchorages. Entrance is between Slate Island Light on the north side and White Reef on the south side. An alternate, if coming from the south, is to pass to the east side of Black Rock Light and White Reef. There are no facilities for boaters in Boca de Quadra. A sport fishing camp is located at the entrance to Mink Bay.

★ **Vixen Bay:** The anchorage is toward the head between Raven Island and Gosling Island, on the east side of the bay in 12 fathoms, soft bottom, good protection.

★ **Mink Bay:** Anchorages are in the cove on the west side at the entrance, just south of Cygnet Island in eight fathoms, mud bottom, good protection, and at the head of Mink Bay in 10 to 15 fathoms. This anchorage is just south of the tidal flat that extends almost across the inlet. Caution must be observed when passing the flats.

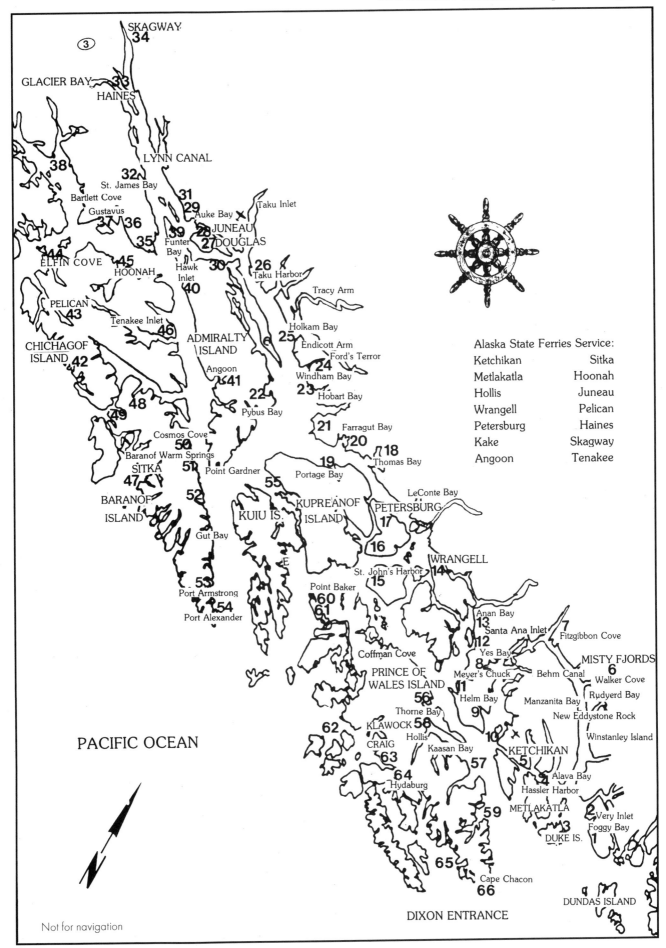

③

SKAGWAY
34

GLACIER BAY
33
HAINES

LYNN CANAL

38

32
St. James Bay
31
Bartlett Cove   29
Gustavus   Auke Bay ✕   Taku Inlet
37 36   28 JUNEAU
35   39   27 DOUGLAS
Funter
Bay   26
ELFIN COVE   45   30   Taku Harbor
HOONAH   Hawk
Inlet
40   Tracy Arm
PELICAN
43   Holkam Bay
Tenakee Inlet   25
46   ADMIRALTY   Endicott Arm
CHICHAGOF   ISLAND   Ford's Terror
ISLAND   42   24
Angoon   Windham Bay
41
22   23 Hobart Bay
48
49   Pybus Bay
Cosmos Cove   21   Farragut Bay
50   20
Baranof Warm Springs   19   18
SITKA   Thomas Bay
47   51 Point Gardner   Portage Bay
BARANOF   55
ISLAND   52   KUPREANOF   LeConte Bay
KUIU IS.   ISLAND   PETERSBURG
Gut Bay   17
16
E   WRANGELL
St. John's Harbor   14
53   15
Port Armstrong   Point Baker
54   60   Anan Bay
Port Alexander   61   13
Santa Ana Inlet   7 Fitzgibbon Cove
12
Coffman Cove   Yes Bay   8 Behm Canal   MISTY FJORDS
PRINCE OF   Meyer's Chuck   6
WALES ISLAND   11   Manzanita Bay Walker Cove
Helm Bay   Rudyerd Bay
56   9   New Eddystone Rock
Thorne Bay   58   Winstanley Island
62 KLAWOCK   Hollis   10
CRAIG   Kaasan Bay   KETCHIKAN
63   57   5
64   Alava Bay
Hydaburg   4 Hassler Harbor
59   METLAKATLA   2 Very Inlet
3   Foggy Bay
DUKE IS.   1
65
Cape Chacon
66   DUNDAS ISLAND

PACIFIC OCEAN

Alaska State Ferries Service:
Ketchikan   Sitka
Metlakatla   Hoonah
Hollis   Juneau
Wrangell   Pelican
Petersburg   Haines
Kake   Skagway
Angoon   Tenakee

DIXON ENTRANCE

Not for navigation

Boca de Quadra and Marten Arm: These two inlets extending 15 and 5 miles respectively from Bactrian Point, are very scenic, but too deep for anchorage.

★ **Weasel Cove:** Good protected anchorage in 16 fathoms, soft bottom with plenty of room.

Ray Anchorage, Duke Island (3): [17434] This anchorage is sheltered from south winds, but open to the northeast. Anchorage is on a hard bottom in 10 to 20 fathoms of water.

★ **Morse Cove:** This cove to the west is protected and has a mud bottom. The entrance is narrow and rock strewn. It is wise to consult the United States Coast Pilot 8 and Chart #17434 before considering anchorage in Morse Cove. Foggy Bay, across Revillagigedo Channel, is a better choice of anchorage.

★ **Moth Bay:** This is a good anchorage at the entrance to Thorne Arm, about 13 miles south of Ketchikan. Relatively protected anchorage in ten fathoms, mud bottom.

★ **Thorne Arm:** [17428] This ten mile long inlet is entered between Moth Point and Cone Point, about 11 1/2 miles southeast of Ketchikan. The head of the arm is broad with relatively low shores. Several anchorages are possible at the head of the arm. The most protected is on the west side of the northernmost of the Minx Islands in eight to ten fathoms, soft bottom. There are two Forest Service buoys, and a Forest Service cabin on the east side of the arm.

★ **Carroll Inlet:** [17428] Twenty miles in length, this inlet is the most scenic of the three inlets on the southwest side of Revillagigedo Island, with high mountains on both sides at its head.

Anchorage is possible in Gnat Cove, six miles up the inlet on the east side in seven to eight fathoms, with good protection. Two more anchorages are two and a half miles farther north. One is in the area just north of Osten Island, protected by an unnamed island to the east and reefs to the west. Anchorage is in six to ten fathoms, soft bottom. The second is 1/2 mile northwest on the Revillagigedo Island shore between two small islands, in three to four fathoms. Anchorage would also be possible off the flats at the head of the inlet, subject to winds up or down the inlet.

★ **George Inlet & Coon Cove:** [17428] This 12 mile long inlet lies north of Mountain Point, four miles southeast of Ketchikan. The best anchorage in the inlet is in the cove north of Bat Point, at the head of the inlet, in ten fathoms, mud bottom, and excellent protection. Anchorage is also possible in Coon Cove on the east side of the inlet in 10 to 13 fathoms, with good protection.

Annette Island & Hassler Harbor (4): [17434]. Located between Pow Island and Annette Island, Hassler Harbor offers shelter from southeast winds, with a good holding bottom in ten fathoms. Page 28 of United States Coast Pilot 8 states that this anchorage may be used only in an emergency, because the old hulk anchored here is used for explosives storage. Metlakatla, also on Annette Island, is the site of a fuel facility. See description of Metlakatla at (67).

Ketchikan
[17420, 17428, 17430]

★ **Ketchikan (5):** See customs and berthage information below. Ketchikan, "Alaska's First City," is located on Revillagigedo Island and is a customs port. Ketchikan Creek, running through the heart of town, was originally the site of a fish camp used by Tlingit Natives. During the 1880's the settlement grew as logging and fishing became lucrative industries. Today, Ketchikan is the state's fourth largest city and is known for its scenic beauty, spectacular sports fishing, rich native culture, and ample "liquid sunshine"--over 160 inches annually! That rainfall helps maintain the lush, green vegetation of the surrounding Tongass National Forest, the United State's largest national forest. The community of Ketchikan is built along the waterfront (often on pilings) and up the hillsides that overlook the channel. There are many things to see and do within the city limits and most are accessible on foot. There is a public bus, as well as several taxi services and even a seasonal horse-drawn trolley ride. Rental cars are also available, 907-225-5000. Downtown Ketchikan offers a number of shops and services including restaurants, cafes, bars, a movie theater, marine hardware store, banks, and library with internet access. Visitors will enjoy the museum, featuring artifacts and exhibits illustrating local history, art, and native culture. 907-225-5600. The Southeast Alaska Discovery Center also has exhibits, as well as a native artist in residence. Here one can obtain trip planning services and information regarding cabin rentals. 907-228-6220. Other downtown attractions include the Great Alaskan Lumberjack Show where log-rolling contestants often take a dip and Dolly's House Museum which offers a glimpse into the days when Creek Street was the town's red light district. From Creek Street, a tram provides panoramic views on its way up to Westmark Cape Fox Lodge and Restaurant. Within walking distance of downtown one can view the Ketchikan Mural or visit the Totem Heritage Center featur-

Totem Bight Park, Ketchikan

ing historic poles and native carvers. 907-225-5900. The nearby city park is the site of the Deer Mt. Tribal Hatchery and Eagle Center. Charters, tours, flight seeing, sightseeing; every activity from A (amphibious tours) to Z (zip line adventures) can be arranged. The Visitor's Bureau on the wooden dock at 131 Front Street, open daily May – September, has information, brochures, maps, coupons and more.   907-225-6166. Ketchikan has the largest collection of totem poles in the world and some of the most magnificent examples are found at Totem Bight Park (10 miles North Tongass Highway) and Saxman Village (2.5 miles South Tongass Highway). Hiking opportunities for all fitness levels abound here. Ward Lake trail, located 8 miles north of town, is great for beginners. Not far from downtown, the Deer Mountain Trail, with its series of switchbacks, poses a much bigger challenge. Local events include the *Fourth of July* celebration with parade, food and game booths, contests, fireworks, and the popular Logger's Timber Carnival. The *Blueberry Festival* occurs each August and features local arts and crafts. Ketchikan has an airport providing jet service and an Alaska State ferry terminal.

★ **Customs Check-in at Ketchikan:** If you are traveling north, you will be re-entering the United States. The captain is required to call U.S. Customs immediately upon arrival. A duty officer is available 24 hours-a-day. If the phone is answered by a message machine, contact information will be provided. The Customs Office is open from 8:00 a.m. to 5:00 p.m. seven days a week. Telephone: 907-225-2254. Customs suggests that, to avoid delays, customs decals be purchased prior to visiting Alaska. The captain may be asked to come to the Customs Office in the U.S. Courthouse and Federal Building, 648 Mission Street, Ste. 101. Be sure to ask for directions. Sometimes, clearance is possible by phone. You will need your boat registration or documentation number, Canadian customs clearance number, pet vaccination records, the number of your current United States Customs decal, and passports or birth certificates.

Berthage Information: See www.city.ketchikan. ak.us for information and site maps. Transient moorage is available in Ketchikan at Thomas Basin, Ketchikan Yacht Club, Casey Moran Harbor (City Float), Hole-In-The-Wall,   Bar Harbor South, and Bar Harbor North. Water and power are not available at all moorages. Call for available power meters. Garbage dumpster provided. All transient moorage (except at the Ketchikan Yacht Club) is parallel to the dock unless a finger slip is assigned by the harbormaster. See paragraphs below. The Ketchikan Harbormaster is located in Bar Harbor, north of town. VHF 16, 73. Telephone: 907-228-5632. If you are moored some distance from Bar Harbor, you can phone in a credit card number to pay for moorage.

Thomas Basin: The historic downtown area of Ketchikan is located between Thomas Basin and Casey Moran Harbor. Thomas Basin has the south side of Float 4, which is the second float inside the breakwater, designated for transient boats. Water & power available in some places. Restaurants, grocery store, laundromat, welding shop all within walking distance. Tidal grid, 2 ton hoist, reservations required. Telephone: 907-228-5632. VHF 16, 73.

Ketchikan Yacht Club (in Thomas Basin): Visitor's moorage is on Float 2, the fourth float inside the breakwater. Call the number posted on the clubhouse wall for assignment.

Ketchikan   *VPLLC Staff Photo*

Hole-In-The-Wall Floats: Moorage to 40-feet. Located seven miles south of the city center. 907-228-5632. VHF 16, 73. No power or water.

Ryus Float: Located at the city center. This is a loading zone.

Casey Moran Harbor (City Float): North of Thomas Basin. Customs check-in. Twenty & 30 ampere power, water, waste oil tank, and a pump-out are available. Exposed to wind, especially if on the outside. There is a great deal of wash here from passing boats. 907-228-5632. VHF 16, 73.

Ketchikan Bar Harbor Facilities: Located one mile north of Casey Moran Harbor (City Float). Close to post office, supermarket, motels, laundry, showers, restaurants and repairs. Moorage to 80-feet, water, some power, telephone at head of ramp. Tidal grid, boat launch nearby. 907-228-5632. VHF 16, 73.

Andres Oil: Gas, diesel, mix, oils, lubricants, filters, batteries, water filters, shower, restroom. 907-225-2163.

Ketchikan Petro Alaska: Gas, diesel, propane, ice, bait, convenience store, liquor. 907-225-1985. VHF 16.

Tongass Narrows: [17428, 17420] Shoals extend from both shores, but they are well marked. This is a busy waterway with an enforced speed limit of seven knots. On shore, Tongass Avenue parallels the channel. The pulp mill in Ward Cove has been shut down. There are no facilities for pleasure craft. A marina is located in Refuge Cove, the next bay to the north.

Air Marine Harbor: Limited moorage, repairs, marine ways, haul-outs to 55-tons, dry storage for airplanes and boats. 907-225-2282. VHF 16, 66.

★ **Misty Fjords National Monument (6):** [17422, 17424, 17434] This is one of 18 National Monuments in Alaska. This area east of Ketchikan includes eastern Behm Canal, Rudyerd Bay and Walker Cove. This is a beautiful area, off the beaten path, and worth taking extra time to explore. There are glaciers, mountain peaks which rise to 3,000 feet, three main rivers and

many small streams, brown bears, black bears, Sitka black tailed deer, wolves, mountain goats, porpoises, whales, sea lions, and seals. A continuation around the north end of Revillagigedo Island and down western Behm Canal will circumnavigate the island, ending in Clarence Strait, just north of Ketchikan. Stops can be made at the many anchorages in the area. There are some mooring buoys and floats. Mooring buoys can be found at Alava Bay, Anchor Pass, Bailey Bay, Blind Pass, Ella Bay, Princess Bay, Winstanley Island, and Burroughs Bay. Check the fishing regulations before fishing in the eastern portion of Behm Canal. Some areas may be closed to salmon fishing. One popular area to fish for Coho, sockeye, pink, king, and chum salmon is the western part of Behm Canal.

★ **Alava Bay:** This is the site of a Forest Service cabin. There is a large white can buoy on which to tie, or there is good anchorage. This is a sheltered spot in a southeast wind.

★ **Sykes Cove:** On the east side of the entrance to the east arm of Behm Canal, this anchorage is in seven fathoms with protection from all but northeast winds.

★ **Winstanley Island:** Anchorage is possible in Shoalwater Pass between the island and the mainland. The best choice is the northern anchorage, where the shoal at the entrance has a least depth of nine feet. Anchorage is on the west side of the passage in seven fathoms, mud bottom, and good protection. A Forest Service cabin and a mooring buoy are located here.

New Eddystone Rock: This prominent feature in Behm Canal was named in 1793 by Captain George Vancouver. The rock's unusual conformation reminded him of Eddystone Lighthouse off Plymouth, England. The rock is 237 feet high. There are shoals extending off the base of the rock.

★ **Rudyerd Bay:** Spectacular cliffs and waterfalls are found here, especially in Punch Bowl Cove. A private mooring buoy is located in Punch Bowl Cove.

McBride Glacier, Muir Inlet. A "giant river of ice moving to the sea."   Betty Guill Photo

★ **Manzanita Bay:** Located on the west shore of Behm Canal, anchorage is possible in 15 fathoms in the cove in the southeast corner. Exposure to northeast winds, soft bottom. The former State of Alaska float and mooring buoy have been removed, but the Forest Service cabin remains on the north shore.

★ **Walker Cove:** Farther along Behm Canal, this is another scenic inlet. Summer anchorage is possible in the entrance to the cove, in six and one-half to twenty fathoms of water. There is usually good bottom fishing to be had on the shoal at the entrance. There is a private buoy in a bight on the south side of the cove.

★ **Fitzgibbon Cove (7):** [17424] At the north end of eastern Behm Canal there is an excellent and beautiful anchorage in 11 to 13 fathoms of water, with a mud bottom. The warnings in the United States Coast Pilot 8 should be noted before entering.

★ **Anchor Pass:** Anchorage is possible in three fathoms, soft bottom, in the little cove on the west side, just south of the restricted north entrance to Anchor Pass. The least depth in this pass is only one and one half feet.

Bell Island: The former resort located on this island is now private, not open to the public.

★ **Bailey Bay:** This deep bay off Bell Arm has a lovely waterfall at the head. Buoys are located here.

★ **Short Bay:** East of Bailey Bay, this bay has good anchorage in 17 to 20 fathoms of water near its head. A privately maintained mooring buoy is near the flat.

★ **Yes Bay (8):** [17422] This bay has anchorage in the cove south of the first narrow spot. Depths are about eight fathoms. The bottom is mud. It is recommended that newcomers navigate the bay at low tide, when the rocks are visible. Enter in mid channel and then favor the north shore. Pass 40 yards south-southwest of the resort and favor the north shore until the basin opens up.

Yes Bay Lodge: Emergency gas, water., lodging,

restaurant, internet, fishing tours.907-247-1575.

★ **Hassler Pass:** The unnamed bay on the east side of this pass has anchorage in 11 fathoms, well protected, and soft bottom. Beware of shoals on all sides of the head of the cove. There are some beautiful tall trees left in this cove.

★ **Spacious Bay:** Anchorage is possible in eight to ten fathoms between Square Island and the mainland. Exposed to north and southeast, but satisfactory in settled weather, soft bottom.

★ **Helm Bay Float (9):** [17422] A 10 by 100 foot state float, located in Helm Bay, 20 miles from Ketchikan, has no facilities and no shore access. It is used as a haven in a storm for layover purposes. Sometimes this float is crowded on weekends. At low tide, the shore side of the float is in shallow moorage depth.

★ **Naha Bay & Loring:** This is a popular sport fishing and hunting area. There are floats without power or water at Loring, the site of a former mining town. The floats are exposed and depths may be shallow. A trail leads through beautiful forests along Roosevelt Lagoon. The lagoon can be entered at high tide, slack water. Anchorage is possible between Dogfish Island and Revillagigedo Island in fifteen fathoms, good protection, or at the head of Naha Bay, where there is also a small Forest Service float. A trail leads to Heckman Lake.

★ **Moser Bay:** Anchorage is possible in the bight on the west side of the entrance to this bay in seven fathoms, soft bottom, and well protected. The small cove is crowded by some old float houses, and there are several houses on shore. A small art gallery features local art work. Walking trails lead through the forest around the bay.

★ **Clover Pass Vicinity (10):** [17422] Fishing resorts and anchorages are located here. Knudson Cove Resort and Clover Pass Resort are connected by highway and by telephone to Ketchikan.

★ **Knudson Cove:** Located 15-miles north of Ketchikan, this small bay on the south side of

Clover Passage offers good anchorage in four fathoms of water. Day beacons mark the entrance. The city of Ketchikan maintains small craft floats on the east side of Knudson Cove. No water or power. They are usually very crowded. Launch ramps nearby. Harbormaster: 907-228-5632. VHF 16.

Knudson Cove Marina: Moorage limited small crafts only. Gas, diesel, water, coffee shop, provisions, lodging. 907-247-8500. VHF 16.

Clover Pass Resort: Moorage, gas, diesel, water, restaurant, laundry, showers, lodging, RV sites. Internet access. fish processing. 907-247-2234.

Clarence Strait
[17420, 17423]

Clarence Strait: This strait can be dangerous in some winds. It is well to check the weather forecasts from Ketchikan, before starting out on the 21 mile trip from Caamano Point to Lemesurier Point, at the entrance to Ernest Sound. Plan ahead for places to hide, if need be, along both sides of the strait. The strait itself is over 100 miles long and about 15 miles wide, at the south end, and five to six miles wide, in the northwest reaches. Flood is from the south, ebb from the northwest. Currents can reach four knots. When wind and strong tidal currents oppose each other, the result can be extremely rough conditions.

★ **Meyers Chuck (11):** [17423] Meyers Chuck is a small harbor 40 miles northwest of Ketchikan, on the east side of Clarence Strait. Its shelter can be a welcome relief if high wind and seas are kicking up in the strait. The narrow entry can be seen by lining up north-northwest of the tall flashing microwave tower (visible from some distance) and north of Meyers Island. Do not enter via shoals south of Meyers Island. Keep "#3" green triangle to port and "#4" red to starboard, turning south just after clearing "#4" red. There is a state operated float with fresh water, a telephone and tidal grid. Anchorage is possible in the arm. The Post Office can be reached by skiff from the state float. By foot, visitors can walk to a unique art gallery that features a wide variety of work from local artisans including homemade crafts, cedar bark baskets, beaded art, wood turned art and more.

★ **McHenry Anchorage:** Indenting Etolin Island, McHenry is 7 1/2 miles north of Ernst Point. It offers shelter except from west winds. Anchor in five to seven fathoms of water in the southeast portion, about 250 yards west of the wooded island. Avon Island, on the north side of the entry, is small and close to shore. Give a wide berth of 250 yards. A reef extends approximately 400 yards southeasterly from the southeast side of Avon Island. Caution advised regarding a rock 1/2 mile west-southwest of Avon Island.

★ **Kindergarten Bay:** [17360, 17382] This deep cove, on Etolin Island, two miles north of Pt. Harrington, is one of the best anchorages in the area. It affords protection in most winds, except when strong winds blow down from the hills. Enter mid-channel to the south of the wooded islet. Anchor in five to seven fathoms of water, soft bottom. Avoid a large rock covered four to six feet at high tide. It is close southwest of the largest islet, near the head of the bay.

Wrangell Area
[17360, 17385]

★ **Wrangell Area:** [17360, 17385] After passing Lemesurier Point, just north of Meyer's Chuck, it is about 52 miles to Wrangell, following the ferry route through Clarence and Stikine Straits. Two alternate routes to the east offer more protection and some inspiring scenery. These are Zimovia Strait between Etolin Island and Wrangell Island, and Blake Channel and Eastern Passage, between Wrangell Island and the mainland. Zimovia is two miles shorter than the Stikine Strait route, and Eastern Passage is about eight miles longer. The chart will help you through either Zimovia Strait or Eastern Passage. Both passages are marked by buoys, day beacons, and lights. Tides run to 1.7 knots in the former, and 2.2 to three knots in the latter. The tides meet from north and south at the narrows in both passages. In making a transit of Zimovia Strait, strict attention must be paid to the channel markers. The course is very crooked and there are shallows on either side.

★ **Vixen Harbor:** A snug little anchorage just southeast of Union Point, about five miles east of Lemesurier Point. It is a very restricted entrance, look out for the submerged ledges if you are not going in at low tide, but it is not difficult if one is cautious. Well protected anchorage is in five fathoms.

★ **Santa Anna Inlet (12):** [17385] This inlet is about midway between Ketchikan and Wrangell. There is excellent anchorage in ten fathoms near the head. Avoid a shoal which extends 200 yards off the southwest shore, one-half mile from the entrance. A river empties from Lake Helen. There is good fishing here for Rainbow trout.

★ **Anan Bay (13):** [17385] Anchorage is fair near the Forest Service cabin. A 30' float is in front of the cabin. The bottom of the bay is sticky mud. A Bear Observatory, built by the Forest Service, is a one mile walk. From here it is possible to watch brown and black bears fishing for salmon in Anan Creek. Late afternoon is a good time to find the bears feeding.

★ **Fool's Inlet:** This inlet is located five miles northeast of Found Island and is acceptable fair weather anchorage when Anan Bay is crowded. Anchor in 11 fathoms to starboard of the north islet at the head. Mud flats extend .9 mile from the head, nearly to the two small islets.

★ **Bradfield Canal:** Bradfield Canal extends 12 miles to the east from Anan Bay with mountains on both sides creating spectacular scenery. Caution must be used in front of Harding River because the shoal in front of it extends much farther across the inlet than one might expect. Waters in the inlet are full of silt and it is impossible to see to any depth. Anchorage is possible at the head of the canal in eight to ten fathoms. The bottom shoals very rapidly and there is no protection from up or down channel winds. The flats are a good place to see both brown and black bears as well as numerous eagles. Anchorage is said to be possible in the cove in the inside of Duck Point, but on inspection it does not look very desirable.

★ **Zimovia Strait, Thom's Place:** On the east side of the strait this bay has protected anchorage in seven to eight fathoms.

★ **Zimovia Strait, Anita Bay:** [17382, 17382] On the west side of the strait this bay affords good anchorage in ten fathoms on a mud bottom

at the head of the bay. This is one of the most beautiful anchorages in Alaska, if the weather lets you see the snow covered mountain tops. It is like being anchored on a mountain lake.

★ **Blake Channel-Eastern Passage:** This is the most beautiful route to Wrangell and the navigation is easier than Zimovia Strait. There are two good anchorages, one on each side of the narrows where the flood tides meet.

★ **Berg Bay:** A well protected anchorage in front of the Forest Service cabin and float. Depths in the bay are from 5-11 fathoms.

★ **Madan Bay:** Good protective anchorage in seven to eight fathoms north of the projecting point on the west side near the head of the bay, soft bottom.

★ **Wrangell (14):** [17360, 17384] The Harbor Master's office is located at the top of the ramp at Reliance Float, the transient float located in Etolin Harbor. Showers and laundry facilities are found within a half a block. A tidal grid is available on a first come, first served basis. Marine way and repairs are accessible. Additional floats include Inner Harbor, Standard Oil, and Fish & Game, which are all located within easy walking distance to downtown Wrangell where pay telephones, grocery stores, restaurants, hotels, library, post office and hardware stores are available. Wrangell Harbor's history of overcrowding is now alleviated due to the completion of Heritage Harbor, a new deep draft harbor located one quarter of a mile from town that provides ample space for transient moorage. A portion of the float structures for transients will be completed by 2006. Additional moorage outside of the harbor basin for 80-200 foot vessels is located on the shore side of the Cruise Ship (City) Dock called Summer Floats. A new marine haul-out/repair facility with a 150-ton travel lift is under development in the downtown port storage yard. The City of Wrangell Port & Harbors Department also manages Shoemaker Bay, located approximately 5 miles south of the city. Shoemaker Bay has RV facilities managed by Parks & Recreation, picnic tables, tent campsites, and access to hiking trails. Wrangell has one FM radio station, at 101.7, which broadcasts news and weather on the hour. Wrangell Harbormaster: 907-874-3736. VHF 16.
Wrangell is 750 miles from Seattle. It is the site of a lumber mill, three seafood processing companies, and other businesses related to the fishing and tourism industries. In 1860 and 1898 Wrangell saw activity during the gold strikes. Today the city is involved with mining exploration activities on nearby islands. Named after an 1831 governor of Russian America, Baron Von Wrangell, it is the only Alaskan city to have been under three flags, Imperial Russian, British, and United States. Ancient Indian rock carvings at Petroglyph Beach State Historic Park show this site to be as much as 8,000 years old. Wrangell is a good place to walk, or for an entirely different experience, take a charter boat day trip up the wild and scenic Stikine River or visit the Anan Bear and Wildlilfe Observatory. Many Forest Service cabins are available in the vicinity of Wrangell. For information call 907-874-2323, 877-444-6777. Other fun activities include golf or a visit to Garnet Ledge, the historic site of an 1880's mine. Hike on the newly renovated trail to the top of Mt. Dewey near downtown. This short, moderate trail has an overlook of town and Zimovia Straits.

Walk-around: The Rainbow Falls Trail, across the road from the boat basin at Shoemaker Bay,

is a one mile hike to the falls. The last portion is very steep and hiking boots are a must.

Walk-around: For a tour of the downtown, walk along Front Street through the business district. Cross the plank bridge in Wrangell Harbor to Shakes Island, the site of the Chief Shakes Community House and collection of totems. This is an entertaining place to look around, however, visiting hours for inside the Tribal House are very restricted. The James & Elsie Nolan Center, located in downtown Wrangell at 296 Outer Drive, houses the Visitor Center, movie theater and meeting rooms, and Museum: 907-874-3770, 907-874-3699.

Walk-around: Walk to Petroglyph Beach State Historic Park, located about 3/4 mile from the ferry dock. Time your walk to arrive at low tide. Walk north on Evergreen Avenue, follow the signs to the accessible boardwalk and interpretive platform. Take the steps to the beach and turn right and walk to the rocks above the high tide line.

Port Of Wrangell: Moorage, power, water. Harbormaster: 907-874-3736. VHF 16.

Wrangell Port and Harbors Delta Western Inc.: Gas, diesel, oils, lubricants, batteries, water, showers, AV -gas. 907-874-2388. VHF 16.

Wrangell Shoemaker Bay: Permanent moorage. Boat launch available.

Wrangell Oil: Gas, diesel, water, lubricants, shower, laundry, restroom, store, bait, ice, marine supplies. 907-874-3276. VHF 16.

Petersburg Area
[17360, 17375, 17382]

Approaching Petersburg: If you did not visit Wrangell, you will be heading for Petersburg, continuing north through Clarence Strait, around Zarembo Island to the south end of Wrangell Narrows. If coming from Wrangell, you will be approaching Wrangell Narrows through Sumner Strait.

★ **St. John Harbor (15):** [17382] Located at the northwest corner of Zarembo Island, St. John Harbor offers good anchorage in 10 fathoms of water on a mud bottom. The harbor is protected from all directions but north. Although it is best to approach the harbor from the north, it is possible to approach from south of Southerly Island. This is a good place to wait for the tide in Wrangell Narrows.

★ **Wrangell Narrows (16):** [17375] Tidal currents enter from both ends and meet just south of Green Point. Transiting either north or south, it is best to start on the end of a rising tide, arriving at Green Point around high slack, therefore having a following tidal current all of the way. Currents can run from five to seven knots on large tides. There are 63 numbered navigational aids in the 21 mile length of the narrows, as well as some unnumbered range markers. Two public floats, 100 and 62 feet in length respectively, are located at Papkes Landing, 13 miles south of Petersburg. These are open for public moorage. There is no water or power. A second public float extends into Wrangell Narrows at West Petersburg.

★ **Petersburg (17):** [17375] The town is decorated with Norwegian rosemal storefront paintings and *Velkommen* signs, which entice visitors into a festive mood. Also found in the downtown shopping area are four large outdoor murals. The first, "Our Town," is a composite of Petersburg. "Flowers" and "Sealife" feature local flora and fauna, while "See't Kwan" depicts the influence of the native Tlingit people. On the third weekend in May, a *Constitution Day* celebration is held. Another celebration takes place on the Fourth of July. The camera buff will enjoy views of the Sons of Norway Hall, Clausen Memorial Museum, the viking ship *Valhalla*, Sing Lee Alley, Eagle's Roost Park, the canneries, the Fiske Fountain, and the homes along Hammer Slough. Fishing is the mainstay of the community's economy. Salmon canneries, and a crab and shrimp cannery are located here. A side trip to Crystal Lake Hatchery, about 17 miles south of Petersburg, is educational. Alaska Airline flies scheduled jet service to Seattle and Juneau. This incorporated city of about 3,400 residents was founded by Peter Buschmann of Tacoma and settled by Norwegians in 1897. The city is still known as *Little Norway*.

Petersburg Harbor: There is a 24-hour Harbor Master on duty for the three boat harbors operated by the city. About one-half hour before arrival, it is advisable to call the Harbor Master for a moorage assignment and directions to find it. Reservations are required for boats over 100-feet. The basin to the south of the large cannery, is home to the world's largest halibut fleet. Unless you are specifically assigned there, transient moorage is not available in that basin. The main harbor for transient moorage is located north of the cannery. Currents in this harbor can be strong and affect landing. Within two blocks of this harbor there are two banks, post office, two food markets, general stores, a laundromat, several restaurants, a drug store, and liquor stores. Internet access is available in town. Taxi service and car rentals are available in the area. Water (at the heads of floats), showers (at the port facility), haul outs, grids, repairs (from off site). Fax: 907-772-4687. Telephone: 907-772-4688. VHF 16, CB-9.

Walk-around: There is a *Heritage of the Sea* wing at the Clausen Memorial Museum, as well as antiques and the world record, 126 pound King salmon, that was caught in a fish trap in 1939. A picturesque street is where the Sons of Norway building sits on pilings over Hammer Slough. Tours of the Coast Guard cutter *Anacapa* and the Buoy Tender *Elderberry*, stationed near the Chevron dock, can be arranged. Be sure to sample the Petersburg shrimp along the way. Several outdoor fishing and picnic spots (handicapped accessble) are found in this community. The Visitor Information Center is at First and Fram Streets. 907-772-4636

Petersburg Petro Marine Services: Gas, diesel, water, batteries, filters, oils, lubricants. 907-772-4251. VHF 16.

Petersburg Bottled Gas: Propane. 907-772-4270.

City of Kupreanof (West Petersburg): Located across the Wrangell Narrows from Petersburg, this community was homesteaded in the late 1890's. Through the years it has been the site of a sawmill, mink farms, gaff hook factory, and clam cannery. It is said that the residents who live here, and commute to their jobs in Petersburg, have an unusual social code. They take pride in having nothing. Independence and self-reliance are prized.The public floats have no power or water and the floats dry at low tides. During the school year, the face of the float is reserved for the school boat.

★ **Thomas Bay & Spray Island (18):** [17360, 17367] There is good anchoring in this bay with its milky-gray glacial silt water. Baird and Patterson Glaciers are at the ends of the arms. Excellent holding bottom with depths of 60 to 70 feet can be found southeast of Spray Island. There is good shrimping here. Another anchorage is in Scenery Cove. It is possible to dinghy to the flats and explore the area of the face of the glacier. Another anchorage is in a bight on the south end of Ruth Island in seven fathoms of water.

★ **Portage Bay (19):** [17367] There is protected anchorage in this bay on the south side of Frederick Sound. The entrance is 150 yards in width. Use directions in United States Coast Pilot 8, which recommends entry at high slack. Anchor in five fathoms of water in mid-channel. Shoals extend from the head and 40-60 feet out from the sides.

★ **Farragut Bay (20):** [17367] This bay is across Frederick Sound from Portage Bay. Best anchorage is in Francis Anchorage, in a small bight on the point on the south side of the anchorage. There is a good holding bottom in 14 fathoms of water. Avoid the mud flats on the east side.

Frederick Sound & Stephens Passage

[17360, 17365]

★ **Nearby Waters:** [17360] At this point some comments may be helpful regarding the waters to the north and west. A glance at Chart #17360 will tell you that Frederick Sound and Stephens Passage have some wide stretches of water. Strong winds can kick up some very rough seas so attention should be paid to the weather reports and forecasts. It is also possible to encounter ice floes from LeConte Glacier to the south and the three glaciers in Holkam Bay to the north.

★ **Cleveland Passage (21):** [17365] Cleveland Passage is located just north of Cape Fanshaw between Whitney Island and the mainland. United States Coast Pilot 8 recommends entering from the north. Anchorages can be found in Cleveland Passage in four to eight fathoms of water near the southeast end behind Whitney Island. Rollers enter Steamboat Bay near Foot Island, however anchorage is possible. The Five Finger Light Station, which was the last manned station in Alaska, is now automated.

Admiralty Island East Side

[17360, 17336, 17362, 17363]

★ **Chapin Bay:** Located on Admiralty Island, this bay has rocks at the entrance. Entry at low tide is recommended to insure locating the channel. The steep-sided indentation has anchorage in the inner bay where a stream enters from the head.

★ **Pybus Bay:** Three channels provide entrance into Pybus Bay. One is through the San Juan Islands. The largest is between the southern San Juan and Elliot Island, and the third is south of Elliot Island. Anchorage can be found in the most northerly entrance, in the small bight in the middle of the south San Juan Islands. Dangers are exposed at low tide making the anchoring basin easier to identify. Kelp marks a shallow patch and foul ground off Pybus Point.

Cannery Cove, the site of a cannery from 1918-1928, affords the most sheltered anchorage. Anchor left of the head in 45 to 50 feet of water. There is good radio reception to Petersburg Operator 28.

★ **Gambier Bay (22):** [17362] Several anchorages are found here. A convenient one is in a small cove east of Good Island, between the island and the peninsula to the east in 10 to 15 fathoms, mud bottom. The Inner Bay or Gambier Bay proper has several excellent protected anchorages. Entry is to the west of Gambier Island with a light at Point Gambier at its south end then northwest three miles to the entrance light, northeast of Gain Island. After passing fairly close to it to avoid the reef to the south head north around the unnamed island north of Gain Island, entering the inner bay. Snug Cove in the southwest corner of the bay offers good anchorage in ten fathoms, mud bottom. There are several other good possibilities for anchoring. We found excellent halibut fishing in the entrance. First on the reef southeast of the Gambier Bay entrance light, and then on the reef north of the unnamed island three miles north where you enter the inner bay. In a short time, we had four halibut on, three were in the 40-50 pound class of which we were able to land two. We were using the large leadhead jigs that are sold for halibut with plastic tails attached.

★ **Hobart Bay (23):** [17363] Found between Port Houghton and Windham Bay, this bay is often the scene of logging operations. Entrance Island, at the entrance has a small niche on the east side with a single state float (remote moorage, no amenities) suitable for six boats. Look for the buildings to port on the island when rounding the south tip of the island. Turn into the bay immediately following this site. The float is on the port side of this niche. The outsides of the floats have water depths of seven feet at a minus two tide at Juneau.

★ **Windham Bay (24):** [17363] This old town site was once a gold mining town. Chum salmon fishing is often excellent here. Some anchorage is possible far into the bay, on the north shore near the town site. The bay is deep, with a sticky mud bottom. Shoal areas are near the head. Another anchorage, on a hard bottom, is found in the small cove inside the entrance on the south side.

★ **Holkham Bay (25):** [17360] Holkham Bay, with its two big arms containing tide water glaciers, plus Ford's Terror, is one of the most spectacular places in all of Southeast Alaska. It is well worth spending several days exploring. Holkham Bay is at the base of Tracy and Endicott Arms. The best anchorage is near the entrance to Tracy Arm, see paragraph on Tracy Arm. In south winds, there is anchorage at Wood Spit in the second niche away from the spit. Anchor in 35 to 50 feet of water at a 13-foot tide at Juneau. The bottom rises quickly to shore. Limit scope accordingly. Sand bottom. Boats also anchor in the niche formed by Point Ashley. Harbor Island sits in the middle of Holkham Bay. In a north wind there is anchorage in a small cove on the south shore of Harbor Island in front of an abandoned fur farm. Anchor just outside the points and about equidistant from them in 25 feet of water, 100- foot rode at 16-foot tide at Juneau. Hard bottom, but good holding. Currents affect the amount of swing. This was once the home of the Sumdum tribe of the Tlingit Indians. They guided John Muir on his exploration in 1897. The word Sumdum comes from the Indian's interpretation of the roar of the icebergs as they calve into the fjords. Views across Holkham Bay to Sumdum Glacier are gorgeous in the late afternoon sun.

★ **Endicott Arm:** Spectacular views and some of the largest icebergs are seen in this fjord that stretches southeast from Holkham Bay. Ford's Terror, opening to port, about 13 miles from Holkham Bay, is one of the must see places for adventuresome boaters. Sumdum anchorage is in Sanford Cove. There appears to be such a limited spot that is suitable for anchorage that it is safer not to recommend anchoring here. Some anchorage has been found near the west shore on line from the unnamed point to Rock Point in about 50 feet of water on a hard bottom. The beach shoals and then drops rapidly, not allowing room for sufficient rode. Sanford Cove is also subject to entry of icebergs and winds. At the turn-of-the-century, the Sumdum Chief Mine was located here. It produced nearly a half- million dollars in gold and silver. Dawes Glacier, at the head of the arm, extends into the water and calves off large amounts of ice that are always present. If one goes in close to the glaciers it will be slow going, because the arms become choked with ice floes. Do not approach the faces of the glaciers too closely, because large chunks of ice fall into the water, creating fairly large swells, as high as 25 feet. The swells are easy to ride if the boat does not get caught between icebergs, and is kept heading into the oncoming swells.

★ **Fords Terror:** [17360] This is one of the most beautiful and isolated fjords in the northwest. If warm days have caused rapid calving off of Dawes Glacier, entry through Endicott Arm may require slow and careful maneuvering through tightly-packed icebergs, Allow three to four hours from Wood Spit to the narrows in Fords Terror, making eight knots when not in congested ice floes. Plan to traverse the narrows on high tide slack with sufficient daylight before and after for navigation. Entry at low slack is not recommended because of a one-quarter fathom controlling depth at zero tide at Juneau. The narrows in Fords Terror are about 1.3 miles inside the inlet. Lay off the largest waterfall, opposite the narrows. Perhaps ten to 25 minutes after high tide at Juneau, the turn in the narrows can be observed by the gradual slowing of the movement of ice and debris. This time will vary depending upon the amount of tidal change for the day. This is the time to enter. While currents in the narrows can run to 15 knots at springs with a seven-foot over fall, high slack passage is easy, with minimum depths of 17 and one-half feet at a 16-foot tide at Juneau, with only slight current and whirlpools.

Once through the narrows, a deep-walled fjord stretches ahead with camera-ready spectacular waterfalls and scenery. At the head of the fjord, the northeast finger is worth viewing, but doesn't have the best anchorage. It is also windy when the west finger is dead calm. A drying bar stretches across the northeast finger where the grassy shore to port on entry juts into the waterway. Minimum depth observed was eight feet at a 15-foot tide at Juneau. The best anchorage is in the west arm, near the waterfall in the northwest corner. Drying flats extend out from the falls and the starboard shore on approach. A quick-rising bottom affords good holding mud off these flats. Anchor in about 55 feet of water at a 14' foot tide at Juneau. Unless there is wind, the force of the current from the falls will keep the boat facing the falls on all tides. Several other falls are visible across the fjord on the south side. There are black bears, seals, plentiful fresh water, and blackberries in season. Plan to spend more than one night in this scenic spot. This is a more isolated location than most boaters have experienced. VHF radio contact will not be possible. It is entirely possible that another boat will not be seen or heard

Margerie Glacier in Glacier Bay National Park   *Gustavus Visitors Association Photo*

during a several day stay here. In the event of the engine not starting when leaving, it would seem wise to take along enough food, water, and cooking fuel to survive for a week. It would also be prudent to notify someone of your plans and expected time of return. The Coast Guard is no longer accepting float plans so this arrangement must be done with a friend. Exit through the Narrows at ten to 25 minutes after high water at Juneau. Fords Terror received its name from navy man H.R. Ford who, in 1889, entered the narrows in a rowboat. After exploring the fjord, the unsuspecting sailor returned to the narrows at a full run and was so frightened by his white water ride that his officers named the fjord accordingly.

★ **Temporary anchorage in the small bight outside Fords Terror narrows:** If necessary to wait until high slack, temporary anchorage is possible in a bight opposite the entry to the narrows, just north of the falls. Shoals and rocks in the west half of this bight are marked by kelp and/or icebergs at most tides. Anchor in 45 to 50 feet of water at a plus 16-foot tide at Juneau. Iceberg fending-off may be required during the last three hours of flood tide and the first three hours of ebb tide. Overnight anchorage in this bight is not recommended because of danger from icebergs.

★ **Tracy Arm:** [17300] Enter by keeping the stern on the Harbor Island Range, the bow on the RW beacon on the east side of Holkham Bay. Markers are about three miles apart, one on the north tip of Harbor Island, the other on a line of about ten degrees magnetic to the mainland shore. The best base-station anchorage for exploring this area is in the unnamed bay about two and one-half miles from Harbor Island on the western shore of the Arm. Turn for entry when depths show that the bar has been cleared. Avoid a rock off the southeast tip of the small island which forms the northeastern shore of the bay. Enter in the center of the bay between the island and the mainland shore. Anchor at the head in 35 feet at a 16-foot tide at Juneau. Hard, rocky bottom. Shoaling near shore. Tracy Arm indents 26 miles and has North and South Sawyer glaciers at the head.

These are both calving glaciers. Icebergs abound, and a day sightseeing excursion from Juneau is often taken by pleasure boaters. The scenery in Tracy Arm surpasses anything found in Glacier Bay in our opinion due to the steep rocky walls on both sides of the arm, as well as the two glaciers at its head.

★ **Taku Harbor (26):** [17300, 17314] Anchorage is found in the south end of the bay in seven fathoms of water on a soft mud bottom. There is also a 400-foot, state-maintained small craft float on the east side of the harbor. Submerged pilings are hazards near the old cannery wharf. This harbor was once the home of both Father Hubbard, The Glacier Priest, and a hermit, Tiger Olson.

Taku Inlet: [17300, 17315] No secure anchorage. This inlet has many shoals and tends to be quite windy. As the Taku Glacier moves, small lakes open up providing resting grounds for geese.

Juneau Area
[17300, 17315]

★ **Douglas (27):** When traversing Gastineau Channel, note that the current floods northwest up Gastineau Channel toward Juneau and ebbs to the southeast. A basin for small craft, operated by the City of Juneau, is located at Douglas, behind Mayflower Island, three miles south of the bridge. When navigating in the Douglas basin, note that in 2003 there is a lighted, temporary breakwater at the entrance. The floats are well maintained and protected. Transient moorage is on the inside of C-float. Year around potable water and electricity are found on all floats. No groceries are available in Douglas. Restaurants are within walking distance. Taxi service is available to downtown Juneau. Douglas was the site of the Treadwell Gold Mine. Once the world's largest, it gave up $66 million in gold before it flooded and caved in.

Douglas Boat Harbor: Moorage, water, power, no reservations. 907-586-5255 VHF16,73.

Diving Humpback Whales in Icy Strait   Gustavus Visitors Association Photo

Walk-around: For a beach walk, try Sandy Beach.

★ **Juneau (28):** See berthage information below. The height of the Juneau-Douglas bridge is 66.4 foot on a 0.0 tide. A gauge on the bridge measures the current height. When approaching Juneau, Alaska's capital city, look to starboard and spot the landmark ruins of the Alaska Juneau Mine. When leaving Juneau, retrace your path and exit down Gastineau Channel. The shallow channel to Auke Bay dries at 10' on Juneau tides.

Juneau Harbor Master: 907-586-5255. VHF 16, 73.

Intermediate Vessel Float: A moorage float provides 800' of moorage at the foot of downtown. Large yachts stay here. Space is reserved ahead of time on a first-come, first-serve basis. See Berthage Information below. Thirty and 100 ampere power, potable water. This is a very busy moorage, used mostly for short stays. Reservations accepted. 907-586-5255, 907-586-0292.

Harris Harbor: The Harbor Master may direct you to this location for transient moorage on a first come, first served basis. Near downtown. Limited moorage may be available when permanent boats are out. Moorage, power, water, tidal grid. 907-586-5255.

Aurora Basin: Located next to Harris Harbor. Limited transient moorage when fishing boats are out. No moorage is allowed here without specific assignment, but be prepared to be sent to this location. This moorage is connected to downtown Juneau by road. Water, power, pump-out. 907-586-5255.

Juneau Aurora Fuel Dock: Gas, diesel, oils, aviation fuel, card lock system. If no card, use phone on dock.

Juneau Petro Marine: Gas, diesel, oils, batteries, ice, water, bait. Located directly across channel from Harris Harbor. 907-586-4400. VHF 16.

Seadrome Marine Complex: Moorage, security gates, power, water, diesel. Reservations preferred. Downtown location. 907-463-8811. VHF 9, 16.

Taku Oil Sales: Gas, diesel, oils, lubricants, water. South of downtown. 907-586-1276.

★ **Exploring Juneau:** Be sure to pick up a free copy of the *Harbor Guide* in the Harbor Master's Office. This busy Alaska capital city and popular cruise ship destination sits amid the scenic backdrop of Mount Juneau and Mount Roberts. Because of its role as the capital and as the center of commerce for outlying communities, Juneau is growing at a steady rate. The economy centers largely around government and tourism; transportation, medical and education services; and as the hub for a growing mining industry that includes the Greens Creek Mine located on nearby Admiralty Island.

When exploring the heart of downtown Juneau, a car is not necessary except to transport provisions back to moorages. Local taxi companies can readily meet this need. There is public bus service connecting downtown Juneau to adjacent Douglas Island and to the Mendenhall Valley, where the airport and Mendenhall Glacier are located. To explore Juneau and the surrounding area, and to avoid walking up the steep hillsides, car transportation should be considered. Rental car agencies, located at or near the airport, are plentiful.

The downtown area, seven blocks of which constitute an historic district, has many attractions. These include the Valentine Building, the Alaskan Hotel, the Emporium Mall with it's impressive turret, government buildings, and the Red Dog Saloon. There are several grocery stores and bakeries found here. Street venders line the narrow streets selling foods representing Cajun, Thai, Vietnamese, Mexican, and Italian specialties in addition to American fare. Guided tours of the Capitol Building are available. Around the downtown core, the hillsides are steep. The Governor's House, with pillared terrace, is easy to locate on the hillside. A few blocks away, the House of Wickersham, built in 1898 in the Victorian style, is being renovated and may be open for tours in 2006. 907-586-9001.

Along Juneau's waterfront are viewing platforms and wide walkways with benches, a marine park, an information kiosk, concessions, picnic sites, public art and memorials, restaurants, and the lower terminal of the Mt. Roberts Tramway.

The Alaska State Museum (907-465-2901) and the Juneau Douglas Museum (907-586-3572) are each just a short walk from the waterfront. Large decorative banners and an abundance of flowers set a pretty stage. The airport and residential area of the Mendenhall Valley are about nine miles north of downtown Juneau, and are connected by road.

One excursion possibility is to the beautiful Mendenhall Glacier. An impressive interpretive center has exhibits, powerful telescopes and staff to explain the facinating qualities of the glacier. 907-789-6640. Easily accessible trails lead to waterfalls, salmon rearing streams, and great photo opportunities. A raft trip down the Mendenhall River leaves from the west side of Mendenhall Lake near the face of the glacier. Many visitors continue by car beyond the glacier to charming Chapel-by-the-Lake, overlooking placid Auke Lake, and further to the serene beauty of the Shrine of St. Therese, 23 miles out the Glacier Highway.

Indoor and outdoor tennis, hiking on well-maintained trails, rock and ice climbing, biking and paragliding are popular local activities. For a game of golf, play the nine-hole Mendenhall Golf Course, located near the airport. 907-789-1221. Flightseeing by helicopter and small planes is also available. Forest Service cabins are a popular way to enjoy wilderness settings. For reservations, 1-877-444-6777 or www.reserveusa.com. The Juneau Ranger District Office of the U.S. Forest Service has cabin information and also issues permits to access the Pack Creek Bear Sanctuary on nearby Admiralty Island. Their office is located at 8465 Old Dairy Road, Juneau 99801. 907-586-8800. If you are visiting during the 4th of July holiday, take in the local parade and enjoy the nation's earliest 4th of July fireworks show, which is held at midnight on July 3.

Walk-around: A downtown map, available at visitor information centers, illustrates a popular walking tour of the city, including such points of interest as museums, historic buildings, public art and facilities.

★ **Auke Bay (29):** Located 12 miles north of Juneau, the Don D. Statter Harbor Facilities at Auke Bay provide 6,000 feet of transient moorage for boats to 200' feet in length. Moorage is on a first come-first serve basis. The breakwater is connected to the float. Water, 20, 30, 50 ampere power, and pump-outs are available. There is no power on the breakwater. Register at the Harbor Master's Office to get current rules and regulations for transient moorage. There is no legal length of stay. Boaters can go back and forth between the 10 day and the 3 day zones. It is alright to understay, but an overstay in any zone will result in a ticket and fine. Staying beyond the maximum legal number of days can result in a ticket and fine of $20 per day. Showers, restrooms, and carts are found at the Harbor Master's office at the head of the floats. Hours: 8:00 a.m. to 6:30 p.m. seven days a week. Harbor Master: 907-789-0819, VHF 16, 74.

Transportation: There is bus service to downtown Juneau. Since there are limited shopping facilities in Auke Bay, you may want to consider a taxi or car rental. There are large shopping centers about seven miles from Auke Bay, along the Auke Bay-Juneau road. The Alaska State ferries stop at Auke Bay, rather than Juneau.

Other Marinas: There are two private marinas nearby, but they do not have transient moorage.

Auke Bay Boatyard: Haul-outs to 15 tons, bottom maintenance, minor repairs. No engine work. 907-789-4225.

Fishermans Bend: Gas, diesel, oils, water. store, tackle, liquor. 907-789-7312.

Petro Marine Services: Gas, diesel, water, oils, 907-790-3030. Free coffee.

★ **Admiralty Cove (30):** Just west of Point Young on the north side of Admiralty Island, this cove offers anchorage to mariners traversing Saginaw Channel. Shoals extend from shore. Fireweed grows profusely in the summer, giving an impression of velvet cloth on a cushion of green. Anchorage is found southwest of the island on the southwest side of Admiralty Cove in five fathoms of water. It is open to the west and somewhat to the north.

Lynn Canal
[17300, 17316, 17317]

Lynn Canal: This body of water, which extends about 85 miles from Icy Strait to Skagway, is often ignored by boaters. This is regretful because it offers some truly beautiful scenery, with high mountains and glaciers on both sides. None of the glaciers reach the salt water, so there is no ice to be concerned about. At the north end you will find one in Skagway at the end of the Inside Passage. Considered the main port for the gold miners in the Klondike Gold Rush of 1898. The only commercial facilities are in Skagway or Haines, about 15 miles south of Skagway. There is a separate VHF weather and wind forecast for Lynn Canal.

★ **Tee Harbor (31):** Tee Harbor is situated on the east side of Favorite Channel, two miles north of Point Lena. There is a private marina here, however, finding moorage might be difficult because it is crowded in the summer. A road connects the harbor to Auke Bay and Juneau. Anchorage is possible in the center of the harbor in 12 to 15 fathoms. The north arm has shallower anchorage in five to ten fathoms, and better protection from north winds.

Donahue's Marina: Gas, diesel, oils. 907-789-7851.

★ **Saint James Bay (32):** Located on the west side of Lynn Canal, Saint James Bay offers anchorage in 40-foot depths. The bottom is sticky mud. This bay is open to winds from the north and southeast. There are shoal areas near the head.

★ **Bridget Cove and Mab Island:** The best anchorage is in the small cove opposite the north end of Mab Island in five fathoms of water. Don't get in too far, because this little cove has large drying flats. Anchorage is also possible in the passage between Mab Island and the mainland. This area is often used by commercial fishermen, especially the gillnetters.

★ **Echo Cove:** Anchorage is possible in ten fathoms near the head of the cove. Enter the cove along the northeast shoreline. Watch charts closely. The entrance is narrow and shallow until past the bar which extends from the southwest shore. Good holding, soft bottom with good protection. Many commercial crab pots affect anchorage. The City of Juneau issues permits for the use of the public boat launch. A small public camp area with seven campsites is available on a first come-first serve basis. Private property adjoins the campsites and is posted.

★ **Haines (33):** [17317] This town, 75 miles northwest of Juneau, has the largest concentra-

tion of American Bald Eagles during the fall and winter months than anywhere in the world. Called Dei-shu, meaning end of the trail, Haines has a population of about 1,500, spectacular mountain scenery, and less rainfall than Ketchikan, Sitka, or Juneau. Restaurants and overnight accommodations are available. There are well-stocked provision stores, laundromats, telephone, and showers. Many local art galleries and shops display works of local artists. Specialties include woodcarving, silver carving, fine art, photography, fiber arts, native Indian artwork and items from Interior Indians. The Sheldon Museum and Cultural Center, located across from the small boat harbor, features other examples of Tlingit art as well as historic pioneer and military pieces illustrating early life in the Chilkat Valley. 907-766-2366. Each May the annual *Great Alaska Craftbeer & Homebrew Festival* highlights local microbrews. June is the month for the *Summer Solstice Celebration.* July 4th is the date for a community *Independence Day Celebration* with parade, races, and a pie eating contest. The *Southeast Alaska State Fair* and the *Alaska Bald Eagle Music Festival* is is also held in July. Car rental gives access by highway to Whitehorse, Haines Junction, and the Alaska Interior. By road it is 19 miles to Weeping Trout Golf Course for a round of golf. 907-766-2827. A very exciting side trip is a scenic flight from the Haines, or Skagway airports over Glacier Bay National Park and Haines' Chilkat Valley. Muir Glacier, in Glacier Bay, is on the other side of the mountains, only about 30 miles from the Haines airport. For the adventurous in spirit, rafting, kayaking, and jet boat excursions can be arranged.

Walk-around: Lookout Park, on the waterfront, has a picnic area and viewing platform. Tlingit Park has a historic cemetery. Visit expansive Chilkat State Park. There are hiking trails and glacier views. It is possible to moor at Haines and walk to Fort William H. Seward, now a center for training Native children in the arts, crafts, and dances of their ancestors. Interpretive signs are provided along the way.

Haines Small Boat Harbor: Transient moorage, gas, diesel, power, water, repairs, sewage pump-out. Located between Port Chilkoot dock and the Army Tank farm at Portage Cove. Fax: 907-766-3010. Telephone: 907-766-2448. VHF 12, 13, 16.

Haines Propane: 907-766-3191.

★ **Letnikof Cove:** At this location, five miles from Haines, there are floats operated by the City of Haines. There is no power or water. 907-766-2448. VHF 12, 16.

★ **Taiasanka Harbor:** [17317] This well protected harbor, located about five miles from Haines, has anchorage in five fathoms of water on a soft bottom. Use the United States Coast Pilot 8.

★ **Skagway (34):** [17317] Moorage is available at this charming town. There is an 80' grid and boat launch. Provisions, fuel, and internet access can be obtained. Some 700,000 tourists visit each year. Activities and attractions include riding in horse drawn wagons, riding in old street cars and trolleys, and visiting museums, gift shops, arts and crafts exhibits, art galleries, the Gold Rush buildings, and dining at the restaurant near moorage. Built in 1899, the building's exterior is covered with thousands of pieces of driftwood. City parks offer tennis, basketball, and softball. A road connects Skagway with Whitehorse, Yukon Territory, Interior Alaska, and the rest of North America. Since the Gold Rush, the 4th of July has been a big holiday. Contests, a barbecue, and a parade

are featured.

Walk-arounds and side trips: In 1898, Skagway had 30,000 residents. By 1900, the Gold Rush had ended and Skagway was nearly a ghost town. Allow plenty of time to learn about the heritage and enjoy the attractions of this historic site. Stroll down the wooden boardwalks of Broadway. There are several good hiking trails close to town. It is possible to rent a car, drive to the ruins of Dyea, at the foot of the Chilkoot Trail, and walk to historic Slide Cemetery. Another side trip would be to ride in one of the vintage parlor cars of the White Pass and Yukon Route narrow gauge railroad. A three hour trip goes over the summit of White Pass and returns. 907-983-2217 ($94.00). Optional would be to continue by bus to Whitehorse. Flightseeing tours of Glacier Bay, Gold Rush sites, or the Juneau Ice Cap are also available.

Skagway Boat Basin: Moorage, crane (2-ton maximum), water, 20-amp/110-volt power, restrooms, showers, haul-outs to 20-tons or 40-feet, sewage pump-out. 907-983-2628. VHF 16.

Skagway Petro: Gas, diesel, batteries, filters, restroom, shower, oils, lubricants. 907-983-2259.

Icy Strait
[17300, 17316]

Couverden Island (35): There is a state float situated in Swanson Harbor near the spit of land connecting the tumbolo off Couverden Island, opposite Ansley Island. No facilities. Designed primarily as protected moorage for refuge in bad weather on Icy Strait. Use extreme caution when navigating the dredged channel and only navigate during the daylight.

★ **Excursion Inlet (36):** There is a small settlement on the east side of the inlet with the same name. It is not shown on Chart #17300, but it is on Chart #17316. An active cannery is located here, and, when operating, fuel, water and some supplies are available. A small craft float is about one-quarter mile north of the cannery dock. The currents can be very strong at the float. When the cannery is not in operation, only a caretaker is present. This is a unique little community in a beautiful setting. Fish traps, now outlawed, are beached at the head of the inlet. The western shore is a park with no facilities.

Excursion Inlet Cannery: Owned by Ocean Beauty Seafoods, this cannery is generally operational from June 1 to September 1. While there are services available if needed, this is a commercial operation and not a boater's destination. All services are limited: gas, diesel, moorage, water, showers, laundry, provisions, propane, stove oil. Call ahead at 907-586-4244, ask for the dock. VHF 11.

★ **Gustavus (37):** [17302] This community on the north side of Icy Strait has a dock and some floats offering temporary tie-ups. No fuel. There are cafes, inns and lodges, a grocery store, gift shops, art galleries, taxi service and rental cars, and a building supply store. The grocery is one and one half miles from the dock. The community's location, adjacent to Icy Straits, places it near some of the best whale watching waters in Alaska. Excursion and charter fishing boats are available for halibut and salmon charters. Guided stream fishing trips by boat or plane can be arranged. Visitors hike on miles of beaches or bike on back roads to Glacier Bay. A 9-hole golf course is also popular. The annual *4th of July* celebration is a highlight with locals and visitors alike. The airport at Gustavus handles jet traffic from Juneau. There are also several small air carriers that service the area. Flights from Gustavus to other Southeast communities, as well as flight seeing tours of Glacier Bay can be arranged with them. A highway connects Gustavus and the airport with park headquarters at Bartlett Cove.

★ ⚓ **Glacier Bay National Park & Bartlett Cove (38):** [17300, 17318] Entry by private vessel into the park, between June 1 and August 31, is by permit only. Internet: www.nps.gov/glba/ E-mail: GLBA_Administration@nps.gov This is a large national park, accessible only by boat or plane. There is a lodge with accommodations, meals, showers, gas, diesel, and water. When approaching, be aware that rips can occur in lower Glacier Bay and there are often swells off the strait. Prevailing winds off Cross Sound are from the southwest. Tidal range is 25 feet. For the protection of the whales and other park resources, there are speed and route regulations within the park and some areas are closed to vessel traffic. Please contact the park for specific information prior to your arrival. Call on VHF 16 or 907-697-2627 up to 48 hours prior to 10am arrival on day of permit to confirm your reservation. Upon arrival in Glacier Bay, permit holders must go ashore at Bartlett Cove and check in at the Visitor's Information Station for a Boaters' Orientation. No overnight moorage is permitted at the dock. Check the dock bulletin board for location of three hour maximum moorage for smaller vessels. The T-shaped head pier is for the National Park Service and the *Daily Tour Boat* and, if space permits, for a three hour visit ashore. Reservations: 888-229-8687. Fuel is available at the Bartlett Cove fuel dock. Pets are not permitted on shore anywhere in the park, except on a leash within 100-feet of roadways in the Bartlett Cove area. Firearms are prohibited within the park, unless they are unloaded and stored aboard your vessel. For shore accommodations, contact the Glacier Bay Lodge for prices and availability. The lodge desk is open 24 hours per day. Staying in the park is by permit only. Between June 1- August 31, only 25 pleasure boats are allowed per day. Applications for permits can be submitted no earlier than 60 days before the date of entry. Permits are valid for seven days. When leaving, boaters are required to clear departure of Bartlett Cove via radio. See contact information below.

Guided tours of the park are available. Glaciers, whales, fish, scenic fjords, and over 200 species of birds and assorted flora and fauna can be seen. Most glaciers within the park are currently receding, but continue to calve into the sea. These are remnants of the little ice age about 4,000 years ago. A Tlingit sea otter hunting canoe is on display in a shelter next to the Visitor Information Station. A camper's laundry is located behind the lodge. You can get a key at the desk. There is no liquor store, even in town. Long periods of wet, cool weather are common. Mosquitoes, deer and horse flies, white sox, and no-see-ums can be ferocious at times. In late summer expect fog and mist. Barlett Cove Headquarters: 907-697-2230.

Walk-around: At Bartlett Cove, well maintained trails near the lodge offer hiking. There is a forest trail of one mile in length, and the Bartlett River Trail, four-mile round trip. Wildlife and water birds are subjects for the camera fan who has a telephoto lens.

Glacier Bay National Park Superintendent: Address: Post Office Box 140, Gustavus, Alaska 99826. Request entry permits or the *Glacier Bay Park Handbook.* 907-697-2627, 907-697-2230. VHF 16, 12.

Glacier Bay Lodge: Operates mid May-mid September. Meals are also available to non-guests. Reservations: 907-697-4000; 1-888-229-8687.

Popular Glacier Bay anchorages and inlets:

★ **North Sandy Cove:** Rarely are icebergs found in this cove which offers good protection in any winds. Watch for bears on the beach. Anchor in four to six fathoms with good holding ground between the mainland and two islands about 1.2 miles east of Sturgess Island.

★ **South Sandy Cove:** Located immediately south of North Sandy Cove, this cove offers excellent anchorage. Try the bight to the southeast of the head in five to eight fathoms on a mud and sand bottom. It is open to southwest winds and the water is more stagnant here. To enter, pass south of the rock 250 yards south of the small islet on the north side entry. Avoid the boulders fringing the southeast shore. Two rocks are .5 mile west of the south entry point. The south rock uncovers 12 feet and the north rock uncovers two feet. Do not try to go between the rocks and the point. Nearby South Marble Islands are closed to hiking to protect nesting bird colonies and sea lions.

★ **Sebree Cove:** There is good holding ground here, although it is exposed to south winds. Ice seldom floats in here. There is an islet at the entry about .5 mile south of Tlingit Point. Small boats may anchor between Tlingit Point and south Sebree Island.

★ **Wachusett Inlet:** Carefully avoid the reef which uncovers nine feet one mile from the entry and 500 yards from the south shore. Favor the north shore. Anchorage is possible in shallow water in a cove two miles west of Rowley Point. The mountains on the south side of this inlet are beautiful and, after the inlet turns northwest seven miles from its entrance, there are also views of Carroll Glacier.

Muir Glacier Face: From the Junction entry it is about 24 miles to Muir Glacier Face. The rapid retreat in the last few decades has exposed a spectrum of glaciated land. Muir Glacier is *grounded out* and does not calve any more.

Berg Bay: This bay is located ten miles above the Glacier Bay entry. To enter pass midway between 3/4 fathoms and the low-water line on the north side of the channel. Be careful until you are past the shoals on the south shore. It is advisable to go in at or near high water. This entry is between the northwest Lars Island and the southeast side of Netland Island. Passage north of Netland Island is not recommended as rocks constrict Glacier Bay end and low water the Berg Bay end of the channel. Strong outflow winds may pour out under some conditions.

★ **Shag Cove:** This two mile long cove is one mile within the entry to Geikie Inlet on the south shore. The inlet extends eight miles southwest from the south shore of Glacier Bay. Protected anchorage is in five to 20 fathoms at the cove head on a soft bottom. Rocks extend 300 yards offshore from the entry point and from a small island at the southwest cove entry. The foul area extends toward a large island .2 mile to the north northeast. Strong outflow winds may pour down Geikie Inlet.

★ **Tyndall Cove:** This is two miles southwest of Shag Cove. Anchor in ten to 20 fathoms at the head, on a soft bottom. Note the comment above that in some summer conditions, strong outflow winds may be expected.

★ **Blue Mouse Cove:** This is a popular anchorage either in the far west corner in five to seven fathoms or on the east side in eight to ten fathoms. Good holding bottom and protection from all but north winds. The cove on the west side one-half mile inside the entrance provides even more shelter. A national park float cabin is moored here.

★ **Reid Inlet:** This anchorage is an excellent base for exploring the huge glaciers in Tarr and Johns Hopkins Inlets, if ice accumulations allow you to enter them. Anchorage is south of the spits on the east and west sides of the inlet at the entrance. Depths are five to seven fathoms on the west side and ten to 12 fathoms on the east side. Less ice was experienced on the east side, although this may vary from time to time. This anchorage should only be used in good weather. Down-inlet winds off Reid Glacier can be severe. Grand Pacific and Margerie Glaciers at the head of Tarr Inlet, and Johns Hopkins Glacier at the head of the inlet with the same name, are truly spectacular and worth visiting. You are asked to go no closer than one-quarter to one-half nautical mile from the face of any glacier.

Admiralty Island West Side
[17300, 17316]

★ **Funter Bay (39):** Two state floats are located here. One is not connected to the shore and lacks protection from north and west winds and seas entering the bay. It has 300 feet of moorage in depths of about 38 feet. The other is connected to shore at the site of the cannery ruins, and has more protection. There is also a seaplane float and water is available. Good anchorage is found in Coot Cove and Crab Cove. There are white sandy beaches and summer cabins on the shores of this bay. In summer, Bare Island is covered with beautiful fireweed wild flowers. It is possible to watch eagles catching fish from the waters of the bay and devouring their treasures on rocky ledges on shore. Funter Bay was a gold mining area from 1877-1920 and also the site of a fish cannery. It has been reported that in unsettled weather wind and swells can enter the bay making it very uncomfortable.

★ **Hawk Inlet (40):** [17316] Give wide berth to foul areas when approaching from the south. Keep the black and green buoy to port to avoid the extensive shoal area. Round the buoy and aim for the port side of the red beacon on the tower, which marks the end of a 200-foot shoal which extends from the starboard side. The old cannery location is now the site of Green's Creek Mine operations. Anchorage is possible here. Continue midchannel up the inlet. Pass two or three float houses. The entry to the basin at the head has shoals marked by kelp. Depths are about ten feet in the channel, which opens to a shoal-surrounded basin. The large basin has extensive shallow areas and care must be taken to locate an anchorage with sufficient depth within swinging room. There is good VHF radio reception to and from Juneau. Seaplane traffic is extensive overhead and a seaplane, if needed, could land easily in this large basin.

★ **Angoon (41):** [17339] Access the boat harbor through the Kootznaho Inlet with a tidal flow of approximately 7 knots. Slack water is the best time to approach. This Tlingit village of 600 residents is located on the west side of Admiralty Island. It has the distinction of being the only community with the status of a National Monument. Angoon petitioned for this status in

Sitka   *Hugo Anderson Photo*

an effort to protect the island from clear-cut logging. Today they are a part of the Admiralty Island National Monument, a 1493 sq. mile preserve. Although it is a National Monument, the city is implementing improvements to water, roads, housing and other infrastructure within the limits allowed by the Alaska National Interest Lands Conservation Act. As stewards of the land, they are watchful of making responsible progress. While making progress, they still preserve the past. Several cultural Tlingit Totem poles stand outside the museum in the downtown area. Part of their history includes the 1862 Angoon Bombardment, when the USS Corwin destroyed the village. This attack resulted when a Tlingit shaman was accidentally killed by a whaling vessel's misfire. As was customary, the Village demanded 200 blankets as payment for the dead man's family. Taken as a threat, the bombardment was the response. In 1973, the Federal Government agreed to an out-of-court settlement for the bombardment.

Lodging is available in town. The Angoon Trading Company sells groceries and supplies. 907-788-3111. Whalers Cove Lodge, a nearby fishing lodge, has a restaurant. This facility can prove to be a safe harbor during rough weather. Angoon is serviced by regularly scheduled air and ferry stops.

Angoon Boat Harbor: Located in the inner harbor by Favorite Bay. Moorage, water, garbage pick-up by arrangement with Harbormaster. New construction at the harbor will include pump-dump facility by 2007. 907-788-3960. VHF 14, 16. CB-5.

Angoon Oil: Gas, diesel, filters, garbage dump. New dock and ramp. 907-788-3436.

Point Gardner: This point at the southwest corner of Admiralty Island, where Frederick Sound and Chatham Strait meet, can be unpleasantly rough at times. When ebbing tides from the north and east meet winds and/or swells from the south, heavy tide rips will form in a large area around Point Gardner. Try to plan so that you round this point at slack water. Murder Cove, adjacent to the point, has been the site of a whaling station, coal mine, and salmon cannery. Anchorage in settled weather only.

Chichagof Island

[17300, 17320, 17321, 17322]

★ **Chichagof Island:** This large island lies south of Glacier Bay, across Icy Strait and Cross Sound. If coming from, or going to Sitka to the south, passage can be on either the east side of the island, through Peril Strait and Chatham Strait, or via Lisianski Inlet down the west side. The course on the west side offers very interesting and beautiful waters with exposure only at the north and south ends of the trip. If you take the "inside passage" behind the islands use the charts.

★ **West Side Chichagof Island (42):** [17303, 17321, 17322, 17323] Beginning from the south, good starting points are two inlets on the north end of Kruzof Island. Sukoi Inlet offers well protected anchorage in eight to 15 fathoms of water on a mud bottom. Kalinin Bay offers well protected anchorage in four to five fathoms of water on a soft bottom, but is more difficult to enter because of rocks in the entrance. A bit of shelter may be used by going inside of Kolkachef Island. Keep well off shore because this is a very rocky coast. A short-cut into Slocum Arm through the islands and rocks northwest of Khaz Head is not worth the risk. The safer route is by way of Khaz Bay, which has a marker in its rocky entrance.

★ **Slocum Arm:** Anchorages are in Waterfall Cove, two miles southeast of Falcon Arm. The west bight, in seven fathoms of water with a good bottom, is best. The east bight dries far out. The head of Falcon Arm has good, protected anchorage on mud in five fathoms of water. Elf Cove in Ford Arm has good anchorage in nine fathoms of water with a soft bottom. Island Cove, four and one-half miles southeast of Falcon Arm, is the location of the abandoned mining town of Cobol. Some buildings remain. Anchorage is in the southeast end of the cove, in 16 fathoms of water. Bears, otter, seals and eagles may be seen in Slocum, with mountains on two sides.

★ **Klag Bay:** [17322] Klag Bay, at the end of Kahz Bay, has a narrow rocky entrance best entered at slack tide and preferably low slack when hazards are visible. The entrance, called The Gate, is well marked and leads into Elbow Passage. The abandoned mining town of Chichagof is at the head of Klag Bay. Several ruins remain. When at its peak of activity in 1938, there were 200 residents. Anchorage is possible at the head of the bay in front of town, but beware of the hazards shown on the chart and especially the unmarked shoals in front of the ruins. There is good halibut fishing off the south end of Borata Island. We let one go that was too big for the boat. It must have weighed over 100 pounds.

★ **Ogden Passage:** Continuing north along the east side of Herbert Graves Island through this passage will bring you into Portlock Harbor.

★ **Kimshan Cove:** [17321] On the east side of Surveyor Passage this cove offers excellent anchorage in seven to ten fathoms, mud bottom, anywhere in the cove. The ruins of the Hirst Mine operation are on the south shore of the cove. In 1938, the town had 100 residents.

★ **Didrickson Bay:** On the east side of Portlock Harbor, there is good anchorage at the head of the bay in 11 fathoms of water, on soft mud. Keep to the west side of the bay, because it shoals very rapidly in front of the waterfalls. Entrance to, or exit from Portlock Harbor is best made through Imperial Passage. There is a light on Hill Island on the north side of the passage. It is nine miles from Imperial Passage to the bell buoy off the entrance to Lisianski Strait. Keep well off the shore because there are many rocks. Turning at the bell buoy into Lisianski Strait, a second marker is on the starboard side, entering the strait. The scenery in both Lisianski Strait and Lisianski Inlet is beautiful, with snow-covered peaks all around.

★ **Pelican (43):** [17303] This supply center for Cross Sound fishermen received its name from a fish packer, The Pelican. The buildings are on stilts, surrounded by boardwalks. The harbor has room for about 98 vessels. Transient floats are between the last two floats. Temporarily unoccupied berths may also be available. Power and water. Moorage is arranged with the Harbor Master, and if not paid prior to departure, the billing amount is doubled. Pelican has two bars and grills, a restaurant, lodging (B & B, inns, cabins and rooms for rent), general store, gift shop, public library with internet access, laundry, showers, public telephone, friendly people, no cars, good moorage, limited repairs, fuel, four tidal grids (up to 50 feet), and a post office. The only vehicles in town are fire, garbage, oil trucks, and a few ATV's and golf carts. A stroll along "Salmon Way" is a pleasant walk. In September the large stream at the end of the boardwalk is full of spawning salmon. There is emergency 911 service and a health clinic. The Alaska Ferry, from Juneau, stops every other week. Scheduled daily air service is available. Fishing, sightseeing, and kayak charters, as well as boat/skiff/kayak rentals are available. Annual community events include the *King Salmon Derby* in June and a downhome *4th of July* celebration. www.pelican.net.

Pelican Harbor Master: water, power. 907-735-2212, VHF 16.

Pelican Fuel Dock: Gas, diesel, propane, provisions. 907-735-2211 or VHF 10.

★ **Elfin Cove (44):** [17302] Moorage can be found on floats in both the outer and inner harbors. Outer harbor moorage has spectacular views, but is susceptible to swells during north winds. The channel to the inner harbor is dredged to eight foot minimum depths. Because of the current, slower boats must enter the inner cove with the flood tide and leave with the ebb. Moorage, for approximately 46 boats, is open on a space available basis. Water is accessible at this location. There is a tidal grid for boats to 60 feet in length. Telephones are located at both the inner and outer floats. Harbormaster stands by VHF 16. Weather information is available by calling 907-586-3997.

Named after a boat owned by a pioneer resident, Elfin Cove is one of the nicest places in all Southeast Alaska. The community is located on a peninsula just behind the outer floats. A boardwalk crosses over the neck of the peninsula to the inner harbor and continues around the outer perimeter of the peninsula, until it reaches the starting point. Along the boardwalk are a fishing lodge (one of several), the post office, several homes, a general store, one restaurant, and a laundry.

Elfin Cove Fuel Dock: Gas, diesel, propane, oils, water. 907-239-2208. VHF 16.

★ **Hoonah (45):** [17302] Enter inside of Pitt Island. Moorage, lodging, restaurants, coffee shop, hotel, hardware, and grocery store. There is ferry service three times a week. The name Hoonah means "village by the cliff" in Tlingit. This is the principal ancestral village of the Huna people from the Tlingit tribe. Residents have always relied on the sea for their livelihood, whether it be commercial or subsistence fishing. A renovated cannery harkens to the years when the salmon industry flourished. Tourism is currently the up and coming industry as a number of cruise ships are making Hoonah a regular stop. The Tlingit Cultural Center is a popular site. Shore and wildlife excursion can be arranged.

Hoonah City Float: Wooden floats located at the city center, a few blocks from Hoonah Harbor. Power, no water. Open to strong northwest winds. 907-945-3670. VHF 16.

Hoonah Harbor: Concrete floats are in the breakwater protected inner harbor, past the Hoonah Cold Storage dock. Moorage, gas, diesel, tidal grid, laundry, showers, power, water, and repairs. Fuel dock in outer harbor. 907-945-3670. VHF 16. Working Channels 9, 14. Email: hoonah_harbor@hoonah.net.

Hoonah Trading Co.: Gas, diesel, oil, lubricants, provisions, hardware. 907-945-3211. VHF 11.

Huna Propane: Lodging, water. 907-945-3389.

Pavlof Harbor: This is on the south shore of Freshwater Bay. A lake is within walking distance.

★ **Tenakee Inlet (46):** [17300, 17302] This long inlet is the site of Tenakee Springs and several bays which permit anchorage. This is a busy place when fishing season is open. Crab Bay, Saltery Bay, Lang Bay, and Seal Bay have anchorage. There is little, if any, radio reception from this area.

★ **Tenakee Springs:** A boat basin, capacity 56, provides moorage one-half mile east of center of town. Power on floats, no water. 16' X 51' grid available. Additional moorage is found on the inside of the floating breakwater with a dinghy ride ashore. There is no formal check-in at the floats. City personnel monitor VHF Channel 16 to assist visiting boaters. A resident certified health aide is in town and the Rescue Boat is a speedy 25 foot Boston Whaler. A fuel wharf with gas and diesel, shops, meals, and groceries can be found. Water at the fuel wharf is non-potable. There are about a hundred residents. Many homes have "shingles" hanging in front which refer to the occupations of owners who come here to vacation. The entire community seems to center around the hot sulfur bath at Dock and Main Streets. Separate bath hours are designated for men and women. Take your own soap to pre-wash. Because of sulfur in the water, remove all jewelry. The oil truck and fire engine are the only vehicles in town. Fishing for halibut, Dolly Varden, cod, salmon, and crab may prove fruitful near the moorage basin. The ferry makes scheduled stops to Tenakee Springs.

Tenakee Fuel Facility: Gas, diesel. 907-736-2288.

Tenakee Springs City Hall: 907-736-2207, VHF 16.

Tenakee Snyder Mercantile: Provisions. 907-736-2205. VHF 16.

★ **Crab Bay:** Good anchorage on the south side of Tenakee Inlet. Anchor in five to 25 fathoms, avoiding mud flats on the south side and at the head.

★ **Saltery Bay:** The narrow entrance opens to a wider basin. Flats extend 1.2 miles from the head. Anchorage is soft mud and gravel bottom. A four fathom shoal is on the north side of the entry.

Seal Bay: This bay is ten miles west northwest of Tenakee Springs on the south side of the inlet. Shoals are at entry at 6¼ fathoms and 1½ fathoms. See Coast Pilot for specifics regarding latitude and longitude. The flat is .8 of a mile from the head, plus a rock near the middle, 1½ miles inside the entry, is covered at high water. Between this rock and the flat, depths are 19 to 29 fathoms on a soft bottom.

★ **Long Bay:** This bay is located 12.5 miles from town on the southwest inlet side. See U.S. Coast Pilot 8 for Pacific Coast Alaska. From the northwest entry point, a reef, covered at half tide,

extends east .5 mile. Depths are five to 15 fathoms, secure mud bottom anchorage. From the head, a mud flat extends .6 mile. On the north shore of upper Tenakee Inlet is a portage 300 yards to Point Frederick in Icy Strait.

★ **Basket Bay:** The cave at the head will be of interest to the explorer in the family. Anchor in about seven fathoms off the flats at the head. Open to southeasterly winds. The tides in Chatham Strait meet near the vicinity of Basket Bay, except during spring tides when the meeting place is farther south.

★ **Sitkoh Bay:** [17320, 17338] Fair anchorage is found off the flats at the head, past the cannery site. Hike four miles to a Forest Service cabin on Sitkoh Lake.

Baranof Island

[17320, 17324, 17326, 17327, 17331, 17336, 17337, 17338]

★ **Baranof Island:** Russian place names predominate on this mountainous island. It was the first place in Southeast Alaska settled by the Russians. The island was named after Alexander Andreievich Baranov, the first governor of the Russian-American colonies.

★ **Goddard Hot Springs Bay & Kluckevoi Bay:** [17326] Located on the east shore of Baranof Island, this is the site of nice hot springs. Kluckevoi Bay is a good anchorage, but be careful in the entrance. Use the east one. Going in, there is a rock sticking up in the entrance. Keep to the right of this, but close to it because the shore to the right is foul. Turn around this rock, keeping to the right of it. There is another submerged rock close beyond the first one, and you have to go between the two. Once inside, there is no problem. The hot springs are to the south, just outside Kluckevoi Bay. You should be able to see a clearing up from the shore and two bath houses. The bay immediately in front of the springs is foul.

★ **Aleutkina Bay:** The inner bay is very protected with good holding. There are many eagles to watch during herring season. Keep well over to the left shore and watch the depth sounder on the way in. Gravel bars extend farther than you might expect, or that is shown on the chart.

★ **Silver Bay:** There is a shallower spot for anchoring at the extreme south end behind the island. Good holding. Several trails lead into the mountains. One takes off slightly towards a power plant, just beyond some old abandoned buildings. It has been marked with surveyor's tape. There are old mines in the vicinity.

★ **Sitka (47):** [17324] This is the oldest city in southeast Alaska. Many believe it also claims the title of being most beautiful. It is possible to see performances of the Tlingit dancers, the New Archangel Dancers (Russian dances in authentic costumes). Other attractions include the National Historic Park, Sheldon Jackson Museum (907-747-8981), and St. Michael's Cathedral. The first cathedral was built in 1844-48, and, although the building was destroyed by fire in 1966, many art and church treasures were salvaged and are in the rebuilt structure. Open when cruise ships are in port. For mor informatin and winter hours: 907-747-8120. Another attraction is the Russian Bishop's House, built in 1842 and the oldest intact Russian building. Sitka National Historic Park: 907-747-0110 for information and reservations. In addition, the landmark Sitka

Pioneer's Home welcomes guests to come and visit, and to explore the handicrafts made by the elderly residents. For those interested in the Native Indian culture, the Sheldon Jackson Museum features one of the oldest collections in Alaska, and the Sitka National Historical Park's 107 acres preserve the site of a Tlingit Indian Fort and the battle grounds of 1804. A fine collection of Haida and Tlingit totem poles were moved to this park from the 1904 Louisiana Exposition in St. Louis. Visitors can watch and talk with Native Indian carvers. Open 8am-5pm daily. A Sitka Historical Walking Trail leads to the area's historic attractions. The Alaskan Raptor Center is about a one mile walk. It offers views of recovering eagles and other wild birds. Call for tour times. 907-747-8662. The *Sitka Summer Music Festival*, which attracts some of the world's classical musicians, takes place, over a three week period in June. For Information call 907-747-6774 during the month of June, at other times of the year call 907-277-4852. The United States Forest Service has campgrounds and recreational cabins in the area. For Forest Service information contact 907-747-6671. Volunteers staff the Visitor Information Desk in the Centennial Hall, mid-May through mid-September.

Sitka's name is said to have come from the Tlingit Indian name for "by the sea." The Natives developed a culture, exemplified by the totem poles which depicted family history and legends, and the creation of baskets, tools, art works, and clan houses. Russian fur traders first visited here in 1741, and returned to settle under the leadership of Alexander Baranov. After a battle at the site of an Indian fort, the Russians took control. Much of the architecture dates to the Russian period. In 1848, Sitka was said to have been the busiest port on the Pacific Coast. Furs, especially sea otter, were the attraction. On October 18, 1867, at the Baranof Castle Hill site, the transfer of Alaska from Russia to the United States was made. Purchase price was $7,200,000. Sitka was the capital of Alaska until it was moved to Juneau in 1912. For more information contact the Sitka Convention & Visitor Bureau 907-747-5940. www.sitk.org.

Berthage: Upon entering the Sitka Channel, contact the Harbormaster on VHF 16 or phone 907-747-3439. All slips are assigned by the Harbormaster, and vessels are required to contact the Harbormaster within eight hours of arrival. The North Thomsen Harbor is the only moorage location in Sitka for transient recreational vessels. Due to construction on the Old Thomsen Harbor, there may be a shortage of available moorge during the 2006 boating season. The inner harbor is a no wake zone, slow to 3 mph.

ANB (Alaska Native Indian Brotherhood) Harbor: ANB Harbor, for commercial boats and permanent moorage is located at the south end of Sitka Narrows, just west of the bridge. Fresh water, power. Groceries, restaurants, and a large tidal grid are nearby. 907-747-3439. VHF 16.

North Thomsen Harbor: Located about ½-mile from downtown Sitka. There is approximately one mile of transient moorage available. About 800' of this moorage has 30 ampere power. Water is available throughout the harbor. There are 244 stalls ranging in size from 32' to 150'. Restrooms and showers are at the head of the ramp. Fish cleaning stations, waste oil and garbage drop on site. This moorage is close to laundry facilities as well as stores providing groceries, supplies, sporting goods, and marine hardware. Call Channel 16 for the Harbormaster. 907-747-3439.

Old Thomsen Harbor: Located directly south of North Thomsen Harbor, this harbor is undergoing a major rebuild during the summer of 2006. When complete, new moorage for transient vessels will likely be added.

Sealing Cove: Located on Japonski Island. Permanent moorage only. Water, power, and launch ramp. Large sailboats may have difficulty getting under the bridge. 907-747-3439, VHF 16.

Sitka Petro Dock: Gas, diesel, propane, water, oils. 907-747-8460. VHF 16.

Sitka Petro Marine: Gas, diesel, water, lubicants. 907-747-3414. VHF 16.

Sitka Service Transfer: Propane. 907-747-3276.

★ **Neva Strait and Olga Strait:** These are on the Alaska State Ferry route to Sitka. They are well marked and boaters should pay close attention to these navigational aids. Also, watch closely for hazards like submerged rocks and floating logs. Currents run to about 1.5 knots. Neva Strait floods to the south, and Olga Strait to the northwest. The ideal situation is to reach Krestof Sound, situated between the two Straits, at high slack. Alaska Ferries give about ten minutes warning on Channel 16 VHF of their approach. There are several spots where one might not want to meet them.

★ **Sergius Narrows:** The channel is 24 feet deep and 450 feet wide. Flood currents set northeast, ebb southwest. Currents can run to 5.9 knots on the flood and 5.5 on the ebb. Use the current tables, and transit at or near times of slack water.

★ **Appleton Cove (48):** [17338] This cove is located on the south side of Rodman Bay, which is on the south side of Peril Strait. Good, well-protected anchorage is available on the east side of the cove in eight fathoms of water, on a soft bottom. Some anchor fouling has been reported. A good anchorage is at the south end of the cove northeast of Andersen Island. Salmon fishing is recommended between Point Benham and the buoy in the mouth of Rodman Bay.

★ **Magoun Islands:** Located in Krestof Sound, the bay formed by these islands is very pretty and well sheltered. Enter through the north passage. There are no obstructions in the entrance, and the holding bottom is good. Keep an eye out for a small wreck on the south shore.

★ **St. John the Baptist Bay (49):** [17323] Located at the north end of Neva Strait, this bay has anchorage in 11 fathoms of water on a soft bottom, near the head of the bay. The publishers caught a ten pound halibut in their crab trap here, for a pleasant surprise. Anchorage is also possible in the bight behind the island off the south side near the entrance, in seven fathoms of water on a soft bottom. However, there is not much room at this second location.

Trader's Islands: This group is located at the eastern end of Peril Strait. The shoreline of Catharine Island is foul. Favor the Traders Islands and anchor in one of the several small bights along the southern shore. This is a good anchorage only in settled weather.

Point Lull: This is open to the southeast, however there is anchorage in six fathoms of water with protection from north winds.

★ **Cosmos Cove (50):** [17337] This is a popular anchorage during the fishing season. Flats extend from the head of the cove.

★ **L Cove:** This is a lovely little nook, adjacent to Takatz Bay. The small indentation, in the shape

Craig Alaska boat harbor   Ralph Mackie Photo

of a reversed L, is unnamed and barely shown on charts. This is an excellent anchorage in about seven fathoms on a rocky bottom.

★ **Baranof Warm Springs (51):** [17337] Located in Warm Springs Bay, on the east side of Baranof Island, is a state maintained 250' small craft float with moorage on both sides. Water is usually available on these floats. Because of currents caused by the falls from Baranof Lake at the head of the bay, landing may be easier on the inside of the floats and heading into the current. Anchorage is possible in the two coves on the south side of the bay. The western most is preferable as it shows shallower water, 12 to 15 fathoms. There are private homes along the boardwalk, at the head of the bay, next to the spectacular waterfalls. A small store was available in 2001. The old tubs for the hot springs are gone, but it is possible to visit the hot springs pools. Walk up the dock onto the wooden boardwalk which, in 2001, was in very good condition. Walk all the way past a two story house with a small store downstairs. Then the walk branches left to dead end, perhaps 200 meters on down in front of three or four houses set well up the hill facing the bay. There are stretches in the boardwalk interspersed with a mud path veined with tree roots. A sign points off to the left down to the hot pools, perhaps 200 meters or so of mud path again veined with tree roots. It is not difficult, just muddy. The lowest pool, in the series of three, is cold. The path continues past the hot pools turnoff to Baranof Lake.

★ **Red Bluff Bay (52):** [17336] Named for the red rock cliffs on the north side, this bay has waterfalls and a river flat at the head. Anchor at the head.

★ **Gut Bay:** Anchor near the head.

★ **Port Armstrong (53):** Use [17333] This was once the site of a whaling plant and, later, a herring oil plant. Good anchorage can be found in the niche near the plant site.

★ **Port Alexander (54):** [17331] Transient moorage is available at the floats in the inner harbor about 1/4 mile from city center. 18 X 48 Grid. No power or water. Fuel and groceries are accessible.

The outer harbor is the site of a Seaplane Float and 400' float. No power, water at head of float. Anchorage in the middle harbor is unadvisable due to seaplane traffic in the area.

Keku Strait: This strait separates Kuiu Island from Kupreanof Island. Navigational aids have been replaced by the Coast Guard and an updated chart is available. However, the passage is narrow and currents can cause problems in some places. Recommended for passage only by skippers with considerable cruising experience. In case of trouble, it could be days before anyone ventures by to offer help.

★ **Kake (55):** [17368] This is a native Tlingit village of about 670 residents, most who are involved in fishing or logging. Like their ancestors, a subsistence lifestyle is also important. Food resources include salmon, halibut, shellfish, deer, bear, berries and more. The world's largest totem, 132 feet, sits on the hill overlooking the harbor. Another totem pole of note, used for EXPO '70 in Japan, was carved by Kake artists. Gannuk Creek Hatchery is an educational stop. Silver Spike Road Bridge is a good spot for bear viewing. A dock, float, and grid are located about two blocks from the city center. No power or water. Be aware of the reef in the general area of the float. Some repairs, fuel, stores, health clinic, library, and a post office are available. The Kake Portage Cove Harbor, located about two miles from town behind a breakwater, is a well protected harbor. Water, grid, and boat launch available. Call on VHF 16 for "WQB 460 Kake," or CB-15, or phone 907-785-3251 for advance information regarding fuel dock hours. or moorage. Kake is connected to other SE Alaska communities by air and state ferry service.

Prince of Wales Island
[17360, 17423, 17426, 17432, 17433, 17436]

★ **Prince of Wales Island:** This island, with 1,000 miles of coastline, is the third largest island in the entire United States. It is 135 miles long and 45 miles across. Eleven islands and several small islets surround Prince of Wales Island. There are many bays, coves, and inlets around this island. Winds flow mainly from the northeast or southwest in the summer. Direction varies with local topography. This area has been populated by Tlingit and Haida Indians. Recently, this has become the home of miners, loggers, and commercial fishermen. The communities of Craig, Klawock, Hydaburg, Coffman Cove, Hollis, and Thorne Bay are connected by road. Prince of Wales Island has a road network of over 1,000 miles, the largest in southeast Alaska. Vehicles can arrive by ferry from Ketchikan to Hollis, or cars can be rented. A picnic site with an outstanding view of Clarence Strait is located at Sandy Beach, six miles north of Thorne Bay. There are tables, fire rings, and toilets. No fresh water. Exchange Cove, 15 minutes by car from the community of Whale Pass, has three campsites. Lake #3, 30 minutes by car from Thorne Bay, has fishing, hiking, canoeing, and two campsites. No developed water supply. All water in these wilderness areas must be boiled at least five minutes before using. Black bears are found on Prince of Wales Island. Make plenty of noise while hiking to warn bears that you are around. A startled bear is a dangerous bear.

East Side Prince of Wales Island

[17360, 17382, 17401, 17420, 17423]

★ **Clarence Strait:** This strait extends about 110 miles along the entire east side of Prince of Wales Island from Dixon Entrance, on the south to Sumner Strait, at the north. Currents run to four knots. The strait is broken by several large sounds and bays in the southern half. Snow Passage, at the north end of Clarence Strait, has strong currents, and can be very uncomfortable when wind is added.

★ **Exchange Cove:** Located on the east side of Prince of Wales Island, about two miles northwest of Kashevarof Passage. Heed the channel marker west of West Island and avoid numerous shoal and rocky areas, when approaching from either north or south. Exchange Cove is the largest well protected anchorage in this area and has room for several boats. The entry depth is ten fathoms, with gradual shoaling toward the head. Avoid the drying mudflat and numbers traps which may, at times, line the sides and head of the cove. Anchor in ten fathoms, excellent holding soft bottom.

★ **Coffman Cove:** This, like Thorne Bay, was a logging camp that received status as a city by the State of Alaska. Moorage, with water, is found at the state float. Transient boats usually moor on the outside. The cove is sheltered and good anchorage is possible. Several tourist oriented businesses are found. Gas and diesel are available although there is no pump at the dock. A general store carries clothing and provisions. The laundry, showers, and the liquor store are accessible, as are rental cabins and car rentals. Library with internet access. Harbor Master: 907-329-2922. VHF 16.

Coffman Cove The Riggin Shack Store: 907-329-2213. VHF 16.

Walk-around: Stroll to Rhody Park within walking distance from moorage, and enjoy a water view from the lookout area or explore other nearby trails.

Ratz Harbor: Fair anchorage, but open to wakes.

★ **Snug Anchorage:** Favor the west shore when entering. Anchor north of the islet.

★ **Thorne Bay (56):** [17423] This large bay is the site of the City of Thorne Bay, McFarland's Floatel, and numerous anchorages. The narrow entrance channel is marked by a light. Floats, located at city center, have power and water. A boat launch is located nearby. This is a friendly town to visit. The residents actively participate in the community events and businesses. Thorne Bay sponsors an annual fishing derby from May - July and the island-wide *Prince of Wales Fair and Logging Show* the last weekend of July. Shopping includes clothing, gifts, groceries, hardware, tackle, liquor, marine supplies, and post office. The Medical Clinic is open four days a week and an excellent Emergency Medical Services program provides care 24/7. For current information regarding local services visit www.thornebayalaska.net.

Thorne Bay is an entry point to the over 1,000 miles of road on Prince of Wales Island. There is scheduled float plane service to Ketchikan. By car, Thorne Bay is reached by the Inter-Island Ferry. For information contact 1-866-308-4848 or 907-826-4848. Both salt and freshwater fishing can be excellent. Thorne Bay was once the largest logging camp in the United States and became a city in 1982. The three major employers are the City of Thorne Bay, the United States Forestry Service, and the Southeast Island School District.

McFarlands Floatel: {55° 40.92' N, 132° 31.47' W} Located two miles by water from the town of Thorne Bay. Lodging, gift store, fishing/hunting licenses, sporting and boating supplies, pop and convenience items. Meeting room with kitchen available for rent. 1-888-828-3335. VHF 16, CB 11. www.mcfarlandsfloatel.com.

Petro Alaska Thorne Bay: Gas, diesel. 907-828-3900.

Tackle Shack: Gas, diesel. 907-828-3333.

The Port: One-half mile past the main dock. Gas, diesel, Post Office, store. 907-828-3995.

Thorne Bay Harbor: Moorage, fresh water, power, garbage drop, pay telephone. Boaters must check in with Harbor Master before plugging into power. Hours: 8am-5pm. 907-828-3380. VHF 16.

Thorne Bay Bayview Fuel & Tire: Gas, propane, batteries. 907-828-3345.

Riptide Liquor: Movie rental. 907-828-8233.

Thorne Bay IGA: 907-828-3306.

★ **Lyman Anchorage:** A small, well protected anchorage. The entrance is narrow, and depths may be minimal at very low tides. Good holding bottom in eight fathoms. This anchorage is on the west side of Clarence Strait, about 22 miles north of Ketchikan.

★ **Kasaan Bay (57):** [17426] This 25 mile long bay is interesting, but the shoreline is relatively flat in comparison to the west side of Prince of Wales Island. Kasaan is a native Haida village with breakwater, floats, and sea plane float. There is a library and health clinic in town. Kasaan has a totem park and Whale Clan House. From the early to mid-1900's this was the site of a busy cannery.

★ **Kina Cove:** Is on the south side of Kasaan Bay, about 15 miles from the entrance. Sheltered

anchorage in seven fathoms is at the head of the cove.

★ **Hollis (58):** [17426] This small residential community is not abandoned, as shown on the charts. There is a 150' moorage float and a separate float for seaplanes. The float approach is quite shallow and restricted, and the float is often full. Anchorage in front of the launching ramp is possible. No services are available. The Prince of Wales Island-Ketchikan Ferry dock is in Clark Bay, not in Hollis anchorage. The ferry link began in 1974. The Alaska Inter-Island Ferry makes daily trips to Ketchikan. 907-530-4848. Twelve Mile Arm continues after Hollis for another 7 miles. There is a Forest Service campground on the east side, at the head of the arm. Access is by road from Craig and Hydaburg. In the early 1900's gold and silver were mined here, later logging fueled the economy.

★ **Skowl Arm:** [17426, 17436] Anchorage is possible in seven fathoms on mud bottom in Saltery Cove. In some places the bottom is rocky. There is a large sport fishing lodge, and several private residences.

★ **McKenzie Inlet:** This is entered at Khayyam Point and extends south for about five miles. McKenzie Rock should be given a wide berth. Anchorage is possible in the cove to the east of Thumb Point, $^1/_2$-mile south of McKenzie Rock, in nine to ten fathoms, soft bottom, and protected from all but north winds. There is also good anchorage near the head of the inlet in seven to ten fathoms, soft bottom on the west side of Peacock Island. The entrance to Polk Inlet, at the west end of Skowl Arm, is foul and entering may not be worth the risks involved.

★ **Cholmondeley Sound:** [17436] Pronounced Chomly, this sound is entered between Chasina Point and Skin Island. This sound extends about 16 miles to the end of its West Arm.

★ **Lancaster Cove:** The first anchorage after entering the sound is in Lancaster Cove, about one mile southeast of Hump Island, and behind the island in the center of the cove. The north cove is the best choice.

Kitkum Bay: This bay lies to the southwest of Lancaster Cove, but because of all the hazards in its entrance, may not be worth exploring.

★ **Dora Bay:** Three miles long, this bay lies off the south side of the sound. The best anchorage is in the tight little cove at the far south end, just before the flats, in eight to ten fathoms, soft bottom. When weather permits there are beautiful views of Mount Eudora.

★ **South Arm:** Seven miles long, the South Arm lies just west of Dora Bay. There are two coves at the head, the one on the east side is probably best, being shallower, and less subject to strong winds coming through from Klakas Inlet on the west side of Prince of Wales Island. Anchorage in the east cove is in seven to eight fathoms, soft bottom, with plenty of room. When the mountains are visible, this is a beautiful place.

★ **West Arm:** Three possible anchorages are found in its six mile length. First is the little cove one and one half miles into the arm on the south side, just past the numerous pilings and an old building or two. They mark the former site of the old town of Chomly. The second anchorage may be the best and is farther west just past the first group of seven or eight islets, in front of the creek that flows into the sound. Anchorage is in eight to ten fathoms, well protected, and a soft bottom.

The third possibility is at the head of the arm in 12-15 fathoms, but it may be subject to winds funneling through from Hetta Inlet. Another anchorage is in Sunny Cove, on the north side of the sound, about five miles west of Hump Island. Protected anchorage in 12-15 fathoms is available.

★ **Port Johnson:** [17432] Entrance is between Wedge Island and Adams Point. Beware of the reef shown off Inner Point, it extends quite far off shore. Port Johnson is three and one half miles long. The cove at the west end is a very nice, protected anchorage in ten to 12 fathoms, soft bottom, just to the south of the small island shown on the chart.

Dolomi Bay: This is a small, narrow inlet, about one and one quarter miles in from the entrance to the inlet, and would be a nice anchorage in eight to ten fathoms at the head. A logging camp and log booms may be present. The abandoned gold mining town of Dolomi is located here.

★ **Moira Sound:** [17432] This sound has beautiful scenery and good anchorages in its seven or more arms. Four mile long North Arm is entered at Point Halliday, three miles west of Moira Rock. This is in the entrance to Moira Sound.

★ **Clarno Cove:** The best anchorages are both in Clarno Cove. The first is at the head of Clarno in eight fathoms, soft bottom, and the second is in the entrance to Aiken Cove in eight to nine fathoms, soft bottom. There is an excellent view of 3,500 foot Mount Eudora. Additional anchorages are in the unnamed cove on the south side of Clarno Cove, with a least depth of one fathom in its entrance, and in Nowiskay Cove and Cannery Cove.

★ **Niblack Anchorage:** Entry is at Safety Rock, three and one half miles west-southwest of Moira Rock. Anchorage is in six to eight fathoms, mud bottom, and good protection in the cove at the head of this inlet. The buildings on shore are those of a mining company doing exploration work in the area. They are on the site of the former copper mining town of Niblack, founded around 1900 and abandoned in 1909.

★ **Kegan Cove:** This is a small scenic cove lying off the north side of Moira Sound. If entering or departing it is best to do so on the top half of a tide, as the chart shows a depth of only five feet at zero tide. Favor the west side when entering. Anchorage in the inner cove is in six to seven fathoms, mud bottom, plenty of room, and well protected. There is a Forest Service cabin on shore, and a buoy in the cove with a sign that says that it should not be used by boats over 26 feet in length. A trail leads from the cabin about a half mile to Kegan Lake, where another Forest Service cabin is located.

★ **Dickman Bay:** This is an inlet in the West Arm of Moira Sound. Dickman Bay extends four miles northwest from its entrance, and is clear of dangers, except for the narrow passage, just prior to entering the cove at the head of the bay. The chart shows seven foot depths in the narrows at zero tide. A fair current flows through the anchorage, but not enough to create a problem. Anchorage is in six fathoms in the far west cove, soft bottom, and good protection. The cove to the south shows a rocky bottom. This is a beautiful anchorage. There are two more anchorages in Dickman Bay, the eastern most has anchorage in 15-17 fathoms, and the western in five to eight fathoms, both with mud bottoms, and good protection.

★ **Frederick Cove:** This inlet extends two and one half miles further west from the west end of Moira Sound. Anchorage near the head is in six to eight fathoms, soft bottom, well protected.

★ **South Arm:** Anchorage is found at the head of this four mile inlet. Anchorage is in seven fathoms, over soft bottom, with protection from all but northeast winds up the inlet. Except for rocky 2,500 foot Bokan Mountain on the east side, the shoreline is low. Beware of the rocks, not visible at high tide, in the center of the inlet about one and one half miles south of the entrance. The best course is along the eastern shore until you are certain that you are past the rocks.

★ **Johnson Cove:** [17432] Johnson Cove lies just east of the South Arm, is two and one half miles long, and has a large, well protected anchorage at its head with depths of ten fathoms, soft bottom. When we were last there, the hulk of the former Washington State Ferry "Vashon", was on the southwest shore near the head of the inlet. It was being converted to a sports fishing camp a few years ago, when it dragged its anchors in a big winter storm, and wound up on the beach. This wreck was not shown on our edition of Chart #17432. Passage from the South Arm to Johnson Cove is possible in the narrow channel south of the largest island on the west side of the entrance to Johnson Cove.

Menefee Anchorage: Located on the south side of the entrance to Moira Sound, this has depths of 25 fathoms, but shallower anchorages can be found around the edges.

★ **Ingraham Bay:** [17432] This bay is located about four miles south of Rip Point on the south side of the entrance to Moira Sound. The best anchorage is in the one mile long north arm in

---

★ **Point Baker:** This secluded harbor at the north end of Prince of Wales Island is a must stop. Halibut, salmon, whale, eagle, and sea otter perform daily for the sportsman and the photographer, and it is the home of the Point Baker Trading Post. While retaining the traditions of previous years, many new additions and improvements have been made to the facilities. In the restaurant, Herb and Judy serve Better Baker Burgers and

homemade pies that have been called the best in SE Alaska. A small convenience store, liquor store, and bar are also on the premises. The bar, the last floating saloon in Southeast Alaska, is complete with Karaoke and three guitars for those so talented. Local artists display their works at the store. Fuel sales, laundry, and shower facilities are located just over the bullrail at the 450' state float. No moorage fees, but you can buy dock power. A recent addition is Ruffies, their Bed and Breakfast Inn. This is a good site for a rendezvous. Visitors arrive by floatplane from Ketchikan, Wrangell, or Petersburg. Some boaters, who arrive via small cruisers, stay in the shore side accommodation, fish all day, and then barbecue their catches on the deck. Daily mail service is provided by floatplane from Ketchikan. If planning your cruise itinerary around the Fourth of July, be sure to visit for the annual Seafest and Independence Day Celebration. This is a great dock party featuring fresh caught salmon and halibut as well as Dungeness crab and oysters, accompanied by all the side dishes and desserts imaginable. The management looks forward to making new friends. **Circle #54 on Reader Service Card at page 251. Websites: www.boattravel.com/pointbaker & www.pointbakeralaska.com Email: ruffies907@aol.com Mailing address: Post Office Box 130, Point Baker, Alaska 99927. Fax: 907-559-2224 Telephone: 907-559-2204. VHF 16.**

---

seven to eight fathoms, mud bottom, good protection, and nice scenery. There are at least six fathoms of water in the entrance to the north arm. The two mile long south arm is so rock infested that entry is not worth the risks involved.

★ **Kendrick Bay:** [17433] Located about six miles south of the entrance to Ingraham Bay, Kendrick Bay can be entered on either the north or south side of the Kendrick Islands. The south side is the easiest. Stay well offshore to avoid the numerous rocks, which afford excellent bottom fishing for large rockfish and ling cod.

South Arm: This has an anchorage in seven to eight fathoms, bottom may be hard. We have only used this as a temporary lunch anchorage.

West Arm: Extreme caution is necessary in entering this arm, because of numerous charted hazards, and some that are not on the chart. The first uncharted rock is in the main part of Kendrick Bay, a short distance to the east of the two islets in the center of the bay. From these islets, or rocks, the course to the West Arm is south of the two small islands in water shown on the chart as 15 fathoms. Just past the second of these islands three underwater rocks are shown extending out into the channel. Two reefs are shown to the west, with above water rocks. They should be passed to the north, giving them plenty of clearance, as there are some uncharted rocks to the north which are only visible at low tide. The Coast Pilot's excellent advice is to traverse this passage near low tide. The best anchorage is found in the bight on the south side in nine to ten fathoms, soft bottom. There is also a large mooring buoy in the bight that visiting boaters may use. The owner, Bob Dotson, says that it is securely anchored. The Dotsons spend part of their summer in the house with the float in front of it, located on the north side of the bay near its head. Visiting boaters are welcome to use the float, as well as get some of the fresh water that is piped to it. The Dotson's work a mine that they own up on Bokan Mountain. They used to mine uranium, but since that market collapsed, they are prospecting for "rare earths minerals". In the winter they move to their house in Ketchikan.

★ **Gardner Bay:** Gardner Bay is entered on the south side of the island in its entrance. There is a good anchorage in 13 fathoms over mud in the basin at the head of the bay. This is a beautiful spot, surrounded by big mountains. Anchorage is also possible in the small bight on the south side, showing six and one half fathoms. This spot is more protected than the head of the bay. The head is subject to "willawaw" winds.

★ **McLean Arm:** McLean Point is about four miles north of Cape Chacon, and McLean Arm is entered north of the light on the point. This four mile inlet is straight, and unencumbered by hazards. Anchorage is possible at the head of either the north or west arms, but they can be subject to "willawaw" winds. The small bight on the south side, just west of the point showing three fathoms has a more protected anchorage in 12 fathoms, soft bottom.

West Side Prince of Wales Island

[17378, 17387, 17400, 17403-17408, 17431-17433]

★ **West Side Prince of Wales Island:** This stretch of water, about 150 miles from Point

Baker on the northwest corner of the island, to Cape Chacon, its southern tip in Dixon Entrance, offers some of the most scenic and protected waters in southeast Alaska. The high, snow-covered mountains and glaciers are lacking, but there are many narrow passages, and untold numbers of anchorages. Good salmon fishing is to be found in several locations, especially along the outer islands.

★ **Point Baker (60):** Located at the north end of Prince of Wales Island, this lovely, sheltered harbor is the site of a float, sea plane float, B & B, and the Point Baker Trading Post. Sport fishing is good in the immediate vicinity as are opportunities for eagle, whale, and dolphin watching. Ask about the World Class caves discovered at nearby El Capitan Mountain. The float accomodates about 27 vessels and has power and seasonal water. Grid nearby.

★ **Point Baker Trading Post and Ruffies Bed & Breakfast:** Moorage available, with no dock fees. Power is accessible. Gas, diesel, laundry, showers, convenience and liquor stores, pub, and restaurant. The last floating saloon in Southeast Alaska. Local artists display their works at the store. Ruffies Bed & Breakfast Inn provides shoreside accommodations. Floatplane service to and from Ketchikan, Wrangell, and Petersburg. Daily mail service from Ketchikan. See our Steering Star description in this chapter. Websites: www.boattravel.com & www.point-bakeralaska.com Circle #54 on Reader Service Card on page 251. Mailing address: Post Office Box 130, Point Baker, Alaska. 99927. Fax: 907-559-2224. Telephone: 907-559-2204. VHF 16.

★ **Port Protection (61):** [17378] This small settlement is in Wooden Wheel Cove on the east side of Port Protection. There is 250-foot, state-maintained float and seaplane float, some houses and private floats. A grid is located near the private floats. Anchorage is found farther into the bay on the east side, south of Wooden Wheel Cove, behind the small islands, in ten fathoms of water on a mud bottom. George Vancouver named this site when he sought refuge from a storm in Sumner Strait.

Wooden Wheel Cove Trading Post: Gas, diesel, showers, laundry, store, groceries, liquor, restaurant (opens after June 20). 907-489-2222. VHF 16.

★ **Shakan Strait:** [17387] Shakan Bay and Shakan Strait lead to the north entrance to El Capitan Passage, between Prince of Wales Island and Koscuisko Island.

Bay at Marble Creek: This bay is being used by commercial boats involved in the mining operations at Maple Creek. If there is room, anchorage is in six fathoms of water on mud.

Calder Bay: This bay has anchorage, on the east side in five fathoms of water on a soft bottom, however, it is open to prevailing winds and can be uncomfortable.

★ **El Capitan Passage:** This is the most spectacular part of this trip. The first three and one-half miles from Shakan Strait to Aneskett Point have been dredged through several shoals. Controlling depth in Dry Pass is seven feet for a width of 70 feet. Currents in Dry Pass run to 1.8 knots to the east on the flood, and 0.9 knots to the west on the ebb. High and low water in this area occur at about the same time as Sitka. El Capitan Passage continues south for 18 miles to Sea Otter Sound.

★ **Sarheen Cove:** This little cove on the east

side of El Capitan Passage offers well protected anchorage in seven to eight fathoms, soft bottom.

Tokeen: A fish processing facility was formerly located here on the west side of El Capitan Island, at the south end of El Capitan Passage. Some floats and a store, where gas may be available, have been at the site.

★ **Sarkar Cove:** This cove is located on the east side of El Capitan Passage, about 18 miles south of Shakan Strait. Anchorage is in seven fathoms of water over a mud bottom. The ruins of the abandoned mining town of Deweyville are on the north side of the cove. Continuing south, the decision must be made as to which side of Tuxekan Island will be traversed. To the west, the route continues in El Capitan Passage and Sea Otter Sound and Karheen Passage. To the east are Tuxekan Narrows and Tuxekan Passage. Both are marked with navigational aids. The two routes join at the south end of Tuxekan Island at Kauda Point. The route continues south through Tonowek Bay and San Cristoval Channel into San Alberto Bay and Klawock Inlet. There are two villages in Klawock Inlet.

★ **Sea Otter Sound:** [17403] Good salmon fishing around Surf Point at the entrance to the sound.

★ **Port Alice:** Anchorage possible near the head in eight to 15 fathoms.

★ **Edna Bay:** When entering the harbor use caution and watch for buoys marking the shoals. There are two state operated floats in the cove in the northeast corner of the bay, one 135 feet long and the other one 150 feet. They are not connected to the shore and have no water, power, garbage or waste oil dump facilities.

★ **Heceta Island:** [17360, 17404] A cove on the northeast side of the island about 1¼ miles southwest at the light on Peep Rock offers well protected anchorage in eight fathoms, mud bottom.

★ **Nossuck Anchorage:** This anchorage, about one mile southwest of Tonowek Narrows, has good anchorage in nine fathoms, on a mud bottom.

Harmony Islands: If the seas are rough in Tonowek Bay, it is possible to avoid some of them by passing to the east of these islands, located about three miles southwest of Tonowek Narrows. At the south end you can come out either between Culebra and St. Philip Islands, or continue east of St. Philip.

★ **Gulf of Esquibel:** Good salmon fishing, coho, at the San Lorenzo Islands on the west side of the sound. The fish were in shallow water along the southeast shore of the eastern most of the two islands. We jigged with buzz bombs and Stingsildas.

★ **Steamboat Bay:** Located on Noyes Island about 20-25 miles from Craig, there are some facilities here for commercial fisherman. Anchorage is possible near the head of the bay in 12-18 fathoms, soft bottom. There is exposure to the north and swells may enter the bay.

★ **Klawock (62):** [17405] This native village of 800 is the site of the first cannery in Alaska, built in 1878. The Tlingit Indians here are friendly and proud of their totem park situated just above the harbor where 21 outstanding poles have been relocated from former villages to the north. Totem restoration is an ongoing process, and the summer of 2005 saw five new replica poles raised amid great ceremony. The public float near the town center has power, and a grid, and water is available at the cannery float. A modern supermarket lies about a mile away on the main highway, and an airstrip lies a few miles to the north.

★ **Craig (63):** [17405] This former native village, now a bustling town of 2,500 residents, was named after turn-of-the-century salmon salter Craig Millar. The use of his first name illustrates the casualness and friendliness of the town. Craig is home to the Healing Heart Totem, carved by Tsimpsian master Stan Marsden. Raised by the community in 1995, this magnificent pole, the tallest in Southeast Alaska, stands in a totem park about one half mile east of the harbors. Craig has a supermarket one block east of the harbors that delivers to the docks at no charge. Call 907-826-3393. The town also has several restaurants, a garage, hardware stores, public swimming pool, library, post office, hotels, medical and dental clinic, banks, rental cars, fiberglass and engine repairs, laundromat, gift shops and internet access. Some cold storage for fish is available, check with Harbor Master. Boat harbor floats are located in the north and south coves, as well as City Float in the old downtown area. About 1,200' of moorage is available for transients, plus assigned slips when the fishing fleet is out. Many improvements have been made in North Cove, including a breakwater (constructed of large concrete pontoons), and floats with water and power. The entrance channel to South Cove has been dredged to minus eleven feet. A marine repair shop is being established. There is no marine ways. Be cautious maneuvering in, and approaching, the harbor. Check your chart carefully. The Harbormaster suggests, "When approaching Craig from the north, pass on the east side (fuel dock side) of green buoy #7 and watch the chart carefully." Heading southwest from Craig, the route is through Ulloa Channel, after rounding Cape Flores.

Craig Harbor Master: 907-826-3404. VHF 16.

Craig Petro Marine: New False Island Dock. Gas, diesel, oils, water, batteries, ice. 907-826-3296. VHF 16.

Port Estrella: About seven miles south of Craig, and just east of Cape Flores, this bay offers anchorage in seven fathoms, mud bottom. It is exposed to west winds, however, and may be uncomfortable under some circumstances.

★ **Port Refugio:** About three miles south of Cape Flores, this bay offers good, well protected anchorage in six to seven fathoms on mud, at the head of the bay, on the south side of the small island.

Waterfall Resort: Private.

Port Real Marina: [17406] This passage between Lulu Island and Baker Island leads to Siketi Sound and the Pacific Ocean. Good salmon fishing reported around south end of Cone Island in Siketi Sound. At the east end the bight between Santa Rita Island and St. Ignace Island offers the best anchorage in the area in ten fathoms, soft bottom. We rode out a 50 knot blow out of the southeast one night with six commercial trollers for company.

★ **North Bay:** [17407] About 2½ miles south of Tlevak Narrows, this anchorage on the east side of Dall Island offers well protected anchorage in ten to 12 fathoms, mud bottom.

★ **Hydaburg (64):** [17407] This hospitable Haida Indian village of 500 has a large harbor with transient moorage which lies about one half mile north of town. Water is available at the head of the dock and there is a grid. No power or fuel. The facility primarily serves the local resident fishing fleet. At present, there is no harbormaster, so check in at the city office in town. There is a grocery store at the south end of town near the cold storage. The cold storage, which is no longer in operation, still affords a good place to tie up. Hydaburg is about 40 miles from Craig by road. After leaving Hydaburg, the course is to Cape Chacon on the southeast tip of Prince of Wales, through Sukkwan Straight and Cordova Bay.

★ **Hetta Inlet (65):** [17431] This 12 mile long inlet starts at Eek Point, about 12 miles southeast of Hydaburg. Around the turn of the century it was the site of several copper mines, and at least one smelter, long ago abandoned. There are two good anchorages. Eek Inlet has well protected anchorage in nine fathoms on mud, and Deer Bay, about 6 miles farther north offers protected anchorage in seven fathoms, good holding.

★ **Kaasa Inlet:** There is good, protected anchorage at the head of the north arm in nine fathoms, soft bottom.

★ **Mabel Bay:** This is an excellent anchorage behind Mabel Island, which is two miles southeast of Mellen Rock light. The anchorage is at the east end of the bay in 12 fathoms of water over a mud bottom. It is attractive as well as being well protected. The final decision in getting to Cape Chacon is whether to go by Round Island light and the outside, or through Eureka Channel in the Barrier Islands. The latter is well marked and offers more protection.

★ **Jackson Island:** [17431] This island in Cordova Bay off the southeast end of Sukkwan Island is a good spot for chinook and coho salmon fishing along its southeast shore. The unnamed bay on Sukkwan Island one mile north of Jackson Island has anchorage in ten fathoms, soft bottom, but open to the southeast. A good temporary anchorage.

★ **Long Island:** [17431] Elbow Bay on the northeast shore of Long Island has an anchorage at the head of its southeast arm in ten fathoms. Soft bottom, good protection. Enter Elbow Bay to the south of the two small islands in the entrance then avoid the shoals on the east side and the center of the bay. Long Island has been heavily logged so the scenery is not the best.

★ **Cape Chacon (66):** [17433] See current table for Wrangell Narrows. The charts have warnings of tide rips in two locations, and they are undoubtedly present under the right conditions when swells, wind, and/or tidal currents oppose each other. When approaching the cape, weather information for Dixon Entrance should be available from both Annette Island (Ketchikan) and Prince Rupert. There are more decisions to be made at Cape Chacon, (1) Prince Rupert is 72 nautical miles to the southeast, (2) Brundige Inlet on the north end of Dundas Island is about 40 miles, both across Dixon Entrance. There are some charted, but unmarked, rocks and shoals to avoid. The third, more protected route is northwest to the end of Annette Island, then along the north side of Duke Island to Danger Passage and into Revillagigedo Channel, where one turns south to Dundas Island and Prince Rupert. A fourth possibility is northeast to Ketchikan, about 45 miles, through Nichols Passage.

Annette Island

★ **Metlakatla (67):** [17434, 17435] In 1884, Father William Duncan and his followers settled this Native Community of Tsimpshian Indians. Located on the south side of Port Chester, which is on the east side of Nicholas Passage, Metlakatla is now home to 1350 permanent residents. Two protected harbors are within the village. The Marine ways is covered and capable of boats to 60', Port Authority can be reached at 907-886-4646 & VHF 80. Local retail shops are convenient to the harbors. Groceries are available at Leask Market and the Mini Mart. The Mini Mart also features fresh baked goods, fast food and videos. Metco is a small hardware/variety store. The Metlakatla Hotel and Restaurant, Ethel's B&B and the Tuck-Em-Inn offer public lodging. Tourism is a new enterprise for Metlakatla. Father Duncan's Cottage and Museum, Duncan Memorial Church, community Totem Poles, Annette Island Packing Company tours and Gift Shop are among the local sights to visit. During the cruise ship season, Metlakatla Tours and Salmon bake offers daily performances of Native Dancers in full regalia and a baked salmon lunch at the Tribal Longhouse. At The Artist's Village, visitors can observe local artists creating their cultural art. Artwork is available for purchase. Metlakatla Tourism Office 907-886-8687. Community-owned Annette Island Packing Company operates a cold storage year round for the Native-owned fishing fleet, which harvests Salmon, Halibut, Sea Cucumbers, etc. Local water from Purple Mountain is bottled by the Metlakatla Water Company and is featured in all village businesses. Metlakatla is accessible from Ketchikan by boat and floatplane. Pacific Air and Promech Air offer the 20-minute plane ride on daily schedules. Metlakatla is homeport to a new Alaska State ferry, the 180' M/V Lituya with scheduled round trips to and from Metlakatla five times a week. Metlakatla has retained Pacific Standard Time, one hour ahead of Ketchikan.

Annette Island Fuels: Delivers gas, diesel and oils to the Port dock with propane also available. 907-886-7851. VHF 72.

Metlakatla Harbor Master: Moorage, power, water at port dock. 907-886-4646. VHF 16, 80.

Duke Island

★ **Ryus Bay (68):** On the north side of Duke Island, Ryus Bay offers a sheltered anchorage in seven to ten fathoms of water over a mud bottom.

VISITOR INFORMATION

Annette Island 907-886-8687
Gustavus..907-697-2245
Haines......................................1-800-458-3579
Juneau 907-586-2201, 1-888-581-2201
Ketchikan......................................907-225-6166
Klawock..907-755-2626
Pelican 907-735-2202
Petersburg.....................................907-772-4636
Prince of Wales Island 907-755-2626
Sitka..907-747-5940
Skagway.......................................907-983-2854
Southeast Alaska 907-228-6220
Stewart/Hyder..............................250-636-9224
Thorne Bay...................................907-828-3380
Wrangell 907-874-3699, 1-800-367-9745

Essential Supplies & Services

AIR TRANSPORTATION
Alaska Airlines 1-800-426-0333
Horizon Air Lines 1-800-547-9308
LAB Flying Service. 907-789-9160
Pacific Air Metlakatla 907-886-3500
Promech Air . . . . .907-225-3845 (Ketchikan)
 . . . . .907-886-3845 (Metlakatla)
Seattle Seaplanes 1-800-637-5553
Skagway Air Service 907-983-2218
Ward Air .907-789-9150
Wings of Alaska. 907-789-0790

BOOKS / BOOK STORES
The Marine Atlas. 541-593-6396
Alaska Natural History Assn. 907-228-6233

COAST GUARD:
Cell Phones *16
All areas: VHF 16, HF 2182 mhz
Ketchikan: VHF 16, ...907-228-0340
Prince Rupert: VHF 16, 11, 71. 250-627-3081

CUSTOMS
Juneau. 907-586-7211
Ketchikan 907-225-2380, 907-225-2254
Prince Rupert 888-226-7277, 250-627-3003

FERRY INFO:
Website: www.state.ak.us/ferry
. . . . **907-465-3941, 800-642-0066**
Inter-Island. 1-866-308-4848

FUELS
Andres Oil: Ketchikan. Gas, Diesel. 907-225-2613
Annette Island: Gas, Diesel 907-886-7851 VHF 72
Angoon: Gas, Diesel. 907-788-3436
Auke Bay: Gas, Diesel . . . . .907-790-3030 VHF 16
Bartlett Cove: Gas, Diesel
Clover Pass Resort: Gas, Diesel 907-247-2234
Coffman Cove: Gas, Diesel.
Craig: Gas, Diesel . . . . .907-826-3296 VHF 16
Donahue's: Tee Harbor. Gas, Diesel. . . .907-789-7851
Elfin Cove: Gas, Diesel . . . . . . .907-239-2208 VHF 16
Excursion Inlet Cannery: Call ahead. Gas, Diesel.
. 907-586-4244
Fisherman's: Auke Bay. Gas, Diesel. . . .907-789-7312
Haines: Gas, Diesel . . . . .907-766-2448 VHF 12, 13, 16
Hoonah: Gas, Diesel . . . . .907-945-3211 VHF 11
Hydaburg Cooperative Pier
Juneau: Gas, Diesel. 907-586-4400
Kake
Ketchikan Petro Alaska: Gas . .907-225-1985 VHF 5, 16
Ketchikan Petro Marine Service:. 907-225-2106 VHF 16
Klawock
Knudson Cove: Gas, Diesel. . . . .907-247-8500 VHF 16
Metlakatla: Gas, Diesel. . . . . .907-886-7851, VHF 72
Pelican: Gas, Diesel . . . . .907-735-2211 VHF 10
Petersburg Petro: Gas, Diesel. . .907-772-4251 VHF 16
Point Baker Trading Post: Gas, Diesel.
. . . . **907-559-2204 VHF 16**
Port Alexander
Port Protection: Gas, Diesel . . . .907-489-2222 VHF 16
Seadrome Marine: Juneau. Diesel. 907-463-8811 VHF 16
Sitka Petro: Gas, Diesel . . . . . . .907-747-3414 VHF 16
Sitka Petro 2: Gas, Diesel . . . . .907-747-8460 VHF 16
Skagway Petro: Gas, Diesel. 907-983-2259
Taku Oil Sales, Juneau: Gas, Diesel. . . .907-586-1276
Tenakee Springs: Gas, Diesel . . .907-736-2288 VHF 16
The Port: Gas, Diesel. 907-828-3995
Thorne Bay Petro: Gas . . . . . . .907-828-3900 VHF 16
Thorne Bay Tackle Shack: Gas. 907-828-3333
Wrangell: Gas, Diesel . . . . .907-874-2388 VHF 16
Wrangell: Gas, Diesel . . . . .907-874-3276 VHF 16
Yes Bay: Gas. . . . . .907-247-1575 VHF 16

HOSPITALS / CLINICS
Craig Clinic 907 826-3257
Haines Clinic 907-766-2521

Juneau. 907-586-2611
Kake Health Center. 907-785-3333
Kasaan Clinic. 907-542-2233
Ketchikan .907-225-5171
Metlakatla Clinic 907-886-4741
Petersburg. 907-772-4291
Queen Charlottes 250-559-4300
Sitka 907-747-3241
Skagway Clinic 907-983-2255
Thorne Bay Clinic 907-828-8848
Wrangell 907-874-7000

INSURANCE
Boat Insurance Agency 206-285-1350
 Or Call 1-800-828-2446

LIQUOR STORES
Craig   Ketchikan
Haines   Meyer's Chuck
Juneau   Petersburg
Point Baker Trading Post. . . 907-559-2204 VHF 16
Sitka   Skagway
Thorne Bay 907-828-8233
Wrangell

LODGING
McFarland's Floatel: Thorne Bay. . 1-888-828-3335 VHF 16
Ruffie's B & B: Point Baker . 907-559-2204 VHF 16

MARINAS / MOORAGE
Air Marine Harbor: Ketchikan. 907-225-2282 VHF 16, 66
Angoon. . . . . .907-788-3960 VHF 14, 16, CB-5
Auke Bay . . . . .907-789-0819 VHF 16
Clover Pass Resort 907-247-2234
Coffman Cove . . . . .907-329-2922 VHF 16
Couverden Island
Craig . . . . .907-826-3404 VHF 16
Douglas 907-586-5255
Edna Bay
Elfin Cove
Excursion Inlet Cannery: Call ahead. Very limited moor-
 age. . . . . .907-586-4244 VHF 11
Funter Bay
Gustavus
Haines. . . . . .907-766-2448 VHF 12, 13, 16
Helm Bay
Hobart Bay
Hollis
Hoonah . . . . .907-945-3670 VHF 16
Hydaburg
Hyder. 250-636-9148
Juneau . . . . .907-586-5255 VHF 16
Kasaan Bay
Ketchikan . . . . .907-228-5632 VHF 16, 73
Klawock
Knudson Cove Marina. . . . . .907-247-8500 VHF 16
Letnikof Cove
McFarland's Floatel: Thorne Bay. . 1-888-828-3335 VHF 16
Metlakatla . . . . .907-886-4646 VHF 16
Meyers Chuck
Papkes Landing: Wrangell Narrows
Pelican . . . . .907-735-2212 VHF 16
Petersburg . . . . .907-772-4688 VHF 9, 16
Point Baker Trading Post . . . 907-559-2204 VHF 16
Port Alexander
Port Protection
Seadrome Marine Complex: Juneau.
. . . . .907-463-8811. VHF 16
Sitka: All moorages. . . . . .907-747-3439 VHF 16
Skagway .907-983-2628
Stewart: British Columbia
Taku Harbor
Tenakee Springs . . . . .907-736-2207 VHF 16
Thorne Bay . . . . .907-828-3380 VHF 16
West Petersburg
Wrangell . . . . .907-874-3736 VHF 16

PROPANE
Annette Island 907-886-7851

Craig
Elfin Cove .907-239-2208
Haines 907-766-3191
Hoonah 907-945-3389
Juneau
Ketchikan
Metlakatla .907-886-7851
Pelican 907-735-2211
Petersburg .907-772-4270
Sitka 907-747-3276, 907-747-8460
Skagway
Thorne Bay 907-828-3345
Wrangell 907-772-4270

RAMPS / HAULOUT
Air Marine Harbor: Ketchikan 907-225-2282
Deharts: Auke Bay. . . . . . . .907-789-4225 VHF 72
Duvals Marina. Auke Bay . . . . . .907-789-7443 VHF 16
Halibut Point Marine: Sitka . . . .907-747-4999 VHF 16
Petersburg Shipwrights. 907-772-3596
Willie's Marine: Juneau 907-789-4831

REPAIRS
Air Marine Harbor: Ketchikan . 907-225-2282 VHF 16, 66
Alaska Outboard: Ketchikan. 907-225-4980
Canal Marine: Haines. 907-766-2437
Deharts: Auke Bay 907-789-4225
Duvals Marine . . . . .907-789-7443 VHF 16
Garrison's Marine: Hoonah 907-945-3722
NC Machinery: Juneau 907-789-0181
Northern Communications: Juneau. 907-789-0008
Petersburg Shipwrights. 907-772-3596
Tanner's Service: Douglas 907-364-2434
Thorne Bay Boatworks . . . . . . .907-828-3947 VHF 16
Willie's Marine: Juneau 907-789-4831

RESCUE COORDINATION
Ketchikan: VHF 22
Petersburg, Sitka: VHF 28

SEWAGE DISPOSAL
Auke Bay: Pump   Juneau: Pump
Aurora Harbor: Juneau: Pump   Skagway: Pump
Haines: Pump   Thorne Bay: Pump
Ketchikan's Casey Moran Harbor: Pump Wrangell: Pump

SHELLFISH INFO: 907-269-7501

SPORTS FISHING
Government Information 907-465-4180
24-hr. Sport Fishing Information
 Ketchikan 907-225-0475
 Juneau 907-465-4116
 Haines 907-766-2625
Point Baker Trading Post: Gas, Diesel.
. . . . **907-559-2204 VHF 16**

STATE PARKS: 907-465-4563

TOWING
C-TOW. 1-888-354-5554

VHF MARINE OPERATOR
Craig VHF 25   Petersburg: VHF 28
High Mountain VHF 87   Ratz Mt: VHF 26
Juneau: VHF 25, 26   Sitka VHF 28
Ketchikan, Sitka: VHF 28

WEATHER (SEE IMPORTANT NOTICES PAGES)
Dundas Island: WX-2
Juneau: WX-1 907-586-3997
Ketchikan: WX-1, KTKN-AM 6:26 a.m. & 12:20 p.m.
NOAA (Juneau) 907-586-3997
Petersburg: WX-1
Sitka: WX-1 907-747-6011
Wrangell: WX-2 907-874-3232
National Weather Service Weatherline . 1-800-472-0391
(Press 4 for SE Alaska, 2 for marine weather and obser-
vations.)

Want to keep yourself & this book up-to-date? Here's How!
Subscribe to Northwest Boat Travel's® CruiseGrams®
Inside Passage News & Information Supplement to this guidebook

❑ **Printed and mailed quarterly** - $18 U.S. per year (includes S&H)

❑ **Available online quarterly AND printable from our website PLUS Northwest Boat Travel Web-Club Membership $15 per year** -This option includes: Access to printable, NBT e-Guide® (this book on our website), *Important Notices, & Directories of Essential Supplies & Services*® (the listings at the end of each chapter in this book), *Picture Of The Day* member archives (over 1200 4-color recreational boating pictures), NBT On-Line Boat Travel Club Membership with cruising articles, family fun, special features, boating logs, recipes, more... PLUS all the features listed at www.nwboat.com#webclub

For gifts, include gift name & address: _____

_____

Total for above choice(s): $___.__ U.S. Funds or Cdn. Equivalent. **WA residents add 8.8% sales tax.**

❑ Check enclosed or Charge my: ❑ Visa ❑ Mastercard

Card number: _____ Expires: _____

Name: _____

Address: _____ City: _____

State/Province: _____ Zip: _____

Telephone: _____ Email: _____
Charging? We MUST have your phone # ----- We never sell or lend our customer files or data.

GREAT BOATING BURGEE & BOOKS FROM NORTHWEST BOAT TRAVEL®

Mail card, or E-mail information below to: Janice@vernonpublications.com, call (425) 488-3211, or fax (425) 488-0946. Order on line at www.boattravel.com/shopping

Please send: **U.S. currency or Canadian Equivalent.**

❑ *Secrets of Cruising: The British Columbia Coast* ($19.50 U.S. **Members: $10.00 U.S.**)

❑ *The Inside Passage to Alaska: A Short History* ($15.95 U.S. **Members: $7.50 U.S.**)

❑ *Northwest Tugboat Captain:* ($12.95 U.S. **Members: $9.95 U.S.**)

Shipping & handling included. **Washington residents add 8.8% sales tax.** Allow two weeks for delivery

We never sell, lend, or rent our membership or sales information to anyone.

❑ Check enclosed. ❑ Charge my: ❑ Visa ❑ Mastercard

Card number:_____ Telephone:_____
(We must have telephone to verify charge.)

Signature _____

Name: _____

Address: _____

City:_____ State/Province:_____ Zip: _____

READER SERVICE CARD FOR FREE ADVERTISER INFORMATION

Name:_____

Address: _____

City:_____ State/Province:_____ Zip: _____

Telephone:_____ Fax: _____

Circle numbers which correspond to the two-digit numbers appearing in display advertisements or descriptions on pages A 12-13 or go to www.boattravel.com/reader/mailform.htm

01	02	03	04	05	06	07	08	09	10	11	12	13	14	15	16	17	18	19	20
21	22	23	24	25	26	27	28	29	30	31	32	33	34	35	36	37	38	39	40
41	42	43	44	45	46	47	48	49	50	51	52	53	54	55	56	57	58	59	60
61	62	63	64	65	66	67	68	69	70	71	72	73	74	75	76	77	78	79	80
81	82	83	84	85	86	87	88	89	90	91	92	93	94	95	96	97	98	99	100

Please provide us with the information below: (We never sell or lend our customer files or data. The information will be made available to participating sponsors in order for them to serve your request.)

1. Misc.: ❑ Making future plans ❑ Immediate Purchase ❑ Own a boat ❑ RV ❑ Use charter boat
2. How will you travel in the Northwest? ❑ Car ❑ RV ❑ Air ❑ Boat Length of trip _____ (days)
3. In the next 12 months do you plan to vacation in: ❑ Washington ❑ British Columbia ❑ Alaska
4. Looking for: ❑ Permanent Moorage ❑ RV Parking ❑ Lodging Information ❑ Tourist Attractions
   ❑ New Equipment, Electronics, Parts, Accessories ❑ Boat Repairs, Renovation ❑ Points of Interest
5. How many people: Travel in your group?_____ Read your copy of Northwest Boat Travel Guide?_____
6. Your Email Address (if available): _____

Vernon Publications, LLC
P.O. Box 970
Woodinville, WA 98072-0970

Vernon Publications, LLC
P.O. Box 970
Woodinville, WA 98072-0970

Vernon Publications, LLC
P.O. Box 970
Woodinville, WA 98072-0970

Crossing The Straits & Other Large Bodies Of Water

Preparing for crossings: There are a few general rules that apply to the crossing of any large body of water, or to preparation for any long cruise. First, it is a good idea for the captain to become familiar with the boat he will skipper, trying her out in local calm and rough waters before tackling unfamiliar seas. The second is to learn to be aware of, and to travel with, the wind and the tide. Waiting for calm weather, not being in a hurry, and being able to time travels to the encountered weather patterns will make the trip both more pleasant and safer. Before and during crossings, weather watches should be maintained on VHF weather channels. The vessel should have plenty of fuel, water, and supplies. Furnishings and gear should be secured and stowed before rough seas are encountered.

Strait of Juan de Fuca: This body of water connects Puget Sound and the Pacific Ocean. It is 12-16 miles wide and extends in length about 80 miles from Whidbey Island to Cape Flattery. Since the winds on this strait tend to rise in the afternoon, the best time of day for crossing this strait is usually in the early morning. Wind flow in the central strait is either east or west. Western entrance weather is more like the west coast of Vancouver Island. This is the Strait of Juan de Fuca forecast and conditions that are given on Canadian weather stations. The inland strait has weather more like that in the lower Georgia Strait. These are the weather forecast and conditions given on American weather stations. Sea fog near the west entrance is caused when northwest air is pulled over the cold water. There are more fog banks on the south side of the entrance than on the Victoria side. Tides for this strait are listed in the Canadian Tide and Current Tables, Volume Five. Between Sooke Inlet and Race Rocks the flood stream is strongest near the Canadian shore. When wind and sea collide, choppy, sometimes dangerous seas result in some areas. Especially heavy rips are found off Cape Flattery, Race Rocks, New Dungeness, Point Wilson, between Beechey Head and Esquimalt, and off the Trial Islands. Note: See Chapter 4 for Makah (Neah Bay) whaling area and regulations.

Strait of Georgia: This body of water, 125 miles long and about 20 miles wide, is not the biggest strait along the Inside Passage, but it is the most traversed by pleasure boaters. While this body of water is certainly deserving of a great deal of respect, the use of knowledge and good judgment is the best assurance of a good crossing. Most boaters take advantage of the protection afforded by Texada Island and use Malaspina Strait, on the east side of Texada, to travel the Sunshine Coast. For this crossing, the problem is getting to the southeast end of Texada Island. Boaters headed north from Vancouver, pass Howe Sound, Gibsons, and Sechelt on their way to Welcome Pass. This does not require crossing the strait, but there is a run of about 16 miles along the northeast shore from Gower Point to Merry Island. Boaters headed north from the Gulf Islands must choose between three routes: (1) Nanaimo to Welcome Pass; (2) Silva Bay to Welcome Pass; and (3) Nanaimo to Ballenas Islands and north about eight and one-half nautical miles to Point Upwood on Texada Island. The first is about five miles shorter than the others. The second has a favorable heading for quartering seas caused by prevailing summer winds out of the northwest. The third avoids military range Whiskey Golf and leads to exploration of the Vancouver Island side of the Strait. When Whiskey Golf is active, this route is being promoted by the Canadian Government, which maintains a non-firing course here for safe passage of vessels. Finally, for those travelling between Vancouver and the Gulf Islands, the Burrard-Point Grey to Silva Bay-Gabriola Pass crossing is about 20 miles and the Burrard-Point Grey to Porlier Pass crossing is about 21 miles.

One complicating factor in the Nanaimo-Welcome Pass area is the Canadian Naval area known as Whiskey-Golf. This area is designated on government charts. In the water, the active area is marked by orange can-buoys. The Canadian and American Armed Forces use this range for firing of non-explosive surface or air launched torpedoes. There are uncharted, lighted and unlighted, buoys within the area, as well as range vessels. During operations, this area is extremely dangerous to mariners because of the possibility of being struck by a torpedo that is rising to the surface after being fired. For a chart of the area, details, and times of operation, see Canadian National Defense Notice in Chapter 11 of this guide. Also see Important Notices between Chapter 7 and Chapter 8. If necessary, call Winchelsea Control on VHF Channel 10 or 16.

It is possible to avoid area Whisky-Golf by crossing from Silva Bay-Flat Top Islands to Merry Island on a heading of 310 degrees magnetic or by leaving Nanaimo on a course heading for Bowen Island, turning to port after passing area Whiskey-Golf. If the latter course is used, care must be exercised to avoid the natural tendency to change course too early and cross the east-ern end of the active area. Another route provided by the operations control is from Departure Bay, passing north of Winchelsea Island and east of Ballenas Island in a designated non-firing area.

Valuable information may be obtained on your VHF marine radio. Boaters who travel regularly in Canadian waters should have installed channels 21B (161.65) in addition to WX-1 (162.55), WX-2 (162.40) and WX-3. These channels have continuous Canadian weather broadcasts and are received at different locations along the coast. Channel 26 is also useful for obtaining information. This is the Canadian Department of Transport, Coast Guard station. Call Vancouver Radio or Comox first on Channel 16 and then switch to Channel 26 to talk to the operator. It is important to note that sea conditions will often vary widely on the two sides of the strait. Thus, you may begin crossing in what appears to be very flat water only to find that about half or two-thirds of the way across you are being battered by seas you did not expect. Getting current sea conditions for both sides of the strait is helpful. The wind and sea conditions at Merry Island, on the Welcome Pass side, and Entrance Island, on the Nanaimo side, will provide information about the two sides of the strait. The wind reports taken at Sisters and Ballenas Islands will describe the middle of the strait. For those making the Burrard Inlet to Silva Bay crossing, the wind and sea conditions at Sand Heads will be helpful on the Burrard side as will the Entrance Island conditions on the Silva Bay side. To enter the Georgia Strait without knowing both present conditions and the forecast is foolhardy indeed.

Wind and sea conditions on the Georgia Strait are quite different from those on the Juan de Fuca Strait or the Queen Charlotte Sound. Developing an adequate plan for crossing requires specific knowledge about the strait. There are a few axioms concerning the Georgia Strait that have served yachtsmen well for some years.

(1). The probability is that the weather tomorrow will be more like the weather today than it will be like any other day.

(2). If the wind comes up in the morning, it will go down in the late afternoon. This illustrates the wisdom of the Indians, who were paddling around the waters of this strait long before white men appeared. In the summer, the prevailing wind on the Georgia Strait is from the northwest. This is a fair-weather wind and must be distinguished from a storm wind which generally flows from the southeast. Many prefer to cross the strait in the afternoon when this fair weather wind goes down. The seas on the Georgia Strait calm down quickly following these warm-weather winds. Once the wind is down in the later afternoon, it is unlikely that it will come up again until after dark. Thus, a boater leaving Nanaimo or Welcome Pass at 5:00 or 6:00 p.m., after having observed that the wind has gone down, is quite likely to have several hours of calm wind during which he may traverse the Strait of Georgia in peace. Some boaters prefer a morning crossing. Indeed, the water is often as smooth as glass at daybreak. But this crossing can be treacherous because the wind will often begin to rise before the crossing is completed.

(3). If the wind does not go down in the late afternoon, it will blow for three days. This is also an Indian axiom. If the northwest fair weather wind has not gone down by 5:00 to 6:00 p.m., the boater can assume that he is probably in for a three-day blow. When this phenomenon occurs, it is unlikely that there will be an opportunity to cross the strait comfortably and safely for the next three, or sometimes four, days. Following such a three-day blow, be alert for the subsiding of the wind in the late afternoon. This is your opportunity to cross, an opportunity that may not come again for another three or four days.

(4). When a southeasterly wind is blowing, there is no preferred crossing time, and it will be best to forget crossing until the storm is over.

(5). If the decks are wet with dew in the evening, it is almost a sure sign that the following day will be bright and clear and that the prevailing fair weather winds will be blowing.

Discovery Passage and Johnstone Strait: Although this strait is only about two to three miles wide, the waters of this 50-mile stretch from Cape Mudge to Blackfish Sound, can be difficult. Tide rips of dangerous proportions may be encountered off Cape Mudge on an flood tide and strong south winds. Seymour Narrows has tides of up to 16 knots at springs. Passage here is recommended near slack waters, using the British Columbia Tide and Current Tables. At Ripple Shoal, Current, and Race Passages, tides can run five to seven knots, with heavy tide rips possible. The main problem in all of these waters is having the tides, which can be strong, and winds opposed to each other, causing very uncomfortable conditions with quite steep seas.

One very popular alternative to Discovery Passage and southeastern Johnstone Strait is to take the more protected eastern route from the Desolation Sound-Discovery Passage area to the Stuart Island area, passing through Yuculta,

Gillard and Dent rapids, Cordero Channel, Green Point Rapids, Chancellor Channel, Wellbore Channel, Whirlpool Rapids, and Sunderland Channel, escaping the lower part of the Johnstone Strait entirely. The rapids are traversed easily at times of slack water, using the Tide and Current Tables. The flood tides come around the north and south ends of Vancouver Island, meeting near Cape Mudge and Stuart Island. Careful planning with the current tables can make it possible to approach either of these points travelling with the flooding tide, crossing the point of the meeting currents near slack water, and proceeding on the other side with the ebbing tide.

From the west end of Hardwicke Island to Broken Islands there is no choice but to tackle the strait for about 12 miles. This area is often windy, acting as a funnel, and tide rips can be encountered. Port Neville offers the best shelter, if escape is needed. The eight miles between Port Neville and the Broken Islands are usually the roughest part of this passage. At the Broken Islands the alternatives are to enter Havanna Channel, and go through Chatham Channel to Clio Channel or Knight Inlet, or to continue on 20 miles west to the end of Johnstone Strait. Weather conditions may make the decision for you.

Queen Charlotte Strait & Queen Charlotte Sound: Queen Charlotte Strait, to the southeast of Queen Charlotte Sound, lies between Queen Charlotte Sound and Johnstone Strait. Weather and wind patterns sometime resemble Queen Charlotte Sound, and sometimes resemble Johnstone Strait. Weather conditions can be determined by listening to WX-1, Alert Bay weather. Queen Charlotte Strait is adjacent to the beautiful islands rimming the mainland in the Fife Sound and Kingcome Inlet areas.

Queen Charlotte Sound is often the most difficult of the Big Waters to traverse safely. There is about a 40 nautical mile stretch that is open to the Pacific Ocean and sizable swells. The topography of the sound is such that the bottom rises from the continental shelf to a depth as shallow as 17 fathoms. This has an amplifying effect upon swells and waves. During the ebbing tide there are currents coming from the straits, sounds, and inlets to the south, north, and east. These ebbing currents collide with each other and with the incoming swells in the sound. This is a recipe for rough waters, even without any wind added. But the wind can blow here, as evidenced by the lethal storm of April, 1984 when several boats and crews were lost. Indeed, unusually strong tidal currents and wave heights have occasionally been observed in this area. The British Columbia Sailing Directions reports observations of waves as high as 90 to 100 feet in

storm and hurricane force winds. Even after the passage of such storms, the effects on the currents in the area can last three to four days.

Fortunately, gale and storm force winds are rare in summer months, so many crossings are made in quiet waters. Fog can be encountered anytime, but is most frequent from August through October. Many sport fishermen put their boats in the water at Port Hardy and make the 50-mile crossing to Rivers Inlet. Port Hardy makes a good starting point to prepare for the crossing and to study the weather reports and patterns. The most critical point is Egg Island. The lighthouse located there gives local conditions on the Alert Bay Radio weather reports on WX-1. When passing Egg Island, may want to call "Egg Yolk" on VHF 16 to say "Hello" to the caretaker. It is also possible to call Alert Bay Radio on Channel 16, switch to Channel 26, and request the latest sea and weather conditions and forecast for the Queen Charlotte crossing.

Nearby provisioning points include Minstrel Island Resort, Alert Bay, Echo Bay Resort, Greenway Sound Marina Resort, Sullivan Bay Marina Resort, Port Hardy, Port McNeill, and Sointula. Starting points include Allison Harbour, Blunden Harbour, Bull Harbour, God's Pocket, Miles Inlet, and Skull Cove. Destination points include Namu, Rivers Inlet, Pruth Anchorage, Safety Cove, and Smith Sound.

Milbanke Sound: The exposure here is for a short duration compared to Queen Charlotte Sound and Dixon Entrance. Most of the direct exposure to the Pacific Ocean is during the seven miles from Ivory Island to Vancouver Rock. This sound can be avoided by travelling through Reid Channel, or partially avoided by heading east-north-east toward Mathieson Channel after rounding Ivory Island.

Dixon Entrance: Topographically, this is a deep trough separating the north end of the Queen Charlotte Islands from Dall and Prince of Wales Islands. Fog plagues these waters from July to October. The crossing is about 20 miles. Nearby starting points are Brundige Inlet or Port Simpson. The closest destination harbor is Foggy Bay in Very Inlet.

Other big southeast Alaska waters: Even though the waters of southeast Alaska are part of the Inside Passage and are "protected" from the Pacific Ocean by one or more islands, there are still some large areas of water where wind and wind against tidal current can cause some very rough seas. Frederick Sound, Chatham Channel, Stephens Passage, Clarence Strait, Lynn Canal, and Icy Strait all deserve respect and careful navigation with an ear and eye to weather and current conditions.

VHF Frequencies for Pleasure Vessels in the Pacific Northwest

Channel Number	Purpose and Use

SAFETY

16   INTERNATIONAL DISTRESS AND CALLING. Used only for distress and urgency traffic, for safety calls and contacting other stations. Listen first to make sure no distress traffic is in progress; do not transmit if a *SEELONCE MAYDAY* or *SEELONCE DISTRESS* is declared. Keep all communications to a minimum. Do not repeat a call to the same station more than once every two minutes. After three attempts wait fifteen minutes before calling the same station. Do not call marinas for moorage on 16 - use 66A.

> Example of proper calling:
> Blue Duck   "Mary Jane this is Blue Duck, WAZ1234."
> Mary Jane   "Blue Duck, Mary Jane."
> Blue Duck   "Reply 68."

Use call sign, vessel name or registration number for identification.
Note: The correct procedure if no response is heard, is silence—no need to say "no contact" or "negative contact."

6   INTERSHIP SAFETY. Only for ship-to-ship use for safety communications. For Search and Rescue (SAR) liaison with Coast Guard vessels and aircraft. All communications not related to the safety of life or property are prohibited.

22A   LIAISON AND SAFETY BROADCASTS U.S. COAST GUARD. A government channel used for Safety and Liaison communications with the Coast Guard. Also known as Channel 22 US. The U.S. Coast Guard does not normally monitor 22A so you must first establish communications on Channel 16.

70   DIGITAL SELECTIVE CALLING ONLY (NO VOICE) FOR DISTRESS, SAFETY AND CALLING

WASHINGTON MARINAS

66A   Port Operations. All marinas in Puget Sound are being encouraged to use this common frequency for arranging moorage. Do not call on 16.

78A   INTERSHIP & SHIP-SHORE FOR PLEASURE VESSELS ONLY. All marinas in Puget Sound are being encouraged to use this as a secondary working channel.

Radiotelephone Procedure Signals:

MAYDAY	Vessel threatened by grave and imminent danger and requests immediate assistance.
PAN PAN	Urgent message concerning safety of vessel or person on board or in sight.
SECURITY	Message concerning safety of navigation or meteorological warning.
SEELONCE MAYDAY OR *SEELONCE DISTRESS*	Mayday in progress, do not transmit normal communications.
SEELONCE FEENE	Resume normal communications.

Recreational Boating Association of Washington

P.O. Box 23601 • Federal Way, Washington 98093-0601
Voice of Northwest Boating
and the

North Pacific Marine Radio Council

11410 NE 122nd Way, Suite 312 • Kirkland, Washington 98034-6927
Dedicated to Improvement of the Maritime Mobile Service

VHF Marine Channels for Pleasure Vessels in Washington

Channel Number	Purpose and Use

SAFETY

16 INTERNATIONAL DISTRESS AND CALLING. Used only for distress and urgency traffic, for safety calls and contacting other stations. Listen first to make sure no distress traffic is in progress; do not transmit if a *SEELONCE MAYDAY* or *SEELONCE DISTRESS* is declared. Keep all communications to a minimum. Do not repeat a call to the same station more than once every two minutes. After three attempts wait fifteen minutes before calling the same station. Pleasure vessels may also use Channel 9 for calling.

6 INTERSHIP SAFETY. Only for ship-to-ship use for safety communications. For Search and Rescue (SAR) liaison with Coast Guard vessels and aircraft.

22A LIAISON AND SAFETY BROADCASTS. A government channel used for Safety and Liaison communications with the Coast Guard. Also known as Channel 22 US. The U.S. Coast Guard does not normally monitor 22A so you must first establish communications on Channel 16.

70 DIGITAL SELECTIVE CALLING ONLY (NO VOICE) FOR DISTRESS, SAFETY AND CALLING

WORKING FREQUENCIES

9 INTERSHIP & SHIP-SHORE ALL VESSELS AND CALLING & REPLY FOR PLEASURE VESSELS (optional, U.S. only).

67 INTERSHIP ONLY FOR ALL VESSELS (U.S. only, Puget Sound).

68 INTERSHIP & SHIP-SHORE FOR PLEASURE VESSELS ONLY.

69 INTERSHIP & SHIP-SHORE FOR PLEASURE VESSELS ONLY.

72 INTERSHIP & SHIP-SHORE FOR ALL VESSELS (U.S. only, Puget Sound).

78A INTERSHIP & SHIP-SHORE FOR PLEASURE VESSELS ONLY (Not available in Canada). All marinas in Puget Sound are being encouraged to use this as a secondary working channel.

NAVIGATION (Use LOW POWER only)

13 Vessel BRIDGE to vessel BRIDGE, large vessels. May also be used to contact locks and bridges *BUT* use sound signals in the Seattle area to avoid dangerous interference to collision avoidance communications between large vessels.

5A VESSEL TRAFFIC SYSTEM—NORTH OF BUSH POINT AND EAST OF WHIDBEY ISLAND. Vessels not required to participate are highly encouraged to maintain a listening watch. Contact with VTS is encouraged if essential to navigational safety.

14 VESSEL TRAFFIC SYSTEM—SOUTH OF BUSH POINT AND WEST OF WHIDBEY ISLAND. Vessels not required to participate are highly encouraged to maintain a listening watch. Contact with VTS is encouraged if essential to navigational safety.

Columbia and the Willamette River

12 Port Operations

14 Corps of Engineers operated locks.

Even though you may use alternate communication means, such as cellular phone, **MONITOR VHF 16.** The safety of yourself, your family and your friends is enhanced by a watch on 16 by *all* vessels.

REDUCE INTERFERENCE—USE LOW POWER

GMDSS IMPLEMENTATION

The USCG plan to implement GMDSS Sea Area A1 is one element of the USCG National Distress and Response System Modernization Project now called "Rescue 21", which replaces the whole USCG VVHF distress system. On 24 September 2002, the Secretary of Transportation announced the award of this $612 million contract to General Dynamics Corp. The Coast Guard will not declare GMDSS Sea Area A-1 operational for several years.
Until this system is installed and Sea Area A1declared operational, the Coast Guard cannot reliably receive VHF DSC distress calls.

VHF CHANNEL 71 DESIGNATED AS A PORT OPERATIONS CHANNEL

The request of the Puget Sound Pilots to have VHF Channel 71 designated as a low power Port Operations Channel for use by Pilots within the area of VTS Puget Sound was approved by the Federal Communications Commission, by Order DA 04-3408, which was released by the Commission on October 28, 2004, published in the Federal Register on December 23, 2004, and became effective on January 24, 2005.

USE OF LOW POWER REQUIRED

When possible, the lowest transmitter power necessary for satisfactory communication should be used.

BRIDGE TO BRIDGE COMMUNICATIONS

In U.S. Navigable Waters, when vessel safety is involved, power driven vessels twenty meters or more in length should be contacted on VHF Channel 13.

MARINE OPERATOR **There are no marine operator stations in Washington. Telus sites in British Columbia are listed at www.npmrc.net and below**

Do not call the marine operator on Channel 16, they do not monitor 16. To place a call, select the telephone channel with the transmitter closest to your vessel location. Listen to see if the channel is clear of traffic, then press the transmit button for about five seconds and give your call sign. There should be a ringing sound. If not, change to another nearby channel or wait until your vessel is in another location.

Location	Ch.	Location	Ch.	Location	Ch.
Alert Bay	86	Estevan Point	23	Noble Mountain	2
Bamfield (Mt. Blenheim)	27	Ganges	64	Patrick Point	24
Bella Bella	25	Gil Isl.	60	Port Hardy	24
Brooks Peninsula	87	Grenville Channel	24	Prince Rupert (Mt. Hays)	27
Burnaby Isl.	3	Griffin Point	85	Rennell Sound	86
Calvert Isl.	23	Holberg	60	Rivers Inlet	3
Cape Caution	2	King Isl.	28	Sayward (Newcastle Ridge)	28
Cape St. James	24	Kincolith (Pearse Is.)	60	Swindle Isl.	87
Coast Cone (Smith Sound)	85	Kyuquot	1	Tasu	25
Denny Isl.	1	Langara	3	Trutch Isl.	86
Dundas Isl.	85	Louise Island	64	Vancouver (Gabriola Isl.)	88
East Thurlow	23	Masset	24	Whidbey Isl. (WA)	87

Tips for US Vessels Cruising in British Columbia Waters:

Ship to Shore Public Correspondence: US vessels in British Columbia may make ship to shore calls through Telus Stations. Contact the station on its working ffrequency as listed above. (Telus stations *do not* monitor channel 16.)

Shore to Ship Public Correspondence: Call your local telephone operator and ask to be connected to the Telus Marine Operator.

Channel Number	Purpose and Use
	CONTINUOUS WEATHER BROADCASTS
WX1	162.55 MHz, in Seattle (Cougar Mt.), Neah Bay and Portland, Or. Canada: Aldergrove, Alert Bay, Eliza Dome, Klemtu, Texada, Van Inlet.
WX2	162.40 MHz, in Astoria, OR. Canada: Barry Inlet, Calvert Island, Dundas Island, Mount Gil, Nootka, Port Alberni.
WX3	162.475 MHz, in Olympia (Capital Peak). *Canada: Bowen Island, Cumshewa, Estevan Point, Mount Helmcken, Naden Harbor, Port Hardy.*
WX4 (US)	162.425 MHz, in Puget Sound (Miller Peak), Forks (Mt. Octopus).
WX7	162.525 MHz, Woodland (Davis Peak).
21b & WX8 (Canada)	*161.650 MHz, Cape Lazo, Discovery, Esperanza, Holberg, Kitimat, Mount Dent, Hays, Mount Ozzard, Mount Parke, Rose Inlet.*
	Note: Some VHF's may number these channels differently. Check your radio manual.

VHF Marine Channels for Pleasure Vessels in British Columbia, Canada

Channel Number	Purpose and Use
16	INTERNATIONAL DISTRESS AND CALLING. Used only for distress and urgency traffic, for safety calls and contacting other stations. Listen first to make sure no distress traffic is in progress; do not transmit if a *SEELONCE MAYDAY* or *SEELONCE DISTRESS* is declared. Keep all communications to a minimum. Do not repeat a call to the same station more than once every two minutes. After three attempts wait fifteen minutes before calling the same station.
6	INTERSHIP SAFETY. Only for ship-to-ship use for safety communications. For Search and Rescue (SAR) liaison with Coast Guard vessels and aircraft.
22A	LIAISON AND SAFETY BROADCASTS. A government channel used for Safety and Liaison communications with the Coast Guard. Also known as Channel 22 US.
70	DIGITAL SELECTIVE CALLING ONLY (NO VOICE) FOR DISTRESS, SAFETY AND CALLING. [Officially monitored by the Canadian Coast Guard.)

WORKING FREQUENCIES

9	INTERSHIP & SHIP-SHORE. ALL VESSELS.
67	INTERSHIP ONLY. ALL VESSELS.
68	INTERSHIP & SHIP-SHORE. PLEASURE VESSELS.
69	INTERSHIP & SHIP-SHORE. PLEASURE VESSELS.
72	INTERSHIP. PLEASURE VESSELS.
78A	INTERSHIP & SHIP-SHORE. PLEASURE VESSELS.

CANADIAN MARINAS

Do not call marinas in Canada on Channel 16—they are not authorized to use 16. All marinas monitor a common frequency, depending upon their geographical location.

66A	Effective January 2004 for all marinas.

Vessel Traffic Service (Pleasure vessels less than 30 meters in length monitor only for vessel traffic.)

5A	SEATTLE—Strait of Juan de Fuca west of Victoria.
11	VICTORIA—Strait of Juan de Fuca east of Victoria; Haro Strait; Boundary Passage; Gulf Islands; Strait of Georgia. PRINCE RUPERT—Queen Charlotte Sound, Hecate Strait.
12	VANCOUVER—Vancouver and Howe Sound.
71	COMOX—East Coast of Vancouver Island, north of Parksville up to Cape Caution. Prince Rupert—Dixon Entrance to Prince Rupert.
74	VICTORIA—Fraser River. TOFINO—West Coast of Vancouver Island.

To contact the Canadian Coast Guard call the station nearest you: Comox, Prince Rupert, Tofino, Vancouver or Victoria.

Even though you may use alternate communication means, such as cellular phone, **Monitor VHF 16.** The safety of yourself, your family and your friends is enhanced by a watch on 16 by all vessels.

REDUCE INTERFERENCE—USE LOW POWER

Marine Distress Communications Form

Complete form now (except for items 5 through 8) and post near your VHF for use in distress.

SPEAK: SLOWLY   —   CLEARLY   —   CALMLY

1. Turn VHF on and select Channel 16 (156.8 MHz).
2. Press and hold microphone button and say: **"MAYDAY—MAYDAY—MAYDAY."**
3. Say: **"This is:** _____ _____ _____."
   Your boat name and call sign or registration number repeated three times.
4. Say: **"Mayday** _____."
   Your boat name.
5. **TELL WHERE YOU ARE** (what navigation aids, landmarks or other vessels are near?).
6. **STATE THE NATURE OF YOUR DISTRESS.** (Taking on water, fire aboard, etc.)
7. **GIVE NUMBER OF PERSONS ABOARD AND CONDITIONS OF INJURED.**
8. **ESTIMATE PRESENT SEAWORTHINESS OF YOUR BOAT.**
9. **BRIEFLY DESCRIBE YOUR BOAT:** _____ **FEET** _____; _____ **HULL;**
   Length   Type   Color

   _____ **TRIM;** _____ **MASTS:** _____.
   Color   Number   Anything else you think will help rescuers find you.
10. **SAY "THIS IS** _____, **OVER."**
    Your call sign/boat name.
11. Release microphone button and listen. Someone should answer.

IF THEY DO NOT, REPEAT CALL, BEGINNING AT ITEM NO. 2 ABOVE.

If there is still no answer, switch to another channel and begin again.

Consider having every one put on their PFD. If you are drifting without power, putting your anchor out may keep you off the shore. Have your flares or other visual signaling items available for use.

VHF Call Sign or Vessel Name _____

Vessel Registration No. _____

> To report any corrections or suggested changes or to request additional copies, contact:
> North Pacific Marine Radio Council
> 11410 N.E. 122nd Way, Suite 312 • Kirkland, WA 98034-6927
> Fax: 425-820-0126

Proper understanding and use of VHF Radio Procedures is essential in order to ensure theat VHF remains a useful and reliable safety and communications tool.

VHF Do's and Don'ts

DO	Use Channel 16 only for Distress and Calling.
DO	Call marinas on the working channel (66A or 78A US only) instead of 16.
DO	Keep all calling to an absolute minimum on Channel 16.
DO	Call coast stations on their working channel and not Channel 16.
DON'T	Try to sneak in short messages on Channel 16.
DO	Listen before transmitting to make sure no distress traffic is in progress.
DO	Stop transmitting when a *SEELONCE MAYDAY* is declared. Resume normal communications when *SEELONCE FEENEE* is declared.
DO	Instruct children on the proper use of the VHF and that it is not a toy.
DO	Call the same station no more than once every two minutes and after three tries wait fifteen minutes.
DO	Use low power at all times. It is required on 13, 14, 5A, and 66A.
DO	Keep all communications to the minimum necessary.
DON'T	Use Channel 16 for radio checks with the Coast Guard. It is not permitted by FCC rules and the Coast Guard doesn't like them on 16. Do your radio checks on a working frequency.
DO	Pick a working channel appropriate to the type of intended communication.
DO	Eliminate idle chit-chat; keep communications to those necessary for the needs of the vessel.
DON'T	Talk on Channel 70—it is reserved for Digital Selective Calling (DSC) for distress, safety and general calling using DSC techniques.
DON'T	Use Channels 1-4 or 60-64 in Puget Sound. They are assigned to land stations only.

For additional information call the FCC Consumer Assistance Branch (888) 225-5322.

DISTANCE TABLES

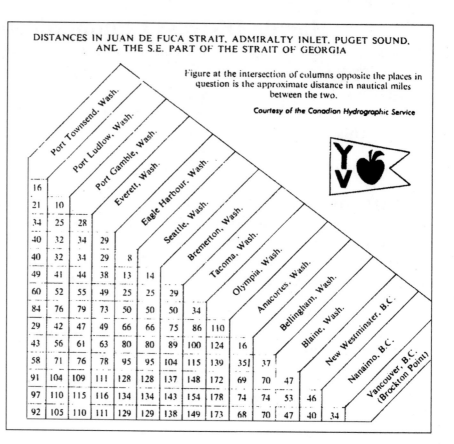

DISTANCES IN JUAN DE FUCA STRAIT, ADMIRALTY INLET, PUGET SOUND, AND THE S.E. PART OF THE STRAIT OF GEORGIA

Figure at the intersection of columns opposite the places in question is the approximate distance in nautical miles between the two.

Courtesy of the Canadian Hydrographic Service

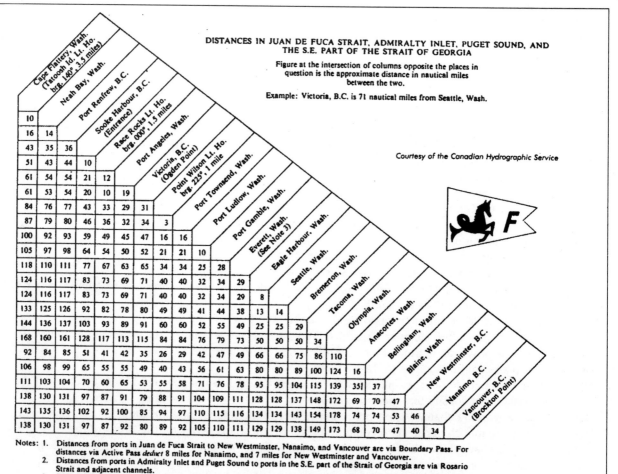

DISTANCES IN JUAN DE FUCA STRAIT, ADMIRALTY INLET, PUGET SOUND, AND THE S.E. PART OF THE STRAIT OF GEORGIA

Figure at the intersection of columns opposite the places in question is the approximate distance in nautical miles between the two.

Example: Victoria, B.C. is 71 nautical miles from Seattle, Wash.

Courtesy of the Canadian Hydrographic Service

Notes: 1. Distances from ports in Juan de Fuca Strait to New Westminster, Nanaimo, and Vancouver are via Boundary Pass. For distances via Active Pass *deduct* 8 miles for Nanaimo, and 7 miles for New Westminster and Vancouver.
2. Distances from ports in Admiralty Inlet and Puget Sound to ports in the S.E. part of the Strait of Georgia are via Rosario Strait and adjacent channels.
3. Distances from Everett, Wash. to Anacortes, Bellingham, and ports in the S.E. part of the Strait of Georgia are by way of Saratoga Passage and Deception Pass. For distances over route west of Whidbey Island and via Rosario Strait *add* 11 miles.

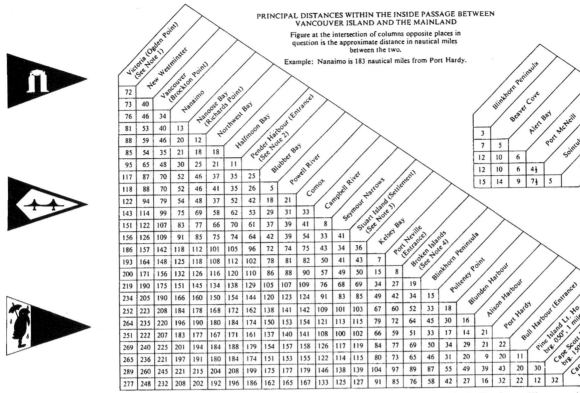

PRINCIPAL DISTANCES WITHIN THE INSIDE PASSAGE BETWEEN VANCOUVER ISLAND AND THE MAINLAND

Figure at the intersection of columns opposite places in question is the approximate distance in nautical miles between the two.

Example: Nanaimo is 183 nautical miles from Port Hardy.

Notes: 1. Distances from Victoria are via Sidney Channel and Active Pass. Via Boundary Pass add 7 miles for New Westminster and Vancouver and 8 miles for the remaining places.
2. For the head of Jervis Inlet, and Porpoise Bay in Sechelt Inlet, add 46 miles and 30 miles respectively.
3. Distances westward from Stuart Island are via Cordero and Chancellor Channels.
4. For Port Harvey, add 3 miles.

Canadian Hydrographic Service

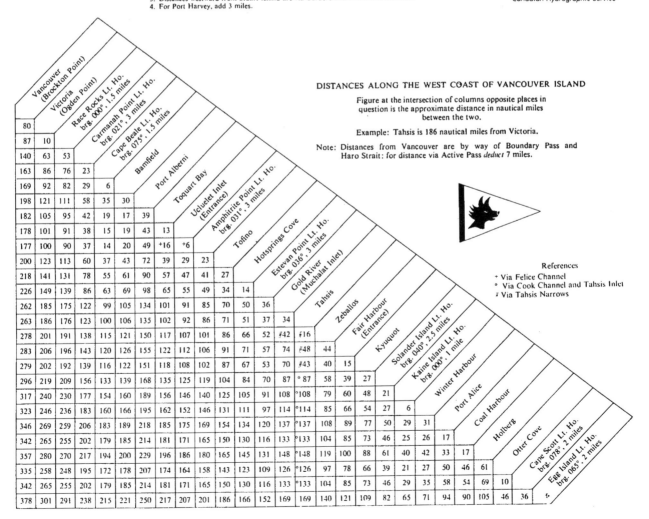

DISTANCES ALONG THE WEST COAST OF VANCOUVER ISLAND

Figure at the intersection of columns opposite places in question is the approximate distance in nautical miles between the two.

Example: Tahsis is 186 nautical miles from Victoria.

Note: Distances from Vancouver are by way of Boundary Pass and Haro Strait: for distance via Active Pass *deduct* 7 miles.

References
+ Via Felice Channel
° Via Cook Channel and Tahsis Inlet
Via Tahsis Narrows

This page continuously updated at Northwest Boat Travel On-line® www.nwboattravel.com

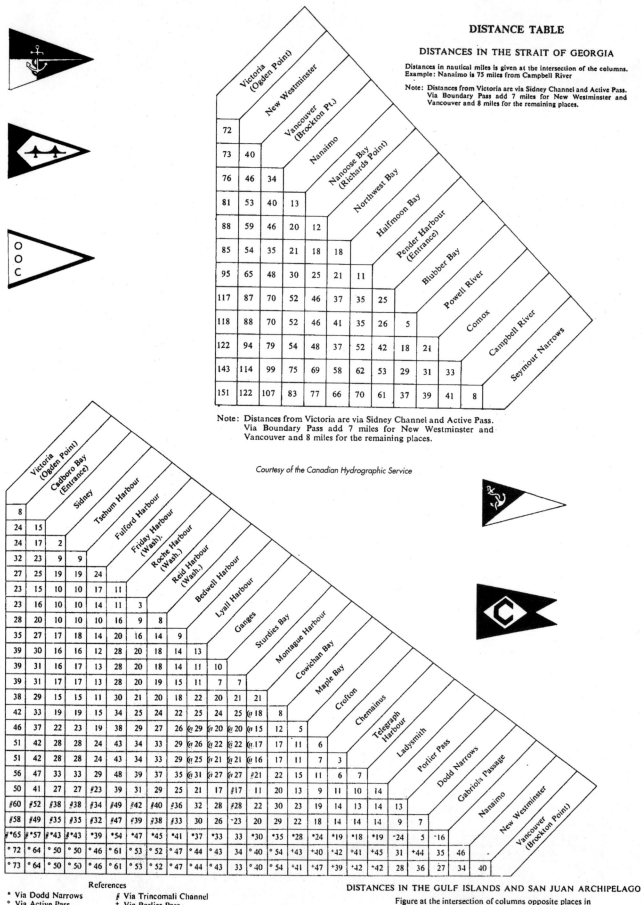

DISTANCE TABLE

DISTANCES IN THE STRAIT OF GEORGIA

Distances in nautical miles is given at the intersection of the columns.
Example: Nanaimo is 75 miles from Campbell River

Note: Distances from Victoria are via Sidney Channel and Active Pass.
Via Boundary Pass add 7 miles for New Westminster and Vancouver and 8 miles for the remaining places.

Note: Distances from Victoria are via Sidney Channel and Active Pass.
Via Boundary Pass add 7 miles for New Westminster and Vancouver and 8 miles for the remaining places.

Courtesy of the Canadian Hydrographic Service

References
* Via Dodd Narrows
° Via Active Pass
@ Via Houston Passage
# Via Trincomali Channel
+ Via Porlier Pass
- Outside the Gulf Islands

DISTANCES IN THE GULF ISLANDS AND SAN JUAN ARCHIPELAGO

Figure at the intersection of columns opposite places in question is the approximate distance in nautical miles between the two.

Example: Victoria is 51 miles from Chemainus.

Please tell our advertisers that you found them in Northwest Boat Travel® & Northwest Boat Travel On-Line®

STRAIT OF GEORGIA

* via Sabine Channel   † via Malaspina Strait

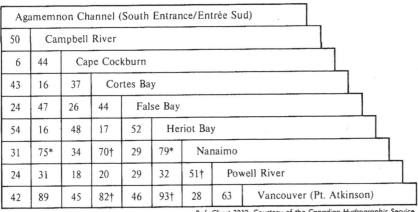

Agamemnon Channel (South Entrance/Entrée Sud)								
50	Campbell River							
6	44	Cape Cockburn						
43	16	37	Cortes Bay					
24	47	26	44	False Bay				
54	16	48	17	52	Heriot Bay			
31	75*	34	70†	29	79*	Nanaimo		
24	31	18	20	29	32	51†	Powell River	
42	89	45	82†	46	93†	28	63	Vancouver (Pt. Atkinson)

Ref. Chart 3312, Courtesy of the Canadian Hydrographic Service

DISTANCES: PENDER HARBOUR TO PORPOISE BAY VIA AGAMEMNON CHANNEL

Pender Harbour Francis Point 1 mile NE							
10.5	Earls Cove						
14.5	4	Egmont					
16	5.5	1.5	Sechelt Rapids				
24	13.5	9.5	8	Kunechin Islets			
25.5	15	11	9.5	1.5	Nine Mile Point		
30.5	20	16	14.5	6.5	5	Four Mile Point	
33	22.5	18.5	17	9	7.5	2.5	Porpoise Bay Anchorage

DESOLATION SOUND

Bliss Landing								
4	Cortes Bay							
13	12	Gorge Harbour						
18	17	8	Heriot Bay					
4	5	15	20	Malaspina Inlet (Entrance/Entrée)				
10	11	21	26	7	Prideaux Haven			
6	6	16	21	4	7	Refuge Cove		
7	7	17	22	6	10	3	Squirrel Cove	
15	13	3	6	16	23	18	19	Whaletown

DISCOVERY PASSAGE - JOHNSTONE STRAIT

Campbell River								
2	Cape Mudge							
38	40	Chancellor Channel (West End/Bout Ouest)						
16	14	54	Cortes Bay					
16	15	54	17	Heriot Bay				
28	30	10	44	44	Mayne Passage (West End/Bout Ouest)			
22	24	16	38	38	6	Nodales Channel (West End/Bout Ouest)		
18	20	20	34	34	10	4	Okisollo Channel (West/Ouest)	
9	11	29	25	25	19	13	9	Seymour Narrows

CORDERO AND/ET NODALES CHANNELS MAYNE PASSAGE

Arran Rapids								
28	Chancellor Channel (West End/Bout Ouest)							
3	25	Dent Rapids						
10	24	7	Frederick Arm (Head/au fond)					
2	27	2	9	Gillard Passage				
16	12	13	12	15	Greene Point Rapids			
20	17	17	16	19	5	Mayne Passage (West End/Bout Ouest)		
15	28	12	12	14	16	20	Nodales Channel (West/Ouest)	
14	22	11	10	13	10	14	14	Phillips Arm (Head/au fond)

POINT ATKINSON TO LUND AND BULL PASSAGE

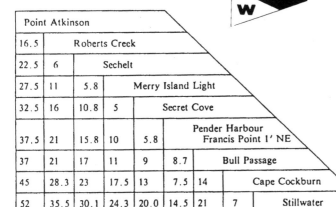

Point Atkinson												
16.5	Roberts Creek											
22.5	6	Sechelt										
27.5	11	5.8	Merry Island Light									
32.5	16	10.8	5	Secret Cove								
37.5	21	15.8	10	5.8	Pender Harbour Francis Point 1' NE							
37	21	17	11	9	8.7	Bull Passage						
45	28.3	23	17.5	13	7.5	14	Cape Cockburn					
52	35.5	30.1	24.3	20.0	14.5	21	7	Stillwater				
60.5	44	39	33	28.8	24	*32 / 28	14.5	9	Vananda			
65	49	44	38	33	29	*30	19	14	5	Blubber Bay		
69	53	48	42	37	33	*34	17	11	4.5	4	Westview	
81	65	60.5	54.5	49	45.5	46.5	29	23	16	13	12.5	Lund

Reference.   * Via Algerine Passage

Inside Passage — Prince Rupert to Cape Caution via Grenville, Princess Royal, and Seaforth Channels, Lama Passage, Fitz Hugh Sound.

Note. — The distances given in the tables on this and subsequent pages are approximate only. They are based on the most frequently used tracks which may not be suitable for all vessels.

Prince Rupert														
72	Sainty Point													
100	28	Butedale												
121	49	67	Kitimat											
158	58	65	57	Kemano										
135	63	35	102	104	Boat Bluff									
161	89	61	126	128	26	Susan Rock								
180	108	80	147	145	45	20	Bella Bella							
190	118	90	157	155	55	30	10	Pointer Island (E. end Lama Pass)						
210	138	110	167	176	63	50	30	20	Ocean Falls					
255	183	165	213	211	119	86	61	56	54	Bella Coola via Burke Chan.				
203	131	103	181	179	68	42	23	12	33	56	Namu			
222	150	122	189	191	87	61	42	32	51	66	20	Safety Cove		
232	160	132	199	201	98	71	52	42	61	86	30	10	Dugout Rocks	
245	173	145	212	214	110	84	65	55	74	99	43	23	13	Cape Caution 078° 2.2 miles

Figure at the intersection of columns opposite places in question is the approximate distance in nautical miles between the two.

Prince Rupert to East Coast Queen Charlotte Islands

Prince Rupert								
9	Holland Rocks							
28	19	Seal Rocks						
95	86	67	Cumshewa Head					
99	90	71	11	Reef Is.				
122	113	94	38	27	Scudder Point			
128	119	100	44	33	6	Copper Is.		
136	127	108	56	45	18	12	Garcin Rocks	
158	149	130	73	62	35	29	17	Cape St. James

Canadian Hydrographic Service

Prince Rupert								
19	Lucy Is.							
37	19	Pointer Rocks						
39	20	5	Port Simpson					
67	49	30	33	Kincolith				
92	74	55	58	27	Brook Shoal Light			
103	85	66	69	37	11	Alice Arm		
95	77	58	61	29	5	16	Anyox	
107	89	70	73	42	15	26	19	Head of Hastings Arm

INSIDE - PASSAGE DISTANCES

Seattle, Wash. to Cape Spencer, Alaska

Figure at intersection of columns opposite ports in question is the nautical mileage between the two. Example: Ketchikan, Alaska, is 220 nautical miles from Juneau, Alaska.

National Oceanic and Atmospheric Administration

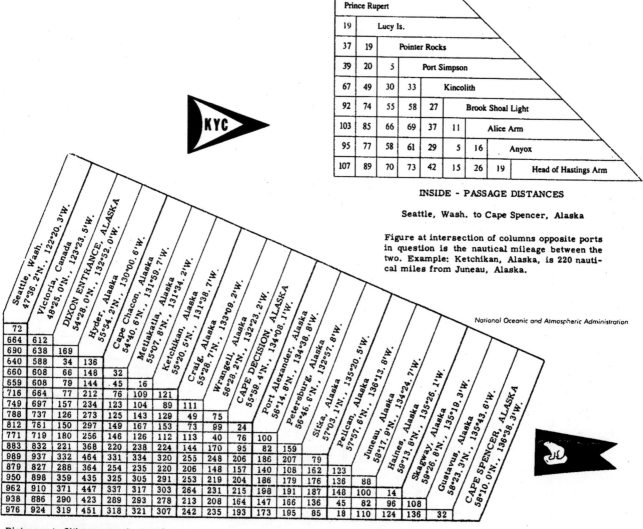

Seattle, Wash. 47°36.2'N., 122°20.3'W.	Victoria, Canada 48°25.0'N., 123°23.51'W.	DIXON ENTRANCE, ALASKA 54°28.0'N., 132°52.0'W.	Hyder, Alaska 55°54.2'N., 130°00.61'W.	Cape Chacon, Alaska 54°40.6'N., 131°59.71'W.	Metlakatla, Alaska 55°07.8'N., 131°34.21'W.	Ketchikan, Alaska 55°20.5'N., 131°38.71'W.	Craig, Alaska 55°28.7'N., 133°09.2'W.	Wrangell, Alaska 56°28.2'N., 132°23.21'W.	CAPE DECISION, ALASKA 55°59.4'N., 134°08.1'W.	Port Alexander, Alaska 56°14.8'N., 134°38.81'W.	Petersburg, Alaska 56°46.6'N., 132°57.81'W.	Sitka, Alaska 57°03.1'N., 135°20.51'W.	Pelican, Alaska 57°57.6'N., 136°13.61'W.	Juneau, Alaska 58°17.91'N., 134°24.7'W.	Haines, Alaska 59°13.8'N., 135°26.11'W.	Skagway, Alaska 59°26.8'N., 135°19.3'W.	Gustavus, Alaska 58°23.3'N., 135°43.61'W.	CAPE SPENCER, ALASKA 58°10.0'N., 136°38.3'W.
72																		
664	612																	
690	638	169																
640	588	34	136															
660	608	66	148	32														
659	608	79	144	45	16													
716	664	77	212	76	109	121												
749	697	157	234	123	104	89	111											
788	737	126	273	125	143	129	49	75										
812	761	150	297	149	167	153	73	99	24									
771	719	180	256	146	126	112	113	40	76	100								
883	832	221	368	220	238	224	144	170	95	82	159							
989	937	332	464	331	334	320	255	248	206	186	207	79						
879	827	288	364	254	235	220	206	148	157	140	108	162	123					
950	898	359	435	325	305	291	253	219	204	186	179	176	136	88				
962	910	371	447	337	317	303	264	231	215	198	191	187	148	100	14			
938	886	290	423	289	293	278	213	208	164	147	166	136	45	82	96	108		
976	924	319	451	318	321	307	242	235	193	173	195	85	18	110	124	136	32	

Distances to Sitka are partly outside.

Index of Advertisers

Index of Anchorages, Parks, Ports-of-Call, Marinas, Moorages, Facilities, & Services

This page continuously updated at **Northwest Boat Travel On-line®** www.nwboattravel.com